P9-APW-830

An official publication of

THE AMERICAN SOCIOLOGICAL ASSOCIATION

RUSSELL DYNES, *Executive Officer*

SOCIOLOGICAL METHODOLOGY

1981

Samuel Leinhardt

EDITOR

SOCIOLOGICAL METHODOLOGY

1981

Jossey-Bass Publishers

San Francisco • Washington • London • 1981

SOCIOLOGICAL METHODOLOGY 1981
by Samuel Leinhardt, Editor

Library of Congress Catalog Card Information

Sociological methodology. 1969–81
San Francisco, Jossey-Bass.

11 v. illus. 24 cm. annual. (Jossey-Bass behavioral science series)

Editor:	1969–70	E. F. Borgatta
	1971, 1972, 1973–74	H. L. Costner
	1975, 1976, 1977	D. R. Heise
	1978, 1979, 1980	K. F. Schuessler
	1981	S. Leinhardt

"An official publication of the American Sociological Association."

1. Sociology—Methodology—Yearbooks. I. American Sociological Association. II. Borgatta, Edgar F., 1924– ed.

HM24.S55 301′.01′8 68-54940

rev.
Library of Congress [r71h2]

International Standard Book Number ISBN 0-87589-490-9

International Standard Serial Number ISSN 0081-1750

Manufactured in the United States of America

JACKET DESIGN BY WILLI BAUM

FIRST EDITION

Code 8105

THE JOSSEY-BASS
SOCIAL AND BEHAVIORAL SCIENCE SERIES

SOCIOLOGICAL METHODOLOGY 1981

EDITOR Samuel Leinhardt

ADVISORY EDITORS David Featherman

Paul W. Holland

Lawrence Mayer

Thomas Pullum

Shelby Stewman

Seymour Spilerman

CONSULTANTS

Alan Agresti
Duane F. Alwin
Ronald Andersen
James W. Balkwell
David J. Bartholomew
Elwood M. Beck
Howard S. Becker
James R. Beniger
Russell Bernard
Brian Berry
Edgar Borgatta
Norman Bradburn
Henry Braun
Ronald Breiger
Michael Capobianco
Andrew Cliff
Clifford C. Clogg
Philip E. Converse
Philip Cook
William Cooley
Herbert Costner
Robert L. Crain
Leslie Curry
James A. Davis
Otto A. Davis
Patrick Doreian
George T. Duncan
Otis D. Duncan
Charles Eastman
William Eddy
Bonnie Erickson
Marcus Felson
Glenn A. Firebaugh
Ove Frank
Steven Garber
Ralph Ginsberg
Terry C. Gleason
Norval Glenn
Erving Goffman
Leo Goodman
Mark Granovetter
Michael Hannan
Eric A. Hanushek
Robert Hauser
James Heckman
Greg Heil
David R. Heise
Neil Henry
Chang-i Hua
Allen Imershein
John M. Johnson
Robert Johnson
Charles Kadushin
David Kenny
Nathan Keyfitz
James R. Kluegel

David Knoke
Kenneth C. Land
Charles Lave
Lester B. Lave
Robert Leik
John Light
Paul Lohnes
Jay Magidson
Colin Mallows
Peter Marsden
William M. Mason
Ralf Meerbote
Edmund Meyers
Donald Morrison
Nicholas Mullins
Daniel Nagin
John K. Ord
George Psathas
Henry T. Reynolds
Morris Rosenberg
Robert Rosenthal
Steven Rytina
Janet Schofield
Peter Schönemann
Karl Schuessler
Joseph Schwartz
Stephen Seidman
Hanan Selvin
Herbert Simon
Burton Singer
Monroe G. Sirken
Robert Somers
Joe L. Spaeth
Ross Stolzenberg
Anselm Strauss
Sheldon Stryker
Seymour Sudman
Garth Taylor
Howard Taylor
Charles Tilly
Robert Townsend
Paul Tukey
Nancy Tuma
Herman Turk
Paul F. Velleman
Stanley Wasserman
Harrison White
Christopher Winship
Sonia Wright

PROLOGUE

The contents of *Sociological Methodology 1981* support three broad inferences: (1) sociologists continue to expand the borders of their discipline creating a collateral pressure on methods and data, (2) the distinction between sociology and related disciplines such as economics is less clear than ever especially in regard to methods of analysis, and (3) methods developed with one data type in mind can prove surprisingly useful in the analysis of seemingly unrelated types.

Not all of the chapters relate directly to these issues. Some continue established lines of research while others provide reviews that detail the state of the art and specify areas where research is needed.

Chapter one by Harrison C. White is certainly nothing less than expansive. He focuses on a topic traditionally reserved to economists: markets, real markets where transactions for goods and services take place. Chapters bearing on the sociological application of economic ideas and results are not a novelty in *Sociological Methodology,* but White is not simply turning developments in economics to advantage in the analysis of a problem in sociology—quite the contrary. The problem he addresses rests securely within the conventional definition of economics while the approach he takes rests solidly in contemporary sociology. In treating the issue as a sociologist, White is saying, in essence, that markets are a sociological phenomenon, too, and that there is a lot to be gained by a sociological analysis. White views markets as a structured system of roles. Differentiated and distinct firms or producers are linked together through communication ties. By virtue of this communication, firms are able to observe each other's production and revenue behavior. Adjustments result from these observations, a market becomes institutionalized as the firms search for optimal niches, and the distribution of market shares equilibrates. White argues that neoclassical economic theory has important failures, including the fact that it cannot specify market boundaries or discriminate a producer's market from an entire industrial economy. These failures can be overcome, however, when markets are understood to be demonstrable social structures built by the interlocking joint perceptions and decisions of actors much as the social structure of affect in a group is a consequence of the interlocking affective choices of the members. White's approach is behavioral and concrete; it is based on the observable, tangible tension between buyers and sellers setting the terms of trade. His approach is in direct contrast to the emphasis on intangible cogitation of utility by producers and consumers that has motivated economic theorists. As a consequence of his focus on tangible interactions, White is able to lay out an eminently sociological research program, one extending traditional sociological field research methods to the study of economic markets.

Charles F. Manski, an economist, returns White's favor by demonstrating in Chapter two how a methodology developed for economic applications can have utility in sociology. He provides an extensive review of the contemporary econometric approach to the modeling, estimation, and forecasting of individuals making choices among discrete, exhaustive, and competing alternatives. Traditionally, this topic has been the province of economists and psychologists. But, as the chapters in this volume make clear, choices—in the form of decisions about who to vote for, where to reside, what work to do, and who to befriend—do interest sociologists. Manski argues that choice-based discrete data can be best analyzed by first positing a structural model of the process generating the responses. The models he describes are familiar to economists but should also have appeal to sociologists. Indeed, the example that he develops—an empirical study of students' college choices—seems, at first glance, to be research in the sociology of education. But besides the potential utility of the methods Manski describes and the substantive interest his example may generate, there is another reason why sociologists should find his chapter exciting. The continuing development of structural models for discrete choices leads naturally to a traditionally sociological issue and to a point where cooperation among members of the two disciplines could be highly productive: the impact of interpersonal relations on an individual's decision. Sociologists often approach this issue from a structural perspective by inquiring into the network that constrains communication on the alternatives and the institutionalized perspectives that cause the options to be valued differentially. Manski's chapter, like White's, is not simply a statement of work done but a call for new joint undertakings.

In Chapter three, Ove Frank surveys statistical methods for the analysis of graphs, a topic of increasing importance. In recent years sociologists have rediscovered an idea originally popularized in the 1930s by the psychiatrist Jacob L. Moreno. He discovered that useful information on the structure of a group's interpersonal relations could be obtained by a simple opinion survey in which each group member was asked to identify the other group members whom he or she preferred on the basis of some affective or activity-oriented criterion. A directed graph representing the group's interpersonal relations was obtained by representing group members by points and their interconnecting choices by arrow-headed lines originating with the chooser and ending on the chosen. Moreno called this graph the sociogram. His work remained specialized until two mathematicians, Frank Harary and Robert Z. Norman, teamed up with a psychologist, Dorwin Cartwright, to write a rigorous introduction to graph theory that has had a tremendous impact on sociologists since its publication in 1965. Graph theoretic concepts are now common devices for organizing relational data and expressing theoretical ideas about social structure. Contemporary applications range from the original substantive context studied by Moreno—small groups of children—to systems of interlocks among the directors of corporations. Although there has been a demonstrable rise in sociologists' interest in structural studies and in their proclivity to use graph theoretic notions in these studies, only marginal progress has been made in improving our theories of social behavior as a consequence. The problem probably lies not so much in the theoretical intent as in the analytic execution. In this regard Frank's chapter may be part of the answer.

Frank points out that empirical measurements on networks, like all data, are subject to sampling variation, measurement error, and other kinds of uncertainty and that they are the result of imperfect observation and other nondeterministic factors that impede observation of the "true" structure of a system of relational ties. The fact that these features of the data are inevitable argues for a statistical approach to their analysis. Surprisingly for a discipline that commonly exploits statistical methods, the statistical approach to the analysis of graph data has yet to gain general acceptance. Frank reviews three kinds of statistical applications: (1) Pure sampling in which various procedural designs are used to acquire information on a portion of the relational ties in a large system, (2) simple transition models for representing uncertain or random graphs, and (3) stochastic models for representing change processes that are subject to nondeterministic transitions. Frank concentrates on what might be called standard topics; methods for answering complex structural questions await additional research efforts.

Stephen E. Fienberg and Stanley S. Wasserman, in Chapter four, demonstrate how the application of an existing method to a data form not ordinarily associated with it can yield dramatic results. They show that the methods now widely used by sociologists to analyze discrete multivariate data can also be used to analyze sociometric data. Although the term *network* is a relatively new addition to sociological jargon, most network data remain similar to the sociometric data originally collected by Moreno. These "who-to-whom" matrices consist of ones and zeros, the ones indicating a directed tie. Fienberg and Wasserman describe how such relational data can be represented as a four-dimensional contingency table. The result is a new way to use discrete multivariate procedures and to estimate the parameters of a multivariate exponential model for digraphs. The model that they estimate places a probability distribution over the dyads of a graph. The parameters of the model represent individual nodal as well as average global effects. The modeling framework has numerous features that make it an appealing method for analyzing relational data. Furthermore, representing network data as a cross-classified table leads directly to a model for subgroups, an extension that has numerous possible empirical applications. Because Fienberg and Wasserman demonstrate how to use standard iterative proportional fitting methods on network data, they make the statistical approach to the analysis of social networks accessible to many investigators.

Leo A. Goodman considers more conventional applications of discrete multivariate statistical methods in Chapter five. In particular, he applies them to two-way cross classifications with ordered categories. By examining applications in three contexts representing three special kinds of data, Goodman argues that one obtains quite different views of the methodological utility and import of these procedures. He chooses three previously analyzed data sets and explores the specification of baseline models and the development of parsimonious models from these null-models. In each case, he links parameters to appropriate quantities, such as frequencies, odds, odds ratios, or their logs. From his elementary approach to the discussion of the models, Goodman is able to draw out the logical relationships in the use of log-linear models to study association, dependence, and structure. Although developed in a context of two-way tables, his approach can be extended to m-way tables.

In Chapter six, Clifford C. Clogg and Darwin O. Sawyer bring rigorous statistical inference to the topic of scalability. They first illustrate the defects of "traditional" or "conventional" nonstatistical scaling methods and then contrast models for assessing the scalability of a set of dichotomous or dichotomized items that have been developed by others. They apply these different models to a cross-classification table of items relating to attitudes about abortion. The results indicate that different conclusions on scalability can follow the application of different models. In an appendix, Clogg and Sawyer demonstrate that a latent structure framework can be constructed to identify different probabilistic scaling models as alternative specifications.

Otis Dudley Duncan, in Chapter seven, presents a study of a single multiway contingency table, a panel consisting of a two-wave, two-variable (religion and party) survey of voting. He points out that there are parallels in the hypotheses related to time that arise in comparative cross-sectional analyses and panel data. He seeks to clarify these parallelisms by stating the hypotheses explicitly and carrying out an analysis of the panel data. But, Duncan asserts, the identification, measurement, and interpretation of across-time interaction is also important. He demonstrates how the construction of a model for these interactions can be facilitated and pursues these interactions in the same data.

The chapter by Duncan introduces a concern with time as a causal factor or, as he describes it, as a "proxy for a collection of indirectly observed causal factors." Duncan explores the use of discrete multivariate techniques to analyze the effect of time on voting choice. Burton Singer, in Chapter eight, also addresses the issue of the impact of time on choice and uses panel data, but he specifies a stochastic model, which involves time explicitly. Like White and Manski, Singer mixes sociology and economics. He develops models of individual employment and intragenerational mobility by joining economic theories of labor force dynamics with sociological theories of occupational mobility. To retain realism and flexibility, he investigates models that are continuous-time, nonstationary Markov chains. The problem, however, is not so much model specification as it is the empirical estimation of the model's parameters. Singer presents a strategy for using multiwave panel data to fit a two-stage model and describes criteria for assessing the fit. Departing from the recent trend toward the use of event-history data, Singer explains that panel data are far more readily obtained and, on many variables of interest, will probably remain the only form of data available.

David D. McFarland, in Chapter nine, is also interested in the analysis of longitudinal data. McFarland develops an analysis of intergenerational occupational mobility and fits a time-stationary Markov model. His objective, however, is not primarily to demonstrate an estimation procedure or to obtain new analytic results for the data but rather to demonstrate how to obtain, interpret, and use the spectral components of stochastic matrices. Nonetheless, in developing an example of eigenvector analysis using transition matrices from models for black and white intergenerational occupational mobility, McFarland obtains some novel insights into the different mobility patterns of these groups.

In Chapter ten, Patrick Doreian raises the question of why sociologists who often analyze data that aggregate regionally do not employ methods that recognize this feature explicitly. Drawing on the work of geographers, regional economists, and social ecologists, Doreian establishes strategies for developing linear structural equation models for data that are spatially distributed; he thereby incorporates geographical space into the analysis of social phenomena. Examples of behavioral data where spatial issues may be central include crime rates in wards, voting, and residential mobility. The important feature of these data is that they are distributed spatially and when taken together comprise a region, which may or may not have holes. In the context of such ordered space, the observations on the areal units are not independent and traditional significance tests are not useful. Two strategies are available: (1) remove the bias introduced by spatial autocorrelation—that is, treat it as a nuisance to be adjusted out of the analysis—and focus on the remaining effects or (2) specify and test a spatial model so that the impact of space can be studied directly.

Much as interest in behavior that is distributed over time has led sociologists to explore models that consider time explicitly, recognition of the role that geographical space plays in influencing social behavior should stimulate the development of explicitly spatial models. One question that remains, however, is to determine whether the spatial dimension is causal or if, as is possible with time, it operates as a surrogate for other substantive features of the social environment.

In Chapter eleven, Charles F. Cannell, Peter V. Miller, and Lois Oksenberg focus on how data are obtained and, in particular, on how the method of obtaining them can influence their content. They explore the sociology of the survey interview, pointing out that survey data are collected through a social process in which interviewer and interviewee interact. Although this is not a novel idea, Cannell, Miller, and Oksenberg present the results of a research program that has led to the development of novel techniques that can exploit this fact to obtain better results and reduce survey error. Concentrating on an understanding of the interviewee's role in performing the reportorial task, they describe research that leads to specific recommendations for procedures that will aid the respondent's memory, increase motivation to cooperate and, potentially, improve the overall quality of the data that are obtained. In effect, they are advising sociologists to be more aware of the roles that are implicit in the survey interview task. Interviewers present alternatives and ask for a reply, which depends in part on the behavioral communication received from the interviewer.

Thus, substantive themes of the other chapters reappear in the detailed analysis of the interviewer-interviewee interaction: the interaction of mutual observations of actions determines roles, and the structure that develops influences the continuing transactional process. Sociologists are naturally concerned with transactions involving choices across time and space and are beginning to be aware that the acquisition of goods, information, careers, friends, and services has costs as well as benefits that individuals recognize and act on. The fact that sociologists, economists, and statisticians find themselves addressing similar issues should come as no surprise. Social behavior is, after all, inherently interdisciplinary, and it is time, as White's work implies, for sociologists to free themselves from artificial disciplinary constraints in their pursuit of productive theories and useful methods.

Each volume of *Sociological Methodology* is the product of cooperative efforts by many people too numerous, unfortunately, to mention by name; the current volume, my first as editor, is no exception. In producing it, I have exploited friendships and pressed colleagues for advice, assistance, and succor. Their willingness to help and the soundness of their ideas have contributed immeasurably to the continuing quality of this series. Special thanks are due to the previous editor, Karl F. Schuessler, for his support and encouragement and to Margie Farinelli, my secretary, for the aplomb and poise with which she ran the editorial office while continuing to respond admirably to the unrelenting pressures of my research and teaching activities.

Pittsburgh, Pennsylvania SAMUEL LEINHARDT
January 1981

CONTENTS

CONTRIBUTORS

Charles F. Cannell, Institute for Social Research, University of Michigan, Ann Arbor

Clifford C. Clogg, Institute of Policy Research and Evaluation, Pennsylvania State University, University Park

Patrick Doreian, Department of Sociology, University of Pittsburgh

Otis Dudley Duncan, Department of Sociology, University of Arizona

Stephen E. Fienberg, Department of Statistics, Carnegie-Mellon University

Ove Frank, Department of Statistics, University of Lund, Sweden

Leo A. Goodman, Department of Sociology, University of Chicago

David D. McFarland, Department of Sociology, University of California, Los Angeles

Charles F. Manski, Department of Economics, Hebrew University of Jerusalem, Israel

Peter V. Miller, Institute for Social Research, University of Michigan, Ann Arbor

Lois Oksenberg, Institute for Social Research, University of Michigan, Ann Arbor

Darwin O. Sawyer, Institute of Policy Research and Evaluation, Pennsylvania State University, University Park

Burton Singer, Department of Mathematics, Columbia University

Stanley S. Wasserman, Department of Applied Statistics, University of Minnesota, St. Paul

Harrison C. White, Department of Sociology, Harvard University

SOCIOLOGICAL METHODOLOGY

1981

1

PRODUCTION MARKETS AS INDUCED ROLE STRUCTURES

Harrison C. White
HARVARD UNIVERSITY

Neoclassical microeconomics (Mansfield, 1975; Scitovsky, 1952; Stigler, 1946) does not look directly at markets. Instead, decisions by typical actors (firms and consumers) are modeled. The theory is unable to specify analytically the boundaries of a market, or to discriminate a production market as such from an entire industrial economy (Kuenne, 1967).

Even the departures from orthodoxy in recent decades share its

Financial support from the National Science Foundation under Grants SOC76-24394, SOC76-24512, and SER76-17502 is gratefully acknowledged. John F. Padgett, Burton Singer, Ronald L. Breiger, and Robert G. Eccles made suggestions that yielded major improvements over preceding drafts. Duane Champagne, Eric Leifer, and Curtis Dombek helped with calculations and ideas. Earlier versions of this material were presented as the A.B. Hollingshead lecture in 1978 at Yale University, and the Snyder lecture in 1980 at the University of Toronto.

individualistic obsessions. In the opening lines of his recent overview of these departures, Herbert Simon (1979) insists that since the time of Alfred Marshall economics could be considered a psychological science. Simon says, like our own George Homans, that the need is to bring men back in again. I argue that the need instead is to focus on markets as such, as social structures built jointly by interlocking perceptions and decisions of actors who can be modeled individually by orthodox archetypes. I introduce one specific theory of market as social structure and indicate from time to time some of the variants possible.

The U.S. government's Standard Industrial Classification (see Shiskin and Peterson, 1972) has been refined in recent decades to the level of five and more digits where "individual products" can be isolated. Most empirical studies in industrial organization, market structure, business planning, and the like use as scaffolding the Standard Industrial Classification (SIC) or another nation's analog to it (as in Porter, 1976; Markham, 1973; Scherer, 1970). Yet most writers on this subject are uneasy, citing its lack of explicit tie to any theory, economic or otherwise, or citing its arbitrary administrative basis—the peculiar mix of past convention, present engineering, sources of materials, and end uses that defines a "product." Like Barber (1977) I say there are puzzles here. Why do particular markets come into existence? Why does a certain market persist? Indeed, what sort of observable social structure is a market?

I propose that market structure derives from feedback on terms of trade between a fully connected clique of producers and aggregate buyers. Feedback can sustain a structure only if terms of trade are observable. Then every choice and every action is based on perceptions that are shared and public. The resulting market is a social structure sustained by the self-interested choices of its constituent actors. Not just the overall structure but also the individual niches within it persist as regular patterns of action.

Terms of trade is the key concept in my approach. It replaces the abstract notion of price with the concept of a schedule specific to the memberships in the market. This schedule combines aspects of price and volume to define a workable interface between pressures from the producers and pressures from the buyers. Each producer chooses a location optimal for itself on this common schedule, thereby assuming a distinctive role that is accepted by the buyers only in the context of what the other producers are doing.

The problem is not which firms and buyers identify with a product defined *culturally* by an essential attribute. Once established, a market defines a product. The problem is which *sets* of producer firms, and of buyers for their outputs, can together sustain a market. Once established, a market is experienced by each actor as an overpowering regimen; the terms of trade are social facts that brook no contradiction. But not just any collection of firms and buyers can put together a market among themselves.

Edward Alsworth Ross in his *Social Psychology* (1921) is one of the great theorists of people's responses to each other's actions as feedback signals. Following Tarde, he confines his interest to imitation; conventions—what he would call "planes" of commonality—are as far as his book would take us. Ross is vague about how imitation contributes to the groups and differentiated structures that are the domain of sociology (see Breiger, 1980b). The general theoretical problem underlying markets is how, from observing others' actions in a common setting, each party evolves its own differentiated behavior—its own role which in turn contributes to the actions that others observe. Hence this chapter's title.

The term *role* usually evokes either examples ingrained in our culture (White, 1963, 1965)—daughter, boss, nurse, and so on—or structures consciously laid out, such as the officials in a bureaucracy or chairmen of congressional committees (Friedell, 1967; Boorman, 1977). But everyday social structure consists in a host of mutual regularities in enacted and perceived behavior that go beyond such ordained roles (Nadel, 1957; Merton, 1959). I shall propose a new set of methods—models plus instructions for field observations—to describe and account for role structures induced in the course of the everyday business of production for sales. In conversations among business people, and in their journals, one hears of many roles that appear to fit my perspective—not only market leader, but also price setter, milk cow, and dog (Abell and Hammond, 1979; *Business Week*, 7 May 1979, pp. 74–78).

One prototype for this view of markets is emergent roles for participants that are common across hundreds of discussion groups (Bales, Cohen, and Williamson, 1980; Breiger and Ennis, 1979). Another is collective behavior models, as in Schelling (1978) and Granovetter (1978). Role models developed earlier for social networks by myself and colleagues provide yet another (White, Boorman, and

Breiger, 1976; Boorman and White, 1976; Schwartz, 1977; and see Breiger, 1980a, 1980b; Bonacich and McConaghy, 1979; Pattison, 1981; Snyder and Kick, 1979).

Other prototypes are implicit in descriptions of a market as stylized interactions among highly individual firms in specific niches affording continuing "excess" profit: accounts from practitioners in marketing (Preston, 1970; Rodger, 1972; Verdoorn, 1956); in business organization (Lawrence and Lorsch, 1967; Burns and Stalker, 1961); in industrial organization (Cowling, 1972; Scherer, 1970); and most clearly of all in business strategy advice (Abell and Hammond, 1979; Cannon, 1968; Hofer and Schendel, 1978; Miles and Snow, 1978; Taylor and Wills, 1969).

The business strategy literature is also a reminder that my proposed approach to markets as role structures should be seen as a new baseline rather than a complete account of a market. I suppress exactly the gaming and arbitrage aspects that obsess economic theorists (among them Riley, 1975); they suppress the persistent structure of roles induced from observable terms of trade in a market. Some businessmen and women not only try to outguess each other but actually take risks on those speculations, but I assume that these are secondary processes in a theory of markets.

Since I appear to intrude on the terrain of economic theory (as I think sociologists should), I clarify the nature of this intrusion in the next section. The simplifications I use are then laid out. Next follows the core of the chapter: One section postulates the process in which both sides of a market test terms of trade; a second supplies the model with a family of possible factual contexts; a third treats what actors do observe and can coordinate. Two other sections spell out formulas and exhibit results for the emergence, main characteristics, and degree of specificity of markets. In the text and accompanying figures special emphasis is given to examples with just three firms. The last section draws implications.

The main issue is not theory but observation. My goal is a handbook for sociologists who wish to apply traditional field research methods in the study of concrete markets. We have too long been hypnotized by what Barber (1977, pp. 15–17) has called the theoretical absolutization of the market, which has seduced economic theorists (among them Becker, 1977). Observation will improve and broaden the theory and methods we start with, and the theory and methods for production markets can lead us to confront some of the most intractable problems in the analysis of social structure.

USING NEOCLASSIC MICROECONOMIC THEORY

Three negative assertions will clear the way for sketching positive uses. First, economic theorists are indebted to Edgeworth for a powerful theory for ad hoc markets, markets of truck and barter, with or without the aid of money. It is called the *pure theory of exchange* (see Newman, 1965). This is the market theory to which Homans (1967), Blau (1964), Cook and Emerson (1978), and many other anthropological, sociological, and social-psychological theorists (among them Ekeh, 1974) turn for analogy and inspiration; there are also some powerful applications (as in Winship, 1978). This theory has nothing to do with industrial economies. In an *exchange* market, everybody comes with some arbitrary collection of goods in order to exchange them for goods of other kinds; the pure theory of exchange shows not only how prices are a sufficient mechanism to clear the market but also that competitive gaming pressures tend to induce such prices. In *production* markets, by contrast, cash is paid by actors on one side of a market in return for—a functionalist would say in order to induce—massive flows of products produced by specialized organizations (producing firms) using roundabout techniques and considerable time.

Second, "supply equals demand" is merely a soothing tautology about production markets except in one idealized case (an asymptotic limiting case in mathematical terms). In this case a given volume of the product of one firm is, in the eyes of all buyers, indistinguishable from the volume of another firm. The problem in any real market is exactly *how* terms of trade establish themselves across differentiated products so as to give meaning to aggregate terms like *supply* and *demand.* This second point deserves emphasis. The supply–demand approach presupposes, takes as given, precisely the chief difficulty: Who is eligible and active in a market? And, even stipulating membership, the approach then proceeds to ignore one of the main reasons a firm's product has value—namely, because it is distinctive from the products of other firms. Textbook statements about price systems (as in Stigler, 1946, p. 16) verge on tautologies (Myrdal, 1928).

Third, it has been a half-century since Chamberlain (1933) and Robinson (1933) independently introduced analysis of competitive markets in distinctive as opposed to homogeneous products. Despite the length and variety of their efforts, economists have concluded that they do not yet have an acceptable theory for application to a production market (Kuenne, 1967; Roberts and Sonnenschein, 1977). Recent reformulations (Lancaster, 1975; Spence, 1976a; Dixit and Stiglitz, 1977) explicitly avoid the problem of descriptive adequacy by focusing on normative implications of the range of deviations from homogeneous markets that their formulations suggest.

What is the difficulty? Since each firm's output is valued differently by buyers, each firm has (and presumably knows it has) a distinctive role. Buyers' purchases of one firm's production depend on the sizes of every other firm's production available. Economists have sought the "reaction functions" of firms in this competitive environment—the rules by which a firm decides what action is optimal given not just its role but also the actions it anticipates from other firms in its hypothesized environment of buyers (Roberts and Sonnenschein, 1977). Economists then assimilate the problem of a production market to Cournot's classic problem of monopoly, duopoly, and the like, which remains indeterminate. I argue that they miss exactly that objective, competitive pressure from other firms too numerous to "psyche out", which guides a real firm in a real market toward volumes and price that demonstrably can be sustained. This problem of multiplicity must be addressed head-on by any sociological theory of social structure.

Business people know the world is much too complex to compute as economic theorists would like them to do and is anyway too opaque to provide enough data to permit such speculative analysis. Instead, businessmen are attuned to tangible evidence from their own specific market as to what volume and value are permitted in their niche among the specific set of producers. Economists assume that producers are speculative virtuosos. I, following Simon (1979), assume they are prudent observers. But economic theorists, especially in the past two decades, provide most of the insights and the technical apparatus I need to specify my approach.

Houthakker (1952) frames my task. Many significant innovations in microeconomic theory that I use—consumers as producers (Lancaster, 1966), the importance of observability and of quality, hedonic prices (Terleckyj, 1976; Griliches, 1971)—seem to stem from this one brief article by Houthakker. Its opening words are "Recent empirical research has drawn attention to the importance of quality variations in consumer demand." The subject as well as the object of this sentence are notable, when coming from a neoclassic theorist. On the second page, Houthakker unveils an ingenious sketch of consumption demand according to quality *and* quantity. On the last page, he insists that further development requires looking also at the supply side and incorporating imperfect competition aspects from the theory of the firm. He points out the main weakness of his brief sketch: "Supply problems were implicitly assumed to be solved in the form of a price schedule which could only shift or tilt."

I present a theory of the sort that Houthakker implies. I use the standard comparative statics tools he advocates. My approach is close to that of Archibald and Rosenbluth (1975), but it avoids the specialized framework they adopt from Chamberlain and drops their requirement of linear cost functions (p. 584).

Neither Houthakker nor more recent workers in this vein (Rosen, 1974; Weitzman, 1974) have suggested a self-sorter mechanism, which is the heart of my terms-of-trade approach. For that I am indebted to another work by Spence (1974a), which does not, however, refer to imperfect competition and is itself not cited in his own later piece on that topic. Using such tools from neoclassic microeconomics, I develop an approach that asks quite different questions and yields differentiated role structures as the answers.

Both questions and answers resemble those of institutional economics and organization sociology. But there are differences. By using neoclassic tools I treat frictional effects as secondary, whereas institutional studies center on friction: Compare the survey of Scherer (1970, p. 3), who argues that the theory of the market is bogged down. Williamson's (1975) integration of market with bureaucracy as a subject of study relies mainly on gaming and legal effects. John Commons' approach to economic institutions, continued vigorously today (as in Horwitz, 1978; Landa, 1976), emphasizes cultural factors, especially the legal system. Economic theory of location effects (Alonso, 1964; Simon, 1978) is a powerful exemplar for study of differentiated products (as in Rosen, 1974), but it builds too closely on the intrinsic logic of spatial geography to be a reliable guide. International trade models of differentiated products are themselves neoclassic theory (Negishi, 1972; Krugman, 1978). Some institutional economists like Leontief (his input/output approach) deliberately neglect market phenomena in favor of an engineering view in terms of cumulative flows. Other institutional economists (Landa, 1979; Porter, 1976) also emphasize the network succession of channels in the economy through which products pass as they transform into forms successively closer to consumption, but unlike Leontief they retain the focus on social transaction: They bet on longitudinal networks, not cross-sectional markets, as the effective unit into which to decompose an economy.

Organization theorists have developed a paradigm of organizations in environment (Burns and Stalker, 1961; Chandler, 1966; Lawrence and Lorsch, 1967; Williamson, 1970; Lorsch and Allen, 1973; and see Caves, 1979). In this paradigm, in contrast with neoclassic economics, a firm does have a role, as do, by implication, its rivals in the market. But the further step is not taken of deriving the market itself as the result of the role behavior of the firms vis-à-vis one another.

Another difference between my approach on the one hand and Chamberlain's, as Spence (1976a), or Dixit and Stiglitz (1977), or Lancaster (1975) present it in neoclassic form, on the other, is their treatment of the long run. Chamberlain makes the standard neoclassic assumption that profits for all firms alike are driven to zero in the long run by the entry of new firms (for a critique see Winter, 1971). My emphasis on roles and their persistence indicates my own inclination. The core of Chamberlain's vision, I think, is the inertial effects of historical experience in the real world. The quality variation emphasized later in this chapter, especially within the range supposed by Chamberlain, reflects primarily the perceptions of consumers. And these are heavily conditioned by loyalty, familiarity with brand names, and the like.

Despite all the differences, however, there is some common ground. In every theory of markets, the cost of additional units must go up faster than value to sustain market equilibrium in a blank context with undifferentiated products—pure or perfect competition, so called. The Chamberlain theory of markets in differentiated products retains this assumption ("decreasing returns to scale"). The Chamberlain theory (1933) also emphasizes a peculiarly modern context of taste and technology—a context in which the representative buyer values as higher quality just those goods that are cheaper to make. Presumably, advertising and the like generate such a paradoxical context. Market equilibria from my models can be matched with the predictions I derive from Chamberlain at every point of a family of situations yielding this paradoxical context. The main differences are the range of payment schedules that I find, depending on historical circumstance, and the indeterminacy I allow in the consumer's exploitation ratio for value received over money paid. Even if arbitrage squeezes out both indeterminacies, the total size and price structure predicted by my theory, in this neoclassic context, differ from those of Chamberlain and Spence. But both theories reduce—in the limiting case where buyers do not distinguish at all between products from different firms—to the conventional theory of pure competition with equilibrium at a unique price (Mansfield, 1975, chaps. 8 and 10).

SIMPLIFICATIONS AND NOTATION

I now set the framework for later operationalizations. The details, however, are less crucial than the perspective.

First, let n index the producers. Each producer in the market makes its own, self-interested decisions. I use the word *firm* whether or not this "business unit" (Abell and Hammond, 1979, pp. 6–9) is a division, a subsidiary, or a census "establishment."

Second, producers in an economy are partitioned into markets, a firm being in exactly one market. In a market all producers offer the same line, which is treated as a single type of flow. The physical volume of flow is represented by y. Precursors of this formulation include:

1. Kalwani and Morrison (1977, sec. 4) gives arguments for the usefulness of partitioning in one form; and see Cannon (1968, chap. 4).
2. Alonso (1964) and Simon (1978) exemplify theories where such separate segregated markets are identified with locations, and their methods also suggest how to allow for overlaps.
3. Markham's (1973) broad study of conglomerates' entry into fresh markets supports the identification of market with product line, as well as the entrenched, rolelike nature of membership in a market; and see Machlup (1952).

Third, one side of the market is aggregated to permit individualized treatment of actors on the other side and still obtain readily interpretable solutions. Here buyers are aggregated. Variants are possible:

1. In earlier working papers (White, 1978, sec. 7; White, 1979, pp. 44–45, 63–64) I develop the dual form in which producers are aggregated; in the latter (1979, p. 44) I show how to partially disaggregate buyers in the present form.
2. The present form is the natural base for studying monopolistic competition (different firms' products differentially evaluated by buyers), and it is used in existing formulations by economists (Spence, 1976a; Dixit and Stiglitz, 1977). The dual form is natural for market segmentation (different products in the line for that market are preferred by different sorts of buyers—Engel and others, 1972).

Fourth, comparative statics is used to assess and compare equilibrium configurations, if any, found for the market. Benassy (1976) develops a disequilibrium approach to Chamberlain competition among differentiated products.

Fifth, each firm in the market makes its decisions with the sole goal of maximizing the resultant net flow of benefits to itself measured in money terms. Specific rationales for this neoclassic tenet are:

1. Herbert Simon's (1979) arguments in favor of satisficing apply better within firms than across firms in a market (see Radner, 1975).
2. I obtain similar results when I assume producers (White, 1976, sec. 3) enforce fixed percentage markups or when buyers (White, 1976, sec. 4) use percentage markups. And see Taylor and Wills (1969, pp. 445–446) on markups.

Sixth, each producer chooses two things simultaneously, using the terms of trade as input: a volume flow y and a revenue flow W. This choice of volume and revenue defines the producer's niche. The variable costs of producer n in producing volume y are a well-defined function $C(y;n)$, given valuations from markets for its supplies.

Variant interpretations are possible:

1. Verdoorn (1956, p. 230) gives a good discussion of the array of other possible decision variables. White (1976, secs. 6 and 7) gives alternative interpretations with y a measure of quality.
2. Scitovsky (1952, pp. 245, 265) exemplifies the mystification about "price-makers" and "price-takers" common in economic theory; see Taylor and Wills (1969, chap. 40) for an antidote.

Seventh, buyers have valuation functions for flows of goods in monetary terms. In a market, the buyers in aggregate have a valuation function **V** (in monetary units) that combines differential evaluations of the goods from each producer, $S(y;n)$. I simplify further by assuming

$$\mathbf{V} = \left[\sum_{n} S(y;n)\right]^{\gamma} \tag{1}$$

with $\gamma < 1$. **V** is the numerical measure of total attractiveness that buyers weigh against their costs, the payments to all producers. Here I have adopted recent conventions in economics:

1. This is Lancaster's (1966) consumer-as-producer paradigm, which replaces older formulations in terms of budget lines and indifference curves. See Triplett's discussion in Terleckyj (1976, pp. 305–323).
2. The form in Equation (1) for **V** will be specialized later in the chapter to a CES (constant elasticity of substitution) function commonly used by economists (as in Spence, 1976a, p. 226).
3. See Spence (1976a, sec. 4), Christensen, Jorgenson, and Lau (1975), and White (1979, sec. 2) for generalizations of the **V** in Equation (1) to allow interaction between specific pairs of products rather than as in Equation (1) between one product and the aggregate.

Eighth, in Equation (1) and subsequent formulas, sharp functional mappings are assumed. I do so to simplify notation and derivations. The main results should not be affected by the introduction of stochastic terms, needed in thorough empirical testing.

TERMS OF TRADE

Producer Side. I assume that every firm can observe the choices of all firms in the market—that is, the revenue each firm n receives for the volume it shipped, $y(n)$—whether learned from a trade association or over lunch. This is the best tangible evidence a firm has on what it could earn from various volumes of production. Figure 1 is an illustrative scatterplot; each point gives the (revenue, volume) pair for each firm in a given market. Any firm can estimate, literally or figuratively, a best-fitting curve through this scatterplot.

Represent this curve by $W(y)$, the total revenue from the aggregate buyer for the volume shipped. Each producer compares $W(y)$ with the cost curve $C(y;n)$, as illustrated in Figure 2, in order to estimate the volume $y(n)$, which yields maximum net returns:

$$y = y(n) \qquad \text{maximizes} \qquad [W(y) - C(y;n)] \tag{2}$$

The market is in equilibrium *on the producer side* when and only when this comparison yields an estimate for each producer identical to the volume it has been shipping.

Buyer Side. The aggregate buyer makes a yes/no decision about each firm: whether or not to accept the (price, volume) pair

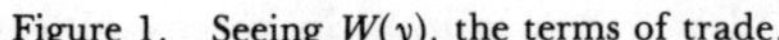

Figure 1. Seeing $W(y)$, the terms of trade.

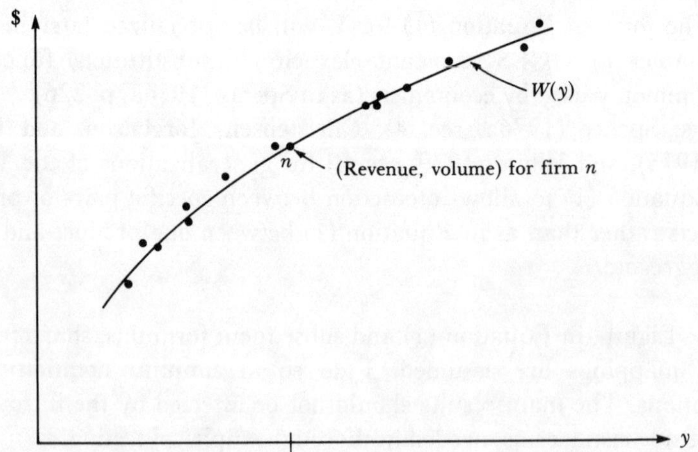

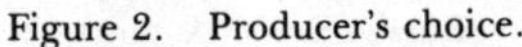
Figure 2. Producer's choice.

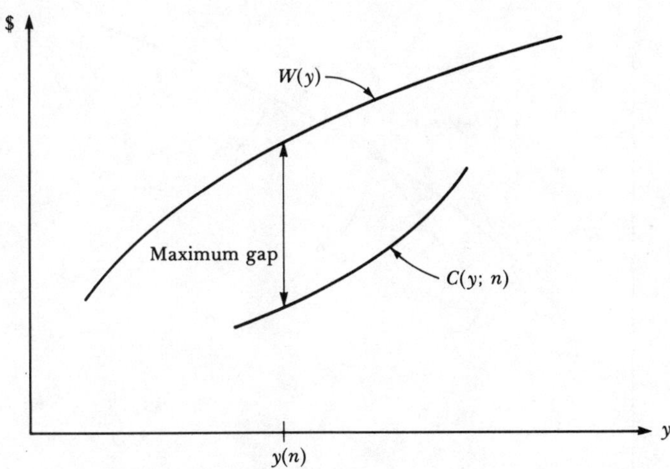

offered. The pair for a given firm n

$$\{W[y(n)], y(n)\}$$

will be accepted only if it is at least as advantageous as that from every other firm. Advantage for the aggregate buyer is judged in the context of aggregate valuation (see Equation 1) less total cost of all payments—that is,

$$\text{Net benefit} = \mathbf{V} - \sum_{n} W[y(n)] \tag{3}$$

But then the market is in equilibrium *on the buyer side* only when for every firm there is the same ratio, call it θ, of additional value contributed to additional cost:

$$S[y(n);n] = \theta W[y(n)] \tag{4}$$

for all n. Figure 3 illustrates the buyer's choices for just three firms but uses the $W(y)$ found in equilibrium on the producer side in Figures 1 and 2. The market in equilibrium imposes a homogeneous regimen such that (Δ value/Δ payment) is the same ratio across the total shipments of each of the market's constituent firms.

If overall equilibrium exists on both the producer and the

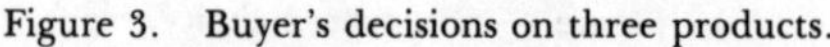
Figure 3. Buyer's decisions on three products.

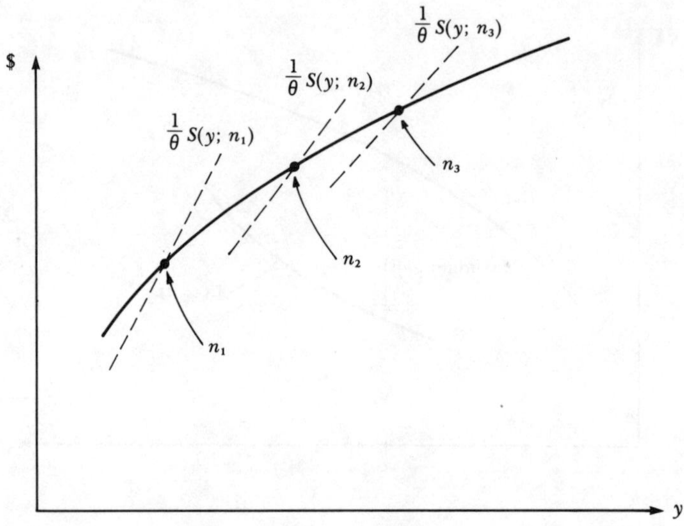

buyer sides,

$$W(y) \text{ defines the terms of trade} \tag{5}$$

To achieve detailed descriptions of possible equilibria, a family of explicit functions for $C(y;n)$ and another for $S(y;n)$ are introduced in the next section. Assuming such specific factual contexts permits study of how terms of trade may change, or become impossible, with changes in the two sides and in their joint context. It permits answers to such questions as whether the terms of trade must be a single-valued function or whether firms with distinctive products can persist in operations at the same volume. But inspection of Figures 1 to 3 already suggests that a variety of different terms of trade $W(y)$ may establish themselves, depending on the detailed history of the dynamics whose outcome is summarized in this comparative statics model. Figure 2 assumes cost per unit increasing with scale; this is the "decreasing returns to scale" assumption mandatory for economists (see Samuelson, 1947). But inspection suggests, and it will later be confirmed, that markets can sustain equilibrium under some circumstances when firms experience *decreasing* costs per unit and that increasing costs per unit do not guarantee the possibility of a market being sustained in equilibrium.

Five points should be made about this terms-of-trade model before we turn to specific assumptions about quality arrays. First, self-sorting is the core. Each firm, by optimizing with respect to the observed schedule, chooses a distinctive volume (and thus a price) that defines its niche or role, which itself is part of the context that induces other firms to their niches. It is evident that no arbitrary collection of cost structures and associated buyer valuations can yield such a schedule—a market. What are observables for various actors? This is a vital question we shall be exploring at length. Self-sorting, within an objective, observable context to which one's own actions contribute, is the core of the model of pure competition (Mansfield, 1975).

Second, a uniform price per item also is defined by the equilibrium schedule $W(y)$ for each firm's goods (specifically the slope of a straight line from the origin to point n in Figure 1). But this conventional price-to-consumer is a secondary matter that follows from the terms of trade established. What buyers are willing to pay depends on how common this brand is seen to be in comparison with other brands: Buyers judge price and volume as a pair, not separately. Similar views can be found in, for example, Bain's treatment of price discrimination (1952, p. 416), in the marketing theory of Verdoorn (1956, pp. 226, 229), and in the work of marketing practitioners Wentz (1966, p. 26) and Taylor and Wills (1969, chap. 40). In the lucid language of Robinson (1933, pp. 87–88):

> The alternative assumptions which make it possible to preserve the appearance of a supply curve on which a given output is associated with a given price are all equally unplausible. . . .
>
> The simple notion of a single price associated with a single output from the industry can only be retained if there is a unique relation which links marginal revenue to price.

Third, second-guessing of the market terms of trade by producers will take place but it suppressed completely in this model as it stands. A firm will be tempted to add or subtract from the terms it reads in the observed schedule $W(y)$ according to its guess about its perception in buyers' eyes in comparison to some median firm. It is such speculation that economic theorists adopt as the main phenomenon. In my approach, the main effort is finding and maintaining a niche: Second-guessing is a perturbation that can be added to this basic terms-of-trade model.

Fourth, buyers in the aggregate exert a severe, knife-edge discipline over producers. If a producer's offer (volume together with cost) is a shade too high, nothing at all is bought—the producer loses his or her place in the market entirely. Knife-edge discipline is a main characteristic of the accepted theory of pure competition, whereas in the existing theory of imperfect competition a producer who chooses the wrong price merely misses the possible optimum results by some percentage (as in Mansfield, 1975, chaps. 8 and 10).

Fifth, aggregation of one side of the market—buyers—is a technical device to simplify the model. This device should not obscure the underlying facts, however. Buyers are not able to coordinate their purchases from all firms; they are not a conspiracy, not a monopsony. Buyers can make only local decisions: They say yes or no to each firm separately. Buyers cannot decide on the whole set of products as an overall package; so "maximization" of net benefit (Equation 3) is operationally meaningless. Existence of two classes of market to be described (crowded and expansive) rests on this fact.

MARKETS AS QUALITY ARRAYS

To see how the terms-of-trade mechanism can ramify, we must specify some factual contexts within which the actors move. The specification should be simple enough to permit full but succinct descriptions of outcomes. Yet it should also promise substantial realism for many current contexts so that it has some use as a guide to field observation.

The central questions are how the various firms indexed by n compare in cost structures $C(y;n)$ and in attractiveness $S(y;n)$. Marketing analysts (for example, Kuehn and Day, 1962) long have urged the importance of perceived quality and how consumers tend to enforce a ranking on quality. It also seems reasonable that production cost structures of different firms should be ordered according to the quality of their respective goods—but in *which* direction is a major question that distinguishes classes of markets. Lancaster (1966) ushered in an era in which economic theorists have paid new attention to the idea of quality. The concept of hedonic prices (see Terleckyj, 1976; Griliches, 1971) is a sophisticated generalization of the quality idea: Customers are paying for a few qualities in a product rather than for its innumerable literal attributes.

Assume that firms can be reindexed such that they fall in a scale by perceived quality, which now increases as n becomes larger. The crucial assumption is that their cost structures $C(y; n)$ are nested one inside another also according to this *same* order. The index n can be treated as a rubber-band scale; so without further loss of generality it can itself be interpreted as an ordinary quantitative variable. (Generalizations of the model can be developed, by analogy with the work on hedonic prices by Lancaster or by Rosen (1974), with n as a two or more dimensional vector of qualities.)

The family of factual contexts with which we deal for the rest of the chapter is

$$C(y; n) = qy^c/n^d \qquad (6)$$

and

$$S(y; n) = ry^a n^b \qquad (7)$$

Equations (1) and (7) are the so-called CES functions commonly used to aggregate preferences by economic theorists (Spence, 1976a; Polemarchakis, Selden, and Pohlman, 1980). Equation (6) is more general than, but contains as a special case, the constant marginal cost assumptions common in economic theory (compare Griliches and Ringstad, 1971). Fuss and McFadden (1978) elaborate Shepard (1970) to an extreme degree and with little attention to the market context as opposed to the firm's technologies.

The important restrictive assumption is that n can function as such an ordering variable with respect to C and S simultaneously. The use of simple powers of y and of n is not essential, since rescaling makes no difference. (The basic results to be presented are unchanged if y and n in Equation 6 or 7 are replaced respectively by any monotone increasing functions, with the former being twice differentiable.) As might be anticipated, outcomes prove to depend essentially only on the two ratios a/c and b/d. In words: The existence and nature of a viable market schedule (terms of trade) depend on trade-offs between cost and valuation across variations in volume (y) and quality (n).

The positive constants r and q are simply convenient scaling parameters to ease discussion of changes in the environment. When the exponent c exceeds unity, costs are increasing with volume; unity exceeds c is the unconventional range of declining costs. Since n is constructed, the exponent b could have been taken as unity (with some occasional loss of convenience), and by the definition of quality it must be positive. Later in the chapter I explain the sign convention for the exponent d (see "Paradox Markets and Failed Markets").

WHAT DO ACTORS KNOW?

Each producer knows its cost for each level of y but need not know either colleagues' costs at any volume or their qualities. Each producer needs to observe, in equilibrium, at least a representative sample of (revenue, output) pairs for producers. (No explicit time frame for observations has been specified, but my view is that the relevant scale is measured in days or weeks and an equilibrium schedule can reestablish itself after a disturbance within a matter of weeks.)

Buyers in aggregate must assess the ratio between incremental value to them from a particular good n in volume $y(n)$ and the payment stream required $W[y(n)]$. This does not require estimating some quality index such as n or even estimating the ratio explicitly. Rather, in equilibrium, for each pair offered in turn, the buyers must verify that the ratio is at least as large as they are getting from any other offer accepted. (A formal derivation is given in White, 1979, pp. 6–8.) Buyers need know nothing about cost.

Buyers in aggregate need not know either the functions S or the overall valuation function $\mathbf{V}$. Nor are producers assumed to know them: Avoiding such assumptions of speculative knowledge is basic to my approach. The producers and buyers need not even be explicitly aware that there is a linear array by quality. I assume specific functions (Equations 6 and 7) with the same motive as the architect who constructs a scale model to illustrate structures and their interconnections. The function $\mathbf{V}$ specifies how buyers have valued various menus of products.

The self-sorting that sustains the terms-of-trade schedule requires the mutual coherence of producers' choices and buyers' perceptions. In later sections I consider what happens when a producer finds no suitable niche. (Strictly speaking, those arguments are not within the basic comparative statics framework and its stipulations of observability.) A schedule may be eliminated as a result, without any actor needing other information.

MARKET PROFILES AND TOTALS

This section contains compressed derivations of general formulas for equilibria in quality arrays: first the terms of trade, then the resulting profiles of volume and payments by quality of firm, then the ranges of quality that can be in the market, and finally aggregate size of payments in a market—which is in a feedback loop with the level of terms of trade. For a first reading it may be sufficient to skim through all but first and last paragraphs while noting the italicized statements. By the end we can identify four major sorts of markets.

Terms of Trade. If terms of trade achieve equilibrium in any of our quality array markets, they take the shape of a displaced power function:

$$W(y) = P(y^{(bc+ad)/b} + K)^{b/(b+d)} \tag{8}$$

This reduces *in the limit of pure competition* to

$$W(y) = Py \tag{9}$$

with P the unique price per unit volume. (Asymptotic analysis is required: $b = 0$ and $a = 1$ in Equations 7 and 1 because of product homogeneity; see de Bruijn, 1961.)

The constant K is not fixed by the attributes of actors and markets; rather, it can take a wide range of arbitrary values. *K thus sums up effects of historical chance on the shape of the tentative terms of trade around which all actors rally.* (Mathematically, the derivation can be recast to show K as a constant of integration, which, as usual in calculus, is fixed by initial conditions.) Whether d is positive or negative, and whether the ratios a/c and b/d are greater or less than unity in magnitude, will prove to block out the main sorts of markets (described in subsequent sections).

Any firm with quality index n will find a proper optimum volume $y(n)$ from equilibrium schedule $W(y)$ only if (Equations 2 and 6)

$$dW(y)/dy\,|_{y(n)} = [c/y(n)]C[y(n);n] \tag{10}$$

On the other side, buyers in aggregate will not say yes to this offer of $y(n)$ volume unless Equation (3) holds, where θ is the common ratio of value to cost that the buyers obtain from the other firms. Treat Equation (8) as a trial solution. Differentiating it, we get

$$dW(y)/dy = (1/y)[(bc + ad)/(b + d)]\,(W^{1+d/b} - PK)/W^{d/b} \quad (11)$$

Substitution of Equations (4) and (11) into Equation (10) yields, after some manipulation,

$$\{W[y(n)]\}^{b+d/b} = [(b + d)c/(bc + ad)]C[y(n);n]\{S[y(n);\mathrm{n}]/\theta\}^{d/b} + KP^{b/b+d} \quad (12)$$

This result confirms Equation (8) as the trial solution only if the right-hand side does not depend explicitly on n, so that terms of trade are common to all firms. Moreover, the power of y must be right; both are in fact the case, from Equations (6) and (7). Inspection yields

$$P = [(b + d)cq/(bc + ad)]^{b/b+d}(r/\theta)^{d/b+d} \quad (13)$$

Market profiles. Market totals depend on the general level of payments P and thus on the ratio θ, whose determination from the number of firms and their distribution over quality n is taken up later. *Profiles do not depend in shape on market aggregates, only in scale,* given the simple power-law dependencies assumed in Equations (6) and (7). Monotonic increase of $W(y)$ with y is guaranteed by Equation (10) since

$$a > 0 \quad \text{and} \quad c > 0 \quad (14)$$

But unit price, $W(y)/y$, need not be monotonic and can either increase or decrease with volume y. The profile of production volume according to quality of firm, $y(n)$, can be specified by substituting Equations (8) and (13), together with (7), into Equation (4):

$$(r/\theta q)[(bc + ad)/(b + d)c]n^{b+d} = y^{c-a} + K/y^{a(b+d)/b} \quad (15)$$

Volume profiles $y(n)$ for positive, negative, and zero values of K are given later for the parameter values used in Figures 1–3. It is then a simple matter to compute profiles versus n of total payments W and profiles versus n of cost C and of profits, $W - C$. The use of Lorenz curves and Gini indices as representations of inequality in such profiles is illustrated extensively elsewhere (White, 1976, sec. 5) for a uniform distribution of firms by quality n.

Ranges. The profiles so far have been screened only by necessary conditions for equilibrium. A firm will not remain in the given market, even at the volume $y(n)$ optimum for it, unless its net income, $W - C$, at this optimum exceeds what it believes it can make elsewhere. The latter depends on time horizon, interest rates, and many other complex factors. I simplify by assuming a firm will continue in the market as long as revenues exceed variable cost:

$$W[y(n)] \geq C[y(n);n] \tag{16}$$

This translates into

$$(c - a)[d/(bc + ad)]y(n)^{(bc+ad)/b} > [(b + d)c/(bc + ad)](-K) \tag{17}$$

in order for firm n to stay in the market. (See Equations 6, 8, 13, and 15.)

To talk about the range of n is to discuss which firms can coexist in a market given the general character of demand and cost there and thus the partition of firms among markets in an economy. It suggests answers to the question, "Where does the partition come from?" The range of n also describes how homogeneous are the various products in the given market: Under what circumstances can a market be sustained across an extremely heterogeneous array of quality in the product?

Profiles for this market may also have the range of n shrunk for another, more subtle reason. Equation (10) only guaranteed that $y(n)$ would be an extremum; $y(n)$ is in fact a proper maximum if the second-order condition is satisfied, which here becomes

$$(c - a)c\,[d/(bc + ad)]y(n)^{(bc+ad)/b} > (ad/b)[(b + d)c/(bc + ad)]K \tag{18}$$

If the inequality is invalid, then that $y(n)$ yields minimum rather than maximum net income for firm n. The firm may well find, for the given $W(y)$, another y (so-called corner maximum) that is attractive. But then there is no reason why its contribution to buyer valuation **V** will satisfy Equation (4), which ensures the self-selecting nature of market equilibrium: Buyers will not accept those offers.

Aggregate Flows. We want to find the sizes of aggregate flows in these markets. The products of different firms are differentiated; so aggregation of cash flows makes more sense than aggregation of physical volumes. Define total cash flow as the sum of payments to all producers:

$$\mathbf{W} \equiv \sum_n W[y(n)] \tag{19}$$

A first and relatively minor problem is the location constant for the schedule, the K defined in Equation (8). It is impossible to derive closed formulas when K is nonzero, although numerical iterative procedures yield solutions for any concrete case. Hereafter I assume

$$K = 0 \tag{20}$$

There is, in general, no substantive significance to this value; for its incidence, see Table A-1, Appendix A.

The important problem, and a much more difficult one, is feedback. Schematically, the feedback loop is

$$\mathbf{W} \rightarrow \theta \rightarrow W(y) \rightarrow y(n) \rightarrow W[y(n)] \rightarrow \mathbf{W} \tag{21}$$

The computation in Equation (19) is involuted. When the general level P of terms of trade $W(y)$ is changed, each firm n will adjust its choice of volume $y(n)$, possibly in the opposite sense, so that the total effect on market aggregate W is not obvious. To disentangle this loop, I calibrate aggregates in terms of size at the buyers' break-even point.

Net benefit to buyers is, after substitutions from Equations (4) and (1),

$$\text{Net benefit} = \theta^{\gamma}\mathbf{W}^{\gamma} - \mathbf{W} \tag{22}$$

which must be positive. The break-even point, indicated by use of subscript zero, is where

$$\theta_0 = \mathbf{W}_0^{1-\gamma/\gamma} \tag{23}$$

Then rescale:

$$\theta \equiv t \cdot \theta_0 \tag{24}$$

Here t is a dimensionless ratio that sums up the effects of historical accident on the money size of the aggregate market. This ratio t determines the height P of $W(y)$ just as K does the location of the terms of trade. And the inequality that bounds t (net benefit positive, Equation 22) is analogous to the two inequalities (Equations 17 and 18) that bound ranges for producer quality n. At the break-even point, where $t = 1$, computation of the sum in (19) can be carried out and the term in θ (now θ_0) transferred to and combined with the left-hand side of (9). The final result is, still for $K = 0$,

$$\mathbf{W}_0 = \{(r^c/q^a)[(bc + ad)/(b + d)c]^a \, (\Sigma\, n^{(bc+ad)/(c-a)})^{c-a}\}^{\gamma/(c-a\gamma)} \tag{25}$$

Here the sum is over the quality level n for each firm in the market. Elsewhere (White, 1979, pp. 54–57) I argue that there will not be a significant interaction effect between aggregate size and limits on the range of quality n (inequalities 17 and 18).

Results can now be given in terms of this calibration (Equations 24 and 25) at the break-even size. Aggregates for other values of payoff ratio θ can be computed as

$$\mathbf{W} = \mathbf{W}_0/t^{c/(c-a)} \tag{26}$$

$$\mathbf{V} = \mathbf{W}_0/t^{a\gamma/(c-a)} \tag{27}$$

Here t is greater, or less, than unity according to whether c is greater or less than a. Finally, terms of trade and also profiles can be calibrated in terms of independent parameters.

To simplify notation, let

$$\phi \equiv r^{\gamma}(bc + ad)/q(b + d)c \qquad \text{and} \qquad \eta \equiv \Sigma\, n^{(bc+ad)/(c-a)} \tag{28}$$

Then the height of $W(y)$ is

$$P = 1/t^{d/(b+d)}\, [(b + d)cq/(bc + ad)]\, (\phi/\eta^{1-\gamma})^{d(c-a)/(b+d)(c-a\gamma)} \tag{29}$$

Effects of the feedback process can be seen by contrasting this result with the earlier form for P (Equation 13). Note in particular that P depends in different ways on the ratio t and on the sum over firms η that together enter the determination of θ (Equation 4). Similarly, the equilibrium profile for volume becomes

$$y(n) = (n^{b+d}/t)^{1/(c-a)}(\phi/\eta^{1-\gamma})^{1/(c-a\gamma)} \tag{30}$$

The main importance of both results is negative: It can be shown that these scale sizes for $W(y)$ and for equilibrium profiles vary differently with parameters such as r, and the sum over n, across market regions. Specifically, both P and equilibrium volume for a given firm, $y(n)$, go down (modestly) as the number of firms (and demand) increases (with the same quality range) and both go up as the level of valuation, r, goes up, but at very different rates as b/d changes.

RESULTS WITH EXAMPLES

Having derived general formulas for profiles and aggregates, I now return to the fundamental question of the factual circumstances—summarized by our parameters—that permit a market to be sustained.

The formulas derived in the preceding pages show, as will become clear, that one fundamental break is whether the power d of Equation (6) is positive. A second fundamental break is whether c is greater than a; the impact here depends not only on the sign of d but also on the size of γ and on the relative magnitudes of b/d and a/c. There prove to be four major regions for success—paradox, grind, crowded, expansive—and two regions for failure of markets. Figure 4 lays out all the regions in parameter space.

Now let us consider the specialized results applicable in each of the main types of markets, with numerical and graphic illustrations in

Figure 4. Market types.

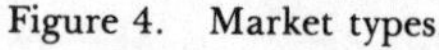

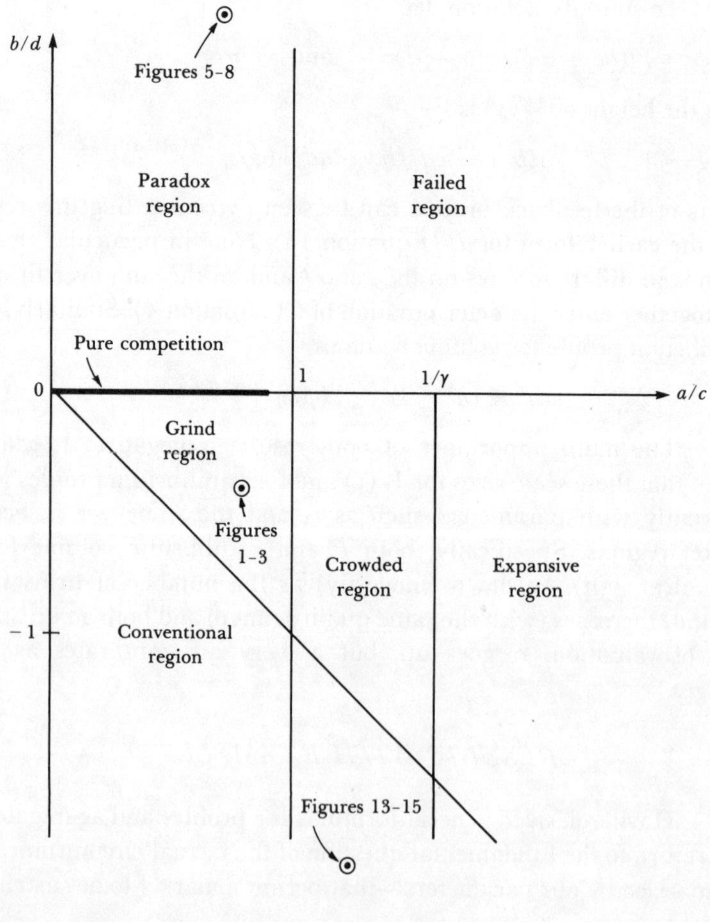

each case. Then we shall take up possibilities for generalization and evidence of robustness. Four very different sorts of markets can build in different factual contexts of production cost structure, number and quality of products, and consumers' valuations. *Crowded* is the most striking market type; it has no analog in microeconomic theory. *Grind* is closest to, though still far from, the microeconomist's model for the same context. *Paradox* is the region that depends most acutely on the buyer's perception of differences among firms. One region (*conventional*) will not sustain markets on my model but will according to Chamberlain's (see Appendix B); another region, labeled *failed,* cannot sustain markets according to either. *Expansive,* the fourth type of market, may be relevant only for earlier centuries.

Calibration, Units, Dimensions. All my figures and tables adopt the same conventions; for details see Appendix A, which also reports (Table A-1) the ranges of K allowed. Until now, parameters have not been merged even though I have just shown in Figure 4 that outcomes often depend only on the ratio of two parameters. Comprehension is aided, and interpretation of fieldwork enhanced, by this separation.

Paradox Markets and Failed Markets. The paradox is that

Figure 5. Producer's optimal volumes from terms of trade $W(y)$.

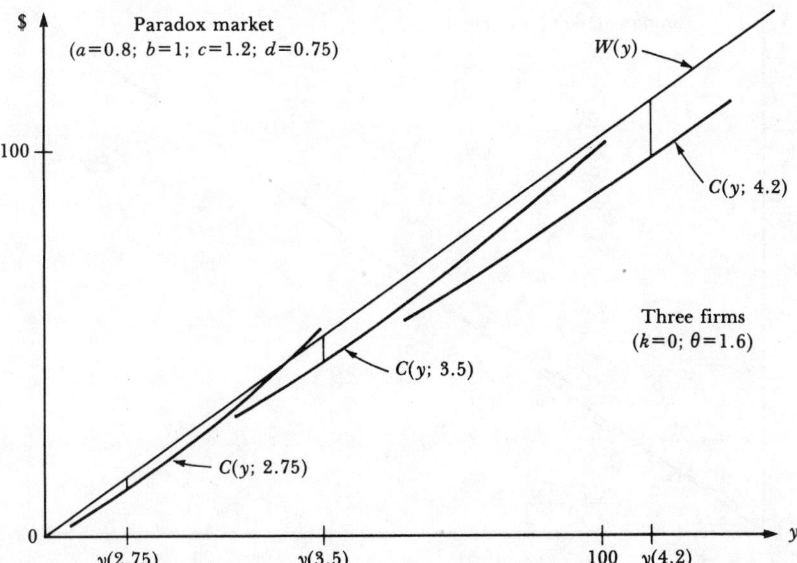

firms with *higher*-quality products (in the eyes of buyers) actually produce a given volume at *lower* cost. The paradox occurs when d is positive: Compare the definitions in Equations (6) and (7). One can argue that differences in fixed costs can remove the paradox—earlier expenditures on large advertising campaigns or superb service guarantees may explain these apparently perverse preferences of buyers. Nonetheless, puzzlement persists and requires still further explanation; perhaps some of the firms in the market (with low n) use outdated facilities. And we shall see that terms of trade are not so easy to establish as they are for d negative. In either my view or Chamberlain's, markets with d positive are likely to be confined to cases where the buyers are individual uninformed consumers rather than industrial purchasers.

Figure 5 exhibits equilibrium terms of trade $W(y)$ for a simplified market of three producers, of qualities $0.8n_0$, n_0, and $1.2n_0$, whose cost curves are also shown together with their respective optimum volumes $y(n)$. The buyers' side, shown in Figure 6, reports the same $W(y)$ together with the valuation contributions $(1/\theta)S[y(n);n]$ from the three volumes of the three respective qualities. One sees the result: Producers of goods regarded as higher quality ship

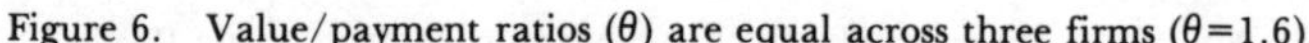
Figure 6. Value/payment ratios (θ) are equal across three firms (θ=1.6).

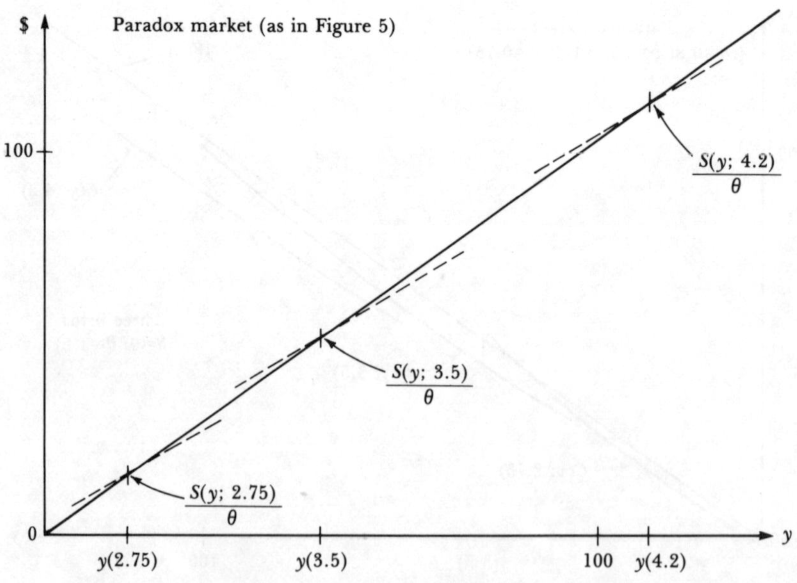

larger volumes. I choose $K = 0$ for this illustration; note that the $W(y)$ terms of trade are close to a linear price schedule.

The whole profile of volume versus quality across the entire possible range of n is traced in Figure 7—first for $K = 0$ (as in Figure 5), then for $K > 0$ and for $K < 0$. For any K, equilibrium volume always increases as n increases, as does revenue $W[y(n)]$. Figure 8 reports the three profiles for net revenue $(W - C)$ versus n at the same values of K. Observe that a given producer works harder for negative K—$y(n)$ is larger—and achieves more revenue but lower net revenue.

When $K > 0$, a place in the equilibrium schedule $W(y)$ cannot be found by firms with low values of n. Firms below the cutoff value

Figure 7. Equilibrium volume by quality: profiles for various K and θ, in paradox region.

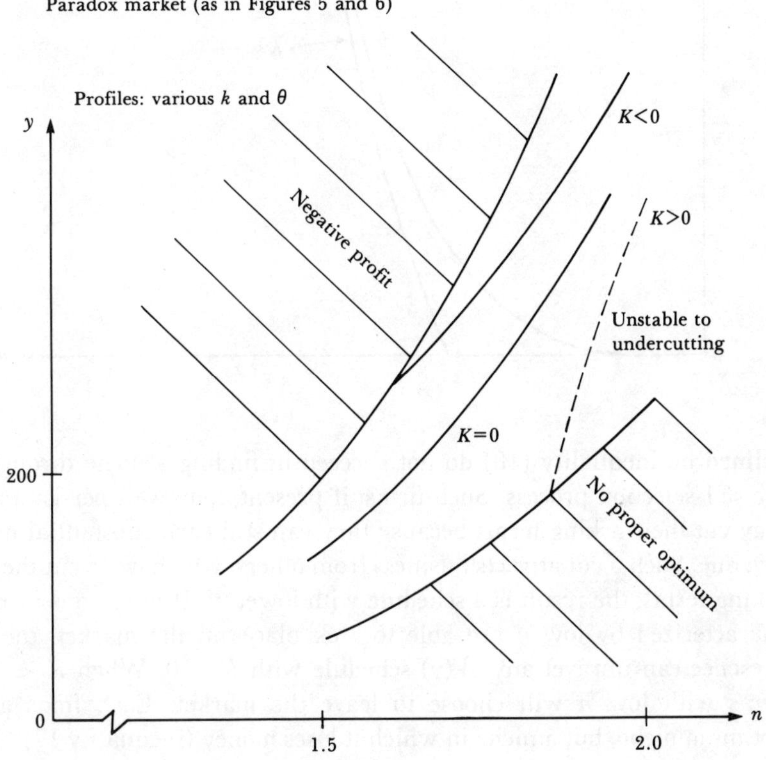

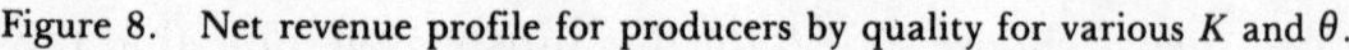

Figure 8. Net revenue profile for producers by quality for various K and θ.

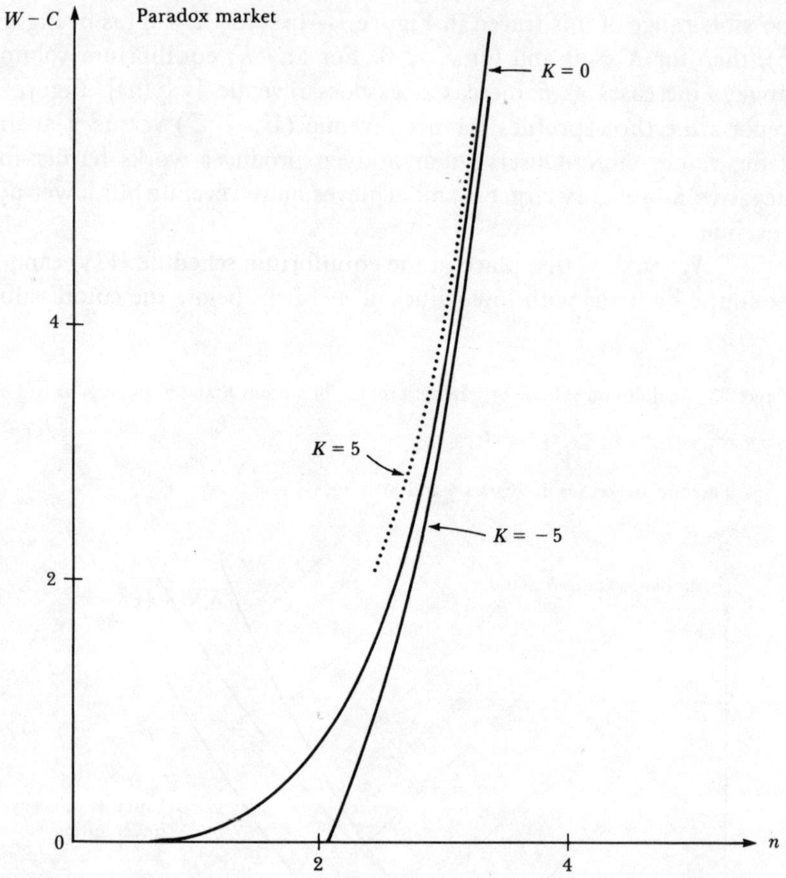

defined by inequality (18) do not succeed in finding a niche through the self-selection process. Such firms, if present, may well persist and may cut their asking terms because they can still earn substantial net revenue. Such a cut attracts business from others, who have to cut their asking terms; the result is a schedule with lower K. If numerous firms characterized by low n are able to seek places in the market, their presence can unravel any $W(y)$ schedule with $K > 0$. When $K < 0$, firms with low n will choose to leave the market: Each finds an optimum niche, but a niche in which it loses money (inequality 17).

These profile results, which screen out values of K or ranges of n or both, are inverted when cost curvature c is less than valuation slope a. And then the self-selection mechanism fails. *This is one set of factual contexts where no market can form (see Figure 4). Thus if $a > c$, markets fail when d is positive, mandating a paradoxical trade-off between actual cost and perceived quality.* When $K \geq 0$, different firms do not identify distinctive optimal volumes $y(n)$ (inequality 18). When $K < 0$, every firm finds that its net revenue is negative at its distinctive optimal volume (inequality 17).

The aggregate size of the market $\mathbf{W}$ (and equivalently the value/cost ratio θ) varies in the same way as the break-even size $\mathbf{W}_0$

Figure 9. Market cash flow at break-even point W_0 for various taste and cost contexts within the paradox region ($b=1$ in all cases).

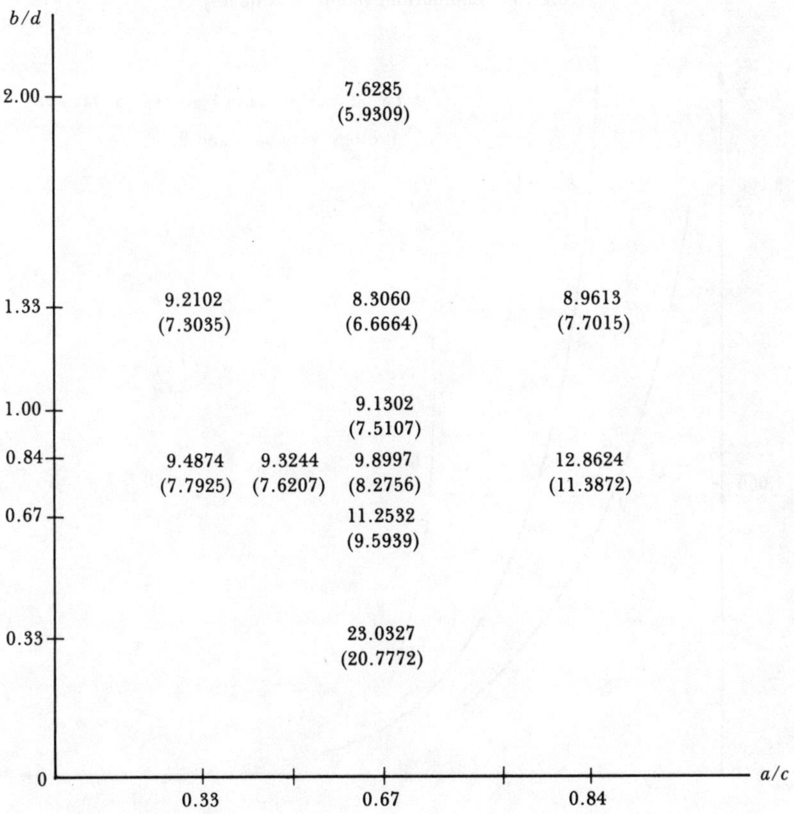

with the facts of the situation (see Equation 26). From inspection of Equations (22), (24), (27), and (26), the aggregate buyers do best when the ratio t equals

$$t_m = (c/a\gamma)^{(c-a)/(c-a\gamma)} \tag{31}$$

Note that at this "best," market size $\mathbf{W}$ always is smaller than $\mathbf{W}_0$. From Equation (25), we are not surprised to learn that $\mathbf{W}$ increases with r, decreases as q increases, increases as the number of firms and associated demand increases (more terms in the sum), and so on. Figure 9 gives numerous examples of aggregate size $\mathbf{W}_0$ for various sets of parameters within the paradox region. This figure assumes $K = 0$ and 20 firms at quality levels evenly spaced between $n = 1.0$ and 2.0 (see Appendix A for units).

Figure 10. Equilibrium volume and quality.

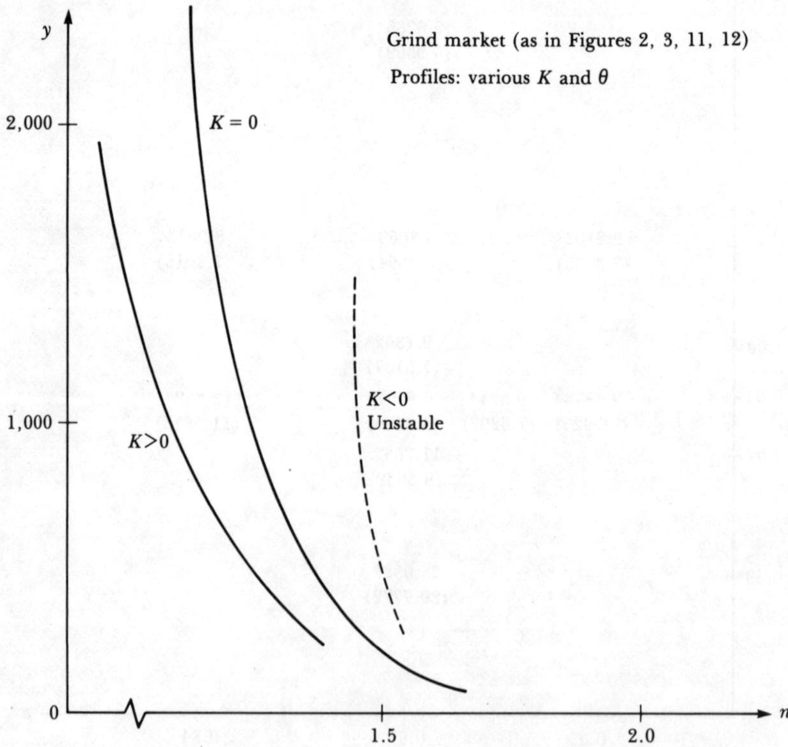

The Chamberlain model, as generalized by Spence (1976a), also predicts market equilibrium in the paradox region (as also in the conventional and grind regions). It predicts a unique outcome, a unique terms-of-trade schedule in my usage, which represents optimization by both producers and buyers. Appendix B supplies derivations and results. These market aggregates are given in parentheses in Figure 9 for comparison.

Grind Markets and the Conventional Region. Conventional wisdom has it that we prefer the things that cost more; so I call the $d < 0$ region *conventional* if $a < c$ (decreasing returns to scale). The form of solution is distinctive in the subregion with b below d in magnitude. I call these *grind* markets because producers grind their teeth: Buyers' evaluations of goods go up less rapidly with increase in quality than do the costs of producing them. In any such grind market a wide range of $W(y)$ schedules can establish itself. Any $K \geq 0$ will do.

At any other point in the conventional region, a market schedule could not be sustained with $K \leq 0$, since firms would then find neither distinctive nor profitable niches. And for $K > 0$, firms with a low value of n would be left out. As they persist, or other low-n firms try to enter, they will drag the schedule down. So in this bottom part of the conventional region any market schedule would be eroded.

Figure 10 reports the profile $y(n)$ for a market in the grind

TABLE 1

Grind Region: Market Cash Flow **W** According to Qualities of the Set of Firms[a]

t	Number of Firms	Set of n Values	**W**
t_m	20	1.05, 1.10, . . . , 2.0	0.236
$0.9\ t_m$	20	1.05, 1.10, . . . , 2.0	0.482
t_m	40[b]	1.05, 1.10, . . . , 2.0	0.079
$0.9\ t_m$	40	1.05, 1.10, . . . , 2.0	0.161
t_m	100	1.01, 1.02, . . . , 2.0	0.348
$0.9\ t_m$	100	1.01, 1.02, . . . , 2.0	0.710
t_m	16	0.5, 0.6, . . . , 2.0	0.509
$0.9\ t_m$	16	0.5, 0.6, . . . , 2.0	1.039
t_m	9	0.2, 0.25, 0.33, 0.5, 1, 2, 3, 4, 5	1.685
$0.9\ t_m$	9	0.2, 0.25, 0.33, 0.5, 1, 2, 3, 4, 5	3.440

[a]As in Figure 10: $a = 0.7 = \gamma$; $c = 0.8$; $b = 1$; $d = -2$. See Appendix A for units: $\mathbf{W}_{t_m} = 0.282\mathbf{W}_0$; t_m is given in Equation (31).

[b]See "Duplication of Producers" subsection.

region; it parallels Figure 7 for a market in the paradox region. As one must insist, the higher the quality of a firm's product, the smaller the volume $y(n)$ that it chooses as its equilibrium niche. Aggregate sizes of markets are exhibited in Table 1 for just the one set of values, a, b, c, d, γ, that identify the market in Figure 10. However, here I explore variations of two kinds:

1. Change in **W** as the number or the set of quality values n (or both) changes
2. Change in **W** when the historical parameter t varies—specifically, at t_m and at $0.9t_m$, where t_m is the value in Equation (31) that maximizes net benefit to buyers (Equation 3)

The sensitivity to t—that is, to the value/cost ratio θ that happens to get established—is surprisingly great. The first kind of variation is discussed later in the subsection on duplication of firms.

The terms-of-trade schedule that underlies Figure 10 is drawn in Figure 11 and repeated in Figure 12: Note that this schedule is identical to the $W(y)$ in Figures 2 and 3. So also are the profiles, the

Figure 11. Producer's optimal volumes for terms of trade $W(y)$.

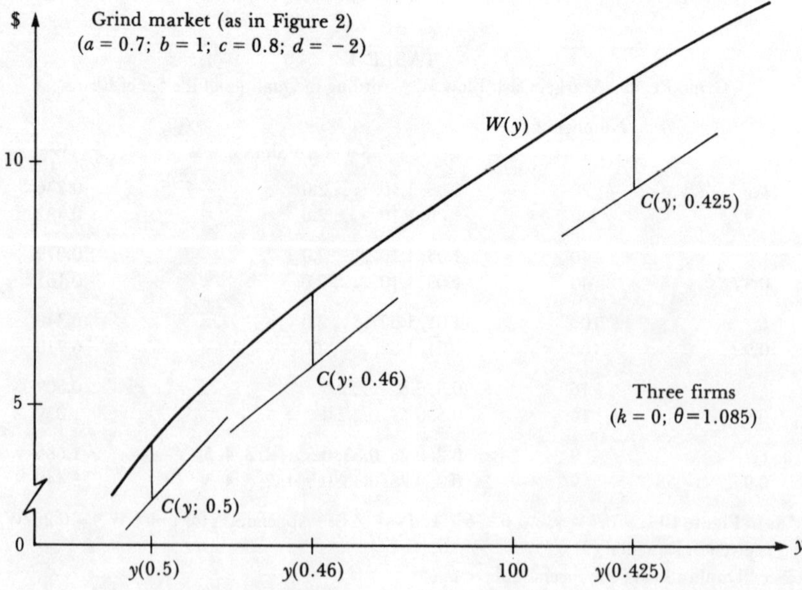

Figure 12. Value/payment ratios equal across firms.

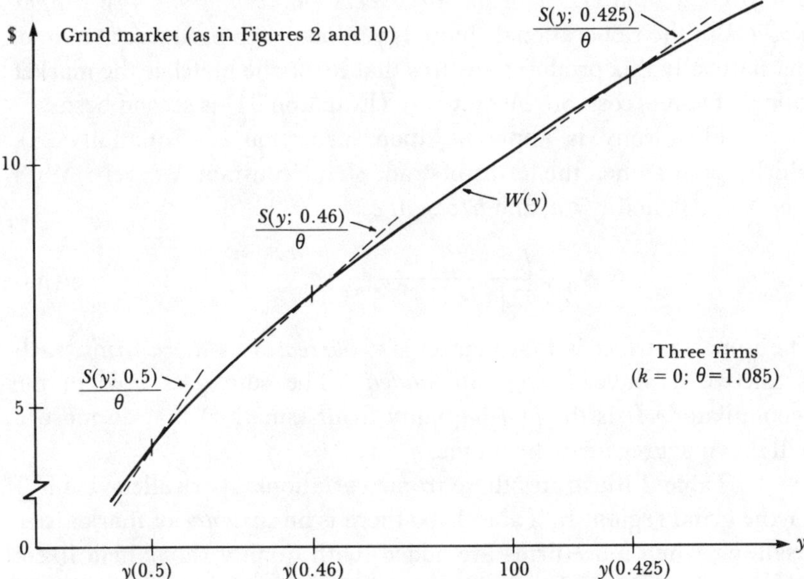

ranges, and the aggregate sizes in equilibrium. The cost schedules do change from Figure 2 to Figure 11, but this change is counterbalanced (given that other parameters are the same—r, q, γ, the n's, and K) by the shift in valuations S shown between Figures 3 and 12.

Crowded Markets

Crowded markets are, I suspect, common around us, and common in other mature economies. Above all this model insists on the lack of conscious coordination among actors. In my terms-of-trade theory, buyers insist upon value for money and can enforce that demand locally, but they cannot change to another set of producers as a whole (any more than producers can create or abolish buyers). Now consider the *crowded* circumstances: Cost goes up with quality of products ($d < 0$), yet there are increasing returns to scale, in that the cost of a given producer does not go up with volume as fast as consumer evaluation does ($a/c > 1$). As I have said, these seem likely enough in an economy with producers rarely operating near capacity. *Under these circumstances buyers would be made better off if they could buy only from a smaller set of the producers—indeed, from any proper subset.* But their operational choice is yes/no to one producer at a time, and naturally this producer ensures that he or she matches the market ratio θ of value/cost. So the best here (Equation 31) is second best.

This irony is apparent upon inspection of Equation (25), which applies when the terms-of-trade shape constant K is zero. With $-\delta \equiv d < 0$, and $c < a$, and $b/\delta > a/c$,

$$\mathbf{W}_0 \sim \left(\frac{1}{\Sigma[1/n^{(bc-a\delta)/(a-c)}]}\right)^{(a-c)\gamma/(c-a\gamma)} \tag{32}$$

The important fact is that market size *decreases* as more firms, each distinctive in buyers' eyes, are *added.* (The sum over n is in the denominator.) It is the *lower*-quality firms (small n) that do most to pull down aggregate cash volume.

Table 2 illustrates these ironic variations. It parallels Table 1 for the grind region. In Table 1 too there is an *instance* of market size declining when more firms are added, with quality range held fixed. But that is a quite different effect, a general one that can also be found in the other regions. Specifically: If more producers come in to match existing products' qualities exactly, and thus induce no distinctive demand from buyers, the result is some decline in aggregate market size. This effect is important enough to warrant a subsection later on. Observe that Table 2, unlike Table 1, can have no size predictions

TABLE 2
Crowded Region: Market Cash Flow at Break-Even $\mathbf{W}_0$ According to Number and Qualities of Firms and Other Parameters[a]

a	b	c	d	γ	$\mathbf{W}_0$
Twenty firms: $1 < n \leq 2$, *uniform distribution*					
1	1	0.8	−0.5	0.7	0.00442
0.8	1	0.5	−0.3	0.5	0.00563
Ten firms: $1 < n \leq 2$, *uniform distribution*					
1	1	0.8	−0.5	0.7	0.0116
0.8	1	0.5	−0.3	0.5	0.0159
Nine firms: $n = (1/5, 1/4, 1/3, 1/2, 1, 2, 3, 4, 5)$					
1	1	0.8	−0.5	0.7	0.00120
0.8	1	0.5	−0.3	0.5	0.00566

[a]See Figure 4. Calculations assume $K = 0$. See Appendix A for units.

Figure 13. Producer's optimal volumes from terms of trade $W(y)$.

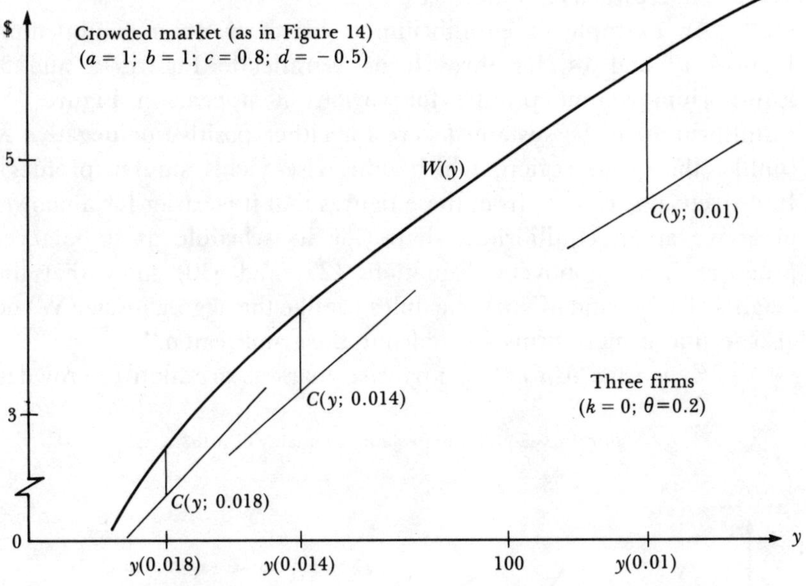

Figure 14. Equal ratios of value to payment across firms.

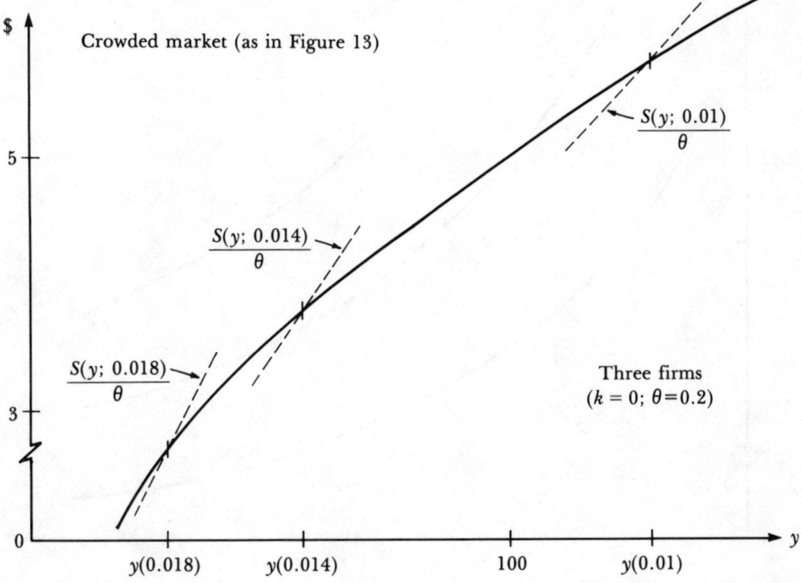

from Chamberlain–Spence theory, which denies the possibility of markets in crowded circumstances.

An example of equilibrium terms of trade is exhibited in Figures 13 and 14, for three firms, parallel to Figures 2 and 3. Equilibrium volume profiles for various K appear in Figure 15. Equilibrium can be sustained here for either positive or negative K (unlike the grind region, which otherwise yields similar profiles). Intuitively, one can see from these figures that it is easier for a market to arrive at an equilibrium shape for its schedule as it balances producers against buyers. Equations (29) and (30) show that the heights of $W(y)$ and of $y(n)$ schedules (unlike the aggregate size $\mathbf{W}$) do also decline as more firms are added in the grind region.

Expansive Markets. Expansive markets are akin to crowded

Figure 15. Equilibrium volume by quality of firm.

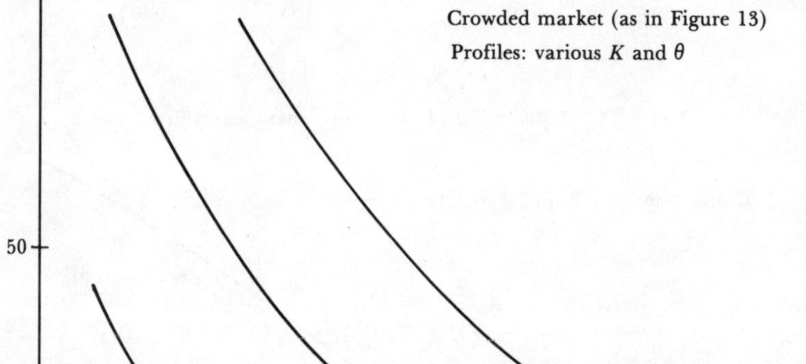

ones, except that the cost structures are much more favorable for producers. Any chance disturbances that raise the $W(y)$ schedule tend to be sustained. I do not develop implications further here, for the parameter region seems implausible for current markets. Elsewhere (White, 1978, sec. 2) I suggest that such markets might be able to represent the early stages of industrialization.

Duplication of Producers. When studying entry and exit of producers from a market, one may wish to consider the possibility that two or more firms are indistinguishable, competing for the same valuation contribution $S(y;n)$ in Equation (1). Duplication is a partial return to pure competition assumptions. (Earlier I cited ways to disaggregate buyers, another partial return to homogeneous competition.) These mixed models raise many complexities, but one extreme form is easy to solve.

Suppose there are f duplicate firms producing at each value of quality n. The derivation of terms of trade is almost unchanged. Buyers continue to say yes/no to the pair (total payment, total volume) for that quality n according to Equation (3). But each firm sees as revenue not $W(y)$ but $(1/f)W(y)$, and it computes optimum volume (Equation 10) accordingly. The new results are obtained simply by replacing q everywhere by $(q \cdot f)$. This procedure was illustrated in Table 1.

Robustness. Advocacy of these models as a guide to field research requires attention to the robustness of their main conclusions (the market types of Figure 4, entry and exit effects, and so on) over variations in the assumptions: the index n of firms as a one-dimensional quality array; the CES form for valuation (Equations 1 and 7); the cost function as a power law (Equation 6). I wish to examine the robustness of my role-structure approach first by testing broad conclusions without need of detailed parameter estimates. A naturalist approach is the first step.

A variety of trials with other functional forms suggest the robustness of the main conclusions and even the shapes of profiles. Consider the profiles for $y(n)$ in Figure 16, where Equations (6) and (7) are replaced by

$$C(y;n) = y + \tfrac{3}{8}(y - n)^2 \qquad (6')$$

$$S(y;n) = y + 2n \qquad (7')$$

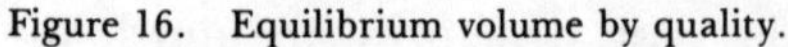

Figure 16. Equilibrium volume by quality.

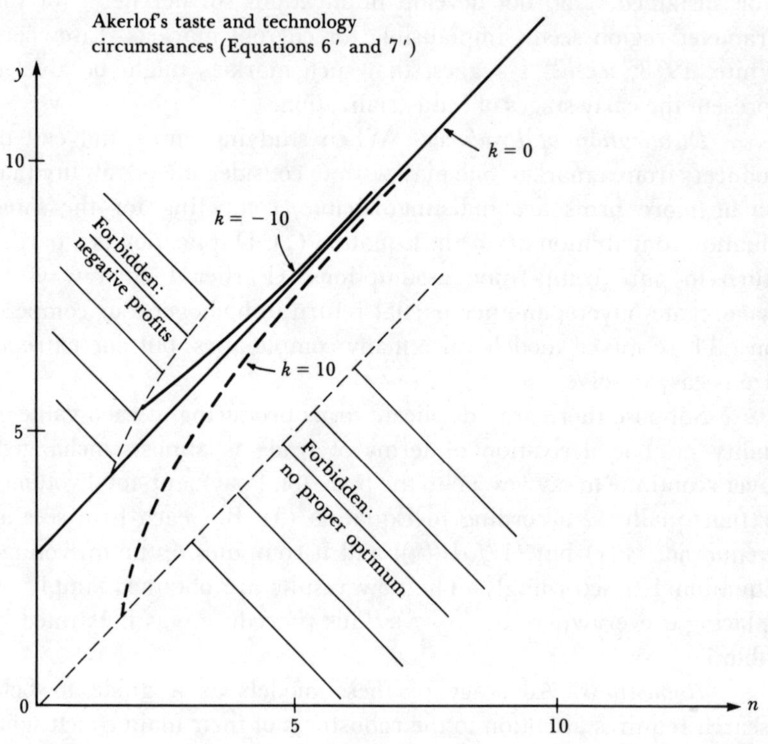

(adapted from Akerlof, 1976). Compare these profiles with those in Figure 7.

Elsewhere (White, 1978, sec. 7) I consider another variant:

$$C(y;n) = q(y - D)^3(1 - n), \tag{6''}$$

where D is an arbitrary constant, and

$$S(y;n) = y(1 - n) \tag{7''}$$

This variant is for the dual form of my terms-of-trade model, where buyers are disaggregated, with the S function for cost and the C function for valuation. Again the equilibrium solutions for the terms-of-trade schedule have the same topology. This example is also important because it is chosen to be plausible for a market situation that is *not* for durable goods—namely, for the insurance markets formulated by Rothschild and Stiglitz (1975) in their analysis of imperfect competition using signaling ideas.

FIELD STUDIES: ANTICIPATIONS AND APPLICATIONS

Massive public depositions on their market practices preceded the 1961 antitrust convictions (Neale, 1970) of GE, Westinghouse, and Allis-Chalmers for conspiring to fix prices of turbine generators sold to electric utilities. (Herling, 1962, pp. 332–333, surveys the range of related indictments.) Just before, Sultan (1974, p. ix) happened to be preparing case studies of GE's management for business school use. His skepticism over the judges' multimillion-dollar guesses about the impact of collusion moved Sultan to conduct extensive interviews—which, in conjunction with the depositions, offer one of the best-documented studies of an industry (Sultan, 1974, 1975). It is a bad case for my theory: The firms are certified as an extreme oligopoly, virtually a triopoly (Sultan, 1975, p. 1). But the case is worth a look, if only to explore the reasonableness of some of my simplifying assumptions and my general view of markets as role structures. Then I shall turn to strategy for field tests of the theory, followed by guesses about particular markets in the United States.

Economies of scale were real and important (Sultan, 1975, pp. 295–296). But Sultan supplies much evidence that producers' major market choices go beyond the (revenue, volume) pair alone. Introduction of technological innovation was a continuing critical choice. Backlogs were important. It was indeed a market of products seen as differentiated according to producer: "In sum, the statistical analysis of brands purchased reveals strong and highly differentiated purchasing loyalties" (Sultan, 1974, p. 299). Cost structures differed as well: GE lowest, then Westinghouse, with Allis-Chalmers highest.

Uniform price per item, a "book price," is a fiction (Sultan, 1974, p. 277). Terms of trade are for a whole transaction between buyer and seller—a (price, volume) pair. The terms established depend on how producers' strategies are *seen* ("transaction visibility"; Sultan, 1974, pp. 248–251).

Buyers' valuation functions (Equation 1) and the consumer-as-producer hedonic prices approach receive support (Sultan, 1974, p. 184):

> One theme runs through General Electric's policy statements, speeches and operating manuals of the 1950's and 1960's: pricing should be value-oriented. Prices were to be based primarily on an exploitation of customers' perceptions of the value of the product. . . . Turbines were priced according to value, and with rapidly rising value, prices could soar. . . . This philosophy was in practice readily accepted by customers: they were paying for kilowatts of output capacity, not for generators.

The three firms and their turbine products can indeed be arrayed in the same order by cost structure and by valuation (although this is hardly a severe test of the idealization of markets as quality arrays). The increasing order for costs (GE, Westinghouse, Allis-Chalmers) is also the decreasing order for valuations (Sultan, 1974, p. 281). I should expect to find a market located within the paradox region. (With more firms this judgment is not so easy: I take this matter up under strategy for field tests in general.)

From my earlier results, given a market in the paradox region, I can venture an opinion contradicting a main judgment of my expert himself (Sultan, 1975, p. 111). I am of course pushing my model (as Sultan does his own model, a half-breed: Schumpeter-plus-multiple-regression). I could select half a dozen other quotes from these two volumes to throw doubt on my model's applicability. The overall balance of Sultan's account is overwhelmingly on the side of a role-structure interpretation, but that does not establish my role model focused on terms of trade.

The judgment I question is that the producers' conspiracy was impotent. The clue I work from is Sultan's repeated emphasis on the use of "buffering," by which the Big Boys took a bigger cut in sales than Allis-Chalmers during a downturn in order to—on Sultan's own account—shelter it. Clue in hand, turn to Figure 8, which portrays two possible equilibrium schedules for a paradox market, corresponding to $K = 0$ and $K < 0$. The third schedule (dotted line), for $K > 0$, cannot continue in a competitive market open to many firms, because the smaller, lower-quality firms will pull down that schedule. Yet that schedule yields enormous increases in net revenue to each firm (n level) large enough to achieve a niche on it. And it is the smallest firm that manages to stay in that benefits most (here Allis-Chalmers).

I need not disagree with Sultan (1975, p. 1) that intense

competition characterizes even this triopoly. The thrust of my model is to show how competitive pressure induces and maintains a role structure.

General Approach. Disappearance of markets under the circumstances I label conventional (lower left region, Figure 4) may be the most surprising prediction, since it is in flat contradiction to the economist's standard view (see Chamberlain–Spence predictions in Appendix B). But a negative prediction is difficult to test from field observation, since it is a statement about circumstances in all the markets that do exist (and also since the model's framework for circumstances is deliberately oversimplified). The most important test, therefore, is searching for any examples of markets in crowded circumstances (lower right, Figure 4), where according to standard economic views there can be no market. Later I offer some guesses.

Likewise difficult to test is my prediction that a great many distinct market schedules could establish themselves in given circumstances—that is, a variety of t and K values for given values of the parameters. This prediction holds for the previous sorts of markets and for the grind region and the paradox region as well. Furthermore, one is unlikely to identify shape and height of profiles and market schedules accurately enough for testing by field observation.

Better candidates for testing are the aggregate sizes of markets. And this is the proper level for supplying answers to the business person's (and the economist's) questions about "what happened to supply and demand?" Cross-sectional comparisons of market cash flows are one possibility—for example, after engineering innovation changes cost scale, q, or shape. Figure 9 and Table 2 also demonstrate how my predictions of aggregate flows differ from those of economists. A second possibility is comparing observations before and after the entry or exit of a firm. A third possibility is comparing observations before and after the entry of a product innovation. These last two require special care, since buyer valuations (Equation 1) are central and are difficult to estimate independently, even roughly for buyers as a whole.

For field testing it is helpful to have guides from the market outcomes themselves to indicate the circumstances that underlie the market. Measurement of cost and value structures is a formidable task, as is assimilating the result to the nearest power-law form stipulated in Equations (6) and (7). Price profiles are one possibility: price per

TABLE 3

Variation of Price p_n with Volume $y(n)$ According to Sign of Historical Constant K and Determinant of Powers, by Three Principal Market Regions[a]

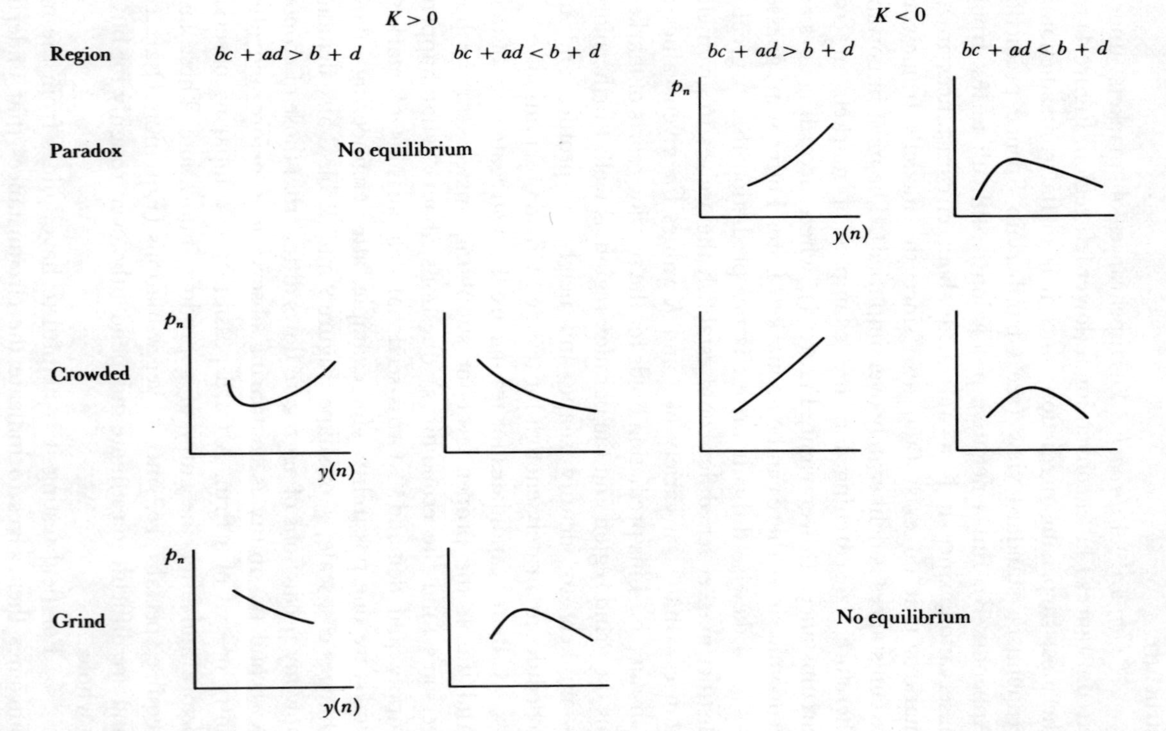

	$K > 0$		$K < 0$	
Region	$bc + ad > b + d$	$bc + ad < b + d$	$bc + ad > b + d$	$bc + ad < b + d$
Paradox	No equilibrium			
Crowded				
Grind			No equilibrium	

[a]Defined in Figure 4.

physical unit versus the market share or the absolute volume of that product variety. Table 3 shows these profiles for absolute volumes, in each of the three market regions (Figure 4), in terms of allowed ranges of the shape measure K and the powers a, b, c, d. (The fact that none of these price profiles has more than one peak or trough is a by-product of the simple power-law forms stipulated in Equations 6 and 7 for C and S.) Only one price profile uniquely identifies which of the three regions the market is in according to my theory, but only one profile can be found somewhere in each of the three regions. As we shall see, qualitative arguments about the likely sizes of the power ratios a/c and b/d will suffice for a first exploration.

Guesses and Advice: Who's Crowded? Suppose you are a chief executive officer considering moving into a new market, perhaps by building upon an existing producer (Markham, 1973). Rough and ready estimates suggest crowded circumstances in this market. You are optimistic that your firm's expertise will elicit a distinctive taste of buyers for the product your new entrance introduces. *Even so, your entrance will cause the total market to shrink (measured by cash volume **W**).* You would be fighting for a market share when your entrance is actually shrinking the total dollar pie! (Only if you were actually bringing in wholly new customers—in effect raising the scale parameter r—would this not be true, but then you would be creating your own market.) To me this scenario is like the one confronting Mr. Whitman in the Mostronics Division of Electro Industries as described by Abell and Hammond (1979, pp. 134–159 and 195–211)—though it cannot be the whole story, which must in addition include continuous technological innovation.

Household appliances may be a grind market; see, for example, the *Business Week* story (7 May 1979, pp. 74–78) on White manufacturers (no relation). I chose the term *grind* because often the circumstances assumed for these markets lead to a struggle for the producers in them. The struggle eases when there is little differentiation, that is, when b approaches zero, leading to pure competition. But in much of the grind triangular area in Figure 4 pickings are slim. The reasons are implicit in the summary of the market mechanism following Equations (6) and (7): The existence and nature of a viable market schedule (terms of trade) depend on trade-offs between cost and valuation across variations in volume (y) and quality (n). Given $d < 0$, when b and $|d|$ are nearly the same size, there is very little leverage for the two trade-offs at the heart of a market. Such parameter values define, as you can see by inspection of Figure 4 and the accompanying solutions, a band of circumstances precluding stable markets, regardless of returns-to-scale parameters (a and c).

CONCLUSIONS

The prominence of general equilibrium theory (Arrow and Hahn, 1971) in economics is testimony to the failure of its mainline theory to replace Alfred Marshall's efforts to model concrete structure at the level of an industry: Roberts and Sonnenschein (1977) justify Triffin's old plaint (see Kuenne, 1967) that there is no place in economic theory proper for any level between whole economy and individual firm (and see Wilson and Andrews, 1951, p. 159). The prominence of multivariate path-analytic models in sociology is testimony to a similar failure.

I hope to have focused your mind on a central weakness of much social science theory: the lack of effective description and accounting of concrete social structure at levels beyond the individual person or group but short of the levels at which culture comes into its own and provides crutches to the analyst. Examples of theory which were developed for just this intermediate level are Coleman (1961), Kuhn (1970), Laumann and Marsden (1979), Mayer (1960), Padgett (1980), Schwartz (1977), Stinchcombe (1968), Tilly (1964), and Williamson (1975).

What I propose is embedding economists' neoclassical theory of the firm within a sociological view of markets. This is almost the inverse of longstanding preconceptions of how sociology relates to economics (Smelser, 1963, chap. 4). Sociology's main concern, I argue, should not be urging a richer view of individual character and of culture upon economics conceived as providing the skeleton of theory. My view, rather, is that a market is a role structure of differentiated firms linked together through an equilibrated set, $W(y)$, of interacting observations. Producers see each other's volume/revenue decisions, and whether or not these observations congeal determines whether or not a market is maintained.

There are two key features: (1) firms are individually distinct in their own and others' eyes, and (2) firms themselves create a market through mutual observation and adjustment—there is no exogenous referee. Interaction among the individual distinctions disciplines the $W(y)$'s allowable under various cost and valuation circumstances. Firm actors do not coordinate their markets when tradeoffs of producers' costs and buyers' valuation cannot balance quality and volume to yield equilibrium terms of trade. But once equilibria are feasible, many different frames (many different values of P and of K) may emerge exactly because there is no referee. Individual distinctions establish the interlock of niches in particular frames of roles.

Neoclassical economics, by contrast, submerges these considerations within the aggregate tautology that "supply equals demand." This tautology suffices to establish unique equilibrium, however, only by denying both of my key features.

The first payoffs to viewing production markets as induced role structures are tentative answers to several major questions. For example, why do so many of our industrial markets have but a dozen or so member firms, several of whom produce substantial shares of the total output? Why, when even the largest of firms wants to offer a product new to it to the public, does it do so by assimilating itself into an existing market by acquiring the *persona* of a firm belonging to that market already? This astonishing fact seems to be overlooked by existing theory.

The next steps, on which associates and I are already working, involve development of detailed procedures for and results from the study of particular industrial markets. It is not just a matter of new results but also of new ideas of what are results: How should one reconceive current concepts like "market share"? Are different kinds of market structure differentially vulnerable to exogenous changes in level of cost or of demand? Do market aggregates change in the same direction as apparent terms of trade?

APPENDIX A: DIMENSIONS, UNITS, AND CALIBRATION

All flows in the market are measured as volumes in a time period of fixed length—call it unity. Each of the volumes of goods, y, is measured as a count and has no dimension but does have a "unit" size—call it y_0. Variables $\mathbf{V}$, $\mathbf{W}$, W, and C have the dimension of money and the same unit size. The exponents a, b, c, d, and γ are pure numbers, as is t.

The quality scale n is arbitrary; it is defined only for purposes of arraying the functions S and C, which are measured across the goods in the given market. Therefore I keep this scale dimensionless: a pure number with unit size always kept unity.

The value scale must have dimension and units consistent with those chosen for the scale constants r and q when fitting data to the functions $\mathbf{V}$ and C. The units of each variable can be expressed as

$$\theta \sim V^{(1-\gamma)/\gamma} \qquad \mathbf{W}, \mathbf{V}, W, C \sim (r^d q^b r_0^{bd+ad})^{\gamma/(b\gamma+d)}$$

and

$$K \sim y^{(bc+ad)/b} \qquad y \sim y_0$$

The *dimension* of q is the same as that of r^γ, V, and C, but q may have its own unit. Choose

$$q = q_0 r^\gamma$$

with q_0 a dimensionless number. The size of q_0 must be related to y_0 by

$$q_0 = 1/y_0^{c-a\gamma}$$

in order for the units of $\mathbf{V}$ and C to agree. Then the units become

$$\mathbf{W}, \mathbf{V}, W, C \sim y_0^{a\gamma} r^\gamma$$

which are used in Figure 9 and Tables 1 and 2 for aggregate cash flows.

There are many ways to calibrate a comparison of two taste-and-technology contexts. I want the heights of equilibrium profiles, $y(n)$ or $W[y(n)]$, to be comparable. In each profile I choose 20 firms spaced at $n = 1.05, 1.10, \ldots, 2.0$. I assert that r^γ should be kept the same for comparability of total demand across contexts. Clearly q, and thus q_0 and y_0, should change radically when d goes from plus to minus, since I keep the quality indexes fixed: Physical volumes from the 20 firms differ by region. The unit size of y, y_0, is the base I adjust to achieve fair comparisons. I choose it for each point to achieve the same total money flow for t (and θ) at optimum (see Appendix B). I use a conventional size of 100 at $K = 0$:

$$\mathbf{W}_{\text{opt}} y_0^{a\gamma} r^\gamma = 100 r^\gamma$$

This optimum is second best for circumstances in the crowded region, and there it and $\mathbf{W}_0$ shrink as the number of firms increases so that in

TABLE A-1
Allowed Range for K by Market Region[a]

Region	Definition by Range for Powers a, b, c, d, γ[b]	Range of K Values in Equilibrium Schedules
Paradox	$d > 0$ $a/c < 1$	$K \leq 0$
Grind	$-\delta \equiv d < 0$ $b < a\delta/c < \delta$	$K \geq 0$
Crowded ($a/c < 1/\gamma$) or Expansive ($a/c > 1/\gamma$)	$-\delta \equiv d < 0$ $b > a\delta/c > \delta$	$-\infty < K < \infty$
	$b < a\delta/c; a/c > 1$	$K > 0$

[a]See Figure 4 for a graphic representation.
[b]By definition, a, b, c, and γ are positive and γ is less than unity. For parameter values precisely on one or more boundaries in Figure 4—such as the pure competition segment—further specialization by asymptotic techniques (see White, 1976, sec. 2; 1978, sec. 1; 1979) is required to obtain solutions and ranges for K.

Figure 15 the base volume of production, y_0, is small. In Figure 10 for the grind region the firms' base volume is very large, whereas in Figures 7 and 8 for the paradox region the y_0 is of intermediate size. My calibration for equilibrium profiles holds fixed the cash size of market at optimum.

Terms of trade, $W(y)$, are graphed only for illustrative markets of three firms each (Figures 1 to 6 and 11 to 14). There aggregate sizes are not computed, the ratio θ is specified arbitrarily, and the height P is computed directly from Equation (13). Neither θ nor P is resolved into its feedback components via Equations (23) to (25) and (29). The n values were chosen outside the range used for the profiles. Heights of these three-firm schedules are calibrated with respect to each other but not with respect to the equilibrium profiles for 20 firms. Table A-1 reports, for each region of Figure 4, the range of values for K that may occur in a schedule sustained in equilibrium by firms of all values of n.

APPENDIX B: CHAMBERLAIN–SPENCE PREDICTIONS

I interpret Spence's (1976a) formulation of Chamberlain (1954) as a three-layer analysis, and I apply it within the quality array context assumed in the chapter proper. Computation for the three levels is straightforward.

First: Each producer n knows the consumer's value function $\mathbf{V}$ of Equation (1). Represent it by

$$\mathbf{V} = \mathbf{S}^{\gamma} \tag{B-1}$$

The consumer, when faced with fixed price p_n, would optimize by choosing $y(n)$ such that

$$(\gamma/\mathbf{S}^{1-\gamma})\,[\partial\mathbf{S}/\partial y(n)] = p_n \tag{B-2}$$

provided the second-order condition is met. This condition can be shown to be equivalent to

$$(a - 1)\mathbf{S} < (1 - \gamma)aS \tag{B-3}$$

so that it is satisfied if $a < 1$ and only then given that S by hypothesis is a negligible fraction of the aggregate $\mathbf{S}$.

Define

$$\phi \equiv \gamma/\mathbf{S}^{1-\gamma} \tag{B-4}$$

which is a measure of overall context depending on the aggregation of all choices. After substitution from Equation (7), Equation (B-2) becomes

$$\phi aS(y,n) = p_n y \tag{B-5}$$

for each firm, which yields as consumer's optimum

$$p_n y(n) = (\phi arn^b/p_n^a)^{1/(1-a)} \tag{B-6}$$

for total payment W_n to firm n.

Second: Producer n now regards y as a function of p_n from (B-5) and now maximizes his or her own profit based on this hypothesized response function of the consumer. The producer maximizes W_n less cost to obtain the optimum price that should be set:

$$p_n^* = [(c/a)(q/n^d)]^{(1-a)/(c-a)}(\phi arn^b)^{(c-1)/(c-a)} \tag{B-7}$$

which yields the ratio (a/c) for cost over payment.

Equation (B-7) holds provided the second-order condition is met. The latter can be reduced to

$$[a/(1 - a)][(a/(1 - a) + 1] < [c/(1 - a)][c/(1 - a) + 1] \tag{B-8}$$

which reduces, whether or not $a < 1$, to

$$a < c \tag{B-9}$$

If (B-9) is violated, each firm will "explode": When $a < 1$, as required to predict consumer response, the price p_n is decreased and the volume $y(n)$ is increased without limit.

Third: Each producer realizes that the actual values of his or her optimum price and volume depend on the values that all the competitors have set. If on the first level each producer has used the same value for ϕ, this common value is fixed uniquely in the equilibrium and optimal market. That is, compute **S** first from Equation (B-4) as a function of ϕ. Then compute **S** from its definition (Equation B-1) as a sum of S's, using (B-5) to compute the latter from (B-7) for optimum price and (B-6) for volume as a function of optimal price. When **S** is denoted $\mathbf{S}(\phi)$, the unique value of ϕ from (B-4) is

$$\phi = (\gamma/\mathbf{S}(1)^{1-\gamma})^{(c-a)/(c-a\gamma)} \qquad \text{(B-10)}$$

(Note that ϕ is analogous to the reciprocal of the multiplier θ for the $W(y)$ model.)

Optimization by producers and by consumers is asserted, of course, but these optimal aggregates can, as for my model, be expressed as a multiple of aggregate size at consumer break-even in the stipulated quality-array context. From the Chamberlain–Spence theory, I derive for break-even cash volume the formula

$$\mathbf{W}_0 = [(a/cq)^a r^c (\Sigma n^{(bc+ad)/(c-a)})^{c-a}]^{\gamma/(c-a\gamma)} \qquad \text{(B-11)}$$

Compare this formula with Equation (25) in the text. The formula for optimum cash volume is

$$\mathbf{W}_{\text{opt}}/\mathbf{W}_0 = (a\gamma)^{c/(c-a\gamma)} \qquad \text{(B-12)}$$

The analogous result from my model is, from Equations (31) and (26),

$$\mathbf{W}_{\text{opt}}/\mathbf{W}_0 = (a\gamma/c)^{c/(c-a\gamma)} \qquad \text{(B-13)}$$

(See White, 1979, pp. 30–32, for various optima with the $W(y)$ model.)

REFERENCES

ABELL, D. F., AND HAMMOND, J. S.
1979 *Strategic Market Planning*. Englewood Cliffs, N.J.: Prentice-Hall.

AKERLOF, G.
1976 "The economies of caste and the rat race and other woeful tales." *Journal of Political Economy* 84:599–617.

ALONSO, W.
1964 *Location and Land Use: Toward a General Theory of Land Rent.* Cambridge, Mass.: Harvard University Press.

ARCHIBALD, G. C., AND ROSENBLUTH, G.
1975 "The 'new' theory of consumer demand and monopolistic competition." *Quarterly Journal of Economics* 89:569–590.

ARROW, K. J., AND HAHN, F. H.
1971 *General Competitive Analysis.* San Francisco: Holden-Day.

BAIN, J. S.
1952 *Price Theory.* New York: Holt, Rinehart and Winston.

BALES, R. F., COHEN, S. P., AND WILLIAMSON, S. A.
1980 *SYMLOG: A System for the Multiple Level Observation of Groups.* New York: Free Press.

BARBER, B.
1977 "Absolutization of the market." In G. Tworkin and others (Eds.), *Markets and Morals.* Washington, D.C.: Hemisphere.

BECKER, G.
1977 "Economic analysis and human behavior." Unpublished manuscript, University of Chicago.

BENASSY, J.-P.
1976 "The disequilibrium approach to monopolistic price setting and general monopolistic equilibrium." *Review of Economic Studies* 43:69–81.

BLAU, P.
1964 *Exchange and Power in Social Life.* New York: Wiley.

BONACICH, P., AND McCONAGHY, M. J.
1979 "The algebra of blockmodeling." In K. F. Schuessler (Ed.), *Sociological Methodology 1980.* San Francisco: Jossey-Bass.

BOORMAN, S. A.
1977 "Informational optima in a formal hierarchy: Calculations using the semigroup." *Journal of Mathematical Sociology* 5:129–147.

BOORMAN, S. A., AND WHITE, H. C.
1976 "Social structure from multiple networks. Part II: Role structures." *American Journal of Sociology* 81:1384–1446.

BREIGER, R. L.
1980a "Structures of economic interdependence among nations." In P. M. Blau and R. K. Merton (Eds.), *Continuities in Structural Inquiry.* Beverly Hills: Sage.

1980b "Social control and social networks: A model from George Simmel." In D. Black (Ed.), *Toward a General Theory of Social Control.* New York: Academic Press.

BREIGER, R. L., AND ENNIS, J. G.
1979 "Personae and social roles: The network structure of personality types in small groups." *Social Psychology Quarterly* 42:262–270.

BREIGER, R. L., AND PATTISON, P. E.
1978 "The joint role structure of two communities' elites." *Sociological Methods and Research* 7:213–226.

BRYSON, A. E., JR., AND HO, Y.-C.
1975 *Applied Optimal Control*. Washington, D.C.: Hemisphere.

BURNS, T., AND STALKER, G.
1961 *The Management of Innovation*. London: Tavistock.

CANNON, J. T.
1968 *Business Strategy and Policy*. New York: Harcourt Brace.

CAVES, R. E.
1979 "Industrial organizations: corporate strategy and structure." Unpublished manuscript, Economics Department, Harvard University.

CHAMBERLAIN, E.
1933 *The Theory of Monopolistic Competition*. [7th ed. 1956] Cambridge, Mass.: Harvard University Press.
1954 *Toward a More General Theory of Value*. Oxford: Oxford University Press.

CHANDLER, A.
1966 *Strategy and Structure*. New York: Doubleday.
1978 *The Visible Hand: The Managerial Revolution in America*. Cambridge, Mass.: Harvard University Press.

CHRISTENSEN, L. R., JORGENSON, D. W., AND LAU, L. J.
1975 "Transcendental logarithmic utility functions." *American Economic Review* 65:367–383.

COLEMAN, J. S.
1961 *The Adolescent Society*. New York: Free Press.

COOK, K. S., AND EMERSON, R. M.
1978 "Power, equity and commitment in exchange networks." *American Sociological Review* 43:721–739.

COWLING, K. (ED.)
1972 *Market Structure and Corporate Behavior*. London: Gray Mills. (Especially chapters by A. Phillips, by G. Yarrow, and by O. Williamson and N. Bhargara.)

DE BRUIJN, N. G.
1961 *Asymptotic Methods in Analysis*. 2nd ed. Amsterdam: North-Holland.

DIXIT, A. K., AND STIGLITZ, J. E.
1977 "Monopolistic competition and optimum product diversity." *American Economic Review* 67:297–308.

EKEH, P.

1974 *Social Exchange Theory*. Cambridge, Mass.: Harvard University Press.

ENGEL, J. F. AND OTHERS (EDS.).

1972 *Market Segmentation*. New York: Holt, Rinehart & Winston. (Especially chapters by J. F. Engel, by N. Foote, by W. Smith, and by R. E. Frank.)

FRIEDELL, M.

1967 "Organizations as semilattices." *American Sociological Review* 32:28–39.

FUSS, M., AND MCFADDEN, D. (EDS.)

1978 *Production Economics*. Amsterdam: North-Holland.

GALBRAITH, J. K.

1952 *American Capitalism: The Concept of Countervailing Power*. Boston: Houghton Mifflin.

GRANOVETTER, M. S.

1978 "Threshold models of collective behavior." *American Journal of Sociology* 83:1420–1443.

GRILICHES, Z. (ED.)

1971 *Price Indexes and Quality Change*. Cambridge, Mass.: Harvard University Press.

GRILICHES, Z., AND RINGSTAD, V.

1971 *Economies of Scale and the Form of the Production Function*. Amsterdam: North-Holland.

HERLING, J.

1962 *The Great Price Conspiracy*. Washington, D.C.: Luce.

HOFER, C., AND SCHENDEL, D.

1978 *Strategy Formulation: Analytical Concepts*. St. Paul: West.

HOMANS, G. C.

1964 "Contemporary theory in sociology." In R. E. L. Faris (Ed.), *Handbook of Modern Sociology*. Chicago: Rand McNally.

1967 *The Nature of Social Science*. New York: Harcourt, Brace & World.

HORWITZ, M.

1978 *The Transformation of American Law: 1780–1860*. Cambridge, Mass.: Harvard University Press.

HOUTHAKKER, H. S.

1952 "Compensated changes in quantities and qualities consumed." *Review of Economic Studies* 19:155–164.

KALWANI, M. V., AND MORRISON, D. G.

1977 "A parisimonious description of the Hendry system." *Management Science* 23:467–477.

KRUGMAN, P.

1978 "Increasing returns, monopolistic competition and international trade." Unpublished manuscript, Department of Economics, Yale University.

KUEHN, A. A., AND DAY, R. L.
1962 "Strategy of product quality." *Harvard Business Review* 40:198–219.

KUENNE, R. (ED.)
1967 *Monopolistic Competition Theory*. New York: Wiley.

KUHN, P.
1970 *Rebellion and Its Enemies in Late Imperial China.* Cambridge, Mass.: Harvard University Press.

LANCASTER, K. J.
1966 "A new approach to consumer theory." *Journal of Political Economy* 74:132–157.
1975 "Socially optimum product differentiation." *American Economic Review* 65:567–585.

LANDA, J.
1976 "An exchange economy with legally binding contract: A public choice approach." *Journal of Economic Issues* 10:905–921.
1979 "The economics of the ethnically-homogeneous middleman group." Working Paper 7924. Institute for Policy Analysis, University of Toronto.

LAUMANN, E. O., AND MARSDEN, P. V.
1979 "The analysis of oppositional structure in political elites: Identifying collective actors." *American Sociological Review* 44:713–732.

LAWRENCE, P.
1980 "The Harvard organization and environment research program." Unpublished manuscript, Harvard Business School.

LAWRENCE, P., AND LORSCH, J.
1967 *Organization and Environment.* Cambridge, Mass.: Harvard University Press.

LORSCH, J., AND ALLEN, S. A.
1973 "Managing diversity and interdependence." Boston: Division of Research, Graduate School of Business Administration, Harvard University.

MACHLUP, F.
1952 *The Economics of Sellers' Competition.* Baltimore: Johns Hopkins Press.

MANSFIELD, E.
1975 *Microeconomics: Theory and Applications.* 2nd ed. New York: Norton.

MARKHAM, J. W.
1973 "Conglomerate enterprise and public policy." Boston: Division of Research, Graduate School of Business Administration, Harvard University.

MAYER, A. C.
1960 *Caste and Kinship in Central India.* Berkeley: University of California Press.

MERTON, R. K.

1959 *Social Theory and Social Structure*. 2nd ed. Glencoe: Free Press.

MILES, R. E., AND SNOW, C. C.

1978 *Organizational Strategy: Structure and Process*. New York: McGraw-Hill.

MYRDAL, G.

1928 *The Political Element in the Development of Economic Theory*. New York: Humanities Press.

NADEL, S. F.

1957 *The Theory of Social Structures*. London: Cohen & West.

NATIONAL BUREAU OF ECONOMIC RESEARCH

1943 *Cost Behavior and Price Policy*. New York: National Bureau of Economic Research.

NEALE, A. D.

1970 *The Antitrust Laws of the United States of America: A Study of Competition Enforced by Law*. Cambridge: Cambridge University Press.

NEGISHI, T.

1972 *General Equilibrium Theory and International Trade*. Amsterdam: Elsevier.

NEWMAN, P.

1965 *The Theory of Exchange*. Englewood Cliffs, N.J.: Prentice-Hall.

PADGETT, J. F.

1980 "Hierarchy and ecological control in federal budgetary decision making." *American Journal of Sociology* in press.

PALDA, K. S.

1971 *Pricing Decisions and Marketing Policy*. Englewood Cliffs, N.J.: Prentice-Hall.

PATTISON, P. E.

1981 "Equating the 'joint reduction' with blockmodel common role structure: A reply to McConaghy." *Sociological Methods and Research* in press.

POLEMARCHAKIS, H. M., SELDEN, L., AND POHLMAN, L.

1980 "Approximate aggregation of diverse homothetic preferences under uncertainty." Unpublished manuscript, Economics Department, Columbia University.

PORTER, M. E.

1976 *Interbrand Choice, Strategy and Bilateral Market Power*. Cambridge, Mass.: Harvard University Press.

PRESTON, L. S.

1970 *Markets and Marketing*. San Francisco: Scott Foresman.

RADNER, R.

1975 "A behavioral model of cost reduction." *Bell Journal of Economics* 6:196–215.

RILEY, J. G.
1975 "Competitive signalling." *Journal of Economic Theory* 10:174–186.

ROBERTS, J., AND SONNENSCHEIN, H.
1977 "On the foundations of the theory of monopolistic competition." *Econometrica* 45:100–113.

ROBINSON, J.
1933 *The Economics of Imperfect Competition*. [2nd ed. 1969] London: Macmillan.

RODGER, L. W.
1972 *Marketing in a Competitive Economy*. 3rd ed. New York: Wiley.

ROSEN, S.
1974 "Hedonic prices and implicit markets: Product differentiation in pure competition." *Journal of Political Economy* 82:34–55.

ROSS, E. A.
1921 *Social Psychology*. New York: Macmillan.

ROTHSCHILD, M., AND STIGLITZ, J.
1976 "Equilibrium in competitive insurance markets: An essay on the economics of imperfect information." *Quarterly Journal of Economics* 90:629–649.

SAMUELSON, P. A.
1947 *Foundations of Economic Analysis*. Cambridge, Mass.: Harvard University Press.

SCHELLING, T. C.
1978 *Micromotives and Macrobehavior*. New York: Norton.

SCHERER, F. M.
1970 *Industrial Market Structure and Economic Performance*. Chicago: Rand McNally.

SCHWARTZ, J. E.
1977 "An examination of CONCOR and related methods for blocking sociometric data." In D. R. Heise (Ed.), *Sociological Methodology 1977*. San Francisco: Jossey-Bass.

SCHWARTZ, M.
1975 *Radical Protest and Social Structure*. New York: Academic Press.

SCITOVSKY, T.
1952 *Welfare and Competition*. London: Allen & Unwin.

SHEPARD, R. W.
1970 *The Theory of Cost and Production Functions*. Princeton: Princeton University Press.

SHISKIN, J., AND PETERSON, M. (EDS.)
1972 *Standard Industrial Classification Manual*. Washington, D.C.: Office of Management and the Budget, Statistical Policy Division.

SIMON, C. P.
1978 "Ellet's transportation model of an economy with differentiated commodities and consumers." Unpublished manuscript, Departments of Economics and Mathematics, University of Michigan.
SIMON, H. A.
1979 "Rational Decision Making in Business Organizations." *American Economic Review* 69:493–513.
SMELSER, N. J.
1963 *The Sociology of Economic Life.* Englewood Cliffs, N.J.: Prentice-Hall.
SNYDER, D., AND KICK, E. L.
1979 "Structural position in the world system and economic growth, 1955–1970: A multiple network analysis of transnational interactions." *American Journal of Sociology* 84:1096–1126.
SPENCE, A. M.
1974a *Market Signalling: Informational Transfer in Hiring and Related Screening Processes.* Cambridge, Mass.: Harvard University Press.
1974b "Competitive and optimal responses to signalling: Analysis of efficiency and distribution." *Journal of Economic Theory* 7:296–332.
1976a "Product selection, fixed costs, and monopolistic competition." *Review of Economic Studies* 43:217–235.
1976b "Informational aspects of market structure: An introduction." *Quarterly Journal of Economics* 91:591–597.
STIGLER, G.
1946 *The Theory of Price.* 2nd ed. New York: Macmillan.
STINCHCOMBE, A. L.
1968 *Constructing Social Theories.* New York: Harcourt, Brace & World.
SULTAN, R. G. M.
1974 *Pricing in the Electrical Oligopoly.* Vol. 1: *Competition or Collusion.* Boston: Harvard Graduate School of Business Administration.
1975 *Pricing in the Electrical Oligopoly.* Vol. 2: *Business Strategy.* Boston: Harvard Graduate School of Business Administration.
TAYLOR, B., AND WILLS, G. (EDS.)
1969 *Pricing Strategy.* London: Staples. (Especially chapters by D. Tull and others, by J. Udell, by G. A. Field and others, and by R. Hapgood.)
TERLECKYJ, N. E. (ED.)
1976 *Household Production and Consumption.* New York: National Bureau of Economic Research–Columbia University Press.

TILLY, C.
1964 *The Vendee.* Cambridge, Mass.: Harvard University Press.

VERDOORN, P. J.
1956 "Marketing from the producer's point of view." *Journal of Marketing* 20:221–235.

WEITZMAN, M. L.
1974 "Prices vs. quantities." *Review of Economic Studies* 41:477–491.

WENTZ, T. E.
1966 "Realism in pricing analysis." *Journal of Marketing* 30:19–26.

WHITE, H. C.
1963 *An Anatomy of Kinship: Mathematical Models for Structures of Cumulated Roles.* Englewood Cliffs, N.J.: Prentice-Hall.
1965 "The cumulation of roles into homogeneous structures." In W. W. Cooper and others (Eds.), *New Perspectives in Organization Research.* New York: Wiley.
1976 "Subcontracting with an oligopoly: Spence revisited." RIAS Program Working Paper 1. Unpublished manuscript, Harvard University.
1978 "Markets and hierarchies revisited." Unpublished manuscript, Department of Sociology, Harvard University.
1979 "On markets." RIAS Program Working Paper 16. Unpublished manuscript, Harvard University.

WHITE, H. C., BOORMAN, S. A., AND BREIGER, R. L.
1976 "Social structure from multiple networks: I. Blockmodels of roles and positions." *American Journal of Sociology* 81:730–780.

WILLIAMSON, O. W.
1970 *Corporate Control and Business Behavior.* Englewood Cliffs, N.J.: Prentice-Hall.
1975 *Markets and Hierarchies: Analysis and Antitrust Implications.* New York: Macmillan–Free Press.

WILSON, T., AND ANDREWS, P. W. S.
1951 *Oxford Studies in the Price Mechanism.* Oxford: Clarendon Press.

WINSHIP, C.
1978 "The allocation of time among individuals." In K. F. Schuessler (Ed.), *Sociological Methodology 1978.* San Francisco: Jossey-Bass.

WINTER, S.
1971 "Satisficing, selection, and the innovating remnant." *Quarterly Journal of Economics* 85:237–261.

2

STRUCTURAL MODELS FOR DISCRETE DATA: THE ANALYSIS OF DISCRETE CHOICE

Charles F. Manski

HEBREW UNIVERSITY OF JERUSALEM

The Prologue to the 1979 volume of *Sociological Methodology* noted both the recent preoccupation of sociologists with categorical data and their growing interest in structural equation theory. Ironically the various chapters in the volume indicate that these two important trends are progressing largely in mutual isolation.[1] On the one hand, the structural equation models that have received attention to date presume continuous endogenous variables. On the other hand, an empirical data-analytic approach has characterized the handling of discrete data.

In many contexts involving discrete data a structural model of the process generating the observations can be specified. One such context is that of discrete choice, in which the data are observations of

[1]An exception is the chapter by Brier (1978) in that volume.

the decisions of persons or groups selecting alternatives from finite sets of mutually exclusive and exhaustive options. Examples of discrete-choice problems abound. The worker mulling alternative job possibilities, the household searching for a residence, the citizen deciding whether to vote and if so for whom, the shopper contemplating various brands of peanut butter, the couple weighing marriage—all may be usefully viewed as facing discrete-choice problems.

Consider an analyst wishing to make sense of observations of the job, housing, voting, shopping, or marriage choices made by a sample of decision makers. A behavioral model explaining how the observed decisions are influenced by observed attributes of the decision makers and their choice sets will generally prove useful in rationalizing the sample data. When the analyst wishes to venture beyond the sample to forecast the choices that would be made by other decision makers facing other options, such a structural model is essential.

Over the past decade a quite extensive body of methodological and empirical research on discrete-choice problems has come into being. The methodological literature, which will be reviewed in this chapter, has had three foci:

1. The development of behaviorally interpretable, computationally convenient, parametric statistical models of discrete choice
2. The development of methods for estimating the parameters of such models from observations of the choices and attributes of a sample of relevant decision makers
3. The development of methods for forecasting aggregate population behavior given an estimated choice model and a description of the environment in which future choices are to be made

The empirical literature will not be surveyed here, but I would like to indicate its range of concerns to date.[2] One broadly and deeply investigated area has been that of transportation choices. Beginning with the relatively simple problem of workers' choice of travel mode for the journey to work (Warner, 1962; Lisco, 1967; Lave, 1969; Daly and Zachary, 1975; Train and McFadden, 1978), attention has spread to other aspects of trip making. These include shopping trip destina-

[2]To lend concreteness to the methodological discussion, however, one empirical study will be described in some detail.

tion and mode (Adler and Ben-Akiva, 1975; Domencich and McFadden, 1975), recreational travel decisions (Kocur and others, 1979), and choice among parking locations (Westin and Gillen, 1978; Fischer and Nagin, 1980). Concern with travel-related mobility decisions has also grown. There have been numerous studies of residential location (Lerman, 1976; Pollakowski, 1980; Quigley, 1973; Li, 1977) and investigations of automobile ownership (Lerman and Ben-Akiva, 1975; Lave and Train, 1979; Manski and Sherman, 1980a). The volumes by Stopher and Meyburg (1976) and Hensher and Stopher (1979) provide state-of-the-art reviews of the literature as well as discussions of outstanding issues.

Outside the realm of transportation, discrete-choice analysis has found an increasing range of applications. In education and labor there have been studies of college-going decisions (Radner and Miller, 1975; Kohn, Manski, and Mundel, 1976; Chapman, 1977; Bishop, 1977; Willis and Rosen, 1979; Fuller, Manski, and Wise, 1980a, 1980b), studies of worker labor-supply choices (Boskin, 1974; Heckman, 1974, 1976), studies of employer screening of job applicants (Swartz, 1976), and studies of physicians' behavior in deciding between private and public practice (Poirier, 1980). McFadden (1976a) and Barton (1979) have studied bureaucratic decision processes: McFadden has examined the selection of highway routes by a state highway department; Barton has investigated the awarding of television licenses by the Federal Communications Commission. Studies of consumer durable choices, beyond the housing and automobile problems already mentioned, have been made by Hausman (1979) and by Brownstonc (1978). Both these authors examine consumer choice among alternative types of air conditioners.

It would seem that a fair number of important sociometric problems could productively be studied from a discrete-choice perspective.[3] In particular, consider the long-standing concern with the interpretation of data on mobility, both geographic and occupational. The prevailing Markov modeling approach, with its generalizations to heterogenous and semi-Markov processes, provides a compact data-analytic tool that occasionally yields useful hints regarding the

[3]In this chapter the term *sociometric* is meant to parallel the terms econometric, biometric, and the like. I recognize that a much narrower usage, referring to sociological network analysis, is prevalent.

underlying determinants of observed mobility patterns. It is probable that a structural approach, explicitly recognizing that observed mobility results from the migration, employment, and hiring decisions of households, workers, and firms, would prove a valuable complement to, if not replacement for, current Markov models. It is worth noting that the potential of a discrete-choice analysis of mobility was actually seen some time ago by Ginsberg (1972). The line of research he initiated has apparently not been followed by others, although its usefulness is recognized by Stewman (1976).

This chapter surveys methodological developments in discrete-choice analysis whose appearance outside the sociological literature may have impeded their diffusion to interested sociometricians.[4] Sections I, II, and III respectively review work in the formulation, estimation, and forecasting application of the classic discrete-choice model. By classic model, I mean one that describes the behavior of members of a population of decision makers, all of whom face exogenously given discrete-choice problems at a certain point in time. Section IV calls attention to four generalizations of the classic model. One of these generalizations is the recurrent-choice model, which describes the behavior of decision makers facing a sequence of discrete-choice problems over time. Another is the endogenous-attribute model in which the characteristics of the alternatives available to each decision maker depend in part on the actions of other decision makers. The third is the analysis of information diffusion in discrete-choice contexts. The fourth generalization is the discrete–continuous model that describes the behavior of decision makers facing both discrete-choice and continuous-choice problems. To balance the abstractness of a purely methodological discussion, Section V describes a recent empirical study of student schooling and work decisions.

Before proceeding, I would like to elaborate on an earlier remark. I have said that the discrete-choice problem constitutes one of many contexts involving discrete data in which a structural model of the process generating observations can be specified. In fact, econometric discrete-choice analysis has numerous connections with other disciplines concerned with the structural treatment of discrete data. One of these is the psychometric literature on probabilistic choice,

[4]An earlier review with somewhat different emphases is McFadden (1976b).

where the notion of a probabilistic discrete-choice model first arose (see Thurstone, 1927; Luce, 1959; Luce and Suppes, 1965; Tversky, 1972). Another is the biometric literature developing specifications and inferential methods for quantal response models (see Berkson, 1944; Finney, 1971; Cox, 1970). Yet another is the econometric work on discrete simultaneous systems modeling—that is, the study of processes that may be described by systems of equations in which some endogenous variables are structurally or observationally discrete (see Tobin, 1958; Amemiya, 1973; Maddala and Nelson, 1974; Heckman, 1978).

I shall not attempt to survey developments of potential interest to sociologists in the foregoing literatures. That task should be left to active contributors. I shall, however, make reference to various literatures dealing with discrete data where such discussion helps clarify the history, concerns, or technical aspects of discrete-choice analysis.

I. DISCRETE-CHOICE MODELS

A. Analytic Framework

The probability model underlying classic discrete-choice analysis is described informally here. A formal treatment is given in Manski and McFadden (1980b). To begin, assume that a decision-making population T has been defined and that each member of this population faces a common, finite set of alternatives C. With each decision maker $t \in T$ and alternative $i \in C$ let there be associated a vector z_{ti} of observable continuous or discrete variables that characterize the pair (t, i). Let $z_t = (z_{ti}, i \in C)$ be the matrix of observable attributes characterizing t's choice problem and let $Z = (z_t, t \in T)$ be the collection of such matrices faced by the various decision makers in T.

In applications, the definition of T, C, and Z varies considerably. In an analysis of choice among travel modes for work trips, for example, T may include all workers traveling on a particular day to or from their place of employment. The choice set C may include modes such as driving alone, transit, and car pooling. The attributes Z may include functions of time, cost, and so forth associated with each mode and functions of decision-maker characteristics such as income and auto ownership. In an examination of intraregional migration, on the other hand, T may include all residents of the region of interest and C

may be a list of counties in the region. In this case Z will include functions of indicators of the job opportunities, environmental features, tax rates, and so forth of the various counties as well as decision makers' socioeconomic and demographic characteristics.

The basic probabilistic assumption of discrete-choice analysis is that the frequency distribution of choices $i \in C$ and attribute matrices $z \in Z$ in the population can be characterized by a generalized probability density

$$f(i, z) \equiv P(i \mid z)p(z) \tag{1}$$

defined over $C \times Z$. The basic structural assumption is that the conditional probability $P(i \mid z)$ is the probabilistic prediction of a behavioral model describing how a decision maker with associated attributes z would select among the alternatives in C. In most applications, $P(i \mid z)$ is *a priori* specified by the analyst to be a member of a restricted family of functions indexed by a real parameter vector θ. Let θ^* be the possibly unknown true value of θ. Then we can write

$$P(i \mid z) = P(i \mid z, \theta^*) \tag{2}$$

I shall momentarily describe the literature on the specification of probabilistic choice models $P(i \mid z, \theta^*)$. Before that, however, three points deserve attention.

First, note that the seemingly restrictive assumption that all members of T face the same choice set C is actually innocuous. To see this, recall that the attribute matrix z_t varies across the decision makers $t \in T$. If some alternative i is known to be unavailable to some decision maker t, this fact can be reflected in the value taken by z_t and we can set $P(i \mid z_t) = 0$.[5]

Second, it is of great interest to place the discrete-choice assumptions within the general framework of the statistical analysis of discrete data. Consider again the joint density $f(i, z)$ describing the joint distribution of choices and attributes in the population. In the absence of any knowledge relating i's to z's one might obtain a random sample of the population and directly examine the features of $f(i, z)$. This exploratory approach is exemplified by the literature on associations in contingency tables, where it is assumed that C and Z are both

[5]A formulation of the model in which each decision maker explicitly faces a distinct choice set C_t can be presented but is notationally more complex than the one given here. See, for example, Manski (1975).

finite. See, for example, Goodman and Kruskal (1954), Haberman (1974), and Bishop, Fienberg, and Holland (1975).

Alternatively, if one believes that the elements of C index conceptually distinct subpopulations of z values, then the natural analytic approach is to decompose $f(i, z)$ into the product

$$f(i, z) \equiv q(z \mid i)Q(i) \tag{3}$$

where $q(z \mid i)$ gives the attribute density in the subpopulation indexed by i and $Q(i)$ is the proportion of the population with this index. This is the approach taken in discriminant analysis. There prior knowledge allows the analyst to specify $q(z \mid i)$ up to a parametric family and a sample suitable for estimating the unknown parameters is obtained from the subpopulation i. See, for example, Anderson (1958), Warner (1963), and Kendall and Stuart (1976).

Finally, if one believes that there exists a causal link from z to i that will continue to hold even if the attribute distribution $p(z)$ should change, then the parametric decomposition

$$f(i, z) = P(i \mid z, \theta^*)p(z) \tag{4}$$

is appropriate. This decomposition and the attendant focus on the structural relation embodied in $P(i \mid z, \theta^*)$ is clearly the natural one for the analysis of choice data.

It is important to recognize that the assumption that $P(i \mid z)$ represents a structural relation and the alternative assumption that $q(z \mid i)$ is structural are generally not consistent with one another. To see this, observe that $P(i \mid z)$ and $q(z \mid i)$ are formally related through Bayes theorem by

$$q(z \mid i) = P(i \mid z)p(z) / \sum_{y \in Z} P(i \mid y)p(y)$$

Suppose that the attribute distribution $p(z)$ changes as a result of population aging or shifts in government policy. If the choice probabilities $P(i \mid z)$ are structural—and hence invariant under the change in $p(z)$—the conditional attribute distribution $q(z \mid i)$ will generally change with $p(z)$. Therefore $P(i \mid z)$ and $q(z \mid i)$ cannot simultaneously be structural.

The third point to be made is that discrete-choice problems certainly do not provide the only context in which a relation taking the form of Equation (4) should serve as the basis for analysis. In particular, the quantal response models of bioassay similarly impose a structural model relating continuous or discrete z variables or both to a discrete i. See, for example, Cox (1970) and Finney (1971). Many of the results described in this chapter have applications in contexts where a structural model other than a discrete-choice model explains the relation between attributes z and the occurrence of an event i.

B. Model Specification

Two paths to the specification of the choice probability $P(i \mid z, \theta^*)$ have been followed. One, appearing in the psychological literature on decision making, begins with the description of mathematical properties that a set of choice probabilities should satisfy and then seeks the form that the function P must have if these properties are to be present. A prominent example of this approach to specification is the work of Luce (1959).

Assume that the attributes (z_{ti} $i \in C$) are scalar indicators with $z_{ti} = 1$ if alternative i is available to person t and $z_{ti} = 0$ otherwise. In its most intuitive form, the Luce "independence of irrelevant alternatives" assumption requires that for any i in C

$$\frac{P\{i \mid z_{ti} = z_{tj} = 1, [z_{tk}, k \in C - (i,j)], \theta^*\}}{P\{j \mid z_{ti} = z_{tj} = 1, [z_{tk}, k \in C - (i,j)], \theta^*\}}$$

should be invariant under alternative values of $[z_{tk}, k \in C - (i,j)]$; $C - (i,j)$ being the choice set elements other than i and j. That is, the odds of choosing i over j should not depend on what other alternatives are available to the decision maker. As is well known, this assumption leads to the very strong result that the choice probability must have the form

$$P(i \mid z_t, \theta^*) = z_{ti}\theta_i^* \Big/ \sum_{j \in C} z_{tj}\theta_j^* \tag{5}$$

where $\theta^* = [\theta_j^*, j \in C]$ is a positive vector defined up to a scale normalization. Luce and Suppes (1965) survey the major developments on the specification of choice models from prior assumptions regarding properties of the choice probabilities. I shall not discuss the approach further.

The second path to model specification begins with an explicit statistical representation of the decision maker's choice process and from this behavioral model derives choice probabilities. By far the most productive application of this approach has been that based on the random utility model.

Random utility models date back as far as Thurstone (1927). They occupy an important position in the modern psychological literature on decision making and are central to the econometric analysis of discrete choice. The psychological interpretation of the models, presented in Luce and Suppes (1965), assumes that each decision maker carries a distribution of utility functions from which one is drawn at random each time a decision must be made. The econometric interpretation, treated in Manski (1977) and McFadden (1973, 1980), assumes that among a population of decision makers there exists a distribution of utility functions. The function associated with each person is fixed but unobserved by the researcher analyzing choice. The two stories are formally indistinguishable and, indeed, can be combined to model a population of decision makers each carrying a distribution of utility functions. Now let us turn to an econometric derivation of the random utility model.

Assume that with every decision maker $t \in T$ and alternative $i \in C$ there is associated a utility value $U_{ti} = U(\chi_i, s_t)$, where χ_i is a vector of attributes of i and s_t is a vector of characteristics of t. That is, $(U_{ti}, i \in C)$ provide a numerical representation of t's preferences over the alternatives in C, with $U_{ti} > U_{tj}$ meaning that i is preferred to j. Let $C_t \subset C$ be the set of alternatives available to person t and assume that t selects an alternative from the choice set C_t that yields maximal utility among the values $(U_{tj}, j \in C_t)$.

Now consider an analyst who knows the structure of function U up to a finite parameter vector, observes a subset of the finitely many alternative attributes $(\chi_i, i \in C)$, and, for each decision maker t, observes a subset of the utility-relevant decision-maker characteristics s_t. Also assume that the analyst knows up to a finite parameter vector the distribution of unobserved s values across the population. Finally, let $z_{ti} = z(\chi_i, s_t)$ designate a vector of utility-relevant functions of observed components of χ_i and s_t.

In this setting the analyst can place a probability distribution on the unobserved utility vector $(U_{tj}, j \in C_t)$ conditioned on the known matrix $z_t = (z_{tj}, j \in C)$ and on an unknown parameter vector θ^*. The vector θ^* includes parameters of the utility function U, parameters of the distribution of unobserved decision-maker attributes s, and unknown elements of the matrix of alternative attributes $(\chi_j, j \in C)$. And from this utility function distribution, assumed to be strictly increasing, the analyst may derive choice probabilities

$$P(i \mid z_t, \theta^*) = \text{Prob}\,[U_{ti} \geq U_{tj}, j \in C_t \mid z_t, \theta^*] \tag{6}$$

for each $i \in C_t$.

In the schooling choice study to be described, for example, χ_i includes observed measures of tuition, academic standards, and location of college i plus unobserved attributes such as programmatic orientation and campus environment. The vector s_t includes observed measures of ability, family income, and race for student t plus unobserved attributes such as career preference and placement among siblings. The set C includes all colleges in the country; C_t is the typically small subset to which student t has applied and been admitted. The choice probability of Equation (6) is the probability that a student prefers a given school to other available alternatives, conditional on the relevant observed attributes.

In applications the observationally random utility function has generally been assumed to have the linear additive form

$$U_{ti} = z_{ti}\phi^* + \epsilon_{ti} \tag{7}$$

with the distribution of $\epsilon_t = (\epsilon_{ti}, i \in C)$ conditioned on z_t specified to lie within a parametric class $F(\epsilon_t \mid z_t, \psi^*)$.[6] Thus $\theta^* = (\phi^*, \psi^*)$. Given (7), the form of the choice probabilities (6) depends on the distributional family F chosen for ϵ.

An ongoing concern of the discrete-choice literature has been to find distributions that yield computationally convenient choice probabilities and at the same time are sufficiently realistic in their behavioral implications. It is worth pointing out that if utilities could be directly observed, then under mild assumptions the parameters of linear models taking the form of Equation (7) could be estimated by regression of U on z. The assumption of the discrete-choice literature, however, is that while choices are observable, utilities are latent, unobservable variables. Hence the literature develops estimation methods predicated on the availability of choice data. This fact motivates the search for tractable forms for choice probabilities. An extensive

[6]In a few recent papers, such as Lerman and Louviere (1978), nonlinear forms for U have been employed.

discussion of the properties of alternative specifications is provided by McFadden (1980). Here I indicate the features of three important cases: the multinomial logit model, the multinomial probit model, and the generalized extreme-value model.

1. *The Multinomial Logit Model.* McFadden (1973) shows that if F is the independent and identically distributed extreme-value distribution

$$F(\epsilon_t \mid z_t, \psi^*) = \prod_{i \in C} e^{-e^{-\epsilon_{ti}}} \tag{8}$$

then the resulting choice probabilities have the form[7]

$$P(i \mid z_t, \phi^*) = e^{z_{ti}\phi^*} \Big/ \sum_{j \in C_t} e^{z_{tj}\phi^*} \qquad i \in C_t \tag{9}$$

Model (9) has been termed *multinomial logit* because formally it is a multinomial generalization of the binary logit model of Berkson (1944). To see this explicitly, observe that when the choice set consists of two alternatives (i, j), then the choice probability for i can be written in the binary logit form $1/[1 + \exp(x\phi)]$, where $x = z_{tj} - z_{ti}$.

The multinomial logit model has the form of the Luce model given in (5). It is also clear that the model has the log linear property so prominent in the literature on discrete multivariate analysis (Bishop, Fienberg, and Holland, 1975). An alternative derivation of the mathematical form (9) begins with the assumption that for each $i \in C$, the conditional distribution $q(z \mid i)$ is multivariate normal with mean $\bar{z}_i$ and common variance Σ. (See Warner, 1963, and Nerlove and Press, 1973.) However, the discrete-choice assumption that $P(i \mid z)$ is a structural relation and the discriminant analysis assumption that $q(z \mid i)$ is structural are generally not compatible, for reasons given in Section I.A. For a statement of the quite restrictive conditions under which the discrete choice and the discriminant analysis derivations of (9) are consistent with one another, see McFadden (1976c).

Because of its relative simplicity, the multinomial logit model has been by far the most widely applied discrete-choice specification. The earliest application of the binary logit model to a discrete-choice

[7]Luce and Suppes (1965) report an independent derivation by Holman and Marley.

problem is generally attributed to Warner (1962). The first multinomial logit application was performed in the late 1960s by McFadden (1976a), although it was published much later. A majority of the empirical studies cited in the introduction make use of the model, as does the case study to be presented in Section V.

While the logit model has proved a valuable empirical tool, it has long been recognized that the model's assumptions are quite restrictive and can lead to counterintuitive behavioral predictions. Early criticisms of the model (Debre, 1960; Tversky, 1972) focused on its independence of irrelevant alternatives property. The classic example concerns a person who must choose between two alternatives i and j for which $z_{ti} \cdot \phi^* = z_{tj} \cdot \phi^*$. Consequently, the logit choice probability for alternative i is one half. Now a third alternative, k, identical to j in all respects, is added to the choice set. Common sense says that the choice probability for i should remain one half. The logit probability, however, is now one third.

It has in recent years come to be understood that such counterintuitive predictions are not traceable to the independence of irrelevant alternatives property per se but rather are common to all random utility models in which the disturbances are assumed independent and identically distributed. In the context of the classic example, the flaw in the logit model is that it assumes ϵ_{tj} and ϵ_{tk} to be statistically independent when really these two disturbances are identical. For an extensive discussion, see Manski (1977).

A consequence of uneasiness regarding the logit model and other specifications assuming independent and identically distributed disturbances has been a search for more flexible, yet tractable, distributional assumptions. Two candidates are now considered.

2. *The Multinomial Probit Model.* An appealing candidate for a flexible specification is to start with the assumption that ϵ has a multivariate normal distribution conditional on z. The resulting choice probabilities are said to have the *multinomial probit* form—a generalization of the classic binary probit model (Finney, 1971).

Multinomial probit choice probabilities have the mathematical form of a multivariate normal tail integral, a form known to have no closed expression. For many years this fact limited application of the probit model to the binary-choice case where a one-dimensional integral must be evaluated and for which good series approximations have long been available. Recently, however, various authors have found computational devices that allow a wider range of applications.

Specifically, Hausman and Wise (1978) have applied series approximation methods to a trinary-choice problem while Lerman and Manski (1980b) have investigated a Monte Carlo simulation approach applicable in a general context. The most cost-effective method found to date, but also one whose accuracy is controversial, is that advanced by Daganzo, Bouthelier, and Sheffi (1977). These authors adapt a procedure, first suggested by Clark (1961), whereby the distribution of the maximal element of a multivariate normal vector is approximated by using a sequence of univariate normal integrals.

It should be noted that the multinomial probit model is actually a class of specifications, the nature of the conditioning of F on z thus far having been left open. One probit specification that seems to have many applications is the random coefficients model

$$U_{ti} = z_{ti}\phi^* + (z_{ti} \cdot \delta_t) \qquad \delta_t \approx N(0, \psi^*) \tag{10}$$

in which preferences across the population T are assumed normally distributed with mean ϕ^* and variance matrix ψ^*. In this case, the disturbance vector $(z_{ti} \cdot \delta_t, i \in C_t)$ is normally distributed with mean zero and covariance matrix $z_t\psi^*z_t'$, where z_t is the attribute matrix having as many rows as there are alternatives in C_t.

As an example of a context in which a random coefficient specification can be useful, consider an examination of residential location. The analyst might think that people differ in their relative preference for urban versus rural living but may be unable to relate such preferences to observed attributes. One might then assume that the strength of preference for urban living is distributed normally across the population with unknown mean ϕ^* and variance ψ^*. Given a sample of decision makers, these parameters of the taste distribution may be estimated.

An early application of a random coefficient model is due to Quandt and Baumol (1966) in a binary-choice setting. More recent binary-choice work has been performed by Daly and Zachary (1975) and by Fischer and Nagin (1980). Hausman (1979) applies the model in a three-alternative context.

3. *The Generalized Extreme-Value Model.* A second approach to the development of flexible discrete-choice models has been followed by McFadden (1978, 1980). Generalizing on the assumptions of his 1973 paper, he posits for F the multivariate extreme-value distribution

$$F(\epsilon_t \mid z_t, \psi^*) = \exp\{-H[(e^{-\epsilon_{ti}}, i \in C), z_t]\} \tag{11}$$

where the function H is nonnegative, linear homogeneous in $(e^{-\epsilon_{ti}}, i \in C)$, and satisfies certain restrictions on its derivatives and on its behavior as elements of the ϵ vector approach $-\infty$. McFadden proves that from (11) one can derive the generalized extreme-value choice probabilities

$$P(i \mid z_t, \theta^*) = e^{z_{ti}\phi^*} H_i[(e^{z_{tj}\phi^*}, j \in C_t), z_t]/H[(e^{z_{tj}\phi^*}, j \in C_t), z_t] \tag{12}$$

$i \in C_t$, where H_i is the partial derivative of H with respect to $e^{z_{ti}\phi^*}$.

The generalized extreme-value model, like the multinomial probit model, is actually a class of specifications, one for each function H satisfying the aforementioned restrictions. Relative to the probit model, the extreme-value case has the advantage of yielding a closed form for the choice probabilities. The substantive content of Assumption (11) has not yet been fully explored, but some interesting special cases are known. In particular the *nested* or *structured* logit case has appeal in the modeling of multidimensional choices.

For concreteness, consider a decision maker selecting a city in which to work and a neighborhood in which to reside. Let A be the set of available cities and let B_α index the set of neighborhoods in city α. Thus the person's choice set is $C = [(a, b), b \in B_a, a \in A]$. Assume that the function H has the form

$$H = \sum_{a \in A} e^{\lambda_a I_a}$$

where

$$I_a = \log \sum_{b \in B_a} e^{z_{ab}(\phi/\lambda_a)}$$

$$0 < \lambda_a \leq 1 \quad a \in A$$

Then the probability of choosing a city–neighborhood pair (α, β) can be shown to have the nested logit form

$$P(\alpha\beta) = e^{z_{\alpha\beta}(\phi/\lambda_\alpha) + (\lambda_\alpha - 1)I_\alpha} \Big/ \sum_{a \in A} e^{\lambda_a I_a}$$

When $\lambda_a = 1$, all $a \in A$, the multinomial logit model results.

Consider, on the other hand, what happens as $\lambda_\alpha \rightarrow 0$. Let

$$b_\alpha = [b \in \beta_\alpha: \quad z_{\alpha b_\alpha}\phi \geq z_{\alpha b}\phi \qquad b \in B_\alpha]$$

That is, b_α is the best neighborhood in city α when only the observed attributes are considered. It can be shown that $\lim_{\lambda_\alpha \rightarrow 0} \lambda_\alpha I_\alpha = z_{\alpha b_\alpha}\phi$ and that

$$\lim_{\lambda_\alpha \rightarrow 0} P(\alpha b_\alpha) = e^{z_{ab_\alpha}\phi} \bigg/ \left[e^{z_{ab_\alpha}\phi} + \sum_{\substack{a \in A \\ a \neq \alpha}} e^{\lambda_a I_a} \right]$$

$$\lim_{\lambda_\alpha \rightarrow 0} P(\alpha\beta) = 0 \qquad \text{for } \beta \neq b_\alpha$$

In other words, in the limiting case of $\lambda_\alpha \rightarrow 0$, the disturbances $(\epsilon_{\alpha b}, b \in B_\alpha)$ have no impact on the choice among $B\alpha$.

This perhaps mystifying result has a simple explanation. The parameter λ_α can be shown to measure the common correlation among the disturbances $(\epsilon_{\alpha b}, b \in B_\alpha)$. When $\lambda_\alpha = 1$, these disturbances are independent; but as $\lambda_\alpha \rightarrow 0$, they become perfectly correlated. In terms of the classic example of the failure of multinomial logit, $\lambda_\alpha \rightarrow 0$ implies that the neighborhoods in city α are increasingly similar along unobserved dimensions. Thus the nested logit model, with the λ's treated as parameters to be estimated, appropriately generalizes the multinomial logit idea so as to escape the latter model's counterintuitive behavior.

The application of nested logit models dates back to Ben-Akiva (1973) and Domencich and McFadden (1975). Independent proofs that the model has a random utility interpretation are given in McFadden (1978) and in Daly and Zachary (1978). Additional results regarding the model are presented in Ben-Akiva and Lerman (1979).

II. MODEL ESTIMATION

Once a discrete-choice model has been specified, it is natural to consider the problem of estimating its parameters. In this section I describe how observations of the choices and attribute matrices of a sample of decision makers can be used to this end.

The estimation theory to be outlined here is quite general in scope. It covers almost arbitrary forms for the choice probabilities, the only requirement being that $P(i \mid z, \theta^*)$ satisfy simple continuity conditions.[8] And it provides methods for utilizing data drawn through a wide variety of sampling processes, including both exogenous and endogenous stratified designs.[9] The focus of the work to date has been on the development of maximum likelihood and related estimators having desirable asymptotic properties under a correct model specification. Present knowledge of the small-sample properties of the available methods and the behavior of these methods when the model is misspecified is quite limited. Comprehensive technical sources on current estimation theory are Manski and McFadden (1980b) and Cosslett (1980).

A. Sampling Processes and the Sample Likelihood

Anyone who has designed, administered, or thoughtfully analyzed the data from a sample survey must recognize the distance separating sampling theory from practice. Consider in particular the stratified process that calls for one to define a population, delineate a set of subpopulations or strata, and then draw at random a specified number of observations from each subpopulation. In applications, the appropriate definition of the population may not be obvious. A practical mechanism to isolate and sample at random from the various subpopulations may be lacking. And the responses obtained may be incomplete or inaccurate. The stratified sampling process assumed in discrete-choice estimation theory ignores these practical difficulties. Nevertheless, the idealized sampling process, like the idealization of a discrete-choice model, proves a useful analytic construct.

The process assumed in current theory begins with the designation by the survey designer of a set of B possibly overlapping subpopulations $T_b \subset T$, $b = 1, \ldots, B$.[10] Each subpopulation T_b comprises those decision makers whose choice-attribute pairs (i, z) lie

[8]In particular, a random utility derivation of the choice probabilities is not required.

[9]Results guiding the survey designer in selecting among the many available sampling processes are much more limited. See the discussion in Lerman and Manski (1979).

[10]In allowing the strata to overlap, the process described here is more general than the usual stratified design where the strata are mutually exclusive and exhaustive.

within a specified subset A_b of the choice-attribute space $C \times Z$. With the stratification defined, the designer establishes a sample size N_b for each stratum T_b.[11] To obtain an (i, z) observation from stratum T_b, the designer samples with replacement at random within this stratum. Note that a simple random sample is the special case $B = 1$ and $A_1 = C \times Z$.

For simplicity, it is assumed here that all observations are retained in their entirety. An alternative possibility is that after (i, z) pairs are drawn, some sort of systematic censoring takes place. Cosslett (1980) treats the case in which each decision maker drawn from some stratum T_b reports only his or her attributes and also treats the symmetric case in which only choices are observed in given strata. McFadden (1980) considers problems in which an observation (i, z) is either totally retained, probability $\gamma(i, z, b)$, or totally lost, with probability $1 - \gamma(i, z, b)$. The literature on discrete simultaneous systems models also contains results on censoring that are relevant to discrete-choice problems. See Section IV.D.

Within the class of all stratification rules, two polar types deserve special mention. In *exogenous* sampling the designer delineates subsets of Z (Z_b, $b = 1, \ldots, B$) and lets $A_b = C \times Z_b$. In *choice-based* sampling the designer specifies subsets of C (C_b, $b = 1, \ldots, B$) and lets $A_b = C_b \times Z$. Less formally, in exogenous sampling the designer selects decision makers with given attributes and observes their choices whereas in choice-based sampling the designer selects persons with given choices and observes their attributes. The general term *endogenous* sampling may be used to describe any sampling process, such as a choice-based process, that is not founded on an exogenous stratification.

Some examples may be helpful. If, in a study of voting patterns, one stratifies the population by neighborhood and then samples at random within each neighborhood, the sample might reasonably be thought exogenous. If this same stratification is used in a study of residential location, however, the sample is clearly choice-based. If, in a study of voting, one surveys people at the polls, the sample is also choice-based in that people who choose not to vote are not surveyed. A sampling process that is endogenous but not purely

[11]The sample sizes N_b may be set directly or may be the result of an auxiliary probabilistic process not involving the unknown parameters θ^*.

choice-based would be one in which the survey is performed at the polls and only men are questioned.

Recall now the density function $f(i, z)$ describing the distribution of choice-attribute pairs in the population. It is easy to see that, conditional on a decision maker having been drawn at random from stratum T_b, the likelihood of observing any given pair (i, z) is

$$\lambda(i, z \mid b) = f(i, z) \Big/ \int_{A_b} f(j, y) d(j, y)$$

$$= P(i \mid z, \theta^*) p(z) \Big/ \int_{A_b} P(j \mid y, \theta^*) p(y) d(j, y) \quad (13)$$

where the denominator of the right-hand-side expression measures the fraction of the decision-making population belonging to stratum T_b. The stratum-conditional sample likelihood is then

$$L = \prod_{b=1}^{B} \prod_{n=1}^{N_b} P(i_n \mid z_n, \theta^*) p(z_n) \Big/ \int_{A_b} P(j \mid y, \theta^*) p(y) d(j, y) \quad (14)$$

Equation (14) is the starting point for the derivation of estimators for the parameters θ^*.[12]

B. Estimation Methods

1. *Exogenous Sampling.* Consider now the likelihood as a function of the unknown parameters θ^* and of the possibly unknown attribute density function p. When an exogenous sampling process has been followed, the expression in the denominator of (14) takes the special form

$$\int_{Z_b} \left[\sum_{j \in C} P(j \mid y, \theta^*) \right] p(y) dy = \int_{Z_b} p(y) dy$$

as the choice probabilities must sum to 1. It follows that the likelihood decomposes into the product

$$L = \prod_{b=1}^{B} \prod_{n=1}^{N_b} P(i_n \mid z_n, \theta^*) \cdot \prod_{b=1}^{B} \prod_{n=1}^{N_b} p(z_n) \Big/ \int_{Z_b} p(y) dy \quad (15)$$

[12]It would be notationally more proper to write (i_{n_b}, z_{n_b}), $n_b = 1, \ldots, N_b$, $b = 1, \ldots, B$. For simplicity, the subscript b on n is omitted.

An immediate consequence is that estimation of the structural parameters can proceed without reference to the nuisance function $p(z)$. In particular, consider the maximum-likelihood estimator

$$\max_{\theta \in \Phi} \sum_{b=1}^{B} \sum_{n=1}^{N_b} \log P(i_n \mid z_n, \theta) \tag{16}$$

where Φ is the designated parameter space for the maximization. Under weak regularity conditions, such as those in Manski and McFadden (1980b), this estimator is consistent, asymptotically normal, and asymptotically efficient.

In general, the maximization must be performed using iterative numerical techniques; the form of the choice probabilities determines the computational burden. A particularly benign case is the multinomial logit case. Here $P(i \mid z, \theta)$ has a simple explicit form and the log-likelihood function is known to be globally concave. Numerous multinomial logit software packages now exist. Two user-oriented packages are McFadden and others (1978), available in CDC and IBM versions, and Cambridge Systematics (1979), available in an IBM version.

It should be noted that when the exogenous stratification is one in which each Z_b, $b = 1, \ldots, B$, consists of a single point, then alternatives to maximum-likelihood estimation exist. In particular the linear regression method of Berkson (1944), extended to the multinomial case by Theil (1970), should be mentioned. These methods are consistent as the number of observations $N_b \rightarrow \infty$ for each stratum b. Unfortunately, in most discrete-choice applications each decision maker has a distinct attribute vector so that the accumulation of multiple choice observations at given z values is not possible. For this among other reasons the maximum-likelihood approach has been prevalent in practice.[13]

2. *Endogenous Sampling.* When the sampling process involves an endogenous stratification, the likelihood (Equation 14) does not decompose in the manner of Equation (15). In the case of choice-based sampling with each alternative defining a separate stratum, for exam-

[13]Other methods applicable when multiple z observations are not available are treated in Manski (1975) and Amemiya (1978a).

ple, the denominator of (14) has the form

$$\int_Z P(i_n \mid y, \theta^*) p(y) dy$$

and thus is a nontrivial function of both θ^* and p. Since the attribute density function p will rarely if ever be *a priori* known, maximization of (14) as a function of θ alone does not constitute a well-defined estimator. Happily, a variety of workable approaches to the estimation of θ^* do exist. I shall discuss three: assumption of a parametric density function; estimators not involving the attribute density; and maximum-likelihood estimation.

a. Assumption of a Parametric Density Function. The first approach begins with the assumption that p, while not known, can be *a priori* restricted to a parametric family of density functions. Then classic maximization of the likelihood as a function of both θ^* and the p parameters can be performed. Assuming a correct specification of the attribute density family, the estimator will be consistent, asymptotically normal, and asymptotically efficient.

For a combination of reasons, this approach has not been favored in practice. One problem is computational; generally the integrals

$$\int_{A_b} P(j \mid y, \theta^*) p(y) d(j, y)$$

are quite costly to calculate. A second concern is with the plausibility of any prior parametric restriction on the function p. In applications, the attribute matrix z is apt to contain at least tens and perhaps hundreds of elements. In the case study of Section V, for example, each schooling alternative is characterized by 25 attributes and students have between 8 and 12 alternatives in their choice sets. Hence p is the density function of a matrix of at least 200 elements for each student. Moreover, theory gives us little guidance regarding the shape of this distribution.

It should be pointed out that in at least one circumstance the objections just voiced disappear. This is the case in which the attribute space Z is finite and multiple observations at given attribute values are obtainable. In that context the usually complex integrals in Equation (15) reduce to sums of the form $\Sigma_{A_b} P(j \mid y, \theta^*) p(y)$ and p can be left as an unrestricted multinomial distribution.

b. Estimators Not Involving the Attribute Density. The failure of the endogenous sampling likelihood to decompose does not imply that every estimator for θ^* must involve p as well. This observation was exploited by Manski and Lerman (1977) in the development of the "weighted exogenous sampling maximum likelihood" estimator. While the method was originally developed for use in choice-based samples, it has since been shown to extend to any endogenous sampling context. The general form of the estimator, treated in Manski and McFadden (1980b), is as follows:

$$\max_{\theta \in \Phi} \sum_{b=1}^{B} \sum_{n=1}^{N_b} (S_b^*/H_b) \log P(i_n \mid z_n, \theta) \tag{17}$$

Here $H_b = N_b/\Sigma_{a=1}^{B} N_a$ is the fraction of the sampled decision makers drawn from stratum b and $S_b^* = \int_{A_b} P(j \mid y, \theta^*)p(y)d(j, y)$ is the fraction of the population belonging to stratum b. Use of the estimator presumes that the stratum shares S_b^*, $b = 1, \ldots, B$, are *a priori* known. This condition is fairly often satisfied in applications, particularly in choice-based sampling contexts. In this case, knowledge of the fraction of the population choosing each alternative suffices to reveal the stratum shares.

Estimator (17) is known to be consistent and asymptotically normal. Within the class of estimators using prior knowledge of the stratum shares, it is not, however, the most efficient. An estimator that is asymptotically efficient will be described later. Computationally, Method (17) is the simplest among the endogenous sampling estimators presently available.

Manski and McFadden (1980b) develop a number of new estimators that do not involve the density p. Among these are methods that also do not suppose prior knowledge of the stratum shares. An important member of this latter class is the estimator

$$\max_{\substack{\theta \in \Phi \\ D \in \Delta}} \sum_{b=1}^{B} \sum_{n=1}^{N_b}$$

$$\log \left[P(i_n \mid z_n, \theta)(H_b/D_b) \Big/ \sum_{a=1}^{B} (H_a/D_a) \sum_{j \in C} P(j \mid z_n, \theta) \cdot \gamma_a(j, z_n) \right] \tag{18}$$

Here $D = (D_b, b = 1, \ldots, B)$ is a set of parameters lying in the unit simplex Δ and $\gamma_a(j, z_n)$ is an indicator such that $\gamma = 1$ if $(j, z_n) \in A_a$

and $\gamma = 0$ otherwise. Estimator (18) is, in general, consistent and asymptotically normal for θ^*. The D estimate converges to the vector

$$S_b^* \Big/ \sum_{a=1}^{B} S_a^* \qquad b = 1, \ldots, B$$

A result of Cosslett (1980) proves that Estimator (18) is asymptotically efficient within the class of consistent asymptotically normal methods not using prior information on S^*.

Criterion (18) simplifies somewhat in the choice-based sampling case where each alternative defines a distinct stratum. There the estimator becomes

$$\max_{\substack{\theta \in \Phi \\ D \in \Delta}} \sum_{i \in C} \sum_{n=1}^{N_i} \log \left[P(i \mid z_n, \theta)(H_i/D_i) \Big/ \sum_{k \in C} P(k \mid z_n, \theta)(H_k/D_k) \right]$$

and the D estimate generally converges to the vector of aggregate choice frequencies $[Q(k),\ k \in C]$. A further, substantial simplification occurs if the choice probabilities have the multinomial logit form. Now the criterion can be written

$$\max_{\substack{\theta \in \Phi \\ D \in \Delta}} \sum_{i \in C} \sum_{n=1}^{N_i} \log \left(e^{z_{ii}\theta + \mu_i} \Big/ \sum_{k \in C} e^{z_{ik}\theta + \mu_k} \right)$$

where $\mu_k = \log (H_k/D_k)$, $k \in C$. Thus the endogenous sampling estimator (18) reduces to the exogenous sampling maximum-likelihood estimator (14) with the added presence of the parameters μ. The reader should be warned that this result is quite special. In general, the exogenous sampling estimator yields inconsistent estimates when applied to a choice-based sample. For a proof of the general result and discussion of the logit special case, see Manski and Lerman (1977).

c. Maximum Likelihood Estimation. Cosslett (1980) has recently confronted head on the problem of joint maximum-likelihood estimation of the choice model parameters θ^* and the attribute density function p. In the first of two stages, he holds θ fixed and conditionally maximizes the likelihood (14) in p. An expression $\hat{p}(z \mid \theta)$ that takes positive values only for z values occurring in the sample is found. In the second stage, Cosslett replaces p in (14) by $\hat{p}(\cdot \mid \theta)$ and maximizes the resulting concentrated likelihood in θ.

In the case where S_b^*, $b = 1, \ldots, B$, are known, the maximum-likelihood estimator is found to be

$$\max_{\theta \in \Phi} \min_{m \in M} \sum_{b=1}^{B} \sum_{n=1}^{N_b}$$

$$\log \left[P(i_n \mid z_n, \theta) \Big/ \sum_{a=1}^{B} m(a) \sum_{j \in C} P(j \mid z_n, \theta) \gamma_a(j, z_n) \right] \quad (19)$$

where

$$M = \left[m(b), b = 1, \ldots, B \;\middle|\; \sum_{b=1}^{B} m(b) S_b^* = 1 \right]$$

This somewhat cumbersome saddle-point problem is derived from a lagrangian representation of the S^*-constrained maximization problem. Although classic proofs do not apply, Cosslett is able to show directly that Estimator (19) is consistent, asymptotically normal, and asymptotically efficient.

When the stratum shares are not known, the maximum-likelihood estimator turns out to be Estimator (18). In this case, maximum-likelihood estimation presents no particular computational problem.

III. FORECASTING

The classic discrete-choice forecasting problem may be described briefly. The usual forecasting objective is to predict the fraction of the population who will, under an exogenously given future environment, select each of the alternatives in C. The first step in forecasting is to characterize the future environment through the attribute density function expected to prevail. Let this density be designated $\tilde{p}$. Then the fraction of the population expected to choose any alternative $i \in C$ is

$$\tilde{Q}(i) = \int_Z P(i \mid z, \theta^*) \tilde{p}(z) dz \quad (20)$$

Given $\tilde{Q}(i)$, one may also forecast the distribution of attributes for the subpopulation of decision makers who will select alternative i.

This is characterized by the conditional density

$$\tilde{q}(z \mid i) = P(i \mid z, \theta^*)\tilde{p}(z)/\tilde{Q}(i) \qquad (21)$$

The practical questions that arise in forecasting concern the construction of the future attribute density $\tilde{p}$, the cost-effective evaluation of the forecast shares $\tilde{Q}$ given in (20), and the assessment of forecasting errors.

The first problem is usually approached by beginning with the current distribution p and modifying it to reflect the expected changes. Thus there is a need to estimate p before forecasting can begin. Lerman and Manski (1979) discuss a number of estimators for p, most of which do not involve use of the choice model.

The evaluation of $\tilde{Q}$ can be achieved through a variety of numerical integration procedures. See Koppelman (1975) for a description of some of these.[14] A particularly useful approach employs a weighted sample of decision makers to represent the population. Specifically, a sample is obtained and its members are given weights so that the attribute distribution in the sample approximates $\tilde{p}$. Let W_n, $n = 1, \ldots, N$, be the weights for the members of a sample of size N. Then the quantity

$$\hat{\tilde{Q}}(i) = \sum_{n=1}^{N} W_n P(i \mid z_n, \theta^*) \qquad (22)$$

is an unbiased, consistent estimate for $\tilde{Q}(i)$. To reduce computation costs further, one may replace the choice probabilities $P(i \mid z_n, \theta^*)$, $n = 1, \ldots, N$, with the results of simulation experiments. Let $\delta(i, n) = 1$ if person n is simulated to choose alternative i and $\delta(i, n) = 0$ otherwise. Then

$$\check{\tilde{Q}}(i) = \sum_{n=1}^{N} W_n \cdot \delta(i, n) \qquad (23)$$

is an unbiased, consistent estimate for $\tilde{Q}(i)$, but one less efficient than $\hat{\tilde{Q}}(i)$.

The assessment of forecasting errors is a difficult matter on which I shall not dwell. Such errors can arise from imperfections in the

[14]In special cases direct evaluation is possible. See, for example, Westin (1974) and McFadden and Reid (1974).

construction of the future attribute density $\tilde{p}$, from approximations made in evaluating the choice frequencies $\tilde{Q}$, from calculation of the choice probabilities using an estimate for θ^* rather than θ^* itself, and, of course, from misspecification of the choice model. Horowitz (1980) discusses the various sources of forecasting error at some length. Later in the chapter I shall summarize an actual forecasting exercise.

IV. GENERALIZATIONS OF THE CLASSIC DISCRETE-CHOICE MODEL

In this section I describe four generalizations of the classic model that may be of interest to sociometricians: recurrent-choice models, endogenous-attribute models, dynamic models of information diffusion and choice, and discrete–continuous choice models.

A. Recurrent-Choice Models

Many of the discrete-choice problems that have received empirical attention are faced by decision makers not once but repeatedly. For example, workers must select a travel mode for the work trip 200 or more times a year. Occupational choice and residential location decisions are faced not once a lifetime nor necessarily on any regular schedule. Individuals might even be thought of as continually updating their occupational and residential location decisions as time passes.

While empirical discrete-choice situations are often recurrent, the classic discrete-choice model predicts the resolution of a single choice problem. Recently Heckman (1980a, 1980b) and others have proposed modeling recurrent choice as a sequence of static utility-maximizing decisions by persons whose utility functions may contain individual, time, and state-dependent effects.[15] This work, which shares features with the discrete-time Markov mobility models of sociometrics, is described presently.

We begin by assuming that at each of an exogenously given sequence of decision moments $m = M, M + 1, \ldots, \bar{M} - 1, \bar{M}$, every

[15]See also Chamberlain (1978) and Manski and Sherman (1980a).

decision maker $t \in T$ must select an alternative i_{tm} from the choice set C. Further assume that the sequence of decisions made by any person is consistent with the period-by-period maximization of an observationally random utility function

$$U_{tim} = z_{tim}\phi^* + \alpha^* g_{tim} + \lambda_{ti} + \epsilon_{tim} \tag{24}$$

over the alternatives $i \in C$.[16]

In Equation (24), z_{tim} is a vector of observed functions of decision maker and alternative attributes that may vary with time. The variable g_{tim} is a state indicator, assumed observed, with $g_{tim} = 1$ if t chose i at period $m - 1$ and $g_{tim} = 0$ otherwise.[17] The variables $(\lambda_{ti}, i \in C)$ are unobserved time-invariant person-specific effects, assumed distributed multivariate normal in the population, independent of the z's. The disturbances $(\epsilon_{tim}, i \in C)$ are, for each t and m, an independent drawing from a multivariate normal distribution. That is, the ϵ's represent white noise.

This model is a simplified version of the one considered in Heckman (1980a) but is nevertheless sufficiently general to reveal the dynamics possible within the effects-model framework. What features an effects model does possess depends crucially on whether neither of, one of, or both of the state-dependent and person-dependent effects are present. There are four cases to be considered: models with temporal independence, recursive models, models with unobserved person-specific effects, and unrestricted models.

1. *Models with Temporal Independence.* If we assume that $\alpha^* = 0$—that is, that no state-dependent effect exists—and that the λ's are degenerate, so that all person-specific effects are observed, then the probability of a sequence of choices decomposes into a product of static

[16]We are *not* assuming here that a person has a one-period planning horizon. Utility function (24) may give the value of choosing alternative i at period m within the context of a multiperiod plan.

[17]There are various reasons why the utility of each alternative in a given period may depend on the past choices of the decision maker. In the analysis of residential location, for example, one should expect such state dependence if only because moving costs, in time and money, are state-dependent. In particular, the option of continuing at period m to live at the $m - 1$ address has the unique advantage over other alternatives of entailing zero moving costs. In terms of equation (24), one should therefore expect that $\alpha^* > 0$. Heckman (1979) discusses sources of state dependence in labor supply; Manski and Sherman (1980a) provide reasons in the case of automobile selection.

choice probabilities. That is:

$$P(i_{tm}, m = M, \ldots, \overline{M} \mid z_t, \theta^*) = \prod_{m=M}^{\overline{M}} P(i_{tm} \mid z_{tm}, \theta^*) \tag{25}$$

where $z_{tm} = (z_{tim}, i \in C)$ and $z_t = (z_{tm}, m = M, \ldots, \overline{M})$.

Under a temporal independence assumption, a time series of choices made by a single decision maker is indistinguishable from a set of choices made by a cross-section of decision makers at a single point in time. The static model formulation, estimation, and forecasting theory described in preceding sections applies without modification.

2. *Recursive Models.* In a recursive model the state-dependent effect is assumed present and the unobserved person-specific effect is presumed absent. The probability of a sequence of choices decomposes into the following product:

$$P(i_{tm}, m = M, \ldots, \overline{M} \mid z_t, \theta^*) = \prod_{m=M}^{\overline{M}} P(i_{tm} \mid z_{tm}, i_{t(m-1)}, \theta^*) \tag{26}$$

where $i_{t(M-1)}$ is an exogenously specified initial condition.

For purposes of model formulation and estimation, the state indicator variables g are statistically predetermined so that static-choice model theory applies pretty much directly. On the other hand, forecasting with a recursive model introduces new issues.

To be concrete, consider the problem of forecasting decision maker t's choice at period $n + 2$ given knowledge of his or her attributes z_t in all periods and his or her choices through period n. The relevant forecast probabilities can be expressed recursively, for $j \in C$, as

$$P(i_{t(n+2)} = j \mid z_t, i_{tn}, \theta^*) = \sum_{k \in C} P(i_{t(n+2)} = j \mid z_{t(n+2)}, i_{t(n+1)} = k, \theta^*) \times P(i_{t(n+1)} = k \mid z_{tn}, i_{tn}, \theta^*)$$

In general, no simpler form exists. Moreover, if we move to forecast behavior at time $n + 3$, another level is added to the recursion. Because direct evaluation of forecast probabilities quickly becomes unwieldly, simulation is the preferred approach to forecasting with recursive models.

3. *Models with Unobserved Person-Specific Effects.* Let us now

consider the case in which $\alpha^* = 0$ but nontrivial person-specific effects λ do exist. Now the effects model does not have the Markov property enjoyed by temporally independent and recursive models. In fact the probability of a sequence of choices does not have any meaningful product decomposition at all.

The mutual statistical dependence of the choices $i_{tm}, m = \underline{M}, \ldots, \overline{M}$, occurs because all choices in the sequence depend on the same unobserved effects λ_{ti}, $i \in C$. This phenomenon should immediately be recognized as the choice model manifestation of the mover-stayer problem. Since the statistical dependence of choices has an observational rather than causal basis, Heckman (1980a) refers to the model under discussion as one having "spurious state dependence."

It should be apparent that in principle the Markov character of the model can be restored if the effects λ are treated as fixed rather than random. In practice, unfortunately, this suggestion can only rarely be acted on. The problem is that estimates in the fixed-effects version of the model are consistent only as the length of the observed choice sequence increases. The typical empirical context, however, is one in which the analyst possesses a short time series for each of a large cross-section of people. The fixed-effects form will not be discussed further here.

The model with unobserved person-specific effects does have one quite useful property. That is, for each period m, the marginal choice probabilities $P(j \mid z_{tm}, \theta^*)$, $j \in C$, have the multinomial probit form described earlier. This fact implies that the parameters θ^* can be estimated from a cross-section of observations using the estimation theory described in the section on model estimation.[18] It also implies that choice behavior in any period n can be forecast without first making forecasts for the prior periods $\underline{M}, \ldots, n - 1$.

4. *Unrestricted Models.* As might be expected, the combination of state effects and unobserved person effects produces a model of complex structure. In this case, there apparently exists no analytic alternative to direct consideration of the joint probability of the choice sequence. Consideration of Equation (24) yields an intuitive explanation for the model's complexity. The explanatory variable g_{tim} is a

[18]The parameters of the distribution of $\lambda + \epsilon$ can be estimated from cross-sectional data, but not those of the λ and ϵ distributions themselves.

function of the utilities $U_{tj(m-1)}$, $j \in C$; the latter depend on the unobserved person-specific effects λ. Hence g_{tim} is correlated with the contemporaneous disturbance $\lambda_{ti} + \epsilon_{tim}$. When the analyst's observations begin after the initial period M, estimation of the unrestricted model poses particular difficulties. For an extensive discussion, see Heckman (1980b).

B. Endogenous-Attribute Models

In the classic discrete-choice model, the alternative and decision-maker attributes that characterize a choice problem are exogenous quantities. While we need not explicitly specify the process generating the attributes, we implicitly assume that this process is not itself related to the choice behavior of the population.

In a variety of contexts the classic assumption breaks down. We have already described one such context—namely, the state-dependent case in which the present utility of an alternative to a decision maker depends on his or her own past choices. In this section I discuss situations in which the attributes characterizing a person's choice problem depends on the behavior of other members of the population.

The empirical importance of endogenous-attribute problems, and the distinct types of choice-to-attribute linkages that may exist, can be highlighted through a series of examples. First consider the student choosing among alternative college opportunities. The set of available schools will depend on, among other things, the admissions decisions made by the colleges to which the student has submitted applications. Admissions decisions in turn will depend on the applications received by each college—that is, on past behavior of the student population. The applications-admissions-enrollment problem is an example of a *sequential process* wherein the prior actions of the decision-making population determine the choice environment each member of the population later faces. Another example of a sequential process is a sports player draft where the decision makers, namely the teams, are ordered and select players in turn.

Next consider the commuter deciding whether to travel by car or by bus to work. The travel time on each mode will in general depend on the volume of traffic on that mode. This congestion problem is an example of a *frequency-dependent process* wherein the attributes of an alternative are functions of the aggregate frequency with which the alternative is selected by members of the population. Another frequency-dependent process occurs in the used automobile market where the equilibrium price of each vehicle type is a function of aggregate vehicle demands and supplies.

Finally, consider the operation of the academic job market. Here prospective faculty and employers are matched in a process that may involve concurrent or sequential one-on-one negotiations. Faculty sorting is an example of a *small-group simultaneous-choice process.* Courting and marriage is a process of the same type. Intrafamily decision making is yet another important case.

These examples distinguish three classes of endogenous-attribute processes—sequential processes, frequency-dependent processes, and small-group simultaneous processes. Of the three, the sequential case is clearly the simplest. In particular, models having the same general structure as the effects models discussed earlier can describe choice behavior at the various stages of such a process.

Relative to sequential-choice models, frequency-dependent models are complex as the choice-attribute interaction is now a simultaneous one. On the other hand, among the class of simultaneous processes, frequency-dependent processes are relatively simple because the link from choices to attributes is channeled through a small set of variables. Analysis of frequency-dependent processes may be equilibrium or dynamic in character. Let $Q = [Q(i), i \in C]$ be the vector of aggregate choice frequencies and assume that frequency-dependent attributes are observed. Then an equilibrium set of choice frequencies satisfies the condition

$$Q(i) = \int_Z P(i \mid z, \theta^*) p(z \mid Q) dz \qquad i \in C \tag{27}$$

There now exists a fairly sizable literature on the analysis of equations of the form (27) in transportation applications. See, for example, Ben-Akiva and others (1977), Sheffi (1978), and Manski and Sherman (1980b). Serious work on the dynamics of frequency-dependent processes out of equilibrium has yet to be performed, however.

The empirical examination of small-group simultaneous-choice processes poses a formidable challenge. Frameworks for the modeling of such processes are not lacking; game theory and social network analysis both are clearly relevant. However, the work of translating theoretical ideas into workable empirical models remains to be performed. Sociologists, with their long history of concern with small-group processes, should be well positioned to contribute in this regard.

C. Dynamic Models of Information Diffusion and Choice

To date, applications of discrete-choice models have universally presumed that the information about alternatives possessed by the decision maker is exogenous. Perceptions of attributes need not be accurate, but they must be known functions of the analyst's measured attribute values.

The classic assumption is often unrealistic. In many cases, one's information about alternatives is not only imperfect but depends on one's own and others' past choices. That is, one learns from personal experience and through communication by others of their experiences. In the language of the preceding two sections, perceptions are often both state-dependent and endogenous.

Once one moves beyond the confines of the idealized world in which choice sets are fixed and attributes known, a vast array of informational situations opens up. To characterize a decision problem, the analyst must specify the decision maker's initial informational conditions, sources of new information, process for integrating prior information with acquired knowledge, and decision rule. The reader familiar with statistical decision theory (for example, DeGroot, 1970) will recognize that decision problems under uncertainty are inherently complex. The experiments of psychologists (such as Kahneman and Tversky, 1979) demonstrate how difficult it is to interpret the observed behavior of decision makers in such contexts.

Nevertheless, some restricted but important problems of imperfect information do yield to analysis. In particular, I shall describe here the recent work of Lerman and Manski (1980a) on the interactive dynamics of information diffusion and population choices after an incompletely anticipated, once-and-for-all change in the attributes of available alternatives.

1. *Assumptions.* Consider a situation in which each of a

population of N decision makers must repeatedly select between the two alternatives i and j. Assume that at time $m = 0$ a steady state prevails; that is, attributes have remained fixed a sufficiently long time that decision makers all have perfect information. Then, at time $m = 1$, a once-and-for-all change occurs in the attributes of either or both alternatives. This attribute change may constitute the introduction of a totally new alternative. Formally, this case is simply one in which the original attributes are so unattractive that the prechange steady-state share is zero.

Some decision makers learn of the changes before they occur through their reception of media reports (advertising, news stories, and the like). For others, however, the changes are unanticipated. A member of the latter group may learn through experience; that is, a person choosing i in period $m = 1$ or later directly observes the new attributes of this alternative. Learning may also be indirect; that is, the person may hear of a change from others who have experienced it or through the media. We assume that the probability of indirect learning does not depend on a person's preferences. Finally, we assume that at each period $m = 0, 1, \ldots$, a person acts according to the most up-to-date information in his or her possession at that time.

Empirical situations at least roughly fitting this scenario abound. After a period of relative stability, the Boston–New York air shuttle fare is raised. A new supermarket is opened in Jerusalem. The medical services offered by a health maintenance organization are improved. The quality of a brand of peanut butter declines. In each case a decision maker faces a repeated choice—how to travel between New York and Boston (if at all); where to shop; what kind of health care plan to use; what peanut butter, if any, to buy. In each case, the decision maker may have prior knowledge of the change, but it is likely that he or she does not. The decision maker may acquire information directly through his or her choices or indirectly through word of mouth or media reports.

2. *Information–Choice Dynamics.* Let Q^i_m be the fraction of the population who select alternative i at time m and let F^i_m be the frequency at time m with which people currently choosing j learn the new attributes of i through word of mouth or media reports. Let K^i be the fraction of the population who would, if given up-to-date information on all attributes, select i. That is, K^i is the postchange steady-state

share for alternative i. Also let K^{ij} be the fraction of the population who select i in the prechange steady state at $m = 0$ but who would, in the postchange steady state, choose j.

Consider first a set of attribute changes in favor *of* alternative i. A set of changes is said to be in favor of i if $K^{ji} > 0$ and $K^{ij} = 0$. Thus such a change includes all situations in which the attractiveness of alternative i unambiguously improves relative to that of j.[19] In this context, it can be shown that for $m \geq 3$, the fraction of the population selecting i is given by the recursion relation

$$Q^i_m = Q^i_{m-1} + F^i_{m-1}\,(K^i - Q^i_{m-1}) \tag{28}$$

Thus the path of Q^i_m over time is monotonic and, assuming the F^i's remain strictly positive, converges to K^i.[20] During the initial periods $m = 1, 2$, the path may be nonmonotonic.

Turn now to the general case in which both K^{ij} and K^{ji} may be positive. Let $K^{i\bar{j}}$ be that subset of K^{ij} who switch to j only *after* learning of changes in the attributes of this alternative.[21] For $m \geq 3$, the time path of Q^i can be shown to be

$$Q^i_m = Q^i_{m-1} + F^i_{m-1}(K^i - Q^i_{m-1}) + (F^i_{m-1} - F^j_{m-1})\left[\prod_{n=0}^{m-2} (1 - F^j_n)\right] K^{i\bar{j}} \tag{29}$$

This path converges to K^i if both F^i_m and F^j_m remain strictly positive over m. The convergence need not be monotonic, however. Note in the case of a change favoring i that $K^{i\bar{j}} = 0$, so Equation (29) reduces to (28).

Equation (29) demonstrates that the time path of aggregate choice frequencies can be characterized without explicitly specifying either a model of individual behavior or a process generating the indirect learning frequencies F. To derive properties of the path beyond convergence and, in the case of favoring changes, monotonicity, however, it is necessary to specify F. Various parametric models for F are posed in Lerman and Manski (1980a).

[19] This does not imply that i must improve in absolute terms. In absolute terms, i and j may both worsen but j more so than i.

[20] Note that the F^j's do not appear in (28).

[21] Some i users may switch to j after learning only that i has become less attractive, unaware that j also has changed.

To close this section, I must emphasize that the strong results obtained here depend crucially on the assumption that the attribute changes are once and for all. If repeated changes take place, the rational decision maker will not simply act according to his or her most up-to-date information but will rather form expectations using all of his or her past observations. He or she may also experiment—that is, select an alternative which appears inferior given his or her expectations expressly for the purpose of learning whether these expectations are accurate or in error.

D. Discrete–Continuous Choice Models

The analysis of discrete choice is a relatively new concern for economists. Much older is the econometric literature on demand that deals with the consumer's or firm's selection of quantities for goods available in continuous amounts. A natural step in the evolution of empirical choice models is the development of models explaining behavior that involves both discrete and continuous choices. The literature on discrete simultaneous systems modeling provides a framework within which such models may be developed. In the following paragraphs I outline the concerns and results of recent work on discrete systems; this work may well be of interest to sociologists. I then describe the application of discrete systems models to the problem of mixed discrete–continuous choices.

1. *Discrete Simultaneous Systems Modeling.* The literature on discrete simultaneous systems modeling is a natural outgrowth of the long-standing concern in econometrics with the estimation of linear model systems. Consider the two-equation linear system

$$\begin{aligned} y_1 &= \beta_1 y_2 + x_1\gamma_1 + \epsilon_1 \\ y_2 &= \beta_2 y_1 + x_2\gamma_2 + \epsilon_2 \end{aligned} \tag{30}$$

where $\begin{bmatrix}\epsilon_1\\ \epsilon_2\end{bmatrix} \approx N(0, \Sigma)$ conditional on $x = [x_1, x_2]$. One major theme of discrete systems analysis concerns the estimation of the parameters $[\beta_1,\beta_2,\gamma_1,\gamma_2]$ when a process is described by this (or a similar multi-equation) system but when observational problems associated with discrete conditions on y_1 and y_2 exist.

To start with some relatively simple cases, Tobin (1958) and

Amemiya (1973) examine maximum-likelihood estimation of γ_1 in the situation where $\beta_1 = 0$, x_1 is always observed, but y_1 is observed only when $y_1 > \alpha_1$, a constant. Heckman (1976) analyzes the version of this situation in which $y_1 \leq \alpha_1$ implies that neither y_1 nor x_1 is observed. The latter problem is one of truncated sampling; the former censoring problem has been termed the *tobit* case. Heckman also provides a computationally convenient estimator usable in tobit and other censoring situations.

Another type of problem is that in which $\beta_1 = \beta_2 = 0$, x_1 and x_2 are always observed, but we only observe whether y_1 is greater or less than y_2. Values for y_1 and y_2 are not observed. The reader will recognize that this is the observational situation faced in discrete-choice analysis when one attempts to infer preferences from choices. That is, if y_1 and y_2 are random utilities for alternatives 1 and 2, a decision maker's choice of alternative 1 over 2 implies only that $y_1 > y_2$.

A third class of problems that has received much attention is the *switching regression*. Here (y_1, x_1) is observed if and only if $y_1 < y_2$; otherwise (y_2, x_2) is observed. Switching regressions, which have been studied by Fair and Jaffee (1972), by Maddala and Nelson (1974), and by others, arise naturally in the analysis of markets in disequilibrium.

Within the last few years, the literature on discrete simultaneous modeling has developed a second major theme. Consider the two-equation mixed discrete–linear system

$$
\begin{aligned}
y_1 &= \beta_1 y_2 + \beta_1^* y_2^* + x_1\gamma_1 + \epsilon_1 \\
y_2 &= \beta_2 y_1 + \beta_2^* y_1^* + x_2\gamma_2 + \epsilon_2
\end{aligned}
\tag{31}
$$

where $y_1^* = 1$ if $y_1 > \alpha_1$ and $y_1^* = 0$ otherwise, where $y_2^* = 1$ if $y_2^* > \alpha_2$, and $y_2^* = 0$ otherwise, and where ϵ is as before. This system is qualitatively different from the one posed earlier because discrete transformations of the endogenous variables are part of the system structure. Consequently, the system now does not have a linear reduced form.

Even when observational problems do not exist, parameter estimation in models such as this one poses difficulties. See Amemiya (1974) and Heckman (1978) for relevant analyses. Note that when $\beta_1 = \beta_1^* = \beta_2 = \alpha_1 = \alpha_2 = 0$ and (y_1, y_2) are unobserved and (y_1^*, y_2^*)

are observed, System (31) may be interpreted as the first two periods of an unrestricted recurrent-choice model in a two-alternative context. In this case, (y_1, y_2) are the differences in utilities between the two alternatives in periods 1 and 2 and (y_1^*, y_2^*) are state indicators for the two periods.

2. *Application.* A number of authors have directly applied Model (30) to mixed discrete–continuous choice problems. In particular, Heckman (1974, 1976) analyzes female labor supply. In his work y_1 is the unobserved difference in utilities between working and not working. The variable y_2 is number of hours worked (always observed). A third equation explains y_3, the woman's market wage. This is observed if and only if the woman works—that is, if $y_1 > 0$.

Westin and Gillen (1978) explain workers' discrete choice of travel mode for the journey to work and continuous choice of a parking location, measured in distance from the workplace, when traveling by private auto. Here y_1 is the difference in utilities between the auto and transit modes and y_2 is the optimal parking distance. The value of y_1 is never observed, but its sign, designating choice of mode, is observed. The optimal parking distance y_2 is observed if and only if $y_1 > 0$.

A further application is by Poirier (1980). He considers the Canadian physician's choice between careers in private and socialized medicine and, when relevant, the physician's continuous choice of fee schedule, number of weekly hours to work, frequency of referrals to other doctors, and other variables.

A disturbing feature of many applications to date is that the model system estimated is not derived from a well-articulated behavioral model. Recently, however, Duncan (1980) and McFadden (1979a) have shown that models of the form (30) and (31) can be derived from utility-maximizing assumptions. These contributions thus strengthen the theoretical justification for use of these models in discrete–continuous choice applications.

V. EMPIRICAL STUDY OF STUDENTS' COLLEGE-GOING DECISIONS

This survey of methodological developments in the analysis of discrete-choice data has, I hope, provided an adequate, if not comprehensive, introduction to the technical literature. The objective of methodological development is, of course, to provide tools for empirical research. In this section, I use a case study to show how the tools of discrete-choice analysis are applied in practice. Since it is easiest to discuss one's own work and most interesting to talk about new findings, I describe here some recently completed work of my own. Specifically, I shall summarize the objectives, execution, and results of an empirical study of students' college-going decisions conducted jointly with Winship C. Fuller and David A. Wise.[22]

A. Background

The research to be described involves the specification, estimation, and forecasting application of a discrete-choice model explaining the high school graduate's initial selection among alternative postsecondary activities, including college, technical school, work, and other options. The development of this model forms part of a larger study of the educational and labor force participation patterns of American young adults during the five-year period following completion of high school.

The problem of modeling college-going decisions has attracted repeated attention over the past decade. Some previous discrete-choice studies were cited in the introduction. All the studies to date have shared a pair of objectives. One goal is to better our understanding of the determinants of college choices. The other is to aid policy formation by predicting student responses to potential changes in the educational environment.

The present effort was initiated in order to exploit a new source of data on college-going behavior, one having qualitative advantages over the surveys previously available. The data set referred to is the National Longitudinal Survey of the High School Class of 1972, commissioned by the U.S. Office of Education. The contents of this survey will be described in Section C. But first our choice model characterizing student behavior must be introduced.

B. The Choice Model

We consider the student at the end of the senior year of high school choosing among postsecondary options conditional on his or her

[22]This study is described in full in Fuller, Manski, and Wise (1980a, 1980b).

previous college applications and colleges' subsequent admissions decisions. In terms of the discussion of recurrent choice in Section IV, the college-going decision can be viewed as one element isolated from a long recursive sequence of career formation decisions during the student's life.

In the model, the choice set facing the student upon completion of high school includes all the colleges and technical schools to which he or she has applied and been admitted plus local community colleges and technical schools having open enrollment policies.[23] The student also has available various nonschooling options including work, the military, and homemaking.[24]

In selecting from his or her choice set, the student is assumed to follow the random utility model of Section IB. The observed utility-relevant attributes characterizing each schooling alternative include measures of academic standards, program length, monthly tuition costs, scholarships offered to admitted students in the sample, monthly dormitory costs when dormitories exist, geographic location of the school, and school control. The utility a student associates with a school depends, of course, on his or her own attributes as well as on those of the school. Specifically, measures of the student's academic ability, family income, home location, race, sex, and high school attributes condition the utility function.

For various reasons the nonschooling alternatives are characterized in a more spartan manner. The work option has as its sole attribute the expected wage (a function of student ability and local labor market wage and unemployment conditions) and the average academic ability of high school graduates choosing to work.[25] The military and homemaking alternatives are represented only by dummy variables.

The utility function disturbances, characterizing unobserved alternative and decision-maker attributes, are assumed independent and identically distributed with the extreme-value distribution. Hence the choice probabilities have the multinomial logit form discussed

[23]Actually, each college having dormitories appears as two alternatives: one for on-campus residence and the other for commuting from home.

[24]With this definition of the choice set, the average student in the sample had about 11 alternatives available.

[25]Distinct occupations are not characterized in the model. Rather, each student has a single "work" alternative.

earlier. This choice of stochastic specification was made primarily for its analytic convenience.

C. Data

As indicated earlier, the Office of Education's National Longitudinal Survey (NLSS) formed the primary data source for the empirical work. The NLSS is an exogenously stratified sample of approximately 22,000 high school seniors first interviewed in Spring 1972 and subsequently followed for a number of years.

For each sampled student, the NLSS provides extensive socioeconomic and demographic background, the results of administered aptitude tests, and high school attribute data. Student reports of colleges applied to, admissions received, and financial aid offers tendered are included, as is the identity of the postsecondary alternative actually chosen[26]

The NLSS does not fully characterize a student's schooling and work options and provides broader, somewhat higher-quality data on the chosen alternative than on nonchosen ones. To fill the gaps we employed a variety of secondary data sources. These included the American Council on Education's Institutional Characteristics File for college attributes, the Office of Education's Vocational Education Directory to identify and characterize voc-tech schools, and Bureau of Labor Statistics reports for local labor market conditions.

D. Empirical Results

The model of college-going decisions was estimated on an exogenous subsample of 4,000 NLSS respondents. The estimator used was the exogenous-sampling maximum-likelihood method of Equation (16). The detailed model specification is presented in Table 1. In the terminology of Equation (7) there are 25 components in each

[26]The existence of applications and admissions data within the NLSS is an important advance over the surveys used in some previous studies of college going, where such data were lacking. It is in fact a common problem in empirical discrete-choice analysis that available surveys provide much detail on respondents' actual behavior but do not even identify alternative, unchosen opportunities.

TABLE 1
Choice Model Parameter Estimates

Variable	Parameter	Asymptotic t
Schooling costs ($ per month/family income)		
1. Tuition if four-year college	−53.6	(−3.3)
2. Scholarship if four-year college	55.1	(2.3)
3. Dormitory cost if four-year college and if student lives on campus	−47.6	(−2.8)
4. Tuition if two-year college	−32.5	(−2.0)
5. Scholarship if two-year college	120.5	(3.7)
6. Tuition if voc-tech school	−42.9	(−4.3)
7. Commuting distance if to four-year college and student lives at home (miles)	−0.00267	(−4.9)
Forgone earnings ($ per month)		
8. Expected income forgone	−0.00206	(−4.8)
Performance standard–ability interaction[a]		
9. $(A + 100)$ if $A \leq -100$	0.00258	(6.3)
10. -100 if $A < -100$, A if $-100 < A < 0$	0.00305	(2.7)
11. A if $0 < A < 100$, 100 if $A \geq 100$	0.00325	(2.9)
12. $(A - 100)$ if $A > 100$	−0.00197	(−4.3)
High school effect (0–100)		
13. If college, percentage of class at student's high school who go on to college	0.0156	(6.2)
14. If voc-tech school, percentage of class who go on to voc-tech school	0.0214	(4.0)
Alternative decision-maker dummies (0–1)		
15. Four-year college: private control	0.169	(0.8)
16. Four-year college: student lives at home	−1.03	(−5.4)
17. Two or four-year college: black student	−0.980	(−5.0)
18. Two-year college	−2.83	(−14.3)
19. Voc-tech school program under a year	−5.01	(−16.5)
20. Voc-tech school program over a year	−4.15	(−14.8)
21. Voc-tech school (industrial trades): male student	1.23	(6.9)
22. Work alternative	−1.54	(−5.3)
23. Military alternative	−3.83	(−13.8)
24. Homemaker alternative	−3.01	(−12.2)
25. Part-time school and work alternative	−3.48	(−14.6)

Sample size: 4,000
Log likelihood at maximum: −4,861
Log likelihood when parameters equal zero: −9,742

Note: When a condition is not satisfied (when the alternative is not a four-year college in variable 1, for example or $A > -100$ in variable 9), the variable takes the value zero.

[a] A = average SAT of people choosing the alternative minus student's SAT. SAT range is 400–1,600.

vector z_{ti} and hence 25 parameters ϕ^* to be estimated. Table 1 gives the estimates and asymptotic t statistics.

The results indicate that schooling costs have the expected negative effect on an alternative's utility and hence, other things being equal, on its choice probability. With the exception of the anomalously large estimate for variable 5, the absolute values of the six cost-related parameters are roughly similar. That is, a dollar seems to be a dollar whether spent for tuition, expended for room and board, or received in scholarship, whether at a four-year college, two-year college, or voc-tech school. In the model, schooling costs are divided by income. This specification expresses the qualitative idea that college expenses are more burdensome to the poor than to the rich and is consistent with earlier work on college choice.[27]

A type of schooling cost not expressible in dollar terms is the commuting cost a college-going student faces if he or she lives at home rather than on campus. In our model this cost is represented by the straight-line distance from home to college. The estimated effect of distance is negative and statistically significant but much smaller in magnitude than expected.[28]

The attractiveness of work as a postsecondary alternative increases as anticipated with expected income. The expected income of a worker is identifiable with the forgone earnings of someone who chooses a schooling alternative. It is of interest to compare the effects of an extra dollar paid in tuition and an extra dollar forgone in earnings. For a student with $10,000 family income (in 1972 dollars), an increase of a dollar per month in tuition at a four-year college lowers the utility of that college relative to the utility of working by 0.00536 unit. For someone with $30,000 family income, the drop is 0.00179 unit. On the other hand, an increase of a dollar in expected monthly earnings raises the utility of working relative to that of the school by 0.00206 unit. Thus the tuition and expected income effects are comparable, the former being the larger at most income levels.[29]

[27]The dormitory cost variable does not appear for two-year college and voc-tech schools because such institutions rarely have these facilities. The scholarship variable does not appear for voc-tech schools for a similar reason.

[28]A distance coefficient could not be estimated for two-year and voc-schools for reasons having to do with our placement of local, open-enrollment two-year colleges and technical schools in students' choice sets.

[29]Note that expected income, unlike school costs, is not divided by family income in the model.

Turn now to the influence of school academic quality on the college-going decision. Earlier work of Kohn, Manski, and Mundel (1976) hypothesized, and tentatively demonstrated, that the effect on utility of increases in school academic standards is first positive and then negative; the modal standard is a function of the student's own ability. This relation was expected as the result of an interplay of two conflicting forces. On the one hand, a high academic standard brings with it prestige and good job opportunities after graduation. On the other hand, a high standard means more competition and a smaller probability of successful completion of the program. The trade-off between these forces depends on the student's ability relative to the institution's standard.

Our findings strongly corroborate those of the earlier paper. Taken together, variables 9 to 12 form a flexible piecewise linear specification of the quality–ability interaction. The set of four coefficients indicates that increases in quality first have a positive effect and then a negative one. The optimal quality for a student appears to lie somewhat above his or her own ability level.[30]

The remaining variables of interest in the model are the high school effects. We find that, all else being equal, the probability a student will go to college or voc-tech school rises with the percentage of his or her high school classmates doing likewise. Whether this result represents a peer group effect or masks high school attributes that affect all students in the school is not known and deserves investigation.

The dummy variables 15 to 25 characterize effects whose structural interpretations are ambiguous. No interpretations for the coefficients will be attempted here.

E. Forecasting Application of the Model

The examination of parameter estimates only partially realizes the value of a structural model. Application of the model to forecast the values of endogenous variables when the exogenous environment differs from that in the sample more fully exercises the power of structural analysis. In this final section, I summarize the application of

[30]It is not possible to determine the exact location of the maximum since the breakpoints in the piecewise linear form were fixed beforehand.

TABLE 2
Predicted Distributions of Enrollments in 1979 With and Without BEOG Program

Income Group	BEOG Status	All Schools (1)	4-Year Schools (2)	2-Year Schools (3)	Voc-Tech Schools (4)
Lower	Yes	590	128	349	113
(<$16,900)	No	370	137	210	23
Middle	Yes	398	162	202	34
	No	354	164	168	22
Upper	Yes	615	377	210	28
(>$21,700)	No	600	378	198	24
Total	Yes	1,603	668	761	174
	No	1,324	679	576	69

NOTE: All numbers are in thousands of students.

the estimated model of college-going decisions to analyze a public issue of some importance. This concerns the efficacy of the Basic Educational Opportunity Grants program in inducing freshman college enrollments. Specifically, we have attempted to answer the following question: Given conditions paralleling those of 1979–1980 except that no BEOG program exists, how would the magnitude and mix of enrollments compare to those actually expected?[31]

The BEOG program, the largest federal student aid instrument in operation, provides awards according to a formula whereby aid increases with school tuition and living expenses, decreases with family income and assets, and is subject to an upper limit. While the original purpose of the program was solely to help low-income students, eligibility criteria have recently been liberalized. The 1979–1980 version of the program incorporates an award ceiling of $1,800 and a family contribution schedule sufficiently flat that a substantial number of upper-income students are eligible for benefits.

The forecasting procedure may be explained briefly. The college-going model can be used to forecast if and how a student admitted to a given set of colleges would react to changes in the cost of enrollment at those schools. Applied to a sample representative of the national population, predictions of aggregate enrollment impact can be produced by using Equation (22). Our forecasts have been obtained by applying the model to the NLSS respondents, suitably weighted to

[31]A detailed report of this application is presented in Fuller, Manski, and Wise (1980b).

TABLE 3
Distribution of BEOG Awards Between Induced and Existing Enrollees

Income Group	Predicted Number of BEOG Recipients	Predicted Induced Enrollments	Number of Awards to Existing Enrollees
Lower	534	220	314
Middle	265	44	221
Upper	296	15	281
Total	1,095	279	816

NOTE: All numbers are in thousands of students.

represent the population of 1979 high school seniors. Specifically, we estimate the BEOG awards for which each student would have been eligible if he or she had been a high school graduate in 1979 and we predict his or her subsequent behavior. These forecasts are compared with forecasts made under the alternative scenario that no BEOG program exists.

The predictions in Table 2 indicate that the program is responsible for a truly substantial increase (30 to 47 percent) in the enrollment rate of low-income students, a moderate increase (38 to 43 percent) in middle-income enrollments, and a minor change (53 to 54 percent) in the rate for upper-income students. Interestingly, the enrollment increases are totally concentrated at the two-year and vocational school levels. Enrollments in four-year schools appear entirely insensitive to BEOG availability.

Table 3 gives the distribution of BEOG awards by income group and the predicted number of induced enrollees in each group. An induced enrollee is defined to be a student who is predicted to enroll in the presence of the BEOG program but would not do so in the program's absence. Table 3 indicates that 25 percent of all awards go to induced enrollees. Disaggregating by income groups, we see that this percentage falls sharply as income rises. Of the low-income awards, 41 percent go to induced enrollees; of the middle-income awards, 17 percent; and of the upper-income awards, only 6 percent. It is thus apparent that a significant fraction of the BEOG budget is spent as a pure subsidy.[32]

It should be pointed out that these forecasts of college-going

[32]Not reported in Table 3 are award sizes. The average low-income recipient receives $1,193, middle income $879, and upper income $628. In total, 40 percent of the approximately $1 billion awarded goes to middle and upper-income students.

decisions may only partially capture the behavioral impacts of the BEOG program. We ignore any effect of the program on application decisions. Likewise, college admissions are assumed insensitive to the existence of the program. A further question regards the reaction of college financial aid offices to students entering with BEOG money. That is, do such awards complement or substitute for college-given aid? The forecasts presented here assume substitution. An alternative set made under the assumption of complementarity is similar.

Also not reported here are the results of a predictive test of the model and forecasting approach. In particular, we obtained the most recent available national statistics on postsecondary activity choices and on freshman BEOG recipients, these being for the high school class of 1977. These data were then compared with predictions we prepared for the 1977–1978 academic year. The outcome of this test, presented in Fuller, Manski, and Wise (1980a, 1980b), was very encouraging.

REFERENCES

ADLER, T., AND BEN-AKIVA, M.

1975 "A joint frequency, destination and mode choice model for shopping trips." *Transportation Research Record* 569.

AMEMIYA, T.

1973 "Regression analysis when the dependent variable is truncated normal." *Econometrica* 41:997–1016.

1974 "Multivariate regression and simultaneous equation models when the dependent variables arc truncated normal." *Econometrica* 42:999–1012.

1978a "On a two-step estimation of a multivariate logit model." *Journal of Econometrics* 8:13–21.

1978b "The estimation of a simultaneous equations generalized probit model." *Econometrica* 46:1193–1206.

ANDERSON, T.

1958 *An Introduction to Multivariate Statistical Analysis.* New York: Wiley.

BARTON, M.

1979 "Conditional logit analysis of FCC decision making." *Bell Journal of Economics* 10:399–411.

BEN-AKIVA, M.

1973 "Structure of passenger travel demand models." Ph.D. dissertation, M.I.T.

BEN-AKIVA, M., AND LERMAN, S.
1979 "Disaggregate travel and mobility choice models and measures of accessibility." In D. Hensher and P. Stopher (Eds.), *Behavioral Travel Modeling*. London: Croom Helm.

BEN-AKIVA, M., AND OTHERS
1977 "Experiments to clarify priorities in urban travel forecasting research and development." Center for Transportation Studies Report 77-24. Cambridge, Mass.: M.I.T.

BERKSON, J.
1944 "Application of the logistic function to bioassay." *Journal of the American Statistical Association* 39:357–365.

BISHOP, J.
1977 "The effect of public policies on the demand for higher education." *Journal of Human Resources* 12:285–307.

BISHOP, Y., FIENBERG, S., AND HOLLAND, P.
1975 *Discrete Multivariate Analysis*. Cambridge, Mass.: M.I.T. Press.

BOSKIN, M.
1974 "A conditional logit model of occupational choice." *Journal of Political Economy* 82:389–398.

BRIER, S.
1978 "The utility of systems of simultaneous logistic response equations." In K. F. Schuessler (Ed.), *Sociological Methodology 1979*. San Francisco: Jossey-Bass.

BROWNSTONE, D.
1978 "An econometric model of consumer durable choice and utilization rate." Paper IP-268. Berkeley: Center for Research in Management Science, University of California.

CAMBRIDGE SYSTEMATICS
1979 "JLOGIT." Computer package. Cambridge, Mass.: Cambridge Systematics, Inc.

CHAMBERLAIN, G.
1978 "On the use of panel data." Paper prepared for the Social Science Research Council Conference on Life Cycle Aspects of Employment and the Labor Market, Mt. Kisco, New York.

CHAPMAN, R.
1977 "Buyer behavior in higher education: An analysis of college choice decision making behavior." Ph.D. dissertation, Carnegie-Mellon University.

CLARK, C.
1961 "The greatest of a finite set of random variables." *Operations Research* 9:145–162.

COSSLETT, S.
1980 "Efficient estimation of discrete choice models." In C. Manski and D. McFadden (Eds.), *Structural Analysis of Discrete Data:*

With Econometric Applications. Cambridge, Mass.: M.I.T. Press.

COX, D.

1970 *Analysis of Binary Data*. London: Methuen.

DAGANZO, D., BOUTHELIER, F., AND SHEFFI, Y.

1977 "Multinomial probit and qualitative choice: A computationally efficient algorithm." *Transportation Science* 11:338–358.

DALY, A., AND ZACHARY, S.

1975 "Commuters' value of time." Report No. T55. Reading: Local Government Operational Research Unit, Royal Institute of Public Administration.

1978 "Improved multiple choice models." In D. Hensher and M. Dalvi (Eds.), *Determinants of Travel Choice*. Farnborough: Saxon House.

DEBREU, G.

1960 "Review of R. Luce, Individual Choice Behavior." *American Economic Review* 50:186–188.

DEGROOT, M.

1970 *Optimal Statistical Decisions*. New York: McGraw-Hill.

DOMENCICH, T., AND MCFADDEN, D.

1975 *Urban Travel Demand: A Behavioral Analysis*. Amsterdam: North-Holland.

DUNCAN, G.

1980 "Formulation and statistical analysis of the mixed continuous/discrete dependent variable model in classical production theory." *Econometrica*, 48:839–852.

FAIR, R., AND JAFFEE, D.

1972 "Methods of estimation for markets in disequilibrium." *Econometrica* 40:497–514.

FINNEY, D.

1971 *Probit Analysis*. Cambridge: Cambridge University Press.

FISCHER, G., AND NAGIN, D.

1980 "Random vs. fixed coefficient quantal choice models: An empirical comparison." In C. Manski and D. McFadden (Eds.), *Structural Analysis of Discrete Data*. Cambridge, Mass.: M.I.T. Press.

FULLER, W., MANSKI, C., AND WISE, D.

1980a "New evidence on the economic determinants of postsecondary schooling choices." Unpublished manuscript.

1980b "The impact of the Basic Educational Opportunity Grants program on college enrollments." Unpublished manuscript.

GINSBERG, R.

1972 "Incorporating causal structure and exogenous information with probabilistic models." *Journal of Mathematical Sociology* 2:83–104.

GOODMAN, L., AND KRUSKAL, W.

1954 "Measures of association for cross-classifications." *Journal of the American Statistical Association* 49:732–764.

HABERMAN, S.

1974 *The Analysis of Frequency Data.* Chicago: University of Chicago Press.

HAUSMAN, J.

1979 "Individual discount rates and the purchase and utilization of energy using durables." *Bell Journal of Economics* 10:33–54.

HAUSMAN, J., AND WISE, D.

1978 "A conditional probit model for qualitative choice: Discrete decisions recognizing interdependence and heterogenous preferences." *Econometrica* 46:403–426.

HECKMAN, J.

1974 "Shadow prices, market wages, and labor supply." *Econometrica* 42:679–694.

1976 "The common structure of statistical models of truncation, sample selection and limited dependent variables and a simple estimator for such models." *Annals of Economic and Social Measurement* 5:475–492.

1978 "Dummy endogenous variables in a simultaneous equations system." *Econometrica* 46:931–961.

1979 "Longitudinal studies in labor economics: A methodological review." Unpublished manuscript.

1980a "Statistical models for the analysis of discrete panel data." In C. Manski and D. McFadden (Eds.), *Structural Analysis of Discrete Data.* Cambridge, Mass.: M.I.T. Press.

1980b "The incidental parameters problem and the problem of initial conditions in estimating a discrete stochastic process and some Monte Carlo evidence on their practical importance." In C. Manski and D. McFadden (Eds.), *Structural Analysis of Discrete Data.* Cambridge, Mass.: M.I.T. Press.

HENSHER, D., AND STOPHER, P. (EDS.)

1979 *Behavioral Travel Models.* London: Croom Helm.

HOROWITZ, J.

1980 "Sources of error and uncertainty in behavioral travel models." In W. Brog, P. Stopher, and A. Meyburg (Eds.), *Proceedings of the Fourth International Conference on Behavioral Travel Modelling.* Lexington: Heath.

KAHNEMAN, D., AND TVERSKY, A.

1979 "Prospect theory: An analysis of decision under risk." *Econometrica* 47:263–292.

KENDALL, M., AND STUART, J.

1976 *Advanced Theory of Statistics.* Vol. 3. New York: Hafner.

KOCUR, G., AND OTHERS
1979 "A model of weekend recreation travel demand." In *PTRC Proceedings*. London.

KOHN, M., MANSKI, C., AND MUNDEL, D.
1976 "An empirical investigation of factors which influence college going behavior." *Annals of Economic and Social Measurement* 5:391–419.

KOPPELMAN, F.
1975 "Travel prediction with models of individual choice behavior." Center for Transportation Studies Paper 75-7. Cambridge: M.I.T. Press.

LAVE, C.
1969 "A behavioral approach to modal split forecasting." *Transportation Research* 3:463–480.

LAVE, C., AND TRAIN, K.
1979 "A behavioral disaggregate model of auto type choice." *Transportation Research* 13B.

LERMAN, S.
1976 "Location, housing, auto ownership and mode to work: A joint choice model." *Transportation Research Record* 610.

LERMAN, S., AND BEN-AKIVA, M.
1975 "A disaggregate behavioral model of automobile ownership." *Transportation Research Record* 569:34–55.

LERMAN, S., AND LOUVIERE, J.
1978 "The use of functional measurement to identify the form of utility functions in travel demand models." *Transportation Research Record* 673:78–85.

LERMAN, S., AND MANSKI, C.
1979 "Sample design for discrete choice analysis of travel behavior: The state of the art." *Transportation Research* 13A:29–44.
1980a "The influence of information on the dynamics of travel demand." Report to the Transportation Systems Center, U.S. Department of Transportation. Cambridge, Mass.: Cambridge Systematics, Inc.
1980b "On the use of simulated frequencies to approximate choice probabilities." In C. Manski and D. McFadden (Eds.), *Structural Analysis of Discrete Data*. Cambridge, Mass.: M.I.T. Press.

LI, M.
1977 "A logit model of home ownership." *Econometrica* 45:1081–1097.

LISCO, T.
1967 "The value of commuters' travel time: A study in urban transportation." Ph.D. dissertation, University of Chicago.

LUCE, R.
1959 *Individual Choice Behavior*. New York: Wiley.
LUCE, R., AND SUPPES, P.
1965 "Preference, utility, and subjective probability." In R. Luce, R. Bush, and E. Galanter (Eds.), *Handbook of Mathematical Psychology*. Vol. 3. New York: Wiley.
MADDALA, G., AND NELSON, F.
1974 "Maximum likelihood methods for markets in disequilibrium." *Econometrica* 42:1013–1030.
MANSKI, C.
1975 "Maximum score estimation of the stochastic utility model of choice." *Journal of Econometrics* 3:205–228.
1977 "The structure of random utility models." *Theory and Decision* 8:229–254.
MANSKI, C., AND LERMAN, S.
1977 "The estimation of choice probabilities from choice based samples." *Econometrica* 45:1977–1988.
MANSKI, C., AND MCFADDEN, D. (EDS.)
1980a *Structural Analysis of Discrete Data: With Econometric Applications*. Cambridge, Mass.: M.I.T. Press.
1980b "Alternative estimators and sample designs for discrete choice analysis." In C. Manski and D. McFadden (Eds.), *Structural Analysis of Discrete Data*. Cambridge, Mass.: M.I.T. Press.
MANSKI, C., AND SHERMAN, L.
1980a "An empirical analysis of household choice among motor vehicles." *Transportation Research* in press.
1980b "Forecasting equilibrium motor vehicle holdings with disaggregate models." *Transportation Research Record* in press.
MCFADDEN, D.
1973 "Conditional logit analysis of qualitative choice behavior." In P. Zarembka (Ed.), *Frontiers of Econometrics*. New York: Academic Press.
1976a "The revealed preferences of a government bureaucracy." *Bell Journal of Economics* 7:55–72.
1976b "Quantal choice analysis: A survey." *Annals of Economic and Social Measurement* 5:363–390.
1976c "A comment on discriminant analysis 'versus' logit analysis." *Annals of Economic and Social Measurement* 5:511–524.
1978 "Modelling the choice of residential location." *Transportation Research Record* 673:72–77.
1979a "Econometric net supply functions for firms with continuous and discrete commodities." Unpublished manuscript.
1979b "Notes for Fisher-Schultz lecture." Paper delivered to the Econometric Society, Athens.

1980 "Econometric models of probabilistic choice." In C. Manski and D. McFadden (Eds.), *Structural Analysis of Discrete Data.* Cambridge, Mass.: M.I.T. Press.

MCFADDEN, D., AND OTHERS
1978 "QUAIL." Computer package. Berkeley: University of California.

MCFADDEN, D., AND REID, F.
1974 "Aggregate travel demand forecasting from disaggregated behavioral models." *Transportation Research Record* 534:24–37.

NERLOVE, M., AND PRESS, J.
1973 "Univariate and multivariate log-linear and logistic models." RAND Report No. R-1306-EDA/NIH.

NOLFI, G., AND OTHERS
1978 *Experiences of Recent High School Graduates.* Lexington: Heath.

POIRIER, D.
1980 "A switching simultaneous equation model of physician behavior in Ontario." In C. Manski and D. McFadden (Eds.), *Structural Analysis of Discrete Data.* Cambridge, Mass.: M.I.T. Press.

POLLAKOWSKI, H.
1980 *Residential Location and Urban Housing Markets.* Lexington: Heath.

QUANDT, R., AND BAUMOL, W.
1966 "The demand for abstract travel modes: Theory and measurement." *Journal of Regional Science* 6:13–26.

QUIGLEY, J.
1973 "Housing demand in the short run: An analysis of polytomous choice." Paper W3-38. Department of Economics, Yale University.

RADNER, R., AND MILLER, L.
1975 *Demand and Supply in U.S. Higher Education.* New York: McGraw-Hill.

SCHUESSLER, K. F. (ED.)
1978 *Sociological Methodology 1979.* San Francisco: Jossey-Bass.

SHEFFI, Y.
1978 "Transportation network equilibration with discrete choice models." Ph.D. dissertation, M.I.T.

STEWMAN, S.
1976 "Markov models of occupational mobility: Theoretical development and empirical support." *Journal of Mathematical Sociology* 4:201–245.

STOPHER, P., AND MEYBURG, A.
1976 *Behavioral Travel Demand Models.* Lexington: Heath.

SWARTZ, B.

1976 "Screening in the labor market: A case study." Ph.D. dissertation, University of Wisconsin, Madison.

THEIL, H.

1970 "On the estimation of relationships involving qualitative variables." *American Journal of Sociology* 76:103–154.

THURSTONE, L.

1927 "A law of comparative judgement." *Psychological Review* 34:273–286.

TOBIN, J.

1958 "Estimation of relationships for limited dependent variables." *Econometrica* 26:24–36.

TRAIN, K., AND MCFADDEN, D.

1978 "The goods/leisure tradeoff and disaggregate work trip mode choice models." *Transportation Research* 12:349–353.

TVERSKY, A.

1972 "Elimination by aspects: A theory of choice." *Psychological Review* 79:281–299.

WARNER, S.

1962 *Stochastic Choice of Mode in Urban Travel.* Evanston: Northwestern University Press.

1963 "Multivariate regression of dummy variables under normality assumptions." *Journal of the American Statistical Association* 58:1054–1063.

WESTIN, R.

1974 "Predictions from binary choice models." *Journal of Econometrics* 2:1–16.

1975 "Statistical models for inter-related discrete and continuous choices." Unpublished manuscript.

WESTIN, R., AND GILLEN, D.

1978 "Parking location and transit demand: A case study of endogenous attributes in disaggregate mode choice models." *Journal of Econometrics* 8:75–101.

WILLIS, R., AND ROSEN, S.

1979 "Education and self-selection." *Journal of Political Economy* 87:S7–S36.

3

A SURVEY OF STATISTICAL METHODS FOR GRAPH ANALYSIS

Ove Frank

LUND UNIVERSITY, SWEDEN

Sociometric problems involving empirical sociograms and more general networks have been one of the major sources of an increasing interest in statistical graph models. The well-known book by Harary, Norman, and Cartwright (1965) has contributed much to the mathematical modeling of social networks, and we now find numerous methodological articles appearing in the literature—for instance, in the *Journal of Mathematical Sociology, Social Networks,* and other professional journals. Nonetheless, while statistical testing and estimation problems are discussed in some reports, statistical issues are all too often ignored or treated in a very elementary way. Only recently have statistical models and methods been developed that begin to meet the need for proper handling of sampling variation, measurement errors, and other kinds of uncertainty in network data.

This survey discusses some of the statistical models and methods for graphs that have been described in the literature and are thought to have potential applications to empirical graph data obtained from social contact networks, paired comparisons, network flows, and the like. Three main types of models are considered: pure sampling models for inference in large graphs, simple transition models for uncertain or randomly deformed graphs, and simple stochastic graph processes for nondeterministic changes in a graph. A unified and systematic way of specifying the models may facilitate the identification of their applicability and limitations in different situations. The specification of simple standard models may also be convenient in initiating development of more sophisticated models by identifying specific assumptions that should be relaxed or changed. I illustrate use of the models by considering various statistical estimation and testing problems. Most of the results are given without proof but with reference to the literature where more details can be found.

The emphasis here is on methods. The problems considered are basic and thought to be of general interest, but they represent, of course, only a beginning of a statistical development in graph theory. The main source of inspiration for the development of statistical graph theory is the problems and achievements reported in applied works in sociology and other fields. Not very much of the applied literature will be covered here, however, and reference should be given to the extensive bibliography by Freeman (1976) and the review chapter by Burt (1980), where further references to sociological applications can be found.

In Section 1 I introduce basic terminology and notation. That section also gives some fundamentals about graphs and graph parameters useful in what follows. Section 2 defines the three main types of statistical graph models: sampling models, transition models, and graph processes. Sections 3 and 4 are devoted to the estimation of various parameters in an unknown graph by using information from a sample-induced subgraph and a sampled star. Section 5 treats estimation based on several sampled subgraphs and discusses comparisons between estimators based on different kinds of samples. Sections 6 and 7 consider transition models for graphs and digraphs and discuss how these models can be used to test various structural hypotheses. Finally, Section 8 discusses the prospects for future development of statistical graph models.

1. BASIC CONCEPTS

1.1 Fundamentals

A *graph* (V, G) consists of a nonempty set V of elements called *nodes* (vertices, points) and a subset G of the class $\mathcal{P}_2(V)$ of unordered pairs of distinct nodes. The elements of G are called *edges* (links, lines). If the node set V of a graph (V, G) is understood from context, then we also simply speak of the graph G.

The numbers of elements in V and G are called the *order* and *size* of the graph, respectively. Figure 1 shows a graph of order 25 and size 19. If a graph has order N, its size can be at most $\binom{N}{2}$. A graph of maximum size is called *complete*.

A graph (V, G) can be represented by its *adjacency matrix* X, which is defined by $X_{vv} = 0$ for $v \in V$ and X_{uv} $(= X_{vu})$ equal to 1 or 0 according to whether or not $\{u, v\}$ belongs to G for $u \neq v$, $u, v \in V$. An edge $\{u, v\}$ is said to be *incident* to u and v; u and v are said to be *adjacent* if $\{u, v\} \in G$.

1.2 Degree Distribution

The *degree* of a node v is defined as the number of edges incident to v; that is,

$$\sum_{u \in V} X_{uv} \tag{1}$$

The *degree distribution* of G is given by the frequencies $F_0, F_1, \ldots, F_{N-1}$ of nodes of degrees $0, 1, \ldots, N-1$, respectively, where $N = |V|$ is the order of the graph. The degree distribution satisfies $0 \leq F_i \leq N$ for $i = 0, 1, \ldots, N-1$ and

$$\sum_{i=0}^{N-1} F_i = N \tag{2}$$

It is convenient to say that G has degree distribution

$$0^{F_0} 1^{F_1} \ldots (N-1)^{F_{N-1}} \tag{3}$$

For instance, the graph in Figure 1 has degree distribution $0^3\ 1^{10}\ 2^9\ 3^2\ 4$.

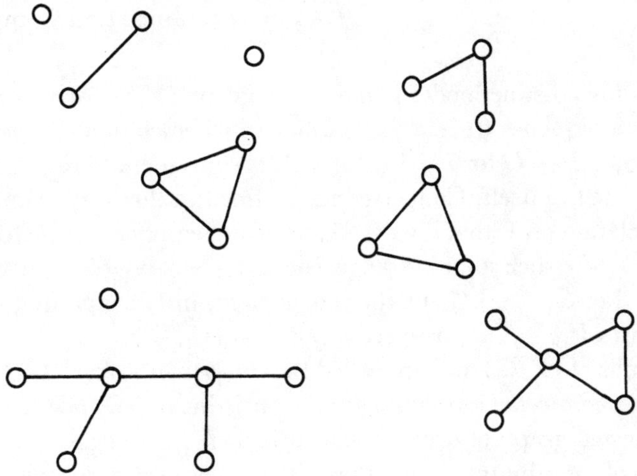

Figure 1. A graph of order 25 and size 19.

Nodes of degree 0 are called *isolates*. The size $R = |G|$ of a graph is given by half the sum of the degrees; that is,

$$2R = \sum_{u\in V} \sum_{v\in V} X_{uv} = \sum_{i=0}^{N-1} iF_i \tag{4}$$

Let Q be the sum of squares of the degrees:

$$Q = \sum_{u\in V} \left(\sum_{v\in V} X_{uv} \right)^2 = \sum_{i=0}^{N-1} i^2 F_i \tag{5}$$

Then the mean μ and variance σ^2 of the degrees are given by

$$\mu = 2R/N \qquad \sigma^2 = Q/N - 4R^2/N^2 \tag{6}$$

1.3 Subgraphs

A *subgraph* of a graph (V, G) is a graph (V', G'), where $V' \subseteq V$ and $G' \subseteq G$. Notice that the requirement that (V', G') is a graph implies that G' has to be a subset of the class $\mathcal{P}_2(V')$ of unordered pairs of nodes in V'. We shall be examining three different kinds of subgraphs: components, induced subgraphs, and stars.

1.4 Connectedness and Components

Two distinct nodes u and v in a graph (V, G) are *connected* if there is a sequence $(v_0, \ldots, v_n)$ of nodes in V such that $v_0 = u$, $v_n = v$, and $\{v_{i-1}, v_i\} \in G$ for $i = 1, \ldots, n$. It is convenient to say that a node is connected to itself. Connectedness defined in this way is an equivalence relation on V that divides V into K nonempty equivalence classes $V_1, \ldots, V_K$ such that no edge connects two nodes from different classes. Let $G_1, \ldots, G_K$ be the sets of edges in G connecting nodes in the classes $V_1, \ldots, V_K$, respectively. Then $(V_1, G_1), \ldots, (V_K, G_K)$ are subgraphs of (V, G) and are called the *components* of (V, G).

A *connected graph* is a graph consisting of only one component. A connected graph of order N has at least $N - 1$ edges. A connected graph of minimum size—that is, a connected graph of size $N - 1$—is called a *tree*. A graph in which all components are trees is called a *forest*. A graph in which all components are complete is called a *transitive graph*.

The *component-order distribution* of (V, G) is given by the frequencies $K_1, \ldots, K_N$ of components of order $1, \ldots, N$, respectively, where $N = |V|$. These frequencies satisfy the equalities

$$K = \sum_{i=1}^{N} K_i \qquad N = \sum_{i=1}^{N} iK_i \tag{7}$$

and the inequalities

$$\sum_{i=1}^{N} (i - 1)\, K_i \leq R \leq \sum_{i=2}^{N} \binom{i}{2} K_i \tag{8}$$

where $R = |G|$. These inequalities can be proved by using the fact that each component of order i has a size which is at least $i - 1$ (which yields a tree component) and at most $\binom{i}{2}$ (which yields a complete component). From (8) it follows (see Frank, 1978c, p. 185) that

$$N - K \leq R \leq \binom{N - K + 1}{2} \tag{9}$$

It is convenient to say that G has component-order distribution

$$1^{K_1} 2^{K_2} \cdots N^{K_N} \tag{10}$$

For instance, the graph in Figure 1 has component-order distribution $1^3\,2\,3^3\,5\,6$.

1.5 Induced Subgraphs

Let $S \subseteq V$ and define the subgraph of (V, G) *induced* by S as the graph with node set S and edge set $G(S)$ consisting of all the edges in G connecting two nodes in S. Induced subgraphs of order 2 and 3 are called *dyads* and *triads*, respectively. There are two different dyads and four different triads (Figure 2).

Induced subgraphs enter naturally in sample investigations of large graphs that are based on a node sample and observations of adjacencies between the sampled nodes. For instance, if the node set of the graph represents a population of people, families, or other units that are sampled and interviewed concerning their adjacency properties, and if adjacency means mutual appreciation, cooperation, or some other sentiment or activity that should be confirmed by both the nodes involved, then the sample information provides an induced subgraph. Even if it is not necessary to have the adjacencies confirmed by both the nodes involved, it might be convenient to restrict interview data to the adjacencies within the sample, since this may make the reliability higher. It might be better to perform the interviews by presenting a list of the nodes in the sample and ask for adjacencies to members of that list than to ask for adjacencies to members of a huge population in which some nodes are probably forgotten in many interviews. Such a

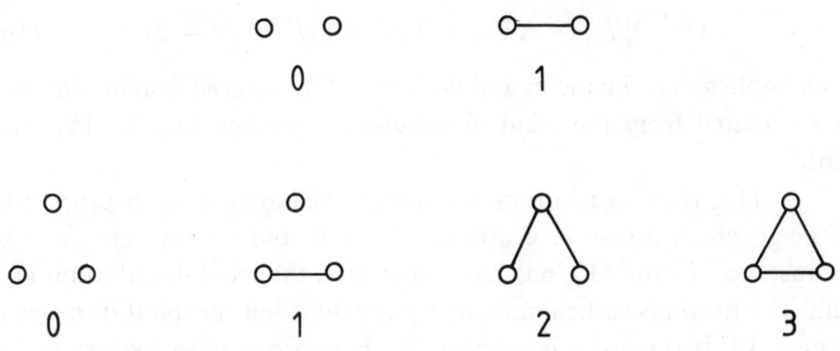

Figure 2. Graph dyads and triads.

restriction to the adjacencies within a sample provides an induced subgraph.

1.6 Dyad and Triad Distribution

A graph (V, G) of order N has $\binom{N}{2}$ dyads and $\binom{N}{3}$ triads. The *dyad distribution* is given by the frequencies (T_{20}, T_{21}) of dyads in G of size 0 and 1, respectively; the *triad distribution* is given by the frequencies $(T_{30}, \ldots, T_{33})$ of triads in G of size $0, \ldots, 3$, respectively. These dyad and triad frequencies satisfy the following relationships:

$$T_{20} + T_{21} = \binom{N}{2} \qquad T_{21} = R = |G| \tag{11}$$

$$T_{30} + \cdots + T_{33} = \binom{N}{3} \qquad T_{31} + 2T_{32} + 3T_{33} = (N-2)R \tag{12}$$

It is possible to deduce properties of the degree distribution $(F_0, \ldots, F_{N-1})$ from the triad distribution. By combinatorial reasoning it can be proved that

$$T_{31} + T_{32} = \sum_{i=1}^{N-1} i(N-1-i)F_i/2 = (N-1)R - Q/2 \tag{13}$$

$$T_{32} + 3T_{33} = \sum_{i=2}^{N-1} \binom{i}{2} F_i = (Q - 2R)/2 \tag{14}$$

where Q is the sum of squares of the degrees. It follows that R and Q are given by the triad distribution according to

$$R = (T_{31} + 2T_{32} + 3T_{33})/(N-2) \tag{15}$$

$$Q = 2[T_{31} + NT_{32} + 3(N-1)T_{33}]/(N-2) \tag{16}$$

This implies that the mean and variance of the degree distribution can be calculated from the triad distribution according to (6), (15), and (16).

The triad distribution can also be used to infer other properties of the graph. A transitive graph has $T_{32} = 0$, and a forest has $T_{33} = 0$, for instance. Frank (1978a) has shown that the triad distribution of a transitive graph is sufficient to determine the whole graph if its order is at most 13. If the order is at most 21, there are at most two transitive graphs with the same triad distribution. In fact, for order 21 there are

694 different triad distributions, each of which is compatible with a unique transitive graph, and 49 different triad distributions, each of which is common to two transitive graphs. The number of graphs in a given class that are compatible with a given triad distribution is called the *multiplicity* of the triad distribution in that class. Table 1 shows the numbers of triad distributions of different multiplicities for transitive graphs of order at most 30. We see that the typical multiplicity grows very slowly with the order and that the triad distribution very often yields a unique graph (at least for the graph orders that are likely to occur in practical paired-comparison experiments).

The triad distribution yields information about the component-

TABLE 1
Number of Triad Distributions of Multiplicity k Among Transitive Graphs of Order N

	k				
N	1	2	3	4	5
3	3				
4	5				
5	7				
6	11				
7	15				
8	22				
9	30				
10	42				
11	56				
12	77				
13	101				
14	133	1			
15	172	2			
16	221	5			
17	283	7			
18	357	14			
19	450	20			
20	561	33			
21	694	49			
22	851	74	1		
23	1,044	104	1		
24	1,253	155	4		
25	1,523	204	9		
26	1,823	279	17	1	
27	2,185	358	35	1	
28	2,596	462	62	3	
29	3,065	597	94	6	
30	3,578	755	153	13	1

order distribution. In particular, we can give lower bounds on the number K of components by using the triad distribution. To see this, we denote by $N_1, \ldots, N_K$ the component orders and introduce the polynomial

$$\prod_{k=1}^{K} (x - N_k) = \sum_{r=0}^{K} (-1)^r C_r x^{K-r} \tag{17}$$

where

$$C_0 = 1 \qquad C_r = \sum_{i_1 < \cdots < i_r} \sum N_{i_1} \cdots N_{i_r} \tag{18}$$

for $r = 1, \ldots, K$. According to a classic result by Newton (see, for example, Hardy, Littlewood, and Pólya, 1952, p. 52), the numbers

$$\overline{C}_r = C_r \Big/ \binom{K}{r} \tag{19}$$

satisfy for each $r = 1, \ldots, K - 1$ the inequality

$$\overline{C}_{r-1}\overline{C}_{r+1} \leq \overline{C}_r^2 \tag{20}$$

with equality if and only if all component orders are equal. The inequality (20) yields the following lower bound on K:

$$K \geq [r^2 C_r^2 - (r-1)(r+1)C_{r-1}C_{r+1}] / [rC_r^2 - (r+1)C_{r-1}C_{r+1}] \tag{21}$$

provided the denominator is positive. By substituting

$$C_1 = N \qquad C_2 = T_{20} = \binom{N}{2} - R \qquad C_3 = T_{30} \tag{22}$$

in (21), we find for $r = 1$

$$K \geq N^2/(N + 2R) \tag{23}$$

and for $r = 2$

$$K \geq [4T_{20}^2 - 3NT_{30}]/[2T_{20}^2 - 3NT_{30}] \tag{24}$$

where, according to (11), (12), and (15),

$$T_{20} = (3T_{30} + 2T_{31} + T_{32})/(N - 2) \tag{25}$$

The lower bound on K given by (23) is better than the lower bound $N - R$ given by (9) if and only if $2R > N$—that is, if and only if the mean degree is larger than 1. The lower bound on K given by (24) is better than the one given by (23) if and only if

$$T_{20}(4T_{20} - N^2) < 3NT_{30} < 2T_{20}^2 \tag{26}$$

1.7 Stars

Let $S \subseteq V$ and define the *star* of (V, G) obtained from S as the subgraph with node set $A(S)$ and edge set $H(S)$, where $A(S)$ consists of all nodes that are either in S or adjacent to some node in S and where $H(S)$ consists of all edges that are incident to some node in S. The set S is called the *center* of the star. If the center has size n, the star is also called an *n-star*.

There is a close relationship between the edge set $H(S)$ and the edge set $G(\bar{S})$ induced by the complement $\bar{S}$ of S with respect to V. If the bar notation is also used for complements of edge sets with respect to $\mathcal{P}_2(V)$, then

$$H(S) = G \cap \overline{G(\bar{S})} \tag{27}$$

That is, the edges in the star with center S are the edges in G that are not in the subgraph of G induced by the complement of S.

Stars enter naturally in sample investigations of large graphs that are based on a node sample and observations of all the adjacencies to the sampled nodes. For instance, contacts between people or transactions between bank accounts might be recorded and accessible in such a way that each node can provide all its adjacencies. A sample of nodes then provides a star with the sample as its center. Stars can also be obtained from interviews with the nodes and considered as alternatives to the induced subgraphs discussed in preceding paragraphs; if both stars and induced subgraphs are possible, a choice between them can be based on decision-theoretic methods using costs for sampling of nodes and observation of edges. I shall illustrate such comparisons between graph sampling designs in Sections 4.2 and 5.4.

1.8 Digraph Concepts

A *digraph* (V, D) consists of a node set V and a subset D of the class $V^{(2)}$ of ordered pairs of distinct nodes. The elements of D are called *arcs* (directed edges). The numbers of elements in V and D are called the *order* and *size* of the digraph. If the order is N, the size is at most $N(N - 1)$. A digraph of maximum size is called *complete*. The *adjacency matrix* X is defined by

$$X_{uv} = \begin{cases} 1 & \text{if } (u, v) \in D \\ 0 & \text{otherwise} \end{cases} \tag{28}$$

for $u, v \in V$. An arc (u, v) is said to be *incident from* u and *incident to* v; u is *adjacent to* v and v is *adjacent from* u if $(u, v) \in D$. The numbers of arcs incident to and from v are called the *in-degrees* and *out-degrees* of v, respectively. Two distinct nodes u and v in a digraph (V, D) are said to be *weakly connected* if there is a sequence $(v_0, \ldots, v_n)$ of nodes in V such that $v_0 = u$, $v_n = v$, and (v_{i-1}, v_i) or (v_i, v_{i-1}) belongs to D for $i = 1, \ldots, n$. If $(v_{i-1}, v_i) \in D$ for $i = 1, \ldots, n$, then u is *unilaterally connected to* v. If u is unilaterally connected to v, and v is unilaterally connected to u, then u and v are said to be *strongly connected*. For convenience, we also say that a node is weakly and strongly connected to itself. Both weak and strong connectedness are equivalence relations on V, and *weak* and *strong components* can be defined from the equivalence classes in a way similar to that described for components of a graph. *Subdigraphs* and *induced subdigraphs* are defined similarly to subgraphs and induced subgraphs in a graph. The induced subdigraphs of order 2 and 3 are called *dyads* and *triads*. For digraphs there are three different dyads and sixteen different triads (Figure 3). For stars in a digraph, it is possible to distinguish between *in-stars* and *out-stars*, but these concepts are not used in the following discussion.

2. STATISTICAL GRAPH MODELS

2.1 General References

Statistical graph models are appropriate for describing and analyzing empirical network data subject to sampling variation, measurement errors, and other kinds of uncertainty. Various graph sampling models are discussed by Goodman (1961), Bloemena (1964), Frank (1969, 1971, 1977a, 1977b, 1977c, 1978b, 1978c, 1979c, 1980a, 1980b), Capobianco (1970, 1972, 1974), Capobianco and Frank

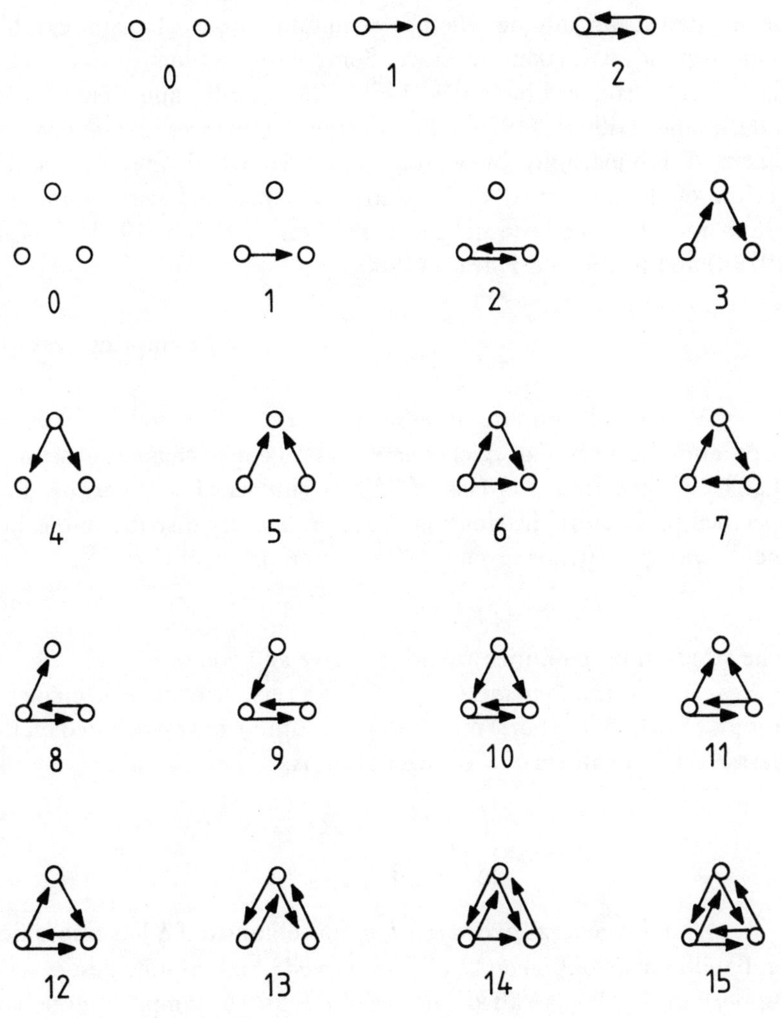

Figure 3. Digraph dyads and triads.

(1979), Frank and Gaul (1979), Frank and Harary (1980), and Frank and Ringström (1979). Several of the topics of these papers are considered in the following paragraphs.

Much of the literature on random graphs deals with models that can be used as interpretations of pure randomness and, thus, can be of interest for judging whether or not an empirical graph exhibits some significant further structure. Some basic random graph models have been introduced by Erdös (1959, 1961), Erdös and Rényi (1959, 1960), and Gilbert (1959). For further references see the recent extensive bibliography by Karoński (1978), which gives a detailed review of the literature. Some statistically oriented uses of random graph models have been described by Frank (1978a, 1979a, 1979b, 1979d) and Frank and Harary (1980).

2.2 Sampling Designs

A general sampling design can be defined as follows. Let the population be a set V of N elements. Let S be a stochastic subset of V that is selected from the class $\mathcal{P}(V)$ of subsets of V according to a specified probability distribution. This probability distribution, called the *sampling design,* is given by 2^N selection probabilities:

$$P(S = A) = p(A) \qquad \text{for } A \in \mathcal{P}(V) \tag{29}$$

The selection probabilities are nonnegative and add to 1.

Simple random sampling without replacement of n elements from V (SRS(n) for short) means that S is uniformly distributed on the class $\mathcal{P}_n(V)$ of subsets of V of size n; that is,

$$p(A) = \begin{cases} \binom{N}{n}^{-1} & \text{for } A \in \mathcal{P}_n(V) \\ 0 & \text{otherwise} \end{cases} \tag{30}$$

A more general *fixed-size design* is obtained if S has a specified probability distribution on $\mathcal{P}_n(V)$ for a fixed n; a sampling design with support in $\mathcal{P}_n(V)$ is called an *n-size design.* A sampling design is called *symmetric* if for each $n = 0, \ldots, N$ the selection probabilities are constant for all $A \in \mathcal{P}_n(V)$. In particular, the only fixed-size designs that are symmetric are the simple random sampling designs.

Another example of a symmetric design is *Bernoulli sampling* with element-selection probability p (Bernoulli(p) design for short); here each element in V is independently selected or not for the sample, and the sample-selection probabilities are given by

$$p(A) = p^n(1 - p)^{N-n} \qquad \text{for } A \in \mathcal{P}_n(V);\ n = 0, \ldots, N \tag{31}$$

If S has a Bernoulli(p) design, the sample size $|S|$ is binomial(N, p), which implies that the expected sampling fraction is p. Therefore the SRS(n) design is sometimes approximated by a Bernoulli(p) design where $p = n/N$. See, for instance, Goodman (1949, 1961) and Frank (1977a, 1978c).

If the Bernoulli(p) design is generalized so that the element-selection probabilities are not required to be equal, the sample-selection probabilities are given by

$$p(A) = \left(\prod_{u \in A} p_u\right)\left[\prod_{v \in \bar{A}} (1 - p_v)\right] \qquad \text{for } A \in \mathcal{P}(V) \tag{32}$$

This general Bernoulli design is symmetric if and only if all the element-selection probabilities are equal. The general Bernoulli design has been used for node sampling in graphs by Frank (1977b).

Another kind of sampling design can be defined by using repeated independent draws of one element from V according to some specified probability distribution given by

$$\begin{gathered} P_v \geq 0 \qquad v \in V \\ \sum_{v \in V} P_v = 1 \end{gathered} \tag{33}$$

Independent sampling of n elements according to P_v for $v \in V$ means that, in each of n independent draws of an element from V, there is a probability P_v that v is drawn. Independent sampling of n elements according to a uniform distribution on V is called *simple random sampling with replacement* of n elements from V, or SRSWR(n) for short. SRSWR(n) is an example of a symmetric design, but it is not a fixed-size design. In fact, if S is the set of distinct elements obtained from the n draws, then the size $|S|$ has a probability distribution given by

$$P(|S| = m) = \binom{N}{m} \sum_{i=0}^{m} (-1)^i \binom{m}{i} [(m - i)/N]^n \tag{34}$$

for $m = 1, \ldots, \min(n, N)$ and, conditioned by $|S| = m$, S has a uniform distribution on $\mathcal{P}_m(V)$. The expected sample size is

$$E|S| = N[1 - (1 - 1/N)^n] \tag{35}$$

and a SRSWR(n) design can sometimes be approximated by a Bernoulli(p) design where $p = 1 - (1 - 1/N)^n$.

For a general probability distribution of S, we define *inclusion* and *exclusion probabilities* of an arbitrary fixed set $A \in \mathcal{P}(V)$ as

$$\pi(A) = P(A \subseteq S) = \sum_{A \subseteq B} p(B) \tag{36}$$

and

$$\overline{\pi}(A) = P(A \subseteq \overline{S}) = \sum_{B \subseteq \overline{A}} p(B) \tag{37}$$

These are the probabilities that all elements in A are included in and excluded from the sample S, respectively. The inclusion and exclusion probabilities are related according to

$$\pi(A) = \sum_{B \subseteq A} (-1)^{|B|} \overline{\pi}(B) \tag{38}$$

and analogously with π and $\overline{\pi}$ interchanged. The selection probabilities can be obtained from the inclusion or the exclusion probabilities according to

$$p(A) = \sum_{B \subseteq \overline{A}} (-1)^{|B|} \pi(A \cup B) = \sum_{B \subseteq A} (-1)^{|B|} \overline{\pi}(\overline{A} \cup B) \tag{39}$$

For a symmetric design, the inclusion and exclusion probabilities of A depend only on the size of A. If we denote $\pi(A)$ and $\overline{\pi}(A)$ by p_m and q_m, respectively, for $|A| = m$, then (38) becomes

$$p_m = \sum_{i=0}^{m} (-1)^i \binom{m}{i} q_i \tag{40}$$

and, by interchanging π and $\overline{\pi}$,

$$q_m = \sum_{i=0}^{m} (-1)^i \binom{m}{i} p_i \tag{41}$$

If S has an SRS(n) design, then

$$p_m = \binom{N-m}{n-m} \Big/ \binom{N}{n} = \binom{n}{m} \Big/ \binom{N}{m} \tag{42}$$

for $m = 0, \ldots, n$ and

$$q_m = \binom{N-m}{n} \Big/ \binom{N}{n} = \binom{N-n}{m} \Big/ \binom{N}{m} \tag{43}$$

for $m = 0, \ldots, N - n$. If S has a Bernoulli(p) design, then

$$p_m = p^m \qquad \text{and} \qquad q_m = (1-p)^m \tag{44}$$

for $m = 0, \ldots, N$.

2.3 Graph Sampling

Frank (1971, 1977c, 1980b) has discussed various graph sampling designs. By distinguishing between sampling units and observation units, it may be possible to give alternative descriptions of the same procedure. For instance, sampling of nodes and observation of the edges that are incident to two distinct sampled nodes can also be described as sampling and observation of dyads or as sampling and observation of an induced subgraph. Another example is sampling of nodes and observation of the edges that are incident to at least one sampled node; this can also be described as sampling and observation of dyads or as sampling and observation of 1-stars. If the nodes are labeled, and if it is possible to observe the labels of all the nodes in the sampled 1-stars, then it is also possible to consider these together as a single sampled and observed star.

The most convenient description of the sampling and observation procedure is not always the one with the simplest sampling design. For some estimation problems it may be advantageous to refer to sampling units that are convenient for a given estimator, even if this means that the sampling design becomes more complicated. For this reason it is important to be able to handle sampling designs that are more general than standard SRS, SRSWR, and Bernoulli designs. Some of the results in Sections 3 to 5 apply to such general designs—for example, to arbitrary symmetric designs.

2.4 Graph Transitions

A simple measurement error model for graphs can be defined as follows. Let (V, G) be a fixed graph with adjacency matrix X and

$(V, \tilde{G})$ a stochastic graph with adjacency matrix $\tilde{X}$. Assume that $\tilde{G}$ is generated from G according to independent dyad transitions with probabilities

$$P(\tilde{X}_{uv} = j \mid X_{uv} = i) = P_{uv}(i, j) \tag{45}$$

for $u < v$ and $i, j \in \{0, 1\}$. This model can be considered if we want to investigate an unknown or partially unknown graph G by means of an observed graph $\tilde{G}$, which is a disturbed or deformed version of G. This model can also be applied to situations where we want to investigate an unknown transition mechanism that, by acting on a known graph G, provides a deformed version $\tilde{G}$ of it. If G is chosen as a complete graph, then $\tilde{G}$ becomes a *Bernoulli graph* with independent edge occurrences with probabilities P_{uv} (1, 1) for $u < v$. In particular, if P_{uv} (1, 1) $= p$ for all (u, v), we say that $\tilde{G}$ is a Bernoulli(p) graph.

The corresponding model for digraphs (V, D) and $(V, \tilde{D})$ with adjacency matrices X and $\tilde{X}$ is given by independent dyad transitions with probabilities

$$P[(\tilde{X}_{uv}, \tilde{X}_{vu}) = (k, l) \mid (X_{uv}, X_{vu}) = (i, j)] = P_{uv}(i, j, k, l) \tag{46}$$

for $u < v$ and $i, j, k, l \in \{0, 1\}$. If D is complete and

$$P_{uv}(1, 1, k, l) = p_{uv}^{k} \, q_{uv}^{1-k} \, p_{vu}^{l} \, q_{vu}^{1-l} \tag{47}$$

where $p_{uv} + q_{uv} = 1$ for $u \neq v$, then $\tilde{D}$ is a *Bernoulli digraph* that has independent arc occurrences with probabilities p_{uv} for $u \neq v$. If $p_{uv} = p$ for all (u, v), we have a Bernoulli(p) digraph.

Bernoulli(p) graphs and Bernoulli(p) digraphs have been much investigated in the literature (see Karoński, 1978, for references). Statistical inference based on Bernoulli graphs and Bernoulli digraphs has been considered by Frank (1978a, 1979a, 1979d). Some of these results are given in Sections 6 and 7.

Related models have been used for statistical inference in a series of papers by Holland and Leinhardt (1970, 1971, 1972, 1975, 1978). They investigate the triad distribution of a Bernoulli digraph conditioned by a fixed dyad distribution, and they also consider conditionings with a fixed size, fixed out-degrees, and fixed out-degrees and in-degrees, separately or in combination with a fixed dyad distribution. They suggest interesting test statistics for structure based on the triad distribution.

2.5 Graph Processes

Graphs or digraphs that change with time in an irregular or uncertain way can be described by stochastic graph processes. A simple markovian model can be defined as follows. Let $[V, G(t)]$ be the graph at time t (or $[V, D(t)]$ the digraph at time t), where $V = \{1, \ldots, N\}$. The adjacency matrix $X(t)$ of $G(t)$ (or $D(t)$) is a Markov process with continuous time and a finite state space consisting of all adjacency matrices for graphs (or digraphs) of order N. The transition intensities for $X(t)$ induce transition intensities for the dyad processes $X_{uv}(t)$ (or $[X_{uv}(t), X_{vu}(t)]$). Conversely, assumptions concerning the dyad processes and their dependencies can be used to derive the transition intensities for $X(t)$.

Holland and Leinhardt (1977a, 1977b) have introduced a markovian digraph process that has independent transitions for transition times tending to zero; that is, the transition probabilities are given by

$$P[X(t+h) = y \mid X(t) = x]$$

$$= \prod_{\substack{u,v \in V \\ u \neq v}} P[X_{uv}(t+h) = y_{uv} \mid X(t) = x] + o(h) \quad (48)$$

for $h \to 0$. They also assume that each dyad process $X_{uv}(t)$ satisfies

$$P[X_{uv}(t+h) \neq x_{uv} \mid X(t) = x] = \lambda_{uv}(t, x)h + o(h) \quad (49)$$

where $\lambda_{uv}(t, x)$ is a transition intensity for change in $X_{uv}(t)$ at time t if $X(t) = x$. By specifying the transition intensities as simple functions that contain parameters for various features of potential interest, such as reciprocity and transitivity, it becomes possible to investigate the effects of these parameters on the graph or digraph process. Some results of this kind are given in Holland and Leinhardt (1977a, 1977b) and Wasserman (1977, 1979).

Simple graph processes and sampling problems are considered by Frank (1979c). Further material on stochastic graph and digraph processes can be obtained from the theory of diffusion and percolation. (See, for instance, Frisch and Hammersley, 1963, and Biggs, 1977.)

Graph processes are also of interest in cluster analysis. A dendrogram produced by a hierarchical clustering method can be represented by a graph process exhibiting a special structure. It is well known that if Y_{uv} is a dissimilarity between objects u and v—that is, $Y_{uv} = Y_{vu}$ for $u, v \in V$ and $Y_{uv} \geq 0$ with equality for $u = v$—and if $X(t)$ is the adjacency matrix of a graph process $G(t)$ defined by

$$X_{uv}(t) = \begin{cases} 1 & \text{for } t \geq Y_{uv} \\ 0 & \text{otherwise} \end{cases} \tag{50}$$

then $G(t)$ is transitive for all t if and only if Y satisfies the ultrametric inequality

$$Y_{uv} \leq \max\,(Y_{uw}, Y_{wv}) \tag{51}$$

for u, v, $w \in V$. A dendrogram produced by a hierarchial clustering method can be represented by an ultrametric (see Jardine and Sibson, 1971) or, alternatively, by its associated transitive graph process. Stochastic graph processes might therefore be a tool for a model-based approach to cluster analysis. Some references in this context are Frank (1976), which discusses comparisons between cluster structures in terms of graph processes, and Frank and Svensson (1980), which uses a simple randomization model to illustrate how statistical inference can be based on dendrogram data.

3. INFERENCE FROM A SAMPLE-INDUCED SUBGRAPH

3.1 The Model

Let (V, G) be a graph with node set $V = \{1, \ldots, N\}$ and parameters denoted as in Section 1—that is, R, Q, K, and so on. Assume that a symmetric data matrix Y is defined that consists of real numbers $Y_{uv} = Y_{vu}$ for all $u, v \in V$. Let

$$T_1 = \sum_{v \in V} Y_{vv} \qquad \text{and} \qquad T_2 = \sum_{\substack{u<v \\ u,v \in V}} \sum Y_{uv} \tag{52}$$

be the node and dyad totals for Y. For instance, Y_{uv} can be time, cost, length, or some other variable defined on the set of nodes and dyads in G. By letting Y be the adjacency matrix X of G, we obtain $T_1 = 0$ and $T_2 = R$. By letting Y be X with all main-diagonal entries replaced by 1's, we obtain $T_1 = N$ and $T_2 = R$. By letting Y_{uv} be 1 or 0 according to whether or not u and v belong to the same component in G, we get

$T_1 = N$ and $T_2 = \Sigma_{i=1}^{N} \binom{i}{2} K_i$. Defining Y_{uv} as zero if u and v do not belong to a common component in G and as the inverted value of the order of the common component otherwise, we find that $T_1 = K$ and $T_2 = (N - K)/2$. And, as a final example, if Y_{uv} is equal to the mean degree of u and v in G, then $T_1 = 2R$ and $T_2 = (N - 1)R$.

Let S be a sample selected from V according to a specified symmetric sampling design. Assume that the subgraph of (V, G) induced by S is observed and that Y_{uv} is observed for $u, v \in S$. It is required to use this subgraph $[S, G(S)]$ and its data $Y(S) = (Y_{uv}{:}u, v \in S)$ in order to make some kind of inference concerning (V, G) and Y. Such inference problems have been considered by Frank (1971, 1977a, 1977c, 1978b, 1978c, 1979c, 1980a) and some of the results are reviewed later on.

For the parameters in $G(S)$ we shall use similar notation as for G—that is, $N(S)$, $R(S)$, $Q(S)$, $K(S)$, and so forth. We also need inclusion and exclusion probabilities for S; these will be denoted by p_m and q_m as in Section 2.

3.2 Estimation of Node and Dyad Totals

Consider the problem of estimating the node and dyad totals T_1 and T_2 of Y in G. The node and dyad totals of Y in $G(S)$ are

$$T_1(S) = \sum_{v \in S} Y_{vv} \qquad \text{and} \qquad T_2(S) = \sum_{\substack{u<v \\ u,v \in S}} \sum Y_{uv} \tag{53}$$

Frank (1971, 1977a, 1977c) has proved that

$$\hat{T}_1 = T_1(S)/p_1 \qquad \text{and} \qquad \hat{T}_2 = T_2(S)/p_2 \tag{54}$$

are unbiased estimators of T_1 and T_2 that have variances and covariance

$$\sigma_{11} = \text{var}\ \hat{T}_1 = \sum_{t=1}^{2} (p_t p_1^{-2} - 1) A_{11t} \tag{55}$$

$$\sigma_{22} = \text{var}\ \hat{T}_2 = \sum_{t=2}^{4} (p_t p_2^{-2} - 1) A_{22t} \tag{56}$$

$$\sigma_{12} = \text{cov}\ (\hat{T}_1, \hat{T}_2) = \sum_{t=2}^{3} (p_t p_1^{-1} p_2^{-1} - 1) A_{12t} \tag{57}$$

where

$$A_{111} = \sum_{v\in V} Y_{vv}^2 \qquad A_{112} = T_1^2 - A_{111}$$

$$A_{222} = \sum\sum_{\substack{u<v \\ u,v\in V}} Y_{uv}^2 \qquad A_{223} = \sum_{u\in V}\Big(\sum_{\substack{v\neq u \\ v\in V}} Y_{uv}\Big)^2 - 2A_{222} \tag{58}$$

$$A_{224} = T_2^2 - A_{222} - A_{223}$$

$$A_{122} = \sum\sum_{\substack{u\neq v \\ u,v\in V}} Y_{uu}Y_{uv} \qquad A_{123} = T_1T_2 - A_{122}$$

Let $A_{rst}(S)$ be defined as A_{rst} in (58) with V replaced by S. Then

$$EA_{rst}(S) = p_tA_{rst} \tag{59}$$

and it follows that an unbiased estimator of σ_{rs} is obtained from Equations (55) to (57) by substituting $A_{rst}(S)p_t^{-1}$ for A_{rst}; that is,

$$\sigma_{rs} = \sum_{t=s}^{r+s} (p_tp_r^{-1}p_s^{-1} - 1)A_{rst} \tag{60}$$

has an unbiased estimator

$$\hat{\sigma}_{rs} = \sum_{t=s}^{r+s} (p_r^{-1}p_s^{-1} - p_t^{-1})A_{rst}(S) \tag{61}$$

for $1 \leq r \leq s \leq 2$.

3.3 Estimation of Order and Size

The results in the preceding section can be used to find estimators of the order N and size R of G. Set Y equal to the adjacency matrix X with the zeros in the main diagonal replaced by 1's. This implies that

$$T_1 = N \qquad T_2 = R$$

$$A_{111} = N \qquad A_{112} = N(N-1)$$

$$A_{222} = R \qquad A_{223} = Q - 2R \qquad A_{224} = R(R+1) - Q \tag{62}$$

$$A_{122} = 2R \qquad A_{123} = (N-2)R$$

and it follows that N and R have unbiased estimators

$$\hat{N} = N(S)/p_1 \qquad \text{and} \qquad \hat{R} = R(S)/p_2 \tag{63}$$

which have variances and covariance

$$\sigma_{11} = \text{var } \hat{N} = (p_1^{-1} - 1)N + (p_2 p_1^{-2} - 1)N(N - 1) \tag{64}$$

$$\sigma_{22} = \text{var } \hat{R} = (p_2^{-1} - 1)R + (p_3 p_2^{-2} - 1)(Q - 2R) + (p_4 p_2^{-2} - 1)(R^2 + R - Q) \tag{65}$$

$$\sigma_{12} = \text{cov } (\hat{N},\hat{R}) = (p_1^{-1} - 1)\, 2R + (p_3 p_1^{-1} p_2^{-1} - 1)(N - 2)R \tag{66}$$

and unbiased variance/covariance estimators

$$\hat{\sigma}_{11} = (p_1^{-2} - p_1^{-1})N(S) + (p_1^{-2} - p_2^{-1})N(S)[N(S) - 1] \tag{67}$$

$$\hat{\sigma}_{22} = (p_2^{-2} - p_2^{-1})R(S) + (p_2^{-2} - p_3^{-1})[Q(S) - 2R(S)] + (p_2^{-2} - p_4^{-1})[R(S)^2 + R(S) - Q(S)] \tag{68}$$

$$\hat{\sigma}_{12} = (p_1^{-1} p_2^{-1} - p_2^{-1})2R(S) + (p_1^{-1} p_2^{-1} - p_3^{-1})[N(S) - 2]R(S) \tag{69}$$

These formulas simplify somewhat if the sampling design is specified as SRS(n); they simplify considerably if it is specified as Bernoulli(p). (See Frank, 1971, 1977a, 1978b.) If the sampling design is not symmetric, it is still possible to use a similar estimation technique. Frank (1977c, 1979c) treats the general case, and Frank (1977b) treats the Bernoulli sampling design with not necessarily equal node-selection probabilities.

3.4 Estimation of Degree Distribution

If N is known, the mean degree μ of G can be estimated from $G(S)$ by using $\hat{\mu} = 2\hat{R}/N$. For SRS(n) we obtain

$$\hat{\mu} = 2R(S)(N - 1)/n(n - 1) = (N - 1)\mu(S)/(n - 1) \tag{70}$$

That is, the mean degree of $G(S)$ is enlarged by dividing it by the modified sampling fraction $(n - 1)/(N - 1)$. More detailed inference about the degree distribution has been considered by Frank (1971, 1980a) for SRS(n) and Bernoulli(p) designs.

Assume that S has a Bernoulli(p) design. An unbiased estimator of the degree distribution ($F_0, \ldots, F_{N-1}$) is given by

$$\hat{F}_i = \sum_j \binom{j}{i} p^{-j-1}(-q)^{j-i} F_j(S) \tag{71}$$

where $q = 1 - p$ and $F_j(S)$ is the number of nodes of degree j in G(S). The variances and covariances of the estimators depend on the numbers $F_{k,r,s,t}$ of ordered pairs of distinct nodes $u, v \in V$ such that

$$X_{uv} = k \qquad \sum_{w \in V} X_{uw} = r \qquad \sum_{w \in V} X_{wv} = s \qquad \sum_{w \in V} X_{uw} X_{wv} = t \tag{72}$$

Refer to Frank (1980a) for further details; here I give results only for the estimator of the number of isolates. The unbiased estimator of the number of isolates is

$$\hat{F}_0 = \sum_{j=0}^{N-1} p^{-j-1}(-q)^j F_j(S) \tag{73}$$

and its variance is equal to

$$\text{var } \hat{F}_0 = F_0 p^{-1} q + \sum_{r=1}^{N-1} (F_r + p\alpha_r + q\beta_r) p^{-r-1} q^r \tag{74}$$

where $\alpha_r = F_{0,r,r,r}$ is the number of ordered pairs of nonadjacent r-degree nodes that have all their adjacent nodes in common and $\beta_r = F_{1,r,r,r-1}$ is the number of ordered pairs of adjacent r-degree nodes that have all their other adjacent nodes in common. Since

$$\alpha_r + \beta_r \leq F_r(F_r - 1) \tag{75}$$

we obtain the following upper bound to the variance:

$$\text{var } \hat{F}_0 \leq F_0 p^{-1} q + \sum_{r=1}^{N-1} F_r^2 p^{-r-1} q^r \tag{76}$$

This bound can be estimated by replacing F_r with $\hat{F}_r$ according to Equation (71).

By using Equations (2) and (4) together with (71), it is possible to obtain unbiased estimators of the order and size of G. These estimators can be shown to be identical to the estimators given by Equations (63).

3.5 Estimation of Component-Order Distribution

The problem of estimating the component-order distribution of G by using a sample-induced subgraph $G(S)$ has been considered by Frank (1971, 1978c). Some progress in this problem can be made if G is assumed to be a transitive graph or a forest. The following results are taken from Frank (1978c), where some alternative estimators are also investigated and computer simulation results are given to illustrate the usefulness of these estimators for a more general graph G.

If G is transitive, its component-order distribution $(K_1, \ldots, K_N)$ has an unbiased estimator that for a Bernoulli(p) design is given by

$$\hat{K}_i = \sum_{r=i}^{N} \binom{r}{i} p^{-r}(-q)^{r-i} K_r(S) \tag{77}$$

for $i = 1, \ldots, N$. The variances and covariances are given by

$$\operatorname{cov}(\hat{K}_i, \hat{K}_j) = \sum_{n=j}^{N} K_n \sum_{r=j}^{n} \binom{r}{i}\binom{r}{j}\binom{n}{r}(-1)^{i+j} p^{-r} q^{n+r-i-j} - K_i \delta_{ij} \tag{78}$$

where $i \leq j$ and δ_{ij} is 1 or 0 according to whether or not $i = j$. Unbiased estimators of the variances and covariances are also immediately obtained by using Equation (77) in (78). In particular, we find that the number K_1 of isolates has an estimator $\hat{K}_1$ that is identical to the estimator $\hat{F}_0$ given by Equation (73). It can further be shown that the estimators of the order and size of G, which can be obtained by substituting (77) in (7) and in the right-hand equality of (8), are identical to the estimators given by (63).

From (7) and 77) we find that the number K of components in a transitive graph G has an unbiased estimator

$$\hat{K} = \sum_{r=1}^{N} [1 - (-q/p)^r] K_r(S) \tag{79}$$

Its variance is

$$\sigma^2(\hat{K}) = \operatorname{var} \hat{K} = \sum_{r=1}^{N} (q/p)^r K_r \tag{80}$$

and an unbiased variance estimator is given by

$$\hat{\sigma}^2(\hat{K}) = \sum_{r=1}^{N} [(-q/p)^{2r} - (-q/p)^r]K_r(S) \tag{81}$$

If G is a forest, then $K = N - R$ and the results in Section 3.3 can be applied to investigate the unbiased estimator

$$\hat{\mathrm{K}} = N(S)/p_1 - R(S)/p_2 \tag{82}$$

for a symmetric sampling design. The variance is found to be

$$\begin{aligned}\sigma^2(\hat{K}) = (p_1^{-1} - 1)(N - 4R) + (p_2p_1^{-2} - 1)N(N - 1)\\ - (p_3p_1^{-1}p_2^{-1} - 1)2(N - 2)R\\ + (p_2^{-1} - 1)R + (p_3p_2^{-2} - 1)(Q - 2R)\\ + (p_4p_2^{-2} - 1)(R^2 + R - Q)\end{aligned} \tag{83}$$

and an unbiased variance estimator is given by

$$\begin{aligned}\hat{\sigma}^2(\hat{K}) = (p_1^{-2} - p_1^{-1})N(S) + (p_1^{-2} - p_2^{-1})[N(S) - 1]N(S)\\ - (p_1^{-1}p_2^{-1} - p_2^{-1})4R(S) - (p_1^{-1}p_2^{-1} - p_3^{-1})\\ \cdot 2[N(S) - 2]R(S)\\ + (p_2^{-2} - p_2^{-1})R(S) + (p_2^{-2} - p_3^{-1})[Q(S) - 2R(S)]\\ + (p_2^{-2} - p_4^{-1})[R(S)^2 + R(S) - Q(S)]\end{aligned} \tag{84}$$

4. *INFERENCE FROM A SAMPLED STAR*

4.1 The Model

From a graph (V, G) with node set $V = \{1, \ldots, N\}$, a node sample $S \subseteq V$ is selected according to a specified symmetric sampling design and the star $[A(S), H(S)]$ obtained from S is observed. Occasionally we shall assume that S is also observed, so that the nodes in S can be distinguished from the other nodes in $A(S)$. Parameters in G will be denoted as in Section 1. Inclusion and exclusion probabilities of S will be denoted by p_m and q_m as in Section 2.2.

4.2 Estimation of Size

It is possible to estimate the size R of G by noting that, according to Equation (27), the size of $H(S)$ is equal to the size of

$G \cap \overline{G(\overline{S})}$; that is,

$$|H(S)| = R - R(\overline{S}) \tag{85}$$

The expected value and variance of $|H(S)|$ can then be obtained by applying to $\overline{S}$ the results in Section 3.3. We find that

$$E|H(S)| = R - Rq_2 \tag{86}$$

and

$$\text{var}|H(S)| = (q_2 - q_2^2)R + (q_3 - q_2^2)(Q - 2R) + (q_4 - q_2^2)(R^2 + R - Q) \tag{87}$$

It follows that

$$\hat{R}' = |H(S)|/(1 - q_2) \tag{88}$$

is an unbiased estimator of R that has variance

$$\text{var}\,\hat{R}' = [(q_2 - 2q_3 + q_4)R + (q_3 - q_4)Q + (q_4 - q_2^2)R^2](1 - q_2)^{-2} \tag{89}$$

To facilitate comparison with the estimator $\hat{R}$ in Section 3.3, we can use the following relationships between inclusion and exclusion probabilities that are instances of (41):

$$\begin{aligned} q_2 &= 1 - 2p_1 + p_2 \\ q_3 &= 1 - 3p_1 + 3p_2 - p_3 \\ q_4 &= 1 - 4p_1 + 6p_2 - 4p_3 + p_4 \end{aligned} \tag{90}$$

In the simple case of a Bernoulli(p) design, we find from (65) that

$$\text{var}\,\hat{R} = p^{-2}q\,(pQ + qR) \tag{91}$$

and from (89) that

$$\text{var}\,\hat{R}' = p^{-1}q^2\,(1 + q)^{-2}\,(pR + qQ) \tag{92}$$

which implies that

$$\text{var}\,\hat{R}'/\text{var}\,\hat{R} \le q/2(1 + q) \le 1/4 \tag{93}$$

That is, the variance of the estimator based on the induced subgraph is at least four times the variance of the estimator based on the star. This comparison refers to subgraphs based on equal sample sizes—that is, an induced subgraph and a star obtained from a Bernoulli(p) sample of nodes. Neither the orders nor the sizes of the subgraphs need be equal. Other comparisons of this kind have been made by Capobianco and Frank (1979).

If the nodes in S can be distinguished from the other nodes in $A(S)$, it is possible to divide the size of $H(S)$ into two observable parts, say r and s, where $r = R(S)$ is the size of $G(S)$ and $s = R - R(S) - R(\bar{S})$ is the size of $H(S) - G(S)$. Since

$$E\,r = Rp_2 \qquad \text{and} \qquad E\,s = R\,(1 - p_2 - q_2) = 2R\,(p_1 - p_2) \tag{94}$$

it will be possible to give a class of unbiased estimators of R by

$$R^* = \theta r/p_2 + (1 - \theta)s/2(p_1 - p_2) \tag{95}$$

for various θ. We obtain $R^* = \hat{R}$ by choosing $\theta = 1$; we obtain $R^* = \hat{R}'$ by choosing $\theta = p_2(2p_1 - p_2)^{-1}$. Another natural estimator of R is obtained by choosing $\theta = p_2 p_1^{-1}$; this yields $R^* = \hat{R}''$, where

$$\hat{R}'' = (2r + s)/2p_1 \tag{96}$$

is an unbiased multiple of the sum of the degrees in $[A(S), H(S)]$. Comparisons between these estimators can be found in Frank (1971) and Capobianco and Frank (1979).

4.3 Estimation of Degree Distribution

Consider the problem of estimating the degree distribution $(F_0, \ldots, F_{N-1})$ in G by using a sampled star $[A(S), H(S)]$. If S can be separated from $A(S)$, so that the degrees of the nodes in S can be observed, then it is possible to use their degree distribution $(f_0, \ldots, f_{N-1})$ in order to estimate $(F_0, \ldots, F_{N-1})$.

If S is selected by an SRS(n) design, then $(f_0, \ldots, f_{N-1})$ has a multivariate hypergeometric distribution with parameters n and $(F_0, \ldots, F_{N-1})$. It follows that F_i has an unbiased estimator

$$\hat{F}_i = Nf_i/n \tag{97}$$

and the variances and covariances of the estimators are given by

$$\operatorname{cov}(\hat{F}_i, \hat{F}_j) = (N - n)F_i(N\delta_{ij} - F_j)/n(N - 1) \tag{98}$$

where δ_{ij} is 1 or 0 according to whether or not $i = j$. See, for instance, Johnson and Kotz (1969, p. 301) for moments of the multivariate hypergeometric distribution.

If S is selected by a Bernoulli(p) design, the frequencies f_i are independent binomial variables with parameters F_i and p. Thus F_i has an unbiased estimator $\hat{F}_i = f_i/p$ that has variance

$$\operatorname{var} \hat{F}_i = F_i q/p \tag{99}$$

5. *INFERENCE FROM SEVERAL SAMPLED SUBGRAPHS*

5.1 Sample-Induced Subgraphs

If n dyads are chosen by SRSWR from (V, G), then the number r of sampled dyads of size 1 is binomially distributed with parameters n and $R/\binom{N}{2}$ and estimation of R is straightforward. Moreover, if n dyads are chosen by SRS, then r is hypergeometrically distributed with parameters n and R and estimation of R is straightforward.

To be able to infer more about G than its size, we need more information than that provided by r. One possibility is to consider dyads with identifiable nodes, so that several sampled dyads can be combined to a subgraph of G. This possibility is considered in Section 6.4. Another possibility, if nodes are not identifiable, is to sample triads. The extension from dyads to triads permits considerably more detailed inference about G.

Assume that n triads are chosen by SRSWR from (V, G) and that $t_0, \ldots, t_3$ are the frequencies of sampled triads of size $0, \ldots, 3$, respectively. Then $(t_0, \ldots, t_3)$ is multinomially distributed with parameters n and $\left[T_0/\binom{N}{3}, \ldots, T_3/\binom{N}{3}\right]$, where $(T_0, \ldots, T_3) = (T_{30}, \ldots, T_{33})$ is the triad distribution of G. This triad distribution can be readily estimated by unbiased estimators

$$\hat{T}_i = \binom{N}{3} t_i/n \qquad i = 0, \ldots, 3 \tag{100}$$

which have variances and covariances

$$\operatorname{cov}(\hat{T}_i, \hat{T}_j) = T_i\left[\binom{N}{3}\delta_{ij} - T_j\right]/n \tag{101}$$

where δ_{ij} is 1 or 0 according to whether or not $i = j$. The triad distribution can be used to estimate various parameters of G according to the relationships mentioned in Section 1.6. For instance, the mean and variance of the degree distribution can be estimated by

$$\hat{\mu} = 2\hat{R}/N \qquad \text{and} \qquad \hat{\sigma}^2 = \hat{Q}/N - 4\hat{R}^2/N^2 \tag{102}$$

where $\hat{R}$ and $\hat{Q}$ are obtained from Equations (15) and (16) by replacing $T_{3i} = T_i$ with $\hat{T}_i$ according to (100).

We can also consider sampling induced subgraphs of arbitrary order. Let $S_1, \ldots, S_n$ be n subsets of V that are independently selected according to a common specified symmetric sampling design. Assume that the induced subgraphs $[S_i, G(S_i)]$ are observed. For each such subgraph the results in Section 3 can be applied and, for instance, the size R of G can be estimated by the average

$$R^* = \sum_{i=1}^{n} R(S_i)/np_2 \tag{103}$$

which is unbiased and has a variance σ^2/n, where σ^2 is the variance of $\hat{R}$ in (65). If an SRS(m) or Bernoulli(p) design is used for the S_i, then it may be of interest to choose m and n or p and n to minimize the variance of R^* subject to some constraint. We shall consider problems of this kind in Section 5.4.

5.2 Sampled Stars

Assume that n 1-stars are selected by sampling their centers from (V, G) using SRS and that f_i of these 1-stars have a center of degree i for $i = 0, \ldots, N-1$. Then it follows that $(f_0, \ldots, f_{N-1})$ has a multivariate hypergeometric distribution with parameters n and $(F_0, \ldots, F_{N-1})$, where $(F_0, \ldots, F_{N-1})$ is the degree distribution of G. This is the same conclusion as that drawn in Section 4.3 for the case with an SRS(n) design for S and observation of the n-star $[A(S), H(S)]$, where S could be separated from the rest of $A(S)$.

If n 1-stars are selected by SRSWR, then $(f_0, \ldots, f_{N-1})$ has a multinomial distribution with parameters n and $(F_0/N, \ldots, F_{N-1}/N)$ and estimation of the degree distribution is straightforward. The unbiased estimators

$$\hat{F}_i = Nf_i/n \tag{104}$$

have variances and covariances given by

$$\text{cov}(\hat{F}_i, \hat{F}_j) = F_i(N\delta_{ij} - F_j)/n \tag{105}$$

If these estimators are substituted for F_i in (4), we obtain an unbiased R estimator

$$\hat{R}'' = \sum_{i=0}^{N-1} i\hat{F}_i/2 \tag{106}$$

which is identical to the estimator given by (96) with an SRSWR(n) design for S.

5.3 Multivariate Graph Sampling

As an example of a multivariate graph problem we consider the following. Assume that there are two graphs (V, G) and (V, H) defined on the same node set $V = \{1, \ldots, N\}$. Let x_v, y_v, z_v be the numbers of nodes connected to v in G, in H, and in $G \cap H$, respectively. Let $A_1, \ldots, A_I$ be the node sets of the components in G, and let $B_1, \ldots, B_J$ be the node sets of the components in H. It follows that the nonnull sets among $A_i \cap B_j$ for $i = 1, \ldots, I$ and $j = 1, \ldots, J$ are the node sets of the components in $G \cap H$. Let K be the number of components in $G \cap H$, and let K_{rst} be the number of these that are of order t and belong to components of orders r and s in G and H, respectively. Set

$$|A_i \cap B_j| = N_{ij} \qquad |A_i| = N_{i\cdot} \qquad |B_j| = N_{\cdot j} \tag{107}$$

Assume now that n nodes are selected by SRSWR from V and that (x_v, y_v, z_v) is observed for each sampled node v. Let f_{rst} be the frequency of sampled nodes having $(x_v, y_v, z_v) = (r, s, t)$. These frequencies, for different possible (r, s, t), are multinomially distributed with parameters n and tK_{rst}/N for different (r,s,t). It follows that

$$\hat{K}_{rst} = Nf_{rst}/nt \tag{108}$$

are unbiased estimators of K_{rst} and their variances and covariances are found from the multinomial distribution. In particular, K has an unbiased estimator

$$\hat{K} = N\sum_r \sum_s \sum_t f_{rst}/nt \tag{109}$$

Moreover, sums of squares of component orders of G, H, and $G \cap H$ can be estimated by using the relations

$$EN\sum_r\sum_s\sum_t tf_{rst}/n = \sum_r\sum_s\sum_t t^2K_{rst} = \sum_i\sum_j N_{ij}^2 \quad (110)$$

$$EN\sum_r\sum_s\sum_t sf_{rst}/n = \sum_r\sum_s\sum_t stK_{rst}$$

$$= \sum_i\sum_j N_{.j}N_{ij} = \sum_j N_{.j}^2 \quad (111)$$

$$EN\sum_r\sum_s\sum_t rf_{rst}/n = \sum_r\sum_s\sum_t rtK_{rst}$$

$$= \sum_i\sum_j N_{i.}N_{ij} = \sum_i N_{i.}^2. \quad (112)$$

Similarly, we have

$$EN\sum_r\sum_s\sum_t tf_{rst}/nrs = \sum_r\sum_s\sum_t t^2K_{rst}/rs$$

$$= \sum_i\sum_j N_{ij}^2/N_{i.}N_{.j} \quad (113)$$

This relationship can be used to find an unbiased estimator of the usual measure of dependence between two categorizations $A_1, \ldots, A_I$ and $B_1, \ldots, B_J$; that is,

$$\psi = N\sum_i\sum_j (N_{ij} - N_{i.}N_{.j}/N)^2/N_{i.}N_{.j} \quad (114)$$

We find, by using (113), that ψ has an unbiased estimator

$$\hat{\psi} = N^2\sum_r\sum_s\sum_t tf_{rst}/nrs - N$$

$$= \sum_r\sum_s\sum_t Nf_{rst}(Nt - rs)/nrs \quad (115)$$

Some further results concerning comparisons between two categorizations can be found in Frank (1976).

5.4 Comparisons Between Sampling Procedures

Consider the problem of minimizing the variance of R^* in (103) subject to a fixed total expected sampling cost. The sampling design is assumed to be Bernoulli(p) and the decision variables are n and p. A sample of size m is assumed to cost

$$c_0 + mc_1 + \binom{m}{2} c_2 \tag{116}$$

where c_0, c_1, c_2 are given costs per sample, per node selected, and per dyad examined, respectively. For n Bernoulli(p) samples the expected cost is

$$c = n[c_0 + Nc_1 p + \binom{N}{2} c_2 p^2] \tag{117}$$

If the variance of R^* is minimized subject to a fixed expected cost, then the optimal n and p are generally dependent on the graph parameters R and Q, and therefore, in practice, the optimal design must be approximated or based on some prior knowledge about R and Q.

Comparisons between a few alternative designs can sometimes be made more easily than optimization. For instance, consider the problem of deciding when a single sample-induced subgraph is preferable to several sampled dyads for estimating the size R of G. Assume that a sample-induced subgraph $[S, G(S)]$ is obtained by using a Bernoulli(p) design for S. Assume further that dyads are sampled according to a Bernoulli(p^2) design, so that the expected numbers of dyads examined will be the same for the two designs. The two estimators of R have variances given by Equation (91) and by $R(1 - p^2)/p^2$. The ratio of these variances is

$$(Rq + Qp)q/R(1 - p^2) \tag{118}$$

and, since $Q \geq 2R$, this ratio is always greater than 1; that is, a sample-induced subgraph is always preferable to a corresponding sample of dyads. Capobianco and Frank (1979) have made similar comparisons between other graph sampling designs.

6. GRAPH MODELS WITH INDEPENDENT DYAD TRANSITIONS

6.1 The General Model

Let (V, G) be a fixed graph thought of as an unknown true structure in a population $V = \{1, \ldots, N\}$. Let $(V, \tilde{G})$ be a stochastic graph obtained from (V, G) by independent dyad transitions with probabilities α and β of changing dyads of size 1 and 0, respectively; that is, an edge in G is deleted in $\tilde{G}$ with probability α, and a nonadjacent pair of nodes in G has an edge in $\tilde{G}$ with probability β. We consider this as a simple model of an observed graph $\tilde{G}$ that is a deformed version of a true structure G. Parameters in G are denoted as in Section 1 by R, Q, and so on; those in $\tilde{G}$ are denoted similarly by $\tilde{R}$, $\tilde{Q}$, and so on.

The size $\tilde{R}$ of $\tilde{G}$ is a stochastic variable that is the sum of two binomially distributed variables with parameters $(R, 1 - \alpha)$ and $\left[\binom{N}{2} - R, \beta\right]$. It follows that

$$E\tilde{R} = R(1 - \alpha) + [\binom{N}{2} - R]\beta \tag{119}$$

and consequently, for $\alpha + \beta \neq 1$,

$$\hat{R} = \left[\tilde{R} - \binom{N}{2}\beta\right]/(1 - \alpha - \beta) \tag{120}$$

is an unbiased estimator of R. The variance of $\hat{R}$ is equal to

$$\sigma^2(\hat{R}) = \left\{R\alpha(1 - \alpha) + \left[\binom{N}{2} - R\right]\beta(1 - \beta)\right\}/(1 - \alpha - \beta)^2 \tag{121}$$

and an unbiased variance estimator is given by

$$\hat{\sigma}^2(\hat{R}) = \binom{N}{2}(1 - \alpha)\beta(1 - \alpha - \beta)^{-2} + \tilde{R}[\alpha(1 - \alpha) - \beta(1 - \beta)](1 - \alpha - \beta)^{-3} \tag{122}$$

To infer more about G than its size, we can use its triad distribution and the relationships mentioned in Section 1.6. Denote by $(T_0, \ldots, T_3)$ and $(\tilde{T}_0, \ldots, \tilde{T}_3)$ the triad distributions in G and $\tilde{G}$. Frank (1978a, 1979a) has shown that the expected value of $\tilde{T}_i$ is given by a linear expression

$$E\tilde{T}_i = \sum_{j=0}^{3} C_{ij}T_j \qquad i = 0, \ldots, 3 \tag{123}$$

where the coefficient C_{ij} is the probability that a triad of size j in G becomes a triad of size i in $\tilde{G}$. According to the model assumptions, this probability can be calculated as the probability that two independent binomial(j, $1 - \alpha$) and binomial($3 - j$, β) variables add up to i; that is,

$$C_{ij} = \sum_{k=0}^{i} \binom{j}{k} (1 - \alpha)^k \alpha^{j-k} \binom{3 - j}{i - k} \beta^{i-k} (1 - \beta)^{3-j-i+k} \quad (124)$$

It can further be shown that the matrix $C = (C_{ij})$ is nonsingular if and only if $\alpha + \beta \neq 1$. Therefore if $\alpha + \beta \neq 1$, T_i has an unbiased estimator

$$\hat{T}_i = \sum_{j=0}^{3} C_{ij}^{-1} \tilde{T}_j \qquad i = 0, \ldots, 3 \quad (125)$$

where $C^{-1} = (C_{ij}^{-1})$ is the inverse matrix of C. These estimators are consistent with the estimator $\hat{R}$ in (120); if we substitute $\hat{T}_i$ for T_i in

$$R = \sum_{i=0}^{3} iT_i/(N - 2) \quad (126)$$

we obtain an estimator of R that is identical to $\hat{R}$. The variances and covariances of the estimators $\hat{T}_i$ can be calculated by applying the general formulas in Frank (1979b) and using the facts that disjoint triads and triads with one common node are stochastically independent and that triads with two common nodes are dependent via their common dyad.

6.2 Cluster Structure

If G is a cluster structure represented by a transitive graph in which the edges indicate similarity, then α and β are the probabilities that a similarity is not observed and that a false similarity is observed, respectively. Frank (1978a, 1979a) has used this model to infer properties of an unknown cluster structure G from an empirical graph $\tilde{G}$ representing independent paired comparisons.

If G is transitive and has component-order distribution $(K_1, \ldots, K_N)$ and triad distribution $(T_0, \ldots, T_3)$, then

$$T_0 = \binom{N}{3} - T_1 - T_3$$

$$T_1 = \sum_{r=2}^{N} (N - r) \binom{r}{2} K_r \qquad T_2 = 0 \tag{127}$$

$$T_3 = \sum_{r=3}^{N} \binom{r}{3} K_r$$

Frank (1978a) has shown that the triad distribution of a transitive graph is sufficient to determine the whole graph if its order is at most 13. Table 1 shows how the number of triad distributions that are compatible with a given number of transitive graphs varies for $N \leq 30$.

6.3 Pure Randomness

To be able to recognize any structure in G by examining the triad distribution in $\tilde{G}$, it is necessary to know what can be expected when no structure is present. No structure in G can be represented by a complete graph or by a graph of size zero. This implies that $\tilde{G}$ becomes a Bernoulli graph: a Bernoulli($1 - \alpha$) graph in the first case and a Bernoulli(β) graph in the second case. Moreover, if G is arbitrary and $\alpha + \beta = 1$, then $\tilde{G}$ becomes a Bernoulli(p) graph, where $p = 1 - \alpha = \beta$.

Frank (1979b) has proved that the triad distribution $(\tilde{T}_0, \ldots, \tilde{T}_3)$ of a Bernoulli(p) graph $\tilde{G}$ has the following moments:

$$E\tilde{T}_i = \binom{N}{3} P_i \tag{128}$$

$$\operatorname{cov}(\tilde{T}_i, \tilde{T}_j) = \binom{N}{3} P_i(\delta_{ij} - P_j) + 12 \binom{N}{4} P_i P_j (p - i/3)(p - j/3)/pq \tag{129}$$

where

$$P_i = \binom{3}{i} p^i q^{3-i} \tag{130}$$

where $0 < p = 1 - q < 1$, and where δ_{ij} is 1 or 0 according to whether or not $i = j$. This result can be used to test the existence of structure in

G against randomness. An appropriate randomness model might be obtained by specifying p as the observed relative edge frequency in $\tilde{G}$.

6.4 Application to Dyad Sampling

If dyads are Bernoulli(p)-sampled from a graph (V, G) with labeled nodes, and the labels on the nodes in the sampled dyads are observed, then it is possible to construct a subgraph $(V, \tilde{G})$ of (V, G) from the sampled dyads. This subgraph can be obtained according to the model in Section 6.1 with $\alpha = q = 1 - p$ and $\beta = 0$. With this specification, the inference from $\tilde{G}$ to G is considerably simplified. For instance, the triad distribution in G can be estimated by $\hat{T}_i$ in (125), where C^{-1} is the inverse of the matrix C given by

$$C_{ij} = \binom{j}{i} p^i q^{j-i} \tag{131}$$

for $i, j \in \{0, 1, 2, 3\}$. This inverse matrix can be shown to be given by

$$C_{ij}^{-1} = \binom{j}{i} p^{-j} (-q)^{j-i} \tag{132}$$

Refer to Frank (1971, chap. 7) for further details concerning this model.

7. DIGRAPH MODELS WITH INDEPENDENT DYAD TRANSITIONS

7.1 The General Model

We now consider the analog for digraphs of the model in the preceding section. Let (V, D) be a fixed digraph and $(V, \tilde{D})$ a stochastic digraph that is a deformed version of (V, D). Let X and $\tilde{X}$ be their adjacency matrices. For a model with independent and identically distributed dyad transitions, we need to specify the transition probabilities

$$P[(\tilde{X}_{uv}, \tilde{X}_{vu}) = (k, l) \mid (X_{uv}, X_{vu}) = (i, j)] = P(i, j, k, l) \tag{133}$$

for $u < v$ and $i, j, k, l \in \{0, 1\}$. It is convenient to consider (V, D) as a labeled digraph with $V = \{1, \ldots, N\}$, where the nodes are labeled according to a *prior order*. An arc from u to v is said to have a *right* or *wrong* direction depending on whether $u < v$ or $u > v$. The dyads consisting of no arc, a single arc in a wrong direction, a single arc in a right direction, a single arc in any direction, and two mutual arcs are called *empty*, *wrong*, *right*, *single*, and *mutual* dyads, respectively.

The 16 transition probabilities $P(i, j, k, l)$ are restricted by four constraints:

$$\sum_{k=0}^{1} \sum_{l=0}^{1} P(i, j, k, l) = 1 \qquad \text{for } i, j \in \{0, 1\} \tag{134}$$

We introduce a transition matrix of $P(i, j, k, l)$ according to

$$\begin{array}{c|cccc} ij \backslash kl & 00 & 01 & 10 & 11 \\ \hline 00 & \alpha_{00} & \beta_{00}q_{00} & \beta_{00}p_{00} & \gamma_{00} \\ 01 & \alpha_{01} & \beta_{01}q_{01} & \beta_{01}p_{01} & \gamma_{01} \\ 10 & \alpha_{10} & \beta_{10}q_{10} & \beta_{10}p_{10} & \gamma_{10} \\ 11 & \alpha_{11} & \beta_{11}q_{11} & \beta_{11}p_{11} & \gamma_{11} \end{array} \tag{135}$$

where we have used the following notation:

$$\begin{aligned} P(i, j, 0, 0) &= \alpha_{ij} \\ P(i, j, 0, 1) + P(i, j, 1, 0) &= \beta_{ij} \\ P(i, j, 1, 1) &= \gamma_{ij} \\ P(i, j, 0, 1) &= \beta_{ij}q_{ij} \\ P(i, j, 1, 0) &= \beta_{ij}p_{ij} \end{aligned} \tag{136}$$

These 20 parameters satisfy the eight constraints

$$\alpha_{ij} + \beta_{ij} + \gamma_{ij} = 1 \qquad p_{ij} + q_{ij} = 1 \tag{137}$$

for $i, j \in \{0, 1\}$. Consider a dyad in D given by $(X_{uv}, X_{vu}) = (i, j)$, where $u < v$. Then α_{ij}, β_{ij}, and γ_{ij} denote the probabilities that this dyad becomes an empty, a single, and a mutual dyad in $\tilde{D}$, respectively, and p_{ij} and q_{ij} denote the probabilities that the dyad becomes right and wrong, respectively, conditioned by the fact that it becomes a single dyad in $\tilde{D}$.

7.2 Transitions Independent of Prior Order

If the prior order is not essential—that is, if (133) holds true for $u \neq v$—then the probability of reversing a single dyad in D should be the same regardless of whether the single dyad is right or wrong; the probability of changing an empty or mutual dyad in D to a right in $\tilde{D}$ should be the same as that of changing it to a wrong in $\tilde{D}$; the probability of changing a right dyad in D to an empty in $\tilde{D}$ should be the same as that of changing a wrong to an empty, and analogously for changes to a mutual. This implies that

$$\beta_{01}p_{01} = \beta_{10}q_{10} \qquad \beta_{00}p_{00} = \beta_{00}q_{00}$$
$$\beta_{11}p_{11} = \beta_{11}q_{11} \qquad \alpha_{10} = \alpha_{01} \qquad \gamma_{10} = \gamma_{01} \tag{138}$$

and so five of the transition probabilities can be eliminated. We then use the notation in the following transition matrix of $P(i, j, k, l)$:

ij \ kl	00	01	10	11
00	α_0	$\beta_0/2$	$\beta_0/2$	γ_0
01	α_1	$\beta_1 q$	$\beta_1 p$	γ_1
10	α_1	$\beta_1 p$	$\beta_1 q$	γ_1
11	α_2	$\beta_2/2$	$\beta_2/2$	γ_2

(139)

The parameters α_r, β_r, and γ_r are the probabilities of obtaining an empty, a single, and a mutual dyad in $\tilde{D}$ from a dyad of size r in D; p and q are the conditional probabilities of reversing and not reversing a single dyad in D that is kept single in $\tilde{D}$. These 11 probabilities satisfy the four constraints

$$\alpha_r + \beta_r + \gamma_r = 1 \qquad \text{for } r = 0, 1, 2$$
$$p + q = 1 \tag{140}$$

7.3 Complete Order

A complete order can be represented by a *transitive tournament*—that is, a digraph D in which all dyads are single and all triads transitive ($X_{uv} = 1$ and $X_{vw} = 1$ implies $X_{uw} = 1$). In this case, the general transition model given by (135) can be specified by using only

$$\begin{gathered} \alpha_{10} = \alpha \qquad \beta_{10} = \beta \qquad \gamma_{10} = \gamma \\ p_{10} = p \qquad q_{10} = q \end{gathered} \tag{141}$$

This model has been investigated by Frank (1979d). If D is considered to be a representation of a true dominance relation between a set of objects, then $\tilde{D}$ is assumed to be the result of a set of independent paired comparisons. The probability of a failing comparison is α, the probability of an observed dominance is β, and the probability of a tie if γ. If a dominance is observed, then it is true with probability p and false with probability q.

In particular, if $\alpha = \gamma = 0$, then $\tilde{D}$ becomes a stochastic tournament in which the probability is p of reversing the prior order of any dyad. This Bernoulli(p) tournament model has been investigated by Frank (1968, 1971), who generalizes some results by Kendall and Babington Smith (1940) and Moran (1947) for $p = ½$. (See also Moon, 1968.) For instance, it is shown that $\tilde{D}$ is a transitive tournament with probability

$$\begin{aligned} &N!2^{-N(N-1)/2} && \text{for } p = 1/2 \\ &(p - q)^{-N} \prod_{k=1}^{N} (p^k - q^k) && \text{for } p \neq 1/2 \end{aligned} \tag{142}$$

and the number of 3-cycles has expected value $\binom{N}{3}pq$ and variance

$$\binom{N}{3} pq(1 - pq) + 2\binom{N}{4} pq(1 - 4pq) \tag{143}$$

7.4 Pure Randomness

The stochastic tournament model and the more general stochastic digraph models may be used for testing transitivity and other structural properties in D. For instance, the hypothesis of transitivity might be tested by comparing the number of transitive triads in $\tilde{D}$ with that expected under randomness. An appropriate randomness model might be obtained by specifying the probabilities in (135) as $\alpha_{ij} = \alpha$,

$\beta_{ij} = \beta$, $\gamma_{ij} = \gamma$, where α, β, and γ are the empirical proportions of empty, single, and mutual dyads, respectively, in $\tilde{D}$.

Frank (1979d) has determined expected values, variances, and covariances of the triad distribution of $\tilde{D}$ for the model given by (141), and I give some of these results here.

Let $(T_0, \ldots, T_{15})$ and $(\tilde{T}_0, \ldots, \tilde{T}_{15})$ be the triad distributions of D and $\tilde{D}$, using the labeling of the digraph triads shown in Figure 3. The expected values of $\tilde{T}_i$ are equal to

$$E\tilde{T}_i = \binom{N}{3} P_i \qquad i = 0, \ldots, 15 \tag{144}$$

where the P_i are given by Table 2. The variances and covariances are given by

$$\text{cov}(\tilde{T}_i, \tilde{T}_j) = \binom{N}{3} P_i(\delta_{ij} - P_j) + 12 \binom{N}{4} (P_{ij} - P_i P_j) \tag{145}$$

where

$$P_{ij} = \Sigma P_{ij}(v_1, \ldots, v_4)/24 \tag{146}$$

is an average over all permutations of four distinct nodes $(v_1, \ldots, v_4)$ and $P_{ij}(v_1, \ldots, v_4)$ is the probability that triad (v_1, v_2, v_3) is of type i

TABLE 2
Probabilities for Random Digraph Model

i	P_i	P_{ii}
0	α^3	α^5
1	$3\alpha^2\beta$	$\alpha^4\beta + 4\alpha^3\beta^2$
2	$3\alpha^2\gamma$	$\alpha^4\gamma + 4\alpha^3\gamma^2$
3	$\alpha\beta^2(1 + 2pq)$	$\alpha\beta^4(1 + 8p^2q^2)/6 + \alpha^2\beta^3(1 + 4pq)/2$
4	$\alpha\beta^2(1 - pq)$	$\alpha\beta^2(1 - 2pq)(\beta^2 + 3\alpha\beta - \beta^2 pq)/6$
5	$\alpha\beta^2(1 - pq)$	$\alpha\beta^2(1 - 2pq)(\beta^2 + 3\alpha\beta - \beta^2 pq)/6$
6	$\beta^3(1 - pq)$	$\beta^5(1 - 2pq) + \beta^5 pq(1 + 2pq)/6$
7	$\beta^3 pq$	$\beta^5 pq(1 + 2pq)/6$
8	$3\alpha\beta\gamma$	$\alpha^2\beta\gamma^2 + \alpha(1 - \beta)\beta^2\gamma(7 - 4pq)/6$
9	$3\alpha\beta\gamma$	$\alpha^2\beta\gamma^2 + \alpha(1 - \beta)\beta^2\gamma(7 - 4pq)/6$
10	$\beta^2\gamma(1 - pq)$	$\beta^2\gamma(1 - 2pq)(\beta^2 + 3\beta\gamma - \beta^2 pq)/6$
11	$\beta^2\gamma(1 - pq)$	$\beta^2\gamma(1 - 2pq)(\beta^2 + 3\beta\gamma - \beta^2 pq)/6$
12	$\beta^2\gamma(1 + 2pq)$	$\beta^4\gamma(1 + 8p^2q^2)/6 + \beta^3\gamma^2(1 + 4pq)/2$
13	$3\alpha\gamma^2$	$\alpha\gamma^4 + 4\alpha^2\gamma^3$
14	$3\beta\gamma^2$	$\beta\gamma^4 + 4\beta^2\gamma^3$
15	γ^3	γ^5

and triad (v_2, v_3, v_4) is of type j. Refer to Frank (1979d) for a proof and to Table 2 for the values of P_i and P_{ii} that are needed to find the variances

$$\operatorname{var}\tilde{T}_i = \binom{N}{3} P_i(1 - P_i) + 12 \binom{N}{4} (P_{ii} - P_i^2) \tag{147}$$

In particular, the number of 3-cycles has expected value $\binom{N}{3} \beta^3 pq$ and variance

$$\binom{N}{3} \beta^3 pq(1 - \beta^3 pq) + 2 \binom{N}{4} \beta^5 pq[1 + 2pq(1 - 3\beta)] \tag{148}$$

For $\beta = 1$, (148) simplifies to Expression (143) for the Bernoulli(p) tournament.

8. PROSPECTS

Since all empirical graph data involve uncertainty because of errors due to measurement, imperfect observation, sampling, or other nondeterministic factors, the development of stochastic graph models is an important field of research for applied graph theory. The interest in graph models, which is growing rapidly in many diverse fields of applications, will presumably also be accompanied by an increasing interest in stochastic graph models and statistical graph methods. It is possible to indicate some lines of progress that are likely to be central for the future development of statistical graph theory.

In pure graph theory, the impact of statistical methods has promoted an interest in graph parameters that can easily be observed and used for graph summarizing purposes. An example is the triad distribution. The range of single or joint triad frequencies is important to know in order to be able to identify extreme graphs. For instance, Frank and Harary (1979) have investigated maximum triad frequencies in general graphs and digraphs and proposed several related extremal problems.

Probabilistic graph theory has had a development that is almost entirely free from explicit statistical concerns. See Karoński (1978) for a review. The future development in this field also will be of fundamental importance for statistical graph theory.

Graph sampling is an extremely rich field which has to be

explored further—both with respect to sampling procedures that exploit the graph structure and with respect to more sophisticated models for combining sample information with various types of prior knowledge.

An interesting kind of sampling in graphs that relies on the graph structure is successive star sampling—that is, an initially sampled star is taken as the center of a new star, which is again taken as the center of a new star, and so forth. This sampling procedure, which has been called *snowball sampling,* has been treated by Goodman (1961) for special graphs and taken up in recent research by Frank (1977c, 1979c). The similarities with models for epidemics and other kinds of spread are evident and must be explored further for sampling procedures.

A way of combining prior graph knowledge with sample information is to use a bayesian approach to graph inference. Frank and Ringström (1979) have initiated work in this field.

The graph and digraph models with independent dyad transitions are too simple for many problems, and more sophisticated stochastic models are needed. It is desirable to relax the independence assumptions and make other general improvements to obtain better models.

There will also be a need to develop specific models for special situations. Some examples of such models are the stochastic signed graph models used by Frank and Harary (1980) for investigating balance in social networks and the stochastic models used by Frank and Karlsson (1980) for investigating a labeled digraph by using all its l-out-stars without center labels.

Many cluster analysis techniques used in explorative multivariate analysis are closely related to graph theory (see, for instance, Ling and Killough, 1976). There is a need for models that would make it possible to base statistical inferences on dendrograms and other output data from intrinsic clustering algorithms. Relevant discussions can be found in Frank (1978a) and Frank and Svensson (1980).

Stochastic graph processes of markovian type are potentially good tools for investigating graph evolution. Graph processes as well as other kinds of multivariate graph models can be defined, for instance, by using log linear models for various transition probabilities. Holland and Leinhardt (1977a, 1977b, 1977c, 1981) and Fienberg and Wasserman (1981) have initiated work of this kind.

REFERENCES

BIGGS, N. L.
1977 *Interaction Models*. Cambridge: Cambridge University Press.

BLOEMENA, A. R.
1964 *Sampling from a Graph*. Amsterdam: Mathematical Centre Tracts.

BURT, R.
1980 "Models of network structure." In *Annual Review of Sociology*. Vol. 6. Palo Alto: Annual Reviews.

CAPOBIANCO, M.
1970 "Statistical inference in finite populations having structure." *Transactions of the New York Academy of Sciences* 32:401–413.
1972 "Estimating the connectivity of a graph." In Y. Alavi, D. R. Lick, and A. T. White (Eds.), *Graph Theory and Applications*. Berlin: Springer Verlag.
1974 "Recent progress in stagraphics." *Annals of the New York Academy of Sciences* 231:139–141.

CAPOBIANCO, M., AND FRANK, O.
1979 "Comparison of statistical graph-size estimators." Statistics Department, Lund University.

ERDÖS, P.
1959 "Graph theory and probability, I." *Canadian Journal of Mathematics* 11:34–38.
1961 "Graph theory and probability, II." *Canadian Journal of Mathematics* 13:346–352.

ERDÖS, P., AND RÉNYI, A.
1959 "On random graphs." *Publicationes Mathematicae Debrecen* 6:290–297.
1960 "On the evolution of random graphs." *Publications of the Mathematical Institute of the Hungarian Academy of Sciences* 5:17–61.

FIENBERG, S. E., AND WASSERMAN, S. S.
1981 "Categorical data analysis of single sociometric relations." In S. Leinhardt (Ed.), *Sociological Methodology 1981*. San Francisco: Jossey-Bass.

FRANK, O.
1968 "Stochastic competition graphs." *Review of the International Statistical Institute* 36:319–326.
1969 "Structure inference and stochastic graphs." *FOA–Reports* 3:1–8.
1971 *Statistical Inference in Graphs*. Stockholm: Swedish Research Institute of National Defense.
1976 "Comparing classifications by use of the symmetric class differ-

ence." In J. Gordesch and P. Naeve (Eds.), *Proceedings in Computational Statistics.* Würzburg: Physica Verlag.

1977a "Estimation of graph totals." *Scandinavian Journal of Statistics* 4:81–89.

1977b "A note on Bernoulli sampling in graphs and Horvitz–Thompson estimation." *Scandinavian Journal of Statistics 4:178–180.*

1977c "Survey sampling in graphs." *Journal of Statistical Planning and Inference* 1:235–264.

1978a "Inferences concerning cluster structure." In L.C.A. Corsten and J. Hermans (Eds.), *Proceedings in Computational Statistics.* Vienna: Physica Verlag.

1978b "Sampling and estimation in large social networks." *Social Networks* 1:91–101.

1978c "Estimation of the number of connected components in a graph by using a sampled subgraph." *Scandinavian Journal of Statistics* 5:177–188.

1979a "Estimating a graph from triad counts." *Journal of Statistical Computation and Simulation* 9:31–46.

1979b "Moment properties of subgraph counts in stochastic graphs." *Annals of the New York Academy of Sciences* 319:207–218.

1979c "Estimation of population totals by use of snowball samples." In P. Holland and S. Leinhardt (Eds.), *Perspectives on Social Network Research.* New York: Academic Press.

1979d "Transitivity in stochastic graphs and digraphs." Statistics Department, Lund University.

1980a "Estimation of the number of vertices of different degrees in a graph." *Journal of Statistical Planning and Inference,* 4:45–50.

1980b "Sampling and inference in a population graph." *International Statistical Review* 48:33–41.

FRANK, O., AND GAUL, W.

1979 "On reliability in stochastic graphs." Applied Mathematics Department, Bonn University.

FRANK, O., AND HARARY, F.

1979 "Maximum triad counts in graphs and digraphs." *Journal of Combinatorics Information and System Sciences* 4:286–294.

1980 "Balance in stochastic signed graphs." *Social Networks* 2:155–163.

FRANK, O., AND KARLSSON, G.

1980 "Inferences concerning interpersonal choices given anonymously." *Journal of Statistical Planning and Inference* 4:51–66.

FRANK, O., AND RINGSTRÖM, J.

1979 "Bayesian graph-size estimation." Statistics Department, Lund University.

FRANK, O., AND SVENSSON, K.
1980 "On probability distributions of single-linkage dendrograms." *Journal of Statistical Computation and Simulation* in press.

FREEMAN, L. C.
1976 *Bibliography on Social Networks*. Montecello, Ill.: Council of Planning Librarians.

FRISCH, H. L., AND HAMMERSLEY, J. M.
1963 "Percolation processes and related topics." *Journal of the Society for Industrial and Applied Mathematics* 11:894–918.

GILBERT, E. N.
1959 "Random graphs." *Annals of Mathematical Statistics* 30:1141–1144.

GOODMAN, L. A.
1949 "On the estimation of the number of classes in a population." *Annals of Mathematical Statistics* 20:572–579.
1961 "Snowball sampling." *Annals of Mathematical Statistics* 32:148–170.

HARARY, F., NORMAN, R. Z., AND CARTWRIGHT, D.
1965 *Structural Models: An Introduction to the Theory of Directed Graphs*. New York: Wiley.

HARDY, G. H., LITTLEWOOD, J. E. AND PÓLYA, G.
1952 *Inequalities*. Cambridge: Cambridge University Press.

HOLLAND, P., AND LEINHARDT, S.
1970 "A new method for detecting structure in sociometric data." *American Journal of Sociology* 76:492–513.
1971 "Transitivity in the structural models of small groups." *Comparative Group Studies* 2:107–124.
1972 "Some evidence on the transitivity of positive interpersonal sentiment." *American Journal of Sociology* 77:1205–1209.
1975 "Local structure in social networks." In D. R. Heise (Ed.), *Sociological Methodology 1976*. San Francisco: Jossey-Bass.
1977a "A dynamic model for social networks." *Journal of Mathematical Sociology* 5:5–20.
1977b "Social structure as a network process." *Zeitschrift für Soziologie* 6:386–402.
1977c "Notes on the statistical analysis of social network data." Paper presented at the Advanced Research Symposium on Stochastic Process Models of Social Structure, Carnegie-Mellon University, Pittsburgh.
1978 "An omnibus test for social structure using triads." *Sociological Methods and Research* 7:227–256.
1981 "An exponential family of probability distributions for directed graphs." *Journal of the American Statistical Association* in press.

JARDINE, N., AND SIBSON, R.
1971 *Mathematical Taxonomy*. London: Wiley.
JOHNSON, N., AND KOTZ, S.
1969 *Discrete Distributions*. Boston: Houghton Mifflin.
KAROŃSKI, M.
1978 "A review of random graphs." Department of Mathematics, Adam Mickiewicz University, Poznań, Poland.
KENDALL, M. G., AND BABINGTON SMITH, B.
1940 "On the method of paired comparisons." *Biometrika* 31:324–345.
LING, R., AND KILLOUGH, G. G.
1976 "Probability tables for cluster analysis based on the theory of random graphs." *Journal of the American Statistical Association* 71:293–300.
MOON, J. W.
1968 *Topics on Tournaments*. New York: Holt.
MORAN, P. A. P.
1947 "On the method of paired comparisons." *Biometrika* 34:363–365.
WASSERMAN, S.
1977 "Stochastic models for directed graphs." Ph.D. dissertation, Statistics Department, Harvard University.
1979 "A stochastic model for directed graphs with transition rates determined by reciprocity." In K. F. Schuessler (Ed.), *Sociological Methodology 1980*. San Francisco: Jossey-Bass.

4

CATEGORICAL DATA ANALYSIS OF SINGLE SOCIOMETRIC RELATIONS

Stephen E. Fienberg
CARNEGIE-MELLON UNIVERSITY

Stanley S. Wasserman
UNIVERSITY OF MINNESOTA

The use of log linear models to summarize and describe categorical data in the form of multiple cross-classifications became increasingly popular in the 1970s. The work of Goodman (see Goodman, 1972) and books by Bishop, Fienberg, and Holland (1975), Fienberg (1980), Haberman (1978, 1979), and Upton (1978) have

Research supported in part by NSF Grant SOC78-26075 to the University of Minnesota and a Postdoctoral Research Training Fellowship from the Social Science Research Council to SW. We thank Paul Holland, Samuel Leinhardt, and Peter Marsden for comments on earlier versions of this chapter, Michael Meyer for research assistance, and Joseph Galaskiewicz for supplying us with his data set.

helped to make these methods more accessible to social science researchers. Because of the flexibility of this new statistical technology, many research problems have been fashioned so that the associated data can be analyzed in the form of a contingency table.

During the same time period, the social network paradigm also grew in popularity due to increasing evidence that networks could be used to quantify structure in social relationships. We use the phrase *sociometric relation* in the broad sense to refer to any set of sociological connections or associations among a group of social actors or entities. For a group of social actors, one can define many sociometric relations; for example, Galaskiewicz (1979) studied three relations: flows of money, information, or support between pairs of organizations in a small midwestern community. The methods discussed in this chapter are appropriate for studying each of these three relations separately.

A social network is one example of a directed graph or digraph. A digraph is a set of g nodes and a set of directed arcs that connect pairs of nodes (Harary, Norman, and Cartwright, 1965). Digraphs are one of the natural mathematical representations for social networks and have been used by sociologists since the pioneering research of Moreno (1934). Many of the mathematical and statistical methods for the analysis of directed graph data are rather elementary and rarely make use of contemporary multivariate statistical analysis. Notable exceptions to this general pattern are the work of Burt (1980), Holland and Leinhardt (1978), and Hubert and Baker (1978). We now describe some new methods for analyzing social networks based on log linear models for multivariate categorical data. Drawing upon the current interest in both categorical data and social networks, we demonstrate the usefulness of these methods in a simple situation—that of a single sociometric relation. These models are versions of a general class of exponential family models for directed graphs developed by Holland and Leinhardt (1977, 1981).

Holland and Leinhardt (1981) suggest the following classification of digraph data:

1. Univariate or single digraphs—single binary relation on a set of nodes
2. Dynamic digraphs, changing over time, and thus involving time-series or longitudinal data
3. Univariate digraphs with data on nodal properties or attributes

4. Multivalued digraphs with degrees of strengths (nonbinary) for one or more relations
5. Multivariate digraphs—more than one binary relation on a set of nodes, possibly with information on nodal attributes

The Holland–Leinhardt p_1 model is appropriate for the study of univariate digraphs with no data on nodal attributes—that is, type 1. They also outline a generalization that deals with bivariate digraphs, also without data on nodal attributes—that is, type 5. In this chapter, we deal primarily with p_1 and extensions to it for univariate digraphs. In addition, we develop methods for incorporating background variables that are used to categorize the nodes in the digraph into distinct subsets—that is, type 3. Fienberg and Wasserman (1980) and Fienberg, Meyer, and Wasserman (1980) describe multivariate versions of the log linear models developed in this chapter and contrast them with the bivariate model outlined by Holland and Leinhardt and with models used by Galaskiewicz and Marsden (1978).

The models discussed in this chapter place probability functions on the links between actors in the group by specifying the probability that a pair of actors has one of four possible dyadic relationships. The entire network of g actors is decomposed into an equivalent set of $\binom{g}{2}$ dyads. To specify the probability distribution of the network, the dyads are assumed to be independent, so that we need merely multiply the dyad probability distributions to obtain their joint distribution. Davis (1968) first proposed the arrangement of data on dyads from one or two relations into a 2^2 (or 2^4) dimensional contingency table. The assumption of independent dyads is common to many of the recent models for networks, although it is, at best, an approximation to reality. But building into the models either a dependence structure among the dyads or probability distributions on larger subgraphs such as triads appears very difficult—in part because some triads have dyads in common. Davis (1977) worked with triads from single relations structured in the form of 2^6 dimensional tables but did not directly address the overlap or dependence problem.

Before we investigate log linear models for analyzing social network data, we review some necessary statistical and graph-theoretic notation. We then present Holland and Leinhardt's p_1 probability model and show through a new representation how this model can be fit by using a version of iterative proportional fitting for multidimensional contingency tables. We then describe several variants of p_1 and extend p_1 to model single relations with data on nodal attributes. Throughout this chapter, we analyze various subsets of the corporate interlock data of Galaskiewicz (1979) and Galaskiewicz and Marsden (1978) to illustrate the methods presented.

SOME MATHEMATICAL NOTATION

Let D_g be a specific digraph on g nodes from a single binary sociometric relation R with at most one arc connecting node i to node j. Let G denote the set of g nodes. We use the mathematical terms *node* to refer to an individual actor and *arc* to refer to the presence of a relation between two individual actors. The digraph D_g is described by means of a sociomatrix or adjacency matrix $\mathbf{X}$ with elements (X_{ij}), where

$$X_{ij} = \begin{cases} 1 & \text{if node } i \text{ "chooses" node } j\,(i \longrightarrow j) \\ 0 & \text{otherwise} \end{cases}$$

Note that by convention we set the g diagonal terms (X_{ii}, $i = 1, 2, \ldots, g$) to zero.

For a single arc X_{ij}—representing the choice of actor j by actor i—the reciprocated choice of actor i by actor j is represented by the arc X_{ji}. We usually label

$$D_{ij} = (X_{ij}, X_{ji}) \qquad i < j$$

as the dyad, or 2-subgraph, involving the pair of actors i and j. Then D_{ij} is a bivariate random variable with $2^2 = 4$ possible realizations. These four realizations and associated labels are

$$D_{ij} = (1, 1) \qquad \text{(mutual)}$$

$$D_{ij} = (1, 0) \text{ or } (0, 1) \qquad \text{(asymmetric)}$$

$$D_{ij} = (0, 0) \qquad \text{(null)}$$

Also, we define

$$X_{i+} = \sum_j X_{ij} \qquad i = 1, 2, \ldots, g$$

$$X_{+j} = \sum_i X_{ij} \qquad j = 1, 2, \ldots, g$$

as the out-degree of actor i and in-degree of actor j, respectively. The *out-degree* of a node is the number of arcs emanating from the node; the *in-degree* is the number of arcs received by the node. A thorough discussion of these and related network summaries can be found in Harary, Norman, and Cartwright (1965).

When discussing networks as categorical data sets, we often work with single observations from multiple relations. For a common set of g individuals and a family of binary relations $R_1, R_2, \ldots, R_n$, we let $\mathbf{X}_r$ be the adjacency matrix for the digraph generated by R_r with elements (X_{ijr}). The collection of the sociomatrices $\mathbf{X}_1, \mathbf{X}_2, \ldots, \mathbf{X}_n$ is denoted by $\mathcal{X}$, the multivariate digraph (see Fienberg and Wasserman, 1980; Fienberg, Meyer, and Wasserman, 1980). In this chapter, we restrict our attention to a single relation.

MODEL FOR DYADIC INTERACTIONS IN A SINGLE RELATION

In the preceding section we described the basic structure for the study of dyads with a single generator. Here we introduce an alternative notation. Consider a four-dimensional $g \times g \times 2 \times 2$ cross-classification $\mathbf{Y} = (Y_{ijkl})$, where the subscripts i and j refer to the two actors in a dyad and k and l refer to the dyad state, so that

$$Y_{ijkl} = \begin{cases} 1 & \text{if } D_{ij} = (X_{ij}, X_{ji}) = (k, l) \\ 0 & \text{otherwise} \end{cases}$$

For example, $Y_{ij11} = 1$ if D_{ij} is a mutual dyad. We have abandoned the X notation in favor of a notation that facilitates analysis of a sociomatrix as a categorical data set. Holland and Leinhardt (1981) prefer to work directly with the X's. The relationship between the X's and Y's can be expressed as follows:

$$\begin{aligned} Y_{ij11} &= X_{ij}X_{ji} \\ Y_{ij10} &= X_{ij}(1 - X_{ji}) \\ Y_{ij01} &= (1 - X_{ij})X_{ji} \\ Y_{ij00} &= (1 - X_{ij})(1 - X_{ji}) \end{aligned}$$

For a given dyad (i, j) we obtain a 2×2 table of counts as in Table 1. Note that $Y_{ij00} + Y_{ij01} + Y_{ij10} + Y_{ij11} = 1$ for all $(i \neq j)$, so that these 2×2 tables contain one 1 and three 0's. Furthermore, $Y_{ijkl} = Y_{jilk}$, and thus we need only consider $i > j$; however, by retaining the

TABLE 1
2 × 2 Dyadic Contingency Table

		Actor $j \rightarrow$ Actor i No	Actor $j \rightarrow$ Actor i Yes	
Actor $i \rightarrow$ Actor j	No	Y_{ij00}	Y_{ij01}	$1 - X_{ij}$
	Yes	Y_{ij10}	Y_{ij11}	X_{ij}
		$1 - X_{ji}$	X_{ji}	1

redundant structure in **Y** we shall be able to provide succinct summaries of important quantities for modeling and estimation. We denote a realization of **Y** by $\mathbf{y} = (y_{ijkl})$ and a realization of **X** by $\mathbf{x} = (x_{ij})$. The marginal totals of this 2 × 2 table, $\mathbf{Y}_{ij}$, correspond to indicator variables for X_{ij} and X_{ji}. Because each of these margins is either (0, 1) or (1, 0), the interior of the table is completely determined by the marginal totals.

Define π_{ijkl} as the probability of the observation (k, l) for the dyad (i, j) and let $\mu_{ijkl} = \log \pi_{ijkl}$ be elements of a table of log probabilities corresponding to the Y_{ijkl}. The Holland and Leinhardt distribution, p_1, for these data begins with the following structure:

$$\begin{aligned} \mu_{ij00} &= \lambda_{ij} \\ \mu_{ij10} &= \lambda_{ij} + \alpha_i + \beta_j + \theta \\ \mu_{ij01} &= \lambda_{ij} + \alpha_j + \beta_i + \theta \\ \mu_{ij11} &= \lambda_{ij} + \rho_{ij} + \alpha_i + \alpha_j + \beta_i + \beta_j + 2\theta \end{aligned} \tag{1}$$

subject to the constraints

$$e^{\mu_{ij00}} + e^{\mu_{ij10}} + e^{\mu_{ij01}} + e^{\mu_{ij11}} = 1 \tag{2}$$

for all dyads and

$$\sum_{i=1}^{g} \alpha_i = \sum_{j=1}^{g} \beta_j = 0 \tag{3}$$

The parameters $\{\alpha_i\}$ measure the "expansiveness" or the "productivity" of the actors, reflecting how likely an actor is to "produce" relational ties. The parameters $\{\beta_j\}$ measure the "popularity" or the "attractiveness" of the actors, reflecting how likely an actor is to "attract" relational ties. The $\{\rho_{ij}\}$ parameters are "reciprocity" measures and specify how likely it is that $i \rightarrow j$ if $j \rightarrow i$—that is, the increase in the probability that an arc exists between two actors if the reciprocated arc is present. The parameters $\{\lambda_{ij}\}$ are "dyadic" effects and are present in (1) to assure that the constraints (2) hold. (Holland and Leinhardt use a slightly different notation for these normalizing constants.)

The p_1 Exponential Family of Distributions

The reciprocity effect for the dyad (i, j) is the logarithm of a cross-product ratio; that is,

$$\rho_{ij} = \log (\pi_{ij11}\pi_{ij00})/(\pi_{ij10}\pi_{ij01})$$

and we observe a single realization for each dyad. Thus the observed cross-product ratios corresponding to the $\{\rho_{ij}\}$ are either 0 or ∞; that is, $\rho_{ij} = +\infty$ or $\rho_{ij} = -\infty$. As a consequence, Model (1) allows us to reproduce the data perfectly but leads effectively to no information about the $\{\rho_{ij}\}$ in a statistical sense. Thus we are forced to use a reduced number of parameters to model the reciprocity effects. The simplest such model is

$$\rho_{ij} \equiv \rho \qquad \text{for all } i \neq j \tag{4}$$

Equation (4), coupled with Equations (1), (2), and (3), is termed the p_1 distribution by Holland and Leinhardt (1981). We later discuss some alternatives to Equation (4).

If we assume that the dyads $\{D_{ij}\}$ are statistically independent, then the log likelihood function for the model p_1 given a realization $\mathbf{y}$ is

$$\begin{aligned}
&\log L(\{\alpha_i\}, \{\beta_j\}, \{\lambda_{ij}\}, \rho, \theta \,|\, \mathbf{y}) \\
&\quad = \log \Pr\{Y_{ijkl} = y_{ijkl}; k, l = 1, 2; i < j = 1, 2, \ldots, g\} \\
&\quad = \rho \sum_{i<j} y_{ij11} + \sum_i \alpha_i (y_{i+10} + y_{i+11}) \qquad (5) \\
&\qquad + \sum_j \beta_j (y_{+j10} + y_{+j11}) + \theta(y_{++10} + y_{++11}) + \sum_{i<j} \lambda_{ij} \\
&\quad = (\rho/2) y_{++11} + \sum_i \alpha_i y_{i+1+} + \sum_j \beta_j y_{+j1+} + \theta y_{++1+} + \sum_{i<j} \lambda_{ij}
\end{aligned}$$

subject to the constraints (Equation 2) that the π_{ijkl} sum to 1 for each dyad. Although the log likelihood is defined for $\{y_{ijkl}, i < j\}$, it can be described as in the last line of (5) through the use of marginal totals of the complete **y** array, which duplicates all counts since $y_{ijkl} = y_{jilk}$. Note that in terms of the original sociomatrix **x**, sufficient statistics or data summaries associated with the parameters of p_1 are

$$1/2\, y_{++11} = \sum_{i<j} x_{ij}x_{ji} \qquad \text{number of mutuals} \qquad (6a)$$

$$y_{i+1+} = x_{i+} \qquad \text{out-degree of node } i \ (i = 1, 2, \ldots, g) \qquad (6b)$$

$$y_{+j1+} = x_{+j} \qquad \text{in-degree of node } j \ (j = 1, 2, \ldots, g) \qquad (6c)$$

$$y_{++1+} = x_{++} \qquad \text{total number of choices} \qquad (6d)$$

General results on maximum-likelihood estimation for log linear models lead to setting these sufficient statistics equal to their expected values under the model. Therefore fitting the p_1 model to an "observed" sociomatrix is equivalent to constructing an "expected" sociomatrix with in-degrees, out-degrees, number of mutuals, and total number of choices identical to those of the observed sociomatrix. We then ask how much the expected and observed sociomatrices differ. A large difference is evidence that one needs a more complex model incorporating parameters for additional structural effects, such as differential reciprocity, choices made only within subgroups or "cliques," and so on. We discuss alternative models later in the chapter.

Fitting p_1 to Data

As we have mentioned, the maximum likelihood estimates for the p_1 model can be found by setting the sufficient statistics (Equation 6) equal to the expected values of the corresponding random variables—that is, setting margins of the **y** array equal to corresponding margins of the $\hat{\pi}$ array:

$$\rho \text{ step:} \qquad \hat{\pi}_{++11} = y_{++11} \qquad (7a)$$

$$\text{Row step:} \quad \begin{cases} \hat{\pi}_{i+10} + \hat{\pi}_{i+11} = y_{i+10} + y_{i+11} & i = 1, \ldots, g \\ \hat{\pi}_{j+10} + \hat{\pi}_{j+11} = y_{j+10} + y_{j+11} & j = 1, \ldots, g \end{cases} \qquad (7b)$$

$$\text{Column step:} \quad \begin{cases} \hat{\pi}_{+i10} + \hat{\pi}_{+i11} = y_{+i10} + y_{+i11} & i = 1, \ldots, g \\ \hat{\pi}_{+j10} + \hat{\pi}_{+j11} = y_{+j10} + y_{+j11} & j = 1, \ldots, g \end{cases} \qquad (7c)$$

$$\text{Normalizing step: } \hat{\pi}_{ij00} + \hat{\pi}_{ij10} + \hat{\pi}_{ij01} + \hat{\pi}_{ij11} = 1 \qquad i < j \qquad (7d)$$

Following Darroch and Ratcliff (1972), one can then specify an algorithm to fit p_1 by iteratively adjusting the elements of the $\hat{\pi}$ table to have the desired margins. Such an algorithm has steps in each cycle corresponding to each set of equations in (7). Because of the symmetries in the **y** array, two sets of equations must be solved for the $\{\alpha_i\}$ (Equations 7b) and two sets for the $\{\beta_j\}$ (Equations 7c). The adjusted fitted values eventually converge to the maximum-likelihood estimates, but only after many iterations.

Holland and Leinhardt (1981) fit p_1 to one half the **y** array by effectively using only y_{ijkl} for $i < j$ and a version of generalized iterative scaling (see Darroch and Ratcliff, 1972). By using the redundant representation of the full **y** array, however, we can transform the statistical problem of fitting p_1 to **x** into an equivalent statistical problem, fitting the "no three-factor interaction" log linear model to **y**. (For further information on the technical details see Meyer, 1980.) Thus one can use a standard iterative proportional fitting computer program for contingency tables, such as BMDP3F (Dixon and Brown, 1979, chap. 11.3), and one need not do any FORTRAN (or other computer language) programming to fit p_1. The size of the data arrays analyzed in this chapter has made the use of an alternative and more efficient algorithm based on a variant of Newton's method infeasible at present.

The no three-factor interaction log linear model[1] simultaneously fits the following margins of **y** to $\hat{\pi}$:

$$[12]\,[13]\,[24]\,[14]\,[23]\,[34] \tag{8}$$

Since $y_{ij++} = 1$, the inclusion of the [12] margin in (8) assures us that the probabilities, $\hat{\pi}_{ijkl}$, add to 1 for each dyad. The [13] and [24] margins are identical and allow for the inclusion of the $\{\alpha_i\}$ and the choice parameter θ in the model. Similarly, the [14] and [23] margins (which are identical) correspond to the inclusion of $\{\beta_j\}$. Finally the [34] margin allows for the inclusion of ρ.

The estimated expected values for the elements of the sociomatrix **X** are then

$$\hat{x}_{ij} = \hat{y}_{ij1+} = \hat{\pi}_{ij1+} = \hat{\pi}_{ij10} + \hat{\pi}_{ij11} \tag{9}$$

[1]The notation here, which follows Fienberg (1980) and others, uses marginal totals to describe log linear models fit to multiway arrays. For example, [12] denotes the two-way marginal totals of the **y** or $\hat{\pi}$ array corresponding to the first two subscripts, i and j, of $\hat{\pi}_{ijkl}$.

Determining the number of degrees of freedom (DF) associated with p_1 requires some care. Each 2×2 table, containing one 1 and three 0's, is determined by its margins. Since both pairs of margins must sum to 1, there are 2 degrees of freedom for each 2×2 table; hence $2\binom{g}{2} = g(g - 1)$ degrees of freedom available for modeling $\boldsymbol{\pi}$—exactly the number of off-diagonal entries in $\mathbf{X}$. In fitting p_1 we use 1 degree of freedom each for θ and ρ and $(g - 1)$ degrees of freedom each for $\{\alpha_i\}$ and $\{\beta_j\}$. Thus we have $g(g - 1) - 1 - 1 - (g - 1) - (g - 1) = g(g - 3)$ DF associated with p_1. Note that the notion of degrees of freedom discussed here is technical, relating to the dimensionality of the subspace of the entire parameter space corresponding to the p_1 model. Because of the sparseness of the $\mathbf{y}$ array, it does not follow that the degrees of freedom are appropriate for use in the context of a standard χ^2 goodness-of-fit test for p_1.

Estimation of the p_1 Parameters

The p_1 distribution is specified by Equations (1) and (4) with constraints (2) and (3). By taking ratios of elements of $\boldsymbol{\pi}$, we get

$$\rho = \log\,(\pi_{ij00}\pi_{ij11}/\pi_{ij10}\pi_{ij01}) \qquad i < j \tag{10}$$

$$\theta + \beta_j + \alpha_i = \log\,(\pi_{ij10}/\pi_{ij00}) \qquad i \neq j \tag{11}$$

Since our iterative procedure is *indirect*—in that it does not work directly with ρ, θ, $\{\alpha_i\}$, and $\{\beta_j\}$—we need to use (10) and (11) to find maximum-likelihood estimates of the parameters. For example, substituting $\{\hat{\pi}_{ijkl}\}$ for $\{\pi_{ijkl}\}$ in Equation (10) yields

$$\hat{\rho} = \log(\hat{\pi}_{ij00}\hat{\pi}_{ij11}/\hat{\pi}_{ij10}\hat{\pi}_{ij01}) \qquad i < j$$

Because the $\{\hat{\pi}_{ijkl}\}$ can be quite close to 0 or 1, *considerable* accuracy in the estimated expected values is required to get identical values of $\hat{\rho}$ for all $i < j$. For this reason, we suggest using an average over all dyads as the estimate of ρ; that is,

$$\hat{\rho} = [2/g(g - 1)] \sum_{i<j} \log(\hat{\pi}_{ij00}\hat{\pi}_{ij11}/\hat{\pi}_{ij10}\hat{\pi}_{ij01}) \tag{12}$$

Similarly, we can average several estimates of the α_i's and β_j's based on differences involving Equation (11) of the form

$$\alpha_i - \alpha_{i'} = \log\left(\frac{\hat{\pi}_{ij10}/\hat{\pi}_{ij00}}{\hat{\pi}_{i'j10}/\hat{\pi}_{i'j00}}\right) \qquad i \neq i' \neq j \tag{13}$$

and

$$\hat{\beta}_j - \hat{\beta}_{j'} = \log \left(\frac{\hat{\pi}_{ij10}/\hat{\pi}_{ij00}}{\hat{\pi}_{ij'10}/\hat{\pi}_{ij'00}} \right) \qquad i \neq j \neq j' \tag{14}$$

Finally we use

$$\hat{\theta} = [1/g(g-1)] \sum_{i \neq j} \{\log (\hat{\pi}_{ij10}/\hat{\pi}_{ij00}) - \hat{\alpha}_i - \hat{\beta}_j\} \tag{15}$$

If the iterative proportional fitting procedure is allowed to run for a sufficiently large number of iterations (until convergence) as in the examples of this chapter, all values of $\hat{\rho}$, $\hat{\theta}$, $\{\hat{\alpha}_i\}$, and $\{\hat{\beta}_j\}$ computed using the $\{\hat{\pi}_{ijkl}\}$ and Expressions (10) and (11) will be virtually identical and will be the maximum-likelihood estimates.

EXTENSIONS AND SPECIALIZATIONS OF p_1

Holland and Leinhardt (1981) discuss special cases of p_1 found by setting various parameters of p_1 to zero. We list most of these cases in Table 2 and specify the marginal totals of **y** required to fit the resulting log linear model using a standard contingency table program. An attractive feature of the approach adopted here is that the same computing algorithm can be used for p_1 and all its special cases. When

TABLE 2
Models for Single Relations Based on p_1

Special Case	Parameters	Margins Fitted from **y**	DF
(i)	ρ, θ, $\{\alpha_i\}$, $\{\beta_j\}$	[12] [13] [14] [23] [24] [34]	$g(g-3)$
(ii)	θ, $\{\alpha_i\}$, $\{\beta_j\}$	[12] [13] [14] [23] [24]	$g(g-3)+1$
(iii)	ρ, θ, $\{\alpha_i\}$	[12] [13] [24] [34]	$g(g-2)-1$
(iv)	θ, $\{\alpha_i\}$	[12] [13] [24]	$g(g-2)$
(v)	ρ, θ, $\{\beta_j\}$	[12] [14] [23] [34]	$g(g-2)-1$
(vi)	θ, $\{\beta_j\}$	[12] [14] [23]	$g(g-2)$
(vii)	ρ, θ	[12] [34]	$(g+1)(g-2)$
(viii)	θ	[12] [3] [4]	$g(g-1)-1$
(ix)	ρ, $\{\rho_i\}$, θ, $\{\alpha_i\}$, $\{\beta_j\}$	[12] [134] [234]	$g(g-4)+1$

closed-form estimates of the $\{\pi_{ijkl}\}$ exist, as in cases (iv), (vi), (vii), and (viii) of Table 2, the iterative proportional fitting procedure will produce them after one cycle.

The last model given in Table 2, special case (ix), is a model for differential reciprocity and an extension of p_1. It takes the full model specified by Equations (1) and specializes it by postulating that

$$\rho_{ij} = \rho + \rho_i + \rho_j \qquad i \neq j \tag{16}$$

where the ρ_i are normalized to sum to zero; that is, the reciprocity parameters depend in a linear fashion on individuals i and j. The $\{\rho_i\}$ parameters measure the rates at which individuals are likely to enter into mutual, symmetric relationships. Fitting this model to the **x** array is equivalent to fitting a log linear model to **y** that, in addition to the dyadic constraints (the [12] margin) fits two three-factor interactions (and implied lower-order terms) corresponding to [134] and [234].

Cases (i) through (viii) of Table 2 are all special cases of the differential mutuality model. To check whether all the parameters in this model are required (are any of the special cases more appropriate?), we can consider testing the hypotheses

$$H_1: \quad \rho_1 = \rho_2 = \cdots = \rho_g = 0$$

$$H_2: \quad \rho = 0$$

$$H_3: \quad \alpha_1 = \alpha_2 = \cdots = \alpha_g = 0$$

$$H_4: \quad \beta_1 = \beta_2 = \cdots = \beta_g = 0$$

By computing likelihood-ratio statistics comparing pairs of models in Table 2, one can obtain test statistics for these four hypotheses. For example, the likelihood-ratio statistic for comparing cases (i) and (ix)—G^2 [(i) | (ix)] in the notation of Fienberg (1980)—can be used to test H_1. This test is conditional on the differential reciprocity model being appropriate for the data. For the four hypotheses, we suggest computing the likelihood-ratio statistics comparing the following pairs of models:

Hypothesis	Models to Be Compared	G^2	DF
H_1	(i) and (ix)	$G^2[\text{(i)}\mid\text{(ix)}]$	$g-1$
H_2	(ii) and (i)	$G^2[\text{(ii)}\mid\text{(i)}]$	1
H_3	(v) and (i)	$G^2[\text{(v)}\mid\text{(i)}]$	$g-1$
H_4	(iii) and (i)	$G^2[\text{(iii)}\mid\text{(i)}]$	$g-1$

Note that the likelihood ratio for comparing models (viii) and (vii) also corresponds to a test of H_2, but it assumes that the model with the $\{\alpha_i\}$ and $\{\beta_j\}$ equal to zero is appropriate for the data. This is far more restrictive than assuming the appropriateness of p_1 and may lead to incorrect inferences. (Note also that the test statistics for H_2, H_3, and H_4 suggested here are not independent.) Holland and Leinhardt (1981) propose an alternative test, based on information on triads, to check on the appropriateness of p_1, but we do not consider their test procedure here.

There is incomplete evidence which suggests that under the appropriate null hypotheses we can treat the conditional test statistics as if they follow χ^2 distributions on the indicated degrees of freedom, even though test statistics for the models themselves may not. This evidence takes two forms.

First, Haberman (1977) has proved the following result. For two sequences of log linear models, both growing in dimension with one sequence a special case of the other, the likelihood-ratio statistic comparing models differing by the same finite number of parameters across sequences will have the usual χ^2 distribution as the dimensions on the models tend to infinity. The dimension of all the models in Table 2 is of the order g^2, and we can think of the structure in terms of a large-sample setting where g, the number of nodes, tends to infinity. The test for H_2 suggested above appears to satisfy Haberman's conditions, but for the other three tests the models differ by $g - 1$ parameters and thus do not satisfy the conditions. But since the dimensions of the models are an order of magnitude larger than the difference in dimensions $g - 1$ (that is, the number of parameters set equal to zero), we might expect that all four test statistics should behave roughly as χ^2 variates with the listed degrees of freedom for moderate-sized g.

Second, Holland and Leinhardt (1981) carried out a pilot simulation study that supports the use of the χ_1^2 distribution for H_2. They also note that for small values of g (such as $g = 10$) the likelihood-ratio test has a slightly heavier tail than the χ_1^2 distribution.

AN EXAMPLE

Here we illustrate the use of p_1 and its relatives on a data set discussed by Galaskiewicz and Marsden (1978). They study the interrelationships among 73 out of a total of 109 organizations in a Midwest community with 32,000 residents in terms of their pairwise or dyadic relationships. These organizations are described in more detail in Galaskiewicz (1979). The three relations analyzed by Galaskiewicz and Marsden are the flow of money, the flow of information, and the flow of "support." In this chapter, we analyze the three relations separately. For more complex analyses linking them together, see Fienberg and Wasserman (1980), Fienberg, Meyer, and Wasserman (1980), and Galaskiewicz and Marsden (1978).

To illustrate the models discussed in preceding sections, we take only a subset of the 73 organizations. Of the 73, there are 16 business organizations and we study the information flows among them. Two questions on information flows were posed to the organizations: (1) Which organizations in the community does your organization rely upon for information regarding community affairs? (2) To which organizations in the community would your organization be likely to pass on important information concerning community affairs? From these lists we get Table 3 in which a "1," denoting the presence of a flow of information from i to j, is recorded if either organization i listed organization j on question 2 or j listed i on question 1. The pseudonyms for the organizations are from Galaskiewicz (1979, p. 47). Note the large amount of symmetry and the near equivalence of the in-degrees and out-degrees; 35.8 percent of the 120 dyads are mutual and only 5.0 percent are asymmetric.

We fit the p_1 distribution to these data by using the approach discussed in the preceding section. This yields the estimated expected values of the entries in the sociomatrix in Table 4. (Recall that $E(X_{ij}) = \pi_{ij1+}$.) For these data, the likelihood-ratio statistic for the fit of the p_1 distribution is

$$G^2 = 2 \sum_{i<j} \sum_{k,l} y_{ijkl} \log (y_{ijkl}/\hat{\pi}_{ijkl}) = 104.8 \tag{17}$$

with 208 degrees of freedom.[2] A stem-and-leaf display of the residuals from the model $x_{ij} - \hat{\pi}_{ij1+}$ is shown in Figure 1. Because of the present

[2]Note that because of the sparseness of the **y** array we do not carry out a formal goodness-of-fit test using G^2 and χ^2_{208} reference distribution. The theory for such situations suggests that G^2 can be less than the degrees of freedom even if the p_1 model does not fit the data (see Koehler, 1977).

TABLE 3

Sociomatrix of Business Organizations Based on Information Flows from Galaskiewicz (1979) and Associated Statistics

	1	2	3	4	5	6	7	8	9	10	11	12	13	14	15	16	Out-degree
1. Farm Equipment Co.		1	1	1	1	1	1	0	0	0	0	0	0	0	0	1	7
2. Clothing Mfg. Co.	1		0	0	0	0	1	0	0	0	0	0	0	0	0	1	3
3. Farm Supply Co.	1	0		0	0	0	0	1	0	1	0	1	0	1	0	1	6
4. Mechanical Co.	1	0	0		0	0	0	0	0	0	0	0	0	0	0	1	2
5. Electrical Equip. Co.	1	0	0	0		1	0	1	0	0	0	0	0	0	1	1	5
6. Metal Products Co.	1	0	0	0	1		0	1	0	0	0	0	0	0	0	1	4
7. Music Equipment Co.	1	1	0	0	0	0		1	0	0	0	0	0	0	0	1	4
8. First Towertown Bank	0	0	1	0	1	1	1		0	1	0	1	0	1	1	1	9
9. Towertown Savings & Loan	0	0	0	0	0	1	0	1		1	0	1	1	1	1	1	8
10. Bank of Towertown	0	0	1	0	0	0	0	1	0		0	1	0	1	1	1	6
11. Second Towertown Bank	0	0	0	0	0	0	0	0	0	0		0	0	0	0	1	1
12. Brinkman Law Firm	0	0	1	0	0	1	0	1	1	1	0		1	1	0	0	7
13. Cater Law Firm	0	0	0	0	0	1	0	1	1	0	0	1		0	0	0	4
14. Knapp Law Firm	0	0	1	0	0	0	0	1	1	1	0	1	0		1	1	7
15. Towertown News	0	0	0	0	1	0	0	1	1	1	0	0	0	1		1	6
16. WTWR Radio	1	1	1	1	1	1	1	1	1	1	1	0	0	1	1		13
In-degree	7	3	6	2	5	7	4	11	5	7	1	6	2	7	6	13	92

NOTE: $\binom{16}{2}$ = 120 dyads; of these, 43 are mutuals, 6 are asymmetric, and 71 are null.

TABLE 4
Expected Values of Information Flows Between Galaskiewicz's Business Organizations

	1	2	3	4	5	6	7	8	9	10	11	12	13	14	15	16
1. Farm Equipment Co.		220	531	128	426	420	321	859	596	582	052	573	170	629	531	960
2. Clothing Mfg. Co.	220		159	024	110	114	073	504	202	189	009	183	033	220	159	801
3. Farm Supply Co.	531	159		090	332	328	240	804	499	483	036	473	121	531	432	942
4. Mechanical Co.	128	024	090		061	065	039	347	117	108	005	104	017	128	090	677
5. Electrical Equip. Co.	426	110	332	061		245	172	728	397	380	024	371	082	426	332	914
6. Metal Products Co.	406	101	309	056	228		158	711	0	360	022	050	001	400	309	900
7. Music Equipment Co.	321	073	240	039	172	174		630	296	280	015	272	054	321	240	871
8. First Towertown Bank	858	501	801	344	726	711	627		008	833	164	724	059	858	801	988
9. Towertown Savings & Loan	616	215	518	127	415	1000	312	998		934	054	552	159	616	518	958
10. Bank of Towertown	581	188	482	108	378	362	279	833	089		043	520	123	581	482	952
11. Second Towertown Bank	052	009	036	005	024	028	015	166	047	043		042	007	052	036	440
12. Brinkman Law Firm	574	184	475	105	372	902	274	852	551	529	042		140	574	475	951
13. Cater Law Firm	171	033	121	018	083	990	054	918	158	261	007	140		171	121	747
14. Knapp Law Firm	629	220	531	128	426	420	321	859	596	582	052	573	170		531	960
15. Towertown News	531	159	432	090	332	328	240	804	499	483	036	473	121	531		942
16. WTWR Radio	960	801	942	677	914	909	871	988	949	952	440	950	744	960	942	

NOTE: Entries are $\times 10^{-3}$

Count	Percent	Stem	Leaf
1	0.4	−9	5
4	1.6	−8	7440
1	0.4	−7	8
4	1.6	−6	4440
8	3.3	−5	98443300
10	4.2	−4	9885333330
17	7.1	−3	98877666543322221
18	7.5	−2	999877553333311110
31	12.9	−1	9998777666666666555544221110000
52	21.7	−0	9999888887555555444444433333333333322222211111100000
18	7.6	0	013333334445556677
14	5.8	1	00022345556677
10	4.2	2	1134666889
7	2.9	3	1144689
17	7.1	4	01111555555566669
12	5.1	5	000112233666
6	2.5	6	266778
2	0.8	7	88
6	2.5	8	555678
2	0.8	9	33
240	100		

Figure 1. Stem-and-leaf display of residuals (differences between observed and fitted values) for Galaskiewicz's data.

lack of asymptotic theory, we do not know of a good way to norm the residuals in order to study their individual magnitudes, but the shape of the display in Figure 1 is suggestive nonetheless. If the p_1 model fit the data well, we would hope that the distribution of residuals would be roughly normal, or at least unimodal without very fat tails. The distribution of residuals is clearly asymmetric, and there appear to be at least two modes, one at zero and the other at 0.4, with a clear abundance of large positive residuals. Large positive residuals correspond to cells with an observed directed arc, but for which the p_1 model predicts that such an arc will occur with low probability. We note that 12 of the 45 residuals in excess of 0.4 are associated with actor 1, Farm Equipment Co.

We can compare the observed and expected values of $\mathbf{x}$ in a second way. Suppose we round the expected values in Table 4 to either 0 (if the entry is <0.50) or 1 (if the entry is ≥ 0.50). Then we can compare the rounded table of expected values to the observed data. A single entry in Table 5 indicates agreement between the rounded

TABLE 5

Rounded Table of Expected Values for Galaskiewicz's Data

	1	2	3	4	5	6	7	8	9	10	11	12	13	14	15	16
1. Farm Equipment Co.		1/0	1	1/0	1/0	1/0	1/0	0/1	0/1	0/1	0	0/1	0	0/1	0/1	1
2. Clothing Mfg. Co.	1/0		0	0	0	0	1/0	0/1	0	0	0	0	0	0	0	1
3. Farm Supply Co.	1	0		0	0	0	0	1	0	1/0	0	1/0	0	1	0	1
4. Mechanical Co.	1/0	0	0		0	0	0	0	0	0	0	0	0	0	0	1
5. Electrical Equip. Co.	1/0	0	0	0		1/0	0	1	0	0	0	0	0	0	1/0	1
6. Metal Products Co.	1/0	0	0	0	1/0		0	1	0	0	0	0	0	0	0	1
7. Music Equipment Co.	1/0	1/0	0	0	0	0		1	0	0	0	0	0	0	0	1
8. First Towertown Bank	0/1	0/1	1	0	1	1	1		0	1	0	1	0	1	1	1
9. Towertown Savings & Loan	0/1	0	0/1	0	0	1	0	1		1	0	1	1/0	1	1	1
10. Bank of Towertown	0/1	0	1/0	0	0	0	0	1	0		0	1	0	1	1/0	1
11. Second Towertown Bank	0	0	0	0	0	0	0	0	0	0		0	0	0	0	1/0
12. Brinkman Law Firm	0/1	0	1/0	0	0	1	0	1	1	1	0		1/0	1	0	1
13. Cater Law Firm	0	0	0	0	0	1	0	1	1/0	0	0	1/0		0	0	0/1
14. Knapp Law Firm	0/1	0	1	0	0	0	0	1	1	1	0	1	0		1	1
15. Towertown News	0/1	0	0	0	1/0	0	0	1	1/0	0	0	0	0	1		1
16. WTWR Radio	1	1	1	1	1	1	1	1	1	1	1/0	1	0/1	1	1	

NOTE: If rounded expected value equals observed value, only one entry is given; otherwise, entry is of the form: observed value/rounded expected value.

TABLE 6
Parameter Estimates for Galaskiewicz's Data

	All Actors	Without Actor 1		All Actors	Without Actor 1
$\hat{\alpha}_1$	0.228		$\hat{\beta}_1$	0.328	
$\hat{\alpha}_2$	−0.455	−0.582	$\hat{\beta}_2$	−0.557	−0.557
$\hat{\alpha}_3$	0.081	0.101	$\hat{\beta}_3$	0.123	0.050
$\hat{\alpha}_4$	−0.725	−1.053	$\hat{\beta}_4$	−0.857	−1.608
$\hat{\alpha}_5$	−0.081	0.064	$\hat{\beta}_5$	−0.089	−0.396
$\hat{\alpha}_6$	−12.670	−13.019	$\hat{\beta}_6$	−12.436	12.411
$\hat{\alpha}_7$	−0.249	−0.278	$\hat{\beta}_7$	−0.312	−0.738
$\hat{\alpha}_8$	−8.290	−8.179	$\hat{\beta}_8$	9.961	10.812
$\hat{\alpha}_9$	12.702	13.121	$\hat{\beta}_9$	−12.224	−12.074
$\hat{\alpha}_{10}$	−5.636	−5.486	$\hat{\beta}_{10}$	6.019	6.368
$\hat{\alpha}_{11}$	−1.143	−1.053	$\hat{\beta}_{11}$	−1.300	−1.608
$\hat{\alpha}_{12}$	6.013	6.218	$\hat{\beta}_{12}$	−5.659	−5.484
$\hat{\alpha}_{13}$	8.632	8.373	$\hat{\beta}_{13}$	−9.922	−9.618
$\hat{\alpha}_{14}$	0.228	0.371	$\hat{\beta}_{14}$	0.328	0.650
$\hat{\alpha}_{15}$	0.081	0.243	$\hat{\beta}_{15}$	0.123	0.311
$\hat{\alpha}_{16}$	1.278	1.288	$\hat{\beta}_{16}$	1.602	2.137

	All Actors	Without Actor 1
$\hat{\theta}$	−15.230	−15.360
$\hat{\rho}$	29.800	29.764

expected value and the observed; double entries indicate a discrepancy—if the residual for the cell is <-0.50, for example, the entry in Table 6 is 0/1. We can see that of the 240 entries, there are 45 "errors" (28 1/0's and 17 0/1's). Moreover, 22 of the 45 involve actor 1, Farm Equipment Co. Actor 1 sends and receives information from corporate actors 2, 3, 4, 5, 6, 7, 16; however, Table 5 indicates that this firm should send and receive information from actors 3, 8, 9, 10, 12, 14, 15, 16. Thus, as we also noted from Figure 1, Farm Equipment Co. behaves contradictorily to the group as a whole. This behavior may be because the company is not locally owned and is located on the outskirts of the community. The company simply may have no need for information from the financial or legal resources in the community. Or perhaps the company interpreted the term *community affairs* (in the questions posed) in a different way and concluded that it had no need for information on "community affairs."

The parameter estimates for the group of 16 business organizations are given at the left of the columns in Table 6. We note the large reciprocity effect ($\hat{\rho} = 29.80$), implying that there is a high probability that a dyad chosen at random is a mutual. This is important—the strongest signal we get from this analysis is that information flows between business firms are *very* likely to be reciprocated. Actors 9, 12, 13, and 16 are likely, and 6, 8, and 10 unlikely, to send information to other actors. Actors 6, 8, 10, and 16 are likely, and 9, 12, and 13 unlikely, to receive information from other actors.

Since Farm Equipment Co. sends and receives information from an unexpected set of firms, we next ignore it and fit the model to the remaining 15. The matrix of rounded expected values is shown in Table 7. There are now 27 errors, 16 1/0's and 11 0/1's, but they are scattered at random throughout the table and 19 of these are in similar positions as the errors in Table 5. The likelihood-ratio statistic for this revised model is $G^2 = 72.7$, with 180 degrees of freedom. The stem-and-leaf display of the residuals from this fitted model is more symmetric than the display in Figure 1, and the tails have lost most of their weight.

The parameter estimates for the reduced set of 15 firms, omitting actor 1, are also given in Table 6. Reciprocity is virtually unchanged ($\hat{\rho} = 29.76$). Actors 9, 12, 13, and 16 are still likely to send information, but now actors 6, 8, and 10 and actors 4 and 11 are unlikely to do so. Actors 6, 8, 10, and 16 are still likely to receive information, but now, in addition to actors 9, 12, and 13, actors 4 and 11 are unlikely to receive any. By ignoring actor 1, we have a more "integrated" network, with nine actors playing essential roles in soliciting and distributing information.

In addition to p_1, we fit other models to the **y** array for the 16 actors. The likelihood-ratio statistics, degrees of freedom, and number of iterations required for the fitted values to converge to the maximum-likelihood estimates for these models are given in Table 8. Note that both p_1 and the differential mutuality model required many, many iterations to achieve accuracy to the third decimal place, while the other four models converged rapidly.

Likelihood-ratio tests for the differential mutuality and p_1 parameters are given at the bottom of Table 8. We see little evidence that any of the parameters in the p_1 distribution are zero, and there is strong evidence that the group of organizations does not exhibit differential mutuality. The conclusion that the $\{\rho_i\}$ are zero may be due to the lack of asymmetric choices in the network. Since virtually all choices are symmetric, the $\{\rho_i\}$ are not needed, given that the $\{\alpha\}$ and $\{\beta\}$ parameters are present in the model.

TABLE 7

Rounded Table of Expected Values for Galaskiewicz's Data Without Actor 1

	1	2	3	4	5	6	7	8	9	10	11	12	13	14	15	16
1. Farm Equipment Co.																
2. Clothing Mfg. Co.			0	0	0	0	1/0	0/1	0	0	0	0	0	0	0	1
3. Farm Supply Co.		0		0	0	0	0	1	0/1	1	0	1/0	0	1	0	1
4. Mechanical Co.		0	0		0	0	0	0	0	0	0	0	0	0	0	1/0
5. Electrical Equip. Co.		0	0	0		1/0	0	1	0	0	0	0	0	0	1/0	1
6. Metal Products Co.		0	0	0	1/0		0	1	0	0	0	0	0	0	0	1
7. Music Equipment Co.		1/0	0	0	0	0		1	0	0	0	0	0	0	0	1
8. First Towertown Bank		0/1	1	0	1	1	1		0	1	0	1	0	1	1	1
9. Towertown Savings & Loan		0	0/1	0	0	1	0	1		1	0	1	1/0	1	1	1
10. Bank of Towertown		0	1/0	0	0	0	0	1	0		0	1	0	1	1	1
11. Second Towertown Bank		0	0	0	0	0	0	0	0	0		0	0	0	0	1/0
12. Brinkman Law Firm		0	1	0	0	1	0	1	1	1	0		1/0	1	0/1	0/1
13. Cater Law Firm		0	0	0	0	1	0	1	1/0	0	0	1/0		0	0	0/1
14. Knapp Law Firm		0	1	0	0	0/1	0	1	1	1	0	1	0		1	1
15. Towertown News		0	0	0	1/0	0	0	1	1	1	0	0/1	0	1		1
16. WTWR Radio		1	1	1/0	1	1	1	1	1	1	1/0	0/1	0/1	1	1	

NOTE: Entries are defined in footnote to Table 5.

TABLE 8
Models Fit to Galaskiewicz's 16 Business Organizations and Related Tests of Hypotheses

	Margins Fitted to y	Parameters	G^2	DF	Iterations
1	[12] [134] [234]	$\theta, \{\alpha_i\}, \{\beta_j\}, \rho, \{\rho_i\}$	102.00	193	350
2	[12] [13] [14] [23] [24] [34]	$\theta, \{\alpha_i\}, \{\beta_j\}, \rho$	104.76	208	350
3	[12] [34]	θ, ρ	207.05	238	1
4	[12] [13] [24] [34]	$\theta, \{\alpha_i\}, \rho$	163.13	223	6
5	[12] [14] [23] [34]	$\theta, \{\beta_j\}, \rho$	154.67	223	7
6	[12] [13] [14] [23] [24]	$\theta, \{\alpha_i\}, \{\beta_j\}$	219.97	209	10

H_1: $\rho_1 = \cdots = \rho_{16} = 0$; $G^2_{(2)} - G^2_{(1)} = 2.76$; DF = 15.
H_2: $\rho = 0$; $G^2_{(6)} - G^2_{(2)} = 115.21$; DF = 1.
H_3: $\alpha_1 = \cdots = \alpha_{16} = 0$; $G^2_{(5)} - G^2_{(2)} = 49.91$; DF = 15.
H_4: $\beta_1 = \cdots = \beta_{16} = 0$; $G^2_{(4)} - G^2_{(2)} = 58.37$; DF = 15.

To summarize our analyses, we find that:

1. Farm Equipment Co. (actor 1) behaves in a "contrary" manner.
2. Towertown Savings & Loan, Brinkman Law Firm, and Knapp Law Firm (actors 9, 12, and 13) are very likely to send information, but unlikely to receive any.
3. Metal Products Co., First Towertown Bank, and Bank of Towertown (actors 6, 8, and 10) are very unlikely to send information, but likely to receive.
4. Mechanical Co. and Second Towertown Bank (actors 4 and 11) are unlikely to either send or receive information.
5. WTWR Radio (actor 16) is a sender and receiver of information.

This accounts for the ten active information-processing organizations; the remaining six organizations, actors 2, 3, 5, 7, 12, and 15, are largely manufacturing firms (except for Brinkman Law Firm and Towertown News). Such organizations, while highly dependent on flows of financial resources, probably have little need for information from the law firms or financial organizations, nor would they have any information to send. It is curious that Towertown News falls into this subgroup, since, like WTWR, it should be very active in disseminating and certainly receiving information. It may be that WTWR functions so well in this regard that Towertown News may exist only for the citizens and not for the corporate world of Towertown.

There is an obvious natural grouping of business organizations into four categories: suppliers and manufacturers; financial institutions; law firms; and media firms. The 16 business firms in Towertown fall neatly into these four subgroups. Based on our analysis, we see that the subgroups in Towertown transmit and receive information in different ways. Law firms are likely to send information, no doubt in the form of legal advice, but have little need for information from the other subgroups except in specific legal cases. Financial institutions are likely to receive information, probably as financial records of the operations of the organizations, but are unlikely to send information. A bank usually dispenses information on rates of return on investments, and interest rates for mortgages, but such information is probably not passed *directly* to the business firms. Other reasons for this behavior cannot be discerned without further knowledge of these financial institutions. Exceptions to this pattern are the savings bank, which behaves not like the other two banks but more like a law firm, and Second Towertown Bank, which neither sends nor receives. We have already noted that the suppliers and manufacturers (with the exception of the outlying Farm Equipment Co. and Mechanical Co.) neither send nor receive and that WTWR, the primary media organization, is very active in sending and receiving information.

MODELS FOR RELATIONSHIPS AMONG ACTORS WITH NODAL ATTRIBUTES

Quite often, information consisting of *individual* measurements on the actors is collected in addition to any sociometric relationships that exist *between* actors. These measurements are nodal attributes and have been treated in past research as exogenous variables since no methods existed for incorporating them into a network study. In our introductory remarks to this chapter, we labeled such digraph data as type 3: univariate digraphs with data on nodal properties or attributes. In this section, we discuss several models for such data and fit these models to the Galaskiewicz data in the next section.

We present a class of models for analyzing the sociometric relationships between the actors, classified into K subgroups, and describe a special case from the general class. The class incorporates a set of parameters for intersubgroup and intrasubgroup choices. We describe the most general model in the class. The special case model is an extension of p_1 where we equate the $\{\alpha_i\}$ and $\{\beta_j\}$ parameters for actors in a given subgroup. This approach is fundamentally different from standard clustering algorithms that find subgroups or cliques solely from the relational data themselves. CONCOR, for example, the basic algorithm for obtaining a blockmodel for a group of actors (Breiger, Boorman, and Arabie, 1975; White, Boorman, and Breiger, 1976), uses only the sociomatrices to find hidden structures. Our approach in this chapter is to postulate the existence of subgroups based on background information on the actors.

Suppose the group of actors, G, has been partitioned into K subgroups $G_1, G_2, \ldots, G_K$ such that subgroup G_m contains g_m actors with $\Sigma_{m=1}^{K} g_m = g$ and that the sociomatrix $\mathbf{X}$ has been rearranged so that the first g_1 rows and columns correspond to the actors in G_1, the next g_2 rows and columns correspond to those in G_2, and so on.

A General Class of Models for Subgroups

We propose using the following model for the logarithms of the probabilities for intrasubgroup and intersubgroup choices for the log probabilities $\mu_{ijkl} = \log \pi_{ijkl}$:

$$\begin{aligned} \mu_{ij00} &= \lambda^{(rs)} \\ \mu_{ij10} &= \lambda^{(rs)} + \theta^{(rs)} \\ \mu_{ij01} &= \lambda^{(rs)} + \theta^{(sr)} \\ \mu_{ij11} &= \lambda^{(rs)} + \theta^{(rs)} + \theta^{(sr)} + \rho^{(rs)} \end{aligned} \tag{18}$$

where $i \in G_r, j \in G_s$, and

$$\lambda^{(rs)} = \lambda^{(sr)} \qquad \text{and} \qquad \rho^{(rs)} = \rho^{(sr)} \tag{19}$$

The normalization constants $\{\lambda^{(rs)}\}$ are chosen to ensure that the sets of four probabilities $\{\pi_{ijkl}$ for $k, l = 1, 2\}$ sum to 1. The $\{\theta^{(rs)}\}$ and $\{\rho^{(rs)}\}$ are subgroup choice and reciprocity parameters, respectively.

To describe the computation of maximum-likelihood estimates for this class of models succinctly, we let

$$w_{rskl} = \sum_{i \in G_r} \sum_{j \in G_s} y_{ijkl} \tag{20}$$

be the sum of quantities y_{ijkl} over all dyads such that the first actor is in subgroup G_r and the second is in subgroup G_s. These w's are the elements of a $K \times K \times 2 \times 2$ dimensional array. Note that the entries in this table are not binary, since $w_{rs00} + w_{rs01} + w_{rs10} + w_{rs11} =$

$g_r(g_s - \delta_{rs})$, where δ_{rs} is the Kronecker delta function:

$$\delta_{rs} = \begin{cases} 1 & \text{if } r = s \\ 0 & \text{otherwise} \end{cases} \tag{21}$$

The elements of the **w** array possess the same symmetries as the elements of **y**; that is,

$$w_{rskl} = w_{srlk} \qquad \text{for } r, s = 1, 2, \ldots, K;\ k, l = 1, 2 \tag{22}$$

As with the other models discussed in this chapter, we assume that the dyads are independent. The log-likelihood function for the subgroup model given by (18) and (19) has two components—one for intrasubgroup choices and another for intersubgroup choices:

$$\log L[\{\lambda^{(rs)}\}, \{\theta^{(rs)}\}, \{\rho^{(rs)}\} \mid \mathbf{y}]$$
$$= \sum_{r=1}^{K} \{[g_r(g_r - 1)/2]\, \lambda^{(rs)} + \theta^{(\mathrm{rs})} w_{rr1+} + (\rho^{(rr)}/2)\, w_{rr11}\} \tag{23}$$
$$+ \sum_{\substack{r,s \\ r<s}} \{g_r g_s \lambda^{(rs)} + \theta^{(rs)} w_{rs1+} + \theta^{(sr)} w_{rs+1} + \rho^{(rs)} w_{rs11}\}$$

There are K intrasubgroup choice components in the log likelihood and $\binom{K}{2}$ intersubgroup choice components. Note that these $K + \binom{K}{2}$ components have no parameters in common and thus can be considered separately. Since the **w** table is an aggregated version of the original **y** table, we must introduce additional notation for the expected value for the (r,s,k,l) entry in **w**. Thus we let

$$m_{rskl} = \sum_{i \in G_r} \sum_{j \in G_s} \pi_{ijkl} = \mathrm{E}(w_{rskl}) \tag{24}$$

The sufficient statistics for the rth intrasubgroup choice component are w_{rr1+} and $\frac{1}{2} w_{rr11}$; for the (r,s)th intersubgroup choice component, the sufficient statistics are w_{rs1+}, w_{rs+1}, and w_{rs11}. Since $w_{rr+1} = w_{rr1+}$, we can re-express the sufficient statistics as the entries in the **w** array. Once again from the general results on log linear models, the maximum-likelihood estimates of the parameters are found by equating the sufficient statistics to their expected values—that is, by solving the equations

$$\hat{m}_{rskl} = w_{rskl} \qquad \text{for } r, s = 1, 2, \ldots, K;\ k, l = 1, 2 \tag{25}$$

We need not iterate to find estimates of the expected values of the **w** array, since Equations (25) constitute an exact solution.

To get the estimated expected values for the original **y** array, we simply divide the $\{\hat{m}_{rskl}\}$ by the number of dyads that have been aggregated:

$$\hat{\pi}_{ijkl} = [g_r(g_r - 1)]^{-1}\hat{m}_{rrkl} \qquad \begin{array}{l} i, j \in G_r \\ r = 1, 2, \ldots, K \end{array} \tag{26}$$

and

$$\hat{\pi}_{ijkl} = (g_r g_s)^{-1}\hat{m}_{rskl} \qquad \begin{array}{l} i \in G_r; j \in G_s \\ r, s = 1, 2, \ldots, K; r \neq s \end{array} \tag{27}$$

Note that this disaggregation reflects the original doubling of the frequencies in the sums for the mutual and null intrasubgroup relationships, w_{rr00} and w_{rr11}, and the duplication in the counting of all asymmetric intrasubgroup relationships, which forces $w_{rr10} = w_{rr01}$. The latter implies that

$$\hat{\pi}_{ij10} = \hat{\pi}_{ij01} \qquad \text{for } i, j \in G_r; r = 1, 2, \ldots, K \tag{28}$$

The degrees of freedom for this model are calculated as follows. In the K diagonal 2×2 matrices in the **w** array, there are $2K$ parameters, K θ's, and K ρ's. In the $\binom{K}{2}$ off-diagonal 2×2 matrices, there are $3\binom{K}{2}$ parameters, two θ's, and one ρ for every matrix. Thus, there are

$$g(g-1) - 2K - 3\binom{K}{2} = g(g-1) - (K/2)(3K+1) \text{ degrees of freedom}$$

The likelihood-ratio statistic is computed as

$$\begin{aligned} G^2 &= 2\sum_{i<j}\sum_{k,l} y_{ijkl} \log (y_{ijkl}/\hat{\pi}_{ijkl}) \\ &= -2\sum_{i<j} \log \hat{\pi}_{ijk'l'} \qquad \text{where } X_{ij} = k' \text{ and } X_{ji} = l' \\ &= -2\Big(\sum_{r<s}\sum_{k,l} w_{rskl} \log (\hat{m}_{rskl}/[g_r g_s]) \\ &\quad + \sum_{r}\sum_{k,l} w_{rrkl} \log (\hat{m}_{rrkl}/[g_r(g_r - 1)])\Big) \end{aligned} \tag{29}$$

The last expression for G^2 in Equation (29) is in terms of the observed and estimated expected entries in the aggregated **w** array.

A Version of p_1 for Subgroups

There are several special cases of the general class of subgroup models defined in Equations (19) and (20). For example, we can postulate a simple additive decomposition of the subgroup choice parameters:

$$\theta^{(rs)} = \theta + \alpha^{(r)} + \beta^{(s)} \tag{30}$$

Or we could decompose the subgroup reciprocity parameters as in the differential mutuality model discussed in earlier sections:

$$\rho^{(rs)} = \rho + \rho^{(r)} + \rho^{(s)} \tag{31}$$

We could also take another simplifying step and assume a constant "force" of reciprocity:

$$\rho^{(rs)} \equiv \rho \tag{32}$$

Equations (30) and (32) specify a model that is equivalent to p_1 but applied to K subgroups rather than g individuals. When $K = g$, the models are identical. All actors in subgroup G_r have a common α value, $\alpha^{(r)}$, and a common β value, $\beta^{(r)}$. In addition to (30) and (32), we let

$$\lambda^{(rs)} = \lambda^{(sr)} \tag{33}$$

and

$$\sum_{r=1}^{K} \alpha^{(r)} = \sum_{s=1}^{K} \beta^{(s)} = 0 \tag{34}$$

We concentrate on this p_1 subgroup model in this section.

The log-likelihood function associated with this model can be written as

$$\begin{aligned}\log L(\{\lambda^{(rs)}\}, \theta, \{\alpha^{(r)}\}, \{\beta^{(s)}\}, \rho \mid \mathbf{w}) \\ = \theta w_{++1+} + \sum_{r=1}^{K} \alpha^{(r)} w_{r+1+} + \sum_{s=1}^{K} \beta^{(s)} w_{+s1+} \\ + (\rho/2) w_{++11} + \sum_{r \leq s} \lambda^{(rs)} w_{rs++}\end{aligned} \tag{35}$$

Because of the symmetries (Equation 22), the minimal sufficient statistics for this subgroup model can be expressed as

$$\begin{aligned} &\lambda: \quad (w_{rs++}) \\ &\rho: \quad (w_{++11}) \\ &\{\alpha^{(r)}\}: \quad (w_{r+1+}), (w_{+r+1}) \\ &\{\beta^{(s)}\}: \quad (w_{+s1+}), (w_{s++1}) \end{aligned} \tag{36}$$

These quantities are equivalent to the six two-way margins of the **w** array, and from the general results on log linear models, the maximum-likelihood estimates of the parameters are found by setting them equal to their expected values. Then, using the results of Meyer (1980), it can be shown that fitting this p_1 subgroup model to a sociomatrix is equivalent to "fitting" the following marginal totals from the **w** table to $\hat{\mathbf{m}}$:

$$[12]\ [13]\ [14]\ [23]\ [24]\ [34] \tag{37}$$

Fitting the two-way margins in (37) yields estimated expected values $\{\hat{m}_{rskl}\}$ for the **w** array, which itself was an aggregated version of the original table. The estimated expected values $\{\hat{m}_{rskl}\}$, defined in (24) for the **w** array, correspond again to an aggregated version of the original sociomatrix **x**. The estimated expected values for the **y** array are found by dividing the $\{\hat{m}_{rskl}\}$ by the number of dyads that have been aggregated as in (26) and (27).

For the p_1 subgroup model given by (30) and (32), we are estimating $2K$ parameters: $K - 1$ for the $\{\alpha^{(r)}\}$, $K - 1$ for the $\{\beta^{(s)}\}$, 1 for θ, and 1 for ρ. Thus there are $g(g - 1) - 2K$ degrees of freedom associated with the model. The likelihood-ratio goodness-of-fit statistic for this model is computed as in (29).

There are other special cases of the general subgroup model containing $\{\theta^{(rs)}\}$ and $\{\rho^{(rs)}\}$, corresponding to other combinations of the additive decompositions (30) and (31), and perhaps involving the setting of some parameters to zero. Some of these special cases will lead to sets of maximum-likelihood equations that can be solved by using the standard iterative proportional fitting algorithm on **w**; other cases will require their own iterative algorithms. We do not discuss any other special cases since it appears that our analysis of the organizational data is quite adequate using just the general subgroup and the p_1

subgroup models. We note that there are more elaborate subgroup models than those discussed in this section, models that combine individual actor with subgroup parameters; however, we do not discuss these generalizations here.

THE EXAMPLE CONTINUED

We partition the 73 organizations in Towertown into $K = 4$ subgroups according to (1) whether each organization is owned by people in the community (*local*) or by people outside the community (*extralocal*) and (2) whether each organization has *public* or *private* ownership. Table 9 lists the organizations in each of the four subgroups. While there are many other ways to partition 73 organizations, the local/extralocal × public/private split is simple enough to illustrate our methods but still of substantive interest. Note that the 16 business organizations analyzed earlier are all private organizations, and all but 5 are locally owned.

Although we do not include the full three 73 × 73 sociomatrices here because of their size, we do report aggregate versions of them in the form of the **w** arrays for our four subgroups. Table 10 gives only the upper triangle of these arrays because of the symmetries shown in Expression (20). The two subgroup models, fitted to each of these arrays, yielded the following values of the likelihood-ratio goodness-of-fit statistics:

	P_1 Subgroup Model		General Subgroup Model	
	G^2	DF	G^2	DF
Information	5,980.9	5,248	4,415.4	5,220
Money	4,018.22	5,248	2,941.0	3,811
Support	5,276.02	5,248	3,965.2	5,225

The values of G^2 are in all cases less or only slightly greater than the degrees of freedom. The degrees of freedom for the general subgroup model vary from one generator to another because we have adjusted them for the zero counts in the **w** arrays. (See the discussion of this point in Bishop, Fienberg, and Holland, 1975, pp. 115–116, and in Fienberg, 1980, pp. 109–110.) These zeros constrain the corresponding π_{ijkl} to be equal to zero, and this must be taken into account in the

TABLE 9
Four Subgroups of the 73 Organizations in Towertown

G_1 Private Local ($g_1 = 26$)	G_2 Private Extralocal ($g_2 = 22$)	G_3 Public Local ($g_3 = 21$)	G_4 Public Extralocal ($g_4 = 4$)
Clothing Mfg. Co.	Farm Bureau	City Council	Highway Authority
Farm Supply Co.	Farm Equipment Co.	City Manager	State University
Chamber of Commerce	Mechanical Co.	County Board	Dept. of Public Aid
Banker's Association	Electric Equip. Co.	Fire Department	Employment Services
First Towertown Bank	Metal Products Co.	Human Relations Committee	
Towertown Savings & Loan	Music Equipment Co.	Mayor's Office	
Bank of Towertown	Music Emp. Union 1	Police Department	
Second Towertown Bank	Music Emp. Union 2	Sanitary District	
Brinkman Law Firm	Teachers' Union	Streets and Sanitation	
Cater Law Firm	League of Women Voters	Park District	
Lenhart Law Firm	First Kiwanis Club	Zoning Board	
Bar Association	Second Kiwanis Club	Hospital Board	
Board of Realtors	Rotary Club	Public Hospital	
Small Business Assoc.	Lions Club	Board of Mental Health	
Central Labor Union	Parent-Teacher Assoc.	County Board of Health	
Democratic Committee	St. Hilary's Catholic Church	School Board	
Republican Committee	First Baptist Church	High School	
Towertown News	First Church of the Light	Local Community College	
WTWR Radio	First Congregational Church	Housing Authority	
Medical Society	First Methodist Church	Towertown Mental Health Center	
Health Services Center	Unity Lutheran Church	Youth Services Bureau	
United Fund	University Methodist Church		
First Assoc. of Churches			
Second Assoc. of Churches			
Family Services			
YMCA			

TABLE 10

w Arrays for Intrasubgroup and Intersubgroup Choices Among the Four Subgroups

Information

	G_1		G_2		G_3		G_4	
G_1	404	44	422	20	365	33	68	4
	44	158	30	100	43	105	2	30
G_2			382	24	356	29	74	3
			24	32	20	57	1	10
G_3					236	33	49	7
					33	118	1	27
G_4							8	0
							0	4

Money

	G_1		G_2		G_3		G_4	
G_1	424	81	433	97	459	43	88	8
	81	64	24	18	30	14	4	4
G_2			454	4	435	0	83	0
			4	0	27	0	5	0
G_3					348	30	74	8
					30	12	2	0
G_4							10	1
							1	0

Support

	G_1		G_2		G_3		G_4	
G_1	484	56	463	44	420	17	80	1
	56	54	34	31	61	48	13	10
G_2			402	26	361	6	73	1
			26	8	60	35	12	2
G_3					254	40	55	8
					40	86	8	13
G_4							6	3
							3	0

computation. The zero problem is especially acute for money because the zeros in Table 10 propagate back to the original sociomatrix for this relation.

While both subgroup models appear to fit the data well for all three relations, a determination of whether or not they provide a reasonable parametric structure for the sociomatrices depends on a direct comparison to the fit of p_1 and the differential mutuality model discussed earlier. Due to computational limitations we have been unable to fit these models to the entire group, and thus our assessment here is more qualitative in nature. The maximum g for which p_1 can be fit is unknown, since it is both program-dependent and machine-dependent. At present, $g = 40$ is possible, and we anticipate being able to increase this limit in the near future. Perhaps even $g = 73$, the size

TABLE 11

Normalized Fitted Values from p_1 Subgroup Model for the Three Generators

Information

	G_1		G_2		G_3		G_4	
G_1	0.638	0.061	0.753	0.041	0.638	0.054	0.627	0.076
	0.061	0.239	0.063	0.142	0.069	0.239	0.050	0.247
G_2			0.839	0.041	0.754	0.056	0.741	0.079
			0.041	0.080	0.047	0.143	0.034	0.147
G_3					0.638	0.061	0.625	0.085
					0.061	0.240	0.044	0.246
G_4							0.619	0.062
							0.062	0.256

Money

	G_1		G_2		G_3		G_4	
G_1	0.643	0.124	0.809	0.150	0.808	0.088	0.822	0.105
	0.124	0.110	0.022	0.018	0.069	0.035	0.046	0.027
G_2			0.948	0.024	0.906	0.014	0.929	0.016
			0.024	0.003	0.075	0.005	0.051	0.004
G_3					0.963	0.044	0.912	0.052
					0.044	0.010	0.029	0.008
G_4							0.925	0.033
							0.035	0.006

Support

	G_1		G_2		G_3		G_4	
G_1	0.785	0.068	0.835	0.070	0.711	0.044	0.742	0.034
	0.068	0.079	0.045	0.050	0.134	0.110	0.138	0.086
G_2			0.877	0.046	0.762	0.029	0.783	0.023
			0.046	0.032	0.138	0.071	0.140	0.054
G_3					0.663	0.089	0.708	0.072
					0.089	0.159	0.094	0.126
G_4							0.750	0.075
							0.075	0.100

of the Towertown network, will be possible by utilizing new Newton-like algorithms currently under development. These algorithms, which have convergence properties and space requirements quite different from those of the iterative proportional fitting algorithms discussed here, should prove to be more efficient on problems such as p_1.

Table 11 contains the estimated dyadic probabilities for the p_1 subgroup model; those for the general, more complex subgroup model can be calculated directly from Table 10 by normalizing each 2×2 table so that its entries add to 1. For flows of information and support, the estimated dyad probabilities for the two models are quite similar except for the mutual and null relationships within G_1 and G_4 and the mutual relations between G_1 and G_3, G_1 and G_4, and G_3 and G_4. There

TABLE 12
Parameter Estimates for the Three Relations

	Information	Money	Support
$\hat{\alpha}^{(1)}$	0.111	0.255	0.249
$\hat{\alpha}^{(2)}$	−0.443	0.220	0.215
$\hat{\alpha}^{(3)}$	−0.010	−0.317	−0.091
$\hat{\alpha}^{(4)}$	0.342	−0.158	−0.373
$\hat{\beta}^{(1)}$	0.047	1.005	−0.266
$\hat{\beta}^{(2)}$	−0.082	−0.973	−0.741
$\hat{\beta}^{(3)}$	0.170	0.193	0.510
$\hat{\beta}^{(4)}$	−0.135	−0.225	0.497
$\hat{\theta}$	−2.504	−2.906	−2.428
$\hat{\rho}$	3.709	1.524	2.589

is considerable reciprocity of information both within and between subgroups except for within G_2. Reciprocity of support is simply much less than information. For money, on the other hand, the estimated dyadic probabilities for choices among and between G_2, G_3, and G_4 are difficult to make because of all the zero counts in Table 10, although we note that most relationships are null (except for possibly within G_1). All in all, the simple model with a constant reciprocity parameter ρ and a simple additive decomposition of $\{\theta^{(rs)}\}$ seems quite reasonable.

To better quantify the subgroup relationships, we examine the maximum-likelihood estimates for the parameters of this simple subgroup model (Table 12). Note that information flows are reciprocated more often than support, and support flows, as noted above, much more often than money. The "productivity" parameters $\{\hat{\alpha}^{(i)}\}$ are not very different for money and support, except for $\hat{\alpha}^{(3)}$ and $\hat{\alpha}^{(4)}$—G_3 is unlikely to send money to the other subgroups and G_4 is likely to send information. The least likely outflow is information from G_2; the most likely, information from G_4. There is also a slight tendency for money and support not to flow from G_4. The remaining $\{\hat{\alpha}^{(i)}\}$ are smaller in magnitude and of little importance.

The "attractiveness" parameter estimates $\{\hat{\beta}^{(i)}\}$ differ even more across groups than the $\{\hat{\alpha}^{(i)}\}$ parameters and, on average, are slightly larger (except for information). We note that support is likely to flow to subgroups G_3 and G_4 and money to G_1. Large negative parameters indicate that neither support nor information is unlikely to flow to G_2.

To summarize, we note that private, local firms are likely to receive money, which is equally likely to come from the other three subgroups. Thus these organizations in G_1, which consist of most of the business firms, labor unions, and *private* charities, are heavily dependent on the receipt of money from other organizations in the community. The private, extralocal organizations, G_2, are active in resource flows in a *negative* sense—they are unlikely to receive money and support and unlikely to send information. This is probably due to the nature of their ownership. The lack of need for money clearly distinguishes the private, extralocal firms from the private, local firms, which are smaller and more dependent on the local community for all their financial resources.

Support is likely to flow to the public organizations, both local and extralocal. Money is unlikely to flow from the public local organizations, G_3, perhaps because they simply have little. Support is unlikely to flow from the public, extralocal organizations, G_4, but information is likely to flow from them. Remember that information and support are *not* likely to flow from the private, extralocal organizations, so that the information and support resources distinguish public from private, extralocal organizations.

SUMMARY

This chapter makes three contributions to sociological methodology. First, we develop an alternative notation for Holland and Leinhardt's p_1 model and a new representation for data on dyadic interactions as a four-dimensional cross-classification that allows for extensions to the basic model. Second, we discuss computation of fitted values and parameter estimates via a simple, widely accessible algorithm: iterative proportional fitting. Third, we present specific details for modeling network subgroupings.

We have illustrated these methods on a large and complex network of organizations in a midwestern town. A study of information flows among the 16 business organizations in the town allowed us to isolate 10 active information-processing organizations and 6 organizations, large manufacturing firms, that have little need for receipt or transmission of information. The 10 active firms fall neatly into three subgroups: financial institutions, law firms, and media firms. We showed that these three subgroups process information in different ways, and we discussed reasons for the differences.

We also grouped all 73 organizations into four subgroups based on ownership and location. An analysis of the three relations separately showed that the four subgroups sent and received resources in very different ways. Private, local firms are likely to send money and support and likely to receive money. Private, extralocal firms also send support, but they are unlikely to receive either support or money. Public firms are most active in receiving support. Public, local firms are unlikely to send money; public, extralocal firms are unlikely to send support or receive information. Overall, information was the most likely resource to be reciprocated, money the least likely.

The methods of this chapter cannot yield a *complete* analysis of this network because they are designed for single relations. Hence substantive conclusions concerning the interrelations among different resource flows are missing. Moreover, as mentioned by Galaskiewicz (1979), the network is even more complex than noted here—since six, not three, questions were posed to the organizations, there are *two* representations for this multiple network. A complete analysis of these data would take many pages and require more complicated methods. Many of the researchers who have studied this network (among them Marsden, 1980) are continuing their efforts using many of the methods described in this chapter.

REFERENCES

BISHOP, Y. M. M., FIENBERG, S. E., AND HOLLAND, P. W.
1975 *Discrete Multivariate Analysis.* Cambridge, Mass.: M.I.T. Press.

BREIGER, R. L., BOORMAN, S. A., AND ARABIE, P.
1975 "An algorithm for clustering relational data with application to social network analysis and comparison with multidimensional scaling." *Journal of Mathematical Psychology* 12:328–383.

BURT, R. S.
1980 "Autonomy in a social topology." *American Journal of Sociology* 85:892–925.

DARROCH, J. N., AND RATCLIFF, D.
1972 "Generalized iterative scaling of log-linear models." *Annals of Mathematical Statistics* 43:1470–1480.

DAVIS, J. A.
1968 "Statistical analysis of pair relations: Symmetry, subjective consistency, and reciprocity." *Sociometry* 31:102–119.
1977 "Sociometric triads as multivariate systems." *Journal of Mathematical Sociology* 5:41–59.

DIXON, W. J., AND BROWN, M. B. (eds.)
1979 *BMDP Biomedical Computer Programs P-Series.* Berkeley: University of California Press.

FIENBERG, S. E.
1980 *The Analysis of Cross-Classified Categorical Data.* 2nd ed. Cambridge, Mass.: M.I.T. Press.

FIENBERG, S. E., AND WASSERMAN, S.
1980 "Methods for the analysis of data from multivariate directed graphs." *Proceedings of the Conference on Recent Developments in Statistical Methods and Applications.* Taipei, Taiwan: Institute of Mathematics, Academia Sinica.

FIENBERG, S. E., MEYER, M. M., AND WASSERMAN, S.
1980 "Analyzing data from multivariate directed graphs: An application to social networks." Paper presented at the Conference on Looking at Multivariate Data, University of Sheffield, March 1980.

GALASKIEWICZ, J.
1979 *Exchange Networks and Community Politics.* Beverly Hills: Sage.

GALASKIEWICZ, J., AND MARSDEN, P. V.
1978 "Interorganizational resource networks: Formal patterns of overlap." *Social Science Research* 7:89–107.

GOODMAN, L. A.
1972 "A general model for the analysis of surveys." *American Journal of Sociology* 77:1035–1086.

HABERMAN, S.
1977 "Log-linear models for frequency tables with small expected counts." *Annals of Statistics* 5:1148–1169.
1978 *The Analysis of Qualitative Data.* Vol. 1. New York: Academic Press.
1979 *The Analysis of Qualitative Data.* Vol. 2. New York: Academic Press.

HARARY, F., NORMAN, R. Z., AND CARTWRIGHT, D.
1965 *Structural Models: An Introduction to the Theory of Directed Graphs.* New York: Wiley.

HOLLAND, P. W., AND LEINHARDT, S.
1977 "Notes on the statistical analysis of social network data." Paper presented at the Advanced Research Symposium on Stochastic Process Models of Social Structure, Carnegie-Mellon University, Pittsburgh.
1978 "An omnibus test for social structure using triads." *Sociological Methods and Research* 7:227–256.

1981 "An exponential family of probability distributions for directed graphs." *Journal of American Statistical Association,* in press.

HUBERT, L. J., AND BAKER, F. B.

1978 "Evaluating the conformity of sociometric measurements." *Psychometrika* 43:31–41.

KOEHLER, K. J.

1977 "Goodness-of-fit statistics for large sparse multinomials." Ph.D. dissertation, School of Statistics, University of Minnesota.

MARSDEN, P. V.

1980 "Methods for the characterization of role structure in network analysis." Paper presented at the Conference on Methods in Social Network Analysis, University of California–Irvine, April 1980.

MEYER, M. M.

1980 "Generalizing the iterative proportional fitting procedure." Technical Report 371. School of Statistics, University of Minnesota.

MORENO, J. L.

1934 *Who Shall Survive?* Washington, D.C.: Nervous and Mental Disease Publishing Co.

UPTON, G. J. G.

1978 *The Analysis of Cross-Tabulated Data.* New York: Wiley.

WHITE, H. C., BOORMAN, S. A., AND BREIGER, R. L.

1976 "Social structure from multiple networks. I: Blockmodels of roles and positions." *American Journal of Sociology* 81:730–780.

5

THREE ELEMENTARY VIEWS OF LOG LINEAR MODELS FOR THE ANALYSIS OF CROSS-CLASSIFICATIONS HAVING ORDERED CATEGORIES

Leo A. Goodman

UNIVERSITY OF CHICAGO

In analyzing a two-way cross-classification table for two qualitative (dichotomous and/or polytomous) variables, we can use log linear models for three purposes: (1) to examine the joint distribution of the variables, (2) to assess the possible dependence of a response variable upon an explanatory or regressor variable, and (3) to study

This chapter is based on a lecture delivered by the author when he received the Outstanding Statistician of the Year Award for 1978–1979 from the American Statistical Association, Chicago Chapter, on 15 May 1979. The research was partly supported by the Division of the Social Sciences, National Science Foundation. For helpful comments, the author is indebted to D. Andrich, C. Clogg, O. D. Duncan, S. Haberman, S. Leinhardt, and P. McCullagh.

the association between two response variables. With each of the three uses of log linear models, a different view of the models will be obtained. Each view will highlight a different class of log linear models, and it will provide a particularly appropriate way to describe the models in that class. The three views will illuminate our understanding of the corresponding three classes of log linear models.

We focus here on cross-classification tables in which the categories of each qualitative variable are ordered. For the two-way table, the corresponding two variables will be called variables A and B. We shall consider first the joint bivariate distribution of variables A and B. This distribution can sometimes be expressed conveniently in terms of the following components: a component pertaining to the univariate distribution of variable A, a component pertaining to the univariate distribution of variable B, and a component pertaining to the association between variables A and B. Expressing the joint bivariate distribution of variables A and B this way is useful when the association between the variables is of special interest. When the association between the variables is of interest but their univariate distributions are not, the log linear models for the analysis of association are particularly useful.

Instead of expressing the joint bivariate distribution of variables A and B in terms of the three components just cited, we can sometimes express it more conveniently in terms of the following two components: a component pertaining to the univariate distribution of variable A and a component pertaining to the possible dependence of variable B on variable A. Expressing the joint bivariate distribution this way is useful when the possible dependence of variable B on variable A is of special interest. When this possible dependence is of interest but the univariate distribution of variable A is not, the log linear models for the analysis of dependence are particularly useful.

Log linear models for the analysis of the association between variables A and B cannot be used to shed light (either directly or indirectly) upon the univariate distribution of variable A or variable B. Similarly, log linear models for the analysis of the dependence of variable B on variable A cannot be used to shed light (either directly or indirectly) upon the univariate distribution of variable A; and log linear models for the analysis of the dependence of variable A on variable B cannot be used to shed light (either directly or indirectly) upon the univariate distribution of variable B. When the interest in the joint bivariate distribution of variables A and B is not confined to the

TABLE 1

Cross-Classification of 7,477 Women According to Right Eye Grade and Left Eye Grade with Respect to Unaided Distance Vision

Right Eye Grade	Left Eye Grade: Best (1)	Second (2)	Third (3)	Worst (4)	Total
Best (1)	1,520	266	124	66	1,976
Second (2)	234	1,512	432	78	2,256
Third (3)	117	362	1,772	205	2,456
Worst (4)	36	82	179	492	789
Total	1,907	2,222	2,507	841	7,477

association between the two variables, or to the possible dependence of one of the variables on the other, then other log linear models for the analysis of the joint distribution will be useful.

To illustrate how log linear models can be used to analyze (1) the joint distribution of the qualitative variables, (2) the possible dependence of a qualitative response variable on a qualitative explanatory or regressor variable, and (3) the association between two qualitative response variables, we shall reanalyze three tables.

Table 1 is the classic 4 × 4 table on unaided vision first analyzed by Stuart (1953, 1955). It cross-classifies the right eye grade and the corresponding left eye grade in unaided distance vision (each eye graded in one of four categories from best to worst) for 7,477 women. These data have been discussed and reanalyzed by many statisticians using various models and methods (see, for example, Kendall and Stuart, 1961; Goodman and Kruskal, 1963; Caussinus, 1965; Bhapkar, 1966, 1979; Ireland, Ku, and Kullback, 1969; Grizzle, Starmer, and Koch, 1969; Koch and Reinfurt, 1971; Plackett, 1974; Wedderburn, 1974; Bishop, Fienberg, and Holland, 1975; Tukey, 1977; Gokhale and Kullback, 1978; Mantel and Byar, 1978; Plackett and Paul, 1978; Agresti, 1980; Anscombe, 1981). By applying an appropriate log-linear model to Table 1 to study the joint distribution of right eye vision and left eye vision, we shall obtain new insight into these data.

Table 2 is a 3 × 3 table describing the length of stay in the hospital for 132 schizophrenic patients classified by the visiting pattern that had been ascribed to the patient and his or her visitors in the hospital. These data were analyzed earlier by Wing (1962), Haberman (1974a), and Fienberg (1977). By applying an appropriate log linear model to study the possible dependence of the patient's length of

TABLE 2
Length of Stay in Hospital for 132 Schizophrenic Patients Classified by Visiting Pattern That Had Been Ascribed in the Hospital

Visiting Pattern	Length of Stay in Hospital 2–10 Years	10–20 Years	20 Years or More	Total
Received visitors regularly or patient went home	43	16	3	62
Received visitors infrequently; patient did not go home	6	11	10	27
Never received visitors; patient did not go home	9	18	16	43
Total	58	45	29	132

hospital stay on the ascribed visiting pattern, we shall obtain some new results that supplement those presented earlier by Haberman (1974a) and Fienberg (1977).

Table 3 is the classic 2 × 3 table first analyzed by Armitage (1955) on the relationship between streptococcus carrier status (noncarrier or carrier) and tonsil enlargement level for 1,398 children. These data have been discussed and reanalyzed by various statisticians (see, for example, Armitage, 1955, 1971; Cox, 1970; Clayton, 1974; Plackett, 1974; Andrich, 1979; Agresti, 1980; McCullagh, 1980), and the data are also included in Holmes and Williams (1954). By applying an appropriate log linear model to Table 3 to study the association between streptococcus carrier status and level of tonsil enlargement, we shall also obtain some new insight into these data.

These three tables have been previously analyzed using a wide variety of models and methods, and comparison of the results presented

TABLE 3
Cross-Classification of 1,398 Children According to Status as Noncarriers or Carriers of *Streptococcus Pyogenes* and Enlargement of Tonsils

Streptococcus Carrier Status	Tonsil Enlargement Level +	++	+++	Total
Noncarrier	497	560	269	1,326
Carrier	19	29	24	72
Total	516	589	293	1,398

in the earlier literature with those presented here will help the interested reader to appreciate the various advantages of the models and methods that will be described here. Our analysis of these classic examples will facilitate this comparison. The three tables will be used here for expository and illustrative purposes.

Tables 1, 2, and 3 are two-way cross-classification tables each of which pertains to two qualitative variables.[1] The methods presented here can be applied to two-way cross-classification tables in which each variable is either polytomous or dichotomous, where the classes of each polytomous variable are ordered, and the classes of each dichotomous variable may be either ordered or unordered.

Variables that have classes (categories) which are ordered abound in sociology, in the social sciences more generally, and in other areas of inquiry as well. Some of the models and methods described here have already been applied to the study of such variables as occupational status, socioeconomic status, and mental health status. (The relationship between socioeconomic status and mental health, and the relationship between father's occupational status and son's occupational status were studied, using log linear models for the analysis of association, in Goodman, 1979a, 1980a. See also Duncan, 1979a, 1979b, Duncan and McRae, 1978, and Goodman, 1980b, for related material.)

Log linear models can be used to analyze two-way cross-classification tables where (1) the number of rows and columns is equal and there is a one-to-one relationship between them (as in Table 1), or (2) the number of rows and columns is equal but there is not a one-to-one relationship between them (as in Table 2), or (3) the number of rows and columns differs (as in Table 3). Each of these kinds of cross-classification tables can be studied by using log linear models to accomplish any of the three general purposes mentioned earlier: analysis of the joint distribution, analysis of dependence, and analysis of association.

On the other hand, if the data in the cross-classification table are such that the row and column marginals are considered to be given (or constant) and these marginals need to be fitted exactly by the

[1]The two qualitative variables are polytomous in Tables 1 and 2, but in Table 3 one of the variables is polytomous (more specifically, trichotomous) and the other is dichotomous.

model, then only models for the analysis of association (or equivalent models) will be relevant (see, for example, Goodman, 1970, 1979a). Similarly, if the data are such that the row marginal is considered to be given (or constant) and this marginal needs to be fitted exactly by the model, then only models that pertain to the dependence of the column variable on the row variable (or equivalent models) will be relevant. Also, if the data are such that the column marginal is considered to be given (or constant) and this marginal needs to be fitted exactly by the model, then only models that pertain to the dependence of the row variable on the column variable (or equivalent models) will be relevant.

With the three views to be presented here, we shall see that there is a hierarchical perspective: The class of models for the analysis of association is, in a certain sense, included within the class of models for the analysis of dependence, which is in turn included within the class of models for the analysis of the joint distribution. This perspective is discussed later.

Although we focus our attention here primarily on the analysis of two-way cross-classification tables and on the use of log linear models to accomplish the three general purposes mentioned earlier, the models and methods presented here can be extended to the analysis of multi-way cross-classification tables, and the corresponding log linear models can be used to analyze such multiway tables in order to accomplish a corresponding set of general purposes. The extensions to the multiway cross-classification table are considered in the final section.

SOME ELEMENTARY NULL MODELS

In our analysis of Tables 1, 2 and 3, we shall use some elementary "null models" as baselines for comparative purposes. Different null models are appropriate in different contexts. In this section, I describe some of the null models appropriate in the analysis of (1) the joint distribution, (2) dependence, and (3) association. Before doing so, I first introduce the notation we shall need to describe the null models.

For the two-way $I \times J$ contingency table pertaining to the joint distribution of two qualitative variables, say, variables A and B, let f_{ij} denote the observed frequency in cell (i, j) of the table ($i = 1, 2, \ldots, I$;

$j = 1, 2, \ldots, J$), and let F_{ij} denote the corresponding expected frequency under some model. In other words, f_{ij} is the observed frequency at level i on variable A and at level j on variable B, and F_{ij} is the corresponding expected frequency.

In the analysis of the $I \times J$ contingency table, the usual null model employed in the past states that variable A and variable B are statistically independent. Under this null model, the expected frequencies F_{ij} are estimated from the observed frequencies pertaining to the univariate distributions of variable A and variable B, using the usual elementary formula for the null model (see, for example, Goodman, 1970). Since the expected frequencies pertaining to the univariate distributions of variable A and variable B are estimated under the null model to be equal to the corresponding observed frequencies pertaining to these two univariate distributions, this null model cannot be used to shed light upon the two univariate distributions (aside from whatever light may be shed by the observed frequencies pertaining to the corresponding univariate distributions). When the interest in the joint bivariate distribution of variables A and B is not confined to the association between the two variables, then other null models should be used as baselines for comparative purposes.

Null Models for Analysis of the Joint Distribution

In our study of the joint distribution of variables A and B in the two-way $I \times J$ contingency table, we could consider various kinds of null models. For the sake of simplicity, we begin here with the most elementary null model: the model which states that all the expected frequencies F_{ij} ($i = 1, 2, \ldots, I; j = 1, 2, \ldots, J$) are equal. Thus under this model

$$F_{ij} = N/(IJ) \tag{1}$$

where N is the sample size. This model states that the probability that an observation will fall in cell (i, j) of the $I \times J$ contingency table is $1/(IJ)$; that is, all the cells (i, j) (for $i = 1, 2, \ldots, I; j = 1, 2, \ldots, J$) are equiprobable.

A null model is used as a baseline for comparative purposes, and in some situations we might begin the analysis of the data by using a null model that is less elementary than Model (1). In some cases, a less elementary null model could provide a more relevant baseline for comparative purposes. For example, in the analysis of the 4×4 table (Table 1) on unaided vision, the possible asymmetry between right eye and left eye vision is of special interest, so we might begin the analysis of these data using the following null model:

$$F_{ij} = F_{ji} \qquad \text{for } i < j \tag{2}$$

This model states that the expected frequencies F_{ij} are symmetric. Model (2) is the usual symmetry model in which the expected frequency in cell (i, j) of the table is equal to the expected frequency in cell (j, i) of the table. Let us call Model (2) the "null asymmetry model."[2] We shall apply Model (2) later in our analysis of the joint distribution of the qualitative variables in Table 1.

Models (1) and (2) serve as examples of the various kinds of null models that could be considered in the analysis of the joint distribution. Other examples could also be presented; in order to save space, I shall not do so here.

Null Models for Analysis of Dependence

We shall now consider the two-way $I \times J$ contingency table for variables A and B in the situation where variable A is viewed as an explanatory or regressor variable and variable B is viewed as the response variable. For adjacent classes pertaining to the response variable B (say, classes j and $j + 1$), we define as follows the odds $\Omega_{ij}^{A\bar{B}}$ based on the expected frequencies:

$$\Omega_{ij}^{A\bar{B}} = F_{ij}/F_{i,j+1} \qquad \text{for } j = 1, 2, \ldots, J - 1 \tag{3}$$

Let $\Psi_{ij}^{A\bar{B}}$ denote the natural logarithm of $\Omega_{ij}^{A\bar{B}}$ (that is, the log-odds). In the present context, the most elementary null model is the following "null log-odds model":

$$\Psi_{ij}^{A\bar{B}} = 0 \qquad \text{for } i = 1, 2, \ldots, I; j = 1, 2, \ldots, J - 1 \tag{4}$$

Model (4) states that $\Omega_{ij}^{A\bar{B}} = 1$, and this is equivalent to the model which states that the classes of variable B are conditionally equiprobable, given the level of variable A (see, for example, Good-

[2]Of course, Model (2) could be called the "symmetry model," but in the present exposition the term "null asymmetry model" turns out to be more felicitous.

man, 1970). This model is the most elementary null model in the present context—that is, analysis of the possible dependence of variable B on variable A.

As we noted earlier, a less elementary null model can sometimes provide a more relevant baseline for comparative purposes. In the present context we also note that a null model less elementary than the null model (4) will sometimes be useful; however, in our analysis of the 3 × 3 table (Table 2) on the possible dependence of length of hospital stay on the ascribed visiting pattern, we shall find that Model (4) can serve as the baseline for comparative purposes. We shall apply it later in our analysis of the dependence in Table 2.

Null Models for Analysis of Association

We shall now consider the two-way $I \times J$ contingency table for variables A and B in the situation where they are viewed as response variables and the association between these variables is of interest. For adjacent classes of variable A (say, classes i and $i + 1$) and adjacent classes of variable B (say, classes j and $j + 1$), we define as follows the odds-ratio Θ_{ij} based on the expected frequencies:

$$\Theta_{ij} = (F_{ij}F_{i+1,j+1})/(F_{i,j+1}F_{i+1,j}) \qquad \text{for } i = 1, 2, \ldots, I-1; j = 1, 2, \ldots, J-1 \quad (5)$$

Let Φ_{ij} denote the natural logarithm of Θ_{ij} (that is, the log-odds-ratio). In the present context, the most elementary null model is the following "null association model":

$$\Phi_{ij} = 0 \qquad \text{for } i = 1, 2, \ldots, I-1; j = 1, 2, \ldots, J-1 \quad (6)$$

Model (6) states that $\Theta_{ij} = 1$, and this is equivalent to the model which states that A and B are statistically independent. This model is the most elementary null model in the present context—that is, analysis of the association between A and B.

In the present context we also note that a null model less elementary than Model (6) will sometimes be useful; but in our analysis of Table 3 on the association between streptococcus carrier status and level of tonsil enlargement, we shall find that Model (6) can serve as the baseline for comparative purposes. We shall apply it later in our analysis of the association in Table 3.

TABLE 4
Chi Square Values for Models Applied to Tables 1, 2, and 3

Model	DF	Goodness-of-Fit Chi Square	Likelihood-Ratio Chi Square
For Table 1: analysis of the joint distribution			
Null asymmetry model (2)	6	19.11	19.25
Fitted asymmetry model	3	0.50	0.50
For Table 2: analysis of dependence			
Null log-odds model (4)	6	44.96	48.24
Fitted log-odds model	5	5.46	5.81
For Table 3: analysis of association			
Null association model (6)	2	7.88	7.32
Fitted association model	1	0.24	0.24

We shall use the null asymmetry model (2), the null log-odds model (4), and the null association model (6) as baselines for comparative purposes in our analysis of Tables 1, 2, and 3, respectively. Each of these models will be applied to the corresponding table, and the observed frequencies in the table will be compared with the expected frequencies estimated under the model using the usual goodness-of-fit and the likelihood-ratio chi-squares. Table 4 gives the chi-square values obtained by using these null models, and it also gives the corresponding chi-square values obtained when the null models are modified in appropriate ways. By using the null models as baselines for comparative purposes, we find that these models can be modified in particularly simple and appropriate ways to obtain models that are more congruent with the observed data and that provide a dramatic improvement in fit.

ANALYSIS OF THE JOINT DISTRIBUTION

In our study of the joint distribution of A and B in the two-way $I \times J$ contingency table, we shall consider models that describe F_{ij} in terms of appropriate multiplicative factors, or equivalently we shall consider models that describe the natural logarithm G_{ij} of F_{ij} in terms of the corresponding additive factors. There are many possible models that could be considered (see, for example, Goodman, 1972, 1979b; Haberman, 1974a, 1974b). Different substantive contexts will suggest

TABLE 5
Rearrangement of Data in Table 1 for Analysis of Symmetry and Related Phenomena

Right Eye–Left Eye Grade Difference	Entries from Table 1			Total
+1	234	362	179	775
−1	266	432	205	903
+2	117	82		199
−2	124	78		202
+3	36			36
−3	66			66

different factors that may affect the F_{ij} (or the G_{ij}). Our analysis of the joint distribution of right eye vision and left eye vision in Table 1 will serve as an example of how multiplicative models for the F_{ij} (or the equivalent additive models for the G_{ij}) can be used to study the joint distribution of two qualitative variables.

In our analysis of Table 1, we begin with the null asymmetry model (2) as the baseline for comparative purposes. To apply this model to Table 1, we can rearrange the data conveniently as presented in Table 5. We can compare f_{21} with f_{12}, f_{32} with f_{23}, f_{43} with f_{34}, f_{31} with f_{13}, f_{42} with f_{24}, and f_{41} with f_{14} to test the corresponding hypothesis that $F_{21} = F_{12}$, $F_{32} = F_{23}$, and so on. Each hypothesis can be tested by using the usual elementary chi-square test with 1 degree of freedom; moreover, since there are six different hypotheses to be tested, and each of the chi-square statistics is statistically independent (asymptotically), the sum of the six chi-square statistics will be distributed asymptotically as chi-square with 6 degrees of freedom, under Model (2). From the chi-square values (with DF = 6) given in Table 4 for Model (2) applied to Table 1, we see that this model does not fit the observed data; however, a dramatic improvement in fit can be obtained with the model we consider next.

Before describing this model, we first express the null asymmetry model (2) as follows:

$$F_{ij} = \rho_{ij} \qquad \text{for } i \neq j \tag{7}$$

where the parameters ρ_{ij} satisfy the condition

$$\rho_{ij} = \rho_{ji} \tag{8}$$

Formula (7) describes the F_{ij} in terms of the symmetry parameters ρ_{ij}.

We now modify Model (7) by introducing into it the diagonals-parameter δ_k for the right eye–left eye grade difference $i - j = k$ (for $k = \pm 1, \pm 2, \pm 3$). Thus we obtain

$$F_{ij} = \rho_{ij}\delta_k \qquad \text{for } i \neq j, k = i - j \tag{9}$$

Although there are six diagonals-parameters δ_k ($k = \pm 1, \pm 2, \pm 3$), without loss of generality we can delete from (9) the three δ_k for $k = -1, -2, -3$; that is, we can set $\delta_k = 1$ for $k = -1, -2, -3$. Having introduced into the null asymmetry model (7) three parameters ($\delta_1, \delta_2, \delta_3$), the number of degrees of freedom for testing Model (9) will be three less than for Model (7). The chi-square values obtained with Model (9) in Table 4 show that introducing these three parameters leads to dramatic results.

Model (9) can be expressed in more elementary terms with the data in Table 1 rearranged as in Table 5. In Table 5, consider the 2×3 table for right eye–left eye grade difference $k = \pm 1$, and the 2×2 table for grade difference $k = \pm 2$. Model (9) applied to Table 1 is equivalent to the model which states that there is statistical independence between the row and column variables in the 2×3 table (for $k = \pm 1$) and also in the 2×2 table (for $k = \pm 2$), in Table 5. To test the hypothesis of statistical independence between the row and column variables in the 2×3 table, the usual chi-square test will have 2 degrees of freedom; the corresponding chi-square test for the 2×2 table will have 1 degree of freedom. The corresponding chi-square statistics for the two tables are statistically independent (asymptotically), and the sum of the two chi-square statistics will be distributed asymptotically as chi-square with $2 + 1 = 3$ degrees of freedom under the null hypothesis. The sum of the chi-square values (with DF = 3) is given in Table 4.

The parameter δ_1 is simply the odds that the right eye–left eye grade difference will be $+1$ rather than -1, and the parameters δ_2 and δ_3 can be defined similarly. These parameters can be estimated directly from the totals column in Table 5. Thus we obtain

$$\hat{\delta}_1 = 0.86 \qquad \hat{\delta}_2 = 0.99 \qquad \hat{\delta}_3 = 0.55 \tag{10}$$

Since $\hat{\delta}_k < 1$ for $k = 1, 2, 3$, a right eye–left eye grade difference of k is estimated to be less likely than a corresponding difference of $-k$; that is, a right eye grade lower than a left eye grade (by k grades) is estimated to be more likely than the reverse.

From the entries in Table 5, in addition to calculating the usual chi-square statistics for testing the hypothesis of statistical independence between the row and column variables in the 2×3 table (for $k = \pm 1$) and for testing the corresponding hypothesis in the 2×2 table (for $k = \pm 2$), as noted above, we can also estimate the expected frequencies under these hypotheses by using the usual elementary formula. Since Model (9) applied to Table 1 is equivalent to the model which states that there is statistical independence between the row and column variables in the 2×3 table ($k = \pm 1$) and the 2×2 table ($k = \pm 2$), the estimated expected frequencies under these hypotheses are also the corresponding estimated expected frequencies under Model (9). These estimates are displayed in Table 6 in a form that facilitates comparison with the observed frequencies in Table 1.

The estimate $\hat{F}_{ij}$ of the expected frequency under Model (9) can also be expressed in terms of the estimate of δ_k ($k = 1, 2, 3$) given in (10) and the corresponding estimate of the symmetry parameter ρ_{ij} in (9). (As was the case for the parameter δ_k, the ρ_{ij} in (9) can be calculated in an elementary way from the entries in Table 5; and it can be easily interpreted in terms of the entries in Table 6.) The asymmetry between right eye and left eye grade, with

$$\hat{F}_{ij} > \hat{F}_{ji} \qquad \text{for } i < j$$

(see Table 6), is a direct consequence of the fact that $\hat{\delta}_k < 1$ (for $k = 1, 2, 3$).

From the $\hat{F}_{ij}$ under Model (9), we can directly calculate the corresponding estimate $\hat{F}_{i.}$ of the expected frequency in the ith row marginal and the estimate $\hat{F}_{.j}$ of the expected frequency in the jth column marginal. (See the totals column and the totals row in Table 6.) The difference between the univariate distribution of the right eye

TABLE 6
Maximum-Likelihood Estimate of Expected Frequencies Obtained When Model (9) Is Applied to Table 1

	Left Eye Grade				
Right Eye Grade	1	2	3	4	Total
1	1,520.0	269.1	121.4	66.0	1,976.5
2	230.9	1,512.0	427.3	80.6	2,250.8
3	119.6	366.7	1,772.0	206.6	2,464.9
4	36.0	79.4	177.4	492.0	784.8
Total	1,906.5	2,227.2	2,498.1	845.2	7,477.0

grade and the univariate distribution of the left eye grade, with

$$\sum_{t=1}^{x} \hat{F}_{t.} > \sum_{t=1}^{x} \hat{F}_{.t} \qquad \text{for } x = 1, 2, 3$$

(see Table 6), is also a direct consequence of the fact that $\hat{\delta}_k < 1$ (for $k = 1, 2, 3$).

The parameter δ_k in Model (9) may depend on k (where $k = i - j$, the right eye–left eye grade difference), but no prior assumptions were made here about the nature of the dependence. Elementary methods can be used to test the hypothesis that δ_k is independent of k—that is, the hypothesis that

$$\delta_k = \delta \ (k = 1, 2, 3) \tag{11}$$

and similar methods are available for testing other related kinds of hypotheses (see Goodman, 1979c). When δ_k is not independent of k, the dependence may be of a rather simple form—for example,

$$\delta_k = \delta^k \ (k = 1, 2, 3) \tag{12}$$

where the superscript k denotes a specified power. The hypothesis that the dependence is of the form (12) can be tested by using log linear methods, and these methods are available for testing other related kinds of hypotheses as well.

For further discussion of the estimate $\hat{\delta}_k$ of δ_k in Model (9), see Goodman (1979c); there Model (9) is called the diagonals-parameter symmetry model, and it is closely related to the diagonals-parameter model introduced in Goodman (1972). Although Model (9) is closely related to the model in Goodman (1972), the former model pertains to the analysis of the joint distribution, whereas the latter pertains to the analysis of association. We shall discuss this point in more detail later when we compare the results obtained in the present section for the analysis of Table 1 with results obtained when models for the analysis of association are applied to this table.

As we noted earlier, Model (9) applied to Table 1 can help to explain the observed asymmetry between right and left eye vision and the difference between the marginal distributions for right eye vision and left eye vision. This model sheds light on the joint bivariate distribution of the variables in Table 1 and on the corresponding univariate distributions. Models for the analysis of association would not shed light on the corresponding univariate distributions.

Model (9) serves as an example of the various kinds of models that could be considered in the analysis of the joint distribution. We shall take note of other examples later when we comment on the analysis of the joint distribution of the variables in Tables 2 and 3.

ANALYSIS OF DEPENDENCE

In our analysis of the possible dependence of variable B on variable A in the two-way $I \times J$ contingency table, we shall consider models that describe the odds $\Omega_{ij}^{A\bar{B}}$ in terms of appropriate multiplicative factors,[3] or equivalently we shall consider models that describe the log-odds $\Psi_{ij}^{A\bar{B}}$ in terms of the corresponding additive factors. Each model can also be reexpressed as an equivalent multiplicative model for the F_{ij} (and/or an equivalent additive model for the G_{ij}). Our analysis of Table 2 will serve as an example of how these models can be used to study the possible dependence of one qualitative variable on another.

In our analysis of Table 2, we begin with the null log-odds model (4) as the baseline for comparative purposes. This model can be applied to the 3 × 3 table (Table 2) using the appropriate chi-square statistic for testing the hypothesis of conditional equiprobability (see, for example, Goodman, 1970), with 3 × 2 = 6 degrees of freedom. From the chi-square values (with DF = 6) given in Table 4 for the null log-odds model applied to Table 2, we see that this model does not fit the observed data, but we obtain better results with the model we consider next.

Table 7 gives the log-odds based on the observed frequencies f_{ij}, and also the standardized value of these log-odds.[4] The data in Table 7

[3]Although our attention here is focused on the odds $\Omega_{ij}^{A\bar{B}}$ pertaining to adjacent classes (classes j and $j + 1$) of variable B (see Formula 3), we could instead have considered more generally the odds pertaining to any two classes (say, classes j and j′) of variable B. The latter odds can be expressed as a product of an appropriate set of $\Omega_{ij}^{A\bar{B}}$; hence any model that describes the $\Omega_{ij}^{A\bar{B}}$ in terms of multiplicative factors will also describe the latter odds in terms of multiplicative factors (see, for example, Goodman, 1979b).

[4]The log-odds in Table 7 are calculated as the natural logarithm of the odds defined by (3), where the expected frequencies in (3) are replaced by a function of the corresponding observed frequencies. The F_{ij} in (3) are replaced by $f_{ij} + \frac{1}{2}$ for reasons explained in, for example, Gart and Zweifel (1967) and Goodman (1970). Each standardized value in Table 7 is calculated by dividing the corresponding log-odds in this table by its estimated standard deviation, where the F_{ij} in the formula for the standard deviation are also replaced by $f_{ij} + \frac{1}{2}$ as in the literature just cited.

TABLE 7
Observed Log-Odds for Adjacent Classes Pertaining to Response Variable in Table 2

Visiting Pattern	Length of Stay in Hospital 2–10 Years vs. 10–20 Years	10–20 Years vs. 20 Years or More
Received visitors regularly or patient went home	0.97 (3.35)	1.55 (2.63)
Received visitors infrequently; patient did not go home	−0.57 (−1.16)	0.09 (0.21)
Never received visitors; patient did not go home	−0.67 (−1.67)	0.11 (0.34)

NOTE: The standardized value of the observed log-odds is given in parentheses.

suggest why Model (4) does not fit the data, and they also suggest a remedy. Consider the modified log-odds model defined as follows:

$$\Psi_{1j}^{A\bar{B}} = \psi \qquad \Psi_{2j}^{A\bar{B}} = \Psi_{3j}^{A\bar{B}} = 0 \tag{13}$$

where ψ is estimated from the data. This model introduces a single parameter into Model (4), and as we have already noted from the results in Table 4, the introduction of this parameter is worthwhile. This model states that the classes of variable B are conditionally equiprobable when variable A is at level 2 or 3; when variable A is at level 1, however, the log-odds $\Psi_{1j}^{A\bar{B}} = \psi$ (for $j = 1, 2$).

Table 8 gives the maximum-likelihood estimate $\hat{F}_{ij}$ of the expected frequencies obtained when Model (13) is applied to Table 2. When variable A is at level 2 and 3, the entries in Table 8 are

TABLE 8
Maximum-Likelihood Estimate of Expected Frequencies Obtained When Model (13) Is Applied to Table 2

Visiting Pattern	Length of Stay in Hospital 1	2	3	Total
1	44.2	13.6	4.2	62.0
2	9.0	9.0	9.0	27.0
3	14.3	14.3	14.3	43.0[a]
Total	67.5	36.9	27.5	132.0[a]

[a]The entry is equal to the sum of summands having more significant digits than are reported here.

calculated in an elementary way; when variable A is at level 1, the calculation of the entries is not so elementary. (I shall describe how these entries are calculated later.) From the $\hat{F}_{1j}$ under Model (13), we find that the maximum-likelihood estimate of the log-odds parameter ψ is $\hat{\psi} = 1.18$. (All calculations in this chapter were made with more significant digits than are reported here.)

The $\hat{F}_{ij}$ under Model (13) can be expressed in terms of the estimate of the log-odds parameter ψ in (13) and the corresponding observed frequency $f_{i.}$ at the ith level of variable A. (For models that pertain to the dependence of variable B on variable A, the estimate $\hat{F}_{i.}$ is set equal to the corresponding observed frequency $f_{i.}$.) The dependence of variable B on variable A, with

$$\hat{F}_{1j}/\hat{F}_{1,j+1} > \hat{F}_{2j}/\hat{F}_{2,j+1} = \hat{F}_{3j}/\hat{F}_{3,j+1} = 1$$

(see Table 8), is a direct consequence of the fact that the estimate of the parameter ψ in (13) is greater than zero.

From the $\hat{F}_{ij}$ under Model (13), we can calculate directly the corresponding estimate $\hat{F}_{.j}$ of the expected frequency in the jth column marginal (see the totals row in Table 8). The particular shape of the corresponding univariate distribution (the distribution of variable B, the length of stay in hospital), with

$$\hat{F}_{.1} > \hat{F}_{.2} > \hat{F}_{.3}$$

(see Table 8), is also a direct consequence of the fact that the estimate of ψ in (13) is greater than zero.

As we have noted, Model (13) applied to Table 2 can help to explain the particular form of the dependence of variable B on variable A and also the particular shape of the corresponding univariate distribution of variable B. Models for the analysis of association would not shed light on the univariate distribution of variable B (or on the univariate distribution of variable A); and models for the analysis of the dependence of variable B on variable A (such as Model 13) do not shed light on the univariate distribution of variable A.

Model (13) is related to but somewhat different from the model described by Haberman (1974a) and Fienberg (1977) for these data. The development of the model in the earlier literature was expressed in terms somewhat different from those used here; the classes of variable B were not conditionally equiprobable at levels 2 and 3 of variable A in the earlier model; moreover, two more parameters were needed in the earlier model than in Model (13) here. The model presented here is more parsimonious than the model in the earlier literature, and it also fits the data well. We shall discuss the advantages of using the more parsimonious model later in a separate section. (The general method used here to obtain a more parsimonious model that fits the data can also be applied in other related contexts; see, for example, Goodman, 1975, 1978, 1979d.)

Before closing this section, we take note of the fact that the odds $\Omega_{ij}^{A\bar{B}}$ defined by (3) and the corresponding log-odds $\Psi_{ij}^{A\bar{B}}$ take account of the order of the classes of variable B, but not the order of the classes of variable A. When the classes of variable B are ordered, models for the odds $\Omega_{ij}^{A\bar{B}}$ or the corresponding log-odds $\Psi_{ij}^{A\bar{B}}$, can be applied both when the classes of variable A are ordered and when they are unordered. Model (13) takes into account to some extent the order of the classes of variable A, and other methods are also available for taking this into account (see, for example, Goodman, 1979e).

As we noted earlier, with models for the odds $\Omega_{ij}^{A\bar{B}}$ or log-odds $\Psi_{ij}^{A\bar{B}}$ (that is, models that pertain to the dependence of variable B on variable A), the univariate distribution of variable A is set equal to the corresponding observed distribution. However, instead of setting the univariate distribution equal to the corresponding observed distribution, we could introduce a model for the univariate distribution, and test this model by comparing the observed frequencies $f_{i.}$ with the corresponding expected frequencies estimated under the model. If the model for the univariate distribution of variable A is then combined with a model pertaining to the dependence of variable B on variable A (for example, Model 13), we obtain a combined model for the joint distribution of variables A and B. The combined model can help to explain the particular form of the dependence of variable B on variable A, the particular shape of the corresponding univariate distribution of variable B, and the univariate distribution of variable A. Models of this kind, together with models of the kind described in the preceding section, can serve as examples of models that could be considered in the analysis of the joint distribution.

ANALYSIS OF ASSOCIATION

In our analysis of the association between variables A and B in the two-way $I \times J$ contingency table, we shall consider models that describe the odds-ratio Θ_{ij} in terms of appropriate multiplicative factors,[5] or equivalently we shall consider models that describe the log-odds-ratio Φ_{ij} in terms of the corresponding additive factors. Each model can also be reexpressed as an equivalent multiplicative model for the F_{ij} (and/or an equivalent additive model for the G_{ij}). Our analysis of Table 3 will serve as an example of how these models can be used to study the association between variables A and B.

In our analysis of Table 3, we shall begin with the null association model (6) as the baseline for comparative purposes. This model can be applied to the 2 × 3 table (Table 3) using the usual chi-square statistic for testing the hypothesis that variables A and B are statistically independent, with 1 × 2 = 2 degrees of freedom. From the chi-square values (with DF = 2) given in Table 4 for the null association model applied to Table 3, we see that this model does not fit the data. We consider next the uniform association model, which does fit the data well.

The uniform association model is defined as follows:

$$\Phi_{ij} = \phi \tag{14}$$

where the parameter ϕ is estimated from the data. Model (14) introduces a single parameter into Model (6), and in this simple way we obtain a model that is congruent with the observed data (see Table 4).

To clarify further our understanding of the uniform association model as defined by (14), Table 9 presents the log-odds-ratios based on the observed frequencies f_{ij}, and also the standardized value of these log-odds-ratios.[6] For the 2 × 3 table (Table 3), there are two observed log-odds-ratios (see Table 9). The difference between them is −0.25

[5]Although our attention here is focused on the odds-ratio Θ_{ij} pertaining to adjacent classes of variable A (classes i and $i + 1$) and variable B (classes j and $j + 1$) (see Formula 5), we could instead have considered more generally the odds-ratio pertaining to any two classes of variable A (say, classes i and i′) and variable B (say, classes j and j′). The latter odds-ratio can be expressed as a product of an appropriate set of θ_{ij}; hence any model that describes the θ_{ij} in terms of multiplicative factors will also describe the latter odds-ratio in terms of multiplicative factors (see, for example, Goodman, 1979a, 1979b.)

[6]The log-odds-ratios in Table 9 are calculated as the natural logarithm of the odds-ratios defined by (5), where the expected frequencies in (5) are replaced by a function of the corresponding observed frequencies. Here, too, the F_{ij} are replaced by $f_{ij} + ½$; see, for example, Goodman (1970). Each standardized value in Table 9 is calculated by dividing the corresponding log-odds-ratio in this table by its estimated standard deviation, where the F_{ij} in the formula for the standard deviation are also replaced by $f_{ij} + ½$, as in, for example, Goodman (1970).

TABLE 9
Observed Association for Adjacent Rows and Adjacent Columns in Table 3

Streptococcus Carrier Status	Tonsil Enlargement Level: + vs. ++	++ vs. +++
Noncarrier vs. carrier	0.29 (0.99)	0.55 (1.93)

NOTE: The standardized value of the observed association is given in parentheses.

[0.295 − 0.547 = −0.252], and the standardized value of this difference is −0.51.[7] This standardized value is rather close to zero, thus helping to explain why the uniform association model (14) fits the data so well.

In the preceding section, we used the observed log-odds in Table 7 to suggest why Model (13) fits the data in Table 2; in the present section we can use the observed log-odds-ratios in Table 9 to suggest why Model (14) fits the data in Table 3. In addition to the observed log-odds-ratios as presented in Table 9, it will often prove enlightening to calculate contrasts among them, and the corresponding standardized value of the contrasts. A similar remark can also be applied to the observed log-odds presented earlier in Table 7.

Table 10 gives the maximum-likelihood estimate $\hat{F}_{ij}$ of the expected frequencies obtained when Model (14) is applied to Table 3. (I shall describe how these entries are calculated later.) From the $\hat{F}_{ij}$ under Model (14), we find that the maximum-likelihood estimate of the log-odds-ratio parameter ϕ in (14) is $\hat{\phi} = 0.43$. Also, the $\hat{F}_{ij}$ under Model (14) can be expressed in terms of the estimate of ϕ in (14) and the corresponding observed frequency $f_{i.}$ at the ith level of variable A and the observed frequency $f_{.j}$ at the jth level of variable B. (For models that pertain to the association between variables A and B, the $\hat{F}_{i.}$ and $\hat{F}_{.j}$ are set equal to the corresponding observed frequencies $f_{i.}$ and $f_{.j}$, respectively.) The association between variables A and B, with

$$(\hat{F}_{11}\hat{F}_{22})/(\hat{F}_{12}\hat{F}_{21}) = (\hat{F}_{12}\hat{F}_{23})/(\hat{F}_{13}\hat{F}_{22}) > 1$$

[7]The log-odds-ratios in Table 9, and the difference between them, are examples of estimated two-factor interactions in the two-way contingency table. The general formula for the estimated standard deviation of an estimated interaction can be applied here; see, for example, Goodman (1970). The standardized value of the estimated interaction is the ratio of the estimated interaction and its estimated standard deviation.

TABLE 10
Maximum-Likelihood Estimate of Expected Frequencies Obtained When Model (14) Is Applied to Table 3

Streptococcus Carrier Status	Tonsil Enlargement Level 1	2	3	Total
1	498.0	558.0	270.0	1,326.0
2	18.0	31.0	23.0	72.0
Total	516.0	589.0	293.0	1,398.0

(see Table 10), is a direct consequence of the fact that the estimate of ϕ in (14) is greater than zero.

The uniform association model (14) provides a simple description of the association between variables A and B in Table 3. This model is useful in the analysis of the association in Table 3, and it can also shed light on the analysis of these data when variable B is viewed as a response variable with variable A a possible regressor and when variable A is viewed as a response variable with variable B a possible regressor. This topic is discussed more fully later. (See also Duncan 1979a; Goodman, 1979a, 1979b.)

As we noted earlier, with models for the analysis of the association between variables A and B, the univariate distributions of variable A and variable B are set equal to the corresponding observed distributions. On the other hand, these models can be modified in various ways to obtain models that do not set the corresponding univariate and observed distributions equal; and the modified models can help to explain the particular form of the association between variables A and B and the shape of the corresponding univariate distributions. An example of such a model is included in the next section.

SOME COMPARISONS

Analysis of Association vs. Analysis of the Joint Distribution

Each model for the analysis of the association between variables A and B can be rewritten in an equivalent form as a special kind of model for the analysis of the joint distribution between variables A and B. For example, the null association model (6) is equivalent to the model which states that variables A and B are statistically independent; that is,

$$F_{ij} = \alpha_i \beta_j \tag{15}$$

where α_i and β_j are parameters pertaining to the ith level of variable A and the jth level of variable B, respectively (with $\alpha_i \geq 0$, $\beta_j \geq 0$). Similarly, the uniform association model (14) is equivalent to the model which states that

$$F_{ij} = \alpha_i \beta_j \theta^{ij} \tag{16}$$

where θ is the odds-ratio parameter (with $\theta > 0$), and the superscripts i and j denote specified powers (see Goodman, 1979a, 1979b). Each model for the analysis of association can be defined as a model for the F_{ij} that includes parameters α_i and β_j pertaining to the ith row and jth column, respectively, in the cross-classification table.

We shall now consider some additional models for the analysis of association defined in these terms, and we shall apply these models to the data in Table 1. The results thus obtained will provide a comparison to the results obtained earlier in the analysis of the joint distribution for Table 1.

As we noted above, Model (15) is the usual model of statistical independence between variables A and B. With respect to Table 1, when the entries on the main diagonal are deleted, the independence model (15) can be modified to obtain the corresponding quasi-independence model:

$$F_{ij} = \alpha_i \beta_j \mu_{ij} \tag{17}$$

where μ_{ij} is a parameter pertaining to cell (i, j) in the cross-classification table, with $\mu_{ij} = 1$ when $i \neq j$. (More generally, when the entries in any given subset of the cells in the cross-classification table are deleted, the quasi-independence model can be defined by (17) with $\mu_{ij} = 1$ for all cells that are not deleted; see, for example, Goodman, 1968.) Earlier we noted that the usual independence model (15) can be expressed in terms of the log-odds-ratios using the formula for the equivalent model (6); similarly, the quasi-independence model (17) can also be expressed in terms of the log-odds-ratios, but the formula for the corresponding equivalent model is not quite so simple. (The formula for the equivalent model can be obtained by applying to (17) the general method used in Goodman, 1979b.)

Table 11 gives the chi-square values obtained when the usual independence model (15) is applied to Table 1 with no entries deleted, and when the quasi-independence model (17) is applied to the

TABLE 11
Chi-Square Values for Some Association Models Applied to Table 1

Model	DF	Goodness-of-Fit Chi Square	Likelihood-Ratio Chi Square
Independence model (15)	9	8,096.86	6,671.50
Quasi-independence model (17)	5	198.01	199.10
Symmetric association model (18)	3	7.26	7.27
Diagonals-parameter model (22)	1	0.22	0.22

cross-classification with the entries on the main diagonal deleted. From the chi-square values in Table 11 we see that, although there is a dramatic improvement in the fit when the independence model is replaced by the quasi-independence model, the latter model still does not fit the data in Table 1 in a satisfactory way. Additional improvement can be obtained with the other two models listed in Table 11; we shall discuss them now.

The symmetric association model in Table 11 can also be defined in terms of the F_{ij} or the corresponding log-odds-ratio Φ_{ij}. With respect to the F_{ij}, we obtain

$$F_{ij} = \alpha_i \beta_j \rho'_{ij} \qquad \text{for } i \neq j \tag{18}$$

where the parameters ρ'_{ij} satisfy the condition

$$\rho'_{ij} = \rho'_{ji} \tag{19}$$

With respect to the corresponding Φ_{ij}, we obtain

$$\Phi_{ij} = \rho^*_{ij} \qquad \text{for } i \neq j \tag{20}$$

where the parameters ρ^*_{ij} satisfy the condition

$$\rho^*_{ij} = \rho^*_{ji} \tag{21}$$

Model (20) states that the log-odds-ratios are symmetric, and the equivalent model (18) is the usual quasi-symmetry model (see, for example, Caussinus, 1965; Goodman, 1979a). The final model in Table 11 is the diagonals-parameter model introduced in Goodman (1972):

$$F_{ij} = \alpha_i \beta_j \delta'_k \qquad \text{for } i \neq j;\, k = i - j \tag{22}$$

This model too can be expressed in an equivalent form in terms of the log-odds-ratios, by applying the general method used in Goodman (1979b). Model (22) states that, aside from the diagonals parameter in the model and the entries on the main diagonal, there is quasi-independence between variables A and B in the cross-classification table.

For a 4×4 cross-classification table, the symmetric association model (18) is equivalent to a model obtained by imposing certain restrictions on the diagonals-parameter model (22). (This can be shown by applying the general method used in Goodman, 1972, to demonstrate such equivalence.) From the chi-square values for Models (18) and (22) in Table 11, we see that the latter model fits the data in Table 1 well, and it is a statistically significant improvement over the former model.

While the diagonals-parameter model (22) fits the data in Table 1 well, the chi-square values pertaining to this model are tested with 1 degree of freedom in the 4×4 cross-classification table (see Goodman, 1972). A more parsimonious model that also fits the data well would be preferable. I shall now present such a model.

All the models described so far in this section pertain to the association in the cross-classification table. (Each of these models can be expressed as a model for the F_{ij} that includes α_i and β_j pertaining to the ith row and jth column, respectively, in the cross-classification table.) We shall now modify the diagonals-parameter model (22) in a way that changes this model for the analysis of association into a model for the analysis of the joint distribution.

For the square $I \times I$ cross-classification table, let us consider the model obtained when the following restriction is imposed on Model (22):

$$\alpha_i = \beta_i = \rho_i \qquad \text{for } i = 1, 2, \ldots, I \tag{23}$$

This restriction states that α_i for the ith row and the corresponding β_i for the ith column are equal to a common unspecified value—say, ρ_i (with $\rho_i \geq 0$). Model (22) with restriction (23) imposed on it is equivalent to the following model:

$$F_{ij} = \rho_i \rho_j \delta'_k \qquad \text{for } i \neq j;\ k = i - j \tag{24}$$

Model (24) states that, aside from the diagonals parameter in the model and the entries on the main diagonal, there is quasi-independence between variables A and B in the cross-classification table, and each row parameter is equal to the corresponding column parameter. For a 4×4 cross-classification table, Model (24) is equivalent to the fitted asymmetry model (9) (see Goodman, 1979c). Thus when this model is fitted to the data in Table 1, the chi-square values reported in Table 4 for Model (9) are obtained. This model fits the data well, and it is more parsimonious than the diagonals-parameter model (22).

Model (22) pertains to the analysis of association, whereas Model (24) pertains to the analysis of the joint distribution. Model (22) sheds light on the association in Table 1, but not on the univariate distribution of variable A or the univariate distribution of variable B in the table. Model (24), however, sheds light upon the association in Table 1 and also upon the corresponding univariate distributions. Under Model (22) and under Model (24), the association in the table can be explained by the diagonals parameter in the model and the entries on the main diagonal. In addition, since α_i for the ith row and the corresponding β_i for the ith column are equal in Model (24), the difference between the corresponding univariate distributions under this model can be explained in terms of the diagonals parameter. With the $\hat{F}_{ij}$ under Model (24) and the corresponding estimates $\hat{F}_{i.}$ and $\hat{F}_{.j}$ pertaining to the univariate distributions (see Table 6), the fact that

$$\sum_{t=1}^{x} \hat{F}_{t.} > \sum_{t=1}^{x} \hat{F}_{.t} \qquad \text{for } x = 1, 2, 3$$

can be explained in terms of the diagonals parameter in the model.

Model (24) was obtained from Model (22) by the imposition of Condition (23). This imposition changes a model for the analysis of association into a model for the analysis of the joint distribution. Any model for the analysis of association can be changed into a model for the analysis of the joint distribution by imposing this kind of condition. I have used the change from Model (22) to Model (24) here as an example to illustrate this general method.

Let us consider for a moment the imposition of Condition (23) on, say, the independence model (15). The model thus obtained states that there is independence between variables A and B in the cross-classification table and that each row parameter is equal to the corresponding column parameter. In other words, this model states that there is both independence and symmetry in the cross-classification table. Thus, the model can be called the "independence and symmetry model" or the "null association and null asymmetry model." If Condition (23) is imposed instead upon, say, the quasi-independence model (17), we obtain the "quasi-independence and symmetry model" or the "null association and null asymmetry model" for the entries not on the main diagonal. With the introduction of the diagonals parameter into this model, we obtain Model (24), the "diagonals-parameter quasi-independence and symmetry model."

Instead of using Condition (23), other conditions can be imposed upon the α_i and β_j in a model for the analysis of association to change it into a model for the analysis of the joint distribution. I have also used Condition (23) as an example to illustrate the general method.

In closing this section, we note that the analysis of the association in Table 1 led us to the diagonals-parameter model (22), and by replacing this model for the analysis of association by a related model for the analysis of the joint distribution, we were led to the more parsimonious model (24). The corresponding analysis of the joint distribution in the earlier section led us directly to Model (9), the diagonals-parameter symmetry model in Goodman (1979c), which is equivalent to Model (24) for the 4 × 4 cross-classification table.

Analysis of Association vs. Analysis of Dependence

Each model for the analysis of the association between variables A and B can be rewritten in an equivalent form as a special kind of model for the analysis of the dependence of variable B on variable A, and in an equivalent form as a special kind of model for the analysis of the dependence of variable A on variable B. For example, the null association model (6) is equivalent to the model which states that the log-odds $\Psi_{ij}^{A\bar{B}}$ is independent of the level i on variable A; that is,

$$\Psi_{ij}^{A\bar{B}} = \psi_j^B \qquad \text{for } i = 1, 2, \ldots, I \tag{25}$$

where ψ_j^B is a parameter pertaining to the jth level of variable B. Similarly, the uniform association model (14) is equivalent to the model which states that

$$\Psi_{ij}^{A\bar{B}} = \psi_j^B - i\phi \tag{26}$$

where ϕ is the log-odds-ratio parameter (see Goodman, 1979b). Each model for the analysis of association can be defined as a model for $\Psi_{ij}^{A\bar{B}}$ that includes a parameter ψ_j^B pertaining to the jth column of the cross-classification table. Similarly, with respect to the log-odds $\Psi_{ji}^{B\bar{A}}$

defined as the natural logarithm of

$$\Omega_{ji}^{B\bar{A}} = F_{ij}/F_{i+1,j} \qquad \text{for } i = 1, 2, \ldots, I-1 \tag{27}$$

(compare Formula 27 witn Formula 3), each model for the analysis of association can be defined as a model for the $\Psi_{ji}^{B\bar{A}}$ that includes a parameter ψ_i^A pertaining to the ith row of the cross-classification table. We shall now see how the association model (14) applied to Table 3 can be interpreted when it is considered as a model for the dependence of variable B on variable A (see Model 26) and when it is considered as a model for the dependence of variable A on variable B.

Model (26) states that the log-odds $\Psi_{ij}^{A\bar{B}}$ is a linear function of the level i on variable A, and the slope of the linear function is equal to $-\phi$, which is the same for each value of j (for $j = 1, 2, \ldots, J-1$). When $J = 2$, this model states simply that $\Psi_{i1}^{A\bar{B}}$ is a linear function of the level i on variable A; when $J > 2$, the model states that the lines obtained for the log-odds, $\Psi_{i1}^{A\bar{B}}, \Psi_{i2}^{A\bar{B}}, \ldots, \Psi_{i,J-1}^{A\bar{B}}$, are parallel. Thus Model (26) can be called the "parallel log-odds model," with variable A having a linear effect on $\Psi_{ij}^{A\bar{B}}$. Since $\hat{\phi} = 0.43$ is the maximum-likelihood estimate of ϕ obtained in the earlier section on the analysis of the association in Table 3, the estimated slope is -0.43 in the linear relationship describing the dependence of $\Psi_{ij}^{A\bar{B}}$ on variable A, and also in the linear relationship describing the dependence of $\Psi_{ji}^{B\bar{A}}$ upon variable B. Thus, from the $\hat{F}_{ij}$ in Table 10, we find that the corresponding estimated log-odds satisfy the following relationships:

$$\hat{\Psi}_{2j}^{A\bar{B}} - \hat{\Psi}_{1j}^{A\bar{B}} = -0.43 \qquad \text{for } j = 1, 2$$

$$\hat{\Psi}_{21}^{B\bar{A}} - \hat{\Psi}_{11}^{B\bar{A}} = \hat{\Psi}_{31}^{B\bar{A}} - \hat{\Psi}_{21}^{B\bar{A}} = -0.43$$

Before closing this section, it may be worthwhile to note that the estimates presented by Andrich (1979) in his analysis of the data in Table 3 (where variable B, tonsil enlargement level, was viewed as a response variable and variable A, streptococcus carrier status, was a possible regressor variable) should have turned out to be equal to the corresponding estimates obtained here when the uniform association model (14) or the equivalent parallel log-odds model (26) is applied.[8]

[8]Andrich (1979) described his model in different terms from those used here to describe Model (14) or the equivalent model (26), but the estimated expected frequencies for the data in Table 3 under his model (and the estimate of the parameter corresponding to the slope) should have turned out to be equal to the corresponding estimates presented here (see Table 10).

However, this was not so. The estimates presented by Andrich (1979) for the data in Table 3 differ from the corresponding estimates presented here because his method for calculating maximum-likelihood estimates was somewhat inaccurate. His method did not provide estimates that satisfy the maximum-likelihood equations.

Analysis of Dependence vs. Analysis of the Joint Distribution

Each model for the analysis of dependence of variable B on variable A can be rewritten in an equivalent form as a special kind of model for the analysis of the joint distribution of variables A and B. For example, the null log-odds model (4) is equivalent to the model which states that the classes of variable B are conditionally equiprobable, given the level of variable A. In other words, this model states that

$$F_{ij} = \alpha_i \tag{28}$$

where α_i is a parameter pertaining to the ith level of variable A (with $\alpha_i \geq 0$). Similarly, if we consider, say, the simple log-odds model

$$\Psi_{ij}^{A\bar{B}} = \psi \tag{29}$$

then we find that this log-odds model is equivalent to the model which states that

$$F_{ij} = \alpha_i / \omega^j \tag{30}$$

where ω is a parameter pertaining to the odds defined by Formula (3) (with $\omega > 0$), and the superscript j denotes a specified power. (Formula 30 can be obtained by applying to Formula 29 the general method used in Goodman, 1979b.) Each model for the analysis of the dependence of variable B on variable A can be defined as a model for the F_{ij} that includes a parameter α_i pertaining to the ith row of the cross-classification table. We shall now see how the model obtained earlier in the analysis of dependence applied to Table 2 can be interpreted when it is considered as a model for the joint distribution of variables A and B in this table.

Let us first consider the following log-odds model:

$$\Psi_{ij}^{A\bar{B}} = \psi_i \tag{31}$$

Model (13) is a special case of Model (31) in which $\psi_2 = \psi_3 = 0$; Model (29) is a special case in which $\psi_1 = \psi_2 = \psi_3$. Model (31) states that the log-odds satisfy the following condition:

$$\psi_{i1}^{\overline{AB}} = \psi_{i2}^{\overline{AB}} = \cdots = \psi_{i,J-1}^{\overline{AB}} \tag{32}$$

Thus Model (31) can be called the "uniform log-odds model," and Model (29) is a special case of this model in which the effect of variable A on the log-odds is nil.

As was the case with Model (29), we find that Model (31) can be expressed in the following equivalent form:

$$F_{ij} = \alpha_i/\omega_i^j \tag{33}$$

where ψ_i is the natural logarithm of ω_i. With respect to the natural logarithm G_{ij} of the F_{ij}, Model (33) can be expressed as

$$G_{ij} = \alpha_i' - j\psi_i \tag{34}$$

where α_i' is the natural logarithm of α_i. Thus the uniform log-odds model (31) is equivalent to the model which states that G_{ij} is a linear function of the level j of variable B, and the slope is $-\psi_i$. Since $\hat{\psi}_1 =$ 1.18 is the maximum-likelihood estimate of the log-odds parameter ψ_1 obtained earlier in the analysis of dependence applied to Table 2 (with $\psi_2 = \psi_3 = 0$), the estimated slope is -1.18 in the linear relationship of G_{1j} on the level j of variable B (see Table 8).

Before closing this section, it might be worthwhile to note that models for the analysis of dependence of variable B on variable A are also models for the conditional distribution of variable B, given the level of variable A. For example, the null log-odds model (4) and the equivalent model (28) state that the classes of variable B are conditionally equiprobable, given the level of variable A; that is, the conditional distribution of variable B is the uniform distribution. Similarly, the uniform log-odds model (31) and the equivalent model (33) state that the conditional distribution of variable B (given the level of variable A) is the truncated geometric distribution. (When the parameter ω_i in Model (33) is greater than or equal to 1, the geometric distribution is defined with the classes of variable B numbered consecutively from $j = 1$ to $j = J$; and when $\omega_i < 1$, the distribution is defined with the classes numbered in reverse order.) Model (29) and the equivalent model (30) state that the conditional distribution of variable B (given the level of variable A) is the truncated geometric distribution, and that the parameter ω_i in this distribution does not depend upon the level i of variable A (that is, $\omega_i = \omega$, for $i = 1, 2, \ldots, I$).

RELATIONSHIPS AMONG MODELS FOR THE ANALYSIS OF ASSOCIATION, DEPENDENCE, AND THE JOINT DISTRIBUTION

We noted earlier that each model for the analysis of the association between variables A and B can be rewritten in an equivalent form as a special kind of model for the analysis of the dependence of variable B on variable A (that is, a model for $\Psi_{ij}^{A\bar{B}}$ that includes the parameter ψ_j^B) and as a special kind of model for the analysis of the dependence of variable A on variable B (that is, a model for $\psi_{ji}^{B\bar{A}}$ that includes the parameter ψ_i^A). Thus these special kinds of models for the analysis of dependence (such as Models 25 and 26) are equivalent to models for the analysis of association. On the other hand, models for the analysis of dependence that are not of this special kind (such as Models 4, 13, 29, 31) are not equivalent to models for the analysis of association.

We also noted earlier that each model for the analysis of the association between variables A and B can be rewritten in an equivalent form as a special kind of model for the analysis of the joint distribution of variables A and B (a model for the F_{ij} that includes the parameters α_i and β_j). Thus, models of this special kind (such as Models 15, 16, 17, 18, 22) are equivalent to models for the analysis of association. On the other hand, models for the analysis of the joint distribution that are not of this special kind (such as Models 1, 2, 7, 9, 24, 28, 30, 33) are not equivalent to models for the analysis of association.

We also noted earlier that each model for the analysis of the dependence of variable B on variable A can be rewritten in an equivalent form as a special kind of model for the analysis of the joint distribution (a model for the F_{ij} that includes the parameter α_i), and each model for the analysis of the dependence of variable A on variable B can be rewritten in an equivalent form as a special kind of model for the analysis of the joint distribution (a model for the F_{ij} that includes the parameter β_j). Thus these special kinds of models for the analysis of the joint distribution (such as Models 15, 16, 17, 18, 22, 28, 30, 33) are equivalent to models for the analysis of dependence. On the other hand, models for the analysis of the joint distribution not of this special kind (for example, Models 1, 2, 7, 9, 24) are not equivalent to models for the analysis of dependence.

The relationships among the models described above are

TABLE 12
Relationships Among Association Models (A Models), Dependence Models (D Models), and Joint Distribution Models (JD Models)

Model	Association Model (A, D, and JD)	Dependence Model (D and JD)	Joint Distribution Model (JD)
Log-odds-ratio	[6,14,20]		
Log-odds	[25,26]	[4,13,29,31]	
Expected frequency	[15,16,17,18,22]	[28,30,33]	[1,2,7,9,24]

summarized in Table 12 and Figure 1. For additional comparisons among these models, see also Table 13.

AN OVERVIEW OF THE MODELS

With respect to the two-way $I \times J$ contingency table, there are four elementary log linear models obtained in the situation where the order of the rows and the order of the columns are not taken into account (see, for example, Goodman, 1970):

1. The usual model H' of statistical independence between variables A and B

Figure 1. Relationships among association models (A models), dependence models (D models), and joint distribution models (JD models).

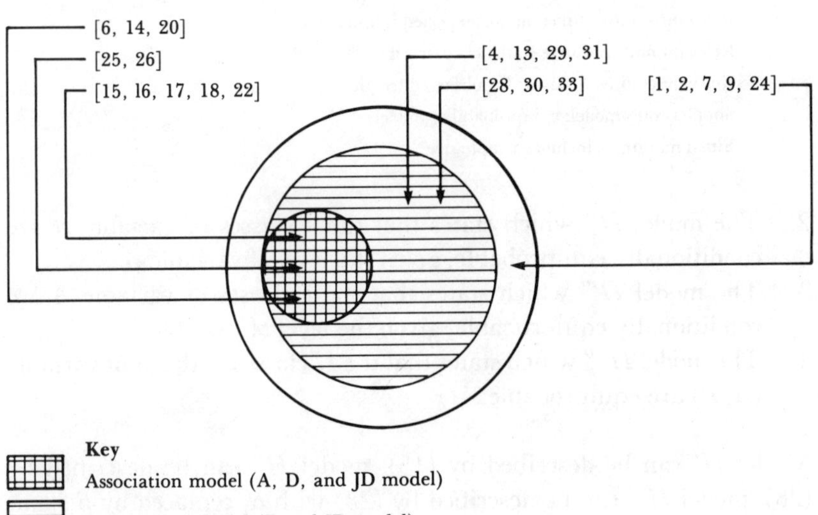

TABLE 13
Models Pertaining to Two-Way Cross-Classification Table

Association models	
Relevant multiplicative function: odds-ratio	Θ_{ij}
Relevant additive function: log-odds-ratio	Φ_{ij}
Relevant multiplicative statistic: observed odds-ratio	θ_{ij}
Relevant additive statistic: observed log-odds-ratio	ϕ_{ij}
Simplest null model: independence model	$\Phi_{ij} = 0$
Fitted marginals include: $\{A\}$, $\{B\}$	
Dependence models for variable B given A	
Relevant multiplicative function: odds	$\Omega^{A\bar{B}}_{i\,j}$
Relevant additive function: log-odds	$\Psi^{A\bar{B}}_{i\,j}$
Relevant multiplicative statistic: observed odds	$\omega^{A\bar{B}}_{i\,j}$
Relevant additive statistic: observed log-odds	$\psi^{A\bar{B}}_{i\,j}$
Simplest null model: conditional equiprobability	$\Psi^{A\bar{B}}_{i\,j} = 0$
Fitted marginals include: $\{A\}$	
Dependence models for variable A given B	
Relevant multiplicative function: odds	$\Omega^{B\bar{A}}_{j\,i}$
Relevant additive function: log-odds	$\Psi^{B\bar{A}}_{j\,i}$
Relevant multiplicative statistic: observed odds	$\omega^{B\bar{A}}_{j\,i}$
Relevant additive statistic: observed log-odds	$\psi^{B\bar{A}}_{j\,i}$
Simplest null model: conditional equiprobability	$\Psi^{B\bar{A}}_{j\,i} = 0$
Fitted marginals include: $\{B\}$	
Joint distribution models	
Relevant multiplicative function: expected frequencies	F_{ij}
Relevant additive function: log expected frequencies	G_{ij}
Relevant multiplicative statistic: observed frequencies	f_{ij}
Relevant additive statistic: log observed frequencies	g_{ij}
Simplest null model: equiprobability model	$F_{ij} = N/(IJ)$
Fitted marginals include: sample size	N

2. The model H'' which states that the J classes of variable B are conditionally equiprobable, given the level of variable A
3. The model H''' which states that the I classes of variable A are conditionally equiprobable, given the level of variable B
4. The model H'''' which states that the IJ classes of the joint variable (A, B) are equiprobable.

Model H' can be described by (15); model H'' can be described by (28); model H''' can be described by (28) with α_i replaced by β_j; and model H'''' can be described by (1).

Model H' can be used in the analyses of association (see Model 6), dependence (see, for example, Model 25), and the joint distribution (see Model 15). Models H'' and H''' can be used in the analyses of dependence (see, for example, Model 4) and the joint distribution (see, for example, Model 28), but not in the analysis of association. Model H'''' can be used in the analysis of the joint distribution (see Model 1), but not in the analyses of association or dependence.

With model H', the marginal for variable A and the marginal for variable B are fitted. With model H'', the marginal for variable A is fitted; with model H''', the marginal for variable B is fitted (see, for example, Goodman, 1970).

Each model for the analysis of the joint distribution that takes into account the order of the rows and/or the order of the columns in the cross-classification table can be formed from the null model H'''' by introducing parameters that take this order into account (see, for example, Models 7, 9, 16, 18, 22, 24, 30, 33). Each model for the analysis of dependence that takes into account the order of the rows and/or columns can be formed from the corresponding null models H'' and H''' by introducing parameters that take this order into account (see, for example, Models 16, 18, 22, 30, 33). Each model for the analysis of association that takes into account the order of the rows and/or columns can be formed from the corresponding null model H' by introducing parameters that take this order into account (see, for example, Models 16, 18, 22).

The class of models for the analysis of association is included in the class of models for the analysis of dependence, which is in turn included in the class of models for the analysis of the joint distribution (see Figure 1). Each model for the analysis of association can be expressed as a special kind of model for the analysis of dependence, and each model for the analysis of dependence can be expressed as a special kind of model for the analysis of the joint distribution. With each model for the analysis of association, the marginals for both variable A and variable B are fitted (see, for example, Goodman 1970, 1979a). With each model for the dependence of variable B on variable A, the marginal for variable A is fitted; with each model for the dependence of variable A on variable B, the marginal for variable B is fitted (see, for example, Goodman 1970, 1979b). On the other hand, there are models for the analysis of the joint distribution that fit neither the marginal for variable A nor that for variable B; there are models for the analysis of the dependence of variable B on A that do not fit the marginal for variable B (although they do fit the marginal for variable A); and there are models for the analysis of the dependence of variable A on variable B that do not fit the marginal for variable A (although they do fit the marginal for variable B).

THE ESTIMATION OF THE PARAMETERS IN THE MODELS

Let us first consider, say, Model (14) for the analysis of association. As we noted earlier, this model is equivalent to Model (16), which is a multiplicative model for the F_{ij}. Model (14) is an example of a more general class of association models that are equivalent to multiplicative models for the F_{ij} (see, for example, Goodman 1979a). The maximum-likelihood estimates of the parameters in the association models, and the corresponding estimates of the F_{ij}, can be obtained by the method presented in Goodman (1979a).

Each of the models considered here for either the analysis of association, the analysis of dependence, or the analysis of the joint distribution is equivalent to a multiplicative model for the F_{ij} and thus to a corresponding additive model for the natural logarithm G_{ij} of the F_{ij}. These are log linear models. The maximum-likelihood estimates of the parameters in these models and the corresponding estimates of the F_{ij} can be obtained by a direct extension of the method presented in Goodman (1979a) or by using general computer programs for log linear models (see, for example, Haberman, 1974a, 1979; Bock, 1975; Nelder, 1975).

For each of the models considered here, the maximum-likelihood estimates can be obtained by the methods described above. However, for some of these models, more elementary methods can be used instead. The methods presented here for the models used in the analysis of the joint distribution for Table 1 serve as an example of this; the methods used with the various null models considered here also serve as an example.

THE MERITS OF PARSIMONIOUS MODELS

Various methods for obtaining parsimonious models that fit the data have been presented here. I shall now comment on some of the advantages of using such models.

Let us first consider, say, the analysis of association. With the models and methods presented here, we obtain asymptotically more powerful methods for testing various hypotheses about the association in the $I \times J$ cross-classification table. For example, with respect to the usual null hypothesis of statistical independence between variables A and B in the $I \times J$ table, if the uniform association model (14) holds true, then instead of using the usual chi-square statistic (with $(I - 1)(J - 1)$ degrees of freedom) to test the null hypothesis, we obtain an asymptotically more powerful test of this hypothesis by using the chi-square statistic (with 1 degree of freedom) pertaining to the hypothesis that the association parameter ϕ in Model (14) is equal to zero. Thus, with respect to the analysis of association presented in Table 4 for the 2×3 cross-classification (Table 3), we see from Table 4 that 7.32 is the numerical value of the likelihood-ratio chi-square (with 2 degrees of freedom) that is obtained in testing the usual null hypothesis of statistical independence in the usual way; but an asymptotically more powerful test of this null hypothesis can be obtained, when the uniform association model (14) holds true, by using the difference between the corresponding chi-squared values—that is, $7.32 - 0.24 = 7.08$, with 1 degree of freedom. This difference provides us with a test of the hypothesis that ϕ in Model (14) is equal to zero (see Goodman, 1979a).

More generally, let us now consider models M and M', where M is more parsimonious than M' (that is, where M can be described in terms of fewer parameters than M'), and M is a special case of M'. (For example, let M be Model 14, and let M' be the usual saturated log linear model for the cross-classification table.) Let H denote a hypothesis within model M' and the equivalent hypothesis within model M. (For example, let H be the usual hypothesis of statistical independence between variables A and B in the saturated log linear model; the equivalent hypothesis within Model 14 is the hypothesis that $\phi = 0$.) The chi-square test of H within the more parsimonious model M will be asymptotically more powerful than the corresponding test of this hypothesis within model M', if model M holds true.

There are also other advantages in using the more parsimonious model M rather than M'. For example, the asymptotic variance of the maximum-likelihood estimates of the parameters in the model M will be less than (or equal to) the asymptotic variance of the corresponding estimates of the same parameters in model M', if model M holds true. (This follows directly from the fact that the maximum-likelihood estimates are fully efficient.) In addition, with respect to the hypothesis that a specified parameter in model M is equal to some specified value (say, zero), the chi-square test of this hypothesis within model M is asymptotically more powerful than the corresponding test of the same hypothesis within model M', if model M is true. (The chi-square tests in the present context are asymptotically equivalent to the usual F tests of linear hypotheses, with an infinite number of degrees of freedom in the denominator; and the usual F tests are uniformly most powerful invariant tests—see Haberman, 1974b, Lehmann, 1959.)

For models M and M' described above, it is preferable to use the more parsimonious model M rather than M' if both models are true. However, it should be noted that if both models are congruent with the observed data, this does not necessarily mean that both models hold true.[9] If more data were obtained, we might find that model M no longer fit the data whereas model M' may continue to fit. With more data, the estimates of the additional parameters in M' (that is, those in M' but not in M) may turn out to be significantly different from zero, and the model that did not include these parameters may no longer suffice. The choice of the more parsimonious model for a given set of data does not imply that the less parsimonious model is dismissed entirely as a possible model for the data (see, for example, Goodman, 1979d).

EXTENSIONS TO MULTIWAY CROSS-CLASSIFICATION TABLES

The models and methods presented here for the two-way table can be extended to the m-way table (for $m = 3, 4, \ldots$), and we can obtain more powerful methods for testing various hypotheses about the m-way table. We shall consider first the $I \times J \times K$ three-way table, in the case where the I levels of variable A, the J levels of variable B, and the K levels of variable C are ordered.

Let f_{ijk} denote the observed frequency in cell (i, j, k) of the three-way table ($i = 1, 2, \ldots, I$; $j = 1, 2, \ldots, J$; $k = 1, 2, \ldots, K$),

[9]Even if both models are congruent with the observed data, and the fit of model M is not significantly worse than the fit of model M', this does not necessarily mean that both models are true.

and let F_{ijk} denote the corresponding expected frequency under some model. Let us now consider models for the analysis of the three-factor interaction in the three-way table.

For adjacent classes of variable A (say, classes i and $i + 1$), variable B (say, classes j and $j + 1$), and variable C (say, classes k and $k + 1$), we define as follows the odds-ratio-ratio Θ_{ijk} based on the expected frequencies:

$$\Theta_{ijk} = \left(\frac{F_{ijk}F_{i+1,j+1,k}}{F_{i,j+1,k}F_{i+1,j,k}}\right) \bigg/ \left(\frac{F_{i,j,k+1}F_{i+1,j+1,k+1}}{F_{i+1,j,k+1}F_{i,j+1,k+1}}\right) \qquad (35)$$

(Compare Formula 35 with Formula 5.) Let Φ_{ijk} denote the natural logarithm of Θ_{ijk} (i.e., the log-odds-ratio ratio). In the present context, the most elementary null model is the following:

$$\Phi_{ijk} = 0 \qquad \text{for } i = 1, 2, \ldots, I - 1;\ j = 1, 2, \ldots, J - 1;\ k = 1, 2, \ldots, K - 1 \qquad (36)$$

(Compare Model 36 with Model 6.) Model (36) is equivalent to the model which states that the three-factor interaction in the three-way table is zero (see, for example, Goodman, 1970).

The uniform three-factor interaction model can be defined as follows:

$$\Phi_{ijk} = \phi \qquad (37)$$

where the parameter ϕ is estimated from the data. (Compare Model 37 with Model 14.) Model (37) introduces a single parameter into the null model (36).

Each model for the analysis of the three-factor interaction between variables A, B, and C can be rewritten in an equivalent form as a special kind of model for the analysis of the joint distribution between variables A, B, and C. For example, the null model (36) is equivalent to

$$F_{ijk} = \alpha_{ik}\beta_{jk}\gamma_{ij} \qquad (38)$$

where α_{ik}, β_{jk}, and γ_{ij} are parameters pertaining to the (i, k) level of the joint variable (A, C), and the (j, k) level of the joint variable (B, C), and the (i, j) level of the joint variable (A, B), respectively (with $\alpha_{ik} \geq 0$, $\beta_{jk} \geq 0$, $\gamma_{ij} \geq 0$). (Compare Model 38 with Model 15.) Similarly, the uniform three-factor interaction model (37) is equivalent to

$$F_{ijk} = \alpha_{ik}\beta_{jk}\gamma_{ij}\theta^{ijk} \tag{39}$$

where θ is the odds-ratio-ratio parameter (with $\theta > 0$), and the superscripts i, j, and k denote specified powers. (Compare Model 39 with Model 16.) Each model for the analysis of the three-factor interaction can be defined as a model for the F_{ijk} that includes parameters α_{ik}, β_{jk}, and γ_{ij} pertaining to the cells (i, k), (j, k), and (i, j) in the two-way marginal tables for the joint variables (A, C), (B, C), and (A, B), respectively, in the three-way cross-classification table.

The null three-factor interaction model (36) can be tested in the usual way by applying Model (38) to the three-way table (see, for example, Goodman, 1970), and the uniform three-factor interaction model (37) can be tested by applying Model (39) to the three-way table, using a generalized form of the method used earlier to test the uniform association model (16) in the two-way table (see Goodman, 1979a).

Consider now the usual null hypothesis that the three-factor interaction in the three-way table is zero. Instead of using the usual chi-square statistic to test this null hypothesis (with $(I - 1)$ $(J - 1)$ $(K - 1)$ degrees of freedom), we can obtain an asymptotically more powerful test of this hypothesis, if the uniform three-factor interaction model (37) holds true. In this case, the null hypothesis can be tested by using the chi-square statistic (with 1 degree of freedom) pertaining to the hypothesis that the three-factor interaction parameter ϕ in Model (37) is equal to zero. To test the latter hypothesis, the appropriate chi-squared statistic (with 1 degree of freedom) is equal to the difference between the corresponding chi-squared statistic for testing the usual hypothesis of zero three-factor interaction and the statistic for testing the uniform three-factor interaction model.

Model (14) is an example of a general class of models pertaining to the association in the two-way table; similarly, Model (37) is an example of a general class of models pertaining to the three-factor interaction in the three-way table (see Goodman, 1979a). Each of the models in this class is equivalent to one formed from the null model (38) by introducing parameters that take into account the order of the rows, and/or the order of the columns, and/or the order of the layers in the three-way table (see, for example, Model 39).

In the overview presented earlier of the models for the two-way table, we noted that each of these models could be viewed as a modification of one of the four elementary log linear models obtained when the order of the rows and the order of the columns are not taken into account. Similarly, each of the corresponding models for the three-way table can be viewed as a modification of one of the 18 log linear models obtained when the order of the rows, the order of the columns, and the order of the layers are not taken into account (see Goodman, 1970, Table 3). The 18 log linear models pertain to the analysis of:

1. The three-factor interaction between variables A, B, and C
2. The conditional association between variables B and C given the level of variable A (there are three models of this general kind obtained by permuting the letters, A, B and C)
3. The association between variable C and the joint variable (A, B) are three models of this general kind)
4. The dependence of variable C upon the joint variable (A, B) (there are three models of this general kind
5. The two-factor interaction (and three-factor interaction) in the three-way table
6. The dependence of variable C upon the joint variable (A, B), and the association between variables A and B (there are three models of this general kind)
7. The dependence of the joint variable (B, C) upon variable A (there are three models of this general kind)
8. The joint trivariate distribution of variables A, B, and C.

Each of these models can be modified by introducing parameters that take into account the order of the rows, and/or the order of the columns, and/or the order of the layers in the three-way table.

The discussion presented earlier in this section pertained to topic 1 in the preceding list. We shall now briefly discuss topic 2. For expository purposes, let us consider the conditional association between variables A and B, given the level of variable C (permuting the letters A, B, and C in the statement of topic 2).

For adjacent classes of variable A (say, classes i and $i + 1$) and variable B (say, classes j and $j + 1$), at level k of variable C, we now define the conditional odds-ratio $\Theta_{ij:k}$ based on the expected frequencies:

$$\Theta_{ij:k} = (F_{ijk}F_{i+1,j+1,k})/(F_{i,j+1,k}F_{i+1,j,k})$$
$$\text{for } i = 1, 2, \ldots, I-1; j = 1, 2, \ldots, J-1 \quad (40)$$

(Compare Formula 40 with Formula 5.) Let $\Phi_{ij:k}$ denote the natural logarithm of $\Theta_{ij:k}$ (that is, the conditional log-odds-ratio). In the present context, the most elementary null model is the following:

$$\Phi_{ij:k} = 0 \qquad \text{for } i = 1, 2, \ldots, I-1; \; j = 1, 2, \ldots, J-1; \; k = 1, 2, \ldots, K \quad (41)$$

(Compare Model 41 with Model 6.) Model (41) is equivalent to the model which states that variables A and B are conditionally independent, given the level of variable C (see, for example, Goodman, 1970).

The model which states that the conditional association between variables A and B is uniform (given the level of variable C) can be defined as follows:

$$\Phi_{ij:k} = \phi_k \quad (42)$$

where the parameter ϕ_k is estimated from the data. (Compare Model 42 with Model 14.) Model (42) introduces into the null model (41) a single parameter ϕ_k at level k of variable C, for $k = 1, 2, \ldots, K$.

Each model for the analysis of the conditional association between variables A and B (given the level of variable C) can be rewritten in an equivalent form as a special kind of model for the analysis of the joint distribution between variables A, B, and C. For example, the null model (41) is equivalent to

$$F_{ijk} = \alpha_{ik}\beta_{jk} \quad (43)$$

where α_{ik} and β_{ik} are parameters pertaining to the (i, k) level of the joint variable (A, C) and to the (j, k) level of the joint variable (B, C), respectively (with $\alpha_{ik} \geq 0$, $\beta_{jk} \geq 0$). (Compare Model 43 with Model 15.) Similarly, the uniform conditional association model (42) is equivalent to

$$F_{ijk} = \alpha_{ik}\beta_{jk}\theta_k^{ij} \quad (44)$$

where θ_k is the conditional odds-ratio parameter (with $\theta_k > 0$), and the superscripts i and j denote specified powers. (Compare Model 44 with Model 16.) Each model for the analysis of the conditional association between variables A and B, given the level of variable C, can be defined as a model for the F_{ijk} that includes α_{ik} and β_{jk} pertaining to the (i, k)

and (j, k) levels in the two-way marginal tables for the joint variables (A, C) and (B, C), respectively, in the three-way cross-classification table.

The null conditional association model (41) can be tested in the usual way by applying Model (43) to the three-way table (see, for example, Goodman, 1970). Similarly, the uniform conditional association model (42) can be tested by applying Model (44) to the three-way table. To apply Model (44), we simply fit the uniform association model at level k of variable C, for $k = 1, 2, \ldots, K$ (see Goodman, 1979a).

Consider now the usual null hypothesis that variables A and B are conditionally independent, given the level of variable C. Instead of using the usual chi-square statistic to test this null hypothesis (with $(I - 1)(J - 1)K$ degrees of freedom), we can obtain an asymptotically more powerful test if the conditional uniform association model (42) holds true. In this case, the null hypothesis can be tested by using the chi-square statistic (with K degrees of freedom) pertaining to the hypothesis that the conditional association parameter ϕ_k in Model (42) is equal to zero (for $k = 1, 2, \ldots, K$). The method described in the preceding section, for obtaining an asymptotically more powerful test (with 1 degree of freedom) of the null hypothesis that variables A and B are statistically independent, can be applied directly at level k of variable C (for $k = 1, 2, \ldots, K$) to obtain the asymptotically more powerful test (with K degrees of freedom) of the null hypothesis that variables A and B are conditionally independent, given the level of variable C.

Consider now the situation where ϕ_k in Model (42) satisfies the following condition:

$$\phi_k = \phi \qquad \text{for } k = 1, 2, \ldots, K \tag{45}$$

where ϕ is unspecified. In this case, the uniform conditional association models (42) and (44) are replaced by

$$\Phi_{ij:k} = \phi \tag{46}$$

and

$$F_{ijk} = \alpha_{ik}\beta_{jk}\theta^{ij} \tag{47}$$

respectively. These models state that the conditional association between variables A and B (given the level of variable C) is uniform and that the three-factor interaction between variables A, B, and C is zero. In this case, the ϕ in Model (46) pertains to the partial association between variables A and B, given the level of variable C (see, for example, Goodman, 1969, 1970; Clogg, 1980). Models (46) and (47) state that the partial association between variables A and B (given variable C) is uniform.

When Model (42) holds true, we can test the usual null hypothesis of zero three-factor interaction by determining whether Condition (45) is satisfied (with $K - 1$ degrees of freedom). This test can be based on the difference between the corresponding chi-square statistics obtained when Models (47) and (44) are applied. Similarly, when Model (47) holds true, we can test the usual null hypothesis of zero partial association between variables A and B (given the level of variable C) by testing (with 1 degree of freedom) whether ϕ in Model (46) is equal to zero. This test can be based on the difference between the corresponding chi-square statistics obtained when Models (43) and (47) are applied. The tests described here for the hypotheses of zero three-factor interaction and zero partial association are asymptotically more powerful than the usual tests.

The parameter ϕ in Model (46) and the corresponding θ in (47) pertain to the partial association between variables A and B, given variable C. Comparing (47) with (38) we see that the model for uniform partial association between variables A and B (given variable C) replaces the two-factor parameter γ_{ij} pertaining to variables A and B in (38) by θ^{ij} in (47), where the superscripts i and j denote specified powers. Similarly, the model for uniform partial association between variables A and B (given variable C), uniform partial association between variables A and C (given variable B), and uniform partial association between variables B and C (given variable A) can be expressed as

$$F_{ijk} = \alpha_i \beta_j \gamma_k \theta_{AB}^{ij} \theta_{AC}^{ik} \theta_{BC}^{jk} \tag{48}$$

where the superscripts i, j, and k denote specified powers. The parameters θ_{AB}, θ_{AC}, and θ_{BC} in (48) pertain to the partial association between variables A and B (given variable C), between variables A and C (given variable B), and between variables B and C (given variable A), respectively. Model (48) is more parsimonious than Model (47), which is in turn more parsimonious than the usual Model (38) for zero three-factor interaction.

When the three-factor interaction is zero, we can consider the more parsimonious models obtained by replacing one or more of the two-factor parameters in (38) by appropriate terms for the situations where the corresponding partial associations are uniform (as in, for example, Model 47 or 48). Models (47) and (48) are examples of a general class of models pertaining to partial association in the three-way table. In this general class, parameters pertaining to uniform partial association (for example, ϕ in Model 46) can be replaced by more general parameters that can take into account the possible effects of rows, columns, and/or layers on the partial association (see, for example, Clogg, 1980). Similarly, with respect to the general class of models pertaining to conditional association between variables A and B (given variable C), parameters pertaining to uniform conditional association (for example, ϕ_k in Model 42) can be replaced by more general parameters that can take into account the possible effects of rows and/or columns on the conditional association (at level k of variable C).

The methods described in this section for the analysis of the three-factor interaction and the conditional association (and the related partial association) can be developed further (see, for example, Clogg, 1980), and they can be extended in a straightforward way to the analysis of the other relationships listed earlier in the section as topics 3 to 8 in the analysis of the three-way table. These methods for the analysis of the three-way table can be explicated in more detail as we did earlier with respect to the two-way table. The various results presented for the analysis of the two-way and three-way tables can also be extended in a straightforward way to the m-way table.

REFERENCES

AGRESTI, A.

1980 "Generalized odds ratios for ordinal data." *Biometrics* 36:59–67.

ANDRICH, D.

1979 "A model for contingency tables having an ordered response classification." *Biometrics* 35:405–415.

ANSCOMBE, F. J.

1981 *Computing in Statistical Science Through APL.* New York: Springer-Verlag.

ARMITAGE, P.

1955 Tests for linear trends in proportions and frequencies." *Biometrics* 11:375–386.

1971 *Statistical Methods in Medical Research.* Oxford: Blackwell.

BHAPKAR, V. P.

1966 "A note on the equivalence of two test criteria for hypotheses in categorical data." *Journal of American Statistical Association* 61:288–235.

1979 "On tests of marginal symmetry and quasi-symmetry in two and three-dimensional contingency tables." *Biometrics* 35:417–426.

BISHOP, Y., FIENBERG, S. E., AND HOLLAND, P. W.

1975 *Discrete Multivariate Analysis: Theory and Practice.* Cambridge, Mass: M.I.T. Press.

BOCK, D. R.

1975 *Multivariate Statistical Methods in Behavioral Research.* New York: McGraw-Hill.

CAUSSINUS, H.

1965 "Contribution à l'analyse statistique des tableaux de corrélation." *Annales de la Faculté des Sciences de l'Université de Toulouse* 29:77–182.

CLAYTON, D. C.

1974 "Some odds-ratio statistics for the analysis of ordered categorical data." *Biometrika* 61:525–531.

CLOGG, C. C.

1980 "Some models for the analysis of association in multiway cross-classifications having ordered categories." Unpublished manuscript.

COX, D. R.

1970 *The Analysis of Binary Data.* London: Methuen.

DUNCAN, O. D.

1979a "How destination depends on origin in the occupational mobility table." *American Journal of Sociology* 84:793–803.

1979b "Constrained parameters in a model for categorical data." *Sociological Methods and Research* 8:57–68.

DUNCAN, O. D., AND MCRAE, J. A., JR.

1978 "Multiway contingency analysis with a scaled response or factor." In K. F. Schuessler (Ed.), *Sociological Methodology 1979.* San Francisco: Jossey-Bass.

FIENBERG, S. E.

1977 *The Analysis of Cross-Classified Categorical Data.* Cambridge, Mass: M.I.T. Press.

GART, J. J., AND ZWEIFEL, J. R.

1967 "On the bias of various estimators of the logit and its variance." *Biometrika* 54:181–187.

GOKHALE, D. V., AND KULLBACK, S.
1978 *The Information in Contingency Tables.* New York: Marcel Dekker.

GOODMAN, L. A.
1968 "The analysis of cross-classified data: Independence, quasi-independence, and interactions in contingency tables with or without missing entries." *Journal of American Statistical Association* 69:1091–1131.

1969 "On partitioning χ^2 and detecting partial association in three-way contingency tables." *Journal of Royal Statistical Society,* series B, 31:486–498.

1970 "The multivariate analysis of qualitative data: Interactions among multiple classifications." *Journal of American Statistical Association* 65:226–256.

1972 "Some multiplicative models for the analysis of cross-classified data." In L. Le Cam and others (Eds.), *Proceedings of Sixth Berkeley Symposium on Mathematical Statistics and Probability.* Berkeley: University of California Press.

1975 "A new model for scaling response patterns: An application of the quasi-independence concept." *Journal of American Statistical Association* 70:755–768.

1978 *Analyzing Qualitative/Categorical Data: Log-Linear Models and Latent-Structure Analysis.* Cambridge, Mass.: Abt Books.

1979a "Simple models for the analysis of association in cross-classifications having ordered categories." *Journal of American Statistical Association* 74:537–552.

1979b "Multiplicative models for the analysis of occupational mobility tables and other kinds of cross-classification tables." *American Journal of Sociology* 84:804–819.

1979c "Multiplicative models for square contingency tables with ordered categories." *Biometrika* 66:413–418.

1979d "The analysis of qualitative variables using more parsimonious quasi-independence models, scaling models, and latent structures." In R. M. Merton, J. S. Coleman, and P. H. Rossi (Eds.), *Qualitative and Quantitative Social Research: Papers in Honor of Paul F. Lazarsfeld.* New York: Free Press.

1979e "Simple log-odds models for the analysis of dependence in cross-classifications having ordered categories." Unpublished manuscript.

1980a "Association models and the bivariate normal distribution in the analysis of cross-classifications having ordered categories." *Biometrika* 67: in press.

1980b "Association models and canonical correlation in the analysis of cross-classifications having ordered categories." *Journal of American Statistical Association* 75: in press.

GOODMAN, L. A., AND KRUSKAL, W. H.
1963 "Measures of association for cross-classifications. III: Approximate sampling theory." *Journal of American Statistical Association* 58:310–364.

GRIZZLE, J. E., STARMER, C. F., AND KOCH, G. G.
1969 "Analysis of categorical data by linear models." *Biometrics* 25:137–156.

HABERMAN, S. J.
1974a "Log-linear models for frequency tables with ordered classifications." *Biometrics* 30:589–600.
1974b *The Analysis of Frequency Data.* Chicago: University of Chicago Press.
1979 *Analysis of Qualitative Data.* Vol. 2: *New Developments.* New York: Academic Press.

HOLMES, M. C., AND WILLIAMS, R. E. O.
1954 "The distribution of carriers of streptococcus pyogenes among 2,413 healthy children." *Journal of Hygiene* (Cambridge) 52:165–179.

IRELAND, C. T., KU, H. H., AND KULLBACK, S.
1969 "Symmetry and marginal homogeneity of an $r \times r$ contingency table." *Journal of American Statistical Association* 64:1323–1341.

KENDALL, M. G., AND STUART, A.
1961 *The Advanced Theory of Statistics.* Vol. 2: *Inference and Relationships.* London: Griffin.

KOCH, G. G., AND REINFURT, D. W.
1971 "The analysis of categorical data from mixed models." *Biometrics* 27:157–173.

LEHMANN, E. L.
1959 *Testing Statistical Hypotheses.* New York: Wiley.

MANTEL, M., AND BYAR, D. P.
1978 "Marginal homogeneity, symmetry, and independence." *Communications in Statistics: Theory and Methods* A7(10):953–976.

MCCULLAGH, P.
1978 "A class of parametric models for the analysis of square contingency tables with ordered categories." *Biometrika* 65:413–418.
1980 "Regression models for ordinal data." *Journal of Royal Statistical Society,* series B, 42:109–142.

NELDER, J.
1975 *General Linear Interactive Modelling.* Release 2. Oxford: NAG.

PLACKETT, R. L.

1974 *The Analysis of Categorical Data.* London: Griffin.

PLACKETT, R. L., AND PAUL, S. R.

1978 "Dirichlet models for square contingency tables." *Communications in Statistics: Theory and Methods* A7(10):939–952.

STUART, A.

1953 "The estimation and comparison of strengths of association in contingency tables." *Biometrika* 40:105–110.

1955 "A test of homogeneity of the marginal distributions in a two-way classification." *Biometrika* 42:412–416.

TUKEY, J. W.

1977 *Exploratory Data Analysis.* Reading, Mass.: Addison-Wesley.

WEDDERBURN, R. W. M.

1974 "Generalized linear models specified in terms of constraints." *Journal of Royal Statistical Society,* series B, 36:449–454.

WING, J. K.

1962 "Institutionalism in mental hospitals." *British Journal of Social and Clinical Psychology* 1:38–51.

6

A COMPARISON OF ALTERNATIVE MODELS FOR ANALYZING THE SCALABILITY OF RESPONSE PATTERNS

Clifford C. Clogg
Darwin O. Sawyer
PENNSYLVANIA STATE UNIVERSITY

A previous version of this chapter was presented at the 1979 annual meeting of the American Sociological Association. The first author was supported in part by Grant SOC78-23759 from the Division of the Social Sciences of the National Science Foundation. The data used in this report were made available by the Inter-University Consortium for Political and Social Research. The data for the Spring 1975 General Social Survey, National Data Program for the Social Sciences, were originally collected by James A. Davis (National Opinion Research Center, University of Chicago) and distributed by Roper Public Opinion Research Center, Williams College. Neither the original collector of the data nor the consortium bear any responsibility for the analyses or interpretations presented here. For helpful comments, the writers are indebted to K. Crittenden, L. A. Goodman, O. D. Duncan, S. E. Fienberg, N. W. Henry, S. Leinhardt, C. H. Proctor, S. A. Tuch, and two anonymous referees.

This chapter compares various models for assessing the scalability of a set of dichotomous or dichotomized items. The formal means of comparison are both theoretical and empirical and emphasize the substantive interpretability of the scaling models considered. Particular attention is paid to the underlying rationale, assumptions, and logic of the models, with primary focus placed on a nonmathematical exposition. An appendix presents a latent-structure framework for all the scaling models of this chapter, a framework that illustrates how the models can be estimated and tested with a single computer program for (restricted) latent-structure analysis.

We begin with Guttman's pure scale model, entirely deterministic in form, and briefly survey and criticize the scalogram methods conventionally used to assess its empirical adequacy. The discussion assumes familiarity with the Guttman model, general accounts of which are provided by Guttman (1950), Edwards (1957), Torgerson (1962), Mokken (1971), Coombs, Coombs, and Lingoes (1978), Kim and Rabjohn (1979), and a variety of standard texts on scaling. Then we consider various probabilistic generalizations of Guttman's model, including Proctor's (1970, 1971) model now widely used in conjunction with conventional scalogram methods (see Barr and others, 1976), Lazarsfeld's latent-distance model often portrayed as a direct probabilistic analog to Guttman's model (see Lazarsfeld and Henry, 1968), Goodman's (1975) model based on the quasi-independence concept, and other relevant models. These probabilistic models have been chosen for consideration because they are all generalizations of Guttman's model that have been suggested in the literature, but they certainly do not exhaust the possible ways that Guttman's model can be generalized.[1] Relationships among the models considered here, and

[1]We actually restrict our attention to models which assume that the trait under consideration can be thought of as a discrete variable. That is, the underlying trait can be regarded as a nominal-level classification (as with the unrestricted latent structure briefly described here), as an ordinal-level classification (as with Proctor's model), or as an interval-level classification (as with Lazarsfeld's latent-distance model). An entirely different class of models arises when it is assumed that the underlying trait is quantitative and continuous, representative examples of which are the factor-analytic models of Christoffersson (1975), Muthén (1979), and Kim and Rabjohn (1979). With the factor-analytic approach, in addition to assuming that the trait in question is continuous, it is also assumed for estimation and testing purposes that this trait is normally distributed. When the underlying trait is not normally distributed, as would be the case if the trait distribution were skewed, these factor-analytic methods are inappropriate. That is, the weaker assumptions concerning the character of the

relationships to other possible generalizations of Guttman's model, will be examined later.

To compare the empirical performance of the various models, we analyze a cross-classification of six items concerning attitudes on legal abortion. These items, or items very similar to them, have been analyzed quite extensively (see, for example, Arney and Trescher, 1976; Jones and Westoff, 1972; and Westoff, Moore, and Ryder, 1969). The inferences to be drawn here concerning the structure of attitudes on abortion are very different from those drawn in most previous work. The usual scalogram methods applied to these data produce an impression that the Guttman model holds admirably well (with, for example, a coefficient of scalability of 0.81). But some of the statistical models lead us to conclude that abortion attitudes depart from the Guttman pattern in serious and statistically important ways. In this context, as well as in others, different models can lead to *very different* conclusions concerning inherent item scalability. In such anomalous circumstances our only recourse is to evaluate formally the logical makeup of the various models from which so much of our understanding of item scalability has in the past been obtained. This chapter offers such a critical evaluation.

Conventional scalogram methods used to evaluate Guttman's model empirically, and widely used in item analysis and scale construction, suffer several limitations. In our view these methods should not now be used, except possibly as an adjunct to some other type of analysis. One purpose of this chapter is to demonstrate the shortcomings of scalogram analysis in a compelling way. These limitations can be enumerated in five not necessarily mutually exclusive statements.

First, the Guttman model is deterministic—that is, entirely nonstatistical in nature. It does not incorporate the notion now fundamental to empirical social research of sampling variability and sampling error. It does not allow for the possibilities of errors of measurement, errors of response, or related nonsampling errors that

underlying trait made with the class of models considered here justify their use in cases where the underlying trait is not quantitative, or is not continuous, or is not normally distributed. There are other differences between the factor-analytic models and the class of models considered here, but it would take us far beyond the scope of this study to describe them.

could presumably be operative in generating the observable cross-classification of items.

Second, relating to the first criticism is the difficulty that Guttman's model does not adequately account for the presence of error responses—that is, the occurrence of response patterns in the cross-classification of items that deviate from the set of response patterns (or scale types) expected under the Guttman model. Error responses could, for example, be due to errors in measuring the "correct" response for some individuals. Alternatively, error responses could arise from population heterogeneity with respect to the trait in question; a subpopulation, for example, might exist that possesses an altogether different ordering of the items than the ordering assumed to describe the scale for the *entire* population under the Guttman model. However, the scalogram methods do not allow the direct examination of either of these possibilities.

Third, stemming from these two fundamental problems we find that applications of scalogram methods are often guided by traditional rules of thumb lacking mathematical justification. For example, the conventions often expressed in textbook accounts that the coefficient of reproducibility should be "greater than 0.9" and the coefficient of scalability should be "greater than 0.6" reflect serious misuse of the scalogram method. These rules of thumb are routinely applied in scale construction, however, regardless of the number of items involved (reflecting, in certain specific senses to be discussed here, the degrees of freedom available to test appropriate scaling hypotheses) or regardless of the sample size (affecting the sampling errors of the coefficients of scalability, reproducibility, and so on).

Fourth, when the Guttman model is judged to be inadequate, it is difficult to provide an explicit quantitative description of alternative scaling models that could describe the data. If the unidimensionality of the scale underlying the items is called into question, for example, perhaps a bidimensional (or biform) scale should be entertained as a possibility. As another example, it could be the case that the Guttman scale would apply to a subset of the items originally chosen for analysis, but the scalogram methods do not allow a rigorous appraisal of which items should or should not be included.

And fifth, as we shall demonstrate, when the Guttman model is judged to be adequate it can nevertheless be the case that, in certain specific senses to be discussed, the actual scale properties of the items need *not* conform in a statistically acceptable way to the predicted Guttman pattern. Even with compelling scalogram results, the assumptions of underlying unidimensionality of scale and cumulativeness of items can still be violated in serious ways, calling into question the very efficacy of the scalogram technique.

In this chapter we survey some of the statistical models that have been proposed as alternatives to the Guttman model and explicate the specific means by which each attempts to address the preceding criticisms. Before discussing the deterministic Guttman model on which all of the models are based, we first present data to be used for the empirical comparison of models.

THE DATA

The 1975 General Social Survey contained six items concerning attitudes on legal abortion, each of which could be answered yes or no. Respondents were asked if abortion should be legally available to a woman:

1. If the woman's own health is seriously endangered by the pregnancy
2. If there is a strong chance of serious defect in the baby
3. If she becomes pregnant as a result of rape
4. If the family has a very low income and cannot afford more children
5. If she is not married and does not want to marry the man
6. If she is married and does not want more children

We assign the mnemonic letters H (health), D (defect), R (rape), P (poverty), S (single), and N (no more) to these six items.

Of the 1,490 cases sampled in the survey, 1,286 (or 86.3 percent) elicited yes or no responses to all six questions. For simplicity it is this part of the sample with complete responses to which we restrict our analysis of item scalability. In effect, inferences to be drawn here pertain only to the scalability of the abortion items in the population of persons who would respond yes or no to all six items. We acknowledge the possibility that this type of inference need not lead to the correct conclusions about the entire population. To save space, the distribution of respondents throughout the 64-fold cross-classification of the six items will not be presented, but enough summary information from that table will be provided to enable the reader to follow subsequent analysis. The initial assumption—of vital importance to all Guttman scale methods but to be considered here as a *tentative* one—is made that the attitude on legal abortion is unidimensional and the six items are cumulative in their indication of different points along a unidimensional scale of that attitude.

The first question to be resolved in an analysis of Guttman scalability is the ordering of items involved. The six items considered here can be ordered from "least difficult" to "most difficult" in a variety of ways (assuming a test theory framework), some of which could reflect *a priori* orderings of theoretical interest or orderings suggested by past research (see, for example, Torgerson, 1962; Lazarsfeld and Henry, 1968). For simplicity we consider the ordering in terms of the marginal distribution of yes/no responses to the individual items. We are thus using the data, rather than strictly *a priori* considerations, to order the six items for subsequent analysis, and this should affect our interpretation of statistical results (for example, significance tests) that follow.

Table 1 presents these marginal distributions for the abortion items. We see that 1,162 respondents, or 90.4 percent, believed it should be legal for a woman to obtain an abortion if her health were seriously jeopardized by pregnancy, implying that of the six items the

TABLE 1
Marginal Distribution of Yes/No Responses to Six Items Concerning Attitudes on Abortion

Item[a]	Yes	No
Health	1,162	124
	90.4%	9.6%
Defect	1,076	210
	83.7%	16.3%
Rape	1,076	210
	83.7%	16.3%
Poor	714	572
	55.5%	44.5%
Single	652	634
	50.7%	49.3%
No more	632	654
	49.1%	50.9%

SOURCE: 1975 General Social Survey.
[a]See text for a full description of the items.

H (health) item was the least difficult to answer in the affirmative. Similarly, 632 respondents, or 49.1 percent, believed that abortion should be legal if the woman is married and wants no more children, implying that the N (no more) item was the most difficult item to answer in the affirmative. If items H and N were Guttman scalable, it would be supposed that all respondents who answered yes to item N would answer yes to item H. Proceeding with similar logic, we deduce the ordering of items in Table 1. If the items were Guttman scalable for all persons in the sample, then on the basis of the item marginals it would be assumed that all individuals answering yes to item N would answer yes to items S, P, R, D, and H; it would be further assumed that all individuals answering yes to item S would answer yes to P, R, D, and H; and so forth. The proposed ordering from least to most difficult is therefore (H, D, R, P, S, N), and we refer to this as ordering *A* in the subsequent discussion.

For k items, there are $k!$ different possible orderings, and with the Guttman scalogram methods only *one* of these orderings is posited to describe the natural ordering of items for the entire population. That this assumption is somewhat dubious is reflected in the fact that many methods have been suggested in the literature to determine the single ordering that is "correct." With the six-item example here, $k! = 720$, implying that 719 possible orderings are ruled out with the Guttman model. Moreover, we note from Table 1 that although most of the items can be tentatively ordered by inspection of the marginals, items R and D cannot be so ordered. Because of a sampling accident both R and D have exactly identical marginals, and in such cases other ordering criteria must be invoked. Here we have selected the ordering that produces the highest coefficient of scalability, but it is easy to see that repeated sampling from the relevant population could lead one to posit an entirely different ordering of the items. For the present argument, however, ordering *A* will be taken as the true ordering; later analysis will further qualify what is meant by this apparently innocuous assumption. We further assume, as is customary in Guttman scaling, that the *entire population* has abortion attitudes which are governed by this ordering. Such an assumption may be designated as the assumption of *population homogeneity:* All persons are assumed to have abortion attitudes that are appropriately described by the ordering considered.

Let 1 refer to the yes response and 2 refer to the no response for any item. Were the six items perfectly Guttman scalable for the entire sample, the seven response patterns

$$\begin{matrix}(1,1,1,1,1,1) & (1,1,1,1,1,2) & (1,1,1,1,2,2) & (1,1,1,2,2,2) \\ (1,1,2,2,2,2) & (1,2,2,2,2,2) & (2,2,2,2,2,2) & \end{matrix} \quad (1)$$

would contain all respondents, and all other response patterns ($64 - 7 = 57$ in number) would contain counts of zero. The response patterns in (1) are denoted as the scale types under ordering A, and we number them 1 through 7 in consecutive order. In general, for k items there will be $k + 1$ scale types, which can be numbered consecutively from $1, \ldots, k + 1$, and the ith scale type will correspond to a certain response pattern where $i - 1$ no responses occur.

Table 2 presents the observed distribution of respondents among the scale types of (1). A full 83.3 percent elicit response patterns corresponding to the scale types, implying a substantial agreement between observation and prediction. But since the conformity of the empirical data to the Guttman pattern is incomplete (that is, less than 100 percent), a rigorous assessment of the extent of the model's failure is needed.

SCALOGRAM ANALYSIS

Scalogram analysis is the conventional approach for assessing item scalability, and it can be easily conducted with the aid of widely

TABLE 2
Distribution of Respondents in Scale Types Corresponding to Ordering (H, D, R, P, S, N)

Scale Type	Response Pattern	Frequency	Percentage
1	(1, 1, 1, 1, 1, 1)	532	41.4
2	(1, 1, 1, 1, 1, 2)	50	3.9
3	(1, 1, 1, 1, 2, 2)	55	4.3
4	(1, 1, 1, 2, 2, 2)	242	18.8
5	(1, 1, 2, 2, 2, 2)	60	4.7
6	(1, 2, 2, 2, 2, 2)	45	3.5
7	(2, 2, 2, 2, 2, 2)	86	6.7
Total in scale types		1,070	83.3
Errors		216	16.8
Total		1,286	100.1[a]

NOTE: A code of 1 denotes yes; a code of 2 denotes no.
[a]Does not equal 100.0 percent due to round-off error.

available computer software (see Nie and others, 1975; Barr and others, 1976). The scalogram compares responses to individual items with the responses expected under the Guttman model, whereas the summary percentages in Table 2 compare respondents' *response patterns* to the response patterns expected under the Guttman model. The number of yes responses to items where no responses were expected, plus the number of no responses to items where yes responses were expected, is defined as the number of error responses in the scalogram, relative to the ordering (say, ordering A) considered. We refer to this number as E_2 and find that $E_2 = 456$ for our sample. The estimated error rate per response, e_2, is given as

$$e_2 = E_2/(kn) \tag{2}$$

where n is sample size. (Note that kn is the number of responses for k items and sample size n.) For our sample we find $e_2 = 456/(6 \times 1{,}286) = 0.059$, yielding a *coefficient of reproducibility,* $1 - e_2$, of 0.941. A coefficient of reproducibility greater than 0.9 is commonly assumed to "indicate a valid scale" (see, for example, Goodenough, 1944; Torgerson, 1962; Nie and others, 1975). Most analysts would therefore conclude that the six items do indeed form a reasonable Guttman scale, although inspection of other indices available from the scalogram would necessarily qualify this conclusion.

Since reproducibility (as defined in scalogram analysis) depends somewhat on the marginal distributions of the individual items, it is common practice to calculate the minimum amount of reproducibility that could be obtained from knowledge of the marginal distributions alone. The maximum number of response errors E_1 that can occur with a given set of item-specific marginals (see Table 1) is equal to the sum of minimums of the respective marginals. And the estimated maximum rate of response error with the given marginals is

$$e_1 = E_1/(kn) \tag{3}$$

From Table 1 we can calculate the sum of the minimum marginals (= 2,382) and so we find $e_1 = 2{,}382/(6 \times 1{,}286) = 0.309$. The *minimum marginal reproducibility* is defined as $1 - e_1$ and turns out to be 0.691 for this sample.

Finally, Guttman's coefficient of scalability is defined as the proportional reduction in error rates,

$$S = (e_1 - e_2)/e_1 \tag{4}$$

and is 0.809 for this sample. Nie and others (1975, p. 533), following the convention established by years of applied work with the scalogram, state that the coefficient in (4) "should be well above .6 if the scale is truly unidimensional and cumulative." Given this convention, we would also be led to conclude that the items were reasonably Guttman scalable.

In Table 3 we present the interitem and the item-scale correlation coefficients commonly used as an adjunct to scalogram analysis. (These were obtained directly from the SAS computer package.) The interitem correlations are phi coefficients for the 2 × 2 cross-classifications of the respective items. The item-scale correlations are the point-biserial coefficients obtained by correlating the particular dichotomous item with the composite scale formed from the remaining items. Since all correlations are positive and at least moderate in size, we would probably not alter our earlier conclusions concerning item scalability. Often an item possessing a negative correlation with one or more of the other items, or an item possessing a negative correlation with the composite scale formed from the items, is deleted from the set of items chosen to construct the scale. Similar procedures are applied when correlations are positive but of negligible magnitude. Using standard statistical methods appropriate for Pearson correlations, it is certainly possible to test the hypothesis that a particular coefficient is zero in the population against the relevant (one-tailed) alternative that it is positive. However, it is not clear to the writers how such a statistical analysis can be brought to bear *in a direct way* on the important question of which items should be included or deleted from

TABLE 3
Interitem and Scale-Item Correlation Coefficients for Guttman Scale Types Corresponding to Ordering *A*

Item	H	D	R	P	S	N
D	0.611					
R	0.497	0.573				
P	0.317	0.400	0.456			
S	0.289	0.381	0.435	0.726		
N	0.274	0.363	0.405	0.748	0.745	
Scale item	0.476	0.563	0.591	0.743	0.723	0.714

NOTE: Interitem correlations are Pearson product-moment correlations, identical to phi for the particular 2 × 2 table. Scale-item correlations are also Pearson correlations, identical to point-biserial coefficients. For the scale-item correlations the assumption is made that the composite scale is quantitative (that is, interval level).

the composite scale. The problem of "collapsing" over items in the analysis of scalability will be taken up in more detail later. In this instance, however, most researchers would not delete one or more of the items, nor would they further question the essential Guttman scalability of the items. The scalogram methods thus produce an impression that a reasonable Guttman scale can be constructed. Indeed, social research is replete with analyses based on less convincing scalogram results.

In summary, we have found that even though conformity of the data to Guttman's pure model is incomplete, the conventional scalogram methods lead us to conclude that the Guttman model nevertheless provides an acceptable summary of the attitude in question. But note that the scalogram analysis was largely divorced from fundamental statistical concepts such as sampling error or the adequacy of fit of a statistical model to data. Indeed, no explicit model accounting for the distribution of respondents throughout the cross-classification of items has been formulated. Even though the data in question are a sample from a well-defined population (the adult U.S. population in 1975) and error responses did occur, the conventional procedures do not incorporate these features into their mode of analysis. Guttman (1950) recognized the need to take account of sampling variability in scalogram work, and Goodman (1959) and others have considered certain statistical inferences for some coefficients used in scalogram work. But as has been expressed repeatedly by various writers (Goodman, 1959, 1975; Lazarsfeld and Henry, 1968; Proctor, 1970), the Guttman model, which is entirely deterministic in form, must first be reformulated to provide an accounting for response errors. Rigorous statistical inference in the analysis of item scalability must be based on an explicit statistical model for the data in the k-way cross-table.

The two broad types of statistical formulations of Guttman's model to be considered explicitly address the criticisms raised in connection with Guttman's model and the scalogram methods associated with it. The first model explains error responses as being due to *errors of measurement* (or response errors) arising from the inability to elicit correct responses for some members of the population. With this type of model, however, the assumption is made that the entire population is "intrinsically" Guttman scalable according to the ordering of items considered. (This assumption was earlier referred to as the assumption of population homogeneity.) A second model assumes that error responses occur as a result of the heterogeneity of the population with regard to the scalability of the trait in question. Under this second formulation, different parts of the population are assumed to have different intrinsic orderings of the items, and error response patterns are then conceived as being scale types for a part of the population where the attitude or trait in question has a different form of item cumulativeness than the *single* form considered under the pure Guttman model. Each type of model is now considered in turn.

MODELS INVOLVING ERRORS OF MEASUREMENT

The simplest model incorporating the notion of measurement error is due to Proctor (1970, 1971). It rests on the assumption that a single parameter governs the expected rate of response error for a homogeneous population that is intrinsically Guttman scalable. For an analysis of k items, Proctor assumes that the relevant statistical population in question consists of $k + 1$ "true" types of individuals; each true type tends to elicit an observable response pattern that corresponds to one of the $k + 1$ scale types under Guttman's pure model. Letting $\pi_1, \ldots, \pi_{k+1}$ refer to the population proportions in the $k + 1$ true types, Proctor's model assumes that $\Sigma_{i=1}^{k+1} \pi_i = 1$—that is, that the $k + 1$ types exhaust the population. The assumption is made that the entire population can be scaled by considering a single, unique ordering of the items, which in turn implies the existence of $k + 1$ true types, and no other ordering is assumed possible.

To account for the existence of response patterns other than the ones corresponding to scale types, Proctor introduced a single error rate α that governs the expected occurrence of response errors for all k items and all $k + 1$ true types of individuals. An individual in the ith true type is assumed to respond to each item with probability α of error, and this response error probability is assumed to be statistically independent of the probability of response error to any of the other items. Any true type of individual can therefore make j response errors (for $0 \leq j \leq k$) with probability $(1 - \alpha)^{k-j} \alpha^j$. In our six-item example ($k = 6$), an individual who is intrinsically a member of true type 3, with expected response pattern (1,1,1,1,2,2), would have a probability $(1 - \alpha)^6$ of being observed in his or her true scale type. The same individual would have a probability $(1 - \alpha)^4(\alpha)^2$ of responding (2,1,1,1,2,1), since there are two response errors in this

TABLE 4
Chi-Square Values for Some Scale Models Involving Response Error

Model	DF	Likelihood-Ratio Chi Square	Goodness-of-Fit Chi Square
Proctor's model	56	174.6	180.6
Item-specific error rates	51	139.6	172.8
True-type-specific error rates	50[a]	115.4	157.6
Lazarsfeld's latent-distance model	57[b]	86.0	106.9

[a]Three error rates were estimated to be zero; thus, strictly speaking, the calculated chi-square statistics do not have 50 degrees of freedom. Following the conventions discussed in Goodman (1974a) we might here consider the *restricted* model where these three error rates are set equal to zero; then the chi-square statistics reported for this model would have 53 degrees of freedom.

[b]The estimated error rates $\hat{\alpha}_{13} = \hat{\alpha}_{23} = \hat{\alpha}_{33} = \hat{\alpha}_{43}$ are zero for this set of data. In such a case we could consider the model as a *restricted* latent-distance model, where we assume that $\alpha_{13} = \alpha_{23} = \alpha_{33} = \alpha_{43} = 0$. In this case the model would have 48 degrees of freedom, one more than for the unrestricted latent-distance model.

response pattern.[2] The single parameter α is thus an important overall index of item scalability in Proctor's model: When α is low, the items are judged to be scalable; when α is high, it is prudent to question the scalability of the items (at least under the ordering considered). When $\alpha = 0$, Proctor's model is easily seen to reduce to Guttman's model where no response errors are expected to occur.

Proctor's model is a special kind of restricted latent-structure model, and so it can be efficiently estimated with a computer program for maximum-likelihood latent-structure analysis (see Clogg, 1977). Alternatively, it can be estimated by the method of scoring considered by Proctor, a method that also produces maximum-likelihood esti-

[2]Note that a response pattern of (1,1,1,2,2,1) and a response pattern of (2,1,1,1,2,1) would under Proctor's model have an identical probability of occurring for members of true type 3 (with expected response pattern (1,1,1,1,2,2)), since both patterns have two response errors. Even though the latter response pattern is much more seriously in error under the hypothesized ordering of items, Proctor's model does not incorporate this information.

mates. (It is this latter method that is used in the SAS package.) Table 4 summarizes the fit of Proctor's model and others to be discussed shortly. We see immediately that Proctor's model does not fit the data to an acceptable degree, since the chi-square statistic based on the likelihood-ratio criterion is 174.6 on 56 degrees of freedom.[3] The failure of the model might be due to (1) an incorrect ordering of items, (2) a departure of the attitude in question from unidimensionality, (3) response error rates that differ by item or latent type of individual or both, (4) the existence of a subpopulation with an entirely different ordering than the one hypothesized to apply to the entire population, or (5) some combination of these factors. Before considering modifications of Proctor's model that take account of these possibilities, we first discuss further aspects of Proctor's model estimated for these data.

The proportion estimated under Proctor's model that intrinsically belong to the scale types—that is, $\pi_1, \pi_2, \ldots, \pi_7$—are as follows:

0.489 0.026 0.046 0.274 0.045 0.039 0.081

A full 48.9 percent are estimated to belong intrinsically to the first scale type (1,1,1,1,1,1), an extreme response pattern indicative of "ideological" attitudes on abortion (see, for example, Duncan, 1979), which is to be compared with an observed proportion in this type of 41.4 percent. Thus Proctor's model states that 7.5 percent more persons are in unqualified support of the "right of choice" than was actually observed. We note further that π_2, the estimated proportion intrinsically belonging to scale type 2, with expected response pattern (1,1,1,1,1,2), is 0.026 and numerically smaller than any of the other estimated proportions. This estimate possesses an approximate standard error of 0.007, so that a confidence interval about π_2 could be constructed and certain hypothesis tests could also be carried out. However, it is not possible with Proctor's methods, which automatically provide large-sample standard errors of the various parameters, to carry out a formal statistical test of whether $\pi_2 = 0$. That is, it is not possible to examine the hypothesis that the *observed* proportion in scale type (1,1,1,1,1,2) is solely the result of response errors on the part of individuals in other true scale types. To facilitate later generaliza-

[3]All chi-square statistics in this chapter have been adjusted for a sampling factor according to guidelines provided in Davis (1975). That is, the General Social Survey has the same efficiency as a random sample approximately two thirds the size of the actual sample. The chi-square statistics were thus deflated by one third.

tion, we now consider why the case where $\pi_2 = 0$ (or the condition where any other $\pi_i = 0$) is an important scaling hypothesis.

When the scale type (1,1,1,1,1,2) does not occur in the population as an intrinsic or true type, then item N (the most difficult item) fails to be important as a discriminator between scale type 1 (with expected response pattern (1,1,1,1,1,1)) and scale type 3 (with expected response pattern (1,1,1,1,2,2)). Item N would in this circumstance contribute nothing to the scale and could thus be deleted from the set of items chosen to measure attitudes on legal abortion. The resulting cross-classification of five items, obtained by collapsing over the N item, could then be used in constructing the scale without any loss of essential information. If π_2 were in fact zero, then the scale types of (1) pertaining to the six items could be replaced by the six scale types

$$\begin{matrix} (1,1,1,1,1) & (1,1,1,1,2) & (1,1,1,2,2) \\ (1,1,2,2,2) & (1,2,2,2,2) & (2,2,2,2,2) \end{matrix} \tag{5}$$

corresponding to the five-way cross-table obtained by deleting the N variable. We see that the justification for collapsing over item N (that is, deleting item N) derives from inspection of the model parameter π_2, and this is to be contrasted with the largely informal methods of collapsing that stem from "looking" at the interitem correlations (see Table 3).

This logic can be extended in several ways. If $\pi_2 = \pi_3 = 0$, for example, then the original six-way cross-table could be collapsed over the categories of *both* N and S, and the scalability of the *six* items could be determined by considering the conformity of the particular *four-way* cross-classification of responses to the response patterns

$$\begin{matrix} (1,1,1,1) & (1,1,1,2) & (1,1,2,2) \\ (1,2,2,2) & (2,2,2,2) & \end{matrix}$$

To take a more extreme example, suppose that $\pi_2 = \cdots = \pi_6 = 0$. In this case only two scale types would be necessary to describe the scalability of the six items:

$$(1,1,1,1,1,1) \qquad (2,2,2,2,2,2)$$

This latter condition implies that any item would be as valid as any other item as an indicator of the trait in question, and this arbitrary dichotomous item alone could be used in further substantive analysis.

To reiterate, the model parameters $\pi_1, \ldots, \pi_{k+1}$, indicating the population proportions intrinsically belonging to the scale types, are important measures of the contribution of individual items (or groups of items) to the composite scale, but Proctor's methods do not allow us to test important statistical hypotheses about them.

Although Proctor's model does not fit the data well, there are nevertheless compelling extrastatistical reasons for using it to infer once again the "essential" Guttman properties of the six items under analysis here. The response error rate α is estimated at 0.042 with approximate standard error of 0.003, signifying a very low rate of response error. The coefficient of scale reliability (Proctor, 1971) is estimated at 0.965, indicating a very reliable scale. Given these indices, it is tempting to conclude that the six abortion items are Guttman scalable to a remarkable degree when a simple model of response errors is assumed, even though in terms of goodness of fit the Proctor model is inadequate.

A natural way to modify the Proctor model is to relax the assumption that the response error rate is constant for each item and each type of individual. The assumption that $k + 1$ types, and *only* these types, exist in the population is still made, however, and the specification of these $k + 1$ types would once again critically depend on the initial ordering of the items considered. We now consider two simple modifications of Proctor's model which still assume that the attribute in question can be scaled for the entire population, but in which simple modifications of assumptions concerning error rates are made. These modified models are in fact suggested by Proctor (1970).

The first generalization of Proctor's model assumes that error rates α_j govern the response errors for the jth item ($1 \leq j \leq k$) and do not vary across the true types of individuals. The assumption that responses to the items are independent of one another for members of each true type is made once again, implying that the probability of any true type of individual being observed in any response pattern can be readily calculated. For an individual whose true type is scale type 3 with expected response pattern (1,1,1,1,2,2), the response pattern (2,1,1,1,2,1) would occur with probability

$$\alpha_1(1 - \alpha_2)(1 - \alpha_3)(1 - \alpha_4)(1 - \alpha_5)\alpha_6.$$

When $\alpha_1 = \cdots = \alpha_k = \alpha$, this model reduces to Proctor's model, and because there are $k - 1$ additional error rates to be estimated, there are

$k - 1$ fewer degrees of freedom for the model relative to Proctor's model. This modification of Proctor's model applied to the abortion data yields a likelihood-ratio chi square of 139.6 on 51 degrees of freedom, a reduction of 35.0 in chi square with the addition of only five parameters. (See Table 4.) Within the context of the models of response error considered in this section, it thus appears plausible to assume that error rates vary by item. The estimated item-specific error rates $(\hat{\alpha}_1, \ldots, \hat{\alpha}_6)$ under this model are

0.019 0.056 0.022 0.031 0.075 0.042

for items H, D, R, P, S, and N, respectively, whereas the estimated error rate $\hat{\alpha}$ under Proctor's model is 0.042. It should be noted, however, that this modification of Proctor's model still fails to describe the data to an acceptable degree as judged by conventional criteria of goodness of fit.

Another straightforward generalization of Proctor's model is obtained in the following way. Instead of assuming that response error rates vary by item but not by true type of individual, assume conversely that the true types have different response error rates that do not depend on the item for which a response error is made. With k items, and hence $k + 1$ true types corresponding to the scale types under the particular ordering, there would be error rates $\alpha_1, \ldots, \alpha_{k+1}$ governing the expected occurrence of response errors, and hence k additional parameters over Proctor's model. As a consequence, there will be k fewer degrees of freedom relative to Proctor's model. This modification of Proctor's model yields a likelihood-ratio chi square of 115.4, a marked improvement (see Table 4). The estimated true-type-specific error rates are

0.017 0.000 0.156 0.098 0.000 0.000 0.004

for true types 1 through 7, respectively, under ordering A.[4]

Other direct generalizations of Proctor's model can certainly be entertained. We could, for example, consider models where response error rates depend (in certain specified ways) on both the item and the true type of individual. One important model of this kind is Lazarsfeld's latent-distance model, long recognized as a probabilistic analog to the pure Guttman scale.

[4]See Table 4 (note a) for a discussion of the consequences of the zero estimates obtained with this model.

Since the latent-distance model is discussed in many sources (see Lazarsfeld and Henry, 1968; Goodman, 1974b; Hays and Borgatta, 1954), only a brief mention of its makeup will be provided here. Let α_{ij} denote the response error rate for the ith true type of individual ($1 \leq i \leq k + 1$) and the jth item ($1 \leq j \leq k$). As with Proctor's model, we once again assume that there are $k + 1$ true types that exhaust the population, each one of which corresponds to a scale type posited to exist with Guttman's model, the designation of which depends critically on the ordering of items used (as in ordering A for the abortion items). Response errors are assumed to obey the following restrictions:

$$\alpha_{11} = \alpha_{21} = \cdots = \alpha_{(k+1)1} \tag{6a}$$

for item 1,

$$\alpha_{1k} = \alpha_{2k} = \cdots = \alpha_{(k+1)k} \tag{6b}$$

for item k, and

$$\alpha_{1j} = \alpha_{2j} = \cdots = \alpha_{(k+1-j)j} \tag{6c}$$

and

$$\alpha_{(k+2-j)j} = \cdots = \alpha_{(k+1)j} \tag{6d}$$

for all items j, where $2 \leq j \leq k - 1$. The restrictions in (6a) to (6d) imply that there will be $2 + 2\,(k - 2) = 2k - 2$ nonredundant error rates α_{ij}. For six items, for example, there are 10 error rates to be estimated from the data. It is easy to see that the latent-distance model (6a) to (6d) is a generalization of all previously considered response error models.

TABLE 5
Error Rates Estimated Under Lazarsfeld's Latent-Distance Model

Intrinsic Type of Individual	Scale Type	Probability of Response Error in Answering Item					
		H	D	R	P	S	N
1	(1, 1, 1, 1, 1, 1)	0.014	0.024	0.000[a]	0.032	0.076	0.047
2	(1, 1, 1, 1, 1, 2)	0.014	0.024	0.000[a]	0.032	0.076	0.047
3	(1, 1, 1, 1, 2, 2)	0.014	0.024	0.000[a]	0.032	0.070	0.047
4	(1, 1, 1, 2, 2, 2)	0.014	0.024	0.000[a]	0.054	0.070	0.047
5	(1, 1, 2, 2, 2, 2)	0.014	0.024	0.279	0.054	0.070	0.047
6	(1, 2, 2, 2, 2, 2)	0.014	0.058	0.279	0.054	0.070	0.047
7	(2, 2, 2, 2, 2, 2)	0.014	0.058	0.279	0.054	0.070	0.047

[a]These error rates were estimated to be zero under the latent-distance model.

The latent-distance model yields a likelihood-ratio chi square of 86.0 (see Table 4)—a substantial improvement over previous models but still unacceptable on conventional statistical grounds. For purposes of illustration, Table 5 presents the error rates estimated under this model. These estimates might lead us to question the role of the R (rape) item in the construction of a composite scale, since the rate governing response errors to this item is estimated at 0.279 for true types 5 through 7. As with earlier models, however, it is tempting to conclude that the essential scalability of the items is reasonably verified, and most researchers would be content to proceed to the estimation of scale scores in a way consistent with the latent-distance model (see Lazarsfeld and Henry, 1968).[5] One cannot help being perplexed, however, over the fact that *none* of the response error models have fit the data to an acceptable degree, even though the earlier scalogram analysis would probably have led us to expect they would fit the data well.

Note that with each of these generalizations of Guttman's pure scale model it has been assumed that (1) a unique ordering of the k items exists and no other ordering is permissible, (2) the population in question is homogeneous with respect to this ordering (that is, no individuals exist for which different orderings are permissible), (3) $k + 1$ true types corresponding to the pure scale types under Guttman's model are assumed to exhaust the population, and (4) only errors of measurement are admitted into the framework of the models in their attempts to account for departures from Guttman's model. The logical development that led from Guttman's model to Proctor's model and from Proctor's model to Lazarsfeld's latent-distance model could have led to further models. In particular, these models, based on the four assumptions just cited, would have led, when pushed to the extreme, to consideration of the unrestricted $(k + 1)$-class latent-structure model, where error rates α_{ij} would be completely unrestricted. But it seems clear from the foregoing analysis that other assumptions besides those made about error rates are at fault (at least for the data on attitudes toward legal abortion), and these other assumptions should be studied analytically. Thus, rather than

[5]The restrictions of (6a) to (6d) are imposed in the latent-distance model so that plausible scale scores can be assigned to each response pattern in the k-way table. The reader can gain further insight into the meaning of these restrictions by inspecting the estimates in Table 5 and consulting Lazarsfeld and Henry (1968).

proceeding with other models of response error, we consider a different generalization of Guttman's model due to Goodman.

THE GOODMAN SCALE MODEL

Goodman's basic model (1975) accounts for the existence of "error response patterns" not by positing stochastic disturbances that result in measurement error but by relaxing the critical assumption of population homogeneity. Given a particular ordering of the items (say, ordering *A* for the abortion items), Goodman assumed that part of the population was *intrinsically scalable* according to the Guttman model, implying that for this part of the population no response errors could occur. The logic is that the Guttman model holds only for *part* of the entire population (that is, for the scalable class), and observed departures from the scale patterns expected under the Guttman model arise from the responses of an *intrinsically unscalable* part of the population. The unscalable class occurs with proportionate frequency denoted by π_0, implying that $1 - \pi_0$ is the proportionate frequency of the scalable class. It is easy to see that when $\pi_0 = 0$ Goodman's model reduces to Guttman's model where no unscalable individuals exist and where consequently no response errors would occur.

The scalable class is defined in reference to the scale types consonant with the particular ordering of items, and as in the previous section we let $\pi_1, \ldots, \pi_{k+1}$ denote the proportions of the population that belong intrinsically to scale types 1 through $k + 1$. For the six-item case, for example, π_1 would correspond to the proportionate frequency intrinsically belonging to scale type 1 with expected response pattern (1,1,1,1,1,1); π_2 would correspond to the proportionate frequency intrinsically belonging to scale type 2 with expected response pattern (1,1,1,1,1,2); and so on. Together with the zeroth class denoting unscalable individuals there are $k + 2$ classes, and these $k + 2$ (*not* $k + 1$) classes exhaust the population—that is, $\Sigma_{i=0}^{k+1} \pi_i = 1$. Goodman's basic model is thus a $(k + 2)$-class model, not a $(k + 1)$-class model as in the case of the response error models of the previous section.

Since for the scalable part of the population response patterns will correspond with certainty to the scale types expected under the Guttman model, no further specification of the model is required for this part. The scalable class is characterized by the same kind of deterministic rules of response that depict Guttman's original concept of a pure scale. "Error response patterns" frequently occur in practice (see Table 2), however, and this implies that an unscalable class with proportionate frequency $\pi_0 > 0$ may be posited to exist. To specify the Goodman scale model completely, assumptions must be made to define expected response patterns for the unscalable class. The working hypothesis is that members of the unscalable class respond to individual items according to a relationship of mutual independence. That is, for members of the unscalable class responses to the k items are mutually independent, and the probability of any response pattern for this class can therefore be calculated from the marginal distributions of the k items in the k-way cross-classification of the items for the unscalable individuals. The assumption of mutual independence among items for members of the unscalable class is critical to the Goodman scale model, and it certainly requires theoretical justification in the present context. Now let us examine one interpretation of this assumption (by no means the only interpretation possible).

In a cross-classification of k items, $k!$ possible orderings (permutations) of the items are possible *a priori*. In typical scalogram work, some of the $k!$ orderings can be ruled out immediately as being logically implausible, but for most empirical situations some or perhaps many of the $k!$ orderings cannot be definitely ruled out on *a priori* grounds. That this is the case is reflected in the history of scalogram work itself, or in the history of the latent-distance model, where considerable effort has been expended with the objective of determining the best "single" ordering of the items involved. Indeed, a variety of methods have been suggested in the literature for finding the best single ordering, the end result of which is to ensure an ordering that essentially maximizes the coefficient of scalability (in scalogram analysis) or the goodness of fit of a latent-distance model (in latent-distance analysis). That such methodology exists, in our view, adds justification to Goodman's conception of the problem, since there appears to be a tacit admission of several rival orderings that must be considered. Unscalable individuals may be taken with the Goodman model as those who possess orderings of the k items that are different from the single ordering which defines the scale types for the scalable part of the population.

Since the number of possible orderings is large for cases when k, the number of items, is large, we expect π_0 to tend to increase with k, as should only be the case when more and more orderings cannot be ruled out *a priori* as describing the actual pattern of scale types for certain parts of the population. And it is here that the assumption of independence for the "unscalable" class can be justified in theoretical terms. Whenever several item orderings can be conceived for part of the population, it is reasonable to assume that the *combined effect* of considering all these other orderings together in one unscalable class is to produce a relationship of mutual independence. For any ordering that pertains to part of the unscalable class, say ordering *B*, the response patterns for persons whose trait "scales" according to this ordering will not produce a relationship of mutual independence. When this ordering is considered jointly with all other plausible orderings (say, orderings *C*, *D*, . . .), then—when the number of potential orderings is large—the response patterns can be assumed to obey a relationship of mutual independence for the *unscalable class as a whole.*[6]

To illustrate these assumptions for the abortion items, it is only necessary to provide a few examples. It is arguable, for instance, that orderings where the H (health) item and the N (no more) item were interchanged are inconceivable; thus all orderings involving this transposition of items could be effectively ruled out. But certainly orderings where the H and D, or the D and R, or the P and S, or the S and N items are interchanged, to take a few examples, are quite conceivable as plausible orderings for *some* individuals. The Goodman scale model does not force us to assume that only one ordering (say, ordering *A*)

[6]That persons whose trait can be scaled according to a particular ordering (say, ordering *B*) will not have a response pattern that can be described by a relationship of mutual independence requires further comment. Suppose we know that a certain individual has response patterns which can be described by this ordering (say, ordering *B*). Then the response to an item depends on, and is not independent of, the response to any other item. For a two-item situation, we might take the response patterns (1, 1), (2, 1), (2, 2) as the scale types of ordering *B*. A response of 2 on the second item would imply that a response of 1 on the first item would be impossible, so mutual independence of responses could not apply for a person known to be a member of the part of the population with this ordering of items. However, if we know that an individual is a member of the part of the population with this ordering—and we know in addition that his or her scale type is (2, 1)—then the response pattern for this individual would in fact obey a relationship of mutual independence with probabilities 0 and 1 of a 1 response on the first and second items, respectively. The assumption is that the *combined* effect of considering so many orderings together (in one unscalable class) produces an overall relationship of mutual independence.

exists to define a unidimensional trait in the entire population; instead it assumes that some, and perhaps many, of the 719 (6! − 1) orderings not considered under the Guttman model are valid orderings for certain parts of the population. The reader will surely conclude, as we have, that the more items involved in the assessment of scalability, the more plausible will this framework appear.

With the Goodman scale model, the parameter π_0 is an important overall index of scalability, a fact that is demonstrated by considering the range of values it might assume. When $\pi_0 = 0$, the population is perfectly Guttman scalable and no response errors (defined relative to a particular ordering of the items) are expected to occur. (See Dayton and Macready, 1979, for methods appropriate for testing whether $\pi_0 = 0$ in the context of a model very similar to the Goodmàn model.) When $\pi_0 = 1$, the entire population is unscalable and the responses to the k items are mutually independent for the entire population. In this latter situation, *no* ordering of the items would produce a set of distinct response patterns that would serve as a scale; equivalently, no single ordering of the $k!$ orderings possible would dominate the others and the population as a whole would be said to be unscalable. When π_0 is small (close to zero), a scalable part of the population exists (with proportionate frequency $1 - \pi_0$) and the ordering chosen to describe the scalable class would be said to dominate the other orderings. When π_0 is large (close to unity), the scalable part of the population is correspondingly small and it would be necessary to conclude that the ordering used to define the scalable class is not substantively important. The parameter π_0 is thus a readily interpretable summary index of the extent to which the ordering producing the scale types of the scalable class is an effective summary of the data. Without further elaboration of model assumptions, we now apply the basic Goodman scale model, and modifications of it suggested in his seminal work, to the abortion items.

Table 6 presents the fit of Goodman's model applied to the six abortion items and some other models directly related to it. Consider first model H_0, where $\pi_0 = 1$, the entire population is assumed intrinsically unscalable, and the responses to the six items are therefore assumed to be mutually independent. For H_0 we find $2^k - 1 - k$ degrees of freedom, or $2^6 - 1 - 6 = 57$ degrees of freedom in this six-item case, as is the situation with a model of mutual independence.

TABLE 6
Estimated Proportion of Intrinsically Unscalable and Chi-Square Values for Some Goodman Scale Models

Model	Number of Scale Types	Estimated Proportion $\hat{\pi}_0$ of Intrinsically Unscalable Individuals	DF	Likelihood-Ratio Chi Square	Goodness-of-Fit Chi Square
H_0	0	1.000[a]	57	1,977.5	15,318.3
H_1	7	0.302	50	96.7	125.0
H_2	6	0.302	51	96.7	125.0
H_3	10	0.239	47	53.2	87.7
H_4	9	0.239	48	53.2	87.7
H_5	8	0.258	49	71.0	106.5
H_6	10	0.192	47	49.7	70.2
H_7	11	0.200	46	41.4	43.9

[a]Under H_0, we set π_0 equal to 1.000; thus it is not *estimated* from the data.

We see that with a likelihood-ratio chi square of 1,977.5, this model is clearly not tenable. This result implies that one or more orderings of the items dominate the other possible orderings, producing this departure from overall independence.

Next consider H_1, a model which says that in addition to the unscalable class there is a scalable class containing seven intrinsic types of individuals. The seven "true" types are chosen to correspond to the response patterns in (1), which again depends on the ordering (ordering A) thought to describe the Guttman scale properties of a large part of the population. We find $\hat{\pi}_0 = 0.302$ for H_1—that is, under ordering A of the items 30.2 percent of the respondents can be regarded as having response patterns that are intrinsically unscalable. Included in this 30.2 percent are persons who have any of the 719 orderings of the six items different from ordering A. Since there are so many possible orderings, we find this estimate of π_0 credible. Note that $\hat{\pi}_0 = 0.302$ is *greater* than the sample proportion 0.168 in the unscalable response patterns (see Table 2). The reason for such a discrepancy is that some unscalable individuals have response patterns identical to the response patterns considered as scale types under ordering A as a result of the random distribution of responses to the items for the unscalable class. Under H_1 we find a chi square of 96.7, which, although still unacceptable, compares favorably with the models considered in previous sections. The latent-distance model has somewhat better fit (see Table 4), but it also has fewer degrees of freedom than H_1.

Before proceeding to other Goodman scale models that will improve the fit, we first consider an aspect of his model which, to our knowledge, has no counterpart in other models for item analysis. In estimating H_1 we found that $\hat{\pi}_3 = 0.00001$, implying that the third scale type, with expected response pattern (1,1,1,1,2,2), is estimated to have only a negligible frequency of occurrence among the scalable part of the population. (The quantity $\hat{\pi}_3/(1 - \hat{\pi}_0)$ is the relevant estimate to describe the relative frequency of occurrence in the scalable population; see Clogg, 1979a.) That is, the S (single) variable is of no consequence in discriminating between scale type 2, with expected response pattern (1,1,1,1,1,2), and scale type 4, with expected response pattern (1,1,1,2,2,2). Model H_2 imposes the restriction that $\pi_3 = 0$ and produces results nearly identical to H_1. If H_1 were true, then the difference $X^2(H_2) - X^2(H_1)$ is a *single degree-of-freedom test* of the distinctness of scale type 3.[7] If H_1 were true, and the difference $X^2(H_2) - X^2(H_1)$ were not significant as judged by a comparison with the tabulated percentiles of the chi-square distribution with 1 degree of freedom, then in these circumstances we could delete the S variable from the cross-classification of items. The model H_2 applied to the five-way table obtained by collapsing the six-way table over the categories of S would also describe the data adequately. Since H_1 would be rejected for these data, we do not here collapse over S, even though the difference in chi-square statistics for H_2 and H_1 produces a negligible value. But *if* the fit of H_1 had been acceptable, then S could have been deleted from the set of items. The scalability of the remaining five items could then have been assessed on the basis of the relevant five-way table, and scale scores could have been calculated from this five-way table. This technique is so important that we develop the rationale for it in Appendix A.

Model H_1 (and H_2) was obtained by assuming that ordering A is correct for the scalable part of the population. Now consider an ordering R, H, D, N, P, S, which we designate as ordering A'. This ordering is obtained from ordering A by placing the R (rape) item in

[7]The chi-square statistic appropriate for these purposes is the likelihood-ratio statistic.

the first (instead of the third) position and by placing the N (no more) item in the fourth (instead of the sixth) position. Under ordering A' we would have scale types $1', 2', \ldots, 7'$, which can be enumerated as:

1′: (1,1,1,1,1,1) (identical to scale type 1)
2′: (1,1,1,1,2,1)
3′: (1,1,1,2,2,1)
4′: (1,1,1,2,2,2) (identical to scale type 4)
5′: (1,2,1,2,2,2)
6′: (2,2,1,2,2,2)
7′: (2,2,2,2,2,2) (identical to scale type 7)

Under ordering A' of the items, scale type 1′ is identical to scale type 1 under ordering A; scale types 4′ and 7′ are also identical to scale types 4 and 7, respectively. Considering both ordering A and A' as part of the scalable class results in a *biform scale*—that is, two different scalable classes exist, each with a different intrinsic ordering of the items. Two possible orderings of items are considered, and the remaining 718 possible orderings are included with the unscalable class. We have considered as model H_3 the hypothesis where scale types 2′, 3′, 5′, 6′ are added to the ones in H_2. (Recall that in H_2, scale type 3 under ordering A was deleted.) Upon estimating H_3 we find that the proportion $\hat{\pi}_{3'}$ approaches zero, so we are led directly to model H_4, where it is assumed that $\pi_{3'} = 0$. We find for H_4 a value $\hat{\pi}_0 = 0.239$ and a likelihood-ratio chi square of 53.2. The general latent-distance model had a chi square of 86.0 on 47 degrees of freedom, so by way of comparison we have obtained a remarkably good fit by taking account of orderings A and A' in the Goodman scale model H_4.

Under H_4 we find that $\hat{\pi}_{6'} = 0.009$, so we next consider H_5, which assumes that $\pi_{6'} = 0$. We find that $X^2(H_5) = 71.0$ and the difference $X^2(H_5) - X^2(H_4)$ is 17.8. Therefore we conclude that scale type 6′ contributes in an important way to explaining the data, implying that (for ordering A') item H is an important discriminator among types.

Model H_6 adds scale type 3 (which was deleted in models H_2 to H_5) to the scale types considered under H_4. That is, the full range of scale types under ordering A, and all the scale types under ordering A' (except scale type 3′), are considered in H_6. We find that $X^2(H_6) = 49.7$, showing only a moderate improvement in fit (over H_4), but we see that $\hat{\pi}_0 = 0.192$. While the improvement in fit is only modest, the reduction in the estimated proportion intrinsically unscalable is substantial; for this reason model H_6 appears preferable to H_4. An additional model was tested that added scale type 3′ in the hope that a biform scale with each dimension complete on all six items would emerge. We found, however, that $\hat{\pi}_{3'}$ was still negligibly different from zero in this modified model, so H_6 is taken as an acceptable summary of the data.

Model H_6 describes the population cross-classification resulting from three distinct kinds of individuals: (1) individuals who are intrinsically scalable under ordering A, (2) individuals who are intrinsically scalable under ordering A' (an ordering that is *very* different from ordering A, but where item S is not important), and (3) individuals comprising an estimated 19.2 percent of the total whose intrinsic orderings of the items are different from orderings A or A'. On the basis of these results we would reject the unidimensionality and cumulativeness of items for the entire population and instead conclude that "bidimensional" or biform scalability is a more plausible possibility for these data. It can be noted that Muthén (1978), using very different methods based on factor analysis, concluded that two different factors appeared to be responsible for the observed association of abortion items. It might be surmised that his finding is in some sense consistent with our own, but this is merely conjecture at the present time.

Before concluding this section we consider model H_7 with a response pattern (2,2,1,1,1,1) included as a scale type. This response pattern would be a scale type (say, type 3″) under an ordering where items H and D were interchanged with items S and N under ordering A. Adding this response pattern to the scale types included in H_6 produces a likelihood-ratio chi square of 41.4 and a nearly identical goodness-of-fit chi square of 43.9 on 46 degrees of freedom. However, we find that $\hat{\pi}_0$ increases from 0.192 to 0.200, so the improvement in fit is in this instance compensated for by an increase in the estimated proportion unscalable. In cases such as these, where there is no clear justification for considering a particular scale type or where the proportion $\hat{\pi}_0$ increases over that obtained in less restrictive models, we recommend that substantive considerations influence the decision concerning alternative models. In this instance we would be led to H_6 once again as an adequate description of the data, since the new scale type in model H_7 appears quite implausible on substantive grounds.

Several other Goodman scale models were considered for the abortion items, but for the sake of brevity we do not discuss them here. Applying these methods to data is, we believe, both simpler and more rigorous than is the case with other methods that might be applied. In our analysis of the scalability of abortion items, we actually began with the ordering suggested by the conventional scalogram methods, and we then used the data to suggest a different ordering (ordering A') that could be given consideration. We have found that model fitting can be greatly simplified by carefully inspecting the standardized residuals associated with particular response patterns. For example, in proceeding from H_2 to H_3, where ordering A' was introduced in a biform scale model, we were led to consider ordering A' by inspection of standardized residuals for the cells corresponding to scale types 2′, 3′, 5′, and 6′. The standardized residuals for these cells were large in magnitude, which suggested model H_3 as an alternative to H_2.

Similar comments apply to our progression from H_6 to H_7. The standardized residual under H_6 for the (2,2,1,1,1,1) cell was 6.58, implying that this response pattern, if included as a scale type in H_7, would produce a great reduction in chi square. (Compare chi-square statistics for H_6 and H_7.) One can indeed use either *forward selection* techniques, using the pattern of standardized residuals as a guide, or *backward elimination* techniques, using the magnitude of the $\hat{\pi}_i$ (for $i > 0$) as a guide; or one could use stepwise techniques that combine the features of both approaches (Draper and Smith, 1966). We believe that the use of these model-fitting procedures can greatly simplify the analysis of the scalability of response patterns while adding rigor to current procedures.

NEW INDICES OF SCALABILITY

To analyze the Goodman scalability of a set of items, the parameter π_0 and the chi-square statistics are important indices. Here we propose two additional indices that can also be used to assess item scalability and are appropriate for all scaling models that can be formulated in terms of latent structure. Under all the probabilistic models considered in this chapter, it is assumed that the population is divided into latent or unobservable classes, and we have denoted the proportions in the latent classes by the parameters π_i. We can consider this categorization of respondents as a latent variable, say variable X, a point to which we return in Appendix B. The first measure we propose as an index of scalability is the lambda measure of association between the latent variable X and the joint variable obtained by considering all k items as a single 2^k-fold variable. The variable X is regarded as dependent, since the k items are conceived as predictors of the classes of the variable, implying that the asymmetric version of lambda is appropriate. This measure has been proposed in a much more general context than this one (Goodman and Kruskal, 1954) and is somewhat analogous to Guttman's coefficient of scalability (see Equation 4). The (asymmetric) lambda measure of association is familiar to social researchers, so we do not discuss it further here.

A second index, closely related to the first, is the percentage of respondents who would be correctly allocated into the classes of the X variable. To illustrate the calculation of this index, consider response pattern (1,1,1,1,1,1)—scale type 1 under all the models of this article. Under model H_6 of the preceding section, we find that an individual who has this observed response pattern has a 0.9879 probability of being a member of the true scale type 1, but a 0.0121 probability of being in the unscalable class—that is, 1.21 percent of the respondents in the (1,1,1,1,1,1) cell actually derive from the unscalable class. Since there are 532 respondents in this cell, we expect to allocate correctly 528.6 ($= 532 \times 0.9879$). The sum of the expected numbers correctly allocated over all the cells in the cross-classification, divided by sample size n, is the expected percentage correctly allocated.

Table 7 presents a comparison of these indices for several models considered in this chapter. We recommend that these indices be used in conjunction with model parameters and chi-square statistics when assessing the overall scalability of a set of items. We see that in terms of these indices the respective models have nearly identical capabilities of predicting the classes of X. These indices are somewhat smaller for the Goodman scale models H_2 to H_7 than for the response error models. The Goodman scale models produce latent X variables with 7 to 12 categories, however, whereas the response error models produce a latent X variable with only 7 categories, so this result is to be expected. These indices are not dependent on sample size (in the way that chi-square statistics are). Thus they might well be used not only in comparing strengths of different models but in comparing results from different samples also. For further details concerning these indices, the reader is referred to Clogg (1977, 1979b, 1980).

TABLE 7
Comparison of Lambda and Percentage Correctly Allocated for Several Models

Model	Lambda	Percentage Correctly Allocated
Proctor's model	0.85	92.5
Proctor's model with equal item-specific response error rates	0.88	93.9
Lazarsfeld's latent-distance model	0.84	91.7
Goodman's model		
H_2	0.85	90.9
H_4	0.83	90.1
H_5	0.82	89.5
H_6	0.84	90.5
H_7	0.83	89.7

It should be noted that, for these data, both the lambda measure and the percentage correctly allocated vary only modestly from one model to the next. The lambdas range from 0.82 to 0.88, while the percentage correctly allocated ranges from 89.5 to 93.9 percent. Two readers of this chapter concluded that since the variability in these new indices of scalability is so modest, it would be inappropriate to use them as criteria for model selection. It appears to us, however, that these indices, in this example at least, are summarizing real scalability properties of the items chosen for analysis, even if they do not discriminate effectively among the statistical models chosen to describe the existence of response errors. That is, the predictability of the classes of the latent variable indicating the scale types is between 82 and 88 percent for these data, depending on the model chosen for analysis.

We are not suggesting that these new indices be used in some ad hoc fashion to accept or reject any of the models considered here. Rather, we are proposing that they be used to construct summary indices of scalability appropriate for models that have been selected on statistical or other grounds. In the present context, for example, all the models except H_6 and H_7 would be rejected on the basis of statistical criteria, but the choice between models H_6 and H_7 might be made in part on the basis of these new indices. While H_7 has a better fit than H_6, its ability to predict the classes of the latent variable is poorer than that of H_6. (The difference is admittedly slight regardless of which index is used.) Using the indices in this way leads us once again to H_6 as an acceptable model.

CONCLUSION

In this chapter several rival models and methods for analyzing the scalability of response patterns were critically compared. Obviously, one cannot accept or reject a model on the basis of analysis of one set of data (such as items on abortion attitudes), but we believe the results do suggest definite advantages of the Goodman scale model over all the others considered here. It would be important in any analysis to consider the relevance of all these models for the substantive issue at hand. In some cases models involving response error parameters might be appropriate; in other cases, the Goodman scale model formulated without reference to response error parameters will be appropriate. It is certainly possible to formulate models with the advantages of both types of models. The Goodman scale model, for example, could easily be modified to incorporate a parameter governing response error rates similar in kind to Proctor's model (Dayton and Macready, 1979). But we believe that the assumption of a *unique* ordering of items for the entire population, made implicitly with all the models except the Goodman model, needs to be carefully examined in each context. On balance, we believe that this critical assumption will be rejected in most cases, and the Goodman model, or extensions of it, should accordingly be given serious attention. Analyzing the scalability of response patterns is only an adjunct to a more fundamental problem of inferring *scale scores* (that is, quantitative scores) to be assigned to each response pattern, and we are currently working on ways to use the Goodman scale model for actually scaling the data.

APPENDIX A: COLLAPSING ITEMS BY USING THE GOODMAN SCALE MODEL

One important technique in item analysis and scale construction is choosing which items should be used to form the scale or, alternatively, choosing which items from a set of items should be deleted or "collapsed" in the analysis. There is a great deal of important work on collapsing variables in contingency table analysis (see Bishop, Fienberg, and Holland, 1975; Whittemore, 1978), and some of these methods can be applied in item analysis. Since the Goodman scale model permits a rigorous statistical approach to this problem, this appendix outlines the procedure in detail. For simplicity, we consider a situation with four items A, B, C, and D, where (i, j, k, l) denotes the response pattern in which responses on these items are at levels i, j, k, and l (for $i = 1, 2$; $j = 1, 2$; $k = 1, 2$; $l = 1, 2$). Results easily generalize to cases where more than four items are involved. We assume that these items are ordered in such a way that the response patterns

$$(1,1,1,1) \qquad (1,1,1,2) \qquad (1,1,2,2) \qquad (1,2,2,2) \qquad (2,2,2,2) \qquad \text{(A-1)}$$

denote the scale types under consideration, and this set of response patterns will be denoted S. The model introduced by Goodman can be expressed in shorthand notation as $H = \{A \otimes B \otimes C \otimes D \mid S\}$, which says that A, B, C, and D are quasi-independent once the response patterns in S have been deleted or blocked out.

Now suppose that H is true; suppose further that item D has been deleted from the cross-classification, so that a three-way cross-classification of items A, B, and C is of interest. The scale types corresponding to the ones in (A-1), but appropriate for this three-way cross-classification, are

$$(1,1,1) \qquad (1,1,2) \qquad (1,2,2) \qquad (2,2,2) \qquad \text{(A-2)}$$

We denote the set of response patterns (scale types) for the three-way table presented in (A-2) as the set S^*. The Goodman scale model for this three-way table can be written as $H^* = \{A \otimes B \otimes C \mid S^*\}$. The basic result is that $H \Longrightarrow H^*$—that is, the truth of H implies the truth of H^*. This result derives from noting that (1) the set S of response patterns for the four-way table is contained in the set S^* for the three-way table and (2) mutual independence among A, B, C, and D implies mutual independence among A, B, and C. Both these facts will be seen to imply that $H \Longrightarrow H^*$.

Let π_{ijkl}^{ABCD} denote the expected proportion in response pattern (i, j, k, l) in the four-way table, and let π_{ijk}^{ABC} denote the expected proportion in response pattern (i, j, k) in the three-way table. Then it is easy to see that π_{111}^{ABC}, the expected proportion in the (1,1,1) pattern in the three-way table, is equal to $\pi_{1111}^{ABCD} + \pi_{1112}^{ABCD}$. This shows that the *two* scale types (1,1,1,1) and (1,1,1,2) in (A-1) are absorbed into the *single* scale type (1,1,1) of (A-2). Similarly, it is obvious that $\pi_{112}^{ABC} = \pi_{1121}^{ABCD} + \pi_{1122}^{ABCD}$—showing that scale types (1,1,2,2) in the four-way table (as well as response pattern (1,1,2,1), which was *not* a scale type) is absorbed into the (1,1,2) scale type in the three-way table, and so on, for each of the scale types in (A-1) and (A-2). This shows that $S \subset S^*$. Blocking out the four response patterns in (A-2) for the three-way marginal table obtained by collapsing over D in the four-way table is thus more restrictive than blocking out the five response patterns in (A-1) for the four-way table.

It is well known that mutual independence among a set of variables implies mutual independence among any subset of those variables (see, for example, Bishop, Fienberg, and Holland, 1975). Moreover, quasi independence among a set of variables implies quasi independence among any subset of those variables, provided that the same cells are blocked out in each case. These results imply that independence of A, B, C, and D (that is, $A \otimes B \otimes C \otimes D$) in the four-way table implies independence among A, B, and C in the marginal table obtained by collapsing over D. Moreover, quasi independence in the four-way table—that is, $H = \{A \otimes B \otimes C \otimes D | S\}$ —implies that A, B, and C are quasi independent in the four-way table where the set of cells in S is blocked out. It further implies that A, B, and C are quasi-independent in the three-way table collapsed over D, whenever the set of cells blocked out in the three-way table includes the set blocked out in the four-way table. The truth of $H^* = \{A \otimes B \otimes C | S^*\}$ is thus implied by the truth of H, since $S \subset S^*$, as was demonstrated in the previous paragraph. These results easily generalize to situations where any item (A, B, C, or D) is deleted or collapsed; they also apply to situations where sets of these items are deleted or collapsed.

To see the relevance of these results for item analysis, consider the situation where π_2 for model H is zero, in which case the scale type (1,1,1,2) does not emerge as an intrinsic scale type. In this case, item D would be of no consequence in discriminating between scale type 1 with response pattern (1,1,1,1) and scale type 3 with response pattern (1,1,2,2). (The reader may verify that item D contributes to the scale *only* if response pattern (1,1,1,2) emerges as a distinct type—that is, when $\pi_2 > 0$.) In this situation, item D could be collapsed and model H^* would be considered for the three-way table. These results show that $H \Longrightarrow H^*$, and so the truth of model H plus the condition where π_2

= 0 together imply that H^* will be true *and* that the D variable can be collapsed without any loss of information to the scale. The results in the body of this chapter show how to test whether $\pi_2 = 0$; this appendix has shown how this result can direct us to consider a collapsed table where one of the items (say, the D item) is ignored. These results extend in a direct way to situations where other items, or sets of items, are judged to contribute nothing to the scale and can thus be collapsed. The reader should compare the simplicity of this statistical approach for the selection of items with the largely informal methods that have arisen to delete items based on analysis of interitem or item-scale correlations (see, for example, Table 3).

APPENDIX B: SCALING MODELS AS RESTRICTED LATENT STRUCTURES

All the scaling models of this chapter can be considered in the framework of the general latent-structure model, a point discussed in Proctor (1970), Goodman (1975), and Clogg (1977). Six items were considered in the example analyzed, and it would have been unwieldy to present the latent-structure notation and formulas appropriate for all the scaling models used. In this appendix the appropriate latent-structure notation is described for a cross-classification of three items; generalization to other situations is immediate. Computer programs like MLLSA (Clogg, 1977) or the somewhat different program listed in Haberman (1979) can be used to obtain maximum-likelihood solutions. Mooijaart (1980) describes methods that can be used to obtain generalized least-squares solutions, which would differ only slightly from those obtained with maximum-likelihood procedures. A survey of relevant latent-structure literature in Clogg (1980) provides comments on the procedures used in these and other latent-structure methods.

For a three-way cross-classification of the dichotomous items A, B, and C, assume that a latent variable X with T classes explains the association among the variables. This means that

$$\pi_{ijk} = \sum_{t=1}^{T} \pi_t^{X} \pi_{it}^{\bar{A}X} \pi_{jt}^{\bar{B}X} \pi_{kt}^{\bar{C}X} \tag{B-1}$$

where π_{ijk} is the expected proportion in the (i, j, k) cell of the observed cross-classification, where π_t^x is the expected proportion in the tth latent class, where $\pi_{it}^{\bar{A}X}$ is the expected conditional probability that variable A takes on level i when X is at level t, and where $\pi_{jt}^{\bar{B}X}$ and $\pi_{kt}^{\bar{C}X}$ are similarly defined conditional probabilities (see Goodman, 1974a). Equation (B-1) is the fundamental equation of latent-structure analysis, and the parameters on the right-hand side are the quantities estimated by latent-structure programs.

Assume that Guttman's model holds, producing four scale types:

$$(1,1,1) \qquad (1,1,2) \qquad (1,2,2) \qquad (2,2,2) \tag{B-2}$$

This means that no other response patterns in the 2^3 table would occur—that is, $\pi_{ijk} = 0$ for all sets (i, j, k) different from the ones in (B-2). Guttman's model is a restricted four-class latent structure, defined in relation to the response patterns in (B-2), with the following restrictions imposed:

$$\pi_{11}^{\bar{A}X} = \pi_{11}^{\bar{B}X} = \pi_{11}^{\bar{C}X} = 1 \tag{B-3}$$

$$\pi_{12}^{\bar{A}X} = \pi_{12}^{\bar{B}X} = \pi_{22}^{\bar{C}X} = 1 \tag{B-4}$$

$$\pi_{13}^{\bar{A}X} = \pi_{23}^{\bar{B}X} = \pi_{23}^{\bar{C}X} = 1 \tag{B-5}$$

$$\pi_{24}^{\bar{A}X} = \pi_{24}^{\bar{B}X} = \pi_{24}^{\bar{C}X} = 1 \tag{B-6}$$

In this situation, where $\pi_{ijk} = 0$ for all response patterns not included in (B-2), we would have $\pi_1^X = \pi_{111}$, $\pi_2^X = \pi_{112}$, $\pi_3^X = \pi_{122}$, and $\pi_4^X = \pi_{222}$. Since response errors typically occur in practice, it is unreasonable to assume that $\pi_{ijk} = 0$ for all response patterns not included as scale types in (B-2). All the statistical models surveyed in this chapter therefore provide an accounting for all the response patterns in the table, in addition to the scale types.

Proctor's model for the three-way table is a restricted four-class latent structure, but it is defined in relation to all the response patterns. His model can be estimated with the MLLSA program by imposing the following equality restrictions:

$$\pi_{11}^{\bar{A}X} = \pi_{11}^{\bar{B}X} = \pi_{11}^{\bar{C}X} =$$

$$\pi_{12}^{\bar{A}X} = \pi_{12}^{\bar{B}X} = \pi_{22}^{\bar{C}X} =$$

$$\pi_{13}^{\bar{A}X} = \pi_{23}^{\bar{B}X} = \pi_{23}^{\bar{C}X} =$$

$$\pi_{24}^{\bar{A}X} = \pi_{24}^{\bar{B}X} = \pi_{24}^{\bar{C}X} .$$

Since all these conditional probabilities are equated, we can denote their common value as $1 - \alpha$. To see why this restricted model is equivalent to Proctor's model, merely note that a response error on any item could occur with a probability of α, the error rate of Proctor's model. (For example, a member of the first intrinsic scale type, with expected response (1,1,1), is defined as the first latent class of X. A response of 2 on item A for a member of this class is regarded as a response error and would occur with probability $\pi_{21}^{\bar{A}X} = 1 - \pi_{11}^{\bar{A}X} = \alpha$.) The restrictions used to define Proctor's model can be laid out as in Table 8, where the conditional probabilities that are restricted to be equal are designated by the integer 2. Conditional probabilities that are not directly restricted (that is, are regarded as "free") are designated by zero. Of course, the explicit equality restrictions imply that the remaining parameters are also restricted implicitly. Since $\pi_{11}^{\bar{A}X} = \pi_{11}^{\bar{B}X} = \pi_{11}^{\bar{C}X}$, and since $\pi_{21}^{\bar{A}X} = 1 - \pi_{12}^{\bar{A}X}$, $\pi_{21}^{\bar{B}X} = 1 - \pi_{11}^{\bar{B}X}$, and $\pi_{21}^{\bar{C}X} = 1 - \pi_{11}^{\bar{C}X}$, we would also have $\pi_{21}^{\bar{A}X} = \pi_{21}^{\bar{B}X} = \pi_{21}^{\bar{C}X}$ and so on. The entries for Proctor's model in Table 8 could be entered directly as the restrictions in the MLLSA program.

To describe other scaling models, the layout in Table 8 for Proctor's model will be used. A zero entry denotes a conditional probability that is free; integers greater than 1 denote equality restrictions. To describe Proctor's model for the three-way table, twelve entries of 2 denote that all the corresponding conditional probabilities of the latent-structure model are equated. To describe the other models in Table 8, other integers are used. The rule is that conditional probabilities corresponding to the same integer are restricted to equal each other. The model of equal item-specific error rates, for example, can be described from Table 8 as a latent structure imposing the following three sets of equality restrictions:

$$\pi_{11}^{\bar{A}X} = \pi_{12}^{\bar{A}X} = \pi_{13}^{\bar{A}X} = \pi_{24}^{\bar{A}X} \qquad \text{(integer 2)}$$

$$\pi_{11}^{\bar{B}X} = \pi_{12}^{\bar{B}X} = \pi_{23}^{\bar{B}X} = \pi_{24}^{\bar{B}X} \qquad \text{(integer 3)}$$

$$\pi_{11}^{\bar{C}X} = \pi_{22}^{\bar{C}X} = \pi_{23}^{\bar{C}X} = \pi_{24}^{\bar{C}X} \qquad \text{(integer 4)}$$

To see how these equality restrictions suffice to produce the model of equal item-specific error rates, consider the first row above pertaining to responses to item A. Since all these conditional probabilities are equated, we could call the common value $1 - \alpha_1$; and a response error

TABLE 8
Restrictions on Conditional Probabilities in Latent-Structure Model Used to Define Response Error Models

	Latent Class t			
	1	2	3	4
Item	(1, 1, 1)	(1, 1, 2)	(1, 2, 2)	(2, 2, 2)
Proctor's model				
$A = 1$	2	2	2	0
2	0	0	0	2
$B = 1$	2	2	0	0
2	0	0	2	2
$C = 1$	2	0	0	0
2	0	2	2	2
Equal item-specific error rates				
$A = 1$	2	2	2	0
2	0	0	0	2
$B = 1$	3	3	0	0
2	0	0	3	3
$C = 1$	4	0	0	0
2	0	4	4	4
Equal true-type-specific error rates				
$A = 1$	2	3	4	0
2	0	0	0	5
$B = 1$	2	3	0	0
2	0	0	4	5
$C = 1$	2	0	0	0
2	0	3	4	5
Lazarsfeld's latent-distance model				
$A = 1$	2	2	2	0
2	0	0	0	2
$B = 1$	3	3	0	0
2	0	0	4	4
$C = 1$	5	0	0	0
2	0	5	5	5

NOTE: An entry of zero denotes a "free" parameter; integers 2, 3, 4, 5 denote that equality restrictions are imposed. See text for details.

on item A would occur with probability α_1, regardless of the intrinsic type of individual considered. Table 8 also presents equality restrictions used in the four-class latent structures to define the true-type-specific error rate model and Lazarsfeld's latent-distance model. If the conditional probabilities were completely unrestricted, then the model would be an unrestricted four-class latent structure; however, the parameters for this model would be unidentifiable.

Goodman's scale model can be viewed as a quasi-independence model (see related comments in Appendix A), and general techniques appropriate for analysis of the quasi-independence model can be directly applied. The model can also be viewed as a restricted five-class latent structure, and the restrictions used to define it are presented in Table 9. Here, as in the body of this chapter, the zeroth class refers to the intrinsically unscalable class and the conditional probabilities $\pi_{i0}^{\bar{A}X}$, $\pi_{j0}^{\bar{B}X}$, $\pi_{k0}^{\bar{C}X}$ are free (unrestricted). The conditional probabilities pertaining to latent classes 1, 2, 3, and 4, corresponding respectively to the four intrinsic scale types, are restricted in the same way as in (B-3) to (B-6), the restrictions used to define Guttman's model. We use the integer 1 in Table 9 to denote that the corresponding conditional probability is set equal to 1. Thus $\pi_{11}^{\bar{A}X} = 1$, $\pi_{12}^{\bar{A}X} = 1, \ldots, \pi_{24}^{\bar{C}X} = 1$ for the Goodman scale model. To consider demiscale types, biform scales, multiform scales, and the like, as was considered at length by Goodman (1975), one merely adds additional latent classes to the model, imposing 0–1 restrictions of the same type.

Dayton and Macready (1979) consider models that combine the features of the Goodman scale model (with intrinsically unscalable individuals) and the response error models considered here. One example of this kind is a "Proctor–Goodman" model, the equality

TABLE 9
Restrictions on Conditional Probabilities in Latent-Structure Model Used to Define Goodman Scale Model and Related Models

	Latent Class t				
	0	1	2	3	4
Item	(Unscalable)	(1, 1, 1)	(1, 1, 2)	(1, 2, 2)	(2, 2, 2)
Goodman's model for a uniform scale					
$A = 1$	0	1	1	1	0
2	0	0	0	0	1
$B = 1$	0	1	1	0	0
2	0	0	0	1	1
$C = 1$	0	1	0	0	0
2	0	0	1	1	1
Proctor–Goodman scale model					
$A = 1$	0	2	2	2	0
2	0	0	0	0	2
$B = 1$	0	2	2	0	0
2	0	0	0	2	2
$C = 1$	0	2	0	0	0
2	0	0	2	2	2

restrictions for which appear in Table 9. Other models that combine the features of the Goodman scale model with various other response error models can be easily devised.

REFERENCES

ARNEY, W., AND TRESCHER, W.

1976 Trends in attitudes toward abortion, 1972–1975." *Family Planning Perspectives* 8:117–127.

BARR, A. J., AND OTHERS

1976 *A User's Guide to SAS 76.* Raleigh, N.C.: SAS Institute.

BISHOP, Y. M., FIENBERG, S. E., AND HOLLAND, P. W.

1975 *Discrete Multivariate Analysis: Theory and Practice.* Cambridge, Mass.: M.I.T. Press.

CHRISTOFFERSSON, A.

1975 "Factor analysis of dichotomized variables." *Psychometrika* 40:5–32.

CLOGG, C. C.

1977 "Unrestricted and restricted maximum likelihood latent structure analysis: A manual for users." Working Paper 1977–09. University Park, Pa.: Population Issues Research Office.

1979a "Characterizing the class organization of labor market opportunity: A modified latent structure approach." *Sociological Methods and Research* 8:243–272.

1979b "Some latent structure models for the analysis of Likert-type data." *Social Science Research* 8:287–301.

1980 "New developments in latent structure analysis." In D. M. Jackson and E. F. Borgatta (Eds.), *Factor Analysis and Measurement in Sociological Research.* Beverly Hills: Sage.

COOMBS, C. H., COOMBS, L. C., AND LINGOES, J. C.

1978 "Stochastic cumulative scales." In S. Shye (Ed.), *Theory Construction and Data Analysis in the Behavioral Sciences.* San Francisco: Jossey-Bass.

DAVIS, J. A.

1975 *Codebook for 1975 General Social Survey.* Chicago: National Opinion Research Center.

DAYTON, C. M., AND MACREADY, G. B.

1979 "A scaling model with response errors and intrinsically unscalable respondents." *Psychometrika* in press.

DRAPER, N. R., AND SMITH, H.

1966 *Applied Regression Analysis.* New York: Wiley.

DUNCAN, O. D.

1979 "Indicators of sex typing: Traditional and egalitarian, situational and ideological responses." *American Journal of Sociology* 85:251–260.

EDWARDS, A. L.

1957 *Techniques of Attitude and Scale Construction.* New York: Appleton-Century-Crofts.

GOODENOUGH, W. H.

1944 "A technique for scale analysis." *Educational and Psychological Measurement* 4:179–190.

GOODMAN, L. A.

1959 "Simple statistical methods for scalogram analysis." *Psychometrika* 24:29–43.

1974a "The analysis of systems of qualitative variables when some of the variables are unobservable. Part I–A: Modified latent structure approach." *American Journal of Sociology* 79:1179–1259.

1974b "The analysis of systems of qualitative variables when some of the variables are unobservable. Part II: The use of modified latent distance models." Unpublished manuscript.

1975 "A new model for scaling response patterns: An application of the quasi-independence concept." *Journal of American Statistical Association* 70:755–768.

GOODMAN, L. A., AND KRUSKAL, W. H.

1954 "Measures of association for cross-classifications." *Journal of American Statistical Association* 49:732–764.

GUTTMAN, L.

1950 "The basis for scalogram analysis." In S. A. Stouffer and others (Eds.), *Measurement and Prediction: Studies in Social Psychology in World War II.* Vol. 4. Princeton: Princeton University Press.

HABERMAN, S. J.

1979 *Analysis of Qualitative Data.* Vol. 2: *New Developments.* New York: Academic Press.

HAYS, D. G. AND BORGATTA, E. F.

1954 "An empirical comparison of restricted and general latent distance analysis." *Psychometrika* 19:271–279.

JONES, E. F., AND WESTOFF, C. F.

1972 "Attitudes toward abortion in the United States in 1970 and the trend since 1965." In C. F. Westoff and R. Parke (Eds.), *Commission on Population Growth and the American Future Research Reports.* Vol. 1. Washington, D.C.: Government Printing Office.

KIM, J., AND RABJOHN, J.

1979 "Binary variables and index construction." In K. F. Schuessler (Ed.), *Sociological Methodology 1980.* San Francisco: Jossey-Bass.

LAZARSFELD, P. F., AND HENRY, N. W.

1968 *Latent Structure Analysis.* Boston: Houghton Mifflin.

MOKKEN, R. J.

1971 *A Theory and Procedure of Scale Analysis.* The Hague: Mouton.

MOOIJAART, A.

1980 "Latent structure analysis for categorical variables." Research Report 80-4. Department of Statistics, University of Uppsala, Sweden.

MUTHÉN, B.

1978 "Analyzing the response structure of dichotomous items." Paper presented at the 9th World Congress of Sociology, Uppsala, Sweden, August 1978.

1979 "A structural probit model with latent variables." *Journal of American Statistical Association* 74:807–811.

NIE, N. H., AND OTHERS.

1975 *SPSS: Statistical Package for the Social Sciences.* New York: McGraw-Hill.

PROCTOR, C. H.

1970 "A probabilistic formulation and statistical analysis of Guttman scaling." *Psychometrika* 35:73–78.

1971 "Reliability of a Guttman scale score." *Proceedings of the Social Statistics Section, Annual Meeting of the American Statistical Association.* Washington, D.C.: American Statistical Association.

TORGERSON, W. S.

1962 *Theory and Methods of Scaling.* New York: Wiley.

WESTOFF, C. F., MOORE, E., AND RYDER, N. B.

1969 "The structure of attitudes toward abortion." *Milbank Memorial Fund Quarterly* 47:11–37.

WHITTEMORE, A.

1978 "Collapsibility of multidimensional contingency tables." *Journal of Royal Statistical Society,* series B, 40:328–340.

7

TWO FACES OF PANEL ANALYSIS: PARALLELS WITH COMPARATIVE CROSS-SECTIONAL ANALYSIS AND TIME-LAGGED ASSOCIATION

Otis Dudley Duncan
UNIVERSITY OF ARIZONA

The two major objectives of this chapter are to clarify the relationships between analyses of panel data and comparative cross-sectional (CCS) data and to describe some specialized models that

This research was supported by National Science Foundation Grant SOC77-27365. Lawrence Santi assisted with computations and analysis. The study is a response to questions raised in correspondence with David Knoke, and his suggestions concerning a previous draft of the chapter were most helpful. Philip Converse also made helpful comments. Neither of them is necessarily in agreement with this chapter's conclusions.

supplement the standard hierarchical models (Goodman, 1978, chap. 4) used in an earlier analysis (Knoke, 1976, chap. 6) of panel data from the 1956/1960 election surveys of the Survey Research Center. Consideration of these methodological matters is timely, inasmuch as a new set of panel data from the 1972/1976 election surveys has recently become available (Converse and Markus, 1979) and will undoubtedly be analyzed intensively. The reader is assumed to be conversant with log linear models, especially as presented by Goodman (1978), because this chapter reviews only a few topics directly related to the new material presented.

As in social indicators research, the results will have some utility for the student of elections interested in "improvement of the record of the past" (Boulding, 1978, p. 136). But no systematic comparison of the present findings with earlier studies of these elections (notably Campbell and others, 1966) is offered. This entire chapter is devoted to a single (albeit complex) multiway contingency table. Clearly, this is no essay in theory construction or theory testing. Nor is it my intention to propose a general model of voters' choices along the lines of Knoke (1976) and Markus and Converse (1979). Instead, my interest here is explicitly historical. The analysis focuses on the thing that most conspicuously set the 1960 election apart from other modern elections—the presidential candidacy of a Catholic on the Democratic ticket. This emphasis on *year* as a causal factor (or, more correctly, a proxy for a collection of indirectly observed causal factors) emerges quite naturally in CCS analysis. But one must look beyond the set of hierarchical models previously suggested (Goodman, 1978, chap. 6) for the causal analysis of panel data if year is to be treated explicitly as a factor. The idea that such a strategy needs to be articulated was slow in dawning on the present writer, for whom it emerged serendipitously as the models discussed here were explored. Hence the reiteration of this point toward the end of the chapter, when relevant empirical results are in hand.

DATA FORMAT AND NOTATION

The data in Table 1 pertain to 786 respondents interviewed twice: once at the time of the 1956 election and again on the occasion of the 1960 election. (There were also interviews with the panel in 1958, but these are ignored here.) A number of respondents voted for the

TABLE 1
Observed Frequencies for Presidential Vote by Party Identification, Religion, and Year: 1956–1960 Panel

	1956		1960					
			Dem Party		Ind		Rep Party	
Religion	Party	Vote	Dem Vote	Rep Vote	Dem Vote	Rep Vote	Dem Vote	Rep Vote
Catholic	Dem	Dem	69	1	2	1	1	0
		Rep	26	4	1	0	0	0
	Ind	Dem	7	0	11	1	0	0
		Rep	12	0	11	7	3	3
	Rep	Dem	1	0	0	0	1	0
		Rep	8	2	6	3	6	15
Non-Catholic	Dem	Dem	127	29	17	2	0	0
		Rep	15	24	4	4	0	3
	Ind	Dem	11	3	9	5	0	1
		Rep	1	6	21	52	1	33
	Rep	Dem	1	0	3	0	1	1
		Rep	2	0	2	16	9	181

SOURCE: 1956 and 1960 election studies, Survey Research Center, tabulated by Knoke (1976, table 6.4).

candidates of different parties in the two years or changed their party identification or both. According to the tabulation, none of them changed from Catholic to non-Catholic religious preference or vice versa. (Such changes, presumably few, either were not identified or were excluded from the tabulation.) Religion, accordingly, is regarded as a fixed factor, so that the analysis pertains to what Lazarsfeld, Pasanella, and Rosenberg (1972, p. 324) called "qualified change." That is, we are prepared for the possibility that the process of changing vote or party or both differs in some respects for Catholics and non-Catholics.

In Table 2 the same data have been used to construct two three-way tables, one for each year, showing religion by party by vote. The juxtaposition of the two cross-sectional tables illustrates the format of CCS data. But Table 2 is a *pseudo* four-way table, inasmuch as the samples for the two years are not independent. Indeed, they are identical. For conceptualizing the analysis of CCS data, Table 2 will be useful. But we must continually remind ourselves that it is not actually a four-way table.

A compact notation will be helpful. Let the letters R, P, V, and Y stand for religion, party, vote, and year. Subscripts 1 and 2 attached

TABLE 2
Two Sets of Three-Way Marginals of Table 1 Arranged as Pseudo Four-Way Table to Illustrate Format of Data for Comparative Cross-Sectional Analysis

Year	Religion	Party	Vote: Dem	Vote: Rep	Total
1956	Catholic	Dem	74	31	105
		Ind	19	36	55
		Rep	2	40	42
		Total	95	107	202
	Non-Catholic	Dem	175	50	225
		Ind	29	114	143
		Rep	6	210	216
		Total	210	374	584
1960	Catholic	Dem	123	7	130
		Ind	31	12	43
		Rep	11	18	29
		Total	165	37	202
	Non-Catholic	Dem	157	62	219
		Ind	56	79	135
		Rep	11	219	230
		Total	224	360	584

to P or V distinguish responses in 1956 from those obtained in 1960. A letter or combination of letters enclosed in braces refers to the (cross) tabulation of sample frequencies for the designated variables, following Goodman's (1978) convention. Thus $\{R\}$ is the one-way table of sample counts for religion—that is, the two counts: 202 Catholics and 584 non-Catholics. The upper half of Table 2 is the three-way cross-classification $\{RP_1V_1\}$, religion by party in 1956 by vote in 1956, and the lower half is $\{RP_2V_2\}$. Table 1 is the five-way table $\{RP_1V_1P_2V_2\}$. Note that $\{RP_1V_1\}$ is one of several possible sets of three-way marginals of $\{RP_1V_1P_2V_2\}$. (There are 10 such sets altogether.) If Table 2 were a genuine set of CCS data, we would label it $\{YRPV\}$. Since it is not, we may write pseudo-$\{YRPV\}$ to designate this pseudo-CCS table.

A set of letters enclosed in parentheses stands for the statistical interaction of the designated variables, and we shall often be interested in the hypothesis that such an interaction is nil or that two (or more) interactions (having the same dimensions) are equal. An interaction may be *marginal* if it is examined without reference to other variables or *partial* (conditional) if it is calculated with one or more other variables entered into a multiway model (Brown, 1976). The table $\{RP_2\}$, for example, can be constructed by collapsing $\{RP_1V_1P_2V_2\}$ over categories of the joint variable $P_1V_1V_2$ if one wishes to examine the marginal two-way interaction (or association) (RP_2). While there is only one such marginal association, there are many different partial associations between R and P_2, depending on the handling of other variables.

A *hierarchical* model for a multiway table may be specified by listing, in the fashion of Goodman (1978), the sets of cross-classifications fitted. Two possible hierarchical models for Table 1 are $\{RP_2\}$, $\{RP_1\}$, $\{RV_1V_2\}$, $\{P_2V_2\}$, $\{P_1P_2\}$ and $\{RP_2\}$, $\{RV_2\}$, $\{RP_1V_1\}$, $\{P_1P_2V_1V_2\}$. The partial interaction (RP_2) estimated from the former might differ considerably from the estimate obtained from the latter. In discussing a partial interaction, therefore, it is necessary to specify the entirety of the model under which it is estimated.

We shall have little occasion to consider one-way interactions, but for completeness we note that hypotheses about them could be tested. The hypothesis $[(R) = 0]$ states that the categories Catholic and non-Catholic are equiprobable. If (R) is taken to refer to the marginal one-way interaction, the test of H is readily accomplished by noting that estimates $\hat{F}$ of expected counts corresponding to the observed counts f of 202 Catholics and 584 non-Catholics are $786/2 = 393$ Catholics and 393 non-Catholics. Hence the likelihood-ratio χ^2 value is $L^2 = 2\Sigma f \log (f/\hat{F}) = 193.8$, DF = 1. Actually, since religion is regarded as a (fixed) factor in the subsequent analysis, there is no occasion to test this hypothesis; it was introduced only for didactic purposes.

CROSS-SECTIONAL INTERACTIONS

CCS and Panel Hypotheses and Tests within Religious Categories

We are now ready to see how hypotheses of interest in CCS analysis suggest *corresponding,* though not identical, hypotheses for panel analysis.[1] To begin with the most elementary problems, we treat

[1]In a single empirical investigation, not all these hypotheses will be of equal substantive interest, nor will they have equally strong theoretical motivation. For the sake of completeness, several hypotheses are mentioned that are of incidental interest in the analysis of the 1956/1960 data.

Catholics and non-Catholics as separate populations and take up hypotheses pertaining to $\{P_1V_1P_2V_2\}$ within each of them. That is, the top and bottom halves of Table 1 are studied in parallel so that the data pertain to a two-wave two-variable panel survey conducted within each of two populations. The pseudo-CCS data are pseudo-$\{YPV\}$ for Catholics and pseudo-$\{YPV\}$ for non-Catholics. We consider only those hypotheses in CCS analysis that involve Y, inasmuch as the whole purpose of CCS analysis is to detect and describe changes in the distributions, associations, or interactions of variables from one year to another.

Consider the CCS table $\{YV\}$ and the hypothesis $[(YV) = 0]$—the hypothesis that the vote distributions of the two years are homogeneous. Since Y and V are both dichotomous, there is 1 degree of freedom for the test of this hypothesis. In the panel format, year is not an explicit variable but a subscript identifying the time at which vote (for example) is observed. The two sample vote distributions are $\{V_1\}$ and $\{V_2\}$, but since they pertain to the same respondents, they appear as the one-way marginals of the two-way cross-classification $\{V_1V_2\}$. The hypothesis that $\{V_1\}$ and $\{V_2\}$ are drawn from the same population distribution of votes is, then, the hypothesis of marginal homogeneity (MH) for the $\{V_1V_2\}$ table. In a 2×2 table the hypotheses of symmetry (Sym) and MH are equivalent, and Sym implies that the (unconditional) probabilities pertaining to change in vote are equal: $\Pr(D \rightarrow R) = \Pr(R \rightarrow D)$. The other two joint probabilities, $\Pr(D \rightarrow D)$ and $\Pr(R \rightarrow R)$, are not relevant, so no assumption is made as to their relative magnitudes. Once the $\{V_1V_2\}$ cross-classification is obtained by the appropriate collapsing of Table 1, we see (Table 3) that for Catholics (for example) f_{12} = frequency of $(D \rightarrow R) = 3$ and f_{21} = frequency of $(R \rightarrow D) = 73$. Corresponding to these observed counts

TABLE 3
$\{V_1V_2\}$ by Religion

Religion	1956 Vote	1960 Vote Dem	Rep	Total
Catholic	Dem	92	3	95
	Rep	73	34	107
	Total	165	37	202
Non-Catholic	Dem	169	41	210
	Rep	55	319	374
	Total	224	360	584

are the estimates of expected counts under the hypothesis: $\hat{F}_{12} = \hat{F}_{21} = (3 + 73)/2 = 38.0$. Calculation of the likelihood-ratio χ^2 statistic takes the same form as calculation for the hypothesis of equiprobability described earlier. For Catholics, we find L^2 (Sym) = 80.08, DF = 1, $P < 0.001$; for non-Catholics, L^2 (Sym) = 2.05, DF = 1, $P = 0.15$. For Catholics there is strong evidence of a change in the vote distribution from 1956 to 1960; for non-Catholics, no such change is detected.

A new problem is raised by the CCS table $\{YP\}$ and the hypothesis $[(YP) = 0]$. The corresponding panel hypothesis is $[(P_1) = (P_2)]$—that is, the hypothesis of MH for the table $\{P_1P_2\}$. But P, unlike V, has three classes, so we must now distinguish Sym and MH. It remains true that Sym $\Rightarrow$ MH, but the converse does not hold. Instead, we take advantage of the theorem MH $\cap$ QSym $\Leftrightarrow$ Sym, where QSym stands for quasi symmetry (Bishop, Fienberg, and Holland, 1975, chap. 8). On the hypothesis of Sym we have the equality of expected frequencies, $F_{ij} = F_{ji}$; QSym means that this condition is approached as closely as possible, given nonhomogeneity of marginals, $F_{i.} \neq F_{.i}$. Since L^2 (MH) + L^2 (QSym) = L^2 (Sym), it is easy to obtain the test statistic for MH as the difference, L^2 (MH) = L^2 (Sym) − L^2 (QSym), after computing the latter two quantities directly. Estimates of expected frequencies under Sym are given by $\hat{F}_{ij} = \hat{F}_{ji} = (f_{ij} + f_{ji})/2$. Under QSym, we again have $\hat{F}_{ij} + \hat{F}_{ji} = f_{ij} + f_{ji}$ and also $\hat{F}_{i.} = f_{i.}$ and $\hat{F}_{.j} = f_{.j}$; the method of iterative proportional fitting (Bishop, Fienberg, and Holland, 1975, sec. 3.5, 8.2.3) is used to obtain $\hat{F}$ under QSym. Actually, it suffices to fit the sums $(f_{ij} + f_{ji})$ and the row marginals $f_{i.}$, since these conditions together imply that the column marginals $f_{.j}$ also are fitted. It should be noted that the diagonal counts are ignored in all these calculations. The $\{P_1P_2\}$ cross-classifications for Catholics and non-Catholics are shown as Table 4. For a $J \times J$ table, degrees of freedom are given by the formulas DF(Sym) = $J(J - 1)/2$, DF(QSym) = $(J - 1)(J - 2)/2$; DF(MH) = DF(Sym) − DF(QSym) = $J - 1$. Note that DF(MH) = $J - 1$ is the same as DF for the hypothesis of homogeneity of response distributions for two years in the CCS $2 \times J$ table $\{YP\}$.

Table 5 reports the statistics for the three hypotheses. We find that the non-Catholic data conform acceptably well to the hypothesis of Sym. This hypothesis has no counterpart in CCS analysis, of course, so we should note that the hypothesis of MH is also acceptable for

TABLE 4
$\{P_1P_2\}$ by Religion

Religion	1956 Party	1960 Party Dem	Ind	Rep	Total
Catholic	Dem	100	4	1	105
	Ind	19	30	6	55
	Rep	11	9	22	42
	Total	130	43	29	202
Non-Catholic	Dem	195	27	3	225
	Ind	21	87	35	143
	Rep	3	21	192	216
	Total	219	135	230	584

non-Catholics. For Catholics, however, both Sym and MH are rejected. As in the analysis of $\{V_1V_2\}$, we find significant (net) change in favor of the Democratic candidate for Catholics but not for non-Catholics.

The techniques discussed thus far are fully described in the literature on log linear models. We come now to a problem only recently discussed (Duncan, 1979b). Consider the three-way CCS table $\{YPV\}$. The salient hypothesis is that the (PV) association is the same in both years; that is, there is no three-way interaction: $[(YPV) = 0]$. The corresponding hypothesis for the panel analysis is $[(P_1V_1) = (P_2V_2)]$. To test it, we must examine the four-way table $\{P_1V_1P_2V_2\}$—that is, for Catholics and non-Catholics, respectively, the top and bottom halves of Table 1. Each of these is a table with six rows (three party by two vote classes) and six corresponding columns. It is obvious that if this 6×6 table had homogeneous margins in the population, the hypothesis just stated would be true, for in that event the distribution of the joint variable P_1V_1 would be the same as that of P_2V_2. But this sufficient condition is not a necessary condition, inasmuch as the two associations (P_1V_1) and (P_2V_2) can be the same

TABLE 5
Likelihood-Ratio χ^2 Statistics, L^2, for Specified Hypotheses Concerning $\{P_1P_2\}$ Table, by Religion

Hypothesis	DF	Catholic	Non-Catholic
Symmetry	3	20.99[a]	4.29
Quasi symmetry	1	0.12	0.69
Marginal homogeneity	2	20.87[a]	3.60

[a]$P < 0.05$. For all other values, $P > 0.1$.

(all odds ratios in the population cross-classification of P_1 by V_1 are the same as the corresponding odds ratios in the population cross-classification of P_2 by V_2) even though none of the expected frequencies for $\{P_1V_1\}$ is the same as for $\{P_2V_2\}$. Thus, while the hypothesis of MH for $\{P_1V_1P_2V_2\}$, regarded as a two-way 6×6 table, is relevant, we shall find it necessary to partition that hypothesis to come to grips with the hypothesis of interest.

Let the observed counts in $\{P_1V_1P_2V_2\}$ be $f_{ijk\ell}$. Here $i = 1, 2, 3$ labels the classes of P_1; $j = 1, 2$ labels the classes of V_1; $k = 1, 2, 3$ labels the classes of P_2; and $\ell = 1, 2$ labels the classes of V_2. We consider a sequence of four models:

1. H_1 This is the hypothesis of Sym for the 6×6 table, P_1V_1 by P_2V_2, expected frequencies under which are estimated by fitting $(f_{ijk\ell} + f_{k\ell ij})$ with the six diagonals $f_{1111}, \ldots, f_{3232}$ deleted.
2. H_2 If, in addition, we fit $\{V_1\}$ (and thereby $\{V_2\}$) so that $\hat{F}_{i1..} = f_{i1..}$ and $\hat{F}_{i2..} = f_{i2..}$, $i = 1, 2, 3$ (entailing $\hat{F}_{..k1} = f_{..k1}$ and $\hat{F}_{..k2} = f_{..k2}$, $k = 1, 2, 3$), we modify the hypothesis of Sym to allow vote to change from 1956 to 1960.
3. H_3 Next we also fit $\{P_1\}$ (and thereby $\{P_2\}$), thus allowing both vote and party, considered separately, to change.
4. H_4 Finally, in addition to the sums already fitted, we fit $\{P_1V_1\}$ (and thereby $\{P_2V_2\}$)—that is, the row marginals (and, thereby, the column marginals) of $\{P_1V_1P_2V_2\}$ regarded as a 6×6 two-way table.[2]

The first and the last models are equivalent, respectively, to the models of symmetry and quasi symmetry for the 6×6 table. The two intermediate models have no recognized names. But the sequence of four models partitions the hypothesis of MH for the 6×6 table, since

$$L^2(H_1) - L^2(H_4) = L^2(\text{MH}) = [L^2(H_1) - L^2(H_2)] + [L^2(H_2) - L^2(H_3)] + [L^2(H_3) - L^2(H_4)]$$

and each of these components has a definite meaning. Degrees of freedom for H_1 are calculated by the usual formula for the hypothesis

[2]We note that fitting the marginals specified in H_3 and then those in H_2 provides an alternative partitioning if one is desired. See Duncan (1979b) for a discussion of these two alternatives.

of Sym. The table $\{P_1V_1P_2V_2\}$, regarded as a two-way table, has $IJ = 6$ rows and $IJ = 6$ columns; hence $IJ(IJ - 1)/2 = 15$ DF for the hypothesis of Sym. However, in the Catholic data we find $(f_{ijk\ell} + f_{k\ell ij}) = 0$ for three pairs of cells, so that the degrees of freedom are diminished by 3. There is a reduction of 1 degree of freedom for the non-Catholic data for the same reason. Since there are $J = 2$ categories of V, the degrees of freedom are reduced by 1 in going from H_1 to H_2. With $I = 3$ categories of P, the degrees of freedom are further reduced by 2 in going from H_2 to H_3. For H_4, the degrees of freedom can be computed by the usual formula for the hypothesis of QSym, $(IJ - 1)(IJ - 2)/2$, but the result is adjusted downward as noted earlier because of the zeros fitted under H_1. Note that DF(MH) = DF(H_1) − DF(H_4) = $IJ - 1 = 5$. This parallels the calculation for the CCS analysis for the hypothesis that the $\{PV\}$ distributions of the two years are homogeneous. To explain this remark and to bring out other correspondences between the CCS and panel analyses, we refer to the following schematic version of a CCS $\{YPV\}$ cross-classification:

	P:	D	D	I	I	R	R
Y	*V*:	D	R	D	R	D	R
1							
2							

We consider three models for this table described in terms of marginals fitted:

Model	Fits	DF
H_a	$\{Y\}$, $\{PV\}$	5
H_b	$\{YV\}$, $\{PV\}$	4
H_c	$\{YV\}$, $\{YP\}$, $\{PV\}$	2

The correspondences are, therefore, as follows:

CCS Test	Panel Test	DF
$L^2(H_a)$	$L^2(H_1) - L^2(H_4)$	5
$L^2(H_a) - L^2(H_b)$	$L^2(H_1) - L^2(H_2)$	1
$L^2(H_b) - L^2(H_c)$	$L^2(H_2) - L^2(H_3)$	2
$L^2(H_c)$	$L^2(H_3) - L^2(H_4)$	2

It is the last of these components that serves as the test statistic for the hypothesis $[(P_1V_1) = (P_2V_2)]$.

The main result, in terms of the question that motivated this work, is that for Catholics $L^2(H_3) - L^2(H_4) = 1.66$ (DF = 2) but for non-Catholics $L^2(H_3) - L^2(H_4) = 17.64$ (DF = 2). (See Table 6.)

TABLE 6
Likelihood-Ratio χ^2 Statistics, L^2, for Specified Hypotheses Concerning $\{P_1 V_1 P_2 V_2\}$ Table, by Religion

		Catholic		Non-Catholic	
Model	Fits	DF	L^2	DF	L^2
H_1	$(f_{ijk\ell} + f_{k\ell ij})$	12	88.58	14	44.89
H_2	H_1 and $\{V_1\}$	11	8.50	13	42.84
H_3	H_2 and $\{P_1\}$	9	5.52	11	39.02
H_4	H_3 and $\{V_1 P_1\}$	7	3.86	9	21.38

Hence there was no significant change in the association of party and vote for Catholics but a highly significant change for non-Catholics. In CCS terms, we would be able to accept $[(YPV) = 0]$ for Catholics but would reject it for non-Catholics.

Some further remarks to clarify the interpretation of these models are needed. The component $L^2(H_1) - L^2(H_2)$ is identical with L^2(Sym) or L^2(MH) for the $\{V_1 V_2\}$ table presented earlier. However, $L^2(H_2) - L^2(H_3)$ is not the same as L^2(MH) for the $\{P_1 P_2\}$ marginal table. Here, by virtue of the order in which $\{V_1\}$ and $\{P_1\}$ are fitted, $L^2(H_2) - L^2(H_3)$ pertains not to the hypothesis concerning the marginal interaction $[\,(P_1) = (P_2)\,]$ but to a similarly stated hypothesis about a partial interaction. Thus there is substantive interest in the finding that $L^2(H_2) - L^2(H_3)$ for Catholics is not significant. Once change in vote has been taken into account, change in party is not significant. For non-Catholics, $L^2(H_2) - L^2(H_3)$ yields the same conclusion as the analysis pertaining to the marginal interaction—to wit, no significant change in party.

The pattern of results described thus far seems fully intelligible in the light of our knowledge that the 1960 election was a contest between a Catholic Democrat and a non-Catholic Republican and was the only presidential election involving a Catholic candidate besides the 1928 election. There is, however, one feature of the results that invites closer scrutiny. Whereas the hypothesis of QSym for the 6×6 $P_1 V_1$-by-$P_2 V_2$ table is quite acceptable for Catholics, $L^2(H_4)$ is highly significant for non-Catholics. Thus, for the latter, the asymmetry of the $P_1 V_1$-by-$P_2 V_2$ table cannot be attributed entirely to the marginal change in the party-by-vote distribution. It turns out that the asymmetry not captured by H_4 can be attributed to the cross-lagged association $(V_1 P_2)$. This is an across-time interaction that has no counterpart in

CCS analysis. Accordingly, its elucidation is postponed to a later discussion.

Changes in Cross-Sectional Interactions Involving Religion

We have found apparently ample evidence of differences between Catholics and non-Catholics in the patterns of change in the distributions of vote and party identification. It might seem redundant, therefore, to inquire whether there was change in the relationship of religion to vote or party or both between 1956 and 1960. After all, in CCS analysis a significant three-way interaction (YRV), or (YRP), is one and the same thing, mathematically, whether we read it as "differential change, by religion, in the vote (or party) distribution" or as "change in the association of religion with vote (or party)." The fact is, however, that none of the work described thus far actually yields *tests* of the apparent differences between the changes noted for Catholics and non-Catholics. To carry out such tests, we now regard religion as one of the two factors in the CCS $\{YRPV\}$ cross-classification, the other being year, and inquire what panel-analysis hypotheses correspond to CCS hypotheses involving this factor. Before studying the complete cross-classification, we examine tabulations involving P and V one at a time.

Beginning with the CCS table $\{YRP\}$ and the hypothesis $[(YRP) = 0]$ of no three-way interaction—that is, no change in the (RP) association—we see that the corresponding hypothesis in panel analysis is $[(RP_1) = (RP_2)]$ and the requisite tabulation is $\{RP_1P_2\}$. To gain insight into this problem, let us momentarily suppose that religion, like party, is a modifiable response rather than a fixed factor. Then we would be working with a four-way cross-classification $\{R_1P_1R_2P_2\}$, so that the entire discussion of $\{P_1V_1P_2V_2\}$ could be carried over with a relabeling of two variables. Indeed we may think of $\{RP_1P_2\}$ itself as the *incomplete* four-way table (Bishop, Fienberg, and Holland, 1975, sec. 5.4) shown as Table 7. Half the cells in the tabulation, those designated by asterisks, are necessarily empty. The consequence is that when we fit the model of Sym for the 6 × 6 table (diagonal cells disregarded), we unavoidably fit $\{R\}$ at the same time. Our earlier sequence of four models collapses to a sequence of three. Model H_5 fits $(f_{ijk\ell} + f_{k\ell ij})$ and, thereby, $\{R\}$ as well. Model H_6 fits in addition $\{P_1\}$ and, thereby, $\{P_2\}$. Model H_7 fits in addition $\{RP_1\}$, alias

TABLE 7
$\{RP_1P_2\}$ Written as Incomplete Four-Way Table

		Religion by 1960 Party					
	1956	Catholic			Non-Catholic		
Religion	Party	Dem	Ind	Rep	Dem	Ind	Rep
Catholic	Dem	100	4	1	*	*	*
	Ind	19	30	6	*	*	*
	Rep	11	9	22	*	*	*
Non-Catholic	Dem	*	*	*	195	27	3
	Ind	*	*	*	21	87	35
	Rep	*	*	*	3	21	192

*Structural zero.

$\{R_1P_1\}$, and thereby $\{RP_2\}$, alias $\{R_2P_2\}$. Results computed for $\{RP_1P_2\}$ follow:

$$L^2(H_5) = 25.27;\ \mathrm{DF} = 6$$

$$L^2(H_6) = 20.91;\ \mathrm{DF} = 4$$

$$L^2(H_7) = 0.81;\ \mathrm{DF} = 2$$

Note that $L^2(H_5) - L^2(H_6) = 4.36$, DF $= 2$, tests the hypothesis of MH for the $\{P_1P_2\}$ table for the aggregate of Catholics and non-Catholics. Earlier, we were able to reject that hypothesis for Catholics but not for the larger population of non-Catholics. But the more interesting result is $L^2(H_6) - L^2(H_7) = 20.10$, DF $= 2$, leading to rejection of the hypothesis $[(RP_1) = (RP_2)]$. In CCS terms, we surmise that the hypothesis $[(YRP) = 0]$ would be rejected. In a CCS analysis, the models of interest would be:

Model	Fits	DF
H_d	$\{YR\}, \{RP\}$	4
H_e	$\{YR\}, \{YP\}, \{RP\}$	2

Hence the following correspondences obtain:

CCS Test	Panel Test	DF
$L^2(H_d)$	$L^2(H_5) - L^2(H_7)$	4
$L^2(H_d) - L^2(H_e)$	$L^2(H_5) - L^2(H_6)$	2
$L^2(H_e)$	$L^2(H_6) - L^2(H_7)$	2

Turning to the other response variable, the three-way table $\{YRV\}$ in a CCS analysis would be of interest—especially in regard to the hypothesis $[(YRV) = 0]$. As before, it is instructive to look at the panel table $\{RV_1V_2\}$ in the spread-out form (Table 8).

TABLE 8
$\{RV_1V_2\}$ Written as Incomplete Four-Way Table

Religion	1956 Vote	Religion by 1960 Vote: Catholic Dem	Catholic Rep	Non-Catholic Dem	Non-Catholic Rep
Catholic	Dem	92	3	*	*
	Rep	73	34	*	*
Non-Catholic	Dem	*	*	169	41
	Rep	*	*	55	319

*Structural zero.

Our sequence of models is further truncated. We first consider model H_8, Sym, diagonals disregarded, fitting $(f_{ijk\ell} + f_{k\ell ij})$ and, thereby, $\{R\}$. We next fit $\{V_1\}$ and, thereby, $\{V_2\}$ to estimate expected frequencies under model H_9. If we then proceed to fit $\{RV_1\}$, as in a supposed model H_9^*, we find that $\hat{F} = f$ in each nondiagonal cell. Model H_9^* is, therefore, just the saturated model. We obtain

$$L^2(H_8) = 82.13;\ \text{DF} = 2$$

$$L^2(H_9) = 39.30;\ \text{DF} = 1$$

Note that $L^2(H_8) - L^2(H_9) = 42.83$, DF = 1, the same as $L^2(\text{Sym})$ for $\{V_1V_2\}$, for Catholics and non-Catholics combined. Thus we reject the hypothesis of no change in vote and the hypothesis of no change in religion-by-vote with the same test. This mathematically degenerate situation is clarified by recognizing that H_8 and H_9 are, in effect, concerned with the 2 × 2 table cross-classifying religion by *change* in vote, with nonchangers disregarded (see Table 9). Model H_8 concerns the hypothesis of equiprobability within rows of Table 9; model H_9 concerns the hypothesis of independence of rows and columns in that table. The hypothesis of Sym for $\{V_1V_2\}$ is then the hypothesis of equiprobability for the row totals; call it H_{10}. Clearly, $H_{10} \cap H_9 \Longleftrightarrow H_8$,

TABLE 9
Religion by Change in Vote: Vote Changers Only

Religion	Change in Vote: Dem → Rep	Rep → Dem	Total
Catholic	3	73	76
Non-Catholic	41	55	96
Total	44	128	172

TABLE 10
Likelihood-Ratio χ^2 Statistics, L^2, for Specified Hypotheses Concerning $\{RP_1V_1P_2V_2\}$ Table

Model	Fits	DF	L^2
H_{11}	$(f_{hijk\ell} + f_{hk\ell ij})$	26	133.47
H_{12}	H_{11} and $\{V_1\}$	25	90.64
H_{13}	H_{12} and $\{P_1\}$	23	88.02
H_{14}	H_{13} and $\{V_1P_1\}$	21	72.27
H_{15}	H_{14} and $\{RV_1\}$	20	34.84
H_{16}	H_{15} and $\{RP_1\}$	18	28.91
H_{17}	H_{16} and $\{RV_1P_1\}$	16	25.24

so that $L^2(H_{10}) + L^2(H_9) = L^2(H_8)$ or, as we just saw, $L^2(H_8) - L^2(H_9) = L^2(H_{10})$.

The CCS hypothesis $[(YRV) = 0]$ would be tested by $L^2(H_f)$, DF = 1, where model H_f fits $\{YR\}$, $\{YV\}$, $\{RV\}$. We note that $L^2(H_f)$ corresponds to $L^2(H_8) - L^2(H_9)$ or, simply, $L^2(H_{10})$.

Our last exercise is suggested by considering the CCS four-way table $\{YRPV\}$ and the CCS hypothesis of no four-way interaction: $[(YRPV) = 0]$. This hypothesis should be rejected if there were changes in the (PV) association differing in form or degree for Catholics and non-Catholics. The corresonding panel analysis pertains to the full table: $\{RP_1V_1P_2V_2\}$ (Table 1). As in the immediately preceding analyses, it is helpful to think about this table in a spread-out form, the typical entry being $f_{hijk\ell}$, as though it had 12 rows defined by the cross-classification $\{RP_1V_1\}$ and 12 columns defined by $\{RP_2V_2\}$. Of course, half the cells in the 12×12 table are empty.

The problem is larger now, but the general strategy is the same as the one that has been illustrated repeatedly. We are testing various possible sources of asymmetry in the 12×12 table, ignoring its diagonal cells, in order to interpret the net changes reflected in the inhomogeneity of the $\{RP_1V_1\}$ and $\{RP_2V_2\}$ marginals. Table 10 lists the models that were fitted. We define the following CCS models, which will be referred to in describing correspondences between CCS and panel analyses:

Model	Fits	DF
H_g	$\{YR\}$, $\{RPV\}$	10
H_h	$\{YR\}$, $\{YV\}$, $\{RPV\}$	9
H_i	$\{YR\}$, $\{YV\}$, $\{YP\}$, $\{RPV\}$	7
H_j	$\{YR\}$, $\{YVP\}$, $\{RPV\}$	5
H_k	$\{YRV\}$, $\{YVP\}$, $\{RPV\}$	4
H_ℓ	$\{YRV\}$, $\{YRP\}$, $\{YVP\}$, $\{RPV\}$	2

(The letter subscripts labeling these hypotheses are not to be confused with the letters used to label cells in multiway tables.)

The following list shows the correspondences between tests of CCS hypotheses and panel hypotheses. In each case, the degrees of freedom are the same.

CCS Test	Panel Test	DF
$L^2(H_g)$	$L^2(H_{11}) - L^2(H_{17})$	10
$L^2(H_g) - L^2(H_h)$	$L^2(H_{11}) - L^2(H_{12})$	1
$L^2(H_h) - L^2(H_i)$	$L^2(H_{12}) - L^2(H_{13})$	2
$L^2(H_i) - L^2(H_j)$	$L^2(H_{13}) - L^2(H_{14})$	2
$L^2(H_j) - L^2(H_k)$	$L^2(H_{14}) - L^2(H_{15})$	1
$L^2(H_k) - L^2(H_\ell)$	$L^2(H_{15}) - L^2(H_{16})$	2
$L^2(H_\ell)$	$L^2(H_{16}) - L^2(H_{17})$	2

We need not review all these tests, since the principle underlying them has become familiar. It is noted that $L^2(H_{15}) - L^2(H_{16}) = 5.93$, DF = 2, is not quite significant at the 0.05 level; nor is $L^2(H_{16}) - L^2(H_{17}) = 3.67$, DF = 2. However, $L^2(H_{15}) - L^2(H_{17}) = 9.60$, DF = 4, is just barely significant at the 0.05 level. Although the decision admittedly rests on a cliffhanger, we conclude that the hypothesis $[(RP_1V_1) = (RP_2V_2)]$ should be rejected or, in CCS terms, that there is a nonzero four-way interaction $(YRPV)$. The change in the association of party and vote was not the same for Catholics and non-Catholics. Later we shall go into the substance of that result in more detail.

It should be noted that $L^2(H_{11}) = L^2(H_1)$ for Catholics + $L^2(H_1)$ for non-Catholics, and $L^2(H_{17}) = L^2(H_4)$ for Catholics + $L^2(H_4)$ for non-Catholics; compare Tables 6 and 10. As we noted earlier, H_4 does not fit well for non-Catholics, since there is an asymmetry in the pattern of changes of party by vote that is not explained by the marginal inhomogeneity of $\{P_1V_1\}$ and $\{P_2V_2\}$. We note that model H_{17} nevertheless has a nominally satisfactory fit: $0.05 < P < 0.1$. But the striking difference in fit for Catholics and non-Catholics in Table 6 should not be disregarded. Bearing this difference in mind makes the decision suggested in the preceding paragraph seem a bit more reasonable.

What Changed: The Association of Vote and Party

We have concluded that a true CCS table $\{YRPV\}$ having the format of pseudo-$\{YRPV\}$ (Table 2) would show a nonzero four-way interaction ($YRPV$). But it is one thing to *detect* an interaction—which is all that has been accomplished thus far—and another thing to interpret or diagnose it or to propose a *structure* for it. The latter, more interesting, task is taken up here.

In Table 2 there are four subtables, each a two-way $\{PV\}$ cross-classification. If the observed odds on voting for the Democratic candidate are computed for all four subtables, it will be found that in each of them the odds are highest for respondents identifying themselves as Democrats, lowest for Republicans, and intermediate for Independents. Although this general pattern is invariant, the contrasts of the odds—that is, the odds ratios—are not the same across the four subtables. All the variation in these odds can be captured with a parameterization of the form suggested by the following display:

V	P: Dem	Ind	Rep
Dem	λ	1	1
Rep	1	1	μ

The subscripts c and d will distinguish parameter estimates for Catholics and non-Catholics, and the context will make clear whether an estimate is for 1956 or 1960.

In contrasting the votes of Democrats and Independents, the odds ratio is λ; for the Ind versus Rep contrast, it is μ; and for the Dem versus Rep contrast, it is $\lambda\mu$. The parameters in the foregoing display pertain, therefore, to the *association* (interaction) of vote and party; parameters pertaining to the one-way distributions of V and P are ignored, since they have no bearing on the (two-way) association. (For other examples of displays like this, see Goodman, 1979.)

It is of interest to determine whether we really need eight different values—two for parameters for two religious groups for two years. Parameter reduction can be defended if we fail to reject hypotheses generated by imposing constraints on the parameters. The graphic plot of observed odds (data points in Figure 1) suggests some plausible constraints. Methods of testing them are discussed by Duncan and McRae (1978).

Table 11 reports the parallel analyses of the cross-sectional data for the two years. In both years we decisively reject the hypothesis H_{18} that P and V are independent within religious groups. At first sight, in view of the results of H_{19}, it may seem that for 1956 (though not 1960) we could accept the hypothesis that the (PV) association is

Figure 1. Odds on voting Democratic as a function of religion and party identification: 1956 and 1960 (cross-sectional relationships).

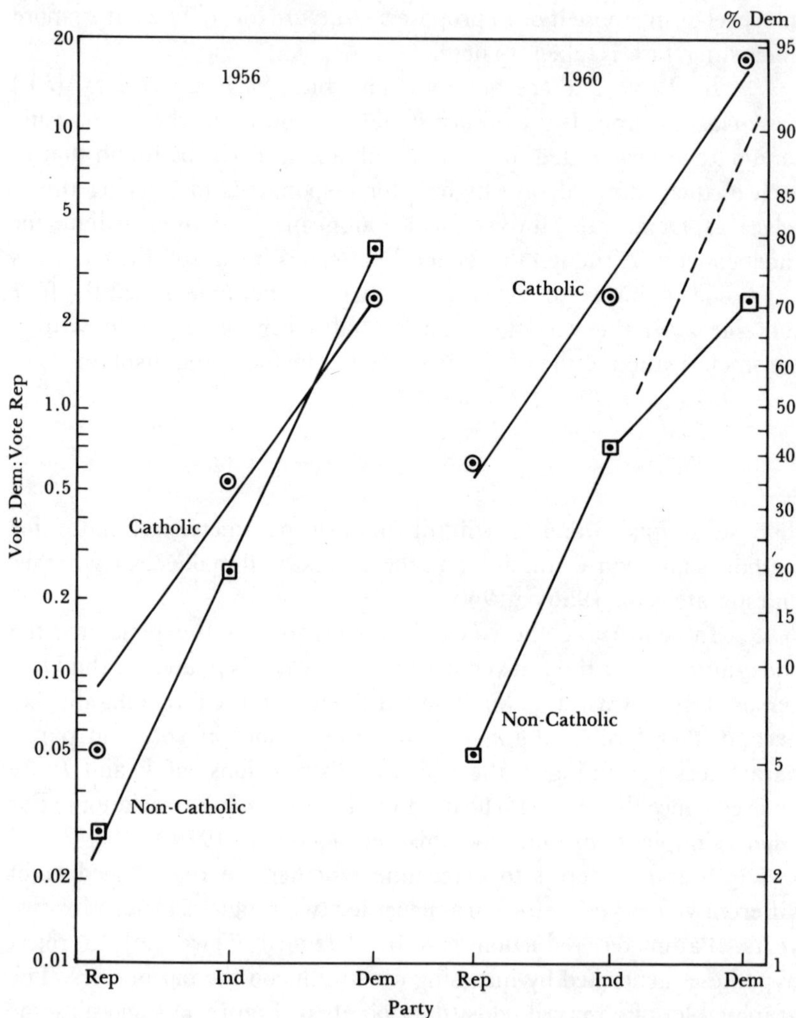

due to a single parameter, common to the Dem, Dem and Rep, Rep cells, and to both religions. However, in 1956 we gain a significant improvement with H_{20}, which relaxes the constraint across religious groups. For 1960, to secure an acceptable fit, we must relax all constraints on the form and level of the (PV) association for non-

TABLE 11
Results of Fitting Alternative Models to 1956 and 1960 Cross-Sectional {RPV} Tables (Table 2)

Model	Marginals and Parameters Fitted	DF	L^2 1956	L^2 1960
H_{18}	{RP}, {RV}	4	390.41	293.52
H_{19}	{RP}, {RV}, $\lambda_c = \mu_c = \lambda_d = \mu_d$	3	6.58	8.62
H_{20}	{RP}, {RV}, $\lambda_c = \mu_c$, $\lambda_d = \mu_d$	2	1.37	8.47
H_{21}	Catholics: {P}, {V}, $\lambda_c = \mu_c$	1	0.87	0.30
	Non-Catholics: {PV} or λ_d, μ_d	0	0.0	0.0

Catholics by fitting H_{21}. This model, however, retains the linear specification for Catholics.

The results are translated into graphic language in Figure 1. There the data points represent observed odds and solid lines signify the odds calculated under the preferred model—model H_{20} for 1956, model H_{21} for 1960. In 1956 our parameter estimates are $\hat{\lambda}_c = \hat{\mu}_c =$ 5.55 for Catholics and $\hat{\lambda}_d = \hat{\mu}_d = 12.1$ for non-Catholics. In 1960, although there is no across-time constraint on parameter values, we find that for Catholics $\hat{\lambda}_c = \hat{\mu}_c = 5.33$, which is very close to the 1956 value. But the regression of vote on party is shifted upward; this shows that Catholics in each party category were much more likely to vote Democratic in 1960 than in 1956. The very substantial shift in the vote left the relationship of party to vote intact.

Something quite different happened among non-Catholics. The 1960 relationship of vote to party was "deformed" by comparison with the 1956 relationship. If only Republicans and Independents are considered, the pattern for the two years is similar, with an upward shift in the odds on voting Democratic superimposed on a regression of vote on party that looked much the same in 1960 as in 1956. But non-Catholic members of the Democratic Party were out of line. Their Democratic vote in 1960 was no higher than in 1956. The dashed line—an extension of the line segment defined by the points for Republicans and Independents—suggests the extent of the shortfall in Democratic voting among non-Catholic members of the Democratic Party. The nonlinearity of the 1960 (PV) interaction for non-Catholics requires rejection of the hypothesis $\lambda_d = \mu_d$. The two parameters are estimated from the observed 1960 odds ratios as $\hat{\lambda}_d =$ 14.1, $\hat{\mu}_d = 3.57$. Note that the 1956 and 1960 values for $\hat{\lambda}_d$, 12.1 and

14.1, are similar, although the estimates are not subjected to an across-time constraint, whereas the two values of μ_d, 12.1 and 3.57, are quite different.[3]

ACROSS-TIME INTERACTIONS

Association Across Time: Stability of Vote and Party Identification

We learned earlier that there was a significant net shift in the Catholic vote; the panel sample showed 47 percent for the Democratic candidate in 1956 but 82 percent in 1960. The net or aggregate shift was not significant, however, for non-Catholics, for whom the panel registered an increase from 36 to 38 percent Democratic between the two elections. These findings are reviewed here—as we initiate our study of stability at the individual level, or across-time association—to call attention to the need for a measure of association that is invariant with respect to adjustments of marginal distributions. It is well known that the cross-product ratio or odds ratio has this property, whereas no other measure of association does (unless it is defined as a function of the odds ratio, like Yule's Q). Accordingly our measure of stability of vote is the odds ratio pertaining to the association of 1956 vote with 1960 vote.

Computing odds ratios from the observed counts in Table 3, we find for Catholics the value $(92)(34)/(3)(73) = 14.3$ and for non-Catholics $(169)(319)/(41)(55) = 23.9$. It would appear that the stability of vote is greater for non-Catholics than for Catholics. And one's first impulse is to link this contrast with the result reported earlier—that the marginal vote distribution for Catholics changed

[3]The foregoing sections provide what I believe is the first coherent account of the formal relationships between CCS and panel analysis. One major limitation of the exposition is obvious but should nevertheless be stated explicitly. The parallels between panel and CCS hypotheses hold only for the population sampled by the panel design. In the present analysis this means, most notably, that the results pertain only to persons who voted in both elections. Moreover, inasmuch as panel studies are notoriously vulnerable to biases arising from failure to maintain contact with all eligible respondents, the population for which inferences are strictly relevant is further circumscribed. This chapter makes no contribution to the resolution of this difficulty. Nor does it consider the interesting but formidable problem of how best to analyze panel and nonpanel samples in tandem (see Fienberg and Picard, 1978).

significantly while the one for non-Catholics did not. But this impulse is mistaken, inasmuch as the marginal distributions do not determine the association between the two variables.

It is only happenstance that the (apparently) lower association occurs for the religious group that has the significant marginal shift. In fact, the ostensible difference between Catholics and non-Catholics with respect to this association is not statistically significant. We establish this result by testing the hypothesis H_{22} of no three-way interaction $[(RV_1V_2) = 0]$ among the variables R, V_1, and V_2. This test requires us to estimate expected frequencies in the three-way table by fitting each set of two-way marginals, $\{RV_1\}$, $\{RV_2\}$, $\{V_1V_2\}$. When this is done, the comparison of observed and expected frequencies is carried out by computing the likelihood-ratio χ^2 statistic, $L^2 = 0.55$, DF $= 1$, $P = 0.46$—an excellent fit. We may, therefore, use the estimates of *expected* frequencies obtained in fitting this model for either Catholics or non-Catholics to estimate the odds ratio for the association of 1956 vote with 1960 vote as 22.7. Without additional evidence, this is our best estimate of the stability of vote (V_1V_2) for both Catholics and non-Catholics. Whether 22.7 represents a high or a low degree of inertia could best be judged by comparing it with odds ratios computed for other periods.

We may regard the odds ratio itself as an estimate of the parameter that measures association (or stability) in the model under study. Or we may consider other (but equivalent) parameterizations if it serves a purpose to do so. In this connection, it is helpful to display the parameters pertaining to association in this fashion:

	1960	
1956	Dem	Rep
Dem	θ	1
Rep	1	1

The odds ratio calculated from this display is, of course, θ. But the same is true of any of a number of alternative displays:

$$\begin{matrix} \theta^{1/2} & 1 \\ 1 & \theta^{1/2} \end{matrix} \qquad \begin{matrix} \theta^{1/4} & \theta^{-1/4} \\ \theta^{-1/4} & \theta^{1/4} \end{matrix} \qquad \begin{matrix} 1 & 1 \\ 1 & \theta \end{matrix}$$

In such tables a parameter is assigned to a particular cell, but its meaning concerns its role in each of the odds ratios into which it enters. A full appreciation of this point should develop when we consider the whole pattern of association in a table larger than 2 × 2.

Table 4 provides the opportunity to do just that, for it juxtaposes two 3 × 3 tables, for Catholics and non-Catholics, pertaining to association of 1960 with 1956 party identification. As before, we could examine hierarchical models, culminating in the model that fits all two-way marginals to test the hypothesis of no three-way interaction, $[(RP_1P_2) = 0]$. But it may save time to consider first the problem of analyzing the structure of the association in a 3 × 3 table. Any such table can be parameterized using three parameters on the main diagonal—in this case (Dem, Dem), (Ind, Ind), and (Rep, Rep)—plus one parameter located in one or more off-diagonal cells in such a way as to produce an asymmetric pattern. Two of the many possible patterns are displayed here:

$$\begin{matrix} \alpha & 1 & \delta \\ 1 & \gamma & 1 \\ 1 & 1 & \beta \end{matrix} \qquad \begin{matrix} \alpha' & 1 & 1 \\ \delta' & \gamma' & 1 \\ \delta' & \delta' & \beta' \end{matrix}$$

It is evident that the analysis of a 3 × 3 table will be simplified if no asymmetry parameter, such as δ or δ', is required. The relevant hypothesis is that of quasi symmetry (QSym) (Ireland, Ku, and Kullback, 1969). In a 3 × 3 table (though not in a larger square table), quasi symmetry is equivalent to quasi independence (QInd) with diagonal cells fixed (Goodman, 1965, 1968). This same hypothesis arose earlier (Table 5), and we found an excellent fit for both Catholics and non-Catholics. Hence the asymmetry parameter can be set to 1.0 for both groups. In that event, our model of association in the $\{P_1P_2\}$ table is represented by this display:

$$\begin{matrix} \alpha_r & 1 & 1 \\ 1 & \gamma_r & 1 \\ 1 & 1 & \beta_r \end{matrix}$$

where $r = c, d$ refers to Catholics and non-Catholics respectively. Now if F_{ij} is the expected frequency in the cell in the ith row and jth column, under the model of QInd, diagonals fixed, we can compute the diagonal parameters from certain odds ratios as follows:

$$\alpha = F_{11}F_{32}/F_{12}F_{31} = F_{11}F_{23}/F_{13}F_{21}$$

$$1/\gamma = F_{12}F_{23}/F_{13}F_{22} = F_{21}F_{32}/F_{22}F_{31}$$

$$\beta = F_{12}F_{33}/F_{13}\mathrm{F}_{32} = F_{21}F_{33}/F_{23}F_{31}$$

Hence inserting into these formulas the maximum-likelihood estimates (MLEs) of expected frequencies obtained in fitting the model, we find MLEs of the parameters α, β, and γ. These estimates are shown in Table 12 (first row). The pattern is reasonably clear: large values for α and β, values closer to unity for γ. However, one is not sure which variations should be taken seriously. Hence it is informative to consider various constraints on parameter values. Maximum-likelihood estimates of expected counts under each of the models listed in Table 12 were obtained by iterative scaling, using a program that allows the user to fit totals for any sets of classes of cells (not merely marginal totals) in a two-way or multiway table where the classes in each set are mutually exclusive and collectively exhaust all cells with expected frequency $F > 0$ in the table. The algorithm is a straightforward extension of the one given for "intrinsically unrestricted" models for the two-way table by Goodman (1972, p. 665).

The trade-off between parsimony and closeness of fit is nicely illustrated with this collection of models. At the 0.05 level, we cannot reject the constraint in H_{27} that all four parameters, α and β for Catholics and non-Catholics, have the same value. But a highly significant improvement in fit is gained by allowing β for Catholics to take a distinct value as in H_{26}. Relaxing other constraints does not, however, produce significant gains in fit, according to comparisons of H_{23}, H_{24}, and H_{25} with H_{26}.

To interpret the parameters of H_{26} we note that for any 2×2 subtable, whether for Catholics or non-Catholics, that involves the (Dem, Dem) but not the (Rep, Rep) cell, the odds ratio is estimated at 34.1. This parameter describes the "inertia" of identification with the Democratic Party. But the corresponding inertia parameter for

TABLE 12

Maximum-Likelihood Estimates of Parameters Under Various Models of (P_1P_2) Association, by Religion, with χ^2 Values for Models

	Catholic			Non-Catholic				
Model	α	γ	β	α	γ	β	DF	L^2
H_{23}	23.3	1.8	6.9	78.0	0.38	58.7	2	0.81
H_{24}	31.6	1.0	8.8	40.5	1.0	29.4	4	7.29
H_{25}	38.2	1.0	8.6	38.2	1.0	29.6	5	7.46
H_{26}	34.1	1.0	8.8	34.1	1.0	34.1	6	7.86
H_{27}	29.8	1.0	29.8	29.8	1.0	29.8	7	13.42

Republican identification is equally high only among non-Catholics. The much lower value among Catholics suggests that there was a loss in holding power of the Republican Party for Catholics in consequence of the religious factor in the 1960 election. Of course, there were few Catholic Republicans before the 1960 election, if even fewer immediately thereafter.

We recall that the hypothesis of MH was rejected (Table 5) for the Catholic but not for the non-Catholic $\{P_1P_2\}$ table. But the marginal shifts do *not* account for the lower inertia parameter for Catholic than for non-Catholic Republicans. That inertia parameter is an aspect of the *association* between 1956 and 1960 party identification—that is, the (P_1P_2) association—and by the definition of association in terms of the odds ratio (or set of odds ratios) the marginals and marginal shifts are rendered irrelevant.

It should be noted that the two parameters of the model are combined in calculating the odds ratio for the four cells pertaining to respondents who gave a definite party identification, Democrat or Republican, in both 1956 and 1960. This odds ratio, computed as the product $\alpha\beta$, is estimated at $(34.1)(8.8) = 300$ for Catholics and $(34.1)^2 = 1{,}163$ for non-Catholics. But this differential in overall stability for the religious groups is seen to be due, exclusively, to the differential in inertia parameter values for the Republican Party.

The absence of an inertia parameter for Independents may be puzzling. But the presence of the other two parameters does imply that there is stability in party identification with respect to either of two subtables: rows Dem, Ind by columns Dem, Ind or rows Ind, Rep by columns Ind, Rep. However, for the other two subtables involving adjacent rows and adjacent columns (rows Dem, Ind by columns Ind, Rep and rows Ind, Rep by columns Dem, Ind), the association is nil—that is, the odds ratio under the model is 1.0. This is not paradoxical if one notes that all respondents in these subtables are party changers or persons declining a definite party identification in either or both interviews. They lack attachment, it would seem.

Perhaps it is emphasizing the obvious to observe that the effort to discern the *structure* of association in the spirit of the present inquiry would be totally frustrated if exclusive reliance were placed on descriptive statistics such as Pearson's correlation or any of the nonparametric (PRE or other) measures of the so-called strength of association over the whole of a two-way contingency table larger than

2×2. In this context as well as others (see, for example, Duncan, 1975, chap. 11), theoretical concerns in research seem to raise questions about structure that call for models explicitly specified for the investigation at hand.

At the same time, it is important not to reify the particular form of the structural model that happens to be easiest to work with. It is generally true that parameters in a model of association can be transformed into the parameters of equivalent models that look, superficially, quite different. Interesting as the topic of equivalent parameterizations may be, however, we cannot explore it here. (But for instructive examples see Goodman, 1972, 1979, and Duncan and Schuman, 1979.)

One further comment concerns the possibility of using an expanded classification of party identification. With, say, five or seven categories in the classification, the variety of possibly relevant structural models is increased. It seems likely that models hitherto found serviceable in analyzing occupational mobility (Goodman, 1972, 1979; Duncan, 1979a) could be used to advantage in studying stability of party identification.

Cross-Lagged Association of Vote and Party

In a two-wave two-variable panel study of vote and party, there are four (PV) associations to examine. We have already studied the cross-sectional associations (P_1V_1) and (P_2V_2). Here we consider the cross-lagged (Campbell, 1963) associations (P_1V_2) and (P_2V_1). Since we have already explored possibilities for parameterizing the cross-sectional (PV) association, the present treatment can be brief. Table 13 displays the relevant marginals of Table 1. The parameters of the (V_1P_2) association are

$$\begin{matrix} \phi_{1r} & 1 & 1 \\ 1 & 1 & \phi_{2r} \end{matrix}$$

where $r = c, d$ labels the religion categories. For the (V_2P_1) association we replace the ϕ's with ψ_{1r} and ψ_{2r}.

For $\{RP_1V_2\}$ we find that a single parameter $\psi_{1r} = \psi_{2r} = \psi$, $r = c, d$, describes the cross-lagged association for both Catholics and non-Catholics. Fitting $\{RV_2\}$, $\{RP_1\}$, and one parameter for associa-

TABLE 13
Party Identification by Vote, Cross-Lagged Relationships, 1956 and 1960, for Catholics and Non-Catholics

Variables	Religion	Vote	Party Rep	Party Ind	Party Dem
1960 vote by 1956 party	Catholic	Dem	22	44	99
		Rep	20	11	6
	Non-Catholic	Dem	18	43	163
		Rep	198	100	62
1956 vote by 1960 party	Catholic	Dem	2	15	78
		Rep	27	28	52
	Non-Catholic	Dem	3	36	171
		Rep	227	99	48

NOTE: Each section of this table represents a different set of three-way {party by vote by religion} marginals of Table 1. Both sections have a total $n = 786$. Hence this is not a four-way table.

tion, we find that $L^2(H_{28}) = 1.80$, DF = 3, $P > 0.5$. The same model for $\{RP_2V_1\}$ is not acceptable, since $L^2(H_{29}) = 16.60$, $P < 0.001$. However, if we allow the parameter to vary by religion, $\phi_{1r} = \phi_{2r} = \phi_r$, the fit is good: $L^2(H_{30}) = 3.31$, DF = 2, $P > 0.1$.

The cross-lagged associations are displayed in Figure 2. We see that the beautifully linear relationship ($\hat{\psi} = 5.1$) of 1960 vote to 1956 party identification was the same for Catholics and non-Catholics, except for an additive effect of the religious factor. In each 1956 party identification category the odds on a Democratic vote in 1960 were 9.3 times as high for Catholics as for non-Catholics.

The other cross-lagged relationship in Figure 2 may be more difficult to appreciate, since it seems somewhat artificial to plot the earlier vote as a function of the later party identification. However, the mathematical representation of the association is not affected by which variable is plotted on the abscissa or by the direction in which odds are computed. From the fitted counts for $\{RV_1P_2\}$ we may compute odds on party identification, conditional on 1956 vote and religion. First, we note that $\hat{\phi}_c = 3.6$ for Catholics, so that among Catholics who voted Democratic in 1956 the estimated odds on Independent, relative to Republican, identification were 3.6 ($= \hat{\phi}_c$) times as high as for 1956 Republican voters. The corresponding odds on Democratic (relative to Republican) identification were 13 ($= \hat{\phi}_c^2$) times as high for 1956 Democratic voters as for 1956 Republican voters. Among non-Catholics, the corresponding figures are $\hat{\phi}_d = 12.5$ and $\hat{\phi}_d^2 = 156$.

Figure 2. Odds on voting Democratic in one year as a function of party identification in the other year (cross-lagged relationships) by religion.

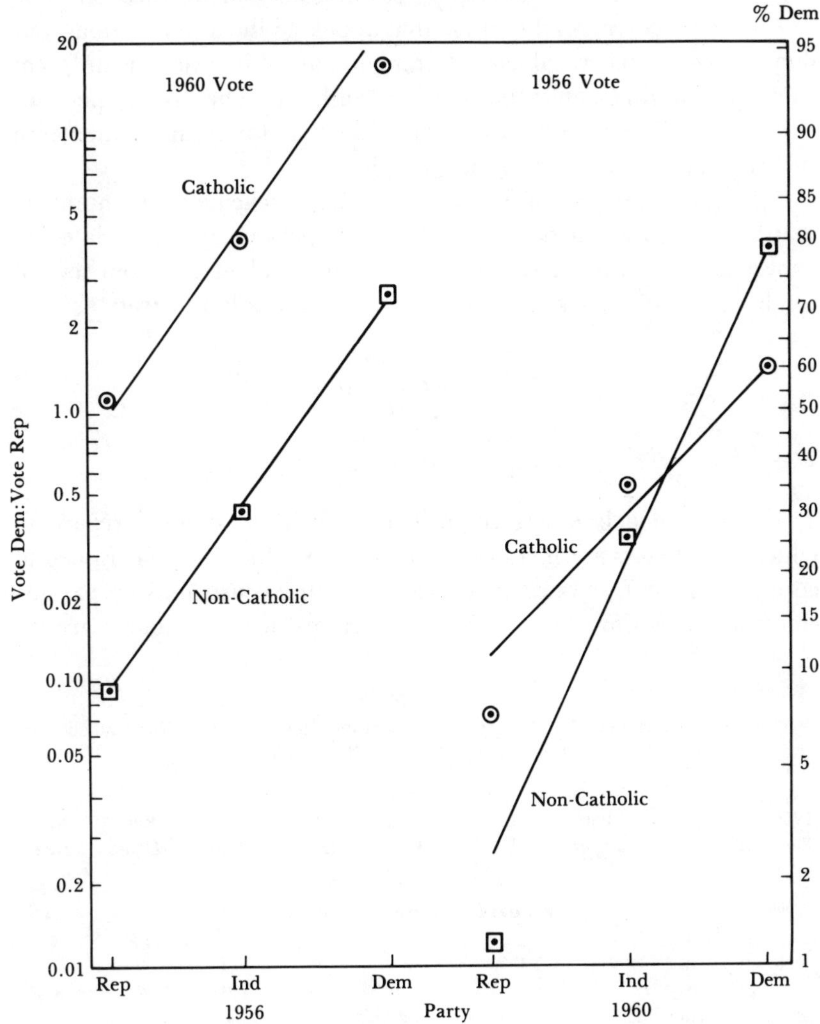

Models for All Across-Time Interactions

We are now ready to assemble the pieces carved out in the earlier analyses. The models considered here focus on across-time relationships, but we take account of the earlier work—which found interactions (RP_1V_1) and (RP_2V_2)—by fitting $\{RP_1V_1\}$, $\{RP_2V_2\}$ in all cases. Table 14 displays the parameters of the across-time interactions that will be the subject of hypotheses and tests in this section. The Greek letters correspond to those that appeared in earlier sections, but they are now interpreted as pertaining to partial interactions different from the marginal interactions studied hitherto. The display pertains either to Catholics or non-Catholics, so that for each parameter a subscript pertaining to religion is implicit.

The lower part of Table 14 provides a scheme of cell numbers that may be used in demonstrating how parameters are related to expected frequencies. Each parameter can be calculated from several combinations of cells, so the ones noted here are only illustrations:

$$\begin{aligned} \alpha &= F_1F_{15}/F_3F_{13} \\ \beta &= F_{22}F_{36}/F_{24}F_{34} \\ \theta &= F_1F_8/F_2F_7 \\ \phi &= F_1F_9/F_3F_7 \\ \psi &= F_1F_{14}/F_2F_{13} \end{aligned}$$

The models described in Table 15 differ, first, in regard to which parameters are included (that is, have values not constrained to equal unity) and, second, in regard to equality constraints on parameter values. We are interested in constraints across religious groups

TABLE 14
Parameters in Models for $\{P_1V_1P_2V_2\}$ Cross-Classification, for Catholics or Non-Catholics, and Cell Numbers in Cross-Classification

1956 Party	1956 Vote	1960 Party: Vote:	Dem Dem	Dem Rep	Ind Dem	Ind Rep	Rep Dem	Rep Rep
					Parameters[a]			
Dem	Dem		$\alpha\theta\phi\psi$	$\alpha\phi$	$\theta\psi$	1	$\theta\psi$	1
	Rep		$\alpha\psi$	α	ψ	1	$\phi\psi$	ϕ
Ind	Dem		$\theta\phi$	ϕ	θ	1	θ	1
	Rep		1	1	1	1	ϕ	ϕ
Rep	Dem		$\theta\phi$	$\phi\psi$	θ	ψ	$\beta\theta$	$\beta\psi$
	Rep		1	ψ	1	ψ	$\beta\phi$	$\beta\phi\psi$
					Cell Numbers			
Dem	Dem		1	2	3	4	5	6
	Rep		7	8	9	10	11	12
Ind	Dem		13	14	15	16	17	18
	Rep		19	20	21	22	23	24
Rep	Dem		25	26	27	28	29	30
	Rep		31	32	33	34	35	36

[a] α, β pertain to (P_1P_2); θ pertains to (V_1V_2); ϕ to (V_1P_2); ψ to (P_1V_2).

TABLE 15
MLEs of Parameters Under Various Models for the $\{RP_1V_1P_2V_2\}$ Cross-Classification (Table 1), with χ^2 Values for the Models

Model[a]	Religion	Parameter α	β	θ	ϕ	ψ	DF	L^2
H_{31}	Catholic	1.0	1.0	1.0	1.0	1.0	25	153.74
	Non-Catholic	1.0	1.0	1.0	1.0	1.0	25	760.63
H_{32}	Catholic	31.6	8.8	1.0	1.0	1.0	23	29.26
	Non-Catholic	40.5	29.4	1.0	1.0	1.0	23	143.26
H_{33}	Catholic	27.8	7.5	6.8	1.0	1.0	22	17.04
	Non-Catholic	32.2	24.2	9.7	1.0	1.0	22	52.04
H_{34}	Catholic	29.6	7.9	7.1	0.85	1.0	21	16.84
	Non-Catholic	21.7	24.0	9.1	3.5	1.0	21	28.07
H_{35}	Catholic	29.3	7.8	6.9	0.85	1.03	20	16.83
	Non-Catholic	21.3	22.1	8.3	4.0	1.4	20	26.47
H_{35}^*	Non-Catholic	25.2	19.7	7.1	2.2	2.2	21	38.26
H_{36}	Catholic	20.5	20.5	8.5	2.2	1.0	47	60.33
	Non-Catholic	20.5	20.5	8.5	2.2	1.0		
H_{37}	Catholic	21.2	21.2	8.7	0.77	1.0	46	48.73
	Non-Catholic	21.2	21.2	8.7	3.5	1.0		
H_{38}	Catholic	29.6	7.9	7.1	0.85	1.0	43	44.96
	Non-Catholic	22.9	22.9	9.1	3.5	1.0		
H_{39}	Catholic	20.7	20.7	8.6	1.0	1.0	47	49.28
	Non-Catholic	20.7	20.7	8.6	3.5	1.0		
H_{40}	Catholic	23.5	7.6	8.7	1.0	1.0	46	45.43
	Non-Catholic	23.5	23.5	8.7	3.5	1.0		

[a]All models fit the marginals $\{RP_1V_1\}$, $\{RP_2V_2\}$, and the parameters whose estimates differ from 1.0.

and also across parameters pertaining to the same interaction ($\alpha = \beta$) or to interactions of the same form ($\phi = \psi$). Where two or more parameters are shown in Table 15 with estimated values the same, this equality results from an explicit constraint imposed in the process of fitting the model (Duncan and McRae, 1978; Duncan, 1979b, 1979c). Models H_{31} through H_{35} and H_{35}^* treat the two religion categories as separate populations. In the remaining models there are one or more across-religion constraints effected in an analysis of Catholics and non-Catholics considered together.

A number of informative comparisons among the models listed in Table 15 can be made. Specific features of the models are tested when two models differ only in that constraints present in one model (say H) are relaxed in another (say H'). In the event, we may write $H \Longrightarrow H'$ and use the χ^2 statistic $L^2(H) - L^2(H')$ with DF = DF(H) − DF(H') to test whether the relaxation of constraints (or the introduction of additional parameters) results in improvement of fit. (This test assumes H' is true; when the assumption is questionable in the light of $L^2(H')$, the "test" should be interpreted with caution.) Relationships among the models in Table 15 are depicted in Figure 3. Implication is transitive, so that if $H \Longrightarrow H'$ and $H' \Longrightarrow H''$, then $H \Longrightarrow H''$ (Goodman, 1978, pp. 456–459).

There are four main results of the comparisons among models. First, inclusion of ψ produces no significant improvement in fit in any relevant comparison, and the constraint $\phi = \psi$ is not an acceptable one for non-Catholics (H_{35} versus H^*_{35}). Second, ϕ is significant and substantial for non-Catholics but is not significant for Catholics (for example, H_{33} versus H_{34} for Catholics only). Constraining ϕ to have the same value in the two religious groups produces an unacceptable

Figure 3. Relationships among models in Table 15. (For Catholics H^*_{35} and H_{35} are the same; the models differ for non-Catholics.)

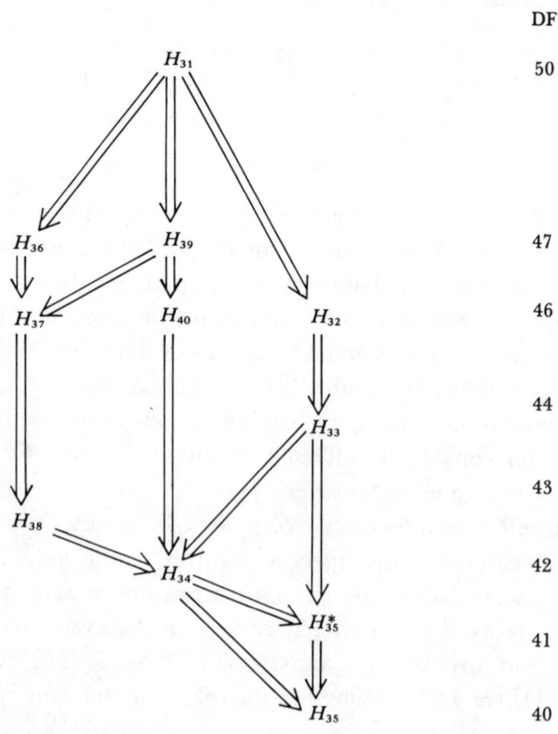

deterioration in fit (H_{36} versus H_{37}). Third, constraining the four parameters, α and β for Catholics and non-Catholics, to take a single common value is undesirable (H_{39} versus H_{40}). Fourth, the remaining constraints in H_{40} are acceptable. Note that $L^2(H_{40}) - L^2(H_{35}) = 2.13$, DF $= 6$, tests all the constraints simultaneously. But the pattern of parameter values highlighted by the constraints of H_{40} is also quite clear in the unconstrained parameter estimates of H_{35}.

By virtue of the constraint $\phi = \psi$, model H_{35}^* for non-Catholics has a symmetric pattern of parameters describing across-time association, although the marginals $\{P_1V_1\}$ and $\{P_2V_2\}$ are not, of course, homogeneous. Hence $H_{35}^* \Longrightarrow H_4$ (see Table 6). We note that for non-Catholics $L^2(H_{35}^*) - L^2(H_4) = 38.26 - 21.38 = 16.88$, DF $= 21 - 9 = 12$, $P > 0.1$. This comparison suggests that the additional symmetric parameters that enter H_4 do not produce a significant improvement in fit. For Catholics a conclusion to the same effect is obtained with $L^2(H_{33}) - L^2(H_4) = 13.18$, DF $= 15$, $P > 0.25$. Strictly speaking, these results do not guarantee that we have not overlooked some significant feature of the across-time interactions. But that inference seems reasonably safe inasmuch as additional work with hierarchical models in the fashion of Knoke (1976, table 6.5) fails to disclose any significant interactions not taken into account in model H_{40}.

A brief comparison with Knoke's results is appropriate. He proposes his model 6 as one that "provides the best fit to the data, since it requires the fewest complex relationships and does not omit any significant relationships." This model, K_6 for short, is specified by the sets of fitted marginals $\{RP_1V_1\}$, $\{RV_2\}$, $\{P_2V_2\}$, $\{V_1V_2\}$, $\{P_1P_2\}$, $\{RV_1P_2\}$. Knoke gives $L^2(K_6) = 44.3$, DF $= 43$. However, Knoke added ½ to each observed frequency before fitting his models. Recomputation without this adjustment (for comparability with all results in this chapter) yields $L^2(K_6) = 50.67$. But this cannot be used in a test of K_6 versus H_{35} or H_{40} because K_6 includes some effects not present in H_{35} or H_{40} and vice versa. The following compilation makes the differences between the two analyses explicit:

Model K_6	Model H_{40}
$\{RP_1V_1\}$	$\{RP_1V_1\}$
$\{RP_2\}$, $\{RV_2\}$, $\{P_2V_2\}$	$\{RP_2V_2\}$
$\{V_1V_2\}$	θ: (V_1V_2)
$\{P_1P_2\}$	α, β: constrained (RP_1P_2)
$\{RV_1P_2\}$	ϕ: constrained (RV_1P_2)

Thus H_{40} detects a three-way interaction (RP_1P_2) missing from K_6 but introduces it in a parsimonious form. Both H_{40} and K_6 recognize the three-way interaction (RV_1P_2), but H_{40} makes its form explicit and parsimonious. Moreover, H_{40} includes $\{RP_2V_2\}$ on the strength of the analysis leading to the right-hand portion of Figure 1. This is one of the cases in which a higher-order interaction is detected when a nonhierarchical approach is taken to the parameterization of the interaction, although it slips through the net of the standard hierarchical models.

It is not to be expected that models of the kind considered here will give dramatically different results from those secured with standard hierarchical models. But when sample size is small (as it almost always is in nonfederal surveys), exercise of finesse in distinguishing pattern from nosie may result in a worthwhile increment of detail in the findings.

Causal Interpretations

The history of attempts at causal interpretation of (categorical) panel data is lengthy and tortuous. Useful though flawed reviews are provided by Lazarsfeld (1972, 1978) and McCullough (1978). McCullough's attempt to revive interest in the "index of relative effect" seems perverse. As Plackett (1974, p. vii) remarked so astringently concerning the whole topic of categorical data analysis, "An earlier negative phase, preoccupied first with the invention of coefficients . . . has been replaced by a positive phase in which models are explored." A somewhat subjective assessment is that most proposals concerning methods of causal interpretation should be forgotten, but three approaches merit further development: (1) use of panel data to estimate parameters of an unobserved Markov process (Coleman, 1964; Singer and Spilerman, 1977); (2) explaining observed interactions of repeatedly measured qualitative variables in terms of latent variables or classes (Goodman, 1978, chap. 8; Duncan, Sloane, and Brody, 1979); (3) causal interpretation of parameters in models pertaining to the observed categorical variables themselves (Goodman, 1978, chap. 6; Knoke, 1976). The following discussion refers only to the third approach.

In Figure 4 we see two diagrams of the kind proposed by

Figure 4. Possible "causal" diagrams for model H_{40}.

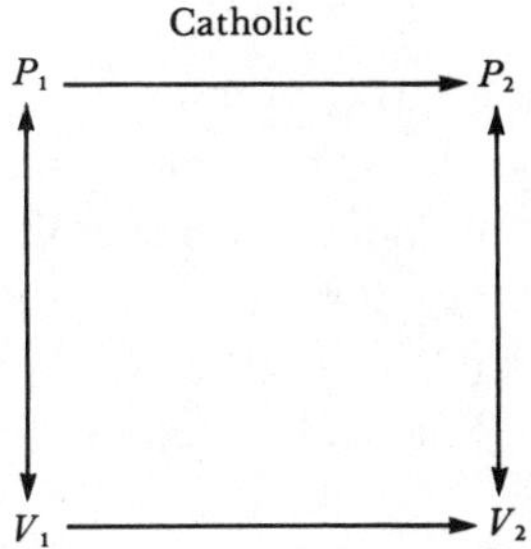

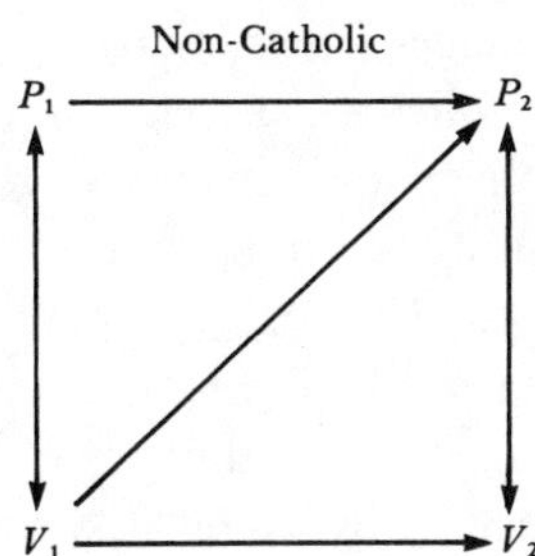

Goodman (1978, chap. 6) for the causal analysis of panel data. The separation by religion suggests that we are studying a causal process in two populations. Indeed, if H_{40} is taken as the preferred model, the form of the process is different for Catholics and non-Catholics; there is no causal path $V_1 \rightarrow P_2$ for the former, but this path is prominent in the model for the latter. Knoke (1976, p. 125) had already observed that "the strength of this cross-lag effect differs between Catholics and non-Catholics," but he did not entertain the possibility that the effect was actually nonexistent for the former. The issue is of some consequence for Knoke's (1976, p. 125) main conclusion: "Except for the unusual impact of religion on party and vote in 1960, . . . the causal model of intrapersonal change over time in the panel may reflect the general process of this period fairly accurately." Which of the two diagrams in Figure 4 depicts the "general process"—the one including $V_1 \rightarrow P_2$ or the one omitting this causal path? Presumably we would want data for another pair of years before deciding which of the two diagrams is to be generalized.

One problem with this kind of diagram is that more than one parameter may be required to describe an interaction involving one or two polytomous variables. In Figure 4 all interactions except $(V_1 V_2)$ are of this complex type. Hence it would be misleading to enter supposed "path coefficients" on these diagrams. There is another feature of these diagrams that distinguishes them from the better-known path diagrams for quantitative variables (Duncan, 1975). In log linear models one cannot separate the paths connecting two endogenous variables. Here this means that $P_2 \rightarrow V_2$ and $V_2 \rightarrow P_2$ are represented by a single interaction, and it makes no sense to inquire which is the "more important" direction of causation. (See Brier, 1978.) An inference of this kind is possible with regard to the cross-lagged interactions, $P_1 \rightarrow V_2$ and $V_1 \rightarrow P_2$. Here the comparison was explicitly carried out for non-Catholics (H^*_{35} versus H_{35}). For Catholics neither cross-lagged association is significant when the remaining parameters, α, β, and θ, are in the model. In general, since P is polytomous, the possibility of making a simple quantitative comparison of the magnitude of two associations, such as (P_1V_2) and (V_1P_2), rests on the prior determination that each of them can be represented by a single parameter.

The diagram suggested by Knoke (1976, fig. 6.2) resembles the one in Figure 4 for non-Catholics. But it also includes the variable R, with arrows connecting R to each of the other four variables. Only with respect to the $V_1 \rightarrow P_2$ path does Knoke's diagram suggest that R enters in other than an additive fashion. But our interpretation requires that four of the five paths among the political variables, all except $V_1 \rightarrow V_2$, be shown in some manner as differing for Catholics and non-Catholics. One could certainly propose a symbol to represent this situation. But the resulting diagram would be so complex as to lose much of its iconic value.

There is a more fundamental shortcoming of this kind of causal diagram. The main *cause* is not even explicitly in the picture at all. The name of this cause, in CCS analysis, is *year*. In panel analysis, year is not even a variable but is reduced to a subscript of the two response variables. How strange to entertain a "causal" diagram that pertains only to responses and makes no explicit reference to stimuli! Of course, "year" is not itself a stimulus but a proxy for the whole collection of relevant stimuli that distinguished the 1960 from the 1956 political environment of the elector. (Our discussion has featured only one of them—the religious preference of the Democractic candidate in 1960.) We could propose a causal diagram to parallel the structure of the hypothetical CCS analysis referred to earlier in the chapter. But the attempt would quickly get out of hand. We have seen that the (PV) interaction was not the same for Catholics and non-Catholics in either year and that it changed between 1956 and 1960 for non-Catholics. We surmised that an actual CCS analysis, using adequate samples, would reveal a four-way interaction $(YRPV)$. A minimal "causal" interpretation, it seems, would run as follows. "Year" (that is, change in political environment) produces changes in the distributions of votes and party identification. But these changes are conditional upon the prior voting behavior and identifications of the electors and on their religious preferences.

I suggest that sensitive analysts (such as Campbell and others, 1966) already knew how to work with heuristic principles at least as rich as these. It is not clear that their interpretations can be improved upon by a "causal" rendering of H_{40} or K_6. The role of formal *statistical* models like these is to provide a consistent framework for describing or analyzing relationships in a set of variables. The analyst will, of course, examine subsets of variables in the process of developing an understanding of the entire structure of interactions. But the ultimate goal of locating every variable somewhere in a final model, while specifying how and why it belongs there, is a powerful incentive for keeping the story straight. Tentative causal interpretations will guide the analyst's work at every stage. But that does not mean that his or her statistical model as such is a causal model.

CONCLUSION

Panel analysis has at least two faces. One is the collection of hypotheses corresponding to those that turn up in a very natural way in CCS analysis. Since CCS analysis leads the investigator to focus on effects of "year," and since year is actually a proxy for the real causes of change in disposition and behavior, it behooves the panel analyst to attend to these CCS-like hypotheses. Failure to do so risks playing Hamlet without the Prince.

The second face of panel analysis is the identification, measurement, and interpretation of across-time interactions. To suppose that this task comes down to nothing more than a decision about which of two response variables has the greater effect on the other is to trivialize the enterprise. Nor, it was suggested, is it good enough (except in the simplest cases) to define the goal as the construction of a "causal" diagram. What we are after is an understanding and explicit quantitative representation of the *structure* (Duncan, 1975, chap. 11) of the process under study. My own belief is that even the most patient and ingenious analysis of the patterns of association among observed variables can yield only preliminary indications and (one hopes) clues concerning the structure. Techniques to be used in such a preliminary analysis are, nevertheless, the sole subject of this chapter. What lies beyond is for others to disclose.

REFERENCES

BISHOP, Y. M. M., FIENBERG, S. E., AND HOLLAND, P. W.

1975 *Discrete Multivariate Analysis.* Cambridge, Mass.: M.I.T. Press.

BOULDING, K. E.

1978 *Ecodynamics.* Beverly Hills: Sage.

BRIER, S. S.

1978 "The utility of systems of simultaneous logistic response equations." In K. F. Schuessler (Ed.), *Sociological Methodology 1979.* San Francisco: Jossey-Bass.

BROWN, M. B.

1976 "Screening effects in multidimensional contingency tables." *Applied Statistics* 25:37–46.

CAMPBELL, A., AND OTHERS.

1966 *Elections and the Political Order.* New York: Wiley.

CAMPBELL, D. T.

1963 "From description to experimentation: Interpreting trends as quasi-experiments." In C. W. Harris (Ed.), *Problems in Measuring Change.* Madison: University of Wisconsin Press.

COLEMAN, J. S.

1964 *Introduction to Mathematical Sociology.* New York: Free Press.

CONVERSE, P. E., AND MARKUS, G. B.

1979 "Plus ça change . . . : The new CPS election study panel." *American Political Science Review* 73:32–49.

DUNCAN, O. D.

1975 *Introduction to Structural Equation Models.* New York: Academic Press.

1979a "How destination depends on origin in the occupational mobility table." *American Journal of Sociology* 84:793–803.

1979b "Testing key hypotheses in panel analysis." In K. F. Schuessler (Ed.), *Sociological Methodology 1980.* San Francisco: Jossey-Bass.

1979c "Constrained parameters in a model for categorical data." *Sociological Methods and Research* 8:57–68.

DUNCAN, O. D. AND MCRAE, J. A., JR.

1978 "Multiway contingency analysis with a scaled response or factor." In K. F. Schuessler (Ed.), *Sociological Methodology 1979.* San Francisco: Jossey-Bass.

DUNCAN, O. D., AND SCHUMAN, H.
1979 "Effects of question wording and context: An experiment with religious indicators." *Journal of American Statistical Association* 75:269–275.

DUNCAN, O. D., SLOANE, D. M., AND BRODY, C.
1979 "Latent classes inferred from response consistency effects." Paper delivered at the conference on Systems under Indirect Observation, Geneva, 18–20 October 1979.

FIENBERG, S. E., AND PICARD, R. R.
1978 "Designing surveys for measuring change in categorical data structures over time." Technical Report 321. St. Paul: University of Minnesota, School of Statistics.

GOODMAN, L. A.
1965 "On the statistical analysis of mobility tables." *American Journal of Sociology* 70:564–585.
1968 "The analysis of cross-classified data: Independence, quasi-independence, and interactions in contingency tables with or without missing entries." *Journal of American Statistical Association* 63:1091–1131.
1972 "Some multiplicative models for the analysis of cross-classified data." In L. M. Le Cam, J. Neyman, and E. L. Scott (Eds.), *Proceedings of the Sixth Berkeley Symposium on Mathematical Statistics and Probability.* Vol. 1. Berkeley: University of California Press.
1978 *Analyzing Qualitative/Categorical Data.* Cambridge, Mass.: Abt Books.
1979 "Multiplicative models for the analysis of occupational mobility tables and other kinds of cross-classification tables." *American Journal of Sociology* 84:804–819.

IRELAND, C. T., KU, H. H., AND KULLBACK, S.
1969 "Symmetry and marginal homogeneity of an $r \times r$ contingency table." *Journal of American Statistical Association* 64:1323–1341.

KNOKE, D.
1976 *Change and Continuity in American Politics.* Baltimore: Johns Hopkins University Press.

LAZARSFELD, P. F.
1972 "Mutual relations over time of two attributes: A review and integration of various approaches." In M. Hammer, K. Salzinger, and S. Sutton (Eds.), *Psychopathology.* New York: Wiley.
1978 "Some episodes in the history of panel analysis." In D. B. Kandel (Ed.), *Longitudinal Research on Drug Use.* New York: Halsted Press.

LAZARSFELD, P. F., PASANELLA, A. K., AND ROSENBERG, M.
1972 *Continuities in the Language of Social Research.* New York: Free Press.

MARKUS, G. B., AND CONVERSE, P. E.
1979 "A dynamic simultaneous equation model of electoral choice." *American Political Science Review,* in press.

MCCULLOUGH, B. C.
1978 "Effects of variables using panel data: A review of techniques." *Public Opinion Quarterly* 42:199–220.

PLACKETT, R. L.
1974 *The Analysis of Categorical Data.* New York: Hafner Press.

SINGER, B., AND SPILERMAN, S.
1977 "Fitting stochastic models to longitudinal survey data—some examples in the social sciences." Discussion Paper 446–77. Institute for Research on Poverty, University of Wisconsin–Madison.

8

ESTIMATION OF NONSTATIONARY MARKOV CHAINS FROM PANEL DATA

Burton Singer
COLUMBIA UNIVERSITY

With a few exceptions (see Tuma, 1976; Littman and Mode, 1977; Pickens and Soyka, 1980), most attempts to model individual choice behavior with Markov and related models have interpreted "Markov" to mean time-homogeneous Markov. Although considerable analytic simplicity is gained via the use of such models, there is a substantial sacrifice in realism and flexibility. Indeed, much of the empirical failure of time-homogeneous chains to provide good descrip-

The work reported here was supported by National Science Foundation Grant SOC76-17706 to the Center for the Social Sciences, Columbia University. I wish to thank Nancy Tuma for critical comments and invaluable suggestions on an earlier draft.

tive models of dynamic choice behavior attests to the limited plausibility of these models.

The purposes of this chapter are:

1. To describe the general continuous-time nonstationary Markov chains and clarify how certain economic theories of labor force dynamics and sociological theories of occupational mobility can be interpreted in this framework.
2. To present—for the first time—a strategy for fitting general *two-state* nonstationary Markov models to multiwave panel data.
3. To present embeddability criteria for assessing whether panel data could have been generated by a continuous-time, nonstationary Markov chain.
4. To present a strategy for detecting with panel data whether observed nonstationarity can be attributed only to nonstationarity in the rate of movement but not in the probabilities of transition between pairs of states. This special form of nonstationarity has been discussed in the intragenerational occupational mobility literature by Mayer (1972) and Sørensen (1975a, 1975b).
5. To present a new interpretation of the widely observed deviations from time-homogeneous Markov models—diagonals of observed transition matrices are underpredicted by diagonals of powers of time-homogeneous Markov transition matrices fit to the first two waves of panel data. This can be accounted for by the class of nonstationary Markov models.

In addition to focusing on continuous-time, nonstationary Markov chains as models of individual choice behavior, a few words are in order about my emphasis on their estimation from panel designs. Although event-history data—as discussed in detail by Tuma, Hannan, and Groeneveld (1979) and Hannan and Tuma (1979)—are vastly superior to the usual panel data for finding classes of stochastic models that can describe a social process, it is nevertheless true that event-history data are currently the exception rather than the rule among longitudinal data sets in sociology. Moreover, event-history data are impossible to collect on many variables of interest: Virtually all studies of attitude change over time and—in a medical context—the intraindividual evolution of chronic diseases.

CONTINUOUS-TIME NONSTATIONARY MARKOV CHAINS

General Specification

Let $w(t)$ be a step function, which we shall interpret as representing an individual's evolution among a finite collection of states. Let $T_1, T_2, \ldots$ be the *waiting* times between successive changes of state. Notice that only T_1 coincides with actual calendar time (or age). These functions will be referred to as sample paths of a general nonstationary continuous-time Markov chain if the evolution proceeds according to the following rules:

1. An individual begins in a state labeled i—where i may be 1, 2, $\ldots, r$—at a reference time $t = 0$. He or she waits there for a random length of time T_1 described by the probability distribution

$$P(T_1 > t) = \exp\left[\int_0^t q_{ii}(u)du\right]$$

where $q_{ii}(u)$ is a negative function of calendar time (or age) after the reference time $t = 0$. Note that the hazard function for state i at calendar time (or age) u is $-q_{ii}(u)$, a positive function. It may be interpreted as the calendar time (or age) u-specific probability per unit time of termination of a spell in state i given that the spell has not terminated prior to calendar time (or age) u.
2. At the end of the spell—at calendar time t_1—the individual moves to state j with probability $m_{ij}(t_1)$. These probabilities must satisfy $\Sigma_{j=1}^{r} m_{ij}(t_1) = 1$ and $m_{ii}(t_1) = 0$.
3. Then he or she waits in state j for a random length of time T_2 that does not depend on the previous state occupied but does depend on the calendar time when the spell is initiated and on the current state. Let T_1+ denote the instant just after T_1 and define $w(T_1+) = \lim_{\epsilon \to 0} w(T_1 + \epsilon)$. The distribution of T_2, conditional on T_1 and the state $w(T_1+)$, is defined to be

$$P[T_2 > t \mid T_1 = t_1, w(t_1+) = j] = \exp\left[\int_{t_1}^{t_1+t} q_{jj}(u)du\right]$$

Here $-q_{jj}(u)$ is the hazard function for state j at age u.

4. At the end of the second spell—at calendar time $t_1 + t_2$—the individual moves to state k with probability $m_{jk}(t_1 + t_2)$.
5. Then he or she waits in state k for a random length of time T_3 described by the probability distribution

$$P\{T_3 > t \mid T_1 + T_2 = t_1 + t_2; w[(t_1 + t_2)+] = k\}$$
$$= \exp\left[\int_{t_1+t_2}^{t_1+t_2+t} q_{kk}(u)du)\right]$$

6. The preceding steps are repeated for subsequent spells.

Steps 1 to 6 describe the evolution of a process that is markovian in the following sense: For times $s < t$, the conditional probability that $w(t)$ is in state j given the list of values of $w(u)$ for all times (ages) u that are less than or equal to time s is the same as the conditional probability that $w(t)$ is in state j given only the value of $w(s)$. Thus probability statements about $w(t)$ depend only on the most recent given value of the process—namely, $w(s)$. However, *unlike* the more familiar time-homogeneous Markov chains, the conditional probabilities

$$P\,[w(t) = j \mid w(s) = i]$$

—hereafter written as $p_{ij}(s, t)$—*depend* on the calendar times s and t and not just on the time difference $t - s$.

For the general nonstationary Markov chains, the transition probabilities $p_{ij}(s, t)$—for $s \leq t$—are entries in stochastic matrices

$$\mathbf{P}(\mathrm{s, t}) = \begin{pmatrix} p_{11}(s, t) & \cdots & p_{1r}(s, t) \\ \cdot & & \\ \cdot & & \\ \cdot & & \\ p_{r1}(s, t) & \cdots & p_{rr}(s, t) \end{pmatrix}$$

That is, $p_{ij}(s,t) \geq 0$ and $\Sigma_{j=1}^{r} p_{ij}(s,t) = 1$ for $i = 1, 2, \ldots, r$. These matrices satisfy the Kolmogorov forward and backward matrix differential equations, respectively,

$$\partial\mathbf{P}(s, t)/\partial t = \mathbf{P}(s, t)\mathbf{Q}(t) \tag{1}$$

$$\partial\mathbf{P}(s, t)/\partial \mathrm{s} = -\mathbf{Q}(s)\mathbf{P}(s, t) \tag{2}$$

subject to $P(s, s) = I$. Moreover, $\mathbf{Q}(\mathbf{t})$ for $t \geq 0$ is a one-parameter family of matrices whose off-diagonal entries are the transition rates

$q_{ij}(t) = -q_{ii}(t)m_{ij}(t)$ and whose diagonal entries are $q_{ii}(t)$, as defined above.[1] Observe that these matrices satisfy the algebraic conditions that $q_{ii}(t) \leq 0$, $q_{ij}(t) \geq 0$ for $i \neq j$ and $\Sigma_{j=1}^{r} q_{ij}(t) = 0$. The matrices $\mathbf{Q}(t)$ are referred to as intensity matrices.

Special Subclasses of Nonstationary Chains

To illustrate the variety of phenomena that can be modeled with nonstationary chains, we specify and interpret some parametric families of intensity matrices $\mathbf{Q}(t)$ that are implicit or explicitly proposed in the sociology and economics literature.

Shifts Between Employment and Nonemployment. In the study of labor force dynamics, where the states are labeled (1 = not employed) and (2 = employed), the property of having an increasing hazard function during a spell of nonemployment is associated with the search-theoretic idea that individuals have a declining reservation wage during such spells (see Kiefer and Neumann, 1979, and Flinn and Heckman, 1980). During a spell of employment a decreasing hazard function is associated with the idea of an increase in firm-specific capital over time (Jovanović, 1979; Tuma, 1976). These economic-theoretic proposals can be formally incorporated in a two-state nonstationary markovian model by introducing the following parametric family of intensity matrices:

$$\mathbf{Q}(t) = \begin{pmatrix} -c_1(1+t)^{\alpha_1} & c_1(1+t)^{\alpha_1} \\ c_2(1+t)^{\alpha_2} & -c_2(1+t)^{\alpha_2} \end{pmatrix} \tag{3}$$

where $\alpha_1 > 0$, $-1 < \alpha_2 < 0$, and $c_i > 0$ for $i = 1, 2$. The specification (3) has the additional feature that the hazards in successive employment spells are not only declining within a spell but also declining across spells. This is an aging effect that is empirically testable. It is identified with an age-dependent decline in the rate of increase of human capital. Similarly, the search times in successive unemployment spells have increasing hazards within spells as well as across spells.

Age Dependence in Occupational Mobility. A restrictive class of nonstationary Markov models has been proposed to account for the

[1]For a rigorous mathematical discussion of Equations 1 and 2 see Goodman (1970) and Goodman and Johansen (1973).

empirically observed decline in occupational mobility rates with age (see, for example, Mayer, 1972, and Sørensen, 1975b). The specification, in terms of the one-parameter family of intensity matrices $\mathbf{Q}(t)$, is that $-q_{ii}(t)$ be a *decreasing* function of t and independent of state i, while $\{m_{ij}(t)\}$ do *not* depend on t and are entries in an upper-triangular stochastic matrix

$$\mathbf{M} = \begin{pmatrix} 0 & m_{12} & m_{13} & \cdots & m_{1r} \\ 0 & 0 & m_{23} & \cdots & m_{2r} \\ & & \ddots & \ddots & \vdots \\ & \mathbf{0} & & \ddots & m_{r-1,r} \\ & & & & 0 \end{pmatrix} \tag{4}$$

In the context of occupational mobility, the states are ordered according to prestige rankings and the upper-triangular restriction represents a population where only upward mobility is possible. Two additional testable restrictions on $\mathbf{M}$ are of interest for an understanding of mobility processes:

1. $m_{ij} > m_{i,j+1}$ for $i + 1 \leq j \leq r$.
2. $m_{12} = m_{23} = \cdots = m_{r-1,r} = 1$ and all other entries are zero.

Restriction 1 corresponds to mobility where the probability of transition across several prestige categories declines as the number of categories traversed increases. Restriction 2 corresponds to a process where only movement to the next highest prestige category is allowed at a single transition.

An alternative mobility proposal (Mayer, 1972) also assumes that $[m_{ij}(t)]$ do *not* depend on t but that $\mathbf{M}$ is of the form

$$\mathbf{M} = \begin{pmatrix} 0 & m_{12} & 0 & 0 & & \mathbf{0} \\ m_{21} & 0 & m_{23} & 0 & & \\ 0 & m_{32} & 0 & m_{34} & & \\ & \mathbf{0} & \ddots & \ddots & \ddots & m_{r-1,r} \\ & & & & m_{r,r-1} & 0 \end{pmatrix} \tag{5}$$

Individuals in such a mobility regime can only move up or down to the nearest-neighbor prestige categories at a single transition. A Markov chain with transitions governed by (5) is referred to as a birth and death process.

These assumptions about $-q_{ii}(t)$ imply that the age-dependent decline in transition rates is the same for all states and that the sample paths of the nonstationary chain may be represented as

$$w(t) = X[\nu(t)] \qquad t \geq 0 \tag{6}$$

Here $X(k)$, $k = 0, 1, 2, \ldots$ is a discrete-time-homogeneous Markov chain with one-step transition matrix **M**. Moreover, $\nu(t)$ is a nonstationary Poisson process with intensity function $\Lambda(t) = \int_0^t q(u)du$, where $q(u)$ denotes the common value of $-q_{ii}(u)$ for $i = 1, 2, \ldots, r$. Thus

$$P[\nu(t) = k] = e^{-\Lambda(t)}\,[\Lambda(t)]^k/k! \qquad k = 0, 1, 2, \ldots$$

and $\nu(t)$ counts the number of transitions made by an individual in the time interval $[0, t]$.

An interesting parametric specification of $q(u)$ has been proposed by Mayer (1972) and used by Sørensen (1975b) in the present context according to

$$q(u) = a \exp(-bu)$$

where $a > 0$ and $b > 0$ are parameters to be estimated. This exponentially declining mobility rate is associated with a defective waiting-time distribution in each state in the sense that

$$P(T_1 < +\infty) = 1 - \exp(-a/b) < 1$$

If this waiting-time distribution were to be converted into a bona fide probability distribution, it would be necessary to assign positive probability to the event $(T_1 = +\infty)$. For such an assignment we set $P(T_1 = +\infty) = \exp(-a/b)$. Then we have

$$\begin{aligned} P(T_1 > t) &= [\exp(-a/b)]\left\{\exp\left[\frac{a}{b}e^{-bt}\right] - 1\right\} \\ &= \exp\left[-\int_0^t h(u)du\right] \end{aligned}$$

and the hazard rate for this distribution is

$$h(u) = a[\exp(-bu)]\left\{\exp\left[\frac{a}{b}e^{-bu}\right] - 1\right\}^{-1} \neq q(u)$$

Intragenerational Mobility. In an interesting discussion of intragenerational occupational mobility, Sørensen (1975a) has proposed the following parameterization of the intensity matrices $\mathbf{Q}(t)$. For $i \neq j$, let

$$q_{ij}(t) = \exp[b_i(t) + c_j(t) - d_{ij}(t)] \tag{7}$$

where $b_i(t)$ and $c_j(t)$ represent calendar time-dependent characteristics of the origin and destination occupation and $d_{ij}(t)$ represents the affinity, or distance, between the two occupations. Then

$$q_{ii}(t) = -\sum_{j \neq i} q_{ij}(t)$$

Specifications of (7) and estimation from panel data on mobility have not been carried out to date. Similar models have been estimated, however, from event-history data (Sørensen and Tuma, 1980).

ESTIMATION FOR TWO-STATE CHAINS FROM PANEL DATA

Parameter estimation within the class of nonstationary continuous-time Markov chains using panel data requires a simple representation of $\mathbf{P}(s, t)$ in Equations (1) and (2) in terms of the intensity matrices $\mathbf{Q}(t)$ for $t \geq 0$. In the time-homogeneous case where $\mathbf{Q}(t) \equiv \mathbf{Q}_0$ = (constant-intensity matrix), it is well known (see Coleman, 1964a, and Singer and Spilerman, 1976) that $\mathbf{P}(s, t)$ may be represented by the matrix exponential

$$\mathbf{P}(s, t) = \exp[(t - s)\mathbf{Q}_0] \tag{8}$$

For the general r-state nonstationary chains, there does *not* exist an analogous formula to represent $\mathbf{P}(s, t)$—primarily due to the fact that for $s \neq t$ the matrices $\mathbf{Q}(s)$ and $\mathbf{Q}(t)$ do not commute.[2] The appropriate mathematical tools for the production of useful formulas for $\mathbf{P}(s, t)$ reside in the theory of Lie algebras (see especially Wei and Norman, 1963, 1964). In this section we restrict our attention to the

[2]Two intensity matrices $\mathbf{Q}(t)$ and and $\mathbf{Q}(s)$ are said to be commutative if $\mathbf{Q}(s)\mathbf{Q}(t) = \mathbf{Q}(t)\mathbf{Q}(s)$.

two-state nonstationary continuous-time chains and exhibit an explicit representation of $\mathbf{P}(s, t)$ of the form

$$\mathbf{P}(s, t) = \exp [\mathbf{A}(s, t)] \tag{9}$$

where $\mathbf{A}(s, t)$ is a simple function of $\{q_{ij}(t), t \geq 0\}$ and of the time points (s, t). This formula and its use in panel-survey estimation strategies is the simplest prototype of a methodology for using continuous-time nonstationary Markov models to study microdynamic processes. A full mathematical discussion of representations of $\mathbf{P}(s, t)$ for the two-state case, as well as for matrices of arbitrary order, will be deferred to another time.

For two-state chains we simplify our notation for the intensity matrices $\{\mathbf{Q}(t), t \geq 0\}$ by writing them in the form

$$\mathbf{Q}(t) = \begin{pmatrix} -q_1(t) & q_1(t) \\ q_2(t) & -q_2(t) \end{pmatrix}$$

where $q_i(t)$, $i = 1, 2$, are arbitrary nonnegative functions that are integrable on finite time intervals. Then let

$$g_1(s, t) = \int_s^t q_2(u) \exp\left\{\int_s^u [q_1(v) + q_2(v)]dv\right\} du \tag{10}$$

and

$$g_2(s, t) = -\int_s^t [q_1(u) + q_2(u)]du \tag{11}$$

In terms of these quantities a somewhat tedious calculation, using the Lie algebraic methods just mentioned, yields the following formula for $\mathbf{A}(s,t)$ in Equation (9):

$$\mathbf{A}(s, t) = \tag{12}$$

$$\frac{-g_2}{\exp(-g_2) - 1} \begin{pmatrix} -[\exp(-g_2) - 1 - g_2] & \exp(-g_2) - 1 - g_2 \\ g_1 & -g_1 \end{pmatrix}$$

Equation (9) with $\mathbf{A}(s, t)$ specified by (12) is the simplest *general* formula for the transition probabilities of the two-state continuous-time nonstationary Markov chains. In the special case where $\mathbf{Q}(s)$ and $\mathbf{Q}(t)$ commute—that is, $\mathbf{Q}(s)\mathbf{Q}(t) = \mathbf{Q}(t)\mathbf{Q}(s)$ for $s \neq t$—we find that $\mathbf{Q}(s) = q(s)(\mathbf{M} - \mathbf{I})$, where $\mathbf{M}$ is a stochastic matrix and $q(s)$ is the intensity rate of a nonstationary Poisson process (as in the subsection

"Age Dependence in Occupational Mobility"). Then, setting $\Lambda(t) = \int_0^t q(u)du$, we have

$$\mathbf{P}(s, t) = \exp\{[\Lambda(t) - \Lambda(s)](\mathbf{M} - \mathbf{I})\} \tag{13}$$

in direct analogy with the time-homogeneous situation where $q(u) =$ constant. For two-state chains Formula (9) *reduces* to (13) whenever $\mathbf{Q}(s)\mathbf{Q}(t) = \mathbf{Q}(t)\mathbf{Q}(s)$ for $s \neq t$. However, Formula (13) is a valid representation of $\mathbf{P}(s, t)$ for matrices of arbitrary order provided the matrices $[\mathbf{Q}(t), t \geq 0]$ commute. Because of the more intricate analytic discussion required, I defer a treatment of formulas analogous to (9) for matrices of order 3 and higher to a separate publication. My emphasis here is on an estimation strategy for the simplest situation: matrices of order 2.

We assume that there are N individuals in the panel at time $t = 0$. The typical data collection strategy for panel studies is to observe

$$[w(0), w(\Delta), w(2\Delta), \ldots, w(K\Delta)]$$

for each individual, where $\Delta =$ (spacing between waves of panel) and $1 + K =$ total number of waves. We confine the discussion in this section to a description of movements of persons present for all $K + 1$ waves. Furthermore we assume that the members of the population begin their evolution simultaneously at $t = 0$ (as in Kuhn and others, 1973, a study of graduate job mobility). A more complex analysis is required for populations where individuals do not initiate a process synchronously. Biases that can enter our estimation procedures due to panel attrition are discussed in Williams and Mallows (1970).

We begin with the set of fitted stochastic matrices

$$\hat{\mathbf{P}}(\mathrm{k}\Delta, \mathrm{l}\Delta) = \| N_{ij}(k\Delta, l\Delta)/N_{i+}(k\Delta, l\Delta) \| \qquad 0 \leq k < l \leq K \tag{14}$$

where

$$N_{ij}(k\Delta, l\Delta) = \text{number of individuals in state } i \text{ at time } k\Delta \text{ and in state } j \text{ at time } l\Delta$$

$$N_{i+}(k\Delta, l\Delta) = N_{i1}(k\Delta, l\Delta) + N_{i2}(k\Delta, l\Delta)$$

Of course, $N_{1+}(k\Delta, l\Delta) + N_{2+}(k\Delta, l\Delta) = N$ for $0 \leq k < l \leq K$.

For arbitrary 2×2 matrices $\mathbf{B}$, represented as

$$\mathbf{B} = \begin{pmatrix} b_{11} & b_{12} \\ b_{21} & b_{22} \end{pmatrix}$$

we introduce the matrix norm

$$\|\mathbf{B}\| = \left(\sum_{i=1}^{2}\sum_{j=1}^{2} b_{ij}^2\right)^{1/2}$$

Then we obtain initial estimates of parameters in $\mathbf{A}(s, t)$ in Formula (12) by minimizing

$$\sum_{0 \le k < l \le K} \|\log \hat{\mathbf{P}}(\mathbf{k}\boldsymbol{\Delta}, \mathbf{l}\boldsymbol{\Delta}) - \mathbf{A}(\mathbf{k}\boldsymbol{\Delta}, \mathbf{l}\boldsymbol{\Delta})\| \tag{15}$$

Here $\log \hat{\mathbf{P}}(\mathbf{k}\boldsymbol{\Delta}, \mathbf{l}\boldsymbol{\Delta})$ means the matrix logarithm. For the *general* 2×2 stochastic matrix

$$\mathbf{P} = \begin{pmatrix} p_{11} & p_{12} \\ p_{21} & p_{22} \end{pmatrix}$$

$\log \mathbf{P}$ is given by

$$\log \mathbf{P} = \frac{\log (p_{11} + p_{22} - 1)}{p_{11} + p_{22} - 1} \begin{pmatrix} p_{11} - 1 & 1 - p_{11} \\ 1 - p_{22} & p_{22} - 1 \end{pmatrix}$$

See Singer and Spilerman (1976) for mathematical details on logarithms for stochastic matrices.

The least-squares estimates obtained by minimizing (15) provide good starting values for steepest-descent algorithms that maximize the likelihood function of the panel observations. For an example of the computer implementation of this kind of strategy on restricted classes of time-homogeneous chains, see Cohen and Singer (1979). Analogous implementation for the parametric family of models in the subsection "Shifts Between Employment and Nonemployment" should be straightforward; however, a working program to deal with $\mathbf{A}(s, t)$ at the full generality of Equation (12) remains to be developed.

INTRINSIC TIME SCALES

A subclass of the general r-state nonstationary chains can be made stationary by a nonlinear change of the time scale. That is, there exists a continuous, strictly increasing positive function $\Lambda(t)$ such that

$$\mathbf{P}(s, t) = \exp [(\Lambda(t) - \Lambda(s))\mathbf{Q}] \tag{16}$$

for some *fixed* intensity matrix Q. A rather striking result of Goodman (1970) can be used to test multiwave panel data for compatibility with representation (16).

> THEOREM (Goodman, 1970): *If a nonstationary continuous-time Markov chain can be made stationary by any continuous strictly increasing time substitution, then it can be made stationary by replacing t by*
>
> $$\Lambda(t) = -\log \det \mathbf{P}(0, t) \tag{17}$$

To employ the time substitution (17) on panel data, we first compute $-\log \det \hat{\mathbf{P}}(0, k\Delta)$ for $1 \leq k \leq K$. Then we check whether there is a single intensity matrix $\mathbf{Q}_0$ on at least one branch of the logarithm of each of the matrices

$$[-\log \det \hat{\mathbf{P}}(0, k\Delta)]^{-1} \log \mathbf{P}(0, k\Delta) \qquad 1 \leq k \leq K$$

If the matrices $[\hat{\mathbf{P}}(0, k\Delta)]$, $1 \leq k \leq K$, can be represented as in Equation (16), we should find that

$$[-\log \det \hat{\mathbf{P}}(0, k\Delta)]^{-1} \log \hat{\mathbf{P}}(0, k\Delta) = \mathbf{Q}_0 \qquad 1 \leq k \leq K \tag{18}$$

Demanding exact equality in (18) with actual data is quite unrealistic because finite samples can lead to tests that yield only approximate equality. Quantitative assessment of these approximate equalities—that is, converting Equation (18) into a formal significance test—requires a distribution theory for $[-\log \det \hat{\mathbf{P}}(0, k\Delta)]^{-1} \log \hat{\mathbf{P}}(0, k\Delta)$ that has yet to be developed. Observe that a verification of (18) and calculation of either upper triangular or Jacobi matrices for log $\hat{\mathbf{P}}(0, k\Delta)$ would imply that the data are consistent with the occupational mobility models in the subsection "Age Dependence in Occupational Mobility."

EMBEDDING CRITERIA

Before using estimation strategies such as those described earlier, it is logical to ask whether transition matrices $[\hat{\mathbf{P}}(k\Delta, l\Delta)$, $0 \leq k < l \leq K]$ could have been generated by sampling *any* continuous-time Markov chain. For two-state processes the answer is affirmative if and only if

$$\hat{p}_{11}(k\Delta, l\Delta) + \hat{p}_{22}(k\Delta, l\Delta) > 1 \qquad 0 \le k < l < K \tag{19}$$

and

$$\hat{\mathbf{P}}(k\Delta, l\Delta)\hat{\mathbf{P}}(l\Delta, m\Delta) \approx \hat{\mathbf{P}}(k\Delta, m\Delta) \qquad 0 \le k < l \le m \le K \tag{20}$$

Singer and Cohen (1980) include formal significance tests of (19) together with an illustration of their use on a panel survey of malaria.

For processes with three or more states, easily applicable necessary and sufficient conditions for a given stochastic matrix $\mathbf{P}$ to be represented as $\mathbf{P}(s, t)$ arising from Equations (1) and (2) for any times $s \le t$ are not known. Two necessary but not sufficient conditions for such an embedding are:

1. $\det \mathbf{P} > 0$.
2. $\Pi_{i=1}^{r} p_{ii} \ge \det \mathbf{P}$.

These conditions—established by Goodman (1970)—represent the only known, easily computable tests for embeddability of single stochastic matrices in arbitrary continuous-time, nonstationary Markov models.

If we restrict consideration to the nonstationary birth and death processes—that is, the intensity matrices $\mathbf{Q}(t)$ satisfy the additional restriction that $q_{ij}(t) = 0$ for $|i - j| > 1$—then we have the following theorem:

> *THEOREM (Frydman and Singer, 1979): A nonsingular stochastic matrix* $\mathbf{P}$ *is embeddable in a two-parameter family of stochastic matrices satisfying Equations (1) and (2), with the additional restriction* $q_{ij}(t) = 0$ *for* $|i - j| > 1$, *if and only if it is totally positive.*

An $r \times r$ stochastic matrix $\mathbf{P}$ is totally positive if for $i_1 < i_2 < \cdots < i_k$ and $j_1 < j_2 < \cdots < j_k$,

$$\det \|p_{i_l, j_m}\| \ge 0 \qquad i \le l \le k; 1 \le m \le k$$

for $k = 2, 3, \ldots, r$.

To facilitate understanding of the notion of total positivity, consider what this means for stochastic matrices of order 3. Let

$$\mathbf{P} = \begin{pmatrix} p_{11} & p_{12} & p_{13} \\ p_{21} & p_{22} & p_{23} \\ p_{31} & p_{32} & p_{33} \end{pmatrix}$$

Setting $k = 2$ in the definition of total positivity, there are nine 2×2 matrices formed from elements of **P**, each of which must have a nonnegative determinant. The row and column indices in **P** which designate the elements of these matrices are listed in the following table.

Row indices		Column indices	
i_1	i_2	j_1	j_2
		1	2
1	2	1	3
		2	3
		1	2
1	3	1	3
		2	3
		1	2
2	3	1	3
		2	3

For example, if $i_1 = 1, i_2 = 3, j_1 = 2$ and $j_2 = 3$ the corresponding 2×2 matrix is

$$\begin{pmatrix} p_{12} & p_{13} \\ p_{32} & p_{33} \end{pmatrix}.$$

Setting $k = 3$, the total positivity criterion simply implies that det $\mathbf{P} \geq 0$.

At present there are no formal significance tests based on multinomial sampling to assess whether estimated stochastic matrices are totally positive. The development of the relevant distribution theory for such tests remains a major challenge.

TRACE INEQUALITIES

Starting with the now classic work of Blumen, Kogan, and McCarthy (1955), multiwave panel data have often been found to be inconsistent with a time-homogeneous Markov model. Frequently

$$\text{trace } \hat{\mathbf{P}}^2(0, \Delta) < \text{trace } \hat{\mathbf{P}}(0, 2\Delta) \tag{21}$$

as explained in Singer and Spilerman (1977, 1978). A common interpretation of (21) has been that this is a characteristic of transition matrices generated by mixtures of time-homogeneous Markov chains. Indeed, such mixtures frequently provide a good description of multi-wave panel data—as in Blumen, Kogan, and McCarthy (1955)—despite the fact that (21) does *not* hold for every mixture of time-homogeneous chains.

Interpreting (21) as a violation of the Markov property is correct only if one means *time-homogeneous* Markov chains. In fact, (21) can arise from a *homogeneous population* model in which individuals evolve according to a nonstationary Markov chain.

EXAMPLE: Let

$$\mathbf{P}(0, \Delta) = \begin{pmatrix} 0.6 & 0.4 \\ 0.3 & 0.7 \end{pmatrix}$$

$$\mathbf{P}(\Delta, 2\Delta) = \begin{pmatrix} 0.8 & 0.2 \\ 0.1 & 0.9 \end{pmatrix}$$

and assume that $\mathbf{P}(0, 2\Delta) = \mathbf{P}(0, \Delta)\mathbf{P}(\Delta, 2\Delta)$. *Then a routine calculation reveals that trace* $\mathbf{P}^2(0, \Delta) = 1.09$, *which is less than trace* $\mathbf{P}(0, 2\Delta) = 1.18$.

The proper analog of (21) that indicates a violation of all Markov chains—time-homogeneous or not—is

$$\text{trace } \hat{\mathbf{P}}(0, \Delta)\hat{\mathbf{P}}(\Delta, 2\Delta) < \text{trace } \hat{\mathbf{P}}(0,2\Delta) \tag{22}$$

Inequality (22) was observed on several hundred transition matrices in a panel survey of malaria in Cohen and Singer (1979). Furthermore, K. Land (private communication, 1980) found that

$$\text{trace } \hat{\mathbf{P}}(0, \Delta)\hat{\mathbf{P}}(\Delta, 2\Delta) > \text{trace } \hat{\mathbf{P}}(0, 2\Delta) \tag{23}$$

in a study of marital formation and dissolution. Characterizations of those mixtures of nonstationary chains that yield (22) and those that yield (23) remain to be developed. Even more pressing is the need for formal significance tests to assess (21) to (23). I know of no research that addresses this topic.

CONCLUSIONS

I have described the general continuous-time nonstationary Markov chains and interpreted special parametric families of them as models of individual employment dynamics and intragenerational occupational mobility. These examples illustrate the wide variety of age and calendar time dependence in the duration distributions of episodes in multistate processes and in the transition probabilities between pairs of states that can be incorporated in nonstationary chains.

I also presented an estimation strategy for fitting two-state, continuous-time, nonstationary Markov models to panel data. This discussion illustrates the feasibility of such modeling in the simplest setting and contains, as a necessary ingredient, the first computationally tractable representation of the transition matrices $\mathbf{P}(s, t)$ in terms of the intensity matrices $[\mathbf{Q}(t), t \geq 0]$.

The discussion of intrinsic time scales contains a new technique for assessing whether multiwave panel data can be represented by the restrictive class of markovian models where the nonstationarity is entirely incorporated in the rate at which transitions occur. Models of this type have a substantial history in the intragenerational occupational mobility literature; the strategy described in this chapter provides the first systematic methods for assessing whether or not panel data on mobility are consistent with such theories.

Finally I showed, by a simple example, that the residuals from time-homogeneous r-state Markov models of the form

$$\text{trace } \mathbf{P}^k(0, \Delta) < \text{trace } \mathbf{P}(0, k\Delta) \qquad k = 2, 3, \ldots \tag{24}$$

can in fact arise from a homogeneous population model where individuals evolve according to a nonstationary Markov chain. This provides a new interpretation of (24) that is quite different from the heterogeneity and response uncertainty interpretations put forth in earlier literature (Coleman, 1964b; Singer and Spilerman, 1977).

The next step, which remains to be carried out, is to develop strategies for introducing independent variables into the general nonstationary chains. This development would allow for the formal incorporation of observed and unobserved heterogeneity in these models and provide possible representations for multiwave panel data that exhibit strong dependencies across time.

REFERENCES

BLUMEN, I., KOGAN, M., AND McCARTHY, P. J.

1955 *The Industrial Mobility of Labor as a Probability Process.* Cornell Studies of Industrial and Labor Relations, vol. 6. Ithaca: Cornell University.

COHEN, J. E., AND SINGER, B.

1979 "Malaria in Nigeria: Constrained continuous-time Markov models for discrete-time longitudinal data on human mixed-species infections." In S. Levin (Ed.), *Some Mathematical Questions in Biology.* Vol. 12 of Lectures on Mathematics in the Life Sciences. Providence: American Mathematical Society.

COLEMAN, J. S.

1964a *Introduction to Mathematical Sociology.* New York: Free Press.

1964b *Models of Change and Response Uncertainty.* Englewood Cliffs, N.J.: Prentice-Hall.

FLINN, C. J., AND HECKMAN, J. J.

1980 "Models for the analysis of labor force dynamics." Discussion paper 80-3. Chicago: Economics Research Center, NORC.

FRYDMAN, H., AND SINGER, B.

1979 "Total positivity and the embedding problem for Markov chains." *Mathematical Proceedings of Cambridge Philosophical Society* 86:339–344.

GOODMAN, G. S.

1970 "An intrinsic time for non-stationary finite Markov chains." *Zeitschrift für Wahrscheinlichkeitstheorie* 16:165–180.

GOODMAN, G. S., AND JOHANSEN, S.

1973 "Kolmogorov's differential equations for non-stationary countable state Markov processes with uniformly continuous transition probabilities." *Proceedings of Cambridge Philosophical Society* 73:119–138.

HANNAN, M., AND TUMA, N. B.

1979 "Methods for temporal analysis." *Annual Review of Sociology* 5:303–328.

JOVANOVIĆ, B.

1979 "Job matching and the theory of turnover." *Journal of Political Economy* 87:972–990.

KIEFER, N., AND NEUMANN, G.

1979 "An empirical job search model with a test of the constant resolution wage hypothesis." *Journal of Political Economy* 87(1):89–108.

KUHN, A., POOLE, A., SALES, P., AND WYNN, H.
1973 "An analysis of graduate job mobility." *British Journal of Industrial Relations* 11:124–142.

LITTMAN, G., AND MODE, C. J.
1977 "A non-Markovian stochastic model for the Taichung medical IUD experiment." *Mathematical Biosciences* 34:279–302.

MAYER, T.
1972 "Models of intragenerational mobility." In J. Berger, M. Zelditch, and B. Anderson (Eds.), *Sociological Theories in Progress*. Boston: Houghton Mifflin.

PICKENS, G., AND SOYKA, M.
1980 "Effects of changed contraceptive patterns on fertility in Taiwan: Applications of a non-Markovian stochastic model." *International Journal of Biomedical Computing* 11:1–19.

SINGER, B., AND COHEN, J. E.
1980 "Estimating malaria incidence and recovery rates from panel surveys." *Mathematical Biosciences* 49:273–305.

SINGER, B., AND SPILERMAN, S.
1976 "The representation of social processes by Markov models." *American Journal of Sociology* 82:1–54.
1977 "Trace inequalities for mixtures of Markov chains." *Advances in Applied Probability* 9:747–764.
1978 "Clustering on the main diagonal in mobility matrices." In K. F. Schuessler (Ed.), *Sociological Methodology 1979*. San Francisco: Jossey-Bass.

SØRENSEN, A.
1975a "Models of social mobility." *Social Science Research* 4:65–92.
1975b "The structure of intragenerational mobility." *American Sociological Review* 40:456–471.

SØRENSEN, A., AND TUMA, N.
1980 "Labor market structures and job mobility." *Research in Social Stratification and Mobility*, in press.

TUMA, N. B.
1976 "Rewards, resources, and the rate of mobility: A non-stationary multivariate stochastic model." *American Sociological Review* 41:338–360.

TUMA, N. B., HANNAN, M., AND GROENEVELD, L.
1979 "Dynamic analysis of event histories." *American Journal of Sociology* 84:820–854.

WEI, J., AND NORMAN, E.
1963 "Lie algebraic solution of linear differential equations." *Journal of Mathematical Physics* 4:575–581.

1964 "On global representations of the solutions of linear differential equations as a product of exponentials." *Proceedings of American Mathematical Society* 15:327–334.

WILLIAMS, W. H., AND MALLOWS, C. L.

1970 "Systematic biases in panel surveys due to differential non-response." *Journal of American Statistical Association* 65:1338–1349.

9

SPECTRAL DECOMPOSITION AS A TOOL IN COMPARATIVE MOBILITY RESEARCH

David D. McFarland

UNIVERSITY OF CALIFORNIA, LOS ANGELES

The dominant left eigenvector (sometimes under other names, such as *equilibrium distribution* or *stable vector*) has long been recognized as providing important information about the mobility process that is characterized by a particular stochastic matrix describing intergenerational or intragenerational occupational mobility.

From its first introduction into the social mobility literature (Prais, 1955a, 1955b), this tool has been found useful in comparative

Revision of a paper presented to the Ninth World Congress of Sociology, Uppsala, Sweden, 14–19 August 1978. I wish to thank O. D. Duncan, G. Erbring, L. Erbring, N. Keyfitz, and S. Spilerman for commenting on an earlier version. Many of their suggestions have been followed, and even some with which I disagree helped by directing my attention to points in the argument that needed to be clarified or elaborated.

analysis. Prais (1955a) used it in comparing observed British mobility patterns with those of a hypothetical baseline known as "perfect mobility," in which a man's occupation is statistically independent of his father's occupation. Matras (1960) used it in comparing mobility patterns observed in different countries. Duncan (1966) used it for comparisons over time in his work on mobility trends in the United States. And Lieberson and Fuguitt (1967) used it in the context of the comparison of racial subpopulations in the United States.

Except in special cases, an $n \times n$ matrix has not just one but n different left eigenvectors corresponding to n different eigenvalues, while only the dominant one, the one corresponding to the largest eigenvalue, has been considered important by mobility analysts. Furthermore, since in the case of a stochastic matrix the largest eigenvalue is necessarily unity, and since multiplication by unity leaves things unchanged, this literature ignores eigenvalues completely.[1] Similarly, while there are n different right eigenvectors corresponding to the n different eigenvalues, the one corresponding to unity is a vector each element of which is unity, a vector of little interest, leading mobility analysts to ignore right eigenvectors completely as well.

The thesis of this chapter is the claim that eigenvalues other than the largest, together with their corresponding left and right eigenvectors, provide important information about a mobility process. In particular, I argue that they are useful in comparative analysis, whether comparison is between observed and hypothetical mobility tables, between observed mobility tables for different countries, or between mobility tables covering different eras or different subpopulations within a single country.

I shall show that eigenvalues other than the largest, together with their corresponding left and right eigenvectors, describe transitory effects that, although negligible in the long run, may be of significant magnitude for the first couple of generations (or other time units). They tell us both the *nature* of these transitory effects (for example, a

[1]Eigenvalues, including those other than the largest, have, however, been used a few times elsewhere in the sociological literature. Keyfitz (1968, chap. 3) and others influenced by him have made extensive use of them in analyses of population projection matrices. Moreover, Singer and Spilerman (1976) make reference to all the eigenvalues of a matrix in their discussion of the conditions under which data collected in a form most suitable for analysis by discrete-time Markov models may, nevertheless, be fitted instead to continuous-time Markov models.

transitory barrier tending to prevent mobility between the skilled and unskilled manual categories) and the *speed* with which the transitory effects are overwhelmed by the main trend contained in the dominant eigenvector (for example, negligible by the third generation).

The substantive insights to be gained by use of these tools are illustrated by reanalysis of the two most dramatically different mobility tables this author has ever examined: the Negro table and the non-Negro table from the Occupational Change in a Generation (OCG) study of occupational mobility in the United States (Duncan, 1968, table 6).

EIGENVALUES AND SPECTRAL COMPONENTS

This section defines and establishes notation for the entities used in spectral decomposition of occupational mobility matrices and states (without proof) some of their mathematical properties. Proofs may be found in books on matrix algebra (Gantmacher, 1959; Seneta, 1973).

Consider a square $n \times n$ stochastic matrix $\mathbf{P}$ whose element $\mathbf{P}_{ij}$ is the conditional probability that a unit of observation (a family line in intergenerational mobility, a person in intragenerational mobility) will be in occupational category j at the end of a time unit, given that the same unit was in category i at the beginning of a time unit. This is the matrix whose square, cube, and successive high powers tell what would happen (under suitable assumptions; see McFarland, 1970) to the individual or family line in the near and remote future.[2]

[2]One reader urged that I state those assumptions explicitly and justify their applicability to the substantive example to be considered. The assumptions are those of a simple Markov chain: that a closed, internally homogeneous population (of family lines, in this example) moves among occupational categories according to probabilities that are stationary (constant from generation to generation) and Markovian (probabilities for the next generation depend only on occupations of current generation, not on occupations of prior generations). Stated more simply (but less precisely), the assumption is that the intergenerational mobility pattern in the given matrix will persist into the future.

The object here is not to predict future mobility, however, but to describe the mobility already observed. An answer to the question "What would happen if current trends were to persist?" tells us something important about current trends and is therefore valuable—quite irrespective of whether or not it tells us anything about the future (see McFarland, 1974).

Nor is this claim a novel one. We go through analogous reasoning each time we

Let **X** denote an $n \times 1$ matrix (a column vector) and **Y** denote a $1 \times n$ matrix (a row vector), both of whose elements are as yet unspecified. Let λ denote a scalar (a real or complex number). Then if $\mathbf{PX} = \lambda\mathbf{X}$, we say that **X** is a *right eigenvector* corresponding to *eigenvalue* λ; and if $\mathbf{YP} = \lambda\mathbf{Y}$, we say that **Y** is a *left eigenvector* corresponding to eigenvalue λ. The corresponding *spectral component* is $\mathbf{Z} = \mathbf{XY}/\mathbf{YX}$, an $n \times n$ matrix.[3]

An $n \times n$ matrix ordinarily has n distinct eigenvalues, which we shall distinguish by different subscripts. When the eigenvalues are distinct,[4] one may decompose the matrix into the sum of its spectral components, each multiplied by the corresponding eigenvalue:

$$\mathbf{P} = \sum_{i=1}^{n} \lambda_i \mathbf{Z}_i \tag{1}$$

---

drive a car. The speedometer reading answers the question "How far would we be an hour hence if we were to continue driving in the current direction and at the current rate?" We take the speedometer reading as descriptive of our current motion, however, not as predictive of our location an hour hence. There are good reasons for expecting that a car's current motion will *not* persist into the future—reduced speed zones, for example—just as there are good reasons for expecting that current mobility patterns will not persist into the future—most notably, lack of closure in the population of family lines, and nonstationarity due to economic shifts. But we do not intend to predict the future, only to describe observed patterns.

[3]Note that the denominator **YX** is a scalar, so the operation indicated is a matrix divided by a scalar. Division by **YX** serves as a norming device that makes the spectral component unique even though the eigenvectors are determined only up to multiplication by a scalar.

[4]It is mathematically possible to have repeated rather than distinct eigenvalues, in which case the spectral decomposition in Equation (1) must be replaced with a somewhat more complex decomposition involving Jordan forms. That mathematical possibility seldom occurs in practice, however, and in particular does not occur for the occupational mobility matrices we have considered.

Gantmacher (1959) and Seneta (1973) give mathematical treatments of the more general case, allowing for repeated eigenvalues. The possibility of repeated eigenvalues for population projection matrices is discussed by Keyfitz (1968, pp. 51, 103), McFarland (1978), and Sykes (n.d.). While Keyfitz and McFarland both give hypothetical examples involving repeated eigenvalues, none of these authors cites any cases of real data matrices with repeated eigenvalues. In a different context (see footnote 1), Singer and Spilerman (1976, p. 28) make the important point that even though an "observed" matrix deriving from empirical data is calculated to have distinct eigenvalues, empirical data are subject to errors (sampling, measurement, rounding), and thus one may sometimes wish to consider whether the corresponding "true" matrix could possibly be one with repeated eigenvalues—that is, whether repeated eigenvalues occur for *any* of the innumerable other matrices within error distance of the "observed" matrix.

Spectral decomposition is desirable because this alternative representation of the original probability matrix greatly facilitates visualization and verbal description of mobility patterns. First, the pattern in any one of the **Z** matrices is particularly simple, because all the rows of a **Z** matrix are proportional to one another and all the columns are proportional to one another. Second, the λ's have a direct interpretation in terms of the persistence or transience of the effects found in the corresponding **Z** matrices (smaller values corresponding to more transient, less persistent effects).

These and other properties of spectral decomposition will be given a more systematic and thorough treatment in a subsequent section, but first we turn to an empirical example to illustrate the substantive insights the technique can provide.

INTERRACIAL OCCUPATIONAL MOBILITY DIFFERENCES

Let us now examine the substantive insights to be gained by spectral decomposition by reanalyzing data on differences in occupational mobility patterns between whites and blacks in the United States. These data, taken from an article by Duncan (1968, p. 19, table 6), originated in the Occupational Change in a Generation study administered as a supplement to the March 1962 Current Population Survey conducted by the U.S. Census Bureau.

While I intend in due course to make other comparisons, including international comparisons, there are several reasons for selecting this comparison for discussion in a chapter concerned primarily with setting forth a particular method of analysis with as few other distractions as possible and in as convincing a form as possible. First, these two mobility matrices display differences more dramatic than those of any other pair of mobility matrices I have examined—and in discussions of differences it is desirable to choose illustrations whose differences are of a magnitude worthy of discussion. Second, the data as published, although requiring some recalculation, still require much less preliminary (that is, prior to spectral decomposition) data manipulation than would most other prospective comparisons. Third, we may with reasonable safety ignore issues of comparability of occupational categories, since occupations of blacks and those of whites were coded at the same time using the same procedures; issues of comparability could not so readily be ignored in comparisons across nations or across time.

In conformity with what I take to be current usage, the term *black* is applied to persons identified as "Negro" in the original study. All others are lumped together under the term *white,* but the reader is hereby warned that this category does include a small proportion of respondents who were identified in the original study as neither Negro nor white—presumably mainly of Hispanic or Oriental background.

Duncan's transition matrices (1968, p. 19, table 6) include five occupational categories: (1) higher white collar, (2) lower white collar, (3) higher manual, (4) lower manual, and (5) farm. I shall use the same five categories in this analysis. However, Duncan's transition matrices also include a sixth category for cases where occupation was not reported. Since cases for which either respondent's occupation or father's occupation is not reported provide no information concerning the relationship between the two, I have eliminated the sixth row and column and recalculated the transition probabilities accordingly. The resulting transition matrices for blacks and for whites (that is, all others) are given in Table 1. These two transition matrices will be spectrally decomposed and comparisons made between corresponding eigenvalues and corresponding spectral components.

The first spectral component gives the stable occupational distribution that would eventually result were current mobility patterns to persist. Were current mobility patterns among blacks to persist, they would eventually have 68.3 percent in lower manual occupations, as contrasted with 21.5 percent of whites in lower manual

TABLE 1
Transition Matrices to Be Analyzed

Black transition matrix				
0.112	0.105	0.210	0.573	0.000
0.156	0.098	0.000	0.745	0.000
0.094	0.073	0.120	0.684	0.030
0.087	0.077	0.126	0.691	0.020
0.035	0.034	0.072	0.676	0.183
White transition matrix				
0.576	0.162	0.122	0.126	0.014
0.485	0.197	0.145	0.157	0.016
0.303	0.127	0.301	0.259	0.011
0.229	0.124	0.242	0.387	0.018
0.178	0.076	0.214	0.311	0.221

TABLE 2
First Components for Blacks and Whites

Black first component (eigenvalue: 1)				
Spectral component				
0.095	0.080	0.122	0.683	0.021
0.095	0.080	0.122	0.683	0.021
0.095	0.080	0.122	0.683	0.021
0.095	0.080	0.122	0.683	0.021
0.095	0.080	0.122	0.683	0.021
Deflated matrix				
0.017	0.025	0.088	−0.110	−0.021
0.061	0.019	−0.122	0.063	−0.021
−0.001	−0.007	−0.002	0.001	0.009
−0.008	−0.003	0.004	0.008	−0.001
−0.060	−0.046	−0.049	−0.007	0.162
White first component (eigenvalue: 1)				
Spectral component				
0.429	0.151	0.186	0.215	0.018
0.429	0.151	0.186	0.215	0.018
0.429	0.151	0.186	0.215	0.018
0.429	0.151	0.186	0.215	0.018
0.429	0.151	0.186	0.215	0.018
Deflated matrix				
0.146	0.011	−0.064	−0.089	−0.005
0.056	0.046	−0.041	−0.058	−0.002
−0.127	−0.024	0.114	0.044	−0.008
−0.200	−0.027	0.056	0.172	0.000
−0.251	−0.075	0.028	0.096	0.202

occupations. (See Table 2, column 4.) Were current mobility patterns to persist, whites would eventually have 42.9 percent in upper white-collar occupations, as contrasted with 9.5 percent for blacks. (See Table 2, column 1.) But these analyses, involving only the first spectral component, have been carried out previously by other authors and will not be belabored here.

A fair summary of the first component would be: A black is quite likely to be in the lower manual category; a white is quite likely to be in the upper white-collar category; and neither is at all likely to be in the farm category—in each case regardless of the occupational categories of one's remote ancestors.

But that is not all that is going on in the data, as the second and subsequent components will show. Consider the white second component in the lower panel of Table 3. Notice the pattern of signs among the elements of the second spectral component:

$$\begin{matrix} + & + & - & - & - \\ + & + & - & - & - \\ - & - & + & + & + \\ - & - & + & + & + \\ - & - & + & + & + \end{matrix}$$

While some of the individual elements are sufficiently small as to be doubtful, the overall pattern seems compelling. Furthermore, it has a straightforward verbal description: The second spectral component for whites signifies a barrier inhibiting movement between the white-collar occupations, on the one hand, and the manual and farm occupations on the other. This is, of course, something one might expect; mobility analysts have, after all, made extensive use of the

TABLE 3
Second Components for Blacks and Whites

Black second component (eigenvalue: 0.1777709681)				
Spectral component				
0.062	0.043	0.034	−0.019	−0.120
0.104	0.072	0.056	−0.032	−0.201
−0.027	−0.019	−0.015	0.008	0.052
−0.002	−0.001	−0.001	0.001	0.004
−0.455	−0.317	−0.247	0.139	0.880
Deflated matrix				
0.006	0.018	0.082	−0.106	0.000
0.043	0.006	−0.132	0.068	0.015
0.004	−0.004	0.000	0.000	0.000
−0.007	−0.003	0.004	0.008	−0.002
0.021	0.011	−0.006	−0.032	0.006
White second component (eigenvalue: 0.3482092556)				
Spectral component				
0.408	0.056	−0.187	−0.272	−0.004
0.243	0.033	−0.111	−0.162	−0.002
−0.317	−0.043	0.145	0.211	0.003
−0.602	−0.082	0.276	0.402	0.006
−1.284	−0.175	0.590	0.858	0.012
Deflated matrix				
0.004	−0.008	0.001	0.006	−0.003
−0.029	0.034	−0.002	−0.002	−0.001
−0.016	−0.009	0.064	−0.030	−0.009
0.009	0.001	−0.040	0.032	−0.002
0.196	−0.015	−0.177	−0.202	0.198

manual/nonmanual dichotomy, especially in analyses performed prior to the advent of modern computing; but here we have empirical evidence that this dichotomy has some basis in fact and is not merely a convenience to an earlier generation of scholars who had to make do with 2 × 2 tables.

These effects are, however, transitory. Since for whites $\lambda_2 = 0.348$, each of these effects influences the first generation attenuated by the factor 0.348, influences the second generation attenuated by the factor $0.348^2 = 0.121$, influences the third generation attenuated by the factor $0.348^3 = 0.042$, and so on—each factor considerably smaller than its predecessor. "Transitory" is an appropriate description of these effects.

White families that have attained white-collar occupations benefit from this spectral component in that the barrier I have

TABLE 4
Third Components for Blacks and Whites

Black third component (*eigenvalue:* 0.05006073023)				
Spectral component				
0.456	0.267	−0.038	−0.815	0.129
0.374	0.219	−0.031	−0.668	0.106
0.005	0.003	0.000	−0.009	0.001
−0.120	−0.070	0.010	0.214	−0.034
0.391	0.229	−0.033	−0.698	0.111
Deflated matrix				
−0.016	0.004	0.084	−0.066	−0.006
0.024	−0.005	−0.130	0.102	0.009
0.004	−0.004	0.000	0.000	0.000
−0.001	0.001	0.004	−0.003	0.000
0.001	−0.001	−0.004	0.003	0.000
White third component (*eigenvalue:* 0.205134913)				
Spectral component				
−0.016	0.001	0.015	0.015	−0.016
−0.005	0.000	0.005	0.005	−0.005
−0.058	0.005	0.055	0.055	−0.057
0.001	0.000	−0.001	−0.001	0.001
0.986	−0.086	−0.934	−0.928	0.962
Deflated matrix				
0.008	−0.008	−0.002	0.003	0.000
−0.028	0.034	−0.003	−0.003	0.000
−0.004	−0.010	0.053	−0.041	0.003
0.009	0.001	−0.040	0.032	−0.002
−0.006	0.003	0.014	−0.012	0.001

TABLE 5
Fourth Components for Blacks and Whites

Black fourth component (eigenvalue: −0.04413588885)

Spectral component				
0.377	−0.188	−1.340	1.067	0.084
−0.557	0.278	1.979	−1.576	−0.124
−0.077	0.039	0.275	−0.219	−0.017
0.027	−0.014	−0.097	0.077	0.006
−0.031	0.016	0.111	−0.088	−0.007
Deflated matrix				
0.000	−0.004	0.025	−0.019	−0.002
0.000	0.007	−0.043	0.032	0.004
0.000	−0.002	0.012	−0.009	−0.001
0.000	0.000	−0.001	0.001	0.000
0.000	0.000	0.001	−0.001	0.000

White fourth component (eigenvalue: 0.08563217598)

Spectral component				
0.003	0.007	−0.036	0.028	−0.002
0.000	−0.001	0.003	−0.002	0.000
−0.050	−0.119	0.614	−0.481	0.035
0.039	0.092	−0.477	0.374	−0.028
−0.014	−0.033	0.173	−0.135	0.010
Deflated matrix				
0.007	−0.009	0.001	0.001	0.000
−0.028	0.034	−0.003	−0.002	0.000
0.000	0.000	0.000	0.000	0.000
0.006	−0.007	0.001	0.000	0.000
−0.005	0.006	−0.001	0.000	0.000

described tends to prevent them from dropping to blue-collar occupations in subsequent generations. Black families that have attained white-collar occupations have no such barrier to protect their subsequent generations. Neither the black second component, in the upper panel of Table 3, nor any of the subsequent black components, in the upper panels of Tables 4, 5, and 6, displays any manual/nonmanual barrier comparable to that in the white second component. Reference to Table 1 shows the result of this difference: Approximately three-fourths of the sons of nonmanual blacks end up in manual occupations, while only approximately one-fourth of the sons of nonmanual whites do so.

Returning to Table 3, note that the second largest eigenvalue for blacks, 0.178, is considerably smaller than the corresponding eigenvalue for whites, 0.348. Furthermore, most of the entries in the

TABLE 6
Fifth Components for Blacks and Whites

Black fifth component (*eigenvalue:* 0.02019439648)

Spectral component

0.009	−0.202	1.223	−0.916	−0.114
−0.016	0.351	−2.125	1.593	0.198
0.005	−0.102	0.619	−0.464	−0.058
0.000	0.006	−0.034	0.026	0.003
0.000	−0.008	0.047	−0.035	−0.004

Deflated matrix

0.000	0.000	0.000	0.000	0.000
0.000	0.000	0.000	0.000	0.000
0.000	0.000	0.000	0.000	0.000
0.000	0.000	0.000	0.000	0.000
0.000	0.000	0.000	0.000	0.000

White fifth component (*eigenvalue:* 0.04190356063)

Spectral component

0.176	−0.215	0.022	0.015	0.003
−0.667	0.816	−0.082	−0.055	−0.012
−0.005	0.006	−0.001	0.000	0.000
0.132	−0.161	0.016	0.011	0.002
−0.117	0.143	−0.014	−0.010	−0.002

Deflated matrix

0.000	0.000	0.000	0.000	0.000
0.000	0.000	0.000	0.000	0.000
0.000	0.000	0.000	0.000	0.000
0.000	0.000	0.000	0.000	0.000
0.000	0.000	0.000	0.000	0.000

black second spectral component are near zero. The first spectral component tells almost the entire story for blacks, although not for whites.

The largest entries in the black second spectral component appear in the bottom row and describe transitory movement by sons of farmers. Specifically, black farmers' sons are more likely than their grandsons and more remote descendants to have farm or lower manual occupations and less likely to have upper manual or nonmanual occupations.

The third component for whites, in the lower panel of Table 4, like the second component for blacks, mainly describes transitory movement by sons of farmers. The third largest white eigenvalue, 0.205, is roughly the same magnitude as the second largest black eigenvalue, 0.178, so that these transitory effects for the two races are attenuated at approximately the same rate. Furthermore, the spectral component entries indicating propensities of sons of farmers to remain in farming, 0.880 for blacks and 0.962 for whites, are of similar magnitudes. However, there is an important difference: While black sons of farmers tend to enter lower manual occupations disproportionately, +0.139 in Table 3, white sons of farmers tend to avoid lower manual occupations, −0.928 in Table 4, and instead enter upper nonmanual occupations disproportionately, +0.986 in Table 4.

The third component for blacks is of considerably less import for the first generation, and is attenuated more rapidly for subsequent generations, than are the components for either blacks or whites discussed thus far: Each element of the spectral component has its contribution to the first generation attenuated by the eigenvalue 0.05, its contribution to the second generation attenuated by $0.05^2 = 0.0025$, and so on. Nevertheless, it does contribute increments or decrements to the transition probabilities—for the first generation, as large as $\lambda_3 \mathbf{Z}_3(1, 4) = (0.05)(0.815) = 0.04$—so it may still be worthy of discussion despite its lesser importance than the components considered earlier.[5]

The largest entries in the third black spectral component (specifically, the entries over 0.2 in magnitude) display the pattern

$$\begin{matrix} + & + & 0 & - & 0 \\ + & + & 0 & - & 0 \\ 0 & 0 & 0 & 0 & 0 \\ 0 & 0 & 0 & + & 0 \\ + & + & 0 & - & 0 \end{matrix}$$

The negative elements in the lower manual column indicate that the long-run proportion in that category is even larger than the proportion there in the first generation, except for family lines originating in that

[5]Two readers of an earlier version of this chapter raised questions concerning statistical inference. "After Z_4 you are probably interpreting noise," suggested one reader. I have not adequately investigated the issue, which really involves complicated questions of simultaneous statistical inference (see Anderson, 1958, sec. 14.6; however, see also footnote 7). However, I offer the following as a preliminary reaction: A sample proportion used to estimate a probability p has variance $p(1 - p)/n$ when based on a sample of size n. From this we can calculate, for example, that a probability increment of 0.04 is two or more standard deviations whenever the sample size is 625 or greater. Thus our preliminary conclusion is in agreement with the rule of thumb that, in large samples, anything large enough to be substantively interesting is also large enough to be statistically significant.

category, while the positive elements in the first two columns indicate that the proportion in the nonmanual categories is larger in the first generation than in the long run—with the proviso, however, that all these increments or decrements are over and above those in the same category that were already covered in the second spectral component.

The white fourth spectral component displays an interesting pattern:

$$\begin{matrix} 0 & 0 & 0 & 0 & 0 \\ 0 & 0 & 0 & 0 & 0 \\ 0 & 0 & + & - & 0 \\ 0 & 0 & - & + & 0 \\ 0 & 0 & 0 & 0 & 0 \end{matrix}$$

This pattern, focusing on the larger elements of the bottom panel of Table 5, indicates a barrier *within* the manual occupations, tending to keep sons of skilled manual workers in the skilled manual category and tending to keep sons of unskilled manual workers in the unskilled manual category. While we have no direct evidence on the mechanisms involved, we may nevertheless note that this is the kind of pattern that would be observed were it in fact the case, as has often been alleged, that the unions in which skilled manual laborers are organized give preference to applicants who are sons of their own members. In any case, spectral decomposition has enabled us to isolate this interesting pattern which, insofar as I can recall, has not been isolated by others using other methods.

Consider next the fifth and final component for whites, given in the lower panel of Table 6. As before, we ignore the smaller elements and find that the larger elements display the pattern

$$\begin{matrix} + & - & 0 & 0 & 0 \\ - & + & 0 & 0 & 0 \\ 0 & 0 & 0 & 0 & 0 \\ 0 & 0 & 0 & 0 & 0 \\ 0 & 0 & 0 & 0 & 0 \end{matrix}$$

Here we have a barrier within the nonmanual occupations, tending to keep sons of professional and managerial fathers in that same category and tending to keep the sons of clerical and sales workers in that same category. Union membership recruitment patterns would not provide an explanation here; however, one might note that colleges as well as unions have been known to inquire whether applicants had parents already affiliated with them.

Consider next the fourth and fifth components for blacks, which include patterns similar to but more complicated than those we have just seen for whites. The black fourth component, in the upper panel of Table 5, introduces something we have not thus far encountered—a negative eigenvalue. In general, eigenvalues may be negative or complex; it is an empirical finding, and not a mathematical necessity, that the mobility matrices considered here have no complex and only one negative eigenvalue. A negative or complex eigenvalue corresponds to a spectral component whose contribution is oscillatory—a positive increment in some generations, a negative decrement in other generations. This is most readily seen in the case of a negative eigenvalue, say $\lambda = -c$, whose odd powers are all negative numbers ($-c$, $-c^3$, $-c^5$, and so on) but whose even powers are all positive numbers ($+c^2$, $+c^4$, $+c^6$, and so on). Thus the black fourth component affects sons and great-grandsons one way but treats grandsons and great-great-grandsons the opposite way—except that the effect on each generation is attenuated relative to the effect on the previous generation, and in this case attenuation is so rapid that the effect on grandsons is already, for most purposes, negligible.

The largest elements of the black fourth component display the pattern

$$\begin{matrix} 0 & 0 & - & + & 0 \\ 0 & 0 & + & - & 0 \\ 0 & 0 & 0 & 0 & 0 \\ 0 & 0 & 0 & 0 & 0 \\ 0 & 0 & 0 & 0 & 0 \end{matrix}$$

Its effect on the first generation, however, will be multiplied by the negative eigenvalue, giving a reversal of signs. Thus the effect, on sons, of the black fourth spectral component *together with its eigenvalue* (an important proviso when the eigenvalue is negative) will have the pattern

$$\begin{matrix} 0 & 0 & + & - & 0 \\ 0 & 0 & - & + & 0 \\ 0 & 0 & 0 & 0 & 0 \\ 0 & 0 & 0 & 0 & 0 \\ 0 & 0 & 0 & 0 & 0 \end{matrix}$$

Substantively, this gives us a finding that has not been noticed by other investigators using other methods of analysis: Among blue-collar sons of white-collar men, the sons of professionals and managers tend to be skilled while the sons of clerical and sales workers tend to be unskilled.

The fifth black component, in the upper panel of Table 6, has its largest elements displaying the identical pattern and thus reinforcing the effect of the fourth component—at least insofar as the first generation is concerned. (Because of the negative eigenvalue accompanying the fourth component, the fourth and fifth components act in opposite directions on the second generation, but we need not consider that matter, since the effects of both are negligible by the second generation.) Apparently there is in fact a tendency for blacks to inherit some aspects of status, but whatever blacks inherit is more along the lines of skill or training and not along the line of the manual/nonmanual distinction and, furthermore, is of a rather small magnitude compared to "inheritance" among whites.

PROPERTIES OF SPECTRAL DECOMPOSITION

Now that we have worked through a substantive example, we return for a systematic discussion of the properties of this technique, properties that thus far I have mentioned only briefly, imprecisely, and incompletely. The spectral components, the **Z** matrices, are, like the **P** matrix from which they derive, square $n \times n$ matrices. However, the spectral components have five convenient properties not shared by the **P** matrix. First, the rows of a spectral component are all proportional to one another. Second, the columns of a spectral component are all proportional to one another. Third, the square, cube, and successive higher powers of a spectral component are all identical to the spectral component itself, an extremely convenient property called *idempotence:*

$$\mathbf{Z}_i^2 = \mathbf{Z}_i \tag{2}$$

Fourth, the product of any two different spectral components is a matrix of zeros, an extremely convenient property called *orthogonality:*

$$\mathbf{Z}_i\mathbf{Z}_j = \mathbf{0} \qquad \text{for } i \neq j \tag{3}$$

Fifth, the sum of all the spectral components is the identity matrix, whose main-diagonal elements are 1's and whose other elements are 0's:

$$\sum_k \mathbf{Z}_k = \mathbf{I} \qquad (n \times n \text{ identity matrix}) \tag{4}$$

In light of these convenient properties, it would be fair to state that the spectral components are much better behaved than the original **P** matrix from which they derive.

The first two properties make spectral components much easier than the original **P** matrix to scan visually and interpret verbally. The third and fourth properties, as we shall see, greatly simplify the analysis of mobility projections over multiple time units. The fifth property, while less important than the other four, still provides a means for checking computational accuracy. These convenient properties, especially those specified in Equations (1), (2), and (3), make spectral decomposition of great significance in the analysis of social mobility data, as well as data on such other sociological topics as population growth and shifts in voters' preferences.

Recall now that the **P** matrix is the one whose square, cube, and successive higher powers are used in projecting mobility over multiple time units. But the powers of a matrix, when expressed alternatively in terms of its spectral components, take on an especially simple form. Consider first the square of the **P** matrix; from Equation (1) it may be expressed in the form

$$\mathbf{P}^2 = \left(\sum_i \lambda_i \mathbf{Z}_i\right)\left(\sum_j \lambda_j \mathbf{Z}_j\right)$$

which may in turn be expanded and simplified. The expansion has n^2 terms, but $(n)(n - 1)$ of the terms drop out because of orthogonality (Equation 3) while the remaining n terms simplify, $\mathbf{Z}_i^2$ reducing to simply $\mathbf{Z}_i$ because of idempotence (Equation 2). The result, after simplification, is

$$\mathbf{P}^2 = \sum_i \lambda_i^2 \mathbf{Z}_i$$

Repeated application of the same argument gives analogous results for higher powers:

$$\mathbf{P}^m = \sum_i \lambda_i^m \mathbf{Z}_i \tag{5}$$

Spectral decomposition simplifies matters, enabling us to avoid raising an entire matrix to powers ($\mathbf{P}^m$) and allowing us instead to raise scalars to powers (λ_i^m), a much simpler operation.

Thus far we have only specified that different eigenvalues will be distinguished by different subscripts on the symbol lambda; now we need further specification of notation. Let the eigenvalues be indexed in order of decreasing magnitude, the largest denoted λ_1, the next largest λ_2, and so forth, with ties (for instance, between the equal magnitudes of a pair of complex conjugate eigenvalues) resolved arbitrarily.

The largest eigenvalue, λ_1, has an interpretation as an overall growth ratio per time unit. For example, in a different substantive context, a recent U.S. population projection matrix based on five-year intervals had 1.0654 as its largest eigenvalue, indicating that the U.S. population was then experiencing an intrinsic growth rate of 6.54 percent per five-year period, or about 1.3 percent per year. But growth or decline in the labor force is impossible in mobility analyses because of the way the data have been collected: A sample of men is asked about occupation and father's occupation and the two are cross-classified; no account is taken of the fact that some fathers, with more than one son employed, had increased probability of being considered in the study, or of the fact that some contemporaries of the fathers in the study were automatically excluded because they had no sons (see Duncan, 1966, p. 57). Thus each respondent who answered both sets of questions provided data on exactly one son and exactly one father, giving a calculated growth ratio of unity. In the case of stochastic matrices, with which we are dealing, λ_1 is necessarily equal to unity. That, however, is an artifact of the study design; it tells us nothing about overall growth or decline of the work force, and it tells us nothing about relative growth and decline of different occupational groups.

The spectral decomposition of $\mathbf{P}^m$, as given in Equation (5), may be rewritten to segregate the largest or "dominant" term from the remaining terms in the summation, and then each term may be divided by λ_1^m, the coefficient of $\mathbf{Z}_1$ in the dominant term. The result is

$$\mathbf{P}^m/\lambda_1^m = \mathbf{Z}_1 + \sum_{i=2}^{n} (\lambda_i/\lambda_1)^m \mathbf{Z}_i \tag{6}$$

This particular formulation is helpful in discussions of convergence to a stable occupational distribution.

Since λ_1 is the largest eigenvalue, each of the factors (λ_i/λ_1) raised to higher powers approaches zero, doing so more rapidly the smaller λ_i is relative to λ_1. As the number of time periods increases, each of the other terms becomes negligible, leaving only the dominant term:

$$\mathbf{P}^m/\lambda_1^m \approx \mathbf{Z}_1 \qquad \text{for } m \text{ sufficiently large} \tag{7}$$

This discussion suggests both the appropriate substantive interpretation of λ_2 and also a method for calculating $\mathbf{Z}_1$.

The second largest eigenvalue, λ_2, tells us about the rate of convergence to the stable distribution—the smaller λ_2, the faster the convergence implicit in the transition matrix $\mathbf{P}$. Specifically, the largest of the nondominant terms in Equation (6) becomes negligible at whatever rate $|\lambda_2/\lambda_1|^m$ becomes negligible. Thus $|\lambda_2/\lambda_1|$ is a natural index for the rate of convergence.[6] Furthermore, we are dealing with stochastic matrices, whose largest eigenvalue is unity; for stochastic matrices this index for the rate of convergence becomes simply $|\lambda_2|$.

Next consider the number of time units required for the process to reach (within some specified tolerance) the stable distribution, where the proportion in each occupational group is as specified in the corresponding column of $\mathbf{Z}_1$ (all rows of which are identical). The rate of convergence, as just discussed, is one, but not the only, determinant of the time required for convergence. The other determinant is the initial distance from stability. These two determinants of time to convergence operate quite differently, and it is important not to confuse them.

Let $\mathbf{N}_0$ denote a $1 \times n$ matrix (row vector) whose elements are the proportions initially in the n occupational groups. Let $\mathbf{N}^*$ denote a $1 \times n$ matrix (row vector) whose elements match those of any row of $\mathbf{Z}_1$ (all rows of which are identical). Then the initial distance from stability, involving $\mathbf{N}_0 - \mathbf{N}^*$, depends on both the initial distribution, through $\mathbf{N}_0$, and the transition matrix, through $\mathbf{N}^*$ and hence $\mathbf{Z}_1$. In

[6]Theil (1972, pp. 263–264) noted earlier that the rate of convergence of a Markov chain depends on the relationship between λ_2 and λ_1. Rather than taking the ratio of their magnitudes itself as an index of rate of convergence, however, he derived an alternative index based on information theory. For earlier use of information-theoretic indices to analyze mobility data, see McFarland (1969). For earlier consideration of λ_2 as affecting the rate of convergence, although in the context of population projection rather than social mobility, see Keyfitz (1968, p. 63).

contrast, the rate at which stability is approached, from whatever distance, of which $|\lambda_2|$ is an appropriate index, depends only on the transition matrix.

This distinction does arise in the analysis of real occupational mobility matrices. Prais and others found that the distribution after one generation already closely approximated the stable distribution when British mobility data were analyzed in this manner. Similarly, the distribution after one generation already closely approximates the stable distribution when Duncan's data for U.S. blacks are analyzed in this manner. The reasons, however, are quite different. In the British mobility study analyzed by Prais, sons were close to the British stable distribution primarily because their fathers too had been close to the stable distribution. In contrast, U.S. black sons were close to the U.S. black stable distribution primarily because the transition matrix they experienced would cause any group to approach the stable distribution rapidly, regardless of that group's initial distribution. Rapid convergence, although occurring in both cases, occurs for quite different reasons.

DISCUSSION

Spectral decomposition enables us to break down the complex pattern of an observed mobility matrix into a number of components, each of which has a considerably simpler pattern, thus facilitating both quantitative comparisons and verbal descriptions of mobility patterns and differences therein. Furthermore, in the comparison of black and white mobility patterns this method has permitted detection of subtle but interesting effects not disclosed by other methods. Information on computing algorithms, including a list of the APL program used for the calculations reported here, is available from the author.[7]

[7]One referee suggested that I discuss how spectral decomposition relates to principal components analysis, which also involves expressing a matrix in terms of its eigenvalues and eigenvectors. There are important differences in presentation of results, and the Z matrices from spectral decomposition are much better suited for our purposes than the results presented from principal components analysis. More important is the limitation of principal components analysis to covariance and correlation matrices (Anderson, 1958, chap. 11). Those matrices have several special mathematical properties, such as symmetry and absence of negative or complex eigenvalues. Some of the theory for principal components analysis depends upon those special mathematical properties of covariance matrices, and will not generalize to other types of matrices such as those treated here (Green, 1978, p. 219).

REFERENCES

ANDERSON, T. W.

1958 *An Introduction to Multivariate Statistical Analysis.* New York: Wiley.

DUNCAN, O. D.

1966 "Methodological issues in the analysis of social mobility." In N. J. Smelser and S. M. Lipset (Eds.), *Social Structure and Mobility in Economic Development.* Chicago: Aldine.

1968 "Patterns of occupational mobility among Negro men." *Demography* 5:11–22.

GANTMACHER, F. R.

1959 *The Theory of Matrices.* 2 vols. New York: Chelsea.

GREEN, P. E.

1978 *Mathematical Tools for Applied Multivariate Analysis.* New York: Academic Press.

KEYFITZ, N.

1968 *Introduction to the Mathematics of Population.* Reading, Mass.: Addison-Wesley.

LIEBERSON, S., AND FUGUITT, G. V.

1967 "Negro-white occupational differences in the absence of discrimination." *American Journal of Sociology* 73:188–200.

MATRAS, J.

1960 "Comparison of intergenerational occupational mobility patterns." *Population Studies* 14:163–169.

MCFARLAND, D. D.

1969 "Measuring the permeability of occupational structures: An information theoretic approach." *American Journal of Sociology* 75:41–61.

1970 "Intragenerational social mobility as a Markov process." *American Sociological Review* 35:463–476.

1974 "Substantive contributions of Markov models to the study of social mobility." In R. Ziegler (Ed.), *Anwendung Mathematischer Verfahren zur Analyse Sozialer Ungleichheit und Sozialer Mobilität.* Kiel: Soziologisches Seminar der Christian-Albrechts-Universität.

1978 "Leslie matrices with eigenvalue multiplicity." Paper presented to the annual meeting of the Population Association of America, Atlanta, 12–15 April.

PRAIS, S. J.

1955a "The formal theory of social mobility." *Population Studies* 9:72–81.

1955b "Measuring social mobility." *Journal of Royal Statistical Society,* series A, 118:56–66.

SENETA, E.

1973 *Non-Negative Matrices*. New York: Wiley.

SINGER, B., AND SPILERMAN, S.

1976 "The representation of social processes by Markov models." *American Journal of Sociology* 82:1–54.

SYKES, Z.

n.d. "A stronger limit theorem for stable population theory." Unpublished manuscript. Department of Population Dynamics, Johns Hopkins University.

THEIL, H.

1972 *Statistical Decomposition Analysis*. Amsterdam: North-Holland.

10

ESTIMATING LINEAR MODELS WITH SPATIALLY DISTRIBUTED DATA

Patrick Doreian

UNIVERSITY OF PITTSBURGH

Sociologists study a wide variety of social, political, and economic phenomena. Many of these phenomena—for example, urbanization, political mobilization, economic development, diffusion of innovations—take place in and are distributed across geographical space. It is reasonable, therefore, to argue that sociologists are interested, indeed have long been interested, in social phenomena distributed in geographical space. Yet, in the main, our theoretical frameworks and data-analytic capabilities do not include the geography of

I am grateful to Norman P. Hummon, who designed and implemented REPOMAT, a matrix algebra package I have used for estimation throughout this chapter, and to Philip Sidel, of the Social Science Computer Research Institute at the University of Pittsburgh, for programming the computation of the spatial autocorrelation statistics. Comments of the anonymous reviewers led to considerable improvements in the chapter and are appreciated.

social phenomena.[1] As a result, the geographical characteristics of social phenomena are overlooked, especially when data analyses are performed. Thus there is a large lacuna in our theoretical frameworks and methodological apparatus. This chapter represents an initial attempt at filling that lacuna. I should make clear that my objective in this chapter is not to claim that geographical space *must* be included; rather, it is to claim that *when* it is appropriate to include geographical space, a variety of conceptual and methodological issues need to be addressed. The following pages outline some of these issues and discuss estimation strategies that are appropriate for linear equations where the data are spatially distributed.

Some examples of the data structure considered in this study are appropriate.[2] Frisbie and Poston (1975), working in the human ecology tradition, analyzed the relationships between sustenance organization and population change. Using data for all nonmetropolitan counties of the 48 contiguous states of the United States, they present regression equations linking population changes to components of sustenance organization and also to other social characteristics that have been hypothesized to account for population change. Inverarity (1976) used a linear model in which the final dependent variables were lynchings and electoral support, the exogenous variables were racial composition, urbanization, and religious homogeneity, and there was an unmeasured endogenous variable of mechanical solidarity. The data were from the (then) 59 parishes of Louisiana. Ragin (1977), using British county data, regressed Conservative and Labour votes on a variety of measures of class composition and two regional dummies. Chirot and Ragin (1975) analyzed the Romanian peasant rebellion of 1907 by using data for counties and multiple-regression methods.

These examples were taken from the *American Sociological Review.* Moving elsewhere, we can find the classic papers of Matthews and Prothro (1963a, 1963b). In the first of these papers, they studied the relationship between social and economic factors and

[1]A stronger argument can be made: Not only is geographical space frequently excluded; so too is consideration of the physical environment (Dunlap and Catton, 1979). The two omissions are not unrelated. While entry into the debate over the "environmental sociology" paradigm would take us too far from our objectives, it can be remarked that the issues discussed here are germane to the empirical study of society–environment interactions.

[2]These examples are not included in a critical vein since the issue of the relevance of geographical space has not been decided.

black voter registration; in the second they extended their analysis to consider political factors. The central workhorse was again multiple regression, and the data were for 997 Southern counties. Salamon and Van Evera (1973) examined three competing explanations of political participation using data for Mississippi's 29 black-majority counties and regression methods. Kernall (1973), in an extended critique of Salamon and Van Evera's thesis, used the same methodology with data for all of Mississippi's counties. Schoenberger and Segal (1971) examined the (linear) relation between voting support for Wallace in 1968 and a variety of socioeconomic characteristics for 77 Southern congressional districts. Wasserman and Segal (1973) performed essentially the same analysis, only they used data for counties and split the South into the Deep South and the marginal South. Capecchi and Galli (1969) presented a linear causal model of voting determinants in Italy using data for 88 territorial units comprising all but four of the Italian provinces. Cox (1969), also employing a linear causal model, analyzed voting participation and the Conservative vote with data for the parliamentary constituencies of London.

In a quite different vein, Aigner and Heins (1967) used regression equations to account for variations in income equality in the 50 states and Washington D.C.; the exogenous variables were a variety of social, demographic, economic, and political variables. Mitchell (1969) adapted econometric procedures to analyze the Huk rebellion in the Philippines, linking insurgent control to a variety of cultural and economic factors; the data were for 57 municipalities in four provinces. Doreian and Hummon (1976) reanalyzed these data with the same objectives as Mitchell.

The list of examples, while long, is far from being exhaustive. These are simply examples of a particular type of data structure; in all cases, the data are defined for areal units and these units together comprise a region.[3] This data structure has prompted the use of multiple-regression analysis to estimate a linear relation. This coupling of a particular data structure and the use of linear structural equations is the focus of this chapter.

[3]There are partial exceptions to this statement. Salamon and Van Evera (1973) did not use all the counties of Mississippi; however, Kernall (1973) did. Matthews and Prothro (1963a, 1963b) did exclude some Southern counties, and Frisbie and Poston (1975) excluded the metropolitan counties. Nevertheless, the general point still stands. Further, the issues and procedures discussed here apply even if there are holes, so to speak, in a region.

The essence of the data structure arises through aggregation. (However, this chapter is *not* about the "aggregation problem.") Whenever data are aggregated to represent areal units, which are usually defined administratively or politically, it is likely that the geography of a social phenomenon has been retained, albeit in an implicit way. Except for the examples represented by Mitchell (1969) and Doreian and Hummon (1976), all the examples cited here ignore geographical space. This is not necessarily meant as a negative appraisal. Whether geographical space should or should not be explicitly included is an issue that hinges on theoretical and methodological considerations. It is these considerations, especially the latter, to which our attention is now directed.

REPRESENTING GEOGRAPHICAL SPACE

The representation of geographical space is not obvious as it involves choices based on substantive concerns and technical constraints. Sociologists can benefit from the efforts of geographers, regional economists, and mathematical ecologists (see Cliff and Ord, 1973; Pielou, 1969) who grapple with representing geographical space. There are two broad strategies: using measurements of distances between geographical locations and partitioning a region into areas.[4] The focus of this chapter is on the latter. In this strategy a region is partitioned into areas and data are recorded for each area. Geographical space is then represented by a $(N \times N)$ matrix where there are N areas in the region. Doreian and Hummon (1976, pp. 117–125) provide a general discussion of this representation of geographical space, and part of their conceptualization is used here.

The overriding reason for deciding on a specific representation is substantive. Generally, an explanation of some phenomenon is sought where the value of a variable of interest in a given area is (systematically) related to the values of that variable in some other areas. That is, observations are presumed to be interdependent rather than independent and this interdependency is presumed to be geographically based. The interdependency, or connectedness in geographical space, determines the representation of geographical

[4]It is possible, of course, to use distances between geographical areas. For example, the distances between area centroids or salient points (such as administrative capitals) can be used.

space. Consider the example of the Huk insurgency (Mitchell, 1969; Doreian and Hummon, 1976). Rebel control (or governmental control) of an area has immediate consequences for adjacent areas. If one side of the conflict can move weaponry and troops into an area, that area becomes a base for attempting to control adjacent areas. Adjacency is then the key geographical characteristic. More generally, accessibility of one area from another may be the key geographical characteristic with adjacency simply being a special case of accessibility. The properties of a transportation network could be used to determine accessibility with respect to each pair of areas that make up a region. Collective violence, as represented by the Romanian peasant rebellion of 1907 (Chirot and Ragin, 1975) or lynchings in the South (Inverarity, 1976), is likely to spread spatially, especially in an era before mass communication. Black enfranchisement in the United States is another process that can be seen to operate in terms of adjacency.[5] More generally, diffusion can be viewed as a spatial process operative over spatial connections between areas.

The first step of spatial representation is deciding which spatial property is to be represented. Even with that choice made, there are further options. Consider adjacency as a spatial property to be represented. Suppose a region R can be partitioned into N mutually exclusive areas. Louisiana is partitioned into 64 parishes, the contiguous United States into 48 states, and so on. Let $\mathbf{S} = [s_{ij}]$ be an $(N \times N)$ matrix, where s_{ij} is 1 if area i is adjacent to area j and 0 otherwise. Throughout, the s_{ii} are taken to be zero. The adjacency characteristics of R are completely specified in terms of $\mathbf{S}$. The entries of $\mathbf{S}$ are either 0 or 1. Such a binary matrix can be converted into a set of weights in the following fashion. Let s_i be the row sum for the ith row of $\mathbf{S}$. Then a matrix, $\mathbf{W} = [w_{ij}]$, can be constructed where $w_{ij} = s_{ij}/s_i$. The entries of $\mathbf{W}$ lie between 0 and 1 (inclusive, although $w_{ij} = 1$ is only possible for a pair of mutually adjacent but elsewise disconnected areas) and are proportions based on the number of other areas adjacent to a specific area. Adjacency could be operationalized slightly differently (Mitchell, 1969). Let b_{ij} be the length of common border between area i and area j. Then define $w_{ij} = b_{ij}/b_{ii}$, where b_{ii} is the total perimeter of area i.

[5]A much more general notion of adjacency could be used such that areas are adjacent if they are sufficiently similar with respect to relevant social, political, or economic characteristics. (See Cliff and Ord, 1970.)

It is clear that in any empirical situation the choice of a matrix **W** to represent geographical space is not obvious. There is, literally, an infinity of possible representations.[6] This infinite number has led some critics, for example, Arora and Brown (1977), to argue that the specification of **W** should be abandoned altogether. Such a judgment is premature. Some representations will be more compelling and soundly based than others. The choice of a representation can be made where the substantive concerns of the investigator will be paramount. A wide range of choice means that care should be exercised in the choice made, not that the investigator should refrain from making choices altogether.

For the following exposition, I assume that geographical space can be represented by a matrix of weights **W**. The elements of **W** are nonnegative and bounded by 0 and 1.

LINEAR EQUATIONS WITH SPATIALLY DISTRIBUTED DATA

Let **Y** be a vector of observations on an endogenous variable; let **X** be a matrix of observations on a set of exogenous variables (including a column of 1's for the intercept term); let $\boldsymbol{\beta}$ be a vector of parameters; and let ϵ be the disturbance term. Then, in abstract terms, the model estimated in most of the preceding examples is

$$\mathbf{Y} = \mathbf{X}\beta + \epsilon \tag{1}$$

where

$$E[\epsilon] = \mathbf{0} \qquad E[\epsilon\epsilon'] = \sigma^2\mathbf{I} \tag{2}$$

and ϵ is multivariate normal. Such is the conventional population regression function. As such, the spatial structure is ignored. The areal units are treated as units of analysis in the conventional sense, and nothing further is done concerning space. However, the spatial structure of the region can be incorporated in a variety of ways. Alternatives have been outlined by Ord (1975), and maximum-likelihood estimation (MLE) procedures have been proposed for each of these. The

[6]Further, a whole variety of distance decay functions could be specified for the elements of **W** (which would introduce the distance approach into this areal partitioning approach).

technical nature and terse presentation of Ord's procedures render them inaccessible to most social scientists, which leads to the need to make them more widely available. Thus this chapter is largely an exegesis of Ord's procedures, presenting derivations of the properties of those procedures and their sociological applications. The chapter is not solely an exegesis, however, for Ord's procedures can be improved and there are cases where much simpler procedures may suffice.

To express the idea of a spatial effect via adjacency,[7] a very simple notion is that Y, for a particular area, is related to, or a function of, the values of Y in adjacent areas. More precisely, Y is related to a weighted combination of values of Y in adjacent areas. If the weights are given in the matrix $\mathbf{W}$, then $\mathbf{Y}$ is a function of $\mathbf{WY}$.

The simplest linear model specifies

$$\mathbf{Y} = \rho\mathbf{WY} + \epsilon \tag{3}$$

where ϵ is as specified in (2). This is a *pure endogenous* model: Only the values of $\mathbf{Y}$ in adjacent areas determine the value of $\mathbf{Y}$ in a given area. Alternatively, we can describe this as a spatially autocovarying model. While such a simple formulation is likely to be of limited sociological utility, extended discussion of this model is warranted, as it underlies the models that do include exogenous variables in their specification. From (3),

$$\epsilon = (\mathbf{I} - \rho\mathbf{W})\mathbf{Y} = \mathbf{AY} \tag{4}$$

where $\mathbf{A} = (\mathbf{I} - \rho\mathbf{W})$. The joint likelihood of the ϵ_i is given by Mead (1967):

$$L(\epsilon) = (1/\sigma^2 2\pi)^{N/2} \exp{(-\epsilon'\epsilon/2\sigma^2)} \tag{5}$$

As Mead observes, however, it is the Y_i that are observed and not the ϵ_i. Thus it is the joint likelihood of the Y_i that needs to be maximized and not the function given in Equation (5). From (4) and (5) we have as the joint likelihood function, given $\mathbf{Y} = \mathbf{y}$:

$$L(\mathbf{y}) = |\mathbf{A}|(1/\sigma^2 2\pi)^{N/2} \exp{[-(\mathbf{Ay})'(\mathbf{Ay})/2\sigma^2]} \tag{6}$$

where $|\mathbf{A}|$ is the Jacobian of the transformation from the ϵ to the $\mathbf{y}$. It is

[7]Adjacency is but one spatial characteristic that can be represented as a matrix $\mathbf{W}$. To avoid cumbersome phrases like "interdependency due to a relevant spatial characteristic," adjacency is used simply as an exemplar.

easier to work with the log-likelihood function,[8] which is obtained from Equation (6) as

$$\begin{aligned} l(\mathbf{y}) &= -(N/2)\ln(2\pi\sigma^2) - [1/(2\sigma^2)]\mathbf{y}'\mathbf{A}'\mathbf{A}\mathbf{y} + \ln|\mathbf{A}| \\ &= \text{const} - (N/2)\ln\sigma^2 - (1/2\sigma^2)\mathbf{y}'\mathbf{A}'\mathbf{A}\mathbf{y} + \ln|\mathbf{A}| \end{aligned} \tag{7}$$

The parameters of the model requiring estimation are ρ and σ^2, so $l(y)$ has to be maximized with respect to these.[9] To simplify notation slightly, $\omega = \sigma^2$ and (7) is rewritten as

$$l(\mathbf{y}) = \text{const} - (N/2)\ln\omega - (1/2\omega)\,\mathbf{y}'\mathbf{A}'\mathbf{A}\mathbf{y} + \ln|\mathbf{A}| \tag{8}$$

We first consider ω and then ρ. Minimizing $l(y)$ with respect to ω is straightforward (Mead, 1967). Differentiating $l(y)$ with respect to ω gives

$$\partial l(\mathbf{y})/\partial\omega = -(N/2\omega) + (1/2\omega^2)(\mathbf{y}'\mathbf{A}'\mathbf{A}\mathbf{y}) \tag{9}$$

Setting this derivative to zero and solving gives

$$\hat{\omega} = \hat{\sigma}^2 = \mathbf{y}'\mathbf{A}'\mathbf{A}\mathbf{y}/N \tag{10}$$

as the estimator of σ^2. As yet, $\hat{\omega}$ is not known, since it depends upon ρ because $\mathbf{A} = \mathbf{I} - \rho\mathbf{W}$. From (10) and (8), however, $\hat{\rho}$ is the value of ρ that maximizes

$$l(\mathbf{y}) = l(\mathbf{y}, \rho; \hat{\omega}) = \text{const} - (N/2)\ln\hat{\omega} + \ln|\mathbf{A}| \tag{11}$$

Computationally this is burdensome, since determining $\hat{\rho}$ rests on the evaluation of $|\mathbf{A}| = |\mathbf{I} - \rho\mathbf{W}|$. Ord, using a simple result in a clever way, reduced the burden of computation and obtained an easier way of estimating ρ. Let $\mathbf{W}$ have $\lambda_1, \ldots, \lambda_N$ as its eigenvalues. Then, by definition of the characteristic equation,

$$|\lambda\mathbf{I} - \mathbf{W}| = \prod_{i=1}^{N} (\lambda - \lambda_i)$$

Further, the determinant of a matrix is equal to the product of its eigenvalues. If $f(\mathbf{W})$ is an algebraic polynomial in $\mathbf{W}$ (Lancaster,

[8]If θ is a parameter being estimated, then, under general conditions, $\partial/\partial\theta$, $(\ln L) = (\partial L/\partial\theta)/L$. Thus L and $\ln L$ will have maxima together, and L is always greater than zero (Kendall and Stuart, 1967, pp. 35–36).

[9]Given $\mathbf{Y} = \mathbf{y}$, $l(\mathbf{y})$ is a function of the parameters to be estimated. I could have written $l(\rho, \sigma^2)$ instead of $l(\mathbf{y})$ to emphasize this.

1971, p. 289), then the eigenvalues of $f(\mathbf{W})$ are $f(\lambda_i)$. Thus the eigenvalues of $\mathbf{I} - \rho\mathbf{W}$ are $\{1 - \rho\lambda_i\}$ and

$$|\mathbf{A}| = \prod_{i=1}^{N} (1 - \rho\lambda_i) \tag{12}$$

The λ_i can be determined once and for all and, from (11), $\hat{\rho}$ is the value of ρ that minimizes

$$-(2/N) \sum_{i=1}^{N} \ln (1 - \rho\lambda_i) + \ln [\mathbf{y}'\mathbf{y} - 2\rho\mathbf{y}'\mathbf{W}\mathbf{y} + \rho^2(\mathbf{W}\mathbf{y})'\mathbf{W}\mathbf{y}] \tag{13}$$

where $\hat{\omega}$ has been substituted from (10). The value of $\hat{\rho}$ that minimizes (13) can be found by a direct-search procedure, and such a procedure is used throughout this chapter.[10] With $\hat{\rho}$ found in this fashion, $\hat{\omega}$ can be obtained from (10). With these estimates established, it is necessary to be able to estimate the variance-covariance matrix of the estimates. In general, the asymptotic variance-covariance matrix is given by $\mathbf{V}$, where

$$\mathbf{V}^{-1} = -E\,[\partial^2 l/\partial\theta_r\partial\theta_s] \tag{14}$$

and where θ_r and θ_s are parameters being estimated (Kendall and Stuart, 1967, p. 55). In the simple model being considered here, there are only two parameters: θ_r is ω and θ_s is ρ. The derivation of this information matrix is given in Appendix A. The asymptotic variance-covariance matrix is

$$\mathbf{V}(\omega, \rho) = \omega^2 \begin{bmatrix} N/2 & \omega \operatorname{tr}(\mathbf{B}) \\ \omega \operatorname{tr}(\mathbf{B}) & \omega^2[\operatorname{tr}(\mathbf{B}'\mathbf{B}) - \alpha] \end{bmatrix}^{-1} \tag{15}$$

As an example of the pure endogenous model, consider the data assembled by Mitchell (1969) on the Huk rebellion in the Philippines. The vector $\mathbf{y}$ is the percentage of barrios in a municipality under Huk control. Using a direct-search procedure, $\hat{\rho} = 0.83$. Use of this

[10]Ord suggests that for more complex models a formal iterative procedure may be preferable. The direct-search procedure is rather cumbersome. It amounts to evaluating the value of the function given in (13) for each value of ρ in a given range and selecting the value of ρ for which the function takes a minimum value. Large increments in ρ can be used to get the minimum value roughly; then smaller increments in ρ can be used in that restricted region.

estimate,[11] together with Equation (10), gives $\hat{\sigma}^2 = 211.4$. Thus the parameters of the (simple) model have been estimated. Using Equation (15), and computing the matrices there, gives

$$\mathbf{V}(\hat{\omega}, \hat{\rho}) = \begin{bmatrix} 1710 & -0.836 \\ -0.836 & 0.005 \end{bmatrix}$$

Straightforwardly, the standard error of $\hat{\rho}$ is 0.07 and the standard error of $\hat{\sigma}$ is 41.36. Thus $\hat{\rho}$ is clearly significantly different from zero and a spatial process could be said to operate if the specification of Equation (3) is accepted. The measure of fit, FIT, is 0.69.[12]

In most social science contexts, however, the pure endogenous model is of limited utility. Exogenous variables must be included in relational specifications, and this leads to

$$\mathbf{y} = \rho\mathbf{W}\mathbf{y} + \mathbf{X}\boldsymbol{\beta} + \boldsymbol{\epsilon} \tag{16}$$

where $\boldsymbol{\epsilon}$ is specified as before. Equation (16) is referred to as the *mixed endogenous-exogenous* model or, in Ord's terms, the regressive-autoregressive model. The joint likelihood function for the ϵ_i is given, as before, by Equation (5). For this specification, however, $\boldsymbol{\epsilon} = \mathbf{Ay} - \mathbf{X}\boldsymbol{\beta}$ and the joint likelihood function for the y_i is given by

$$L(\mathbf{y}) = |A|(1/2\pi\sigma^2)^{N/2} \exp\{-(1/2\sigma^2)[\mathbf{Ay} - \mathbf{X}\boldsymbol{\beta}]'[\mathbf{Ay} - \mathbf{X}\boldsymbol{\beta}]\} \tag{17}$$

Equation (17) points out the error in the establishment of the estimation procedure of Doreian and Hummon (1976, p. 138), as they omitted $|\mathbf{A}|$, the Jacobian of the transformation from $\boldsymbol{\epsilon}$ to $\mathbf{y}$. The

[11]Actually, the estimation and inference statistics were computed by using the results of the following section. Rather than estimate the model of (3) directly, the estimation was done for $\mathbf{Y} = \alpha + \rho\mathbf{W}\mathrm{Y} + \epsilon$, where α is an intercept term. For simplicity, the pure endogenous model is discussed here without the intercept term. If α is significantly different from zero, then $\hat{\rho}$ will be biased; if $\hat{\alpha} > 0$, then $\hat{\rho}$ will be biased upwards; and if $\hat{\alpha} < 0$, then $\hat{\rho}$ will be biased downward. In the estimation, $\hat{\alpha} = 2.67$ with a standard error of 2.22; in this case, therefore, omission of α would not have been problematic. Indeed, estimation with α omitted leads to only small modifications of the estimates.

[12]The measure of fit (FIT) is the square of the correlation between y and the fitted value, $\hat{y}$. For OLS this is equivalent to the coefficient of determination (see Johnston, 1963, p. 58). However, R^2 does not have meaning here due to the interdependence of the observations. For this reason, the notation of R^2 has been avoided and the measure of fit used here cannot be interpreted as the proportion of variance explained. One hopes that a more adequate measure of the goodness of fit of these spatial models will be developed.

log-likelihood function is given by

$$l(y) = \text{const} - (N/2)\ln\omega - (1/2\omega)$$
$$(\mathbf{y}'\mathbf{A}'\mathbf{A}\mathbf{y} - 2\boldsymbol{\beta}'\mathbf{X}'\mathbf{A}\mathbf{y} + \boldsymbol{\beta}'\mathbf{X}'\mathbf{X}\boldsymbol{\beta}) + \ln|\mathbf{A}| \quad (18)$$

which has to be minimized with respect to ω, ρ, and $\boldsymbol{\beta}$. As before, we start by minimizing $l(y)$ with respect to ω:

$$\partial l/\partial\omega = -(N/2\omega)$$
$$+ (1/2\omega^2)(\mathbf{y}'\mathbf{A}'\mathbf{A}\mathbf{y} - 2\boldsymbol{\beta}'\mathbf{X}'\mathbf{A}\mathbf{y} + \boldsymbol{\beta}'\mathbf{X}'\mathbf{X}\boldsymbol{\beta}) \quad (19)$$

Setting (19) to zero gives

$$\hat{\omega} = \hat{\sigma}^2 = (1/N)(\mathbf{y}'\mathbf{A}'\mathbf{A}\mathbf{y} - 2\boldsymbol{\beta}'\mathbf{X}'\mathbf{A}\mathbf{y} + \boldsymbol{\beta}'\mathbf{X}'\mathbf{X}\boldsymbol{\beta}) \quad (20)$$

Of course, $\hat{\omega}$ is numerically unknown since $\hat{\rho}$ and $\hat{\beta}$ have not been determined. Define $\mathbf{z} = (\mathbf{I} - \rho\mathbf{W})\mathbf{y} = \mathbf{A}\mathbf{y}$. Then $\epsilon = \mathbf{z} - \mathbf{X}\boldsymbol{\beta}$ and $\epsilon'\epsilon = \mathbf{z}'\mathbf{z} - 2\boldsymbol{\beta}'\mathbf{X}'\mathbf{z} + \boldsymbol{\beta}'\mathbf{X}'\mathbf{X}\boldsymbol{\beta}$, which begins to look like the situation of ordinary least squares (OLS) of $\mathbf{z}$ on $\mathbf{X}$. With this change, we can write

$$l(\mathbf{y}) = \text{const} - (N/2)\ln\omega$$
$$- (1/2\omega)(\mathbf{z}'\mathbf{z} - 2\boldsymbol{\beta}'\mathbf{X}'\mathbf{z} + \boldsymbol{\beta}'\mathbf{X}'\mathbf{X}\boldsymbol{\beta}) + \ln|\mathbf{A}| \quad (21)$$

Differentiating (21) with respect to $\boldsymbol{\beta}$ gives

$$\partial l/\partial\beta = -(1/2\omega)[-2\mathbf{X}'\mathbf{z} + 2(\mathbf{X}'\mathbf{X})\boldsymbol{\beta}] \quad (22)$$

Setting this to zero gives

$$\hat{\boldsymbol{\beta}} = (\mathbf{X}'\mathbf{X})^{-1}\mathbf{X}'\mathbf{z} \quad (23)$$

as the estimator of $\boldsymbol{\beta}$, which, if ρ were known, would be given by OLS of $\mathbf{z}$ on $\mathbf{X}$. Substituting (23) into (20) gives

$$\begin{aligned}\hat{\omega} &= (1/N)[\mathbf{z}'\mathbf{z} - 2\mathbf{z}'\mathbf{X}(\mathbf{X}'\mathbf{X})^{-1}\mathbf{X}'\mathbf{z} + \mathbf{z}'\mathbf{X}(\mathbf{X}'\mathbf{X})^{-1}\mathbf{X}'\mathbf{z}] \\ &= (1/N)\mathbf{z}'[\mathbf{I} - \mathbf{X}(\mathbf{X}'\mathbf{X})^{-1}\mathbf{X}']\mathbf{z} \quad (24) \\ &= (1/N)\mathbf{z}'\mathbf{M}\mathbf{z}\end{aligned}$$

where $\mathbf{M} = \mathbf{I} - \mathbf{X}(\mathbf{X}'\mathbf{X})^{-1}\mathbf{X}'$ is a symmetric, idempotent matrix. While (24) and (23) give estimation equations for ω and $\boldsymbol{\beta}$, ρ is, as yet, unknown. As before, it has to be found by a direct-search procedure. Equation (13) is replaced by another expression to be minimized that takes into account the exogenous variables. As before, $\hat{\rho}$ maximizes

$$l(\mathbf{y}) = l(\mathbf{y}\colon \quad \rho, \hat{\omega}, \hat{\beta}) = \text{const} - (N/2)\ln\hat{\omega} + \ln|\mathbf{A}|$$

Using the simplified expression for $\ln|\mathbf{A}|$, ρ minimizes

$$-(2/N)\sum_{i=1}^{N}\ln(1-\rho\lambda_i) + \ln\hat{\omega}$$

But

$$\begin{aligned}\hat{\omega} &= (1/N)\mathbf{z}'\mathbf{M}\mathbf{z}\\ &= (1/N)\mathbf{y}'\mathbf{A}'\mathbf{M}\mathbf{A}\mathbf{y}\\ &= (1/N)\mathbf{y}'(\mathbf{I}-\rho\mathbf{W})'\mathbf{M}(\mathbf{I}-\rho\mathbf{W})\mathbf{y}\\ &= (1/N)[\mathbf{y}'\mathbf{M}\mathbf{y} - 2\rho\mathbf{y}'\mathbf{M}\mathbf{W}\mathbf{y} + \rho^2(\mathbf{W}\mathbf{y})'\mathbf{M}\mathbf{W}\mathbf{y}]\end{aligned}$$

Thus $\hat{\rho}$ minimizes

$$-(2/N)\sum_{i=1}^{N}\ln(1-\rho\lambda_i) + \ln[\mathbf{y}'\mathbf{M}\mathbf{y} - 2\rho\mathbf{y}'\mathbf{M}\mathbf{W}\mathbf{y} + \rho^2(\mathbf{W}\mathbf{y})'\mathbf{M}\mathbf{W}\mathbf{y}] \tag{25}$$

and this is again done by a direct-search procedure. From Appendix A,

$$\mathbf{V}(\hat{\omega}, \hat{\rho}, \hat{\boldsymbol{\beta}}) = \omega^2\begin{bmatrix} N/2 & \omega\,\text{tr}(\mathbf{B}) & \mathbf{0}' \\ \omega\,\text{tr}(\mathbf{B}) & \omega^2\,\text{tr}(\mathbf{B}'\mathbf{B}) + \omega\beta'\mathbf{X}'\mathbf{B}'\mathbf{B}\mathbf{X}\beta - \alpha\omega^2 & \omega\mathbf{X}'\mathbf{B}'\mathbf{X}\beta \\ \mathbf{0} & \omega\mathbf{X}'\mathbf{B}\mathbf{X}\beta & \omega\mathbf{X}'\mathbf{X}\end{bmatrix}^{-1} \tag{26}$$

is the asymptotic variance-covariance matrix for the estimators of the parameters of the mixed endogenous-exogenous model specified in (16). Before providing examples of these estimation procedures, I take a brief digression into the topic of spatial autocorrelation.

In the specification of the classic linear regression model, we have $E[\epsilon\epsilon'] = \sigma^2\mathbf{I}$, which indicates that the disturbance term is homoskedastic and not autocorrelated. If some off-diagonal elements of the variance-covariance matrix are nonzero, we have autocorrelation. The realm in which this has been most extensively discussed is time-series analysis. In that context a disturbance term is autocorrelated if $E[\epsilon_t\epsilon_{t-t_1}] \neq 0$ for $t > t_1$. A variety of tests have been used to detect the presence of (temporal) autocorrelation; of these, the

Durban–Watson statistic is the most widely used. Once the autocorrelation is detected, its form can be diagnosed and estimation strategies can be devised that take into account the autocorrelation that has been empirically diagnosed. (See, for example, Hibbs, 1974.) Of course, any variable of direct interest (endogenous or exogenous) in a model may be autocorrelated. Temporal interdependencies amount to temporal autocorrelation and, by the same token, spatial interdependencies amount to spatial autocorrelation. However, spatial autocorrelation is far more than a simple spatial analog of temporal autocorrelation. Cliff and Ord, in a series of publications culminating in their book (1973), have dealt extensively with this problem by reviewing earlier efforts, providing an exhaustive account of measures of spatial autocorrelation, and applying these measures to a variety of empirical situations.

Given a spatially distributed variable **y**, an initial question is whether or not **y** is spatially autocorrelated. This technical issue is dealt with by defining an appropriate test statistic. Moran (1950) proposed such a statistic that was modified by Dacey (1965). The test statistic proposed by Dacey was generalized by Cliff and Ord (1973, p. 12) as

$$I = (N/T)(\mathbf{y}'\mathbf{W}\mathbf{y}/\mathbf{y}'\mathbf{y}) \tag{27}$$

for a spatially distributed variable where N is the number of areas, T is the sum of the weights of **W**, and **W** is an appropriate matrix of spatial weights.[13] Cliff and Ord (1973, pp. 13–15, 29–33) establish the distribution theory for I to test for spatial autocorrelation by treating $(I - E[I])/(V[I])^{1/2}$ as a standardized normal deviate with E and V the expected value and variance operators respectively. They extend this approach (1973, pp. 87–97) to deal with residuals from a regression analysis. While the details are omitted here, some computational formulas are included in Appendix B. On the basis of their work it is possible to test for spatial autocorrelation either in a variable of interest or in a residual resulting from a regression analysis.

In the empirical examples that follow, the analysis of spatial autocorrelation is undertaken and reported. It is only of secondary interest to my objectives, however. In one respect, spatial autocorrelation can be viewed as an annoying technical problem. By the nature of

[13]Cliff and Ord discuss other measures that are not considered here.

the models discussed earlier, it is clear that the endogenous variable **y** is hypothesized as spatially autocorrelated due to a well-defined spatial process specified in (3) or in (16). As the estimation procedures detailed earlier and in Appendix A are complex and computationally burdensome, it is reasonable to test for spatial autocorrelation prior to such an analysis. If **y** is not spatially autocorrelated, it is not fruitful to proceed further. If spatial autocorrelation does exist in **y**, it is reasonable to perform the regression analysis implied by (1) and assess the residual for spatial autocorrelation in **y** to see if it is removed by the regression analysis. If it is removed, the estimation of (16) is not warranted; but if it has not been removed, it is appropriate to proceed to the estimation of (16).[14]

EMPIRICAL EXAMPLES

To illustrate the mixed endogenous-exogenous model, we consider first the Huk example of Mitchell. The exogenous variables are:

- P Proportion of the population speaking the Pampangan dialect
- FMP Farmers as a percentage of the population
- OWN Owners as a percentage of farmers
- SGR Percentage of cultivated land given over to sugarcane
- MNT Presence of mountainous terrain (dummy)
- SWP Presence of swamps (dummy)

For further details on these variables, and on the rationale for their inclusion, see Mitchell (1969) or Doreian and Hummon (1976). The actual specification of the linear model uses *P* multiplicatively with the other variables so that the exogenous variables are P*FMP, P*OWN, P*SGR, P*MNT, and P*SWP.

Table 1 gives the results of three estimations for a linear model linking insurgent (Huk) control to the cultural, demographic, economic, and physical exogenous variables. Panel 1 gives the result of OLS applied to the specification of the standard population regression

[14]If the analysis were approached from the viewpoint of spatial autocorrelation and OLS did not remove the spatial autocorrelation, then it would be necessary to ask how the spatial autocorrelation could be removed. Given the formulation of the models in the previous section, it is obvious how the (nonspatial) OLS model should be reformulated.

function (Equation 1) where geographical space is ignored. Panel 2 gives the outcome of the MLE procedure given in the preceding pages. As far as the primary objective of this chapter is concerned, the major comparison is made between these two panels. Panel 3 gives the OLS procedure suggested (incorrectly) by Doreian and Hummon, where **Wy** is simply included as another exogenous variable.[15] However, the practical question behind the comparison of panels 2 and 3 is whether the much simpler OLS procedure (with a spatial term) will suffice as a surrogate for the more complicated and computationally burdensome MLE procedure. In each case, the figures in parentheses are estimated standard errors.

TABLE 1
Alternative Estimations for Multiplicative Model of Huk Insurgent Control

Nonspatial Model

$$
\text{1: OLS}\left\{\begin{array}{l}
Y = \underset{(2.94)}{1.15} + \underset{(0.94)}{3.79}\text{P*FMP} - \underset{(0.44)}{1.91}\text{P*OWN} + \underset{(0.16)}{0.46}\text{P*SGR} \\
\qquad + \underset{(7.02)}{38.38}\text{P*MNT} + \underset{(7.94)}{17.17}\text{P*SWP} \\
R^2 = 0.73 \quad (0.94)
\end{array}\right.
$$

Spatial Model

$$
\text{2: MLE}\left\{\begin{array}{l}
Y = \underset{(2.48)}{-0.88} + \underset{(0.11)}{0.47}WY + \underset{(0.81)}{2.27}\text{P*FMP} - \underset{(0.38)}{1.07}\text{P*OWN} + \underset{(0.14)}{0.178}\text{P*SGR} \\
\qquad + \underset{(5.89)}{30.46}\text{P*MNT} + \underset{(6.52)}{12.43}\text{P*SWP} \\
(\text{FIT} = 0.80)^{a} \qquad \hat{\sigma}^2 = 126.4\,(23.9)
\end{array}\right.
$$

$$
\text{3: OLS}\left\{\begin{array}{l}
Y = \underset{(2.62)}{-1.38} + \underset{(0.14)}{0.59}WY + \underset{(0.93)}{1.89}\text{P*FMP} - \underset{(0.45)}{0.86}\text{P*OWN} + \underset{(0.16)}{0.11}\text{P*SGR} \\
\qquad + \underset{(6.51)}{28.49}\text{P*MNT} + \underset{(7.01)}{11.26}\text{P*SWP} \\
R^2 = 0.80
\end{array}\right.
$$

[a]The measure FIT is not strictly comparable to R^2 (see footnote 12).

For the MLE procedure, $\hat{\rho} = 0.47$ with a standard error of 0.11. This indicates that a spatial process is operative and that the mixed endogenous-exogenous specification is appropriate. There are dramatic numerical and, more important, inferential differences between the spatial model and the nonspatial model.[16] Apart from the

[15]The estimates differ from those of Doreian and Hummon (1976) and Mitchell (1969) since a different matrix W is used in this case. Here **W** is normalized to have row sums of unity rather than using a binary matrix.

[16]The term *spatial model* refers to the specification of the mixed endogenous-exogenous model.

intercept (which is not significantly different from zero in either approach), all the numerical estimates of the regression coefficients for the nonspatial model are inflated. Moreover, the estimates, for all coefficients, of the standard errors are also inflated. These are serious deficiencies in the nonspatial model and the application of OLS when geographical space is ignored. The nonspatial model would lead to the inclusion of all the exogenous variables (defined interactively with *P*) whereas the spatial model, together with the use of the appropriate MLE procedure, would lead to the inclusion only of P*FMP, P*OWN, P*SGR, and P*MNT. There are clear, substantive differences in the outcomes of the two specifications and their corresponding estimation procedures.

When we turn to the two estimation alternatives for the spatial model, there appear to be few differences. The numerical values of the estimated coefficients are close. The only systematic difference is that the estimates of the standard errors of the coefficient estimates are smaller under the MLE procedure than under the OLS approach. In this case, there is one inferential difference under the two approaches: P*OWN would not be included if the OLS estimates were used whereas it would be included with the maximum-likelihood estimates.

Further examples are merited, and all are taken from the context of Louisiana politics.[17] The dependent variable is support for the Democratic presidential candidate at various elections, and the exogenous variables are limited to:

B	Percentage black (in a parish)
C	Percentage Catholic (in a parish)
U	Percentage urban (in a parish)
BPE	Measure of black political equality

The data are for all 64 Louisiana parishes (counties), and BPE operationalizes the extent to which blacks are enfranchised in a parish in relation to their numbers there. Again our attention is confined to estimation problems rather than the setup of models or their detailed interpretation.

In the tables that follow, there are again two comparisons being made: between a spatial model and a nonspatial model and between

[17]The author, in collaboration with Charles Grenier, is analyzing the dynamics of Louisiana politics from 1932 to 1976. The examples used here are for illustrative purposes only, since our concern is with estimation procedures.

TABLE 2
Alternative Linear Equations Predicting Support for Democratic Presidential Candidate (Kennedy) 1960: Louisiana

Nonspatial Model

$$\text{1: OLS}\left\{\begin{array}{l} Y = 21.03 + 0.01\text{B} + 0.30\text{C} - 0.11\text{U} + 0.39\text{BPE} \\ \quad (4.40) \quad (0.08) \quad (0.04) \quad (0.04) \quad (0.06) \\ R^2 = 0.88 \end{array}\right.$$

Spatial Model

$$\text{2: MLE}\left\{\begin{array}{l} Y = 13.78 + 0.31WY - 0.004\text{B} + 0.22\text{C} - 0.10\text{U} + 0.29\text{BPE} \\ \quad (4.67) \quad (0.09) \quad (0.07) \quad (0.05) \quad (0.04) \quad (0.06) \\ (\text{FIT} = 0.90)^{a} \quad \hat{\sigma}^2 = 49.78 \quad (8.83) \end{array}\right.$$

$$\text{3: OLS}\left\{\begin{array}{l} Y = 12.34 + 0.37WY - 0.007\text{B} + 0.21\text{C} - 0.10\text{U} + 0.28\text{BPE} \\ \quad (4.99) \quad (0.12) \quad (0.08) \quad (0.05) \quad (0.04) \quad (0.07) \\ R^2 = 0.90 \end{array}\right.$$

[a]The measure FIT is not strictly comparable to R^2 (see footnote 12).

two alternative ways of estimating the spatial model. Table 2 presents the equations for the 1960 presidential election. As before, the coefficient estimates for the nonspatial model are inflated relative to the maximum-likelihood estimates for the spatial model. The estimates for the standard errors of the coefficient estimates are close to each other. However, no inferential differences occur save the obvious inclusion of a spatial term for the spatial model. Percentage Catholic and BPE are positively related to percentage support for Kennedy whereas percentage urban is negatively related to support for Kennedy. Percentage black is not relevant as a predictor of that support. (The coefficient sign difference for this variable is irrelevant as it is not significant.)

Comparing the two estimation approaches for the spatial model, we see that the coefficient estimates for the exogenous variables are very close. As before, the maximum-likelihood estimates of the standard errors of the coefficient estimates are smaller than the corresponding OLS estimates (where there are differences). However, these make no difference so far as inferential decisions and substantive interpretations are concerned. In this instance, the OLS procedure is a perfectly good surrogate for the more involved MLE procedure.

The next example is for the 1972 election; Table 3 gives the estimated linear equations. As before, the OLS estimates of the coefficients and the standard errors of the estimates for the nonspatial model are inflated (with one exception) relative to the maximum-likelihood estimates for the spatial model (although the differences are very small). The one exception is the intercept, which (in magnitude) is deflated in the nonspatial model. This exception leads to the one inferential difference. For the nonspatial model, the intercept is not significant whereas it is in the spatial model. And, in the equation specified, the intercept term has a perfectly reasonable interpretation. Those (hypothetical) parishes with no blacks, no Catholics, no urban dwellers, and no black political equality were predisposed against the Democratic candidate in 1972. When the two estimation procedures are compared for the spatial model, the same pattern as for 1960 can be seen. The coefficient estimates are virtually identical; the maximum-likelihood estimates of the standard errors of the estimates are smaller; and no inferential differences exist. Again, for the spatial model, the OLS estimators are satisfactory surrogates for the maximum-likelihood estimators.

TABLE 3
Alternative Linear Equations Predicting Support for Democratic Presidential Candidate (McGovern) 1972: Louisiana

Nonspatial Model

$$\text{1: OLS}\begin{cases} Y = -7.36 + 0.41\text{B} + 0.09\text{C} + 0.001\text{U} + 0.29\text{BPE} \\ \quad\;\;(4.32)\quad(0.05)\quad(0.03)\quad(0.022)\quad(0.07) \\ R^2 = 0.75 \end{cases}$$

Spatial Model

$$\text{2: MLE}\begin{cases} Y = -11.44 + 0.29WY + 0.39\text{B} + 0.07\text{C} + 0.01\text{U} + 0.24\text{BPE} \\ \quad\;\;(4.18)\quad(0.10)\quad(0.04)\quad(0.02)\quad(0.02)\quad(0.06) \\ (\text{FIT} = 0.78)^{a} \quad \hat{\sigma}^2 = 163.2 \quad (2.9) \end{cases}$$

$$\text{3: OLS}\begin{cases} Y = -12.51 + 0.37WY + 0.39\text{B} + 0.07\text{C} + 0.01\text{U} + 0.22\text{BPE} \\ \quad\;\;(4.50)\quad(0.13)\quad(0.04)\quad(0.02)\quad(0.02)\quad(0.07) \\ R^2 = 0.78 \end{cases}$$

[a]The measure FIT is not strictly comparable to R^2 (see footnote 12).

The final example concerns the 1968 presidential election; the estimated equations are shown in Table 4. The comparisons between the nonspatial model, with its OLS procedure, and the spatial model, with its MLE procedure, are similar to the previous case. However, both the coefficient estimates and the standard error estimates are much closer. The coefficient for the spatial term in the spatial model is rather small, and one would expect that as $\hat{\rho}$ tends to zero, and no spatial process operates, the two procedures will tend to give the same results. This is, of course, obvious, since the crucial difference between the two models is the specification of the spatial term. In the 1968 election, there is again an inferential difference concerning the intercept term: It is included in the spatial model but excluded from the nonspatial model (as before). Both models judge percentage urban not to be a significant predictor of Democratic presidential support in 1968.

TABLE 4

Alternative Linear Equations Predicting Support for Democratic Presidential Candidate (Humphrey) 1968: Louisiana

Nonspatial Model

$$\text{1: OLS}\begin{cases} Y = -4.54 + 0.59B + 0.12C + 0.04U + 0.11BPE \\ \quad\;\;\; (3.0) \quad\;\; (0.05) \quad\; (0.03) \quad\; (0.03) \quad\; (0.04) \\ R^2 = 0.76 \end{cases}$$

Spatial Model

$$\text{2: MLE}\begin{cases} Y = -6.12 + 0.12WY + 0.58B + 0.11C + 0.05U + 0.10BPE \\ \quad\;\;\; (3.67) \quad\; (0.12) \quad\;\; (0.05) \quad\; (0.03) \quad\; (0.03) \quad\; (0.04) \\ (\text{FIT} = 0.76)^{a} \quad \hat{\sigma} = 22.9 \quad (4.1) \end{cases}$$

$$\text{3: OLS}\begin{cases} Y = -6.83 + 0.12WY + 0.58B + 0.11C + 0.05U + 0.10BPE \\ \quad\;\;\; (4.26) \quad\; (0.15) \quad\;\; (0.05) \quad\; (0.03) \quad\; (0.03) \quad\; (0.04) \\ R^2 = 0.76 \end{cases}$$

[a]The measure FIT is not strictly comparable to R^2 (see footnote 12).

In this final example, the OLS and MLE procedures return the same estimates of ρ. For the previous examples, $\hat{\rho}$ via OLS was higher than the corresponding maximum-likelihood estimate. The pattern is maintained: The OLS estimate of the standard error of $\hat{\rho}$ is greater than the corresponding maximum-likelihood estimate. The OLS bias of tending to overestimate the magnitude of ρ is offset by the OLS bias of tending to overestimate the magnitude of the standard error of the estimate of ρ. The nature of the two biases makes it difficult to state a general conclusion on the merits of OLS for the spatial model versus the MLE procedure. If the two procedures were to lead to different inferential processes concerning ρ, then obviously the OLS procedure would not be a good surrogate for the MLE procedure.[18]

DISCUSSION

Given that social scientists do consider social phenomena that are distributed in geographical space, this chapter has addressed three

[18]In part, this issue can be assessed in terms of spatial autocorrelation. For each of the foregoing examples, the spatial autocorrelation statistic I was computed. In all cases, the dependent variable y was spatially autocorrelated.

issues. First, should geographical space be included in modeling efforts when linear equations are used? Second, if geographical space should be included, how can we include it parsimoniously? And, third, given the inclusion of geographical space in linear models, what estimation procedures should be used?

The first issue arose in the context of the use of aggregated data for areal units. As such, geography is implicitly included in the data structure and whether or not geographical space should be included depends on whether or not some spatial process is operative. Such a decision is a theoretical one, and several examples were given in which a spatial process was at least plausible.

With regard to the second issue, we have explored a straightforward way of including geographical space by means of a matrix **W** of weights representing a spatial property. The exemplar spatial property was that of adjacency. Representing space in this fashion is, however, only one alternative. Coelen (1976) has argued that use of a single ρ means that the autocorrelation is either positive or negative across all observations and has suggested that this use is too restrictive. There may be different spatial effects in different local subregions. Specification of a differential ρ complicates the estimation procedure considerably, as the simplification provided by Equation (12) is not available; this research problem merits further attention. Another line of inquiry is to specify multiple spatial effects with multiple ρ's and **W**'s. However, the use of multiple ρs also means that the simplification found in (12) would no longer be available.

As there are difficulties in specifying **W**, Arora and Brown (1977) have proposed abandoning such an approach and have suggested, instead, using econometric methods. They outline the procedures of joint generalized least squares, equicorrelated error terms, random error component models, and random coefficient regression models. As they make no attempt to apply these approaches empirically, their suggestions remain speculative. The reader is referred to their article for details, but some preliminary remarks are in order here. The method of joint generalized least squares (see Theil, 1971) requires panels of observations. Further, distinct β's are specified for each area, which greatly enlarges the number of parameters to be estimated. For the situations discussed in this chapter, the method is not applicable. If there are a sufficiently large number of panels of observations, and if the β_i are fixed through time, the method has some appeal. Both Swamy's (1970) and Hsiao's (1975) approaches to the random coefficients model also require panels of observations. The equicorrelated error term models (without the spatial term) for a single cross-section amount to OLS if an intercept is specified (Theil, 1971, p. 243). If there are good grounds for anticipating a spatial process, however, the methods described here are preferable to OLS. Arora and Brown propose the random error components model for interaction (between areas) variables, but since the dependent variables discussed here are not such interaction variables, the approach does not appear relevant in this context. On the other hand, for interaction variables this approach can be explored further.

With regard to the third issue, given the specification of a (linear) spatial process, the mixed endogenous-exogenous model, the chapter has detailed a maximum-likelihood procedure for estimating such a model. We also discussed a test for spatial autocorrelation that can be used to guide the researcher in assessing the need to incorporate spatial characteristics into the formulation of a model.

In the examples we have used, it is clear that important differences do exist between the spatial model and the nonspatial model. This was most dramatically the case in the Huk insurgency example. While there was an instance in the set of Louisiana examples where the two models led to substantively the same conclusion, the nonspatial model is unreliable as a means of coupling endogenous variables to exogenous variables when a spatial process operates. In the nonspatial model, both coefficient estimates and estimates of the standard errors of those estimates are inflated. The examples make clear that when a spatial social process is operative, a spatial model should be specified and the MLE procedures detailed in the preceding pages should be used.

The MLE procedure is not straightforward, however, and it is computationally burdensome. If a simpler procedure will work, it seems preferable to use it. To this end, a second line of inquiry was to see if OLS applied to the spatial model would be an adequate substitute for the MLE procedure. The results of this inquiry were mixed for the Louisiana data. In most instances, it appears that OLS is satisfactory as a surrogate for MLE when a spatial process is *clearly* operating. The OLS coefficient estimates are always close to, if not identical to, the maximum-likelihood estimates. However, the OLS estimates of the standard errors of the coefficient estimates are inflated. In general, this inflation is problematic for OLS unless ρ is likely to be relatively low. In such cases, the greater precision of the maximum-likelihood estimators makes them preferable. For the Huk data, OLS is not an adequate surrogate for the MLE approach detailed here. The **W** matrix for the Huk data is more densely connected in the sense that many areas are connected to a large number of other areas relative to the Louisiana examples. It seems that the structure of **W** and the true value of ρ are critical in deciding whether OLS can be used as a surrogate for maximum-likelihood estimators. This is something that can best be investigated via Monte Carlo simulations, and such studies are under way. The clear, and perhaps conservative, advice is that for the spatial processes considered here, the MLE approach should be used. For regions with "less connected" areas and high values of ρ, OLS should probably suffice.

One further option outlined by Ord, but not discussed here, is to retain the usual population regression function $\mathbf{y} = \mathbf{X}\boldsymbol{\beta} + \boldsymbol{\epsilon}$ but to incorporate the spatial effects into the disturbance term via $\boldsymbol{\epsilon} = \rho\mathbf{W} + \boldsymbol{\nu}$, where $\boldsymbol{\nu}$ is a white noise term. This is a way of dealing with spatial autocorrelation and represents another method of incorporating geographical space into the analysis of social phenomena.

This chapter advocates that geographical space be at least explicitly considered for some social phenomena. For many social, political, and economic phenomena, geographical space may not be relevant. But for the cases where it is relevant, the procedures outlined here should lead to richer and more substantive analyses of those phenomena.

APPENDIX A: DERIVATION OF VARIANCE-COVARIANCE MATRICES FOR ESTIMATORS

Purely Endogenous Model

The log-likelihood function is given by

$$l(\mathbf{y}) = \text{const} - (N/2)\ln\sigma^2 - (1/2\sigma^2)\mathbf{y}'\mathbf{A}'\mathbf{A}\mathbf{y} + \ln|\mathbf{A}| \quad \text{(A-1)}$$

From Equation (9) we have, writing l for $l(\mathbf{y})$,

$$\partial l/\partial\omega = -N/2\omega + (1/2\omega^2)\mathbf{y}'\mathbf{A}'\mathbf{A}\mathbf{y} \tag{A-2}$$

Differentiating (A-1) with respect to ρ gives

$$\partial l/\partial\rho = (\partial/\partial\rho)\ln|\mathbf{A}| - (1/2\omega)(\partial/\partial\rho)\mathbf{y}'\mathbf{A}'\mathbf{A}\mathbf{y}$$

Using the form of $|\mathbf{A}|$ given in (12),

$$(\partial/\partial\rho)(\ln|\mathbf{A}|) = (\partial/\partial\rho)\sum_{i=1}^{N}\ln(1-\rho\lambda_i) = -\sum_{i=1}^{N}\lambda_i/(1-\rho\lambda_i)$$

and

$$\begin{aligned}(\partial/\partial\rho)(\mathbf{y}'\mathbf{A}'\mathbf{A}\mathbf{y}) &= (\partial/\partial\rho)[\mathbf{y}'\mathbf{y} - 2\rho\mathbf{y}'\mathbf{W}\mathbf{y} + \rho^2(\mathbf{W}\mathbf{y})'(\mathbf{W}\mathbf{y})]\\ &= -2\mathbf{y}'\mathbf{W}\mathbf{y} + 2\rho(\mathbf{W}\mathbf{y})'\mathbf{W}\mathbf{y}\end{aligned}$$

Hence

$$\partial l/\partial\rho = -\sum_{i=1}^{N}\lambda_i/(1-\rho\lambda_i) + (\mathbf{y}'\mathbf{W}\mathbf{y}/\omega) - (\rho\mathbf{y}'\mathbf{W}'\mathbf{W}\mathbf{y}/\omega) \tag{A-3}$$

We turn now to the second derivatives of $l(\mathbf{y})$. From (A-2):

$$\begin{aligned}\partial^2 l/\partial\omega^2 &= (N/2\omega^2) - (2/2\omega^3)\mathbf{y}'\mathbf{A}'\mathbf{A}\mathbf{y}\\ &= (1/2\omega^2)[N - (2/\omega)\mathbf{y}'\mathbf{A}'\mathbf{A}\mathbf{y}]\\ &= (1/2\omega^2)[N - 2N] \qquad \text{(at the minimum)}\\ &= -N/2\omega^2 \end{aligned} \tag{A-4}$$

From (A-3):

$$\begin{aligned}\partial^2 l/\partial\rho^2 &= (\partial/\partial\rho)\left(-\sum_{i=1}^{N}\lambda_i/(1-\rho\lambda_i)\right)\\ &\quad + (1/\omega)(\partial/\partial\rho)(\mathbf{y}'\mathbf{W}\mathbf{y} - \rho\mathbf{y}'\mathbf{W}'\mathbf{W}\mathbf{y})\\ &= -\sum_{i=1}^{N}\lambda_i^2/(1-\rho\lambda_i)^2 - (1/\omega)\mathbf{y}'\mathbf{W}'\mathbf{W}\mathbf{y}\\ &= \alpha - (1/\omega)\mathbf{y}'\mathbf{W}'\mathbf{W}\mathbf{y}\end{aligned} \tag{A-5}$$

where

$$\alpha = -\sum_{i=1}^{N}\lambda_i^2/(1-\rho\lambda_i)^2$$

From (A-2):

$$\begin{aligned}\partial^2 l/\partial\omega\partial\rho &= (1/2\omega^2)(\partial/\partial\rho)(\mathbf{y}'\mathbf{A}'\mathbf{A}\mathbf{y}) \\ &= (1/2\omega^2)[-2\mathbf{y}'\mathbf{W}\mathbf{y} + 2\rho(\mathbf{W}\mathbf{y})'(\mathbf{W}\mathbf{y})] \\ &= -(1/\omega^2)[\mathbf{y}'(\mathbf{I} - \rho\mathbf{W}')\mathbf{W}\mathbf{y}] \\ &= -\epsilon'\mathbf{W}\mathbf{y}/\omega^2 \qquad \text{(by 4)}\end{aligned} \tag{A-6}$$

To obtain the information matrix, we need to take the expected values of these second derivatives. For (A-4):

$$E[-N/2\omega^2] = -N/2\omega^2 \tag{A-7}$$

For (A-5):

$$E[(1/\omega)\mathbf{y}'\mathbf{W}'\mathbf{W}\mathbf{y}] = (1/\omega)E[\epsilon'\mathbf{A}^{-1\prime}\mathbf{W}'\mathbf{W}\mathbf{A}^{-1}\epsilon]$$

Define $\mathbf{B} = \mathbf{W}\mathbf{A}^{-1}$; then

$$\begin{aligned}(1/\omega)E[\epsilon'\mathbf{A}^{-1\prime}\mathbf{W}'\mathbf{W}\mathbf{A}^{-1}\epsilon] &= (1/\omega)\mathrm{E}[\epsilon'\mathbf{B}'\mathbf{B}\epsilon] \\ &= (1/\omega)E[\mathrm{tr}\ \epsilon'\mathbf{B}'\mathbf{B}\epsilon] \\ &= (1/\omega)E[\mathrm{tr}\ \mathbf{B}'\mathbf{B}\epsilon\epsilon'] \\ &= (1/\omega)[\mathrm{tr}\ (\mathbf{B}'\mathbf{B})E\epsilon\epsilon'] \\ &= (1/\omega)[\mathrm{tr}\ (\mathbf{B}'\mathbf{B})\sigma^2\mathbf{I}] \\ &= \mathrm{tr}\ (\mathbf{B}'\mathbf{B}) \qquad \text{as } \omega = \sigma^2\end{aligned}$$

Therefore

$$E[\partial^2 l/\partial\rho^2] = \alpha - \mathrm{tr}(\mathbf{B}'\mathbf{B}) \tag{A-8}$$

For (A-6):

$$\begin{aligned}E[-(1/\omega^2)\epsilon'\mathbf{W}\mathbf{y}] &= -(1/\omega^2)E[\epsilon'\mathbf{W}\mathbf{A}^{-1}\epsilon] \\ &= -(1/\omega^2)E[\mathrm{tr}\ \epsilon'\mathbf{B}\epsilon] \\ &= -(1/\omega^2)[\mathrm{tr}\ (\mathbf{B})E\epsilon\epsilon'] \\ &= -(1/\omega^2)[\mathrm{tr}\ (\mathbf{B})\sigma^2\mathbf{I}] \\ &= -\mathrm{tr}\ (\mathbf{B})/\omega\end{aligned} \tag{A-9}$$

The expressions in (A-7) to (A-9), when substituted into (14), yield

$$\mathbf{V}(\omega, \rho) = \begin{bmatrix} N/2\omega^2 & \text{tr}\,\mathbf{B}/\omega \\ \text{tr}\,\mathbf{B}/\omega & \text{tr}(\mathbf{B}'\mathbf{B}) - \alpha \end{bmatrix}^{-1}$$

$$= \omega^2 \begin{bmatrix} N/2 & \omega\,\text{tr}\,(\mathbf{B}) \\ \omega\,\text{tr}\,(\mathbf{B}) & \omega^2(\text{tr}\,\mathbf{B}'\mathbf{B} - \alpha) \end{bmatrix}^{-1} \qquad \text{(A-10)}$$

The expression given in (A-10) is the asymptotic variance-covariance matrix for the parameters estimated for the pure endogenous model.

Mixed Endogenous-Exogenous Model

The expressions for $\partial^2 l/\partial\omega^2$, $\partial^2 l/\partial\rho^2$, and $\partial^2 l/\partial\omega\partial\rho$ remain exactly as for the pure endogenous model. It is now necessary to obtain $\partial^2 l/\partial\beta^2$, $\partial^2 l/\partial\beta\partial\rho$, and $\partial^2 l/\partial\beta\partial\omega$. From (22), which gives $\partial l/\partial\beta$, we have

$$\partial^2 l/\partial\beta^2 = -\,(1/\omega)(\mathbf{X}'\mathbf{X}) \qquad \text{(A-11)}$$

From (22) we also have

$$\begin{aligned} \partial^2 l/\partial\beta\partial\omega &= (1/\omega^2)[(\mathbf{X}'\mathbf{X})\boldsymbol{\beta} - \mathbf{X}'\mathbf{z}] \\ &= (1/\omega^2)[\mathbf{X}'\mathbf{z} - \mathbf{X}'\mathbf{z}] \\ &\quad \text{as } \boldsymbol{\beta} = (\mathbf{X}'\mathbf{X})^{-1}\mathbf{X}'\mathbf{z} \text{ at the minimum} \\ &= 0 \end{aligned} \qquad \text{(A-12)}$$

From (22):

$$\begin{aligned} \partial^2 l/\partial\beta\partial\rho &= (1/\omega)(\partial/\partial\rho)(\mathbf{X}'\mathbf{z}) \\ &= (1/\omega)(\partial/\partial\rho)[\mathbf{X}'(\mathbf{I} - \rho\mathbf{W})\mathbf{y}] \\ &= -\,(1/\omega)\mathbf{X}'\mathbf{W}\mathbf{y} \end{aligned} \qquad \text{(A-13)}$$

We now consider the expected values of the second derivatives in order to obtain the information matrix. As before,

$$E[\partial^2 l/\partial\omega^2] = -\,N/2\omega^2 \qquad \text{and} \qquad E[\partial^2 l/\partial\omega\partial\rho] = \text{tr}(\mathbf{B})/\omega$$

From (A-12), $E[\partial^2 l/\partial\omega\partial\beta] = 0'$ (as a row vector). The result for $\partial^2 l/\partial\rho^2$ is not identical to the result for the purely endogenous model.

From (A-5):

$$\begin{aligned}\partial^2 l/\partial\rho^2 &= \alpha - (1/\omega)\mathbf{y}'\mathbf{W}'\mathbf{W}\mathbf{y}\\ &= \alpha - (1/\omega)[(\epsilon'\mathbf{A}^{-1\prime} + \beta'\mathbf{X}'\mathbf{A}^{-1\prime})\mathbf{W}'\mathbf{W}(\mathbf{A}^{-1}\mathbf{X}\beta + \mathbf{A}^{-1}\epsilon)]\\ &= \alpha - (1/\omega)[\epsilon'\mathbf{A}^{-1\prime}\mathbf{W}'\mathbf{W}\mathbf{A}^{-1}\mathbf{X}\beta + \beta'\mathbf{X}'\mathbf{A}^{-1\prime}\mathbf{W}'\mathbf{A}^{-1}\epsilon\\ &\quad + \epsilon'\mathbf{A}^{-1\prime}\mathbf{W}'\mathbf{W}\mathbf{A}^{-1}\epsilon + \beta'\mathbf{X}'\mathbf{A}^{-1\prime}\mathbf{W}'\mathbf{W}\mathbf{A}^{-1}\mathbf{X}\beta]\\ &= \alpha - (1/\omega)[\epsilon'\mathbf{B}'\mathbf{B}\epsilon + \beta'\mathbf{X}'\mathbf{B}'\mathbf{B}\mathbf{X}\beta + 2\epsilon'\mathbf{B}'\mathbf{B}X\beta]\end{aligned}$$

as $\epsilon'\mathbf{A}^{-1\prime}\mathbf{W}'\mathbf{W}\mathbf{A}^{-1}\mathbf{X}\beta = (\beta'\mathbf{X}'\mathbf{A}^{-1\prime}\mathbf{W}'\mathbf{A}^{-1}\epsilon)'$, a scalar. Thus

$$E[\partial^2 l/\partial\rho^2] = -\alpha + \mathrm{tr}(\mathbf{B}'\mathbf{B}) + (1/\omega)\beta'\mathbf{X}'\mathbf{B}'\mathbf{B}\mathbf{X}\beta \quad \text{(A-14)}$$

From (A-13):

$$\begin{aligned}E[\partial^2 l/\partial\beta\partial\rho] &= -(1/\omega)\mathbf{X}'E[\mathbf{W}\mathbf{y}]\\ &= (1/\omega)\mathbf{X}'\mathrm{E}[\mathbf{W}\mathbf{A}^{-1}\mathbf{X}\beta + \mathbf{W}\mathrm{A}^{-1}\epsilon] \quad \text{(A-15)}\\ &= (1/\omega)\mathbf{X}'\mathbf{B}\mathbf{X}\beta\end{aligned}$$

Finally, from (A-11),

$$E[\partial^2 l/\partial\beta^2] = -(1/\omega)(\mathbf{X}'\mathbf{X}) \quad \text{(A-16)}$$

Substituting all the expressions for the expected values and noting the negative signs gives

$\mathbf{V}(\omega, \rho, \beta)$

$$= \omega^2\begin{bmatrix} N/2 & \omega\,\mathrm{tr}\,(\mathbf{B}) & \mathbf{0}' \\ \omega\,\mathrm{tr}\,\mathbf{B} & \omega^2(\mathrm{tr}\,\mathbf{B}'\mathbf{B} - \alpha) + \omega\beta'\mathbf{X}'\mathbf{B}'\mathbf{B}\mathbf{X}\beta & \omega\mathbf{X}'\mathbf{B}\mathbf{X}\beta \\ \mathbf{0} & \omega\mathbf{X}'\mathbf{B}\mathbf{X}\beta & \omega\mathbf{X}'\mathbf{X}\end{bmatrix}^{-1} \quad \text{(A-17)}$$

APPENDIX B: TESTING FOR SPATIAL AUTOCORRELATION

Suppose a residual, $\hat{\epsilon}$, has been returned from a (nonspatial) regression analysis. To test for spatial autocorrelation, the following test statistic is defined:

$$I = (N/T)(\hat{\epsilon}'\mathbf{W}\hat{\epsilon}/\hat{\epsilon}'\hat{\epsilon}) \quad \text{(B-1)}$$

where

$$T = \sum_{\substack{i,j\\ i\neq j}} w_{ij}$$

Cliff and Ord (1973) derive expressions for $E[I]$ and $V[I]$ in order to construct a standardized normal deviate. Define $\mathbf{D} = [d_{ij}] = \mathbf{X}(\mathbf{X}'\mathbf{X})^{-1}\mathbf{X}'$. Then

$$E[I] = [1 + (N/T)\sum_{\substack{i=1\\i\neq j}}^{N}\sum_{j=1}^{N} w_{ij}\, d_{ij}]/(N - K) \tag{B-2}$$

where there are K exogenous variables (including the column of 1's for the intercept). The expression for $V[I]$ is considerably more complex. The following preliminary definitions are required:

$$w_{i.} = \sum_{j=1}^{N} w_{ij}$$

$$w_{j.} = \sum_{i=1}^{N} w_{ij}$$

$$S_1 = \frac{1}{2}\sum_{\substack{i=1\\i\neq j}}^{N}\sum_{j=1}^{N} (w_{ij} + w_{ji})^2$$

$$S_2 = \sum_{i=1}^{N} (w_{i.} + w_{.i})^2$$

With these definitions,

$$\begin{aligned} V[I] = [N/(N-K)T^2]\Bigg\{&(N^2S_1 - NS_2 + 3T^2)/N^2 \\ &+(1/N)\sum_{i=1}^{N}\sum_{j=1}^{N} (w_{i.} + w_{.i})(W_{j.} + w_{.j})\, d_{ij} \\ &+ 2\Bigg(\sum_{\substack{i=1\\i\neq j}}^{N}\sum_{j=1}^{N} w_{ij}d_{ij}\Bigg)^2 \\ &- \Bigg[\sum_{i=1}^{N}\sum_{\substack{j=1\\i\neq j\neq k}}^{N}\sum_{k=1}^{N} (w_{ik} + w_{ki})(w_{jk} + w_{kj})d_{ij} \\ &+ \sum_{\substack{i=1\\i\neq j}}^{N}\sum_{j=1}^{N} (w_{ij} + w_{ji})^2\, d_{ii}\Bigg] \\ &+ (1/N)\sum_{i=1}^{N}\sum_{\substack{j=1\\i\neq j\neq k}}^{N}\sum_{k=1}^{N} (w_{ij} + w_{ji})(w_{ik} + w_{ki})(d_{ii}d_{jk} - d_{ij}d_{ik})\Bigg\} \\ &- [1/(N-K)^2] \end{aligned} \tag{B-3}$$

Note that when there are no exogenous variables $E[I] = -(1/N)$ and

$$V[I] = N/(N-K)T^2\,[(N^2S_1 - NS_2 + 3T^2)/N^2]$$

which can be used to assess the spatial autocorrelation of **y**.

REFERENCES

AIGNER, D. J., AND HEINS, A. J.

1967 "On the determinants of income equality." *American Economic Review* 57:175–184.

ARORA, S. S., AND BROWN, M.

1977 "Alternative approaches to spatial autocorrelation: An improvement over current practice." *International Regional Science Review* 2:67–78.

CAPECCHI, V., AND GALLI, G.

1969 "Determinants of voting behavior in Italy: A linear causal model of analysis." In M. Dogan and S. Rokkan (Eds.), *Social Ecology*. Cambridge, Mass.: M.I.T. Press.

CHIROT, D., AND RAGIN, C.

1975 "The market, tradition and peasant rebellion: The case of Romania in 1907." *American Sociological Review* 40:428–444.

CLIFF, A. D., AND ORD, K.

1970 "Spatial autocorrelation: A review of existing and new measures with applications." *Economic Geography* June(Supplement):269–292.

1973 *Spatial Autocorrelation*. London: Pion.

COELEN, S. P.

1976 "Book review: Spatial autocorrelation by Cliff and Ord." *Journal of Economic Literature* 14:924–925.

COX, K. R.

1969 "Voting in the London suburbs: A factor analysis and a causal model." In M. Dogan and S. Rokkan (Eds.), *Social Ecology*. Cambridge, Mass.: M.I.T. Press.

DACEY, M. F.

1965 "A review on measures of contiguity for two and *k*-color maps." Technical Report 2, Spatial Diffusion Study. Department of Geography, Northwestern University.

DOREIAN, P., AND HUMMON, N. P.

1976 *Modeling Social Processes*. New York: Elsevier.

DUNLAP, R., AND CATTON, W.

1979 "Environmental sociology." *Annual Review of Sociology* 5:243–273.

FRISBIE, W. P., AND POSTON, D. L.
1975 "Components of sustenance organization and non-metropolitan change: A human ecological investigation." *American Sociological Review* 40:773–784.

HIBBS, D.
1974 "Problems of statistical estimation and causal inference in time series regression models." In H. L. Costner (Ed.), *Sociological Methodology 1973–74*. San Francisco: Jossey-Bass.

HSIAO, C.
1975 "Some estimation methods for a random coefficient model." *Econometrica* 43:305–325.

INVERARITY, J. M.
1976 "Populism and lynching in Louisiana 1889–1896: A test of Erikson's theory of the relationship between boundary crises and repressive justice." *American Sociological Review* 41:262–280.

JOHNSTON, J.
1963 *Econometric Methods*. New York: McGraw-Hill.

KENDALL, M. G., AND STUART, A.
1967 *The Advanced Theory of Statistics*. Vol. 2. London: Hafner.

KERNALL, S.
1973 "Comment: A re-evaluation of black voting in Mississippi." *American Political Science Review* 67:1307–1318.

LANCASTER, K.
1971 *Mathematical Economics*. New York: Macmillan.

MATTHEWS, D. R., AND PROTHRO, J. W.
1963a "Social and economic factors and Negro voter registration in the south." *American Political Science Review* 57:24–44.
1963b "Political factors and Negro voter registration in the south." *American Political Science Review* 57:355–367.

MEAD, R.
1967 "A mathematical model for the estimation of interplant competition." *Biometrics* 23:189–205.

MITCHELL, E. J.
1969 "Some econometrics of the Huk rebellion." *American Political Science Review* 63:1159–1171.

MORAN, P. A. P.
1950 "A test for the serial independence of residuals." *Biometrika* 37:178–181.

ORD, K.
1975 "Estimation methods for models of spatial interaction." *Journal of American Statistical Association* 70:120–126.

PIELOU, E. C.
1969 *An Introduction to Mathematical Ecology*. New York: Wiley.

RAGIN, C.
1977 "Class, status, and reactive ethnic cleavages: The social basis of political regionalism." *American Sociological Review* 42:438–450.

SALAMON, L. M., AND VAN EVERA, S.
1973 "Fear, apathy, and discrimination: A test of three explanations of political participation." *American Political Science Review* 67:1288–1306.

SCHOENBERGER, R. A., AND SEGAL, D. R.
1971 "Ecology of dissent: The southern Wallace vote in 1968." *Midwest Journal of Politics* 15:583–586.

SWAMY, P. A. V. B.
1970 "Efficient-inference in a random coefficient regression model." *Econometrica* 38:311–323.

THEIL, H.
1971 *Principles of Econometrics*. New York: Wiley.

WASSERMAN, I. M., AND SEGAL, D. R.
1973 "Aggregate effects in the ecological study of presidential voting." *American Journal of Political Science* 17:177–181.

11

RESEARCH ON INTERVIEWING TECHNIQUES

Charles F. Cannell
Peter V. Miller
Lois Oksenberg
INSTITUTE FOR SOCIAL RESEARCH, UNIVERSITY OF MICHIGAN

The survey interviewer, as gatekeeper to the attitudes, experiences, and perceptions of respondents, occupies a prominent position in survey research and has been a subject of concern since the emergence of systematic survey research. Recognition of the interviewer's potential for manipulating or distorting responses has generated numerous approaches aimed at controlling the interviewer's influence on responses. Over the years, rules for interviewer behavior have evolved

This material is based on work funded by the following organizations: contracts with the National Center for Health Statistics, a program grant (P01-00624) from the National Center for Health Services Research, and a grant (SOC78-07287) from the National Science Foundation. Findings and conclusions do not necessarily reflect the views of these organizations.

from the work of researchers studying survey methodology and from the practices of survey organizations. These rules appear to have solved some of the problems of bias that were the focus of earlier investigation, but they fail to address other sources of survey error whose importance has only recently begun to be recognized and understood.

In this chapter we address sources of survey error inherent in the reporting task itself and examine the interactive nature of the interview. Our aim is to find ways to enhance the respondent's role of providing full and accurate information. A concept of the interview is presented that emphasizes, on the one hand, the difficulty of many reporting tasks and, on the other, the need to improve the respondent's understanding of these tasks and increase motivation to perform them. We report research on new interviewing techniques that promise to improve the quality of survey data.

PERSPECTIVES

Historical Perspective

A series of studies in the early decades of survey research raised the issue of interviewer effects on responses. A classic demonstration was Rice's 1929 study of the causes of destitution. Comparing the results obtained from poverty-stricken respondents by two different interviewers, he discovered that the data collected by one interviewer showed overindulgence in alcohol as the most common cause of destitution while the other interviewer found social and economic conditions the most frequent causes. The case for *interviewer bias* appeared to be established when it was learned that the first interviewer was a prohibitionist and the second a socialist (Rice, 1929). Because of this and other studies, the problem of interviewer bias became a major concern of early opinion polls, especially preelection polls. (See Cantril, 1947, and Cahalan, Tamulonis, and Verner, 1947).

A second early trend focused on interviewers as a source of bias through the effects on the respondent of the interviewer's expectations about the response. (For example, see Stanton and Baker, 1942.)

Concern about the interviewer's expectations stimulated the first systematic research into interviewer influence by Hyman and his colleagues at the National Opinion Research Center (NORC) (Hyman and others, 1954). These sophisticated investigations established the potential importance of interviewer expectations. The researchers identified three kinds of expectations: role expectations, in which the interviewer expects certain responses from individual members of certain population groups (women, businessmen, blacks, and so on); attitude structure expectations, in which the interviewer expects respondents' views to be internally consistent; and probability expectations, in which the interviewer expects certain responses because of his or her beliefs about sentiments prevailing in the population.

More recent work by Rosenthal and colleagues (1966, 1969) on experimenter effects in laboratory studies emphasized possible interviewer effects—both related to their own opinions and to their expectations for the respondent. There are, of course, several avenues by which the interviewer could bias data. Rice, for example, assumed that the interviewer's own opinions were somehow communicated to the respondent, who then tailored his or her own responses accordingly. Alternatively, the interviewer might ask leading questions in an attempt to probe the respondent's replies or might be biased in which replies are probed and how. The interviewer might be selective in recording responses, might distort the actual responses in writing them down, or even might falsify responses outright. (It should be noted that "interviewer bias" was not, broadly speaking, presumed to be conscious or deliberate, though in some instances it might be.) Finally, early surveys often used quota sampling, thereby giving interviewers the real possibility of biasing survey results through their choices of whom to interview.

Despite the potential for interviewers to bias data somehow, concern over interviewer effects has lessened in recent years. (See, for example, Sudman and others, 1977.) Paralleling this decrease in concern have been improvements in survey practice. Interviewer training now typically stresses the importance of appearing neutral and accepting toward all responses. Questionnaire wording and administration have been standardized; nondirective probing procedures have been developed. It is probable that these improvements have reduced the potential for interviewers to influence adversely the validity of data through their personal attitudes and beliefs. There remains one important exception: Respondents sometimes modify answers in reaction to the *appearance* of the interviewer. Robinson and Rohde (1946) found that fewer anti-Semitic opinions were expressed to interviewers who appeared to be Jewish; Katz (1942) found that the interviewer's apparent social class influenced reporting of social and political opinion by working-class respondents; Schuman and Converse (1971) found that the interviewer's race influenced reporting of racial attitudes by black respondents. Interviewing techniques cannot be expected to overcome such reporting problems.

Current Perspectives

Question wording, an important determinant of the nature of the reporting task, has received considerable attention in the past four decades. Cantril (1947) addressed this problem in his book on social surveys. Payne (1951) produced an extensive discussion of question wording and its pitfalls. The relative merits of open and closed response formats have been much discussed. Recently, Schuman and his associates have undertaken systematic investigations of several question-wording issues (Schuman and Presser, 1977, 1978, 1979).

Except for this attention to the variable of question wording, reporting task variables are only now receiving attention as important elements in determining the accuracy of survey results. Evidence is growing that the nature of the respondent's task in processing and reporting the information asked for by the interviewer may impose demands the respondent is unwilling or unable to meet (Sudman and Bradburn, 1974; Oksenberg and Cannell, 1977; Bradburn, 1977).

Key variables in the reporting task appear to be the burden placed on the respondent's memory to produce the information requested of him or her and problems faced by the respondent in self-presentation in the interview. The research in interviewing techniques presented here was inspired primarily by the dramatic evidence of the importance of these factors, and our orientation to them is guided by a diagram of the response process.

Figure 1. Diagram of respondent's (*R*) question-answering process.

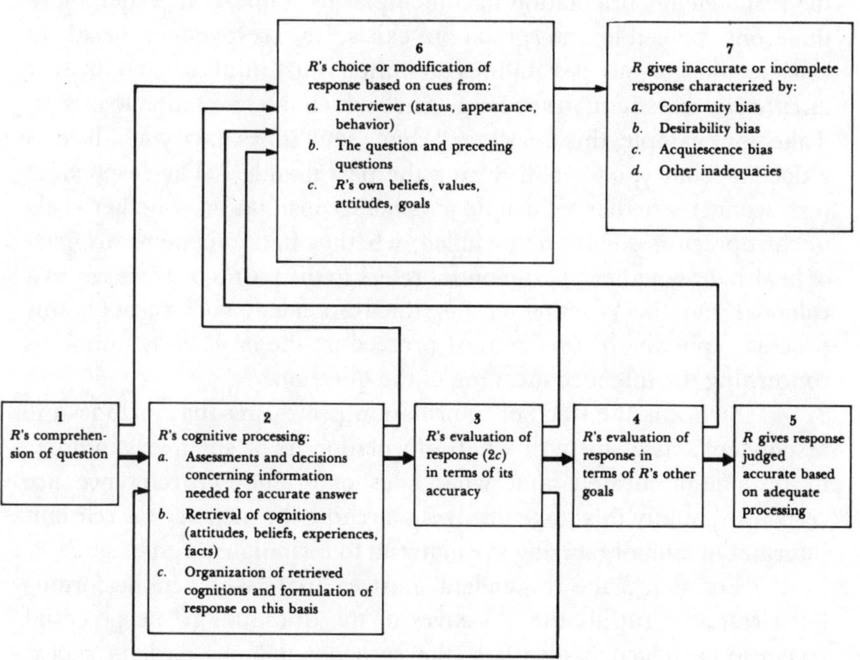

Question-Answering Process

To help structure our examination of the reporting process in detail, Figure 1 is useful.[1] We begin by following the route taken by a conscientious respondent who proceeds appropriately through steps 1 to 5 without detouring at any point to inappropriate processing (represented by steps 6 and 7).

The response process begins with comprehending the question (step 1). Comprehension includes issues of vocabulary level, clarity of concept, complexity of sentence structure, and other familiar issues of

[1]This diagram was developed originally by Marquis, appeared in Cannell, Marquis, and Laurent (1977), and has undergone several revisions. The latest, by Oksenberg and Cannell (1977), has been further revised for this chapter.

question wording discussed in texts on survey methods. In this chapter, however, we are interested in broader issues of question interpretation: the respondent's orientation in contemplating a question. When more than one plausible interpretation exists, the respondent needs to consider the various possibilities and often must think up and answer an *internal* questionnaire to help decide which interpretation to accept. Take, for example, this question: "How many times have you talked to a doctor about your health during the past month?" The respondent may wonder whether to include telephone consultation, whether visits to chiropractors should be included, whether immunizations are part of health, or whether "past month" refers to the past four weeks or to a calendar month. Whether or not the respondent goes through this process explicitly, he or she must proceed on the basis of assumptions concerning the intended meaning of the question.

Step 2 is the stage of information processing that includes the respondent's assessment of what information he or she needs in order to respond accurately and what cues or frames of reference are relevant. Usually this stage involves searching the memory for relevant information and organizing the material to formulate a response.

For step 3 the respondent must evaluate whether the formulated response fulfills the objectives of the question. If the potential response is judged inadequate, the respondent loops back to repeat some or all of the preceding activities (step 2).

At step 4 a second kind of evaluation occurs as the respondent evaluates the psychological meaning of the response in relation to personal goals extraneous to the survey. Some respondents, however well intentioned, will probably evaluate an intended answer in terms of its potential threat to their personal goals—for instance, self-esteem—in addition to the goal of giving accurate responses. If the potential response is evaluated as nonthreatening, the respondent states the response (step 5).

This brief description of the question-answering process, when it is proceeding ideally, illustrates the demands placed on respondents and the potential complexity of responding to questions. Carrying out this process can be difficult, especially when the question requires considerable effort to produce an accurate response or when the respondent regards the accurate response as embarrassing or otherwise personally uncomfortable. Undoubtedly, there are respondents who accept this task only provisionally; they will attempt to produce accurate responses as long as this does not require much effort on their part and does not embarrass them.

Figure 1 also suggests ways in which the responding process may go awry. While the ideal respondent follows steps 1 through 4 and eventually produces an adequate response (step 5), at any step he or she may deviate to other response modes (step 6) and produce a response (step 7) that is, to some degree, inadequate.

For the respondent who has not understood the question or is not sufficiently skilled or motivated to go through the retrieval and organizational processes, the extraneous situational cues suggested in step 6 are more likely to be the basis for response selection. Even respondents who proceed adequately through step 3 (that is, who formulate a response they judge to be adequate) will undoubtedly evaluate the response further to determine whether it threatens or is incompatible with some other personal goal (step 4). If a threat emerges at this step, the respondent may deviate (steps 6 and 7) and modify his or her potential response or substitute another.

Once the respondent departs from the appropriate answering process (steps 1 to 5) and relies on other situational cues (steps 6 and 7), the response will exhibit some kind of invalidity (step 7). Researchers have labeled the effects on responses of such situational cues as *social desirability bias, acquiescence bias,* and the like. It is sometimes argued that these biases result from the respondent's personality characteristics—such as an "acquiescence trait," a "social desirability trait," or a need for approval—but we assume that the response process is most likely to be shaped by situational cues in the interview itself: from the interviewer, the questionnaire, or the organization for which the research is being conducted. While it may be possible to differentiate people by their willingness to agree or give a socially appropriate response, for our purposes agreeing responses and socially desirable responses are best understood in terms of their perceived appropriateness in the immediate interview situation.

We think that cognitive and motivational difficulties in answering questions are more common and more serious than is generally realized. Questions are often ambiguous in ways that can have important implications for interpreting research data. Questions may make excessive demands on the cognitive skills of respondents by making unrealistic demands on the respondent's memory or ability to process and integrate retrieved information. Finally, the psychological implication of providing responses that truly reflect the respondent's beliefs or experience may lead to suppressing the information or distorting it into a more acceptable response.

The mechanisms of the responses when adequate processing fails are identified in step 7. Their effect is to distort survey data. That is, the reported information varies from truth in some predictable direction. Perhaps the most common distortion is a failure to report information—that is, making "false negative" reports—because of a failure of retrieval and processing (step 2), which may reflect true memory lapse or carelessness and unwillingness to make the effort necessary to retrieve the information. This form of inadequate response is probably the most frequent in reporting of past events and behavior. We shall see several examples of this form of response error in the following pages.

Another common distortion involves making "false positive" reports—that is, falsely reporting events, behavior, or other information. This distortion may occur frequently when a time reference is specified in the question. For example, in answering a question about events occurring within the past month, the respondent may report things that occurred before that month. Such false reports may reflect faulty recall or may be more purposeful. (The respondent may falsely report information that seems to reflect to his or her credit, for example, or seems to meet some other goal.)

Some Data on Response Errors

The purpose of our research has been to develop and test methods for encouraging a smooth progression from comprehending the question to giving a valid response. We are interested in enhancing the respondent's answers to survey questions. What evidence do we have of the prevalence and magnitude of such errors? What are the common detours to response error?

Findings from a number of validity studies may be summarized as follows: Underreporting rates are related to the *elapsed time* between events to be reported and the interview, to the *salience* of events for respondents, and to respondent's *perceptions of the social desirability* of the events. (See, for instance, Sudman and Bradburn, 1974, chap. 3.)

Our own findings, reported here, are obtained from household interviews concerning hospitalization. The existence and availability of independent medical records permitted validation of responses about hospitalization and provided evidence on the reporting of factual information about medical treatment. Other studies support our own findings—for example, studies by Ferber (1966) and Neter and Waksberg (1965) on the reporting of factual information about personal finances and household repairs. Our findings are summarized in the following three paragraphs.

Elapsed Time. As the time between an event and the interview increases, there is increased underreporting of information about that event. This finding will surprise no one; what is unexpected is the *rapidity* with which the failure to report the event increases with time. For visits to physicians, the failure to report the visit increased over a two-week period from 15 percent in interviews one week after the visit to 30 percent in interviews two weeks after (Cannell and Fowler, 1963). Table 1 shows how reporting of hospitalization decreases as the time between the event and the interview increases.

Salience. Events that are important to the individual are reported more completely and accurately than those of less significance. Salience probably reflects the psychological presence of past events or their impact on life at present. Research findings about salience make use of observable characteristics of events that are assumed to be related to the importance of the event to the individual.

TABLE 1
Percentage of Hospitalizations Not Reported in Household Interviews: By Number of Weeks Between Discharge and Interview

Weeks Between Discharge and Interview	Number of Recorded Hospitalizations	Percentage Not Reported in Household Interviews
1–10	114	3
11–20	426	6
21–30	459	9
31–40	339	11
41–50	364	16
51–53	131	42

SOURCE: Cannell, Fisher, and Bakker (1965).

TABLE 2
Percentage of Hospitalizations Not Reported in Household Interviews: By Duration of Hospitalization

Duration of Hospitalization in Days	Number of Recorded Hospitalizations	Percentage Not Reported in Household Interviews
1	150	26
2–4	646	14
5–7	456	10
8–14	352	10
15–21	111	6
22–30	58	1
31 and over	46	8

SOURCE: Cannell, Fisher, and Bakker (1965).

For example, the study of hospitalization reporting found that the longer the hospital stay, the better the reporting (Table 2). Hospitalizations involving operations were better reported than those not involving operations. Similarly, Madow (1967) found that the more visits made to a clinic for a health condition, the better the reporting about the condition.

Social Desirability. Reporting of an event is likely to be distorted in a socially desirable direction. If the event is perceived as embarrassing, sensitive, threatening, or divergent from one's self-image, it is likely not to be reported at all or to be distorted in a desirable direction. To explore the impact of social desirability in reporting hospitalization, a "threat scale" for diagnoses was created to distinguish three levels of threat or embarrassment. All diagnostic classifications that, in the opinion of the raters, would be very embarrassing or threatening were placed in level 1. Level 3 included classifications judged neither embarrassing nor threatening. Level 2 contained a mixture of classifications that were thought to be somewhat threatening, or possibly threatening, to some persons but not to others. Comparisons of underreporting rates for hospitalization associated with conditions classified in the three threat-scale levels of embarrassment revealed threat to be an important predictor. As Table 3 shows, hospitalizations associated with clearly embarrassing conditions were underreported at twice the rate as hospital stays for less threatening maladies.

These findings for social desirability in health reporting are similar to effects found for reporting of other types of experiences. For

TABLE 3
Percentage of Hospitalizations Not Reported in Household Interviews:
By Diagnostic Threat Rating

Diagnostic Threat Rating	Number of Recorded Hospitalizations	Percentage Not Reported in Household Interviews
Very threatening (level 1)	235	21
Somewhat threatening (level 2)	421	14
Not threatening (level 3)	1,164	10

SOURCE: Cannell, Fisher, and Bakker (1965).

example, Lansing, Ginsberg, and Braaten (1961) found that primary car loans are reported well but secondary loans are greatly underreported. Conversely, desirable behavior tends to be overreported: Voting is one such act (Parry and Crossley, 1950); saving money is another (Ferber, 1966). Bradburn and others (1979) find underreporting of bankruptcy and drunken driving and overreporting of possession of library cards and voting in primary elections.

To summarize these findings, the combined effects of threat, salience, and elapsed time since the event on reporting of hospitalization is presented in Table 4. In line with the earlier findings, hospital stays that were short, occurred a long time before the interview, and were associated with embarrassing illnesses were the ones most underreported.

Underreporting is only one type of response error. As

TABLE 4
Percentage of Hospitalizations Not Reported in Household Interviews:
By Duration of Hospitalization, Number of Weeks Between Discharge and Interview, and Diagnostic Threat Rating

Number of Weeks Between Discharge and Interview	Number of Recorded Hospitalizations	Diagnostic Threat Rating		
		Most Threatening	Somewhat Threatening	Least Threatening
Duration 1–4 days				
1–20	223	7	9	7
21–40	355	26	16	9
41–53	219	56	27	27
Duration 5 days or more				
1–20	308	0	7	3
21–40	442	15	5	3
41–53	273	33	22	17

SOURCE: Cannell, Fisher, and Bakker (1965).

mentioned, characteristics and events that appear to be socially desirable may be exaggerated. But the magnitude of the underreporting problem suggests the potentially larger extent of the response error in general, considering the fact that the variable we have focused on here—hospitalization—seems to be a straightforward issue when compared to the many other questions asked in surveys. The demonstration that survey reports of hospitalization experiences differ from the recorded events in predictable, significant ways gives one pause about the quality of survey measures generally. Morover, it buttresses the conclusion that the response task is likely to be much more difficult for respondents than survey practitioners commonly believe.

Time lapse, salience, and social desirability are terms that describe the undoubtedly complex response process diagrammed in Figure 1. The problems presented by time lapse involve cognitive processing of the question demands, defining what information is relevant, recalling it, and organizing it (step 2). The errors in response could come at any or all of these stages. Additionally, when the demands of these retrieval tasks become too difficult, other response sources, such as norms of self-presentation or reaction to interviewer cues (step 6), may come into play. Salience describes the psychological importance of experiences and feelings; the most prominent are the most easily recalled and reported. Asking questions about nonsalient events may place such a burden on memory that other means for producing a response come into play. Finally, when cognitive tasks posed by questions exceed the effort exerted by respondents, or when an accurate response is perceived as conflicting with a norm of self-presentation, a socially desirable response may be given instead of the accurate answer. Respondents may, in fact, filter their veridical responses to give only those that are not ego threatening (as described by the line from step 4 to step 6 in Figure 1).

In summary, then, elapsed time, lack of salience, and social desirability are factors that, when involved in the response tasks we present to respondents, influence the departure from the straight-and-narrow route to veridical answers presented in the model. These issues appear to be embodied in many cases of response error.

Standard Interviewing Practice

How are interviewers trained to reduce response errors stemming from the sources we have just outlined? One important aspect of interviewer training is inculcating the idea that the interviewer should be nondirective: He or she should not provide respondents with cues about the "correct" answers and certainly should not express any opinions to the respondent. This basic component of interviewer neutrality grew out of the recognition of the potential for interviewer bias in early surveys. The idea of rapport is often mentioned in discussions of interviewing technique as well. By establishing friendly contact, the interviewer is supposed to gain the respondent's confidence so that self-disclosure is less threatening. The combination of a nondirective approach and rapport is supposed to reduce response error by removing the pressure from the respondent to maintain a totally positive self-presentation and by motivating the respondent to work hard. Overall, the respondent is supposed to get the message that it is all right to reveal himself or herself accurately.

The problem with this notion is that the neutral, or nondirective, interviewer style frequently does not sufficiently motivate or inform respondents. The survey interview is a rare experience for most people, and they need guidance to appropriate response behavior. The cues to the respondent for deciding when an adequate response has been rendered are obscure; and they are likely to remain so if the interviewer sticks to the simple rules of being nondirective and friendly. In fact, respondents in many studies may be ignorant of the most simple facts concerning the interview—the purpose of the investigation and the auspices under which the survey is conducted.

In a survey of 412 respondents following their participation in a National Health Survey interview (Cannell, Fowler, and Marquis, 1968), it was found that although respondents had been informed that the survey was being conducted for the U.S. Public Health Service by the Bureau of the Census, nearly half (45 percent) said they did not know what agency was doing the survey or the agency for which it was done, and only 11 percent identified the Census Bureau. The others who made any identification did so only vaguely—"some government agency," "a state agency," and so forth. When asked why they thought the information was being collected, respondents were also very vague; more than half said they had no idea. Of those who did report something, most answered only in general terms, such as "for statistical purposes."

Moreover, the study examined respondents' perceptions of the interviewers' expectations and goals. A major part of the health interview consisted of questions of specific health conditions such as illnesses, days of disability, medication taken, and chronic conditions. Other questions concerned health events such as the number of physician visits and hospitalizations. Although the questionnaire had been set up to obtain specific and complete reports, only about half the respondents said the interviewer wanted exact information; the others thought that general ideas were adequate. Three quarters of the respondents thought the interviewer wanted a report of everything; the rest thought only the important things were to be mentioned. Such findings suggest reasons for poor respondent performance. The respondents do not know what is expected of them. They understand neither the general goals of the survey nor specifically what they are supposed to do on particular questions.

The argument can be made that, while extrinsic motives seem to be absent from respondents' retrospective reports, forces are generated in the interview that help to establish goals and produce motivation. To learn what messages, instructions, or cues are directed to the respondent and how the interviewer performs the task—both in terms of communicating expectations and in motivating good reporting performance—several hundred interviews were analyzed (Marquis and Cannell, 1969). The analyses were based on tape recordings of household interviews. Of particular interest was the frequency of different interviewer behaviors and when they occurred. Table 5 shows a typical distribution of frequencies.

Most surprising was the finding that, with the exception of asking or repeating questions from the questionnaire, the most frequent interviewer behavior was to give the respondent some type of

TABLE 5
Percentages of Different Interviewer Behaviors Coded from Tape-Recorded Interviews

Interviewer Behavior	Percentage
Question-asking activity	37
Probing (includes repeating questions)	22
Clarifying and providing information	9
Feedback	26
Irrelevant activity (conversations, humor)	4
Other	2
	100

NOTE: Number of interviews = 181.
SOURCE: Marquis and Cannell (1969).

feedback. As defined in the study, feedback consisted of any evaluative or affective response by the interviewer to a respondent behavior. In these interviews the feedback—frequently a short comment ("um-hum, I see," "all right," "okay," "that's interesting," "that's good")—was inevitably a positive evaluation. Other types of feedback were more elaborate, consisting of summaries of the respondent's replies, statements of how well the respondent was performing, and so on.

As Table 6 shows, interviewers delivered such feedback indiscriminately for both good and poor respondent behavior. Adequate or appropriate answers (that is, desirable behavior) received proportionately fewer positive feedback responses than did several other less desirable answers. In fact, refusal to answer a question, the worst possible behavior, received proportionately the greatest verbal rewards ("that's OK," "you're doing fine"). Interviewers delivered these statements to maintain a positive relationship with respondents, but the comments can also be seen as reinforcing undesirable response performance. We questioned whether this self-styled, friendly approach by the interviewers was necessary, given its potential drawbacks.

Feedback, properly used, is an effective means of influencing behavior in desired directions. If the behavior of the interviewers in this study can be taken as a guide, the techniques are not being used by survey interviewers in ways that promote good respondent behavior. Rather, interviewers appear to use it primarily to reassure the respondent (and themselves) by indicating receptivity and approval of

TABLE 6
Probability of Interviewer Feedback After Different Respondent Behaviors

Respondent Behavior	Probability of Feedback
Adequate answer	0.28
Inadequate answer	0.24
"Don't know" answer	0.18
Refusal to answer	0.55
Other answer	0.34
Elaboration	0.30
Repeats answer	0.32
Gives suggestion	0.33
Other behavior	0.21

NOTE: Number of interviews = 181.
SOURCE: Marquis and Cannell (1969).

any response—including refusal to respond. Thus a potentially powerful technique for influencing behavior is used inappropriately. Neither the Survey Research Center's program for training interviewers, nor any other the authors know of, includes specific training in feedback techniques. Interviewers have been doing what they think best, or what comes naturally, with virtually no guidance from research staff.

The data illuminate another weakness. Interviewers demonstrated considerable variability in the frequency and contingency with which they used various techniques. Not only were techniques often used ineffectively, but the variability threatened the goal of uniform procedures.

What do these observations imply for the question-answering process outlined in Figure 1? Adequate responding requires that respondents understand the response task well enough to proceed from step 1 to step 5, avoiding steps 6 and 7; and further, it requires that they be motivated to do an adequate job of carrying out the activities described in steps 1 through 5. The observations of typical interviewing suggest that these conditions are not met: Respondents often do not understand task requirements and often are not motivated to undertake them. Most respondents may accurately report information that is readily accessible and nonthreatening. As tasks become more demanding, however, respondents may not comprehend the reporting task adequately, may not work hard enough to retrieve information from memory and organize it efficiently, and may not accept even a minimal risk of embarrassment. Two statements summarize our ideas about the response task in survey interviews:

1. The task demand level (difficulty) is the sum of the cognitive demands imposed by the requirements for information retrieval and processing and the affective demands imposed by the threat of the information requested.
2. The quality of respondent performance is a function of the difficulty of the task and the level of effort achieved by the respondent.

Current interviewing procedures do not adequately take into account the difficulty of many reporting tasks, nor do they adequately motivate respondents to undertake them. Further, the variability in interviewers' use of techniques threatens the comparability of data from different interviews. To improve the validity of the survey interview, new techniques and new standards of measurement are required. To translate these objectives into operations, one can say that the questionnaire and interviewing techniques should:

1. Teach the respondent what is expected of him or her in general in order to perform the task properly.
2. Inform the respondent and provide cues as to how to be most efficient in answering specific questions.
3. Encourage the respondent to work diligently to recall and organize information and to report even potentially embarrassing material.
4. Ensure standard techniques for greater comparability among interviews.

IMPROVING INTERVIEWING TECHNIQUES

Question Length and Response Modeling

Question Length. Our finding that respondents did not have a clear idea of the role they were supposed to play in the interview led to an exploration of several avenues of providing this information. One of the techniques we tried was based on work by Matarazzo, Wren, and Saslow (1965) on the effect of long questions in interviews. The hypothesis was that the extra cues given by the longer questions might help to communicate to respondents the nature of their role and how to perform it. Matarazzo's studies demonstrated that respondents in personnel interviews tended to adjust the length of their responses to the length of the interviewer's inquiries, a finding that challenged the usual principle of making questions short and simple. We experimented with questions that were two or three times as long as a control, using redundancies to avoid introducing additional content. Example:

Short question: What health problems have you had in the past year?

Long question: The next question asks about health problems during the last year. This is something we are asking everyone in the survey. What health problems have you had in the past year.?

Results showed that while the *length* of the response to the longer questions was not significantly greater, a greater number of relevant health events were reported. Since a questionnaire consisting only of long questions is oppressive, we interspersed long and short questions. We found that not only did the longer questions obtain more reporting of health events, but the short questions did also (Cannell, Marquis, and Laurent, 1977).

There are at least three possible interpretations of the findings: (1) The long question is essentially stating the question twice, and this may improve the respondent's understanding of what is wanted; (2) the question is actually stated in the first sentence but cannot be answered until it is completed, thus enforcing a response time lag that the respondent may use to consider the question and think about a response; and (3) a motivational interpretation suggests that the long question indicated the serious intention and interest of the interviewer, encouraging greater attention and effort by the respondent.

Modeling. Another line of investigation focused on direct modeling of response behavior as a means of giving respondents an idea of how to behave in the interview (Henson, 1973). Short recorded excerpts of a "model respondent" replying to questions were played for the respondent at two points during the interview. In the recording a respondent answered questions similar to those being asked in the interview. The model respondent was depicted as considering each question carefully, asking the interviewer for clarification, and providing detailed responses.

This cumbersome technique had mixed results. Some respondents showed significant improvement in reporting; others reacted negatively to what they regarded at patronizing. Whether the result was effective or not appeared to depend on the interviewer's attitude. In a poststudy survey of interviewers, some reported that they found the procedures oppressive and perceived respondents as being negative. Other interviewers were interested in the experimental procedures. Results tended to conform to these interviewers' attitudes.

Instructions

Both the investigations of question length and modeling, though strictly exploratory and, in the second case, tentative in the findings, seemed to support the notion that respondent behavior could be improved by a technique which attempted to increase knowledge of the reporting task—either indirectly or directly. Ruminating on these results, it seemed that both the advantages of the long questions and the directness of the modeling approach could be captured simply by adding instructional passages to the interview. Such additions would, in effect, alter the question length and provide direct information on role performance at the same time.

The idea behind the use of instructions is simple. To perform a task adequately, one needs to know what is expected: what the task is and how to perform it. If this is not known already, an efficient way to transmit this information for many tasks is through explicit, verbal instructions that clarify goals by specifying what is to be accomplished and by setting forth the criteria for good performance. Moreover, instructions clarify the specific actions involved in achieving the goals (Gagné, 1964; Hackman, 1969).

The goal of a survey interview is to obtain complete and accurate answers from the respondent. Yet respondents often appear not to understand this, and interviews often do not adequately communicate this information. Information about goals, if imparted at all, is usually limited to a general statement of the survey's purpose (for example, "to find out about the health of the American population"). It appears that respondents often do not connect the survey goal to their behavior in the interview.

One function of instructions, then, is to clarify for the respondent the purpose of the interview. This includes not only a statement of the goal of the research, but also a statement of the respondent's behavior in relation to this goal—that is, to provide complete and accurate information. As a further aid, instructions may clarify for respondents what should *not* be their goal—for example, that the interviewer is not from the welfare department, so they need not be concerned about appearing to be a worthy recipient. A study of health reporting by Oksenberg, Vinokur, and Cannell (1979b) provides an example of the "global" instruction. After introducing the topic of the interview, interviewers told respondents:

> In order for your answers to be most helpful to us, it is important that you try to be as accurate as you can. Since we need complete and accurate information from this research, we hope you will think hard to provide the information we need.

A second function of instructions in the interview is to detail how the respondent should go about producing complete and accurate information. As is true for the goal of the interview, respondents typically are given very little information about *how* to answer questions adequately. Instructions about the operations needed for adequate performance include such things as carefully considering each question, being diligent in retrieving and organizing information needed for responding, and requesting clarification if a question is not understood. Instructions may also point out the importance of considering various frames of reference and taking all the time necessary to answer adequately. For example, interviewers in the health study gave respondents the following specific advice:

> Some people want to know what they can do to give accurate and complete information. We know that people do better when they think carefully about each question, search their memory, and take their time in answering. People also do better if they give exact answers and give as much information as they can. This includes important things as well as things which may seem small or unimportant. Please tell me when a question is not clear, and I will read it again. For some questions you may want to take time out and look for the answer by checking whatever is available to you in the house, so we can be sure we get complete and accurate answers.

In addition to these general guides, instructions can be tailored to the needs of specific questions. Such instructions can clarify the objective of a question or suggest efficient ways to retrieve relevant information for a particular question. One question might specify that we want to find out *exact* dates of doctor visits; another might suggest that respondents think of each TV program viewed in the evening before to help them recall the total amount of time spent viewing. Instructions in the interview help to establish a clear goal for the respondent and provide guidance for performance.

Apart from these directive functions, instructions may have an instigative function (Marlatt, 1972). That is, instructions can help to motivate performance. The inclusion of instructions in a question lengthens the question and, as described earlier, lengthening questions has been shown to increase the amount of information given by respondents. One hypothesis is that the effect is generated by communicating to the respondent an atmosphere of serious intent and interviewer involvement.

Reinforcement and Feedback

The extensive theoretical frameworks dealing with the effects of reinforcement on learning and performance provide one of the cornerstones of psychology. These theories are associated with the work of Pavlov and Hull and the research of Skinner (1957), Dollard and Miller (1950), and Ullman and Krasner (Krasner, 1958). The last four researchers are known for their work in psychotherapy and behavior modification. In the past 25 years, many researchers have used verbal reinforcers to alter verbal behavior. Researchers have demonstrated that simple verbal pronouncements such as "um-hmm" or "all right" in response to certain words or statements have reinforcement effects that increase production of such words or statements (Taffel, 1955; Greenspoon, 1955; Verplanck, 1955; Centers, 1964).

Reinforcement appeared to have considerable potential for improving responses in the survey interview. Several studies (ours and those of other investigators such as Hildum and Brown, 1956) have demonstrated that verbal reinforcement can significantly alter respondent behavior. Our first studies programmed typical verbal reinforcers for use after each "good" report. A list of chronic conditions and symptoms was administered, and a positive reinforcement was given for each yes response ("thanks," "that's useful," "OK"). When reporting an illness in answer to an open question was similarly reinforced, reporting increased significantly (Marquis and Cannell, 1969). In general, the findings were that reinforcement increases respondent activity and usually increases the reporting level.

We were concerned, however, that respondents might be learning the wrong lesson from the reinforcing patterns. They might have thought that the interviewer was indicating approval of the *content* of the response or approval of the respondent's behavior, or that the interviewer was only indicating interest. Since our goal was not simply to obtain higher frequencies but more valid reporting, we had to be certain that the reinforcing technique was not just introducing new biases into the reporting process. What we required were techniques that would teach the respondent what was expected and reward proper performance. That is, it was essential to reward for good respondent *role performance,* not for content or kind of information reported. This concern led to a broad consideration of feedback techniques. The combination of instructions to inform the respondent of what was expected and feedback to inform and reinforce good role performance was essential. Instructions established the contingency for the reinforcement.

Feedback is, of course, widely used in teaching task performance in a wide variety of activities. This is particularly true for tasks that are hard to perform, tasks for which the goals or necessary behaviors are difficult to describe, or tasks that involve behavior the respondent may be reluctant to carry out. To complete the picture one needs some type of information that helps respondents to apply the instructions to their own performance and to evaluate their success. Verbal feedback about performance *efforts* can serve the valuable function of further specifying and confirming the performance *criteria.* It can also help to motivate good performance through its reinforcing properties. When a person succeeds in performing a task or part of a task, the approval contained in the feedback can act as an incentive for further good performance. As behavior modification theorists have long argued, such reinforcements have an impact on behavior apart from their teaching value.

Most interviewers do not exploit these potential uses of feedback. To be sure, interviewers are trained to probe individual responses that do not appear to meet study objectives, using nondirective probes such as "Can you tell me more about that?" or "Is there anything else?" While these probes elicit more information from respondents, they may not communicate task requirements efficiently and may even misdirect respondents if used indiscriminately.

Because an interview is an ambiguous situation for the respondent and because of the possibilities for misinterpreting the object of the feedback, the feedback needs to be carefully constructed and applied so the respondent perceives the underlying intent—to encourage good performance, for example, or to correct poor performance and redirect it appropriately.

Coordination of the content and timing of instructions and feedback is essential. For example, a question requiring the respondent to recall information about events in the past may include the instruction, "For this question you may need to take some time before answering." Responses preceded by several seconds of thought can be followed by feedback such as "Thanks, we appreciate your effort." Instructions linked to specific questions and closely followed by relevant feedback can help respondents to understand just what their task is, to determine how well they are performing, and to become motivated to perform it.

In contrast to instructions, which are standardized for all respondents, feedback is contingent on the assumed quality of their reporting performance. Interviewers are provided with objective criteria and a set of appropriate feedback statements, all of which are printed in the questionnaire. Interviewers judge the quality of the respondent's performance by these criteria and select the feedback statements appropriate to the performance. Feedback is contingent on amounts of information, precision, deliberateness in answering, or use of specified answer categories—measures of apparent effort and attention to the task requirements. Positive or negative feedback is used to indicate adequate or poor performance to the respondent. The following are examples of positive feedback:

Uh-huh. I see. This is the kind of information we want.
Thanks. You've mentioned ______ things.
Thanks, we appreciate your frankness.
Uh-huh. We are interested in details like these.

These are examples of negative feedback:

You answered that quickly.
Sometimes it's easy to forget all the things you felt or noticed here.
Could you think about it again?
That's only ______ things.

The following example from the Oksenberg, Vinokur, and Cannell study (1979b) illustrates how feedback works. Preceding a question on recent bodily injuries was a brief instruction: "Let me just say that it helps to think back carefully over the time period we are talking about." Then came the question: "People often get injuries such as cuts, bruises, burns, and so on. Have you been injured in any way within the last two weeks?" Any report of an injury was taken as evidence that the respondent had made an effort to do a good job of reporting, and respondents making such a report were told, "Uh-huh. We are interested in getting details like this." This was followed by a standard probe question: "Was there anything else, even something small?" In contrast to this sequence, respondents who quickly replied that they had no injuries were judged not to have made enough effort to recall possible injuries and were told, "You answered that quickly." This comment was followed by the standard probe question: "Was there anything at all, even something small?"

Putting instructions and contingent feedback statements in a questionnaire involves some assumptions about the extent and direction of response error. In the preceding example, we assume that injuries are underreported (as validity studies in health indicate). Therefore the instruction for this question asked the respondent to consider the matter carefully before answering in order to recall any nonsalient events. The feedback approach follows directly from the instruction. Respondents who take time and produce an affirmative response are told that they have met the expectations; the others receive messages tailored to their response style. We deliberately manipulate the communication from interviewer to respondent in line with our expectations about response error.

The feedback is programmed into the questionnaire, and interviewers practice delivering these statements until they can give them in a way that sounds spontaneous. By means of contingent feedback such as this, the expectations for complete and accurate reporting are related to the respondent's behavior in answering particular questions. Respondents are coached on specific ways they might improve their reporting performance and are rewarded when they appear to be making an effort to do a good job. The combination of instructions and contingent feedback serves the dual function of establishing performance standards and increasing the respondent's motivation to perform well.

Commitment

Another technique for motivating performance is to obtain a formal commitment from the respondent to be diligent in performing the task. This technique appears to be a valuable complement to the use of instructions and feedback for improving the respondent's question-answering performance.

Despite the oft-discussed proliferation of surveys, being interviewed is still a novel experience for most people. In the absence of behavioral norms, they are likely to treat the event as a lark—an unimportant and uninvolving activity. The effectiveness of instructions and, to a certain extent, the effectiveness of feedback are based on the assumption that the individual is motivated to conform to the interviewers' expectations for performance. The commitment technique represents one approach to the problem of motivating respondents to devote the effort necessary for accurate and complete reporting. The technique involves having the respondent make an overt agreement to work hard to provide complete and accurate information during the course of the interview.

The idea behind the use of such an agreement is that stating one's intention to behave in a certain way *commits* the person to carry out the terms of the agreement. Even in the absence of the enforcement measures found in formal contracts and treaties, the act of agreement itself apparently commits the actor to carry out the agreement. The research most relevant to the commitment technique includes some of the classic studies in social psychology, most of which were undertaken within the theoretical framework associated with Kurt Lewin (Lewin, 1951; Bennett, 1955). The studies suggest that if one wants an individual to perform a certain task, it is necessary to gain his or her acceptance of task completion as the goal or as a necessary step on the path to that goal. The studies further suggest that implicit or explicit agreement to carry out the task is an effective means of gaining goal acceptance and that a decision to perform a task is, in itself, motivating. The concept has received considerable attention in social psychology and sociology. In sociology, commitment has been used to account for the fact that people can persist in consistent goal-related activity even in the face of adverse experiences that could be expected to discourage them from further effort (Becker, 1960; Goffman, 1961; Johnson, 1973). In social psychology, commitment has become a key concept for theoretical positions growing out of cognitive dissonance theory (Brehm and Cohen, 1962; Gerard, Conolley, and Wilhelmy, 1974; Kiesler, 1971).

In the application to interviewing, the concept of commitment is valuable in clarifying why the respondent's agreement to carry out the activities that result in good respondent performance should lead to improved performance. The goal the respondent has agreed to pursue is to furnish complete and accurate answers to the interviewer's questions. The goal-related activities include diligent application of the respondent's cognitive skills and resistance of impulses to alter responses because of anticipated undesirable effects. Explicit agreement to carry out these activities binds the respondent to such actions.

In line with this theory, we have asked respondents in personal interviews to sign an agreement (after a few introductory questions) promising to do their best to report accurately. In telephone interviews, we have elicited a verbal promise. The interviewer, in turn, gives a written or verbal promise to keep all information gained in the interview confidential. Interviews with respondents who refuse to commit themselves to accurate reporting are terminated. Although one might think that such cases are numerous, in the various studies we have conducted using this technique, all but about 5 percent of the respondents have completed the agreement.

Thus instructions, feedback, and commitment are features of the questionnaire as we design it for interviewers. Exhibits 1 and 2 illustrate how these procedures look in practice. In Exhibit 1, two instruction-feedback linkages are presented: one dealing with health and the other with mass media. The instructions, appearing before the major questions, are italicized, as are the various contingent feedback statements. Exhibit 2 details the interviewer's scripted statement introducing the commitment and a copy of the agreement signed by respondents and interviewers in personal interviews.

Pace

Having discussed three new experimental interviewing methods, we need to add another technique that is not new but is certainly a valuable complement to the new procedures—the pace at which the interview is conducted. In our experience, nearly all interviewers

EXHIBIT 1
Instruction-Feedback Examples

SICKNESS EXPERIENCES

Q1. *Let me just mention that, to be most accurate, you may need to take your time to think carefully before you answer.* (PAUSE) Have you been sick in any way within the last two weeks?

If R says yes:
1a. In what ways were you sick?
1b. *Uh-huh, I see. This is the kind of information we want.* Were you sick in any other ways within the last two weeks?

If R says no within 5 seconds:
1c. *You answered that quickly.* Were you sick in any way at all in the last two weeks?
1d. (ANY MENTION) *Thanks, this is the kind of information we want.*

If R says no after 5 seconds:
1e. Were you sick in any way at all within the last two weeks?
1f. (ANY MENTION) *Thanks, this is the kind of information we want.*

TELEVISION WATCHING

Q2. *On this next question, we'd like to get numbers as exact as possible.* How many hours did you personally spend watching television yesterday?

Exact number:
2a. *I see . . . thanks.*

Approximation:
2b. Can you be any more exact about the number of hours?
2c. (EXACT NUMBER) *I see . . . thanks.*

No response, don't know:
2d. Let me repeat the question. How many hours did you personally spend watching television yesterday?
2e. (EXACT NUMBER) *I see . . . thanks.*

proceed through the interview too quickly; they ask questions at a rapid rate, permit no pause between response and the next question, and jump into the interaction with fast feedback. The atmosphere created is hasty and casual. The interviewer's major goal seems to be to finish the interview.

For instructions, commitment, and feedback to be effective, they must be delivered in an atmosphere that supports their use. We have trained interviewers to ask questions slowly and with proper phrasing and inflection. The recommended pace is, on the average, two words per second.

EXHIBIT 2
COMMITMENT PROCEDURE EXAMPLE

That's the last of this set of questions. The rest of the questions are on how media like newspapers, TV, and radio fit into your daily life. We are asking people we interview to give us extra cooperation and that they try hard to answer accurately so we can get complete and accurate information about this topic. You are one of the people we hope is willing to make the extra effort.

Here is an agreement that explains what we are asking you to do. (HAND AGREEMENT) As you can see, it says, "I understand that the information from this interview must be very accurate in order to be useful. This means that I must do my best to give accurate and complete answers. I agree to do this."

We are asking people to sign an agreement and keep it for themselves so that we can be sure they understand what we are asking them to do. It is up to you to decide. If you are willing to agree to do this, we'd like you to sign your name here. (POINT OUT LINE) Down below there is a statement about confidentiality, and I will sign my name there. (POINT OUT LINE)

(IF R HAS NOT ALREADY SIGNED) Are you willing to make the extra effort to continue the interview?

AGREEMENT

I understand that the information from this interview must be very accurate in order to be useful. This means that I must do my best to give accurate and complete answers. I agree to do this.

____
Signature of Respondent

All information that would permit identification of the people being interviewed as part of this project will be held in strict confidence. No information that would allow identification will be disclosed or released to others for any purpose.

____
Signature of Interviewer

Rapport

Programming and standardizing the interviewer's array of techniques into the questionnaire gives the interview a less chatty quality than is ordinarily present. While there are clear advantages to standardizing these procedures, an interview structured in this way, focusing on task performance rather than on the personal components of the interaction, might not be well received by respondents. One of the mainstays of theories about good interviewing has been the concept of establishing rapport between the interviewer and the respondent. Although there is considerable lack of agreement on what rapport *is* (Weiss, 1970), the term usually implies a positively affective and personalized interactive style. The power of rapport to stimulate good respondent behavior is so widely accepted that we could not afford to abandon it without some evidence that it was unnecessary.

Preliminary investigations showed that respondents tolerated a variety of techniques without negative reactions and without apparent deterioration of the quality of reports (Henson, 1973). We then conducted a study designed to answer the question of whether a personal interactive style was necessary or whether respondents performed as well in a task-oriented interview. We studied a sample of people who had had an automobile accident within the past three years resulting in some bodily injury. Half the sample was interviewed using a rapport-type interview—the interviewer made personal references, expressed positive affect, smiled, nodded, made supportive comments, and so forth. The other half was given an interview in which *research* goals were stressed. While the rapport interviewer said, "You are doing a good job; you are a good respondent," the other's comments were task-oriented: "That's the kind of information we need. This helps our research." The task-oriented interviewer was not permitted to socialize. The results showed no significant difference in completeness or accuracy of reporting for the two groups. In fact, there was some tendency for the task-oriented group to report accidents occurring three years prior to the interview more accurately (Henson, Cannell, and Lawson, 1976).

When asked their reactions to the interview, respondents in the rapport interview were somewhat more likely to report that the interviewer was friendly, but neither group showed any negative reactions to the interview. Based on these findings, we abandoned the rapport style and began to substitute techniques that are certainly not cold or unfriendly but do focus attention on performance of the response task rather than on personal affect. In the remainder of this chapter we present a series of experimental tests of the three interviewing techniques just described.

EXPERIMENTS WITH THE NEW TECHNIQUES

With the development of the ideas of instructions, contingent feedback, and commitment as applied to survey interviewing, a series of studies was undertaken to assess their effectiveness in improving reporting performance.

First Study: Contingent Feedback and Commitment

The combination of contingent feedback and commitment received our first attention (Oksenberg, Vinokur, and Cannell, 1979a; Vinokur, Oksenberg, and Cannell, 1979). The procedures were developed and tested in a study of the reporting of a variety of health-related information.

The Sample. Respondents in this experimental survey were 515 white women between the ages of 18 and 64 from suburban Detroit. The entire sample was asked the same set of questions but was divided randomly into three groups (two experimental and one control) according to which interviewing techniques were used: contingent feedback (153 respondents), commitment (184 respondents), and control (170 respondents).

In the contingent feedback condition, respondents received positive or negative feedback depending on how closely they conformed to desirable question-answering performance. In the commitment condition, respondents were asked to sign an agreement promising to do their best to give accurate and complete answers. Both the feedback and the commitment procedures included some task and role instructions. In the control condition, respondents received neither the feedback nor the commitment procedures; otherwise, their interviewing conditions were the same as for the two experimental groups. It should be noted that for the control condition, as for the other two, the interview was highly structured, restricting the interviewer to specific behavior, and thus did not represent "typical" interviewing conditions versus "feedback" and "commitment" conditions.

Experimental Procedures and Measures. Fourteen women were employed as interviewers. Each was trained in all three procedures, and interviewing behavior was closely controlled in all three conditions. For the feedback and commitment conditions, separate versions of the questionnaire were provided, each specifying the interviewer behavior appropriate to the condition. For all three conditions, the questionnaire provided a script that the interviewer was instructed to follow without deviation. The techniques in all three conditions differed from typical interviewing practice in several ways. Interviewers did not probe at their own discretion but used standard probe questions incorporated in the questionnaire. Unless it was scripted as part of the feedback procedure, no feedback was allowed. Interviewers could not smile or nod the head or offer comments such as

"Uh-huh," "I see," "OK." Moreover, personal or other irrelevant conversation was to be avoided. Other interviewer behavior, such as responses to respondents' requests for clarification, was carefully standardized. A large part of interviewer training was devoted to achieving a high degree of conformity to these rules.

The questionnaire was designed to tap a wide range of respondent experience and to allow good reporting behavior to be identified. It contained both closed and open questions, the latter including open questions about physical condition, episodes of illness, symptoms, medication taken, and other health-related matters. It was assumed that the more information given in response to such open questions, the more accurate and complete the responses were likely to be (Table 7). One measure was the number of ideas reported in response to each of the 18 open questions. A second open-question measure was the total number of doctor visits reported for a certain time period.

It was also assumed that good reporting behavior is evidenced by precision in reporting. Thus additional measures were based on the precision with which certain information was reported to questions asking about visits to doctors and dentists, dates of activity curtailment, and recent medical events. Responses were scored for preciseness—how close the report was to specifying a single day. For each event reported, a respondent was given a score of 1 if the date was precise and 0 if it was not. For questions about visits to doctors and dentists, as well as instances of recent health-related activity curtailment (both limited to a short reporting period), a reported date was considered precise if the day and month were given ("May 28"). For questions about five medical events (x-rays, shots, and the like) with long reporting periods, a date was considered precise if the month and year were given ("June 1973"). For each respondent, a precision score (the proportion of dates reported precisely) was computed; the results are presented in Table 7.

Another measure of effort was based on responses to an open question asking for a report of everything the respondent had eaten or drunk the previous day. One of the measures based on these responses was specification of *amounts* of foods or beverages consumed ("two cups of coffee"). Such specifications were considered more precise than mentions of food or beverages without specific amounts ("coffee"). The precision index for this measure was the number of times the respondent mentioned specific amounts.

TABLE 7
Mean Scores on Measures of Respondent Performance by Experimental Condition: First Study—Contingent Feedback and Commitment

Performance Measure	Experimental Condition		
	Control	Feedback	Commitment
Amount of information			
No. of items to 18 open questions	61.76	71.96**	70.00**
No. of doctor visits	1.45	1.84	1.96
Indices of precision			
Dates of doctor visits[a]	0.54	0.58	0.63
Dates of activity curtailment[a]	0.54	0.38	0.64
Dates of dentist visits[a]	0.61	0.51	0.69
All three of above[a]	0.55	0.49	0.64*
Dates of five medical events[b]	0.44	0.53*	0.47
Specification of amounts of food eaten	4.19	4.66	5.12*
Checking outside information sources	0.61	0.65	0.72*
Reporting treatment for nervous condition	0.22	0.27	0.29
No. of items reported for pelvic region	0.44	0.75**	0.86***

NOTE: For the control, feedback, and commitment groups, $N = 170$, 153, and 184, respectively. For the indices of precision labeled "dates of doctor visits," "dates of activity curtailment," "dates of dentist visits," and "all three of above," N ranged from 53 to 163 for the three experimental treatments. Only respondents who reported at least one appropriate event for each measure received a precision index score, resulting in the reductions in N. For "dates of five medical events," $N = 183$ for the commitment group.

[a]Precise-to-day index.

[b]Precise-to-month index.

*Differs significantly from control group mean, $p < 0.05$, two-tailed t test.

**Differs significantly from control group mean, $p < 0.01$, two-tailed t test.

***Differs significantly from control group mean, $p < 0.001$, two-tailed t test.

SOURCE: Based on analyses reported in Oksenberg, Vinokur, and Cannell (1979a) and Vinokur, Oksenberg, and Cannell (1979).

On the assumption that accurate reporting should sometimes involve consulting outside sources of information, we included as a measure the number of times the respondent checked such sources (medical records, medicine cabinet, refrigerator) in response to questions for which such behavior would be helpful in answering.

Finally, on the assumption that good reporting behavior includes disclosing potentially embarrassing or threatening personal information, we included two questions: One asked whether the respondent had ever been treated for a mental or nervous condition of any kind; the other asked for reports of symptoms and conditions in the pelvic region.

Results. Compared to control respondents, commitment and contingent feedback respondents performed better on a number of these measures (Table 7). First, both the feedback and commitment groups reported significantly more information than the control group in response to the 18 open questions—the most general performance measure. Both the feedback and commitment groups reported significantly more presumably embarrassing information about the pelvic region than the control group. Although both commitment and feedback respondents reported about 30 percent more recent doctor visits than control respondents, the differences ($p < 0.10$ in both instances) missed the conventional 5 percent level of significance.

The indices of precision presented a mixed picture. Only an index combining the three "precise-to-day" indices yielded significant increases, and the increase was only for the commitment group. In contrast, only the contingent feedback group showed significantly better reporting of the dates of five medical events where the "precise-to-month" index was applied. Moreover, as shown in Table 7, the commitment group specified *amounts* of food eaten significantly more often than the control ("two cups of coffee" scored 1; "coffee" scored 0). Likewise, the commitment group was significantly more likely to check some external source of information to help in answering.

While reporting performance did not improve on every measure, there were enough shifts to indicate the value of both the commitment and the feedback procedures. Two questions, however, remained. The first was whether combining both procedures in the same interview would lead to even greater improvements. The second was whether the feedback and commitment techniques could be made even more effective by combining them with substantial task instructions. The second study investigated these topics.

Second Study: Combining Instructions, Contingent Feedback, and Commitment

For the second study, we used different combinations of the three techniques—task instructions, contingent feedback, and commitment—and compared reporting performance in interviews using each combination (Oksenberg, Vinokur, and Cannell, 1979b).

The Sample and Experimental Conditions. From a sample of about 900 white women, approximately equal numbers of respondents were interviewed in each of five conditions (see Table 8 for details).

TABLE 8

Mean Scores on Measures of Respondent Performance by Respondent Education and Condition: Second Study—Instructions, Contingent Feedback, and Commitment

Performance Measure	*A* Control	*B* Instructions	*C* Instructions + Feedback	*D* Instructions + Commitment	*E* Instructions + Feedback + Commitment	Increase in Reporting (%) (*E* − *A*)
Low-Education Respondents (High School Grad or Less)						
Amount of information						
No. of items to 16 open questions	61.63	63.14	64.73	72.04	71.90	17
No. of doctor visits	1.31	1.15	1.01	1.26	1.35	3
Indices of precision						
Dates of doctor visits[a]	0.52	0.54	0.78	0.71	0.77	48
Dates of activity curtailment[a]	0.48	0.50	0.56	0.67	0.62	29
Dates of 7 medical events[b]	0.52	0.50	0.54	0.54	0.62	19
Specification of amounts of food eaten	5.09	4.84	5.56	5.83	6.04	19
Checking outside sources of information	0.70	1.21	1.66	1.45	2.27	224
Reporting treatment for nervous condition	0.34	0.37	0.23	0.20	0.36	6
No. of items reported for pelvic region	0.63	0.58	0.61	0.82	0.91	44

High-Education Respondents (Some College or More)						
Amount of information						
No. of items to 16 open questions	64.05	73.50	78.36	72.62	79.30	24
No. of doctor visits	1.14	1.19	1.30	1.63	1.55	36
Indices of precision						
Dates of doctor visits[a]	0.60	0.73	0.88	0.78	0.82	37
Dates of activity curtailment[a]	0.50	0.61	0.71	0.70	0.85	70
Dates of 7 medical events[b]	0.46	0.60	0.66	0.61	0.65	41
Specification of amounts of food eaten	5.28	6.05	5.90	6.24	6.60	25
Checking outside sources of information	0.81	1.45	2.31	1.90	2.29	183
Reporting treatment for nervous condition	0.21	0.17	0.26	0.24	0.26	24
No. of items reported for pelvic region	0.69	0.77	0.80	0.77	0.87	26

NOTE: Except for several instances of missing data, scores on the performance measures for experimental treatments *A* through *E* are based on 99, 92, 113, 103, and 99 low-education respondents, respectively, and on 95, 84, 81, 71, and 84 high-education respondents. For the indices of precision labeled "dates of doctor visits" and "dates of activity curtailment," *N* ranged from 30 to 59 for the 10 experimental groups. Only respondents who reported at least one appropriate event for each measure received a precision index score, resulting in the reductions in *N*.

[a]Precise-to-day index.

[b]Precise-to-month index.

SOURCE: Adapted from Oksenberg, Vinokur, and Cannell (1979b).

The five conditions included four combinations of the three techniques and a control:

Condition *A*: None of the three techniques (control)
Condition *B*: Instructions only
Condition *C*: Instructions and feedback
Condition *D*: Instructions and commitment
Condition *E*: Instructions, feedback, and commitment

The feedback technique included negative feedback similar to that used in the feedback procedure in the first study; the commitment procedure included an agreement similar to that used in the commitment procedure in the first study (see Exhibit 2); and task instructions represented an expansion and further development of the role and task instructions that had accompanied the commitment and feedback procedures in the first study (see Exhibit 1). The usefulness of task instructions by themselves—the first question underlying the study—can be assessed by comparing reporting in condition *B* with that in condition *A*. Whether adding performance feedback or a commitment agreement to task instructions improves reporting performance beyond that achieved by task instructions alone and whether adding both feedback and commitment is better than adding just one of them—the second and third questions underlying the study—were assessed by comparing reporting by respondents interviewed under conditions *B*, *C*, *D*, or *E*.

We were interested in discovering whether the new interviewing techniques had different effects for respondents of different educational levels. A major concern was whether respondents with high education might react negatively to the use of the techniques (might find them patronizing, for example, or even insulting) and for this reason do a poor job of reporting. Consequently, we assessed reporting performance separately for high-education and low-education respondents.

Procedures. The questionnaire was quite similar to that used in the preceding study. As before, the experimental techniques were designed as part of the questionnaires, resulting in five different forms of the questionnaire for the five interview conditions. Each of the 19 interviewers was assigned to all five interview conditions. The interviewer's behavior was controlled as in the first study, and similar measures of reporting performance were used.

To obtain adequate numbers of highly educated respondents, the sample was drawn from census tracts known to have relatively high levels of education and income. As a result, 55 percent of the respondents fell into the low-education category (high school graduate or less), and 45 percent fell into the high-education category (some college or more).

The effects of instructions, commitment, feedback, and respondent's educational level on the major dependent variables were assessed through unweighted-means analyses of variance. One set of analyses involved treatment groups *B, C, D,* and *E* (see Table 8). With respondents classified as low or high education, this set yielded a 2 × 2 × 2 design (feedback × commitment × education). These analyses gave information concerning the effects of commitment, feedback, and respondent's education in the presence of instructions. The second set of analyses involved treatment groups *A* and *B* (see Table 8), which, with respondent's educational level, yielded a 2 × 2 design (instructions × education). These analyses gave information concerning the effects of instructions and education in the absence of feedback and commitment.

Results. The results from these analyses, too numerous to present in detail here, are summarized. To provide an overview, Table 8 displays the mean scores on the measures of reporting performances for the five experimental conditions, for both high-education and low-education respondents. As this table illustrates, each of the three experimental techniques leads to improvement in reporting and the combination of all three techniques (column *E*) generally leads to the best reporting. These results are confirmed by the analyses of variance summarized here for instructions, feedback, and commitment, as well as for respondent's educational level. Results from the analyses of variance reported here are significant at $p < 0.05$ or better.

The results for the commitment technique were similar to those for the commitment procedure in the first study. Commitment increased the amount of information reported—both the number of items reported to the 16 open questions and the number of doctor visits reported (Table 8). It also improved the precision with which dates of activity curtailment were reported and the specification of amounts of foods eaten. Moreover, commitment increased the checking of outside information sources and the number of items reported for the pelvic region.

The feedback technique was somewhat more successful in this

study than in the first. As before, feedback increased the amount of information reported to open questions; it also increased the precision of reporting dates of doctor visits and dates of seven medical events. These new successes may have resulted from improvements in the instructions and the wording of the date questions, improvements that appear to have clarified the reporting tasks. Finally, feedback increased checking of outside sources of information.

Instructions, by themselves, increased the number of items reported to the 16 open questions, improved the precision of reporting dates of seven medical events, and increased the amount of checking of outside sources of information. The successes indicate that instructions aid in improving task performance by themselves, in addition to the supporting role they play for the feedback and commitment techniques.

Anlayses of variance revealed no differences in effectiveness of the feedback technique for high-education and low-education respondents; however, there were differences with both instructions and commitment techniques. For the amount of information reported to open questions (considered the most general performance measure), use of instructions markedly improved performance only for high-education respondents. Adding commitment to instructions markedly improved reporting by low-education respondents on this measure but did not further improve reporting by high-education respondents. While not all performance measures showed these differential effects—for example, the effects of the two techniques on checking outside sources of information were the same for the two educational levels—there was enough evidence to indicate their importance. The techniques may well be meeting different respondent needs related to educational level.

Although we were concerned that high-education respondents might react negatively to the experimental techniques, both educational levels appeared to tolerate the experimental techniques equally well. When asked at the close of the interview how interested they were in the interview, respondents in the group with all three techniques reported the greatest interest: 60 percent of both high-education and low-education respondents claimed to have been "very interested" in the interview (Table 9). Analyses of variance similar to those performed for the performance measures yielded significant main effects for the feedback and commitment techniques used in

TABLE 9
Proportion of Respondents "Very Interested" in the Interview by Respondent Education and Experimental Condition

	Experimental Condition				
	A	*B*	*C*	*D*	*E*
Respondent Education	Control	Instructions	Instructions + Feedback	Instructions + Commitment	Instructions + Feedback + Commitment
Low	0.51	0.43	0.50	0.56	0.60
High	0.39	0.36	0.51	0.46	0.60

NOTE: *N* is given in Table 8. Proportions are based on responses to the question "How much did the interview interest you? Were you very interested, somewhat interested, or not very interested?"
SOURCE: Oksenberg, Vinokur, and Cannell (1979b).

conjunction with instructions but not for the instruction technique by itself. Thus there is no evidence that the experimental techniques led either educational group to have less positive reactions to the interview. Moreover, there is some evidence that they led to more positive reactions.

An Experiment on Media-Use Reporting

Shortly after completing the second study, we had an opportunity to apply the new techniques to another area of inquiry in a pilot study of users of various mass media. In contrast to health surveys for which reporting errors are usually in the direction of underreporting, media-use surveys can be expected to produce overreporting in some aspects of media use that are socially valued. Thus the media-use pilot study allowed us to test whether the new techniques could reduce the amount of information reporting in those areas expected to be overreported by respondents.

The study also allowed a comparison of the new techniques with more typical interviewing practice. In the two preceding studies, strict control over behavior of interviewers in the control groups was necessary to the development and evaluation of each of the new techniques, and thus the studies did not provide a true comparison of reporting using the new techniques versus reporting using typical interviewing procedures.

The media-use study compared two types of interviews: experimental and control. The experimental interview combined the three new techniques. As before, interviewers were trained to treat the experimental questionnaire as a complete script for the interview. The control interview involved none of the new techniques in the questionnaire, but in contrast to previous experimental studies, interviewers were given basic training in interviewing and were exhorted to get good data by applying the general rules of interviewing as they saw fit.

Respondents in this study were 209 white, middle-class women in Lafayette, Indiana. Of these, 102 received the experimental interview and 107 the control interview. Interviewers, each of whom conducted both kinds of interviews, were college students studying interviewing techniques or interpersonal communication. (In previous studies, interviewers were employed on a professional basis.)

The questionnaire focused on amount of contact with television, radio, books, newspapers, and movies and on details about programs and articles. Reports of incidence of media contact and amounts of contact, as well as the number of details reported about the contact, were compared for the two types of interviews. As in the two health studies, most of the information reflected by these measures was expected to be underreported because of poor recall, lack of salience, or social undesirability. And, as before, it was expected that this information would be reported more completely in experimental interviews than in the control interviews. However, the media-use questionnaire also asked about two things that respondents were expected to overreport in the interest of presenting themselves in a favorable light. These were questions about reading the editorial page of newspapers and about the number of books read recently. Because the experimental interviews in the health studies did not include any measures on which overreporting was expected, we were particularly interested in whether the media-use survey would produce lower levels of reporting in the experimental interviews than in the control interviews for the measures on which overreporting was expected.

As Table 10 shows, in comparison with the control interviews in which interviewers were essentially on their own, the experimental interviews yielded increased reporting of information likely to be underreported and decreased reporting of information likely to be overreported. Where underreporting was expected because of elapsed time or lack of salience (as for most reporting of media contact and related details) or because of social undesirability (admission of having seen an X-rated movie), reporting in experimental interviews was uniformly superior. The differences for the two types of interviews were significant on a number of the separate measures (see Table 10). On the two measures on which overreporting was expected because of social desirability ("editorial page" and "book" reading), respondents in the experimental interviews had significantly *lower* levels of reporting than respondents in the control interviews. (See Miller and Cannell, 1977).

One additional piece of data supports the interpretation that reporting by experimental-interview respondents was less affected by social desirability than was reporting by control-interview respondents: The former reported titles for 97 percent of the books they claimed to have read (2.8 titles for 2.9 books on the average); the latter reported titles for only 40 percent of the books they claimed to have

TABLE 10
Reported Media Use by Interview Procedure

Reports of Media Contact	Interview Procedure: Experimental		Control	
Percentage of respondents				
Watched TV previous day	86**	(102)	66	(107)
Listened to radio previous day	67	(102)	65	(107)
Read newspaper previous day	83	(102)	77	(107)
Read editorial page previous day[a]	38*	(84)	55	(70)
Had seen an X-rated movie	61	(101)	51	(106)
Mean amount of contact claimed[b]				
Minutes watched TV previous day[c]	197**	(88)	157	(71)
Minutes listened to radio previous day[c]	157**	(68)	89	(69)
Minutes watched TV on average day[c]	215*	(98)	177	(106)
Minutes listened to radio on average day[c]	151	(97)	138	(106)
Number of books read in last three months[a]	2.9*	(99)	5.3	(104)
Mean amount of information mentioned in response to open questions				
Details about media contact	30.71*	(102)	22.39	(107)
Titles of books read in last three months[c]	2.8	(61)	2.14	(65)

NOTE: *N* are in parentheses. Except where noted, higher levels of reporting are assumed to indicate better reporting performance.
[a]Lower levels of reporting are assumed to indicate better reporting performance.
[b]Respondents reported numbers, rather than names of specific programs or books.
[c]Calculated only for respondents reporting any time.
*Experimental group differs significantly from control group, $p < 0.05$.
**Experimental group differs significantly from control group, $p < 0.01$.
SOURCE: Adapted from Miller and Cannell (1977).

read (2.14 titles for 5.3 books on the average). This finding suggests that the control-interview respondents' claims about number of books read were in fact somewhat inflated and that when asked to back up their claims with titles, they were unable to do so.

The new techniques focusing on the nature of the task the respondent is expected to perform appear to lead to more accurate reporting, whether the expected error is in the direction of under-reporting or overreporting. The results of this study indicate that interviewers obtain more accurate reports using the new, standardized approach than they do using a more flexible, discretionary approach to obtaining the best reporting.

Application to Telephone Interviews

In view of the growing use of the telephone for survey data collection, a question naturally arises about the application of these techniques to telephone interviewing. At this writing, we have two major studies under way to investigate this issue. Although data are just beginning to be analyzed, indications are that the new techniques are as effective in telephone interviews as they are in personal interviews.

SUMMARY AND CONCLUSIONS

This chapter reports results of some new techniques designed to improve the validity of responses in survey interviews and to reduce variability among interviewers. These techniques were developed after studies of health variables showed that poor information reporting often seemed attributable to the fact that respondents did not understand what was expected of them and did not exert the effort necessary to retrieve or organize material for satisfactory reporting.

We hypothesized that techniques to increase the respondent's understanding of the interview goals, to enhance the respondent's motivation to exert the effort required for the response task, and to reduce the variability of interviewing conditions would lead to improved validity of survey results. To test this hypothesis, three techniques—instructions, contingent feedback, and commitment—were adapted for use in the survey interview. Each has both cognitive and motivational objectives; that is, each provides information on goals and expected behavior, and each supplies cues for specific questions. All are directed to stimulating the respondent to meet the task demands. The techniques employ a highly structured or "scripted" interview format and thus reduce variability that may be introduced by the interviewer's discretion from one interview to the next.

We must remind the reader that, in order to evaluate these new techniques in experimental settings, we have made assumptions about the nature of measurement error in survey questions. We anticipated that events or experiences for some questions will be underreported, and we expected an overreporting bias on others. The efficacy of the interviewing techniques was assessed within this framework; where more valid reporting is anticipated, it is on the basis of these assumptions about the direction of error.

In some cases, data from validity studies back up these ideas. Health variables, for example, have provided fertile ground for identifying measurement error because of the availability of validating medical records. Matching many survey reports to records makes visible the patterns of invalidity in the responses. For this reason, the health field presented an ideal environment for developing and testing the interviewing procedures discussed here.

But in health and other fields there are many variables to be measured about whose error structures little or nothing is known. These variables involve not only hard facts but attitudes, perceptions, expectations, and so forth. For these concepts, notions of response validity depend on our reasoning about the nature of the reporting task. If, for example, the question seems to demand considerable recall effort, or if it asks the respondent to admit to something we think may be embarrassing, it is anticipated that the error tendency will be to underreport. We have no external information to justify these suppositions, and the conclusions about the effects of the interviewing techniques in such cases must be tempered by this fact. Even in those cases where the error structure has been researched and identified, we are still uncertain about the distance between the responses and the truth.

Nonetheless, it seems that investigators should make reasoned attempts to anticipate error in their measures, and try to reduce it through modifications in the interviewer procedure. One of the chief benefits of work in this area is that the researcher must give considerable thought to ways in which measures go awry. Rather than relying on interviewers to compensate for poorly constructed questions, the investigator must assume full responsibility for measurement in the survey and structure the questionnaire to remove this burden from the interviewer's shoulders.

Future research on interviewing techniques should address a number of salient issues. First, replication of the findings presented here is needed, particularly concerning variables for which an overreporting tendency is expected. Second, research is needed on the effects of the techniques on *random* measurement error, as well as on bias. Third, we need to understand how the effects of the procedures extend to findings of relationships among variables. To this point, the focus has been almost exculsively on measures of univariate effects. It would be interesting now to find out under what circumstances altering univariate distributions changes measures of relationships. There is also a need to understand fully how the techniques work. How do respondents learn appropriate behavior, and which cues are most salient for them? For this understanding, an individual analysis is needed, rather than reliance on group differences. Finally, it is important to document the costs of the techniques in training time and interview time relative to their benefits in improved reporting. Our experience with the research thus far leads to some optimism about the potential for this approach to survey measurement. Nevertheless, the preceding list of unanswered questions emphasizes that there is a long way to go.

REFERENCES

BECKER, H. S.

1960 "Notes on the concept of commitment." *American Journal of Sociology* 66:32–40.

BENNETT, E. B.

1955 "Discussion, decision, commitment, and consensus in 'group decision'." *Human Relations* 8:251–273.

BRADBURN, N.

1977 "Respondent burden." *Research Proceedings Series.* Second Biennial Conference, National Center for Health Services Research.

BRADBURN, N., SUDMAN, S., AND ASSOCIATES.

1979 *Improving Interview Method and Questionnaire Design:*

Response Effects to Threatening Questions in Survey Research. San Francisco: Jossey-Bass.

BREHM, J. W., AND COHEN, A. R.
1962 *Explorations in Cognitive Dissonance.* New York: Wiley.

CAHALAN, D., TAMULONIS, V., AND VERNER, H. W.
1947 "Interviewer bias involved in types of opinion survey questions." *International Journal of Opinion and Attitude Research* 1:63–77.

CANNELL, C. F., AND FOWLER, F. J.
1963 "A study of the reporting of visits to doctors in the National Health Survey." Research report. Ann Arbor: Survey Research Center, University of Michigan.

CANNELL, C. F., FISHER, G., AND BAKKER, T.
1965 "Reporting of hospitalization in the health interview survey." *Vital and Health Statistics,* series 2, no. 6, i–71.

CANNELL, C. F., FOWLER, F. J., AND MARQUIS, K. H.
1968 "The influence of interviewer and respondent psychological and behavioral variables on the reporting in household interviews." *Vital and Health Statistics,* series 2, no. 26, i–65.

CANNELL, C. F., MARQUIS, K. H., AND LAURENT, A.
1977 "A summary of studies of interviewing methodology: 1959–1970." *Vital and Health Statistics,* series 2, no. 69, i–78.

CANTRIL, H.
1947 *Gauging Public Opinion.* Princeton: Princeton University Press.

CENTERS, R.
1964 "A laboratory adaptation of the conversational procedure for the conditioning of verbal operants." *Journal of Abnormal and Social Psychology* 67:334–339.

DOLLARD, J., AND MILLER, N. E.
1950 *Personality and Psychotherapy.* New York: McGraw-Hill.

FERBER, R.
1966 *The Reliability of Consumer Reports of Financial Assets and Debts.* Urbana: Bureau of Economic and Business Research, University of Illinois.

GAGNÉ, R. M.
1964 "Problem solving." In A. W. Milton (Ed.), *Categories of Human Learning.* New York: Academic Press.

GERARD, H. B., CONOLLEY, E. S., AND WILHELMY, R. A.
1974 "Compliance, justification, and cognitive change." In Leonard Berkowitz (Ed.), *Advances in Experimental Social Psychology.* Vol. 6. New York: Academic Press.

GOFFMAN, E.
1961 *Encounters.* Indianapolis: Bobbs-Merrill.

GREENSPOON, J.

1955 "The reinforcing effect of two spoken sounds on the frequency of two responses." *American Journal of Psychology* 68:409–416.

HACKMAN, J. R.

1969 "Toward understanding the role of tasks in behavioral research." *Acta Psychologica* 31:97–128.

HENSON, R. M.

1973 "Effects of instructions and verbal modeling on health information reporting in household interviews." Research report. Ann Arbor: Survey Research Center, University of Michigan.

HENSON, R. M., CANNELL, C. F., AND LAWSON, S. A.

1973 "Effects of interviewer style and question form on reporting of automobile accidents." Research report. Ann Arbor: Survey Research Center, University of Michigan.

1976 "Effects of interviewer style on quality of reporting in a survey interview." *Journal of Psychology* 93:221–227.

HILDUM, D. C., AND BROWN, R. W.

1956 "Verbal reinforcement and interviewer bias." *Journal of Abnormal and Social Psychology* 53:108–111.

HYMAN, H., AND OTHERS

1954 *Interviewing in Social Research.* Chicago: University of Chicago Press.

JOHNSON, M. P.

1973 "Commitment: A conceptual structure and empirical application." *Sociological Quarterly* 14:395–406.

KATZ, D.

1942 "Do interviewers bias poll results?" *Public Opinion Quarterly* 6:248–268.

KIESLER, C. A.

1971 *The Psychology of Commitment.* New York: Academic Press.

KRASNER, L.

1958 "Studies of the conditioning of verbal behavior." *Psychological Bulletin* 55:148–170.

LANSING, J. B., GINSBERG, G. P., AND BRAATEN, K.

1961 "An investigation of response error." *Studies in Consumer Finances,* 2. Champaign: Bureau of Economic and Business Research. University of Illinois.

LEWIN, K.

1951 *Field Theory in Social Science.* New York: Harper & Row.

MADOW, W. G.

1967 "Interview data on chronic conditions compared with information derived from medical records." *Vital and Health Statistics,* series 2, no. 23, i–84.

MARLATT, G. A.
1972 "Task structure and the experimental modification of verbal behavior." *Psychological Bulletin* 78:335–350.

MARQUIS, K. H., AND CANNELL, C. F.
1969 "A study of interviewer-respondent interaction in the urban employment survey." Research report. Ann Arbor: Survey Research Center, University of Michigan.

MATARAZZO, J. D., WREN, A. N., AND SASLOW, G.
1965 "Studies in interview speech behavior." In P. Krasner and L. P. Ullman (Eds.), *Research in Behavior Modification: New Developments and Clinical Implications.* New York: Holt, Rinehart & Winston.

MCNEMAR, Q.
1946 "Opinion-attitude methodology." *Psychological Bulletin* 43:289–374.

MILLER, P.V., AND CANNELL, C. F.
1977 "Communicating measurement objectives in the survey interview." In P. M. Hirsch, P. V. Miller, and F. G. Kline (Eds.), *Strategies for Communication Research.* Vol. 6. Beverly Hills: Sage.

NETER, J., AND WAKSBERG, J.
1965 "Response errors in collection of expenditures data by household interviews: An experimental study." Technical Paper 11. Washington, D.C.: U.S. Bureau of the Census.

OKSENBERG, L., AND CANNELL, C. F.
1977 "Some factors underlying the validity of response in self report." *International Statistical Bulletin* 48:324–346.

OKSENBERG, L., VINOKUR, A. AND CANNELL, C. F.
1979a "Effects of commitment to being a good respondent on interview performance." In C. F. Cannell, L. Oksenberg, and J. M. Converse (Eds.), *Experiments in Interviewing Techniques.* Ann Arbor: Survey Research Center, University of Michigan.
1979b "The effects of instructions, commitment and feedback on reporting in personal interviews." In C. F. Cannell, L. Oksenberg, and J. M. Converse (Eds.), *Experiments in Interviewing Techniques.* Ann Arbor: Survey Research Center, University of Michigan.

PARRY, H., AND CROSSLEY, H.
1950 "Validity of responses to survey questions." *Public Opinion Quarterly* 14:61–80.

PAYNE, S. L.
1951 *The Art of Asking Questions.* Princeton: Princeton University Press.

RICE, S. A.
1929 "Contagious bias in the interview: A methodological note." *American Journal of Sociology* 35:420–423.

ROBINSON, D., AND ROHDE, S.
1946 "Two experiments with an anti-semitism poll." *Journal of Abnormal and Social Psychology* 41:136–144.

ROSENTHAL, R.
1966 *Experimenter Effects in Behavioral Research.* New York: Appleton-Century-Crofts.

ROSENTHAL, R., AND ROSNOW, R. L. (EDS.)
1969 *Artifact in Behavioral Research.* New York: Academic Press.

SCHUMAN, H., AND CONVERSE, J. M.
1971 "The effects of black and white interviewers on black responses in 1968." *Public Opinion Quarterly* 35:44–68.

SCHUMAN, H., AND PRESSER, S.
1977 "Question wording as an independent variable in survey analysis." *Sociological Methods and Research* 6:151–170.
1978 "The assessment of 'no-opinion' in attitude surveys." In K. F. Schuessler (Ed), *Sociological Methodology 1979.* San Francisco: Jossey-Bass.
1979 "The open and closed question." *American Sociological Review* 44:692–712.

SKINNER, B. F.
1957 *Verbal Behavior.* New York: Appleton-Century-Crofts.

STANTON, F., AND BAKER, K. H.
1942 "Interviewer bias and the recall of incompletely learned materials." *Sociometry* 5:123–135.

SUDMAN, S., AND BRADBURN, N.
1974 *Response Effects in Surveys: A Review and Synthesis.* Chicago: Aldine.

SUDMAN, S., AND OTHERS
1977 "Modest expectations." *Sociological Methods and Research* 6:171–182.

TAFFEL, C.
1955 "Anxiety and the conditioning of verbal behavior." *Journal of Abnormal and Social Psychology* 51:496–501.

VERPLANCK, W. S.
1955 "The control of the content of conversation: Reinforcement of statements of opinion." *Journal of Abnormal and Social Psychology* 51:668–676.

VINOKUR, A., OKSENBERG, L., AND CANNELL, C. F.
1979 "Effects of feedback and reinforcement on the report of health information." In C. F. Cannell, L. Oksenberg, and J. M.

Converse (Eds.), *Experiments in Interviewing Techniques*. Ann Arbor: Survey Research Center, University of Michigan.

WEISS, C. H.
1970 "Interaction in the recent interview: The effects of rapport on response." *Proceedings of the American Statistical Association*, Social Statistics Section. Washington, D.C.: American Statistical Association.

NAME INDEX

M

N

T

U

V

W

SUBJECT INDEX

C

D

F

G

H

I

N

O

P

Q

R

S